全国高等中医药院校中药学类专业双语规划教材
Bilingual Planned Textbooks for Chinese Materia Medica Majors in TCM Colleges and Univers

中药商品学

The Chinese Materia Medica Commoditology

（供中药学、药学、药物制剂、市场营销及相关专业使用）

(For Chinese Materia Medica, Pharmacy, Pharmaceutical Preparations, Marketing and other related majors)

主　编　蒋桂华　都晓伟

副主编　杨扶德　李宝国　李昌勤　兰志琼　王添敏　吴军凯

编　者（以姓氏笔画为序）

王少男（河北中医学院）　王明伟（甘肃中医药大学）
王添敏（辽宁中医药大学）　兰志琼（成都中医药大学）
曲中原（哈尔滨商业大学）　苏雪慧［山东第一医科大学（山东省医学科学院）］
杨　烨（贵州中医药大学）　杨扶德（甘肃中医药大学）
杨青山（安徽中医药大学）　杨枝中（云南中医药大学）
杨晶凡（河南中医药大学）　李昌勤（河南大学）
李宝国（山东中医药大学）　连　艳（成都中医药大学）
吴军凯（黑龙江中医药大学）　吴志瑰（江西中医药大学）
张　璐（浙江中医药大学）　张文奕（甘肃中医药大学）
陈　嵩（黑龙江中医药大学）　胡　静（天津中医药大学）
侯　嘉（甘肃中医药大学）　都晓伟（黑龙江中医药大学）
盛　琳（海南医学院）　蒋运斌（西南大学）
蒋桂华（成都中医药大学）　谢军丽（贵州中医药大学）

中国健康传媒集团
中国医药科技出版社

内容提要

本教材是“全国高等中医药院校中药学类专业双语规划教材”之一。全书中英文对应，促进中药经销国际化。总论部分主要介绍了中药商品学的含义与任务、中药商品学的起源与发展、中药资源与道地药材、药材商品的采收与产地加工、中药商品的包装、中药市场、中药商品的经营及管理等。各论部分主要介绍了常见中药材商品，以著名药材产区为特点介绍川、广、云、贵、怀、浙、南、关、北、西等道地药材。本教材为书网融合教材，即纸质教材有机融合电子教材、教学配套资源和数字化教学服务。

本教材实用性强，主要供中药学、药学、药物制剂、制药工程、中药资源与开发等专业必修课程或选修课使用，也可作为市场营销学、管理学、商品学、医学等相关专业学习使用，还可以作为中药商品市场的购、销、运、贮等经营与行业培训等的参考书。

图书在版编目（CIP）数据

中药商品学：汉英对照 / 蒋桂华，都晓伟主编．—北京：中国医药科技出版社，2020.11

全国高等中医药院校中药学类专业双语规划教材

ISBN 978-7-5214-1874-3

Ⅰ．①中…　Ⅱ．①蒋…②都…　Ⅲ．①中药材－商品学－双语教学－中医学院－教材－汉、英　Ⅳ．① F762.2

中国版本图书馆 CIP 数据核字（2020）第 097265 号

美术编辑　陈君杞

版式设计　辰轩文化

出版　**中国健康传媒集团** | 中国医药科技出版社

地址　北京市海淀区文慧园北路甲 22 号

邮编　100082

电话　发行：010-62227427　邮购：010-62236938

网址　www.cmstp.com

规格　889 × 1194 mm 1/16

印张　21 1/8

彩插　1

字数　575 千字

版次　2020 年 11 月第 1 版

印次　2020 年 11 月第 1 次印刷

印刷　三河市万龙印装有限公司

经销　全国各地新华书店

书号　ISBN 978-7-5214-1874-3

定价　68.00 元

获取新书信息、投稿、为图书纠错，请扫码联系我们。

出版说明

近些年随着世界范围的中医药热潮的涌动，来中国学习中医药学的留学生逐年增多，走出国门的中医药学人才也在增加。为了适应中医药国际交流与合作的需要，加快中医药国际化进程，提高来中国留学生和国际班学生的教学质量，满足双语教学的需要和中医药对外交流需求，培养优秀的国际化中医药人才，进一步推动中医药国际化进程，根据教育部、国家中医药管理局、国家药品监督管理局等部门的有关精神，在本套教材建设指导委员会主任委员成都中医药大学彭成教授等专家的指导和顶层设计下，中国医药科技出版社组织全国50余所高等中医药院校及附属医疗机构约420名专家、教师精心编撰了全国高等中医药院校中药学类专业双语规划教材，该套教材即将付梓出版。

本套教材共计23门，主要供全国高等中医药院校中药学类专业教学使用。本套教材定位清晰、特色鲜明，主要体现在以下方面。

一、立足双语教学实际，培养复合应用型人才

本套教材以高校双语教学课程建设要求为依据，以满足国内医药院校开展留学生教学和双语教学的需求为目标，突出中医药文化特色鲜明、中医药专业术语规范的特点，注重培养中医药技能、反映中医药传承和现代研究成果，旨在优化教育质量，培养优秀的国际化中医药人才，推进中医药对外交流。

本套教材建设围绕目前中医药院校本科教育教学改革方向对教材体系进行科学规划、合理设计，坚持以培养创新型和复合型人才为宗旨，以社会需求为导向，以培养适应中药开发、利用、管理、服务等各个领域需求的高素质应用型人才为目标的教材建设思路与原则。

二、遵循教材编写规律，整体优化，紧跟学科发展步伐

本套教材的编写遵循“三基、五性、三特定”的教材编写规律；以“必需、够用”为度；坚持与时俱进，注意吸收新技术和新方法，适当拓展知识面，为学生后续发展奠定必要的基础。实验教材密切结合主干教材内容，体现理实一体，注重培养学生实践技能训练的同时，按照教育部相关精神，增加设计性实验部分，以现实问题作为驱动力来培养学生自主获取和应用新知识的能力，从而培养学生独立思考能力、实验设计能力、实践操作能力和可持续发展能力，满足培养应用型和复合型人才的要求。强调全套教材内容的整体优化，并注重不同教材内容的联系与衔接，避免遗漏和不必要的交叉重复。

三、对接职业资格考试，“教考”“理实”密切融合

本套教材的内容和结构设计紧密对接国家执业中药师职业资格考试大纲要求，实现教学与考试、理论与实践的密切融合，并且在教材编写过程中，吸收具有丰富实践经验的企业人员参与教材的编写，确保教材的内容密切结合应用，更加体现高等教育的实践性和开放性，为学生参加考试和实践工作打下坚实基础。

四、创新教材呈现形式，书网融合，使教与学更便捷更轻松

全套教材为书网融合教材，即纸质教材与数字教材、配套教学资源、题库系统、数字化教学服务有机融合。通过“一书一码”的强关联，为读者提供全免费增值服务。按教材封底的提示激活教材后，读者可通过PC、手机阅读电子教材和配套课程资源（PPT、微课、视频等），并可在线进行同步练习，实时收到答案反馈和解析。同时，读者也可以直接扫描书中二维码，阅读与教材内容关联的课程资源，从而丰富学习体验，使学习更便捷。教师可通过PC在线创建课程，与学生互动，开展在线课程内容定制、布置和批改作业、在线组织考试、讨论与答疑等教学活动，学生通过PC、手机均可实现在线作业、在线考试，提升学习效率，使教与学更轻松。此外，平台尚有数据分析、教学诊断等功能，可为教学研究与管理提供技术和数据支撑。需要特殊说明的是，有些专业基础课程，例如《药理学》等9种教材，起源于西方医学，因篇幅所限，在本次双语教材建设中纸质教材以英语为主，仅将专业词汇对照了中文翻译，同时在中国医药科技出版社数字平台“医药大学堂”上配套了中文电子教材供学生学习参考。

编写出版本套高质量教材，得到了全国知名专家的精心指导和各有关院校领导与编者的大力支持，在此一并表示衷心感谢。希望广大师生在教学中积极使用本套教材和提出宝贵意见，以便修订完善，共同打造精品教材，为促进我国高等中医药院校中药学类专业教育教学改革和人才培养做出积极贡献。

全国高等中医药院校中药学类专业双语规划教材
建设指导委员会

数字化教材编委会

主　编　蒋桂华　都晓伟

副主编　杨扶德　李宝国　李昌勤　兰志琼　王添敏　吴军凯

编　者（以姓氏笔画为序）

王少男（河北中医学院）

王明伟（甘肃中医药大学）

王添敏（辽宁中医药大学）

兰志琼（成都中医药大学）

曲中原（哈尔滨商业大学）

苏雪慧［山东第一医科大学（山东省医学科学院）］

杨　烨（贵州中医药大学）

杨扶德（甘肃中医药大学）

杨青山（安徽中医药大学）

杨枝中（云南中医药大学）

杨晶凡（河南中医药大学）

李昌勤（河南大学）

李宝国（山东中医药大学）

连　艳（成都中医药大学）

吴军凯（黑龙江中医药大学）

吴志瑰（江西中医药大学）

张　璐（浙江中医药大学）

张文奕（甘肃中医药大学）

陈　嵩（黑龙江中医药大学）

胡　静（天津中医药大学）

侯　嘉（甘肃中医药大学）

都晓伟（黑龙江中医药大学）

盛　琳（海南医学院）

蒋运斌（西南大学）

蒋桂华（成都中医药大学）

谢军丽（贵州中医药大学）

前言

中药商品学是一门具有中医药特色的以中药商品质量和经营管理为核心内容研究中药商品的应用学科，是中药学类、管理学类、中医学类以及相关学科的必修课或专业基础课。本书由成都中医药大学、黑龙江中医药大学、山东中医药大学、甘肃中医药大学、河南大学、辽宁中医药大学、浙江中医药大学、安徽中医药大学、天津中医药大学、山东第一医科大学（山东省医学科学院）、江西中医药大学、河南中医药大学、海南医学院、西南大学、河北中医学院、云南中医药大学、贵州中医药大学、哈尔滨商业大学的25位教师，根据专业教学和英语教学经验共同编写而成。

本教材以“博采众长，突破创新；注重实践，突出商品；双语对照，促国际化”为编写理念。教材编写注意参考吸收了现有各个版本中文《中药商品学》教材的优点，以及《商品学》《营销学》《中药鉴定学》《中药资源学》《中药制剂学》《医学英语》等相关教材的内容。教材牢牢把握“中药”“商品”和“双语”三个关键点，通过中英文对照形式，突出中药的商品特色，注重中药在商品流通环节的各种变化，注意近年来中药材市场、商品规格、等级的新变化、新动态和新趋势。

全书分总论和各论两部分，共十八章。总论部分主要介绍了中药商品学的含义与任务、中药商品学的起源与发展、中药资源与道地药材、药材商品的采收与产地加工、中药商品的包装、中药市场、中药商品的经营以及中药商品的管理。各论部分主要介绍了常见中药材商品，采用以中药材道地产区如川、广、云、贵、怀、浙、南、关、北、西药为常见中药商品各论分类依据，另增设进口药部分，独立成章。

本教材充分体现教科书的特点，重点突出，层次分明，为帮助学生更好地学习掌握中药商品学的基本理论、基础知识和基本技能，在每章之前设立了“学习目标”；在每章之后总结归纳出“重点小结”；对重点知识内容通过“目标检测”等方式在教材中给予提示，以满足教师教学和学生学习的需要。本教材为书网融合教材，即纸质教材有机融合电子教材、教学配套资源和数字化教学服务。

本教材由主编和副主编分工负责各章的审稿，第一章由蒋桂华、王少男编写，第二章由李宝国、吴志瑰编写，第三章由兰志琼、胡静编写，第四章由蒋桂华、杨枝中编写，第五章由蒋桂华、蒋运斌编写，第六章由吴军凯、曲中原编写，第七章由杨扶德、谢军丽编写，第八章由兰志琼、连艳、杨青山编写，第九、十四章由王添敏、盛琳编写，第十章由都晓伟、杨晶凡编写，第十一章由兰志琼、杨烨编写，第十二、十三章由李昌勤、张璐编写，第十五章由都晓伟、吴军凯编写，第十六章由李宝国、苏雪慧编写，第十七章由杨扶德、王明伟编写，第十八章由杨扶德、侯嘉编写，药材图片由蒋桂华提供，药材中、英文名和原植物、动物拉丁文名检索由都晓伟、吴军凯编写。英文由张文奕、陈嵩审校。总论由蒋桂华负责统稿审校，各论由都晓伟负责统稿审校。

本教材适用于中药学、药学、药物制剂、制药工程、中药资源与开发等专业必修课程或选修课使用，也可作为市场营销学、管理学、商品学、医学等相关专业的学习使用，还可以作为中药商品市场的购、销、运、贮等经营与行业培训等的参考书。

本教材编写过程中，由于水平所限，难免有不妥之处，欢迎批评指正，以利于今后修改完善。

编　者

2020年6月

Preface

The Chinese materia medica commoditology (CMMC) is an applied discipline with the characteristics of Chinese materia medica (CMM), whose core content is the quality and management of Chinese materia medica commodities(hereinafter abbreviated as CMMCs). It is a compulsory course or professional basic course of Chinese pharmacy, management, traditional Chinese medicine and related disciplines. It is jointly compiled by 25 teachers majoring in CMMC and medical English from Chengdu University of Traditional Chinese Medicine, Heilongjiang University of Chinese Medicine, Shandong University of Traditional Chinese Medicine, Gansu University of Chinese Medicine, Henan University, Liaoning University of Traditional Chinese Medicine, Zhejiang Chinese Medical University, Anhui University of Chinese Medicine, Tianjin University of Traditional Chinese Medicine, Shandong First Medical University & Shandong Academy of Medical Sciences, Jiangxi University of Traditional Chinese Medicine, Henan University of Chinese Medicine, Hainan Medical University, Southwest University, Hebei University of Chinese Medicine, Yunnan University of Chinese Medicine, Guizhou University of Traditional Chinese Medicine and Harbin University of Commerce.

Taking "absorbing others' advantages, breaking through innovation; focusing on practice, highlighting commodities; bilingual control, promoting internationalization" as the compiling concept, the compilation of this textbook focuses on absorbing the advantages of the existing various Chinese versions of *Chinese Materia Medica Commoditology*, along with reference to the contents of related textbooks such as *Commodity science*, *Marketing Science*, *Identification of Chinese Materia Medica*, *Resource Science of Chinese Materia Medica*, *Preparation Science of Chinese Materia Medica*, *Medical English*. The textbook firmly holds the three key points of "Chinese materia medica" "commodity" and "bilingual", which is in the form of Chinese English parallel texts, highlighting the commodity characteristics of CMM, focusing on various changes of CMM in the commodity circulation link, and paying attention to the new changes, new situation and new trends in the market and the commodity specifications and grades of CMM in recent years.

It consists of two parts: the general part and the special part, totaling 18 chapters. The general part mainly introduces the meaning and tasks of CMMC, the origin and development of CMMC, CMM resources and authentic medicinal, the collection and processing of CMMCs, the packaging of CMMCs, the CMM market, and the management of CMMCs. The special part mainly introduces common CMMCs, and introduces authentic medicinal according to famous medicinal material producing areas such as Chuan, Guang, Yun, Gui, Huai, Zhe, Nan, Guan, Bei, and Xi. In addition, the imported medicines are added to form an independent chapter.

It fully reflects the characteristics of the textbook, with distinct emphasis and levels. Aiming at helping students better acquire the basic theory, basic knowledge and skills of *Chinese Materia Medica Commoditology*, the "Learning targets" are set up at the beginning of each chapter, and the "Key points" is summarized at the end of each chapter. Meanwhile, the key knowledge content thereof is prompted in the textbook by means of "Object detection" to meet the needs of teachers' teaching and students' learning. Being a book-network integration textbook, it includes an integration of published textbooks and electronic textbooks, teaching supporting resources, and digital teaching services.

The editors in chief and deputy editors in chief have a clear division of the compilation and revision of each chapter. The first chapter is written by Jiang Guihua and Wang Shaonan, the second by Li Baoguo and Wu Zhigui, the third by Lan Zhiqiong and Hu Jing, the fourth by Jiang Guihua and Yang Zhizhong, the fifth by Jiang Guihua and Jiang Yunbin, the sixth by Wu Junkai and Qu Zhongyuan, the seventh by Yang Fude and Xie Junli. The eighth chapter is written by Lan Zhiqiong, Lian Yan and Yang Qingshan, the ninth and the fourteenth by Wang Tianmin and Sheng Lin, the tenth by Du Xiaowei and Yang Jingfan, the eleventh by Lan Zhiqiong and Yang Ye, the twelfth and the thirteenth by Li Changqin and Zhang Lu, the fifteenth by Du Xiaowei and Wu Junkai, the sixteenth by Li Baoguo and Su Xuehui, the seventeenth by Yang Fude and Wang Mingwei and the eighteenth by Yang Fude and Hou Jia. The pictures of Medicinal materials are provided by Jiang Guihua. The Chinese name and Latin name indexes of Medicinal materials, and their original plants and animals are compiled by Du Xiaowei and Wu Junkai. Zhang Wenyi and Chen Song are English editors. The reviewer and reviser for the general part is Jiang Guihua, and the counterpart for the special part is Du Xiaowei.

It is mainly used for compulsory or optional courses in specialties such as traditional Chinese medicine, pharmacy, pharmaceutical preparations, pharmaceutical engineering, Chinese materia medica resources and development, and can be selected and used to meet different teaching needs. It can also be used as a textbook of marketing, management, merchandising, medicine and other related specialties. What's more, it can also be used as a reference book for the purchase, sale, transportation, storage and other business and industry training of CMMCs market.

Because of hasty time and limited capacity, inevitable deficiencies may exist in this version. Your comments and suggestions are appreciated for our future revision and perfection.

Editor

June 2020

目录 | Contents

总　论
Overview

各　论

Monograph

总　论
Overview

第一章　绪　　论
Chapter 1　Introduction

学习目标 | Learning targets

知识目标：

1. **掌握**　中药商品学的定义和中药商品学的任务。

2. **熟悉**　中药商品学的研究对象以及商品、中药商品、中药、中药材、中药饮片、中成药等名词术语。

能力目标：

能够阐述中药商品学的特点，了解中药商品学的起源和发展。

Knowledge targets:

1. **Proficiency**　The definition and tasks of Chinese materia medica commoditology (CMMC).

2. **Familiarity**　The research objects of CMMC and terminology such as commodities, Chinese materia medica commodities (CMMCs), Chinese materia medica (CMM), Chinese medicinal material, Chinese decocting pieces, Chinese patent medicine.

Skill targets:

Learning to set forth the characteristics of CMMC and familiarizing the origin and development of it.

第一节　中药商品学的含义与任务
Section 1　The Definition and Task of CMMC

PPT

一、中药商品学的定义
I. Definition of CMMC

中药商品学是一门以研究中药商品质量和经营管理为中心内容的应用学科。它是在继承中药商品传统经营管理和质量控制经验的基础上，以商品学的理论与方法为指导，运用现代科学技术研究中药商品在流通领域中的来源、产地、购销、贮存、商品规格、商品质量及经营管理规律，从而促进中药商品的生产、经营、管理和发展，保证中药商品安全有效，提高人民的健康水平。中药商品学是研究在商品流通领域中如何保证中药商品质量和提高经营管理水平的学科。

Chinese materia medica commoditology (hereinafter abbreviated as CMMC) is an applied discipline which focuses on the study of the quality and management of Chinese materia medica commodities (hereinafter abbreviated as CMMC). Inheriting from the traditional management and quality control experience of CMMC and guided by the theory and method of commodities science, CMMC uses modern science and technology to study the place of origin, producing areas, purchase and sale, storage, commodities specification, commodities quality and management rules of CMMC in the field of circulation. Through these means, CMMC was able to promote the production, management and development of CMMC, ensure the safety and effectiveness of CMMC and improve the health level of the people. In short, the purpose of CMMC is to study how to ensure the quality of CMMC and improve the level of management in the field of commodities circulation.

中药是指在中医药理论和临床经验指导下用于防治疾病和医疗保健的药物总称，包括中药材、中药饮片和中成药以及中药提取物等。中药材是取自天然的、仅经过产地简单加工的原料药，简称“药材”，按其来源可分为植物药、动物药和矿物药三大类。中药饮片是根据治疗疾病的需要，将中药材经过净制、切制或炮制后可直接用于临床配方使用的加工品。中成药是以中药饮片为原料，根据中医处方的要求，采用相应的制备工艺和加工方法制成一定剂型的中药制品。

Chinese materia medica (hereinafter abbreviated as CMM) refers to the general name of drugs used for the prevention, treatment of diseases and medical care under the guidance of CMM theory and clinical experience, including Chinese medicinal material, Chinese decocting pieces, Chinese patent medicine, as well as CMM extract and so on. CMM is a kind of raw material medicine which is taken from nature and simply processed in the producing areas, which is abbreviated as “medicinal material”. According to its source, CMM can be divided into three categories: plant, animal and mineral as medicinal materials. According to the needs of the treatment of diseases, Chinese decocting pieces can be directly used in clinical formula after purification, cutting or stir-bake with adjuvant processing of Chinese medicinal materials. According to Chinese medicine prescription, Chinese patent medicine is a certain dosage form of CMM made by adopting corresponding preparation technology and processing methods, using Chinese decocting pieces as raw materials.

商品是用来交换的劳动产品。它具有使用价值和价值二重属性。使用价值是物品能够满足人们某种需要的属性，它是商品的自然属性，如粮食可以充饥，衣服可以保暖，药品可以治病等。价值是凝结在商品中的无差别的一般人类劳动，它是商品的社会属性，也是商品所特有的属性。

Commodities are labor products for exchange. It has dual attributes of use value and value. The use value is the property of goods that can meet people’s needs. It is the natural property of goods. For example, food can satisfy hunger, clothing can keep warm, medicine can cure diseases and so on. Value is the general human labor that condenses in the commodities, it is the social attribute of commodities, and it is also the unique attribute of commodities.

中药商品是在中医药理论指导下，用于防病治病、康复保健的传统药物商品，属于市场流通、交换和经营中的特殊商品。国家及有关药品标准中规定使用的中药均为中药商品。中药商品是康复保健、防病治病的物质基础，属于特殊的商品，除具备一般商品的使用价值和价值二重属性外，还具有如下特点。

Under the guidance of TCM theory, CMMCs are used for disease prevention and treatment, rehabilitation and health care, as a special commodity in market circulation, exchange and management. CMMs conforming to the national and related drug standards are all CMMCs. CMMC is the material basis of rehabilitation, health care, disease prevention and treatment, which belongs to a special commodity. In addition to its dual attributes of use value and value, it also has the following characteristics.

（一）质量特点

（I） Quality characteristics

中药商品的使用价值就是对人有治疗、预防、保健等作用，中药质量的优劣将直接影响中药商品的使用价值。中药作为特殊的商品，其质量涉及到疗效、毒性、稳定性三个关键点。质量合格的中药，可以用于防治疾病和卫生保健；质量不合格的中药，不但延误病情还有可能对身体造成损害。也就是说，药品的质量不合格，就失去了使用的价值。所以，要严格中药商品的质量管理制度，以保障临床用药的安全与有效。

The use value of CMMCs is to treat, prevent disease and protect people. The quality of CMM will directly affect the use value of CMMCs. As special commodities, the quality of CMM involves three key points: curative effect, toxicity and stability. Qualified CMM can be used for disease prevention and health care; unqualified CMM can not only delay the illness, but also cause damage to the body. In other words, if the quality of the medicinal is not up to standard, it will lose the value of use. Therefore, we should strictly enforce the quality management system of CMM to ensure the safety and effectiveness of clinical medication.

（二）经营特点

（II） Management characteristics

中药商品的经营活动与医疗卫生领域有直接或间接的联系，其社会效益重于经济效益。药品经营的品种、数量和价格取决于临床需要。所以，中药商品的生产和储备需要在医疗和保健需求信息的指导下进行。

The business activities of CMMCs are directly or indirectly related to the field of medical and health care, whose social benefits outweigh economic benefits. And the variety, quantity and price of CMM are determined by clinical needs. Therefore, the production and storage of CMMCs need to be conducted under the guidance of demand information on medical and health care.

（三）来源特点

（III） Source characteristics

中药商品既有来源于自然界的植物、动物和矿物，又有经过中药炮制、制剂加工的产品，来源复杂，品种繁多，管理困难。正确的中药来源是保证中药商品质量的基础。

CMMCs include plants, animals and mineral medicinal materials from the nature, as well as processed and prepared products, with complex source and various variety, which leads to difficult management. Thus the correct source is the basis for ensuring the quality of CMMCs.

（四）生产特点

（IV） Production characteristics

中药商品既有中药材，又有中药饮片、中成药等多种类型。目前中药材生产属于农副产品，仍以野生为主，家种、家养的药材约 200 多种，大宗者占 100 余种。无论家种、家养或野生，药材生长均需要一定的生长年限和生态环境。因此，药材生产常常具有一地生产供全国，一季生产供全年的特点。另外，由于中药野生资源日趋减少，亟待中药材规范化种植。在国家积极推广的

《中药材生产质量管理规范》(GAP)中，中药材种植需规范各生产环节乃至全过程，使生产出的药材“真实、优质、稳定、可控”。中成药、中药提取物均是制药企业工业化生产，其生产需符合《中药生产质量管理规范》(GMP)。

CMMCs include Chinese medicinal material, as well as Chinese decocting pieces and Chinese patent medicines. At present, the production of Chinese medicinal material belongs to agricultural and sideline products, and its source is mainly wild. There are more than 200 kinds of medicinal materials from family cultivation or breeding, and more than 100 species are produced in large quantities. Whether they are planted in the family, raised in the family or grown in the field, the growth of medicinal materials needs a certain period and ecological environment. Therefore, the production of medicinal materials often has the characteristics of one place for the whole country and one season for the whole year. In addition, due to the decrease of wild resources of CMM, it is urgent to standardize the cultivation of CMM. In *Good Agriculture Practice* (GAP) actively promoted by China, all the production links and even the whole process in the cultivation of CMM need to be regulated, to ensure that the produced medicinal materials are “authentic, high-quality, stable and controllable”. Both Chinese patent medicine and Chinese herbal extract are industrialized production of pharmaceutical enterprises, and their production needs to conform to *Certification of Good Manufacturing Practice* (GMP).

(五)“道地”特点

(V) Characteristics of “authenticity”

中药材商品最讲究“道地性”。道地药材是指产于一定地区、历史悠久、质量优良、加工技术成熟、疗效显著的优质药材。如东北人参、内蒙甘草、宁夏枸杞、山东金银花、江苏薄荷、四川贝母、甘肃当归、河南四大怀药、浙江浙八味等。道地药材商品的产生以大量的临床实践经验为依据，经得起临床的考验，有着丰富的科学内涵。道地药材在国内外享有很高的信誉，发展道地药材不仅有利于提高中药材的质量，还有利于巩固、提高和加强中药在国际市场的竞争力。

CMMCs focus on “authenticity”. Authentic medicinal refers to high-quality medicinal materials with a long history, good quality, mature processing technology and significant curative effect, which are produced in a certain area, namely northeast Ren Shen, Inner Mongolia Gan Cao, Ningxia Gou Qi, Shandong Jin Ying Hua, Jiangsu Bo He, Sichuan Bei Mu, Gansu Dang Gui, Henan with the four major Huai medicines, Zhejiang with the eight Zhe medicines, etc. The authentic medicinal is based on a large number of clinical practice experience, which can stand the clinical test and has rich scientific connotation. Authentic medicinal enjoys a high reputation in China and at abroad. Developing authentic medicinal is not only conducive to improving the quality of CMM, but also to consolidating, improving and strengthening the competitiveness of CMM in the international market.

二、中药商品学的任务

II. The task of CMMC

中药作为一种特殊商品，从生产领域进入流通领域，除具一般商品的共性外，还具有被动购买性和社会福利性。中药商品品种规格多而复杂，生产涉及面广，因此中药商品的经营、管理、质量控制、价格制定等方面都比一般商品复杂而特殊。中药商品学的研究范围涵盖了中药商品的名称、来源、产地、生产工艺或加工方法、商品鉴别、商品规格、主要化学成分、质量标准、商品包装、商品流通、商品贮藏及商品用途和商品信息等方方面面。

As a special commodity, CMM has entered the circulation field from the production field, with both common characteristics of general commodities and special characteristics of passive purchasing and social welfare. CMM has many varieties and specifications, produced in a wide range, so the operation, management, quality control, price setting and other aspects of CMM are more complex and special than general commodities. The research scope of CMMC covers the name, source, producing areas, production process or processing method, commodities identification, commodities specification, main chemical composition, quality standard, commodities packaging, commodities circulation, commodities storage, commodities use and commodities information.

中药商品的特殊性，中药商品学研究范围的广泛性，决定了中药商品学任务的重要性和复杂性。

The particularity and universality of the research scope of CMMC determine the importance and complexity of its task.

（一）研究和掌握中药商品的流通、经营和管理规律，构建现代中药商品体系

(I) To study and master the law of circulation, operation and management of CMMCs, and to build a modern commodities system of CMM

中药商品在传统市场经营活动中具有特定的规律性，研究和掌握这些规律，是做好中药商品流通和管理的基本条件。购、销、运、存是商品流通领域中的四个重要环节，深入研究中药商品在这四个环节的基本内容和相互间的内在联系，应用科学的管理方法，按照市场经济规律做好流通过程，构建现代化中药体系，保证中药的质量，减低商品损耗，实现科学化的经营管理，为研制和开发新药奠定基础，以满足市场的需要和人们用药的需求，这是中药商品学的基本任务。

CMMCs has the special regularity in the traditional market management activity. It is the basic condition for the circulation and management of CMMCs to study and master these regularity. Purchase, sale, transportation and storage are four important links in the field of commodities circulation. The basic task of CMMCs is to study the basic contents and internal relations of CMMCs in these four links: to apply scientific management method; to build a modern system of CMM according to the law of market economy; to ensure the quality of CMM; to reduce the loss of commodities; to realize scientific management, to lay the foundation for the research and development of new medicinal, so as to meet the market demand and people's medicines demand.

（二）制订和完善中药商品规格、等级标准

(II) To formulate and improve the specifications and grade standards of CMMCs

中药是防病治病的特殊商品，其质量的优劣关系到人民身体健康和生命安全。制定中药商品质量标准，是保证人们用药安全有效，促进中药生产、经营、发展的重要措施。目前中药商品，除中成药和部分药材、饮片有全国统一的质量标准外，大部分药材及饮片都无统一的商品规格、等级标准。少数已有标准，如 1984 年，由原国家医药管理局联合原卫生部制订的《七十六种药材商品规格标准》，因其年代过于久远，亟需修订；2018 年，中华中医药学会发布的《中药材商品规格等级（226 种）》，为常用的 226 种中药材制订了团体标准。所以，制订和完善全国统一的中药商品规格、等级标准，提高中药商品质量是本学科的首要任务。制订、完善和修订中药商品规格、等级标准总要求，是要有利于发展生产、保证供应、提高质量、保证疗效以及符合按质论价原则。同时应逐步以中药商品内在质量指标和临床疗效的好坏作为制订、完善和修订中药商品规格、等级标准的主要依据，以克服单纯地把外观质量作为主要依据的经验标准不规范的缺点。

其主要方法是在深入调查分析和广泛征求意见的基础上，组织有关科研、教学单位协作攻关，有计划地分期分批地进行中药商品规格、等级标准的研究，在取得大量外观的和内在的质量指标数据后，制订出标准，并经过一段时间试用、修改补充后，以法定标准的形式颁布，实现全国各类中药商品的规格、等级标准的规范化和标准化。

CMM is special commodities for disease prevention and treatment. People's health and life safety is related to its quality. The establishment of the quality standard of CMM is an important measure to ensure the safety and effectiveness of people's medication and to promote the production, management and development of CMM. At present, in addition to the unified national quality standards for Chinese patent medicine and some medicinal materials and decocting pieces, most of the medicinal materials and decocting pieces have no unified commodities specifications and grade standards. A few of CMM have existing standards, A few of CMM have existing standards, such as *The Standard for the Specifications of 76 kinds of Medicinal Materials*, formulated by the National Administration of Medicine and the Ministry of Health in 1984, which is too old to be revised.*The Commodity Specification Grade of Chinese Medicinal materials* (*226 kinds*), formulated by the China Association of Traditional Chinese Medicine (CMCA) in 2018, which sets group standards for 226 kinds of commonly used Chinese medicinal materials. Therefore, the primary task of this discipline is to formulate and complete the national unified specifications and grade standards of CMMCs and improve its quality. The formulation, improvement and revision of the general requirements of commodities specifications and grade standards of CMM are conducive to the development of production, supply assurance, quality improvement, efficacy assurance and compliance with the principle of pricing according to quality. The main method is to organize relevant scientific researches and teaching units to work together to tackle key problems on the basis of in-depth investigation and analysis and extensive consultation, to carry out the research on the commodities specifications and grade standards of CMM by stages and batches in a planned way, to work out the standards after obtaining a large number of external and internal quality index data, and to use legal standards after trial, modification and supplement for a period of time. The standardization of the specifications and grade standards of all kinds of CMMCs across the country will be realized.

同时应逐步以中药商品内在质量指标和临床疗效的好坏作为制订、完善和修订中药商品规格、等级标准的主要依据，以克服单纯地把外观质量作为主要依据的经验标准不规范的缺点。

Meanwhile, we should gradually take the internal quality index and clinical efficacy of CMMCs as the main basis for formulating, improving and revising the specifications and grade standards of CMMCs, so as to overcome the shortcomings of the experience standards which simply take appearance quality as the main basis.

（三）研究中药商品的价值规律，制订合理的价格

（III）To study the law of value of CMM and make price reasonable

长期以来，由于忽视价值规律的作用和一些历史原因，造成了中药商品的价格体系严重偏离其药用价值的不正常现象。这种不正常现象表现在质量差价没拉开，优质不优价；不同药材商品之间的比价不合理；道地与非道地药材商品的价格差别不大，同种药材商品的价格大起大落等。所以研究中药商品的价值规律，改革不合理的价格体系，促使价值与价格的统一，制订合理的药品价格是本学科重要任务。

For a long time, due to the neglect of the law of value and some historical reasons, the price system of CMM has deviated from its medicinal value seriously. This abnormal phenomenon is manifested in the small difference in prices between different quality medicinal materials, the unreasonable price comparison between different medicinal materials, the small difference in prices between authentic and unauthentic medicinal materials, and the big difference in prices of the same kind of medicinal materials. Therefore, it is an important task for the discipline to study the law of value of CMM, reform the unreasonable price system, promote the unity of value and price, and formulate a reasonable medicinal price.

（四）加强中药市场的调查与预测，积极推进现代中药商品贸易

(IV) To strengthen the investigation and forecast of CMM market and actively promote the modern trade of CMMCs

中药市场是指中药商品交换的场所或中药商品交换关系的总和，市场调查是指对市场信息的收集、整理、传递和贮存。市场预测是指在市场调查分析的基础上，运用数学或逻辑学的方法，对未来市场发展变化趋势做出的估计，是中药商业企业制订经营决策和经营计划的科学依据。因而加强市场调查与预测不仅是中药商业企业急需解决的问题，也是本学科的核心任务。

The market of CMM refers to the exchange place of CMMCs or the sum exchange relations of CMMCs. Market investigation refers to the collection, arrangement, transmission and storage of market information. Market prediction refers to the estimation of future market development trend based on market investigation and analysis by using mathematical or logical methods. It is the scientific basis for Chinese medicine commercial enterprises to make business decisions and business plans. Therefore, it is not only an urgent problem for Chinese medicine commercial enterprises to strengthen market investigation and prediction, but also the core task of this discipline.

同时中药商品是我国具有自主知识产权的国内外医药贸易中的重要组成部分。全面地了解国际市场对中药需求和动态变化及信息，根据国内外市场的需求而采取相应的对策，积极开展以电子商务、网络营销为代表的现代中药商品营销和国际贸易方式，大力促进中药商品的国内外贸易，使中药商品走向全世界、造福全人类是中药商品学的又一重要任务。

Meanwhile, CMMCs is an important part of domestic and foreign pharmaceutical trade with independent intellectual property rights in China. It is another important task of CMMC to understand the international market's demand for CMM and its dynamic changes and information comprehensively, to take corresponding countermeasures according to the demand of domestic and international markets, to actively carry out the modern marketing and international trade mode of CMMCs represented by e-commerce and Internet Marketing, to vigorously promote the domestic and foreign trade of CMMCs, and to make its products go to the whole world and benefit the whole mankind.

第二节　中药商品学的起源与发展

Section 2　The Origin and Development of CMMC

PPT

中药作为商品在市场上进行交换，已有几千年的历史。随着社会的发展，中药商品交换日益频繁，研究中药商品交换为主要内容的中药商品学也应运而生，并在各个历史时期都有不同程度的发展。

As commodities, CMM has been exchanged in the market for thousands of years. With the development of society, the exchange of CMM is becoming more and more frequent. CMMC forms gradually with the main content of CMMCs exchange and develops to some extent in different historical periods.

早在原始社会的末期，就开始出现了以物易物的商品交换。夏商时代（公元前 2070 年 ~ 公元前 221 年），我国由原始社会进入奴隶社会，商品交换有了进一步发展，并出现了市场。如《史记》中有："日中有市，至天下之民，聚天下之货，交易而退，各得其所"的记载，说明那时的商业已相当发达。同时在"至天下之民，聚天下之货"的商品交换中，中药作为人们生活中的特殊用品，也必在其中了。

As early as the end of the primitive society, the commodities exchange of barter began to appear. In the Xia and Shang Dynasties (2070 B.C.~221 B.C.), China entered the slave society from the primitive society. As commodities exchange developed further, market appeared. For example, there is a record in *The Records of History* that "Where markets open at noon, gather people and goods from all corner of the country. After exchanging, off they go with what they purchase", indicating that the commerce was quite thriving at that time. Meanwhile, as a special product in people's life, the sale of CMM no doubt belongs to a commodity exchange, which ever appears in the vivid description of "people and goods gather from all corner of the country".

货币的出现，极大地推动了商业的发展，中药商品贸易也随之日益发展起来。并受其他商品（农业、畜牧业、手工业商品等）在交换中分等分级、按质论价的影响，中药商品也开始分等分级，按质论价出售，于是中药商品学开始萌芽。

The emergence of currency has greatly promoted the development of commerce, followed by the boom of the trade of CMMCs. Influenced by other commodities (agriculture, animal husbandry, handicraft industry, etc.), CMMCs also began to be classified and graded with price based on quality, hence the bud of CMMC.

秦汉时代（公元前 221 年 ~ 公元 220 年），我国由奴隶社会进入封建社会，经济、文化的发展促进了中医药学的发展。这一时期医药学家辈出，医药著作增多。如《伤寒论》《金匮要略》《神农本草经》等先后问世。《神农本草经》是我国最早的药学专著，在序录中始有："土地所出，真伪新陈，并各有法"的论述，强调了药物产地、真伪、新陈的重要性，对后世本草学的发展有深远的影响。书中还引录了《范子·计然》一书论及的药价，谓："柏脂出三辅，上，升价七千，中，三千一斗。螵蛸出三辅，上，价三百。皂荚出三辅，上，价一枚一钱。"同时其他典籍也记载了中药或中药采集与销售的情况。如《诗经》记载了菟丝子、远志、泽泻等几十种中药；《后汉书》记载了韦彪、张楷等采药、卖药的情况；东汉恒帝时霸陵人韩康（字伯林）常采药于名山，在长安卖药三十多年；三国时期名医华佗既行医诊病又配方售药，在其故里（今安徽亳州）还保留有华佗当时诊病售药的"元化堂"。

During the Qin and Han Dynasties (221 B.C.~220 A.D.), China evolved into the feudal society from the slave society. The progress of economy and culture promoted the development of Chinese medicine. This era witnessed a galaxy of medical scientists and a pile of medical works. A good case in point was the publishing in succession of *Treatise on Cold Damage Diseases*, *Synopsis of Prescriptions of the Golden Chamber* and *Shennong's Classic of Materia Medica* (the earliest pharmaceutical monograph in China), etc. As the preface says "producing areas, authenticity and counterfeit, freshness and staleness, all of which must conform to the criterion of processing." This book emphasizes the importance of producing areas and authenticity of CMM, and has a profound impact on the development of CMM in the future. In addition, it quotes the medicinal prices stated in *Fanzi*: "*Jiran*, which says that in term of the prices for Bo Zi Ren beyond the areas of capital city, the prime quality of which is 7,000 for 1 *dou*, and the medium quality is 3,000; for Sangpiaoxiao, the prime quality of which is 300; for Zaojiao, the prime quality of which is 1 *qian* for 1 *mei*." Meanwhile, other ancient books also recorded the collection and sale of CMM. Take *The Book of Songs* as an example, in which records dozens of CMM, namely Tusizi, Yuanzhi and Zexie, etc.; *The History of the later Han Dynasty* records the situation of collecting and selling medicine by Wei Biao and Zhang Kai; in the Eastern Han Dynasty (Emperor Heng period), Han Kang (style name Bolin), a Baling local, used to collect herbs in famous mountains and sell them in Changan for more than thirty years; Hua Tuo, a famous doctor in the Three Kingdoms period, not only practised medicine but also sold medicine in accordance with formula. In his hometown (today's Bozhou, Anhui Province), there still exists a "Yuanhua Drugstore" where Hua Tuo diagnosed and sold medicine at that time.

综上所述，中药商品学于夏商时代开始萌芽，在秦汉时代有较大发展。

To sum up, CMMC started to bud in Xia and Shang Dynasties and developed greatly in the Qin and Han Dynasties.

晋唐时代（265~960年），特别是唐代，是我国封建社会的鼎盛时期，政治、经济、文化高度发展，中医药学也加速发展。这一时期对外贸易和中外医学的交流频繁，医药学著作不断增多。如雷敩的《雷公炮制论》，论述约300种药物的炮制加工方法和药材商品真伪鉴别，发展了药材加工技术，提高了饮片商品的质量。又如葛洪的《肘后备急方》，是我国早期的方书专著。书中记载了硬膏、干浸膏、蜡丸、锭剂、条剂、饼剂等多种剂型，并将成药列为专章论述。这些都说明饮片、成药已成为中药商品的组成部分，是中医临床用药方法的发展，为中药商品学的形成与发展提供了依据。

The Jin and Tang Dynasties (265~960), especially the Tang Dynasty, were the heyday of China's feudal society, along with the development of politics, economy, culture and Chinese medicine. During this period, foreign trade and medical exchanges between China and foreign countries were frequent, hence the increasing number of medical works. Take the example of *Master Lei's Discourse on Medicinal Processing* by Lei Xiao, in which discusses the processing methods of about 300 kinds of medicinals and the identification of the authenticity of medicinal products, develops the processing technology of medicinal materials, and improves the quality of decocting pieces. Another example is *Handbook of Prescriptions for Emergencies* by Ge Hong, which is a monograph of the early Chinese medical formulary. In the book, many kinds of dosage forms, such as hard paste, dry extract, wax pill, pastille, medicated roll and medical cake, were recorded, and the Chinese patent medicine was listed as an exclusive chapter. All of these show that Chinese decocting pieces and patent medicine have become a component of CMMCs, which is the development of Chinese medicine clinical medication, providing a basis for the formation and development of CMMC.

梁代陶弘景编著的《本草经集注》，是魏晋以来300多年药学发展的总结。书中首次记载了火试、对光试等中药商品鉴别方法，为中药商品的质量控制增加了手段。书中还记载了一些中药商品的价格，如在牛黄项下谓："药中之贵，莫复过此，一子及三二分，好者值五六千至一万也。"这些记载也为中药商品学的形成和发展提供了宝贵的资料。

Variorum of the Classic of Materia Medica, compiled by Tao Hongjing in Liang dynasty, is a summary of the development of pharmacy for more than 300 years since Wei and Jin Dynasties. For the first time, the book records the identification methods of CMMCs such as fire test and light test, which increases the means of quality control of CMMCs. The book also records the prices of some CMMCs. For example, there is a record under the item of Niu Huang: "This is the most expensive one among CMM, some of which are only 2 or 3 *fen*, and the good ones range from 5,000 to 10,000." These records also provide valuable information for the formation and development of CMMC.

隋唐时期，我国社会经济发展迅速，朝廷对医药十分重视，组织编撰了几部重大的医药专著，推动了全国医药业大发展。唐代李勋、苏敬等22人奉命编著的《新修本草》（唐本草）由唐朝政府颁发全国，是我国也是世界上最早的国家药典。本书首创图文对照的编著方法，对后世本草有深远的影响。特别是该书极为重视道地药材商品，对此有精辟的论述："离其本土，则质同而效异"。书中收载的外来药物，如血竭、安息香、龙脑、诃黎勒、阿魏等，说明中药商品贸易在国内外都有很大的发展。随着国内药材产地扩大，品种增加，外来药物交流增多，中药商品日趋兴旺，使全国市场进一步扩大，出现了定期专业中药市场。如在四川梓州出现了一年一度的定期药市，唐末传到成都，在五代时成都药市已有较大规模。边疆及少数民族聚居地药材贸易也有较大发展。药市的出现对中药业发展起到了极大的促进作用。

During the Sui and Tang Dynasties, with the rapid development of China's social economy, the court attached great importance to medicine, organized and compiled several major medical monographs, which greatly push forward the national medical and pharmaceutical industry. *Newly Revised Materia Medica* (Tang materia medica), written by 22 people including Li Xun and Su Jing in the Tang Dynasty, was issued by the Tang government. It is the earliest national pharmacopoeia in both China and the world. This book took initiative in compilation method of illustration accompanying with text, which has profound impact on materia medica of the later generation. In particular, it attaches great importance to authentic medicinal commodities, upon which it expounds that"Far from its original habitat, the same medicinal has different effect".The foreign drugs included in the book, namely Xuejie, Anxixiang, Longnao, Helile, Awei etc., showed a great development of CMM in China and at abroad. With the expanding producing areas and increasing varieties of domestic CMM, the boosting foreign medicinal exchanges, and the growing prosperity of CMMCs, the national market had been further expanded, and the regular professional CMM market had emerged. For example, the annual regular medicinal market appeared in Zizhou, Sichuan Province, and spread to Chengdu at the end of Tang Dynasty. In the Five Dynasties, Chengdu medicinal market had a large scale. The trade of Chinese materia medica in border areas and ethnic minority areas had also developed greatly. The emergence of drug market had greatly promoted the development of CMM industry.

宋代经济、文化交流和商品贸易发达，海外贸易达50余个国家和地区。宋开宝四年（971年），宋政府在广州设置了"市舶司"统管对外贸易。据《宋会要》记载，通过市舶司由阿拉伯商人运往西方（包括今亚洲西部、非洲和欧洲）各国的中药商品有朱砂、人参、牛黄等58种。北宋朝廷十分重视医学，国家开办官药局，防止药商投机；中药商品经营体制出现了官营和民营两种，医药商品经营方式有了批发、零售之分；经营品种分生、熟两类。宋朝兴起的"太医局卖药所"是我国官办的第一个中药经营机构，在全国陆续推广，形成了庞大的官营中药工商体系。另外，民营药铺几乎遍及各大集市。至南宋迁都杭州，有名的药铺有20余家，并出现专事经营川广道地药材的"川广生药市"。河南禹州（今河南禹州市）形成中原地区药材集散的常年大市，不少外地药商都到此采购。江西建昌府（今江西南城县）发展为赣东地区的药材市场。

In the Song Dynasty, economic and cultural exchanges and commodities trade were booming, and overseas trade reached more than 50 countries and regions. In the fourth year of Kaibao era in the Song

Dynasty (971), the government of the Song Dynasty set up a "Shi Bo Si" in Guangzhou to manage foreign trade. According to *Song Huiyao*, there were 58 kinds of CMMCs, such as Zhusha, Renshen and Niuhuang, which were transported to the West (including the west of Asia, Africa and Europe) by Arabian merchants supervised by Shi Bo Si. The imperial court of the Northern Song Dynasty attached importance to medicine, and the state set up the official medicine bureau to prevent drug merchants from speculating. There were two kinds of management systems of CMMCs, official and private. And the management methods of medicine commodities were divided into wholesale and retail. The management varieties were divided into two types: crude and prepared. As the first Chinese medicine business organization run by the government in China, the "Taiyi Bureau pharmacy", which was popularized in succession all over the country, formed a huge industrial and commercial system of CMM run by the government. In addition, private pharmacies were almost all over the market. After the Southern Song Dynasty moved its capital to Hangzhou, there were more than 20 famous pharmacies, and there was a "Chuanguang crude drug market" specializing in the management of Chuanguang authentic medicinals. Yuzhou, Henan Province (today's Yuzhou City, Henan Province) had formed a perennial large market of drug distribution in the Central Plains, where many foreign drug manufacturers purchased. Jianchang Prefecture of Jiangxi Province (now Nancheng County of Jiangxi Province) has developed into the medicinal material market in the eastern Jiangxi Province.

宋代官药局颁行的《太平惠民和剂局方》，可视为当时中成药配制的国家标准，为宋代及后世的中成药生产、宣传推广起到了巨大的推动作用。当时还在京城和州县开办医学教育，广泛培养医学人才。北宋元丰五年（1082 年），唐慎微编著的《证类本草》，是我国自唐《新修本草》后五百多年药学发展的又一次总结。该书不仅为道地药材商品的生产、销售、应用提供了依据，而且为后世保存了宋以前许多珍贵的医药史料，在中医药史上占有重要地位。

Prescriptions from the Great Peace Imperial Grace Pharmacy issued by the official pharmaceutical Bureau of the Song Dynasty was the national standard for the production of Chinese patent medicine at that time, which played a huge role in pushing forward the production and promotion of Chinese patent medicine in the Song Dynasty and later generations. Then the medical education was initiated in the capital, prefectures and counties to train medical talents. In the fifth year of Yuanfeng in the Northern Song Dynasty (1082), *Classified Emergency Materia Medica* by Tang Shenwei is another summary of the development of pharmacy in more than 500 years since *Newly Revised Materia Medica* in Tang Dynasty. This book not only provides a basis for the production, sale and application of authentic medicinal materials, but also preserves many precious medical historical materials before Song Dynasty for later generations, which occupies an important position in the history of Chinese medicine and CMM.

元代疆土幅员广大，地跨欧亚大陆，各民族接触频繁，促进了东西方的医药交流，中药商品贸易在此期间也有所发展。《元史》记载了一些中药商品的价格，如矾价 30 斤值（银）五两，白药 14 锭值（银）二十五两等。

Yuan Dynasty witnessed the development of the trade of CMMCs, thanks to the vast territory across Eurasia and frequent contacts between different nationalities, which promoted the exchange of medicine between the east and the west. *History of Yuan Dynasty* records the prices of some CMMCs, namely 30 *jin* of alum worth (silver) five *liang*, 14 *ding* of Baiyao worth (silver) twenty-five *liang*, etc.

综上所述，宋元时代中药商品学随中药商业的发展而有较大的迈进，并为本学科的形成和发展提供了新的依据。

To sum up, the CMMC in Song and Yuan Dynasties has made great strides forward with the development of CMM business, and provides a new basis for the formation and development of this discipline.

明清时代（1369-1911 年），尤其是明代，由于郑和十次奉命率领船队下南洋，与所到之国建立了外交和贸易关系，打通了我国与国外的海上通道，促进和扩大了医药的对外交流和外贸的发展。这一时期，医药人才辈出，据有关资料的统计，中医药著作多达 100 种以上，其中最著名的是李时珍编著的《本草纲目》。该书集我国历代本草之大成，载药 1892 种，其中新增药 374 种；附药图 1109 幅，附方 11096 首，剂型 40 余种。本书对中药商品质量与产地、水土、采收时节的关系也有精辟的论述，谓："性从地变，质与物迁……沧卤能盐，阿井能胶""生产有南北，节气有早迟，根苗异采收。"《本草纲目》还记载了当时新进口的药物，如曼陀罗、番木鳖、阿芙蓉等。这些记载都为中药商品学的形成和发展积累了丰富的资料。明代的中药药铺业发展也很快，如山西的文盛号药铺、广州的陈李济药铺规模均较大，享誉全国。全国药材交流市场初步形成，首先在药业发达的河南禹州出现，以后有百泉、祁州、樟树等药市形成，除上述四大药市外，还有河南马山口药市和云南大理药市等。

In Ming and Qing Dynasties (1369-1911), especially in Ming Dynasty, Zheng He was ordered ten times to lead ships down to southeast Asia, established diplomatic and trade relations with the countries he visited, opened up the sea passage between China and foreign countries, promoted and expanded the foreign exchange and trade development of medicine. During this period, there sprang up a galaxy of medical talents. According to the statistics of relevant documents, there were up to 100 kinds of TCM works, the most famous of which was *Compendium of Materia Medica* compiled by Li Shizhen. It contains 1, 892 kinds of CMM, including 374 kinds of new ones, 1,109 illustrations, 11, 096 prescriptions and more than 40 kinds of dosage forms. This book also has an incisive discussion on the relationship between the quality of CMMCs and the producing areas, soil and water, and harvest season, which says: "nature varies from place to place, quality changes from material to material...the brine in Cangzhou can be used to produce salt, while the well in E Jiao can be used to boil E Jiao " "There are North and South production, early and late solar terms, and different harvest of roots and seedlings". *Compendium of Materia Medica* also records the newly imported medicinals at that time, namely Man Tuo Luo, Fan mubie, and Afurong etc., which have accumulated rich data for the formation and development of CMMC. The development of Chinese materia medica pharmacy in Ming Dynasty was also very fast, such as Wenshenghao pharmacy in Shanxi Province, and Chenliji pharmacy in Guangzhou, both of which had a large scale and were well-known all over the country. The national exchange market for medicinal materials was initially formed, first in Yuzhou of Henan Province, where the pharmaceutical industry developed well, and then in Baiquan, Qizhou, Zhangshu and other pharmaceutical cities. In addition to the above four pharmaceutical cities, there were also Mashankou pharmaceutical city in Henan Province and Dali pharmaceutical city in Yunnan Province and so on.

继明代李时珍的《本草纲目》之后，清代赵学敏对民间药物也进行了广泛地收集和整理，编著了《本草纲目拾遗》，新增药物达 716 种之多，极大地丰富了我国传统的药学宝库。书中又记载了新进口的药物如番红花、丁香油、金鸡纳、西洋参等，并收载了浙贝母、川姜、银柴胡等新增的道地药材。这些记载都反映了中药贸易的发展。此时期中药商业的规模更加扩大，出现了区域性、垄断式的药品经营组织"十三邦"。在此基础上，形成了一批全国性的中药集散地，规模较大的有河北祁州（安国）、河南百泉（辉县）、江西樟树（清江市）、安徽亳州等地。随着交通的发达，中药市场不断繁荣，中药商品的经营方式出现了多样化。有主要经营帮货和道地药材的

"生药行"、既销药材又售饮片的"拆货棚"、专营饮片的"片子棚"、经营炮制品和中成药的"熟药行"、专门生产和销售中成药的"成药业"等，流通渠道多样，信息网络广泛。随着海上航道的开通，我国与东南亚及欧美等国的中药贸易也日趋频繁。

After Li Shizhen's *Compendium of Materia Medica* in the Ming Dynasty, Zhao Xuemin in Qing Dynasty extensively collected and sorted out folk medicines and compiled *Supplement to the Compendium of Materia Medica*. There were 716 new medicinals added in this book, which greatly enriched the traditional pharmaceutical treasure house of Chinese medicine. This book also recorded the newly imported drugs, such as Fanhonghua, oil of Dingxiang, Jinjina, Xiyangshen, and collected the new authentic materials, namely Zhebeimu, Chuanjiang, Yinchaihu, etc. These records reflected the development of CMM trade. At this time, the scale of CMM business became larger, and the regional and monopolistic medicinal trade organization "thirteen group" appeared. On this basis, a number of national CMM distribution centers have been formed, including Qizhou (Anguo) of Hebei, Baiquan (Huixian) of Henan, Zhangshu (Qingjiang) of Jiangxi, and Bozhou of Anhui, etc. With the development of transportation and the prosperity of CMM market, the management of CMMCs has diversified. There were "crude medicinal material shop" mainly engaged in authentic medicinal materials, "detachable shop" which sold both medicinal materials and decocting pieces, "pieces shop" which specialized in pieces of decoction, "prepared medicinal shop" which dealt in processed products and Chinese patent medicines, "patent medicine shop" which specialized in the production and sale of Chinese patent medicines, etc. During this period, there were various channels of commercial circulation of CMM and extensive information networks. With the opening of sea channel, the trade of CMM between China and Southeast Asia, Europe and America had been more and more frequent.

鸦片战争后，西方教会在我国沿海和内地城市纷纷建立医院和诊所，从清末起，中国药业已不是中药业的一统天下，萌芽的西药业以近代医学和科技为基础，显露出蓬勃的生机。

After the Opium War, Western churches set up hospitals and clinics in coastal and inland cities. Since the end of the Qing Dynasty, Chinese pharmaceutical industry did not dominate the whole country any longer. The burgeoning western pharmaceutical industry, based on modern medicine, science and technology, has shown vigorous vitality.

民国元年（1912年1月），北洋政府颁布《医学教育规程》，将中医药教育拒之门外，西医药业借此迅速发展，给传统的中医药业带来了巨大的冲击和挑战。中国药业从此形成两种不同科学体系药业并存的局面，共同占有中国市场。但是民国时期的中国药业，从药业户数、从业人数、地域布点、出口贸易和经营效益等方面看，中药业仍占主导地位。中药经营性商号在清末的基础上有所发展，如天津的达仁堂、北京的同仁堂在全国各大城市建立了分号；具有一定规模的药市如河北的安国、江西的樟树、安徽的亳州等都有所发展；广大农村及中小城市主要使用的药物，仍是中药行业提供的传统中药。

In the first year of the Republic of China (January 1912), the Beiyang government promulgated the medical education regulations, which excluded the education of Chinese medicine. The western medicine industry took this opportunity to develop rapidly, which brought great impact and challenges to the CMM industry. Since then, China's pharmaceutical industry had formed a situation in which two different scientific medical systems coexisted and jointly occupied the Chinese market. However, in this period of the Republic of China, the Chinese pharmaceutical industry still dominated in terms of the number of business users and employees, geographical distribution, export trade and operating efficiency. Based on the late Qing Dynasty, CMM business firms developed, such as Daren Drugstore in Tianjin and Tongren Drugstore in Beijing, which established sub branches in the major cities of the country; drug markets with certain scale, such as Anguo in Hebei, Zhangshu in Jiangxi and Bozhou in Anhui, all developed to some extent. The medicinals mainly used in rural areas, small and medium-sized cities are still CMM provided by the CMM industry.

中华人民共和国成立后，国家成立了专门的中药机构和医药行政管理部门，对中药商品的产、供、销实行统一管理。中药生产、经营企业遍及全国。形成了一批全国性的现代大型中药交易市场，并定期召开中药商品交易大会。在计划经济时期，中药的生产、加工、销售均在国家商业机构和医药行政管理部门监管下进行，按需定量、计划生产、统一调拨。改革开放后的市场经济时期，在国家药品监督管理部门管理下，依据药品管理法，中药商品主要根据市场需求和经济规律调控生产、购销和使用。市场经济给中药商品带来了活力，有力地推进了中药现代化和国际化的发展进程。我国的中药商品在长期的发展过程中，积累了丰富的商品知识经验，为中药商品学的形成奠定了坚实的基础。

After the founding of The People's Republic of China, the state had established a special organization and the administrative department for CMM to exercise unified management over the production, supply and sale of CMMCs. By then, CMM production and enterprises were all over the country. A number of national modern large-scale CMM trading markets had been formed, and regular CMMCs trading conferences had been held. In the period of planned economy, the production, processing and sales of CMM were all supervised by the state commercial institutions and the pharmaceutical administrative departments, on-demand quantity, planned production and unified allocation. In the period of market economy after the reform and opening up, under the administration of the State Drug Administration and according to the drug administration law, the production, purchase, sale and use of CMMCs were mainly regulated based on the market demand and economic laws. The market economy had brought vitality to the CMMCs and effectively promoted the modernization and internationalization of CMM. In the long-term development of CMMCs, we had accumulated rich commodities knowledge and experience, which has laid a solid foundation for the formation of CMMC.

20 世纪 60 年代中期，我国中等中医药学校最早开设了《中药材商品学》课程。1965 年，原商业部据全国中药商业工作和中药商品技术人员培养的需要，责成四川省中药学校编写了《中药商品学》教材。自此《中药商品学》教材不断推陈出新，促进了中药商品学学科的建设与发展。进入 21 世纪，全国大部分高等中医药院校均开设了《中药商品学》课程。《中药商品学》课程的开设，对于培养中医药商业高层次人才，发展中药商品学学科和中医药贸易经营管理事业，具有十分重要的意义。

In the mid-1960s, the secondary specialized school of Chinese medicine in China first set up the course of CMMC. In 1965, the Ministry of Commerce invited Sichuan secondary specialized school of CMM to compile the textbook of "Chinese Materia Medica Commoditology" according to the needs of the national Chinese medicine commercial work and the cultivation of CMMC technicians. Since then, the textbook of "Chinese Materia Medica Commoditology" has been constantly innovating and promoting the construction and development of the discipline of CMMC. In the 21st century, most colleges and universities of Chinese medicine have set up the course of Chinese materia medica commoditology. It is of great significance to the cultivation of high-level talents of Chinese medicine business, the development of the discipline and the management of Chinese medicine trade.

重点小结
Key points

绪论	中药商品学定义	中药商品学是一门以研究中药商品质量和经营为中心内容的应用学科
	中药商品学的研究范围	中药商品在流通领域中的来源、产地、购销、贮存、商品规格、商品质量及经营管理规律
	中药商品学的研究目的	促进中药商品的生产、经营、管理和发展，保证中药商品安全有效，提高人民的健康水平
	中药商品学任务	1. 研究和掌握中药商品的流通、经营和管理规律，构建现代中药商品体系 2. 制订和完善中药商品规格、等级标准 3. 研究中药商品的价值规律，制订合理的价格 4. 加强中药市场的调查与预测，积极推进现代中药商品贸易

Introduction	The definition of CMMC	It is an applied discipline which focuses on the study of the quality and management of CMMCs
	The scope of CMMC	The place of origin, producing areas, purchase and sale, storage, commodities specification, commodities quality and management rules of CMMCs in the field of circulation
	The Research Purpose of CMMC	To promote the production, management and development of CMMCs, ensure the safety and effectiveness of it, and improve the health level of the people
	The task of CMMC	1. To study and master the law of circulation, operation and management of CMMCs, and to build a modern commodities system of CMMs 2. To formulate and improve the specifications and grade standards of CMMs 3. To study the law of value of CMMs and make reasonable price 4. To strengthen the investigation and forecast of CMM market and actively promote the trade of modern CMMs

目标检测
Object detection

一、填空题（Fill in the blanks）

1. 中药商品学是一门以研究________和________为中心内容的应用学科。

Chinese materia medica commoditology(CMMC) is an applied discipline which focuses on the study of the ______________ and ________________of CMMCs.

2. 中药商品学是在继承中药商品传统________和________经验的基础上，以商品学的理论与方法为指导，运用现代科学技术研究中药商品在流通领域中的来源、产地、________、________、________、商品质量及__________，从而促进中药商品的生产、经营、管理和发展，保证中药商品安全有效，提高人民的健康水平。

Inheriting from the traditional ________________and ______________of CMM, and guided by the theory and method of commodities science, CMMC uses modern science and technology to study the place of origin, producing areas, ________________, ________________, ________________, commodities quality and ________________of CMMCs in the field of circulation. Through these means, CMMC was able to promote the production, management and development of CMMCs, ensure the safety and effectiveness of CMMCs, and improve the health level of the people.

3. 中药是指在________和________指导下用于________的药物总称，包括中药材、中药饮片和中成药，以及中药提取物等类型。

Chinese materia medica (CMM) refers to the general name of drugs used for the ________________ under the guidance of ________________ and ________________, including Chinese medicinal material, Chinese decocting pieces, Chinese patent medicine, as well as CMM extract and so on.

4. 中药材是取自天然的________的原料药，简称“药材”，按其来源可分为植物药、动物药和矿物药三大类。

CMM is a kind of raw material medicine which is taken from natural and ________________, which is abbreviated as “medicinal material”. According to its source, CMM can be divided into three categories: plant, animal and mineral medicinal materials.

5. 中药商品学研究范围包括中药商品在流通领域中的________、产地、________、______、________、________及经营管理规律。

The scope of CMMC includes ________________, producing areas, ________________, ______________, ________________, ________________ and management rules of CMMCs in the field of circulation.

6. 首次记载了火试、对光试等中药商品鉴别方法的是梁代陶弘景编著的__________。

For the first time, the identification methods of CMM such as fire test and light test were recorded in the book of________, which was written by Tao Hongjing in Liang Dynasty.

二、选择题（Choice question）

1. 以下属于中药商品学任务的有（　　）

A. 研究和掌握中药商品的流通、经营和管理规律，构建现代中药商品体系

B. 制订和完善中药商品规格、等级标准

C. 研究中药商品的价值规律，制订合理的价格

D. 加强中药市场的调查与预测，积极推进现代中药商品贸易

E. 以上都不是

Which of the followings belongs to the task of CMMC（　　）

A. To study and master the law of circulation, operation and management of CMMCs, and to build a modern commodities system of CMMCs.

B. To formulate and improve the specifications and grade standards of CMMCs.

C. To study the law of value of CMMCs and make reasonable price.

D. To strengthen the investigation and forecast of CMM market and actively promote the modern trade of CMMCs.

E. None of this.

2. 中药商品学研究目的有（　　）
   A. 促进中药商品的生产、经营、管理和发展
   B. 保证中药商品安全有效
   C. 提高人民的健康水平
   D. 鉴别中药的真伪优劣
   E. 以上都是
   Which of the followings belong to the research purpose of CMMC（　　）
   A. To promote the production, management and development of CMMCs
   B. To ensure the safety and effectiveness of CMMCs
   C. To improve the health level of the people
   D. To identify the authenticity of CMM
   E. All above
3. 中药商品的经营活动都直接或间接地与医疗卫生领域相关，下面表述中正确的是（　　）
   A. 中药商品的社会效益重于经济效益
   B. 中药商品也是商品，所以其经济效益重于一切
   C. 药品经营的品种、数量和价格取决于临床需要
   D. 中药商品的生产和储备需要在医疗和保健需求信息的指导下进行
   E. 以上都是
   The business activities of CMMCs are directly or indirectly related to the field of medical and health care. Which of the following statements are correct（　　）
   A. For the CMMCs, social benefits are more important than economic benefits.
   B. CMMCs is also commodities, so its economic benefits are more important than all
   C. The variety, quantity and price of CMM are determined by clinical needs.
   D. The production and storage of CMMCs need to be conducted under the guidance of medical and health care demand information.
   E. All above
4. 以下属于中药商品特点的有（　　）
   A. 质量特点
   B. 经营特点
   C. 来源特点
   D. 生产特点
   E. “道地”特点
   Which of the followings are the characteristics of CMMCs（　　）
   A. Quality characteristics
   B. Management characteristics
   C. Source characteristics
   D. Production characteristics
   E. Characteristics of “authenticity”

第二章　中药资源

Chapter 2　Resources of Chinese Medicinal Materials

学习目标 | Learning Targets

知识要求：

1. 掌握　中药资源、道地药材的概念。

2. 熟悉　道地药材的分类和中成药的概况。

3. 了解　成方资源。

能力要求：

1. 学会区分中药资源、道地药材；

2. 熟悉道地药材的分类和中成药的概况。

Knowledge requirements:

1. Proficiency　The concept of resources of Chinese medicinal materials and authentic medicinal materials.

2. Familiarity　The classification of authentic medicinal materials and the overview of Chinese patent medicines.

3. Understanding　Set prescription resources.

Skill requirements:

1. Learn to distinguish between resources of Chinese medicinal materials and authentic medicinal materials.

2. To be familiar with the classification of authentic medicinal materials and the overview of Chinese patent medicines.

中药资源是指在一定时间、空间（一定地区或范围内）、人文背景和经济技术条件下分布的各种药用植物、药用动物、药用矿物及其蕴藏量的总和。我国历史悠久，土地辽阔，地跨寒、温、热三带，受第四纪冰川影响较小，地形错综复杂，气候、土壤条件多种多样。从东部的沿海之滨到西部的帕米尔高原，从南部炎热的南海诸岛到北部寒冷的黑龙江，从高山到平原，从陆地到江河湖海，都蕴藏着极为丰富的中药资源，其种类之多、贮量之大，均为世界之冠。根据我国第三次中药资源普查（1983~1988 年）显示，我国中药资源（包括民族药和民间药）有 12807 种，其中，植物药 11146 种，动物药 1581 种，矿物药 80 种。2017 年正式启动第四次全国中药资源普查，截至 2019 年 8 月，共获得全国近 1.3 万种野生药用资源、500 多种栽培药材、1600 多种市场流通药材、563 种《中国药典》收载药材的种类、分布、蕴藏量信息。

Resources of Chinese medicinal materials refer to the total amount of various medicinal plants, medicinal animals, medicinal minerals and their reserves which distributed in a certain time, space (a certain region or scope), cultural background and economic and technological conditions. China has a long history and stretches across vast area covering the cold, temperate and tropical three zones, less affected by quaternary glaciers with complex topography and diverse climate and soil conditions. From the coastal areas in the east to the Pamirs plateau in the west, from the hot Nanhai islands in the south to the cold Heilongjiang Province in the north, from the mountains to the plains, from the land to the rivers, lakes and seas, there are all extremely rich resources of Chinese medicinal materials, which is the largest in the world. According to the third national census of resources of Chinese medicinal materials(1983-1988), there are 12,807 kinds of resources of Chinese medicinal materials (including ethnic medicines and folk medicines), among which 11,146 are plant-based medicines, 1,581 are animal-based medicines and 80 are mineral-based medicines. Information had been obtained by August 2019, which include the types, distribution and reserves of nearly 13,000 wild medicinal resources, more than 500 cultivated medicinal materials, more than 1,600 medicinal materials in circulation, and 563 medicinal materials recorded in the Chinese pharmacopoeia, since the fourth Chinese Materia Medica (CMM) Resources Investigation was officially launched in 2017.

第一节 药材资源与道地药材

Section 1 Medicinal Materials Resources and Authentic Medicinal Materials

PPT

药材资源是指经过简单产地加工的中药原料及其蕴藏量的总和，包括植物药、动物药、矿物药三大类。药材资源是中药资源的基础，是中药饮片、中成药与中药提取物的源泉。

Medicinal materials resources refer to the total amount and their reserves of raw materials of Chinese medicine simply processed in producing areas, including plant-based medicines, animal-based medicines and mineral-based medicines. The medicinal materials resources are the basis of the resources of Chinese medicinal materials, and are the source of the Chinese decocting pieces, the Chinese patent medicines and the Chinese medicine extracts.

道地药材是药材资源的重要组成部分，药材资源与道地药材有着极为密切的关系。道地药材是具有中国特色、根植于中医药理论体系、来源于生产和用药实践、世所公认的特定产区的名优正品药材的代名词。

Authentic medicinal materials are an important part of the medicinal materials resources, which are closely related to each other. Authentic medicinal materials are synonymous with the best quality and quality medicinal materials from specific area with Chinese characteristics, rooted in the theoretical system of Chinese medicine, derived from production and drug use practice, and recognized by the world.

药材资源的开发利用和保护，可以更好发展道地药材和开发出更多更好的新型中成药，保证中药饮片供应临床配方的需要。

With the development, utilization and protection of medicinal materials resources, authentic medicinal materials, as well as more and better new Chinese patent medicines, can be well developed so as to ensure the supply of Chinese decocting pieces for clinical formulations.

一、药材资源

I. Medicinal material resources

目前市场流通的常用药材1200余种。药材资源按生产方式和来源不同，分为野生资源和家种养殖资源两大类。这两类资源大多数属于可再生资源，只要管理、保护得好，可循环开发，永续利用。

At present, there are more than 1,200 kinds of common medicinal materials in circulation. According to different production methods and sources, medicinal materials resources are divided into wild resources and cultured or planted medicinal material resources. Most of these two types of resources belong to renewable resources. As long as they are well managed and protected, they can be developed in a circular way and used sustainably.

（一）野生资源

(I) Wild medicinal material resources

野生资源又叫天然资源，是药材资源的重要组成部分，其品种占药材资源总数的80%，产量占总产量的60%，如冬虫夏草、麻黄、羌活等药材多属野生资源，其中不少是有名的道地药材。

Wild medicinal material resources, also known as natural resources, are an important part of the medicinal materials resources, which account for 80% of the total medicinal materials resources and 60% of the total production, such as Dongchongxiacao, Mahuang, Qianghuo and most of them are famous authentic medicinal materials.

随着医疗保健事业的发展，野生资源日益减少，不能完全满足市场需要。国家为了解决中药供需矛盾，一方面制订药源开发利用和保护计划；另一方面组织了几次全国性的大普查，加强了药源开发利用的研究，以寻求新药源。以前一贯依靠进口的马钱子、胡黄连、安息香、血竭、阿魏等也分别在云南、西藏、广西、广东、海南、新疆、内蒙古等省区发现了国产资源，有的已引种成功，并已开发利用，提供了商品，摆脱了全依赖进口的局面。

With the development of medical and health care, wild resources are decreasing day by day and cannot completely meet the needs of the market. To solve the contradiction between supply and demand of CMM, the government made plans for the exploitation, utilization and protection of medicinal sources on one hand, and organized several CMM Resources Investigation to strengthen the research on the development and utilization of medicinal sources so as to seek for new medicinal sources on the other hand. Some natural resources previously dependent on imports, such as Maqianzi, Huhuanglian, Anxixiang, Xuejie, Awei have also been found in Yunnan, Tibet, Guangxi, Guangdong, Hainan, Xinjiang provinces and Inner Mongolia autonomous region. Some of them have been introduced successfully, and have been developed and utilized, also can provide commodities and then get rid of the situation of total dependence on imports.

通过药源普查和开发利用研究，部分紧缺药材商品找到了基原相近、功效相似的新药源，保证了市场供应。如冬虫夏草，通过调查研究，在湖南发现的亚香棒虫草 *Cordyceps hawkesii*（BerK.）Sacc.，四川发现的凉山虫草 *Cordyceps liangshanensis* Zang, Hu et Liu 的主要成分、药理作用、功效与正品冬虫夏草 *Cordyceps sinensis*（BerK.）Sacc. 相似，分别在湖南、四川以亚香棒虫草和凉山虫草药用。

Through resources investigation and research on development and utilization, some new medicinal sources with similar bases and similar functions were found for the replacement of those scarce medicinal materials, which ensured the market supply. For example, *Cordyceps* hawkesii (BerK.) Sacc. found in Hunan, and *Cordyceps liangshanensis* Zang Hu et Liu found in Sichuan, are used as medicinals because of similarity to the authentic *Cordyceps sinensis* (BerK.) Sacc. in main ingredients, pharmacological actions and effect.

（二）家种养殖资源

（II）Cultured and planted medicinal material resources

我国家种养殖药用动植物已有几千年的历史，近几十年来，为了发展药材商品生产，进一步扩大了家种家养的面积和场所，目前全国家种养殖药材多为大宗药材，如三七、茯苓、天麻、鹿茸、珍珠等。这些药材除内销外，还出口外销，为国家积累了不少资金。家种养殖资源对保护和增加药源，保证市场供应，发展农村经济都起到了积极作用。

With a history of several thousand years in planting medicinal plants and breeding animals, China has expanded the area and place of breeding and planting in recent decades in order to develop medicinal material commodity production. At present, most of cultured and planted medicinal materials are bulk medicinal materials, namely Sanqi, Fuling, Tianma, Lurong, Zhenzhu etc. These medicinal materials are not only sold domestically, but also exported, which has accumulated a lot of funds for the state. The resources of cultured and planted medicinal materials play a positive role in protecting and increasing the sources of medicine, ensuring market supply and developing rural economy.

多年来，由于资源的利用，一些野生药材资源濒临枯竭，有些品种由野生资源为主转向了栽培品为主，加之可能受无序引种，过量施肥施药，使用植物生长激素等促进药材高产以及不规范的采收加工等诸多因素影响。在这期间中药材商品规格也发生了较大的变化，导致药材性状与质量均发生了较大的改变，我们应引起重视。

Over the years, due to the utilization of resources, some wild medicinal materials resources are on the verge of exhaustion, and some varieties have turned from wild resources to cultivated products, which may be affected by some factors such as disordered introduction, excessive application of fertilizers, the use of plant growth hormone to promote the high yield of medicinal materials, non-standard harvesting and processing. During this period, the commercial specifications of Chinese medicinal materials also changed greatly, resulting in great changes in the characters and quality of medicinal materials, and thereby we should pay attention to it.

二、道地药材

II. Authentic medicinal materials

（一）道地药材的含义

（I）Definition of authentic medicinal materials

《中华人民共和国中医药法》第二十三条明确指出道地中药材是经过中医临床长期应用优选出来的产在特定地域，与其他地区所产同种中药材相比，品质和疗效更好，且质量稳定，具有较高知名度的中药材。历史形成的道地药材约 200 余种。

It is clearly stated in the 23rd article of *Law of the People's Republic of China on Traditional Chinese Medicine* that the authentic medicinal materials which are optimized from long-term clinical application of Chinese medicine and produced in specific regions have better quality and curative effect, stable quality and high popularity, compared with the same Chinese medicinal materials produced in other regions. There are more than 200 kinds of authentic medicinal materials formed in history.

（二）道地药材的形成进展

(II) Formation progress of authentic medicinal materials

成书于东汉时期的《神农本草经》所收载的365味药物中，不少从药名上就带有道地性，如巴戟天、蜀椒、秦艽、秦皮、吴茱萸、代赭石等。巴、蜀、秦、吴、代都是周朝前后的古国地名，间接地界定了这些药物的道地产地。同时代的专著《伤寒论》是医方中最早应用道地药材较多的医书，巴豆、代赭石、阿胶等道地药材被广泛应用。

Among the 365 medicines collected in *Shen Nong Ben Cao Jing* in the Eastern Han Dynasty, many of them were authentic in name, namely Bajitian, Shujiao, Qinjiao, Qinpi, Wuzhuyu, Daizheshi etc. Ba, Shu, Qin, Wu and Dai were all names for ancient countries before and after Zhou Dynasty, which indirectly defined the origin of these medicines. The contemporary monograph treatise *Shang Han Lun* was the earliest medical book in which more authentic medicinal materials, namely Badou, Daizheshi and Ejiao were widely used.

南北朝时期陶弘景所著《本草经集注》中谓"诸药所生，皆有境界……多出近道，气力性理，不及本邦，所以疗病不及往人，亦当缘此故也。蜀药及北药，虽有去来，亦复非精者……上党人参，始不复售。华阴细辛，弃之如芥。"该书在前人的基础上，进一步论述了药物道地性的重要性，第一次阐述了道地药材与非道地药材对临床疗效的影响，对60余种中药的道地性用"第一""最佳""为佳"等加以描述。

It says that "all kinds of medicines have their own origin... most are from nearby, whose flavour and nature is not as good as those from the origin, so the treatment is superior to that in the past.Shu medicines and Bei medicines are not the best in quality although in circulation, Renshen from Shangdang is no longer sold. Xixin from Huayin is discarded like mustard." in *Ben Cao Jing Ji Zhu*, compiled by Tao Hongjing in NanBei Dynasty. On the basis of predecessors, it further discussed the importance of the authenticity of medicinals, expounded the influence of authentic medicinal materials and non-authentic medicinal materials on clinical efficacy for the first time, and described the authenticity of more than 60 kinds of Chinese medicinals with the words "the first" "the best" " better" and so on in this book.

隋唐时代更加重视道地药材的研究。《新修本草》中谓："离其本土，则质同而效异。"《千金翼方》中，最先按当时行政区划的"道"来归纳药材的产地，特别强调"用药必依土地"，这些为道地药材的研究奠定了基础。

More attention is paid to the study of authentic medicinal materials in Sui and Tang dynasties. *Xin Xiu Ben Cao* says "the same species have different effect if away from its native place." In *Qian Jin Yi Fang*, the origin of medicinal materials was first summarized according to the "dao" of administrative division at that time, with special emphasis on "the use of medicine must be based on the land", which laid the foundation for the study of authentic medicinal materials.

宋元时代的医药学家在前人基础上对药材的道地性从理论上加以阐述，有了进一步的研究。《证类本草》中附图的图题都冠以产地名称，如"神州半夏""银州柴胡"等。《本草衍义》谓："凡用药必须择州土所宜，则药力具，用之有据。"《用药法象》谓："凡诸草木昆虫，产之有地，失其地则性味少异"。

In the Song and Yuan dynasties, pharmacists theoretically expounded the authenticity of medicinal materials on the basis of predecessors and made further research. The title of the attached pictures in the book are named after the origin, such as "Shenzhou Banxia" and "Yinzhou Chaihu" in *Zheng Lei Ben*

Cao. *Ben Cao Yan Yi* says: "the use of medicinals must choose the appropriate state soil, so the effect is good and use on good grounds." *Yong Yao Fa Xiang* says: "all plants and insects have their producing areas, and the loss of authentic area, will make the flavor and nature weak".

明清时代对道地药材的研究更深入。《本草品汇精要》收载的药物中269种有明确道地优劣记载，其中川药32种，广药27种，怀药8种。《本草蒙筌》谓："各有相宜产地，气味功力自异寻常……一方土地出一方药也。"《本草纲目》谓："性从地变，质以物迁……沧卤能盐，阿井能胶。"许多药物项下记载了其最佳产地，如麦冬强调了以浙中来甚良，薄荷以苏州为胜。《牡丹亭》中首次出现了"道地药材"一词。《药性变迁论》中指出："当时初用之始，必有所产之地，此乃本身之土，故气厚而力全。以后移种他方，则地气移而薄矣。"到这一时期，对道地药材的研究基本形成了其理论体系并贯穿于整个中医药的生产、流通、临床用药中。

In Ming and Qing dynasties, the research on authentic medicinal materials was more in-depth. The pros and cons of 269 medicinals are clearly recorded in *Ben Cao Pin Hui Jing Yao*, including 32 Chuan medicines, 27 Guang medicines and 8 Huai medicines. *Ben Cao Meng Quan* says:"each has its own appropriate producing area, and its own unique flavor and nature... A special land produces a unique drug." *Ben Cao Gang Mu* says: "nature can change with land, quality can change with medicinal...... salt can be made from Canglu, Ejiao can be made from Ejing." The best place of producing area has been recorded in each entry of medicinals. For example, it is emphasized that Maidong from central Zhejiang and Bohe from Suzhou are better. The word "authentic medicinal materials" appeared for the first time in *Mu Dan Ting*. It is pointed out in *Yao Xing Bian Qian Lun* that "when it was first used, it must have its own area. Owing to its own native soil, the flavor is strong and the nature is comprehensive. Later, when moved to another place, the nature will become less." By this time, the theoretical system of the research on authentic medicinal materials had been basically formed, and it ran through the whole production, circulation and clinical use of Chinese medicine.

中华人民共和国成立以后，政府高度重视道地药材的研究发展。道地药材受到广大医药学者的推崇，不少学者对道地药材科学性相关问题展开研究。近年来，道地药材的研究与创新取得了一系列成果。

After the founding of new China, the government attached great importance to the research and development of authentic medicinal materials, which are highly respected by the majority of medical scholars, and many scholars have carried out research on the scientific issues related to them. In recent years, a series of achievements have been made in the research and innovation of them.

（三）道地药材的形成因素

(III) Formation factors of authentic medicinal materials

道地药材的形成主要是优良种质资源的选育、适宜生态环境的选择、规范的生产加工、显著的临床疗效等综合作用的结果。

The formation of authentic medicinal materials is mainly the result of the comprehensive effects of the selection and breeding of excellent germplasm resources, the selection of suitable ecological environment, the standardized production and processing, and the significant clinical effect.

1. 优良种质资源的选育

1. Selection and breeding of excellent germplasm resources

中药种质资源多数为野生种，栽培种仅占20%~30%。优良种质资源是道地药材形成的内在基础。道地药材的种质资源是优质的遗传资源，主要包括栽培品种或类型、野生品种和选育的良种等。如东北的人参，其栽培品种从茎果色泽分为紫茎红果、青茎黄果、紫茎黄叶红果；以根形状分为大马牙、二马牙、长脖、圆膀圆茎。其中，大马牙植株高大，茎杆粗壮，人参产量高，被选为主要栽培品种。

Most of the germplasm resources of CMM are wild species, while cultivated species only account for 20%~30%. Excellent germplasm resources are the internal basis for the formation of authentic medicinal materials. The germplasm resources thereof are high quality genetic resources, mainly including cultivated varieties or types, wild varieties and selected varieties. For example, the cultivated varieties of Renshen in northeast China are divided into purple stem red fruit, green stem yellow fruit and purple stem yellow leaf red fruit based on the color of stem and fruit. Based on the shape of the root, it can be divided into "Damaya, Ermaya, Changbo, and Yuanbangyuanjing". Among them, the plant "Damaya" with high height, strong stem and high yield, is chosen as the main cultivar.

物种的优良特性是人们通过长期栽培、养殖、选育和环境条件的影响下逐渐形成的，但内在的遗传特性是重要的因素。建立道地药材种质资源库，将物种优良的遗传物质基因及其本身进行收藏保存，不仅有利于保持道地药材的优良性状，提供丰富的遗传资源和研究材料，而且有利于培育新的优良品种。

The excellent characteristics of species are gradually formed under the influence of long-term cultivation, breeding, seed selection and environmental conditions, but the inherent genetic characteristics are important factors. The establishment of the germplasm resource bank of authentic medicinal materials and the collection and preservation of the excellent genetic material genes of the species as well as themselves are not only conducive to maintaining the excellent characters of authentic medicinal materials, providing abundant genetic resources and research materials, but also conducive to the cultivation of new excellent varieties.

2. 适宜环境的选择

2. Selection of suitable environment

每一种生物与周围环境之间的相互联系，都有其适宜的环境、最佳的环境。环境是影响生物有机体生命、生存与发展的所有外部条件的总体。

Every kind of organism has its own suitable environment and the best environment in relation to its surroundings. Environment is the totality of all external conditions that affect the birth, living and development of organisms.

道地药材的生长、发育、繁殖都离不开生存的环境条件。特定的生态环境条件，是形成道地药材重要的外在因素，中药材对特定的生态环境能够适应，又因其适应特点而产生获得性遗传的种内变异。如著名的广药道地药材阳春砂，系热带、亚热带雨林植物，喜温暖潮湿的气候，适宜生长的温度为22℃~28℃，相对湿度为75%~90%，土壤含水量为25%~35%。忌阳光照晒，苗期荫蔽度以70%~80%为宜，开花结果荫蔽度以50%~60%为宜。对土壤要求不严，多种类型的土壤都能种植。但土层肥沃、疏松、富含腐殖质，保水保肥能力强，pH值为4.8~5.6中性或微酸性的黑色砂质壤土或黏质壤土为佳，适宜生长在一面开阔、三面环山的坡地，广东阳春县为其道地产地。

The growth, development and reproduction of authentic medicinal materials are inseparable from the living environment condition. Specific ecological environment conditions are important external factors for the formation of them. Chinese medicinal materials can adapt to specific ecological environment and produce intraspecific variation of acquired heredity due to its adaptive characteristics. For example, Yangchunsha, a famous authentic medicinal material of Guangdong, is a tropical and subtropical rain forest plant. It likes a warm and humid climate. The temperature suitable for growth is 22℃-28℃, the relative humidity is 75%~90%, and the soil moisture content is 25%~35%, percentage of seedling shade 70%~80%, percentage of flowering and fruit shade 50%~60%, avoiding the sunlight. With no severe limitation of soil requirements, many types of soil can be planted in for Yangchunsha. However, the soil layer is fertile, loose, rich in humus, with strong ability of water and fertilizer conservation. The neutral or slightly acidic black sandy loam or clayey loam with pH value of 4.8~5.6 is the best, which is suitable for growing on a slope with one side open and three sides surrounded by mountains. Yangchun county in Guangdong province is its best production area.

3. 规范的种植和产地加工

3. Standardized planting and origin processing

种植和产地加工主要包括栽培、采收、加工、贮藏和养护等方面。规范的种植及产地加工是道地药材形成的重要技术保障。千百年来，我国人民在道地药材的生产实践中，不断总结道地药材的规范生产加工技术方法。如江油附子的栽培，分为两个阶段：第一阶段选择较高的海拔，气候凉爽的山区栽培乌头以培育栽培附子的种源“乌头”，这一过程称为“乌药生产”；第二阶段将“乌药”运到海拔较低、气候相对温暖、地势平坦、向阳、土层深厚、肥沃、灌溉排水方便的坝区栽培以生产附子，这一过程称为“附子生产”，从选地整地、种植、田间管理、病虫害防治、采收、加工等为附子的生产提供了高产、优质的技术保障。

Planting and processing in producing area mainly include cultivation, harvesting, processing, storage and conservation. Standardized planting and processing are important technical guarantee for the formation of authentic medicinal materials. For thousands of years, Chinese people have been summing up the standardized production and processing methods of authentic medicinal materials in the production practice thereof. For example, the cultivation of Fuzi in Jiangyou can be divided into two stages: in the first stage, which is called “production of Wu medicine”, the higher altitude and the cool mountain area is selected to cultivate the seed origin of Fuzi “Wu Tou”. In the second stage, which is called “ production of Fuzi”, “Wu medicine” is transported to the dam areas, with the low altitude, relatively warm climate, flat terrain, sunny exposure, deep soil layer, fertile soil, easy irrigation and drainage, to cultivate and produce Fuzi, which are applied to the selection of land, planting, field management, pest control, harvesting, processing and so on.

规范的种植和产地加工技术，是影响道地药材的重要因素。因此，我们需要加强对道地药材的规范生产加工技术研究。

The normative technology in planting and processing of producing area is an important factor affecting authentic medicinal materials. Therefore, we need to strengthen the research on the standardization of technology in production and processing of authentic medicinal materials.

4. 显著的临床疗效

4. Significant clinical efficacy

质优效佳是道地药材的标志，临床疗效是判断和评价道地药材品质的最终标准。中药材的“道地”性是古人在中医临床实践中优化筛选出来的。历代中医药学家十分重视道地药材产地与疗效的关系。现代研究也证明，同一种药材，由于产地不同，质量有差异，作用有不同。如不同产地黄芩的抑菌、抗炎、解热和镇静的药效作用研究表明道地产区河北围场（位于承德市北部）所产黄芩其作用较为突出。

High quality and good effect is the mark of authentic medicinal materials, and clinical efficacy is the final standard to judge and evaluate the quality thereof. The “authentic” nature of Chinese medicinal materials was optimized and screened by the ancients in the clinical practice of Chinese medicine.

Chinese medicine scholars in past dynasties attached great importance to the relationship between the producing area and their curative effect of authentic medicinal materials. Modern research has also proved that there are differences in quality and effects due to the different producing area even for the same kind of medicinal materials. For example, studies on effects about the antibacterial, anti-inflammatory, antipyretic and sedative function of Huangqin from different areas indicate that Huangqin from Weichang, Hebei Province (located in the north of Chengde city) has a prominent effect.

（四）道地药材的分类

(Ⅳ) Classification of authentic medicinal materials

历史形成的道地药材分布于全国各地，几乎各省都有。根据各种道地药材分布省区在我国所处的地理位置不同，按照历史习惯形成的分类方法，将道地药材分为以下 10 大类。

The authentic medicinal materials formed in history distributed in different parts of the whole country, almost every province. According to the different geographical location of the distribution of various authentic medicinal materials in China, based on classification method formed from historical habits, the authentic medicinal materials are divided into ten categories as follows :

1. **川药类** 指分布于四川、重庆产区的道地药材。四川道地药材呈明显的区域性和地域性。如有高原地区的川贝母、冬虫夏草、麝香；岷江流域的干姜和川郁金；江油的附子；都江堰的川芎；绵阳的川麦冬；石柱的味连；遂宁的川白芷；合川的使君子和补骨脂；汉源的花椒；中江的丹参和白芍；通江的银耳；天全、乐山金口河的川牛膝。其他还有著名的“三木”药材厚朴、杜仲、川黄柏，以及川乌、川木香、川木通、川射干、川续断、乌梅、半夏、姜黄、独活、莪术、羌活等。

1. Chuan medicines Refer to the authentic medicinal materials distributed in the producing areas of Sichuan and Chongqing. The authentic medicinal materials in Sichuan are characterized for their region, such as Chuanbeimu, Dongchongxiacao, Shexiang in the plateau areas; Ganjiang and Chuanyujin in Minjiang River basin; Fuzi in Jiangyou; Chuanxiong in Dujiangyan; Chuanmaidong in Mianyang, Weilian in Shizhu; Chuanbaizhi in Suining; Shijunzi and Buguzhi in Hechuan; Huajiao in Hanyuan; Danshen and Baishao in Zhongjiang; Yin’er in Tongjiang; Chuanniuxi in Tianquan, Leshan Jinkou River. It also includes famous “three woods” medicinal materials (Houpo, Duzhong, Chuanhuangbo), and Chuanwu, Chuanmuxiang, Chuanmutong, Chuanshegan, Chuanxuduan, Wumei, Banxia, Jianghuang, Duhuo, Ezhu, Qianghuo.

2. **广药类** 指分布于广东、广西、海南产区的道地药材。该产区的主要特点是水、热资源丰富，土壤呈强酸性，适于热带、亚热带动植物的生长。主要道地药材有著名的槟榔、砂仁、巴戟天、益智被称作“四大南药”（和本书的南药概念不一样），珠江流域出产广藿香、高良姜、广防己、化橘红等，桂南一带出产鸡血藤、广豆根、广金钱草、桂莪术、石斛、肉桂等，海南主产槟榔、胡椒等。

2. Guang medicines Refer to the authentic medicinal materials distributed in the producing areas of Guangdong, Guangxi and Hainan. The main characteristics of this region are abundant water and thermal resources, and strong acid soil, suitable for the growth of tropical and subtropical plants and animals. The main authentic medicinal materials are famous Binglang, Sharen, Bajitian, Yizhi known as “four Nan medicines”(it is not the same concept in this book); Guanghuoxiang, Gaoliangjiang, Guangfangji, Huajuhong in the Zhujiang River basin; Jixueteng, Guangdougen, Guangjinqiancao, Gui’e’zhu, Shihu, Rougui in south Guangxi; Binglang and Hujiao in Hainan.

3. **云药类** 指分布于云南、西藏南部包括滇北、滇南和西藏的江南察隅、墨脱等地产区的道地药材。道地药材主要有文山、砚山的三七，滇北的云苓、云木香、冬虫夏草，滇南的诃子、槟榔、儿茶、木蝴蝶，丽江地区的云当归、云龙胆，德钦的云连，麻栗坡的云南马钱，昭通的云天麻等。

3. Yun medicines Refer to the authentic medicinal materials distributed in Yunnan and southern Tibet, including northern and southern of Yunnan, and the producing areas such as Chayu and Motuo in Tibet. Main authentic medicinal materials are Sanqi in Wenshan and Yanshan, Yunling, Yunmuxiang and Dongchongxiacao in northern Yunnan, Hezi, Binglang, Ercha, Muhudie in southern Yunnan, Yundanggui and Yunlongdan in Lijiang District, Yunlian in Deqin, Yunnanmaqian in Malipo, and Yuntianma in Zhaotong.

4. 贵药类 指分布于贵州产区的道地药材。贵州全省冬无严寒、夏无酷暑。贵药主要分布在地形崎岖的高原、山岭、河谷、丘陵和盆地，尤以苗岭、梵净山、大娄山为多。道地药材主要有贵天麻、朱砂（辰砂）、杜仲、吴茱萸、半夏、雄黄、天冬、白及、石斛、艾片、通草、黄精、猪苓、南沙参等。

4. Gui medicines Refer to the authentic medicinal materials distributed in Guizhou producing areas. There is no severe cold in winter nor severe heat in summer in Guizhou. Gui medicines are mainly distributed in the plateau, mountain ridge, valley, hill and basin with rugged terrain, especially in Miaoling, Fanjing mountain and Dalou mountain. The famous authentic medicinal materials are Guitianma, Zhusha, Duzhong, Wuzhuyu, Banxia, Xionghuang, Tiandong, Baiji, Shihu, Ai'pian, Tongcao, Huangjing, Zhuling, Nanshashen, etc.

5. 怀药类 指分布于河南产区的道地药材。“怀”是古代怀庆府的简称，即是指产于怀庆府所管辖的博爱、武陟、孟县、沁阳等地。本书所指的怀药范围稍广，包括了河南的其他道地药材。道地药材主要有著名的“四大怀药”（怀山药、怀牛膝、怀地黄、菊花），新密的密银花，禹州的禹白附、禹白芷，沁阳的怀红花，此外，还有全蝎、辛夷、何首乌、旋覆花、款冬花、千金子、茜草等。

5. Huai medicines Refer to the authentic medicinal materials distributed in Henan producing areas. “Huai” is the abbreviation of the ancient Huaiqing government, that is, the areas in the jurisdiction of the government of Huaiqing including Bo'ai, Wuzhi, Meng county, Qinyang and other places. It refers to a slightly wider range of Huai medicine in this book, including other Henan medicines. Authentic medicinal materials mainly have the famous “four Huai medicines” (Huaishanyao, Huainiuxi, Huaidihuang, Huaijuhua), Miyinhua in Xinmi, Yubaifu and Yubaizhi in Yuzhou; Huaihonghua in Qinyang; in addition, Quanxie, Xinyi, Heshouwu, Xuanfuhua, Kuandonghua, Qianjinzi, Qiancao etc.

6. 浙药类 指分布于浙江产区的道地药材，以产“浙八味”为代表。浙江山多地少，素有“七山一水二分地”之说，地处亚热带。道地药材主要有著名的“浙八味”（杭白术、杭白芍、杭白菊、杭麦冬、浙玄参、浙贝母、温郁金、延胡索），此外还有天台乌药、山茱萸、温厚朴、女贞子、乌梢蛇、白前、前胡、桑叶等。

6. Zhe medicines Refer to the authentic medicinal materials distributed in the producing areas of Zhejiang province, represented by “eight Zhe medicines”. Zhejiang, known as “seven mountains, one water and two lands”, is located in the subtropical zone. The authentic medicinal materials mainly include the famous “eight Zhe medicines” (Hangbaizhu, Hangbaishao, Hangbaiju, Hangmaidong, Zhexuanshen, Zhebeimu, Wenyujin, Yanhusuo), in addition to Wuyao in Tiantai, Shanzhuyu, Wenhoupo, Nüzhenzi, Wushaoshe, Baiqian, Qianhu, Sangye, etc.

7. 关药类 指分布于山海关以北的东三省及内蒙古东部产区的道地药材，以“东北三宝”为代表。道地药材主要有著名的东北三宝（人参、五味子、鹿茸）以及黄柏、关龙胆、关防风、辽细辛、辽藁本、刺五加、升麻、桔梗、蛤蟆油、西洋参等。

7. Guan medicines Refer to the authentic medicinal materials distributed in the three northeast provinces and the eastern producing areas of Inner Mongolia located at the north of Shanhaiguan, represented by "the three treasures of northeast China". The authentic medicinal materials mainly include "the famous three treasures of northeast China"(Renshen, Wuweizi, Lurong), Huangbo, Guanlongdan, Guanfangfeng, Liaoxixin, Liaogaoben, Ciwujia, Shengma, Jiegeng, Hamayou, Xiyangshen, etc.

8. 北药类 指分布于华北大部分省区，包括河北、山东、山西、内蒙中部产区的道地药材。道地药材主要有山西的潞党参、浑源的北黄芪、五灵脂，山东东阿的阿胶、莱阳的北沙参、济南的济银花，河北易县的知母（西陵知母）、酸枣仁、连翘，内蒙中部的麻黄、甘草，此外还有北板蓝根、北柴胡、北葶苈子、黄芩、小茴香、远志等。

8. Bei medicines Refer to the authentic medicinal materials distributed in most provinces and regions of north China, including Hebei, Shandong, Shanxi and central Inner Mongolia. There are many authentic medicinal materials such as Ludangshen, Beihuangqi in Shanxi and Wulingzhi in Hunyuan; Ejiao in Dong'e, Beishashen in Laiyang, Jiyinhua in Jinan from Shandong; Zhimu, Suanzaoren, Lianqiao in Hebei; Mahuang, Gancao in central Inner Mongolia; and Beibanlangen, Beichaihu, Beitinglizi, Huangqin, Xiaohuixiang, Yuanzhi.

9. 西药类 是指分布于西安以西的广大地区，包括陕西、甘肃、宁夏、内蒙古西部、新疆及青藏高原的道地药材，以"西北四大药材"为代表。道地药材主要有著名的西北四大药材（西大黄、岷归、黄芪、西党参），以及陕西的秦艽、秦皮、西茵陈、西天麻、党参，甘肃的岷归、大黄、党参、羌活，宁夏的枸杞子、银柴胡，青海的贝母、冬虫夏草、大黄、羌活、大青盐、硼砂，新疆的阿魏、紫草、伊贝母、甘草、大黄、肉苁蓉、马鹿茸、雪莲花、红花等，内蒙古西南部的黄芪、甘草、麻黄等。

9. Xi medicines Refer to the authentic medicinal materials distributed in the vast west areas of Xi'an, including Shaanxi, Gansu, Ningxia, western Inner Mongolia, Xinjiang and Tibetan Plateau, represented by "four major medicinal materials in the northwest". There are many authentic medicinal materials such as four major medicinal materials in the northwest (Dahuang, Mingui, Huangqi, Xidangshen, as well as Qinjiao, Qinpi, Xiyinchen, Xitianma, Dangsheng in Shaanxi; Mingui, Dahuang, Dangshen, Qianghuo in Gansu; Gouqizi and Yinchaihu in Ningxia, Beimu, Dongchongxiacao, Dahuang, Qianghuo, Daqingyan, Pengsha in Qinghai; A'wei, Zicao, Yibeimu, Gancao, Dahuang, Roucongrong, Malurong, Xuelianhua, Honghua in Xinjiang; Huangqi, Gancao, Mahuang in southwest of Inner Mongolia.

10. 南药类 是指分布于长江以南的湖南、湖北、江苏、安徽、江西、福建、台湾等省区的道地药材，即长江以南除川、广、云、贵、浙药产区以外均属于"南药"。道地药材主要有安徽铜陵的凤丹皮、亳州的亳菊、亳白芷、亳芍、亳桑白皮、滁州的滁菊花、黄山歙县的贡菊、宣城的宣木瓜、霍山的石斛等，江苏的苏薄荷、苏枳壳、茅山的茅苍术、太子参、蟾酥等，福建的建泽泻、建曲、建乌梅、建青黛、蕲蛇，江西樟树的江枳壳、宜春的江香薷、丰城的鸡血藤、泰和的乌鸡，湖北大别山的茯苓、应城的石膏、板桥党参、江汉平原的龟甲、鳖甲、鄂西的味连和厚朴，湖南平江白术、沅江的枳壳、邵东的湘玉竹、湘乡的木瓜，零陵薄荷、零陵香、湘红莲等，台湾地区的樟脑、槟榔、胡椒等。

10. Nan medicines Refer to the authentic medicinal materials distributed in Hunan, Hubei, Jiangsu, Anhui, Jiangxi, Fujian, Taiwan and other provinces in the south of the Yangtze River, namely

"Nan medicine" except the producing areas of Sichuan and Guangdong, Guangxi, Yunnan, Guizhou and Zhejiang. There are many authentic medicinal materials such as Fengdanpi in Tongling, Boju, Bobaizhi, Bobaishao, Bosangbaipi in Bozhou, Chuju in Chuzhou, Gongju in Shexian of Huangshan, Xuanmugua in Xuancheng, and Shihu in Huoshan in Anhui; Subohe, Suzhiqiao, Maocangzhu, Taizishen, Chansu in Maoshan in Jiangsu; Jianzexie, Jianqu, Jianwumei, Jianqingdai, Qishe in Fujian; Jiangzhiqiao in Zhangshu, Jiangxiangru in Yichun, Jixueteng in Fengcheng, Wuji in Taihe in Jiangxi; Fuling in Dabieshan, Shigao in Yingcheng, Dangshen in Banqiao, Guijia and Biejia in Jianghan plain. Weilian and Houpo in Exi in Hubei; Baizhu in Pingjiang, Zhiqiao in Yuanjiang, Yuzhu in Shaodong, Mugua in Xiangxiang, Bohe in Lingling, Linglingxiang, Xianghonglian in Hunan; Zhangnao, Binglang and Hujiao in Taiwan.

第二节　成方资源与中成药

Section 2　Set prescription resources and Chinese patent medicine

PPT

一、成方资源

I. Set prescription resources

成方是指现成的处方，一般来源于历代方书著作和民间单方、验方及秘方。中成药的生产必须按照一定的处方规定，这样成方就成了中成药生产的源泉。这与中药材商品大多来源于天然药源的情况相似，是我国中药资源的重要组成部分，称为成方资源。

Set prescription refers to the ready-made prescription, which is generally derived from the works of ancient prescription books and folk single recipe, proved recipe and secret recipe. The production of Chinese patent medicine must be in accordance with certain prescription regulations, so that set prescription becomes the source of the production of Chinese patent medicine. This is similar to the situation that most of the commodities of Chinese medicinal materials come from natural medicinal sources. It is an important part of the resources of Chinese medicinal materials in China, which is called set prescription resources.

我国中成药的制作生产历史悠久，可追溯到战国时期。在长沙马王堆汉墓中发现的《五十二病方》中，记载医方 283 首，并有丸、散等古老的剂型。在我国现存的第一部医学经典著作《黄帝内经》中，记载 13 个方剂，9 种成药，包括丸、散、膏、丹、酒等剂型。

The manufacturing and producing of Chinese patent medicine in our country has a long history, which can be traced back to the Warring States period. There are 283 prescriptions and ancient dosage forms such as pill and powder recorded in *Wu Shi Er Bing Fang*, which was found in Mawangdui Han Tomb of Changsha. There are 13 prescriptions and 9 kinds of patent medicines, including pill, powder, paste, pellet, medicated wine and other dosage forms, recorded in the first existing medical classic book *Huang Di Nei Jing*.

我国历代的方书著作浩如烟海。从汉代《伤寒论》的 113 方，到唐代《备急千金要方》的 5300 余方，到宋代《太平惠民和剂局方》的 788 方，再到明代《普济方》的 61739 方和《本草纲目》的11096方。1983年出版的《中药制剂汇编》收载实用的成方制剂4000个，剂型30种。1993年出版的《中医方剂大辞典》收载9万余方。历代方书收载的中成药品种繁多，剂型多样，应用广泛。

The works of Chinese prescription books in the past dynasties are as vast as a misty ocean. From 113 prescriptions of *Shang Han Lun* in Han Dynasty, to more than 5,300 prescriptions of *Bei Ji Qian Jing Yao Fang* in Tang Dynasty, to 788 prescriptions of *Tai Ping Hui Min He Ji Ju Fang* in Song Dynasty, to 61,739 prescriptions of *Pu Ji Fang* and 11,096 prescriptions of *Ben Cao Gang Mu* in Ming Dynasty. *Zhong Yao Zhi Ji Hui Bian* published in 1983 contains 4,000 practical prescriptions and 30 dosage forms. *Zhong Yi Fang Ji Da Ci Dian* published in 1993 contains more than 90,000 prescriptions. There are many kinds of Chinese patent medicines, various dosage forms and wide application of the prescription books in the past dynasties.

成方是生产中成药的依据，成方资源是一种不可再生的资源。我国的成方资源经过不断的整理、挖掘与发展，内容极为丰富。随着现代社会的进步、科学技术的发展，以及中医药理论和诊疗技术水平的提高，成方资源的进一步开发利用价值巨大。

Set prescription is the basis for the production of Chinese patent medicine, and the resource thereof is a kind of non-renewable resources. Chinese set prescription resources have been continuously sorted out, excavated and developed, and the content is extremely rich. With the progress of modern society, the development of science and technology, as well as the improvement of the theory of traditional Chinese medicine and the level of diagnosis and treatment technology, the further development and utilization of set prescription resources is of great value.

二、中成药的含义与特点
II. The meaning and characteristics of Chinese patent medicine

中成药是在中医药理论的指导下，以中药饮片为原料，按照规定的处方和标准，采用相应的制备工艺和质量标准，依据病情需要制成具有一定规格剂型，可以直接应用于预防、治疗和保健的中药制剂。中成药有着悠久的历史，近年来其剂型、制备工艺技术、质量标准都得到了较大的发展。中药剂型不但有传统的丸、散、膏、丹等剂型，还包括了片剂、胶囊剂、颗粒剂、注射剂等现代剂型。目前我国现有中成药8000余种，剂型40余种，涉及内、外、妇、儿、骨伤、皮肤、五官等科别。中成药应用广泛，在保障人们健康方面发挥了巨大的作用。

Under the guidance of the theory of traditional Chinese medicine, using Chinese decocting pieces as raw materials, according to the stipulated prescriptions and standards, adopting the correspondent preparation process and quality standards, and making a certain dosage form according to the needs of the disease, Chinese patent medicine is a kind of traditional Chinese medicine preparation which can be directly used in prevention, treatment and healthcare. Chinese patent medicine has a long history, and its dosage form, preparation technology and quality standard have been greatly developed in recent years. Traditional Chinese medicine dosage forms not only have traditional pill, powder, paste, pellet and other dosage forms, but also include tablet, capsule, granule, injection and other modern dosage forms. At present, there are more than 8,000 kinds of Chinese patent medicines and more than 40 kinds of dosage forms in China, involving internal medicine, surgery, gynecology, pediatrics, orthopedics, dermatology, ophthalmology and otorhinolaryngology and other departments. Chinese patent medicine is widely used and plays a gigantic role in protecting the people's health.

中成药是我国传统的特有药品，具有独有的特点。中成药的处方必须符合传统中医药的组方配伍原则，疗效确切，应用广泛；在剂型选择上注重中药功效和疾病性质的相互结合；在生产和管理上与药品相同，有药品监督管理部门的批准文号和生产批号，生产工业化和机械化，产品具有特定的质量标准和准确的质量检测方法，质量稳定，安全有效，贮藏、运输、携带和服用方便；在临床应用中注重中医特色的辨证论治；在商品化方面，中成药产品本身就是一种商品，不仅可以作为医生的处方用药，患者也可以根据自己的医疗经验和中医药常识在非处方药中选购使用。但是，中成药也有不足，主要表现在处方组成和剂型的固定不变上，不能随证加减。

Chinese patent medicine is a specific traditional Chinese medicine with unique characteristics in China. The prescription of Chinese patent medicine must conform to the principles of prescription compatibility of traditional Chinese medicine, definite curative effect and extensive application. In the choice of dosage form, we should pay attention to the mutual combination of the efficacy of traditional Chinese medicine and the nature of disease. In terms of production and management, it is the same as the medicine, with the approval number and production batch number of the drug supervision and administration department, industrialization and mechanization of production, specific quality standards and accurate quality inspection methods, stable quality, safety and effect, convenient storage, transportation, carrying and taking. We should pay attention to Syndrome Differentiation Treatment of TCM characteristics in clinical application. In terms of commercialization, Chinese patent medicine product is a kind of commodity in itself, which can not only be used as a prescription medicine for doctors, but also be purchased on selection by patients in over-the-counter medicine according to their own medical experience and common sense of Chinese medicine. However, Chinese patent medicine also has deficiencies, which mainly manifests in the fixed composition of the prescription and dosage form, and cannot be added or subtracted with the symptoms.

三、中成药商品的分类
III. Classification of Chinese patent medicine commodities

中成药至宋代以前尚未自成体系，自《太平惠民和剂局方》问世以后，中成药才始有专集，有了独立分类方法，分类多以临床各科为纲，以病证为目，便于查找应用。

Chinese patent medicine had not formed its own system until Song Dynasty. Since the publication of *Taiping Huimin Heji Ju Fang*, Chinese patent medicine has begun to have a special collection, with an independent classification method. Most of the classification is based on clinical departments and the purpose of disease syndromes, which is easy to search and apply.

采用按功效分类的方法，便于临床应用，以中成药的主要功效为分类依据，分为解表、泻下、和解、清热、祛暑、温里、补益、安神、开窍、固涩、理气、理血、祛湿、治风等不同种类。

The method of classifying according to efficacy is convenient for clinical application. According to the main efficacy of Chinese patent medicine, it is divided into different kinds, such as relieving the external symptoms, purgation, reconciliation, clearing away heat, dispelling summer heat, warming the interior, tonic, tranquillizer, resuscitation, astringent, regulating qi, regulating blood, removing dampness and expelling wind.

近年的中药成药制剂手册，多采用按剂型分类的方法，常见传统的有丸剂、散剂、膏剂、丹剂、露剂、胶剂、酒剂、酊剂等，现代的有片剂、颗粒剂、糖浆剂、注射剂、滴丸剂等许多新剂型。

In recent years, the preparation manual of traditional Chinese medicine mostly adopts the method of classification according to the dosage form. The common traditional dosage forms are pill, powder, plaster, pellet, dew, gelatin, wine, tincture, etc., while the modern ones are the forms of tablet, granule, syrups, injection, dripping pill and many other new dosage forms.

中成药按照临床使用可以分为内科用药、外科用药、妇科用药、儿科用药、五官科用药、骨伤科用药、皮肤科用药等。

Chinese patent medicine can be divided into internal medicine, surgical medicine, gynecological medicine, pediatric medicine, ENT medicine, orthopedic medicine, dermatology medicine, etc.

四、中成药的贮存保管
IV. Storage and preservation of Chinese patent medicine

中成药由于其特殊性，较之化学药物制剂更易于发霉、变质、沉淀、虫蛀等，尤其是合剂、浸膏剂、蜜丸等剂型的中成药不易贮存保管。因此，为了防止变质损失，对于中成药应注意贮存保管方法。中成药的分类贮存保管应注意：

Owing to its distinctiveness, Chinese patent medicine is more prone to mildew, deterioration, precipitation, and insect damage than chemical pharmaceutical preparations, especially the Chinese patent medicine with mistura, extract, honeyed pill and other dosage forms is uneasy to store and preserve. Therefore, in order to prevent the loss of deterioration, we should pay attention to the storage and preservation methods of Chinese patent medicine. Attention should be paid to the classified storage and preservation of Chinese patent medicines:

（1）易生虫中成药：水丸、蜜丸、糊丸、散剂、片剂、颗粒剂如贮存不当容易生虫。这些中成药应贮存在干燥阴凉的库房，库房内的温度不超过 28℃，相对湿度不超过 70%，如温度过高、湿度过大，应及时做好降温吸潮措施。经常做好库房的清洁卫生工作。

Moth-prone Chinese patent medicine: If stored improperly, water-paste pill, honeyed pill, pasted pill, powder, tablet and granule are prone to moth. These Chinese patent medicines should be stored in a dry and cool storehouse, where the temperature should not exceed 28℃ and the relative humidity should not exceed 70%. If the temperature or the humidity is excessive, measures of cooling and absorbing moisture should be taken in time. Always keep the warehouse clean and sanitary.

（2）易发霉中成药：使中成药库内温度以保持在 28℃以下、相对湿度不超过 68% 为宜。要勤加检查，一般以 5~7 天检查一次为宜。

Mildew-prone Chinese patent medicine: It is better to keep the temperature below 28℃ and the relative humidity no more than 68% in the storehouse of Chinese patent medicine. For frequent inspections, it is advisable to inspect once every 5 to 7 days.

（3）易挥发散失气味中成药：应贮存在既凉爽干燥又不通风的库房里，库内温度应保持在 28℃以下，相对湿度以不超过 70% 为宜。同时采用按件密封，以防气味散失。

Volatile-prone and lost odor Chinese patent medicine: It should be stored in a cool, dry and unventilated storehouse, where the temperature should be kept below 28℃ and the relative humidity should not exceed 70%. At the same time, it should be sealed according to the pieces to prevent the odor from being lost.

（4）易融化、泛油中成药：应贮存在低温、干燥、通风和阳光不能直射的库房内。库内温度不高于 25℃，相对湿度以 70%~75% 为宜。

Melt-prone and extensive diffusion of oil Chinese patent medicine: It should be stored in a storehouse with low temperature, dryness, ventilation and indirect sunlight. The temperature in the storehouse should not be higher than 25℃, and the relative humidity should be 70%~75%.

（5）易发酵、变味中成药：应贮存在低温通风的库房内，库内温度应保持在 28℃以下，相对湿度在 75% 左右，不要使阳光直接照射。

Ferment-prone and changed flavor Chinese patent medicine: It should be stored in a low-temperature and ventilated storehouse, where the temperature should be kept below 28℃, the relative humidity should be about 75%, away from the direct sunlight.

重点小结
Summary

中药资源	药材资源与道地药材	药材资源	野生资源	
			家种养殖资源	
		道地药材	道地药材的含义	
			道地药材的形成进展	
			道地药材的形成因素	优良种质资源的选育
				适宜生态环境的选择
				规范的种植和产地加工
				显著的临床疗效
			道地药材的分类	川药
				广药
				云药
				贵药
				怀药
				浙药
				关药
				北药
				西药
				南药
	成方资源与中成药	成方资源		
		中成药的含义与特点		
		中成药商品的分类		
		中成药的贮存保管		

<table>
<tr><td rowspan="22">Resources of Chinese medicinal materials</td><td rowspan="18">Medicinal Materials Resources and Authentic Medicinal Materials</td><td rowspan="2">Medicinal materials resources</td><td colspan="2">Wild resources</td></tr>
<tr><td colspan="2">Cultured and planted resources</td></tr>
<tr><td rowspan="16">Authentic Medicinal Materials</td><td colspan="2">Definition</td></tr>
<tr><td colspan="2">Formation progress</td></tr>
<tr><td rowspan="4">formation factors</td><td>The selection and breeding of excellent germplasm resources</td></tr>
<tr><td>The selection of suitable ecological environment</td></tr>
<tr><td>The standardized production and processing</td></tr>
<tr><td>The significant clinical effect</td></tr>
<tr><td rowspan="10">classification</td><td>Chuan medicines</td></tr>
<tr><td>Guang medicines</td></tr>
<tr><td>Yun medicines</td></tr>
<tr><td>Huai medicines</td></tr>
<tr><td>Zhe medicines</td></tr>
<tr><td>Guan medicines</td></tr>
<tr><td>Xi medicines</td></tr>
<tr><td>Bei medicines</td></tr>
<tr><td>Gui medicines</td></tr>
<tr><td>Nan medicines</td></tr>
<tr><td rowspan="4">Set prescription resources and Chinese patent medicine</td><td colspan="3">Set prescription resources</td></tr>
<tr><td colspan="3">The meaning and characteristics of Chinese patent medicine</td></tr>
<tr><td colspan="3">Classification of Chinese patent medicine commodities</td></tr>
<tr><td colspan="3">Storage and preservation of Chinese patent medicine</td></tr>
</table>

题库

目 标 检 测
Object Detection

一、选择题 (Choice question)

(一) 单项选择题 (One-choice question)

1. “道地药材”一词首次出现于（　　）

A. 新修本草　　B. 证类本草　　C. 千金翼方
D. 牡丹亭　　E. 本草纲目

The word “authentic medicinal materials” first appeared in (　　)

A. *Xin Xiu Ben Cao*　　B. *Zheng Lei Ben Cao*　　C. *Qian Jin Yi Fang*
D. *Mu Dan Ting*　　E. *Ben Cao Gang Mu*

2. 道地药材形成的内在基础是（　　）

A. 优良种质资源的选育　　B. 适宜环境的选择
C. 规范的种植和产地生产加工　　D. 显著的临床疗效

E. 社会环境的影响

The inherent important factor of authentic medicinal materials formation is (　　)

A. selection and breeding of excellent germplasm resources

B. selection of suitable environment

C. standardized planting and origin processing

D. significant clinical efficacy

E. effect of social environment

3. 道地药材形成的外在因素是（　　）

A. 优良种质资源的选育　　B. 适宜环境的选择

C. 规范的种植和产地生产加工　　D. 显著的临床疗效

E. 社会环境的影响

The external factor of authentic medicinal materials formation is (　　)

A. selection and breeding of excellent germplasm resources

B. selection of suitable environment

C. standardized planting and origin processing

D. significant clinical efficacy

E. effect of social environment

4. 不属于“四大南药”道地药材资源的是（　　）

A. 巴戟天　　B. 砂仁　　C. 槟榔

D. 益智　　E. 附子

Which of the following drugs **does not** belong to the four famous Nan medicine (　　)

A. Bajitian　　B. Sharen　　C. Binglang

D. Yizhi　　E. Fuzi

5. 下列不属于成方资源的是（　　）

A. 历代方书著作　　B. 民间单方　　C. 验方

D. 秘方　　E. 医生临时处方

Which of the following does not belong to the set prescription Resources (　　)

A. the works of ancient prescription books

B. folk single recipe

C. proved recipe

D. secret recipe

E. Doctor's temporary prescription

（二）多项选择题 (Multiple choice questions)

1. 道地药材的形成因素有（　　）

A. 优良种质资源的选育　　B. 适宜环境的选择

C. 规范的种植和产地生产加工　　D. 显著的临床疗效

E. 社会环境的影响

Formation factors of authentic medicinal materials include (　　)

A. selection and breeding of excellent germplasm resources

B. selection of suitable environment

C. standardized planting and origin processing

D. significant clinical efficacy

E. effect of social environment

2. 下列属于川药道地药材资源的是（　　）

A. 川贝母　　B. 川乌　　C. 巴戟天

D. 蛤蚧　　E. 干姜

Which ones in the following authentic medicinal materials are from Sichuan. (　　)

A. Chuanbeimu　　B. Chuanwu　　C. Bajitian

D. Gejie　　E. Ganjiang

3. 四大怀药包括（　　）

A. 山药　　B. 牛膝　　C. 地黄

D. 菊花　　E. 栀子

The four famous Huai medicines include (　　)

A .Shanyao　　B. Niuxi　　C. Dihuang

D. Juhua　　E. Zhizi

4. 下列按照剂型分类的有（　　）

A. 解表剂　　B. 丸剂　　C. 泻下剂

D. 散剂　　E. 膏剂

Which of the following are classified by dosage form (　　)

A. relieving the external symptoms　　B. pill

C. cathartic　　D. powder

E. plaster

5. 下列对中成药的描述错误的是（　　）

A. 中成药不需要中医药理论的指导　　B. 中成药服用和携带方便

C. 中成药疗效好，无毒副作用　　D. 临床可直接应用，不需要辨证论治

E. 中成药处方组成固定不变

Which of the following descriptions of Chinese patent medicine are wrong（　　）

A. Chinese patent medicine does not need the guidance of traditional Chinese medicine theory.

B. Chinese patent medicine is easy to take and carry.

C. Chinese patent medicine has good curative effect and no toxicity or side effects.

D. It can be used directly in clinic without Syndrome Differentiation Treatment of TCM characteristics.

E. The prescription composition of Chinese patent medicine is fixed.

二、解答题 (Thinking question)

1. 举例说明道地药材形成的因素。

Please illustrate the formation factors of authentic medicinal materials with examples.

2. 举例说明道地药材的分类。

Please illustrate the Classification of authentic medicinal materials with examples.

第三章　中药材商品的采收与产地加工

Chapter 3　Collection and Primary Processing of Chinese Materia Medica

学习目标 | Learning Target

知识要求：

1. 掌握　中药材适宜采收时间和常用的产地加工方法。

2. 熟悉　中药材产地加工的要求。

3. 了解　中药材产地加工的目的。

能力要求：

1. 掌握不同药用部位中药材的适宜采收时间规律及采收方法。

2. 学会根据中药材种类、质地及加工要求，因地制宜采用不同的加工方法。

Knowledge requirements:

1. Proficiency　Appropriate collection time and primary processing methods of Chinese Materia Medica (CMM).

2. Familiarity　Requirements of primary processing of CMM.

3. Awareness　Purposes of primary processing of CMM.

Skill requirements:

1. To master appropriate collection time and methods of CMM for different medicinal parts.

2. To learn how to apply different processing methods of CMM depending on their different varieties, textures, preparation requirements, and local conditions.

中药材商品质量的优劣和规格等级的划分与药材的采收时节和产地加工有着密切的关系。所以在中药材商品生产中，必须十分注意采收时间、采收方法和及产地加工方法。

The quality of CMM and division of specifications and grades are closely related to the collection and primary processing in producing areas. Therefore, in the course of the production of CMM, great attention must be paid to the collection time, collection method, and primary processing in producing areas.

第一节　中药材的采收

Section 1　Collection of CMM

PPT

中药材的品种繁多，家种、野生不一，产地分散，加上药用部位各不相同，其成熟期也不一样，采收时节很不一致，因此适时合理地采收药材，对保证药材商品质量，保护和扩大药用资源均有重要意义。目前大多数药材是根据我国历代药农的采药实践经验，结合现代研究对药用动植物生长发育过程中营养物质消长的一般规律，来确定较合理的采收期、采收方法。

There are many varieties of CMM, with domestic and wild species, scattered producing areas, different medicinal parts, mature periods, and collection seasons. Therefore, timely and reasonable collection is of great significance for the quality of CMM and protection and expansion of medicinal resources. At present, the reasonable collection time and methods of most CMM are based on the practical experience of medicinal farmers and modern research on the general laws of nutrient fluctuations in the growth and development of medicinal plants and animals.

除特殊的种类外，一般中药材的采收期及采收方法按药用部位的不同而异，现分述如下。

Except for special types, the collection time and methods of CMM vary from different medicinal parts, which are described as follows.

一、植物类药材

I. Plant medicinal materials

1. 根及根茎类

1. Roots and rhizomes

根及根茎类药材一般都在秋冬季地上部分刚枯时或新春刚发苗时采收。这时植物生长缓慢，基本上处于休眠状态，各种营养物质大部分贮存在根或根茎内，有效成分含量较高，所以此时采收药材的质量好。如天麻冬末春初采收的“冬麻”比春末夏初茎杆出土再采收的“春麻”的质量优。其他如黄连、木香、当归、前胡等也都宜在秋季或冬季采收。如果植物体枯萎较早的，就在夏季采收，如浙贝母、川贝母、延胡索等。所以对根及根茎类药材的采收期应具体分析，区别对待。

Roots and rhizomes as medicinal materials are generally collected in autumn or winter when the aerial parts appear to wither or in early spring when the seedlings are just emerging. At this time, the plants grow slowly or remain dormant and put their energy into roots or rhizomes. Meanwhile, the content of effective components is higher and the quality of medicinal materials collected at this time is better. For example, the quality of Tianma collected in late winter or early spring known as “Dongma” is better than that of “Chunma” collected in late spring or early summer when the stems have grown out from soil. Others should be collected in autumn or winter, namely Huanglian, Muxiang, Danggui, Qianhu, etc. Some plants wither earlier, and they should be collected in summer, namely Zhebeimu, Chuanbeimu, Yanhusuo, etc. Therefore, the collection time of roots and rhizomes as medicinal materials should be specifically analyzed and treated differently.

2. 茎木类

2. Stems and woods

茎类药材一般在秋季或冬季采收，如鸡血藤、川木通等；木类药材一年四季可采或结合伐木工作进行，如苏木、降香等。

Stems as medicinal materials are generally collected in autumn or winter, namely Jixueteng, Chuanmutong, etc. Woods as medicinal materials are collected all the year around or combined with logging, namely Sumu and Jiangxiang, etc.

3. 皮类

3. Plant corks

树皮类药材以清明到夏至间采收最好，此时皮部与木部易分离，如厚朴、杜仲、黄柏等；但肉桂宜在秋分前后采收，此时药材气香味甜、质量好。根皮类药材大多在秋末冬初挖根后剥取，如地骨皮、牡丹皮等。

Plant corks as medicinal materials are usually collected between Qingming Festival and the summer solstice. At this time, the corks and woods are easily separated, namely Houpo, Duzhong, and Huangbai, etc. However, Rougui should be collected before or after autumnal equinox, during which it has a sweet smell and good quality. Most plant corks as medicinal materials are stripped from their roots after the roots are dug up in late autumn or early winter, namely Digupi and Mudanpi, etc.

4. 叶类

4. Leaves

叶类药材一般在花将开放时至刚结果时采收，此时植物生长旺盛，叶的光合作用强，叶内养分丰富。如荷叶在其花蕾含苞欲放或盛开时采收，叶片肥厚、清香气浓郁，质量较好。又如薄荷多在小暑至大暑的盛花期选晴天采收的，此时叶大、香气浓郁，薄荷脑和油的含量最高，而阴雨后 2~3 日采收的，挥发油含量降低了 25%。另有少数叶类药材在霜降后叶落时采收的质量较好，如桑叶、枇杷叶。

Leaves as medicinal materials are generally collected from the early flowering stage to the beginning of yielding fruit, during which plants grow vigorously, the photosynthesis is strong and the nutrients of leaves are rich. For example, Heye is collected when the buds are ready to bloom or in full bloom, during which the leaves are thick, the clear aroma is strong and the quality is good. Bohe is collected on sunny days in full bloom from slight heat to great heat, during which the leaves are large and fragrant, and menthol and oil content is highest, but volatile oil content will decrease by 25% in those collected 2~3 days after rainy days. In addition, a few leaves as medicinal materials are collected with better quality when the leaves fall after Frost’s Descent, such as Sangye and Pipaye.

5. 花类

5. Flowers

花类药材一般在花蕾含苞欲放时或初开时采收。盛开后采收的花不但有效成分含量降低，而且花瓣易脱落，气味较弱，质量降低。如金银花应在花蕾期或刚开时采收，其清热解毒有效成分绿原酸花蕾期含量高。其他如红花、菊花、旋覆花在花盛开时采收。

Flowers as medicinal materials are generally picked when the flowers are in bud or open at the beginning. Not only does effective component content decrease for flowers picked after full bloom, but also the petals fall off easily, with weak odor and quality degradation. For example, Jinyinhua should be picked in bud or at the beginning of open, and the content of chlorogenic acid thereof is highest in bud stage, which is an effective component for clearing heat and detoxifying. Other flowers are picked in full bloom, such as Honghua, Juhua and Xuanfuhua.

6. 果实种子类

6. Fruits and seeds

果实类药材一般都在自然成熟或近成熟时采收，此时营养物质或有效成分的含量相对较高，药材质量好，如山楂、香橼、五味子、枸杞子、桑椹等。有的则在果实未成熟时采收，如枳壳、青皮等。种子类药材须在果实成熟后采收，如决明子、牵牛子等。

Fruits as medicinal materials are generally collected when the fruits are ripe or nearly ripe. At this time, the content of nutrients and effective components is higher and the quality is better, namely Shanzha, Xiangyuan, Wuweizi, Gouqizi, Sangshen, etc. However, some medicinal materials are collected when the fruits are unripe, namely Zhiqiao and Qingpi, etc. Seeds as medicinal materials are collected when the fruits are ripe, namely Juemingzi and Qianniuzi, etc.

7. 全草类

7. Herbs

全草类药材一般在植物茎叶茂盛时采收，此时是植物新陈代谢旺盛的时期，有效成分含量高，如薄荷、益母草、穿心莲、广藿香等。

Herbs as medicinal materials are generally collected when the stems and leaves are luxuriant, during which the plants have a faster metabolism and the content of effective components is higher, namely Bohe, Yimucao, Chuanxinlian, Guanghuoxiang, etc.

8. 树脂类

8. Resinae

树脂类药材随种类不同，其采收部位与采收时间也不同。如乳香多在春季采收，安息香多在四月至秋末，于树干上切成倒三角形的口子，待其汁凝固后采收。

To resinae as medicinal materials, when and what part to collect vary depending on its varieties. For example, Ruxiang is generally collected in spring and Anxixiang is collected from April to late autumn, during which a worker cuts into an inverted triangle on the trunk of a tree and harvests after its juice has solidified.

二、动物类药材

II. Animal medicinal materials

动物类药材宜根据药用动物生长习性和活动规律不同，进行适时合理的捕取。如蛤蚧多在夏、秋二季捕取；全蝎宜在春、夏、秋三季捕取；有翅昆虫如斑蝥，应选早晨露水未干时捕捉；桑螵蛸应在二月中旬前采收，过时卵已孵化，失去药效；动物的生理或病理产物应在宰杀时收集，如牛黄、鸡内金等。

Animal medicinal materials should be collected timely and reasonably depending on the growth habits and activities of medicinal animals. For example, Gejie is generally collected in summer or autumn. Quanxie is collected in spring, summer or autumn. Ptilota such as Banmao should be collected before the dew is dry in the morning. Sangpiaoxiao is collected before mid-February. Later the eggs will hatch and the drug will lose efficacy. Physiological or pathological products of animals should be collected on the spot that the animals are killed, namely Niuhuang, Jineijin, etc.

三、矿物类药材
III. Mineral medicinal materials

矿物类药材全年均可采收，大多应结合开矿或兴修各种工程时收集，如石膏、滑石、龙骨等。

Most mineral medicinal materials are collected all the year round according to mining or construction of various projects, namely Shigao, Huashi, Longgu.

第二节　中药材的产地加工
Section 2　Primary processing of Chinese Materia Medica

PPT

一、产地加工的目的和要求
I. Purpose and requirements of primary processing

产地加工是指中药材采收后，在产地进行净选、清洗、切片、干燥等的初步加工。这种加工与使用前的炮制加工不同，所以称为产地加工。除少数药材要求鲜用外，绝大多数药材均需在产地进行不同的加工，其目的一是除去杂质和非药用部位，保持中药材的纯净度；二是进行初步的蒸、煮、烫，杀死虫、菌、利于干燥，防止进入流通领域后产生虫蛀、霉变等变质现象，确保中药材质量；三是便于对中药材进行分等分级、包装和贮运保管。

Primary processing refers to the preliminary preparation after collection in producing areas, including selecting, washing, cutting, drying, etc. The preparation is different from the CMM processing, so it is called primary processing. Except for a few medicinals requiring fresh use, most medicinals need to be prepared differently in producing areas. The first purpose of primary processing is to remove impurities and non-medicinal parts to maintain the purity of CMM. The second purpose is to conduct preliminary steaming, boiling, and blanching to kill insects and fungus, facilitate drying, prevent damage from insects, fungus and others in the circulation field, and ensure the quality of CMM. The third purpose is to facilitate the classification, packaging, storage and transportation of CMM.

中药材的品种繁多，药用部位各不相同，其形、色、气、味、质地及所含物质差异很大，因而对加工的要求各异。但一般都要达到外形完整，含水量适度、色泽鲜艳、气味正常，有效物质损失少的要求，从而确保中药材商品的质量。

There are many varieties of CMM, different medicinal parts, appearance, color, flavor, taste, texture and components, the processing requirements vary thereby. However, it is generally required to meet the requirements of complete appearance, moderate water content, bright color, normal odor and less loss of effective substances, to ensure the quality of CMMCs.

二、常用的产地加工方法
II. Methods of primary processing

选择加工方法时要考虑中药材种类、质地及加工要求，同时还要注意因地制宜。常用的加工方法主要有：

The selection of primary processing methods depends on the varieties, texture and preparation requirements of CMM, and more attention should be paid to the local conditions. The main primary processing methods are described as follows:

1. 净制

1. Cleansing

将采收的新鲜药材，除去杂质和非药用部位，用水洗去泥沙，如牛膝去芦头、须根，桔梗、白芍等药材去皮，牡丹皮、地骨皮、五加皮等药材去心，杜仲、关黄柏等树皮类药材产地加工时应刮去粗皮。有些含挥发油的药材如薄荷、细辛等不宜水洗，以免损失有效成分，影响质量。

Cleansing is to remove impurities and non-medicinal parts from the collected fresh medicinal materials, and then wash away the mud and sand with water. For example, Niuxi is removed from residual parts of stem and fibrous roots. Jiegeng and Baishao are peeled outer bark. Some medicinal materials are removed from woody part, namely Mudanpi, Digupi, Wujiapi, etc. The coarse outer part of stem corks as medicinal materials is removed in producing areas, namely Duzhong, Guanhuangbai, etc. Some medicinal materials containing volatile oil should not be washed to avoid the loss of effective components and affect the quality, namely Bohe, Xixin, etc.

2. 切片

2. Cutting

肉质的果实类、坚硬的藤木类、较大的根及根茎药材大多宜趁鲜在产地进行切制，以便干燥和包装。如木瓜纵切成瓣；鸡血藤、大血藤横切成片；大黄、何首乌、葛根切成厚片或块。对含挥发性成分的芳香药材或有效成分易氧化变质的药材如川芎、当归、白芷、槟榔，切片后会加大有效成分的损失，影响药材质量，宜以完整药材保存，使用前切片或粉碎。

Most of the fleshy fruits, hard lianoid stems, larger roots and rhizomes should be cut in producing areas for drying and packaging. For example, Mugua is rip cutting into petals; Jixue teng or Daxueteng is crosscutting into slices; Dahuang, Heshouwu or Gegen is cut into thick slices or cubes. Fragrant medicinals such as Chuanxiong, Danggui, Baizhi and Binglang, which containing volatile or effective components that are easy to oxidize and deteriorate should be cut before use, and cutting will decrease the content of effective components and affect the quality. It should be preserved with complete medicinal materials, sliced or crushed before use.

3. 蒸、煮、烫

3. Steaming, Boiling and Blanching

含浆汁、糖分、淀粉多的药材，使用普通方法难以干燥，需将药材装入容器内进行加热处理，同时杀灭酶的活性，有利于保存有效成分，保证药材质量。如含淀粉多的白芍、明党参等根类药材，可用煮法。天麻、红参要蒸透，使药材外观饱满、色泽明亮。五倍子、桑螵蛸需蒸后杀死虫卵，便于贮存。此外，盐水煮全蝎有利于其保存，煮芒硝、硼砂是为纯净药物。对肉质含水量较高的根及根茎类药材，如百合、百部、太子参等，采收后放入沸水略烫，再晒干。

Some medicinals containing a high amount of juice, sugar and starch are difficult to dry by common processing methods. They should be put into containers and then heated to kill the enzyme activity, which could preserve the effective components and ensure the quality of CMM. For example, some roots as medicinal materials high in starch are boiled, namely Baishao and Mingdangshen, etc. Tianma or Hongshen is steamed thoroughly to be externally plump and bright. Wubeizi or Sangpiaoxiao is steamed to kill the insects for storage. In addition, Quanxie is boiled in salt water for storage. Mangxiao or

Pengsha is boiled for purification. High-moisture fleshy root and rhizome as medicinal materials should be heated in boiling water for a while and then dried in the sun, namely Baihe, Baibu, Taizishen, etc.

4. 发汗

4. Sweating

有些药材在加工过程中经过微煮或蒸后，堆积起来发热，使其内部水分外溢，变软、变色，增加气味，以利于干燥，称为“发汗”。如厚朴、杜仲、玄参、茯苓、巴豆、续断等。发汗能够加快药材干燥速度，但应掌握好“发汗”的时间和次数，并及时摊开晾晒，防止药材堆积发霉变质。

Some medicinals, namely Houpo, Duzhong, Xuanshen, Badou, Xuduan, etc., should be slightly decocted in boiling water or steamed in primary processing and piled up to accumulate heat until the internal water overflows. Then the medicinals become soft and dark and smell strongly, which may be beneficial to drying. The method has capability to accelerate the drying process and shorten production time, which is known as sweating. The sweating time and frequency should be controlled and the medicinals should be spread out timely to prevent mildew and deterioration.

5. 干燥

5. Drying

干燥是药材产地加工最普遍、最主要的加工方法。干燥能使药材水分降低，体积缩小，重量减轻，避免发霉、虫蛀以及有效成分的分解和破坏，便于运输、贮藏，使药材的含水量达到10%~15%的安全范围，保证药材的质量。常见的干燥方法主要分为：

Drying is the most common and main method in producing areas. Drying could reduce moisture, size and weight of medicinal materials and thereby protect against mold, insects or destruction of effective components, which could make medicinal materials easy to transport or store. Drying could make the moisture content reach a safe range of 10% to 15% and ensure the quality of CMM. The main drying methods are described as follows:

（1）自然干燥

(1) Air Drying

自然干燥是指利用天然太阳辐射、风及干燥空气除去药材中过多水分的加工方法。有不需特殊设备，节约能源的特点。具体分阴干法和晒干法两种。晒干法适于多数普通药材。阴干法适于芳香类和颜色鲜艳的药材，如薄荷、香薷、细辛、红花。

Air drying refers to the processing method of using natural solar radiation, wind and dry air to remove too much moisture from medicinals. It could save energy without special equipment. It can be divided into drying in sunshine and drying in shade. Drying in sunshine is suitable for most medicinals, while drying in shade is suitable for medicinals containing fragrant components or bright-color medicinals, such as Bohe, Xiangru, Xixin and Honghua.

（2）人工干燥

(2) Artificial Drying

人工干燥是指利用人工热能除去药材中过多水分的加工方法，包括烘干、远红外干燥、微波干燥、真空干燥等。烘干是将药材置于烘房、火炕上加热干燥，此法适合大多数药材的干燥，特别适用于阴湿多雨的季节，具有干燥快、清洁卫生、不受场地、气候限制等优点。在烘干时，应严格控制温度，适时翻动，以防烘枯烤焦，影响药材质量。一般药材烘干温度控制在50℃~60℃；芳香性药材控制在30℃~40℃；含维生素C的多汁果实类如山楂、木瓜等可用70℃~90℃的温度迅速干燥。远红外干燥是利用远红外线辐射药材进行干燥的方法，具有速度快，能杀虫灭菌，便于自动化生产等优点。微波干燥是由微波能转变为热能使药材干燥的方法，具有速度快，加热均匀，效率高，能杀灭微生物的优点。

Artificial drying refers to the processing method of using artificial heat energy to remove too much moisture from medicinals, namely baking, far-infrared drying, microwave drying, vacuum drying, etc. Baking is to heat and dry the medicinals in the drying room and on the hot Kang, which is suitable for the drying of most medicinals, especially in wet and rainy seasons. It has the advantages of fast drying, cleanliness, not limited by place and climate. The temperature should be strictly controlled in baking and turned timely to prevent scorching. The baking temperature of most medicinals is controlled at 50℃~60℃, the fragrant medicinals is controlled at 30℃~40℃, and the succulent fruit medicinals containing vitamin C could be dried rapidly at 70℃~90℃, such as Shan zha and Mugua. Far-infrared drying is a method of drying medicinals with far-infrared radiation, which has the advantages of high speed, killing insects and bacterium, and which is convenient for automatic production. Microwave drying is a method of drying medicinals from microwave energy to thermal energy, which has the advantages of high speed, uniform heating, high efficiency and killing microorganisms.

重点小结
Summary

<table>
<tr><td rowspan="12">中药材商品的采收与产地加工</td><td rowspan="3">采收</td><td colspan="2">植物药</td><td>按药用部位分成根及根茎、茎木、皮、花、叶、果实及种子、全草、树脂类等，按类采收</td></tr>
<tr><td colspan="2">动物药</td><td>根据动物种类、生长习性和活动规律实施合理采收</td></tr>
<tr><td colspan="2">矿物药</td><td>一般无季节性限制，多结合矿藏的开采进行</td></tr>
<tr><td rowspan="9">加工</td><td>净制</td><td>除去药材表面的泥沙和非药用部位</td><td>牛膝、桔梗、白芍、牡丹皮、地骨皮、五加皮、杜仲、关黄柏</td></tr>
<tr><td>切片</td><td>肉质的果实类、坚硬的藤木类、较大的根及根茎药材</td><td>木瓜、鸡血藤、大血藤、大黄、何首乌、葛根</td></tr>
<tr><td>蒸煮烫</td><td>含浆汁、糖分、淀粉多的药材</td><td>白芍、明党参、天麻、红参、五倍子、桑螵蛸，全蝎、芒硝、硼砂，百合、百部、太子参等</td></tr>
<tr><td>发汗</td><td>将药材经过微煮或蒸后，堆积起来发热，使其内部水分向外溢</td><td>厚朴、杜仲、玄参、茯苓、巴豆、续断等</td></tr>
<tr><td rowspan="5">干燥</td><td>晒干：利用天然太阳辐射、风及干燥空气</td><td>多数普通药材</td></tr>
<tr><td>阴干：利用风及干燥空气</td><td>薄荷、香薷、细辛、红花</td></tr>
<tr><td>烘干：将药材置于烘房、火炕上加热干燥</td><td>一般药材温度控制在 50℃~60℃；芳香性药材控制在 30℃~40℃；含维生素 C 的多汁果实类如山楂、木瓜等可用 70℃~90℃的温度迅速干燥</td></tr>
<tr><td>远红外干燥：利用远红外线辐射</td><td>干燥速度快，杀虫灭菌，便于自动化生产</td></tr>
<tr><td>微波干燥：利用微波能转变为热能</td><td>干燥速度快，加热均匀，效率高，且能杀灭微生物</td></tr>
</table>

Collection and Primary Processing of Chinese Materia Medica	Collection	Plant medicinal materials		The collection varied from different medicinal parts, namely root, rhizome, stem, lignum, cork, leaf, flower, fruit, seed, herb, resinae, etc.
		Animal medicinal materials		Medicinal materials of animal should be collected timely and reasonably depending on the varieties, growth habits and activities of animals
		Mineral medicinal materials		Most mineral as medicinal materials are collected all the year round according to mining or construction of various projects
	Primary Processing	Cleansing	Remove mud and non-medicinal parts from the collected fresh medicinal materials	Niuxi,Jiegeng,Baishao, Mudanpi,Digupi,Wujiapi, Duzhong,Guanhuangbo
		Cutting	Most of the fleshy fruits, hard lianoid stems, larger roots and rhizomes	Mugua,Jixueteng, Daxueteng, Dahuang Heshouwu, Gegen
		Steaming, Boiling and Blanching	Medicinal materials containing a high amount of juice, sugar and starch	Baishao,Mingdangshen, Tianma,Hongshen,Wubeizi, Sangpiaoxiao, Quanxie, Mangxiao, Pensha, Baihe, Baibu, Taizishen, etc.
		Sweating	Medicinal materials are slightly decocted in boiling water or steamed in primary processing and piled up to accumulate heat until the internal water overflows	Houpo, Duzhong Xuanshen,Badou, Xuduan, etc.
		Drying	Drying in sunshine: using natural solar radiation, wind and dry air	most medicinal materials
			Drying in shade: to use natural solar radiation, wind and dry air	Bohe, Xiangru, Xixin, Honghua
			Baking: to heat and dry the medicinal materials in the drying room and on the hot Kang	The baking temperature of most medicinal materials is controlled at 50℃~60℃, the fragrant medicinal materials are controlled at 30℃~40℃, and the succulent fruit medicinal materials containing vitamin C could be dried rapidly at 70℃~90℃, such as Shanzha and Mugua
			Far-infrared drying: to use far-infrared radiation	High speed, killing insects and bacterium, convenient for automatic production
			Microwave drying: to change microwave energy to thermal energy	High speed, uniform heating, high efficiency and killing microorganisms

题库

目 标 检 测
Object Detection

一、选择题（Choice question）

（一）单项选择题（One-choice question）

1. 根及根茎类药材商品的采收期通常是（　　）

A. 春季　　B. 夏季　　C. 春末夏初
D. 秋冬季　　E. 植物茎叶茂盛时

Roots and rhizomes as medicinal materials are generally collected in（　　）

A. spring　　B. summer
C. late spring or early summer　　D. autumn or winter
E. when the stems and leaves are luxuriant

2. 全年可采收的药材是（　　）

A. 皮类药材　　B. 茎类药材　　C. 根类药材
D. 矿物药　　E. 花类药材

Which of the following is collected all the year round（　　）

A. cork　　B. stem and lignum　　C. root
D. mineral　　E. flowe

3. 肉桂药材商品的适宜采收期为（　　）

A. 秋分前后　　B. 春末夏初　　C. 清明到夏至
D. 冬季　　E. 春季

Rou Gui should be collected（　　）

A. before or after autumnal equinox
B. late spring or early summer
C. between Qingming Festival and the Summer Solstice
D. winter
E. spring

4. 桑叶药材商品的适宜采收期为（　　）

A. 秋季　　B. 霜降后　　C. 春季　　D. 夏季　　E. 冬季

Sangye should be collected（　　）

A. autumn　　B. after Frost's Descent　　C. spring
D. summer　　E. winter

5. 以下药材商品产地加工需要发汗的是（　　）

A. 大黄　　B. 当归　　C. 厚朴　　D. 灵芝　　E. 枳壳

Which of the following is required for sweating in producing areas（　　）

A. Dahuang　　B. Danggui　　C. Houpo
D. Lingzhi　　E. Zhiqiao

（二）多项选择题（Multiple choice question）

1. 中药材商品产地加工的目的是（　　）

A. 去除杂质
B. 促使药材干燥
C. 防止有效成分散失
D. 控制药材含水量
E. 去除非药用部位

The purposes of primary processing are to (　　)
A. remove impurities
B. facilitate drying
C. prevent decrease of effective components
D. control moisture content
E. remove non-medicinal parts

2. 以下药材商品适宜在花蕾期采收的是(　　)
A. 红花　B. 菊花　C. 金银花
D. 丁香　E. 旋复花

Which of the following are collected in the bud stage (　　)
A. Honghua　B. Juhua　C. Jinyinhua
D. Dingxiang　E. Xuanfuhua

3. 自然干燥法包括(　　)
A. 烘干　B. 微波干燥　C. 阴干
D. 晒干　E. 真空干燥

Air drying includes (　　)
A. baking　B. microwave drying　C. drying in shade
D. drying in sunshine　E. vacuum drying

4. 以下为果实未成熟时采收的中药材商品有(　　)
A. 枳实　B. 青皮　C. 五味子
D. 枸杞子　E. 桑椹

Which of the following are collected when the fruit is unripe (　　)
A. Zhishi　B. Qingpi　C. Wuweizi
D. Gouqizi　E. Sangshen

二、解答题(Thinking question)

举例说明中药材采收、产地加工与其商品规格等级形成的关系?

Give examples to illustrate the relationship between the collection and primary processing of CMM and their specifications and grades?

第四章　中药商品的包装

Chapter 4　Packaging of Chinese Materia Medica Commodities

学习目标 | Learning Target

知识要求：

1. 掌握　中药商品包装的含义及作用；药材、饮片及中成药商品包装材料的分类；中药商品包装的分类。

2. 熟悉　中药商品包装的标志。

能力要求：

1. 学会区分广义、狭义的中药商品包装。
2. 认识中药商品包装的意义。

Knowledge requirements:

1. Proficiency　The meaning and role of packaging of Chinese materia medica commodities (CMMCs). The classifications of the packaging materials of Chinese medicinal materials, Chinese decocting pieces and Chinese patent medicine commodities. The classifications of the packaging of CMMCs.

2. Familiarity　The marking of the packaging of CMMCs.

Skill requirements:

1. Learning to distinguish the packaging of CMMCs in broad and narrow sense.
2. Recognizing the significance of the packaging of CMMCs.

中药商品的包装是实现其商品价值和使用价值，以及增强市场竞争能力的有效手段。包装质量的好坏、商标图案及其装潢是否精美、有无吸引力，直接影响中药商品的价格和市场竞争能力，直接关系到中药商业企业经营工作成败的大事。所以中药商业企业和生产企业应把中药商品的包装质量视为产品质量的一部分，花大力气把中药商品的包装搞好，以适应国内外市场的需要。

The packaging of CMMCs is an effective means to realize its commodity value and use value, as well as enhance market competitiveness. There are the quality of the packaging, the attractiveness of the trademark logo, and the refinement of the decoration, all of which have a significant impact on the price and market competitiveness of CMMCs, even on the enterprises future in CMMCs. Therefore, commercial and manufacturing enterprises dealing in CMMCs should regard the packaging quality of

CMMCs as a part of product quality, take great efforts to do the packaging well, to meet the needs of domestic and foreign markets.

第一节 中药商品包装的含义与作用

Section 1 The meaning and role of packaging of Chinese Materia Medica Commodities

PPT

一、中药商品包装的含义

I. The meaning of packaging of Chinese Materia Medica Commodities

包装的概念分狭义和广义。我国国家标准 GB/T4122.1-2008 中规定，包装的含义是："为在流通过程中保护产品，方便贮运、促进销售，按一定技术方法而采用的容器、材料及辅助物等的总体名称"，即是包装的狭义概念。广义的包装是指一切能改变事物的外观形象的方法和手段等。本章所讲的是狭义的包装概念，即盛装商品的容器、材料及辅助物品。

The concept of packaging has both broad and narrow sense. The meaning of packaging is: "the overall name of the container, material, and auxiliary that are used according to a certain technical method, and that are used for protecting the product during circulation, facilitating storage and transportation, and promoting sales", which is the narrow concept of packaging, derived from Chinese national standard (GB/T 4122.1-2008). The broad concept of packaging is all methods and means that can change the appearance of things. This chapter is about the narrow concept of packaging, that is, containers, materials and auxiliary items for commodities.

药品包装必须适合药品质量的要求，方便储存、运输和医疗使用。

The packaging of medicines must be suitable for the quality of medicines, and convenient for storage, transportation and medical use.

二、中药商品包装的作用

II. The role of packaging of Chinese Materia Medica commodities

中药商品包装作用较多，主要作用有：

The packaging of CMMCs has many functions. The main effects are:

1. 确保中药商品的质量

1. To ensure the quality of CMMCs

中药是防治疾病和康复保健的特殊商品，如不加包装，易受空气、日光、温度、湿度等自然条件的影响和虫霉等的污染而变质。因此必须进行严密的包装。包装后，有密封、防潮、隔热、避光和防虫、防霉等作用，从而确保中药商品的质量。如党参，若不包装，在夏天一个月之内就会霉烂或被虫蛀空，不能药用，应按贮存要求，处理后包装于厚型塑料袋内，置阴凉干燥处。

CMM are special commodities for prevention and treatment of diseases and rehabilitation and health care of human. Without packaging, CMM are vulnerable to the natural conditions as air, sunlight, temperature, humidity, and damaged by insects and molds resulting in metamorphism. With packaging, they have the functions of sealing, moisture-proof, heat-insulation, light-proof, insect-proof and mildew-proof, so as to ensure the quality of CMMCs. Take the example of Dangshen, without packaging, it will rot or be damaged by worms within one month in the summer, and cannot be used for medicine. According to storage requirements, Dangshen should be packaged in a thick plastic bag and stored in a cool and dry place.

2. 防止损耗，保持数量

2. To prevent loss and maintain quantity

中药商品要满足市场需要，必须有足够的数量。尽可能减少流通过程中的损耗，保持足够数量是提高经济效益的必备条件，如不加包装，在流通中的损耗过大，就必然影响市场供应，降低经营效益。因此对中药商品必须进行严密的包装，从而达到减少损耗，保证供应，提高经营效益的目的。为此国家有关主管部门对中药商品流通中各个环节的损耗规定了一定的比例。

To meet the needs of the market, CMMCs must have sufficient quantities. It is a necessary condition for improving economic benefits to reduce the losses and maintaining a sufficient quantity in the circulation process. Without packaging, the heavy loss of CMMCs in the circulation will inevitably affect market supply and reduce operating efficiency. Therefore, CMMCs must be tightly packed to reduce loss, ensure supply, and improve business efficiency. Thus the proportion of losses in various links in the circulation of CMMCs have been stipulated by the relevant national authorities.

3. 美化外观，指导消费，促进销售

3. To beautify appearance, guide consumption, and promote sales

中药商品的种类繁多，形态多样，大小不一，如不包装或包装外观不美，难以达到商品包装标准化、规范化和美观化的质量要求，因此必须有精美的包装。并要求在包装上有美观的商标装潢图案，附有必要的说明，使药品的名称、功效、主治、用法用量及其他注意事项都一目了然。这样的包装外形美观、整齐，又指导了消费，方便消费者识别、选购，从而促进销售，提高经营效益。

There are many kinds of CMMCs with various forms and different sizes. Without packaging nor beautiful packaging, it is difficult to meet the quality requirements of standardization, normalization and aesthetics of commodities packaging. So an exquisite package is essential for CMMCs. In addition, an elegant trademark and a clear instruction on name, efficacy, indications, dosage and other precautions of the drug are required to be printed on the package. Such package has a beautiful and neat appearance, which guides consumption, facilitates consumer identification and purchase, thereby promoting sales and improving business efficiency.

4. 方便运输、有利于贮存

4. To be convenient for transportation and storage

中药商品包装成一定的包件后，同类商品的外形、大小、重量都是固定的，便于在运输、转运中进行装卸、搬运和清点，便于在贮存中进行计量、堆码、出库、转仓倒垛、盘点等工作，也便于在销售中进行计量管理。

After CMMCs are packaged into certain packages, the appearance, size and weight of commodities in the same catalogue are fixed, which is convenient for loading, unloading, handling, and inventorying during transportation and transshipment, for measurement, stacking, delivery from storage, transfer warehouse inversion, inventorying and other tasks, and for measurement management in sales.

总之，对中药商品进行包装后，为整个流通环节的规范化管理提供了有利条件，减少了差错

事故的发生，省时省力，降低了管理费用，对提高中药商业企业的经营效益起着重要作用。

In short, the packaging of CMMCs is conducive to the standardized management of the entire circulation, to reduce the occurrence of accidents, to save time and effort, and to lower management costs, which plays an important role in improving the operating efficiency of CMM enterprises.

第二节　包装材料的分类

Section 2　Classifications of the packaging materials

PPT

中药商品的包装必须与药品性质相适应，直接接触药品的包装材料，必须符合药用要求和保障人体健康、安全的标准，并经国务院药品监督管理部门批准注册。中药商品的包装材料种类繁多，性能不一，规格不等，各有其适用范围。同时各类中药商品对包装材料的要求差异很大。现分类简介如下。

Packaging materials selected for CMMCs shall accommodate to medicinal properties. The immediate packaging materials shall meet the requirements for medicinal use and the standards for ensuring human health and safety, and be subject to registration upon approval by the drug regulatory department under the state council. There are many kinds of packaging materials for CMMCS, with different properties and specifications, each of which has its scope of application. Meanwhile, various types of CMMCs have different requirements for packaging materials. The classification is as follows:

一、药材及其饮片商品的包装材料

I. Packaging materials for Chinese medicinal materials and decocting pieces

1. 布袋和麻袋

1. Cloth bags and sacks

布袋和麻袋是传统的包装材料之一，其质地细软，有一定的耐压耐磨性能和防潮、避光作用。除贵重药品外，都可选用。布袋适用于粉末状药材的包装，如蒲黄、松花粉、海金沙、珍珠母粉、海蛤壳粉及矿物药粉末等；细麻袋适用于包装细小的果实种子类药材商品，如紫苏子、芥子、茺蔚子、车前子、青葙子、葶苈子、菟丝子等；粗麻袋适用于大部分药材或中药饮片的包装，如何首乌、苍术、白术、常山、山楂、金樱子、厚朴、黄柏、桑寄生及其饮片等。

Cloth bags and sacks are two types of traditional packaging materials, texture soft, pressure and abrasion resistant, moisture preventing and light-proof. Except for costly medicines, they are all optional. The cloth bags are suitable for the packaging of powdered Chinese medicinal materials, such as Puhuang, Songhuafen, Haijinsha, powder of Zhenzhumu and Haigeqiao, and mineral powder as medicinal materials. The fine linen sacks are suitable for the packaging of small fruits and seeds as Chinese medicinal materials, such as Zisuzi, Jiezi, Chongweizi, Cheqianzi, Qingxiangzi, Tinglizi, and Tusizi. The railway sacks are suitable for the packaging of most Chinese medicinal materials or Chinese decocting pieces, such as Heshouwu, Cangzhu, Baizhu, Changshan, Shanzha, Jinyingzi, houpo, Huangbo, Sangjisheng, and decocting pieces thereof.

2. 编织袋

2. Woven bags

编织袋是近三十多年开发的包装材料，质地坚韧、具良好的耐磨耐压和抗腐蚀的性能，有好的密封、避光作用，是较理想的外包装材料，除适用于大多数药材和饮片包装外，尤适用于矿物药材如芒硝、大青盐等，和极易吸潮变质药材及饮片如生地黄、黄精、天冬、盐附子、盐苁蓉、制何首乌等。

As packaging materials, the woven bags have a history of more than 30 years, with tough texture, good abrasion resistance, pressure resistance and corrosion resistance, along with good sealing and light protection. So, the woven bags are ideal outer packaging materials. In addition to the packaging of most Chinese medicinal materials and decocting pieces, it is especially suitable for the packaging of mineral as medicinal materials such as Mangxiao, Daqingyan, and highly hygroscopic and deteriorating Chinese medicinal materials and decocting pieces such as Shengdihuang, Huangjing, Tiandong, Yanfuzi, Yancongrong, and Zhi Heshouwu.

3. 筐、篓和苇席

3. Bamboo baskets and reed mats

筐和篓为竹类编织品，质量粗韧、耐压耐磨、透气性能好，适用于条形或块段状药材的包装，如黄芪、甘草、赤芍、白芍、大黄、黄芩、牛膝等。苇席是苇茎的编织品，质地较柔软，弹性弱，易打包成型，适用于花、叶、全草类等轻泡药材机械包装。不仅可使包件形成大小一致，外形整齐，而且可增加车船和仓库的容量，节约费用，如菊花、金银花、旋覆花、桑叶、枇杷叶、大青叶、番泻叶、金钱草、紫花地丁、蒲公英、广藿香、佩兰等。

The woven bamboo baskets are coarse and tough in quality, resistant to pressure and wear, and have good air permeability, which are suitable for packaging of strips or blocks of Chinese medicinal materials, such as Huangqi, Gancao, Chishao, Baishao, Dahuang, Huangqin, and Niuxi. The reed mats which are reed stems weaving with soft texture and weak elasticity, are easy to be packaged and suitable for mechanical packaging of flowers, leaves, and whole grasses. Using reed mats as packaging materials is not only conducive to the formation of packages with a uniform size and a neat appearance, but also helpful to increase the capacity of vehicle, ship and warehouse and save costs, such as Juhua, Jinyinhua, Xuanfuhua, Sangye, Pipaye, Daqingye, Fanxieye, Jinqiancao, Zihuadiding, Pugongying, Guanghuoxiang, and Peilan.

4. 木箱和纸箱

4. Wooden cases and cartons

木箱质地坚实，密封性能好、耐压耐磨、有较好承压能力。在内壁衬垫防潮纸或塑料袋作内包装，有良好防潮、避光、密封作用，适用于细贵药材如天麻、鹿茸、人参、阿胶、龟甲胶、川贝母等药材的包装，也适用于绝大部分中药商品的外包装。纸箱的包装性能较木箱差一些，但造价低，较轻便，适用于一般细贵药材和中成药的外包装。

The wooden cases have solid texture, good sealing, pressure resistance, wear resistance, and good pressure bearing capacity. Padded with moisture-proof paper or plastic bags as inter packaging on the inner wall of the wooden cases, it has good moisture-proof, light-proof and sealing effects. It is suitable for packaging of costly fine Chinese medicinal materials such as Tianma, Lurong, Renshen, Ejiao, Guijiajiao, and Chuanbeimu. The wooden cases are also suitable for the outer packaging of most CMMCs. The packaging properties of the cartons are worse than those of the wooden cases, but with lower cost and lightweight. The cartons are suitable for the outer packaging of general costly fine Chinese medicinal materials and Chinese patent medicine.

5. 厚型塑料袋

5. Thick plastic bags

质地薄韧，轻便，有良好的密封防潮作用，除做细贵药材和中成药的内包装或中包装材料外，主要适宜做中药饮片的定量包装材料，也适用于果实种子类药材的中、小定量包装材料，如大枣、枸杞子、五味子等。

The thick plastic bags have thin and tough texture, lightweight, and good sealing and moisture-proof effects. In addition to being used as the inner packaging or the medium packaging of fine costly Chinese medicinal materials and Chinese patent medicine, it is mainly suitable for quantitative packaging of Chinese decocting pieces, also suitable for the small and medium quantitative packaging of fruits and seeds as Chinese medicinal materials, such as Dazao, Gouqizi, and Wuweizi.

6. 铁器制品（铁桶、铁箱、铁盒）和陶瓷制品（瓷缸、瓷罐）

6. Iron products (iron drums, iron boxes, tins) and ceramic products (porcelain jars, porcelain pots)

这类制品质地坚重，耐磨耐压，密封性能好，主要适用于液体和浸膏状药品如水银、蜂蜜和芳香药材如麝香、西红花、苏合香、冰片、樟脑、薄荷脑的包装。

This type of products have heavy texture, wear-resistant, pressure-resistant, and good sealing performance, which are mainly suitable for the packaging of liquid and extract-like medicinal materials such as Shuiyin, Fengmi, and aromatic medicinal materials such as Shexiang, Xihonghua, Suhexiang, Bingpian, Zhangnao, Bohenao.

二、中成药商品的包装材料

II. Packaging materials for Chinese patent medicine commodities

（一）外包装材料

(I) Outer packaging materials

中成药商品的外包装材料主要是纸箱，其性能与上述相同。近几年来也有用塑料桶、塑料盒作外包装材料的。

Cartons are the main outer packaging material of Chinese patent medicine commodities, and the performance of cartons is the same as above. Plastic buckets and plastic boxes have also been used as the outer packaging materials in recent years.

（二）内包装材料

(II) Inner packaging materials

中成药商品的内包装材料又分为盛装包装材料与装潢包装材料两种。

The inner packaging materials of Chinese patent medicine commodities include into two types: the packaging materials for containing and for decoration.

1. 盛装包装材料

1. Packaging materials for containing

是指直接盛装药品的包装材料，再分为中包装和小包装两种，常见的有以下几种。

It refers to the packaging materials for directly containing medicines, which include into two types of the medium packaging and the small packaging. The popular types are as follows:

（1）玻璃瓶和塑料瓶：玻璃瓶和塑料瓶规格繁多，大小不一，广泛用于片剂、丸剂、胶囊剂、散剂、丹剂、露剂、酒剂、糖浆剂等固体或液体药剂的盛装，如银翘解毒片、补中益气丸、七厘散、金银花露、舒筋活络酒、川贝枇杷糖浆、复方鲜竹沥液等。

(1) Glass bottles and plastic bottles: There are many kinds of glass bottles and plastic bottles with various forms and different sizes. They are suitable for containing tablets, pills, capsules, powders, elixirs, lotions, liquors, syrups and other solid or liquid medicines, such as Yinqiao Jiedu Pian, Buzhong Yiqi Wan, Qili San, Jinyinhua Lu, Shujin Huoiuo Jiu, Chuanbei Pipa Tangjiang, Fufang Xianzhuli Ye.

（2）安瓿：有玻璃的和塑料的两种安瓿。安瓿的密封性能好，塑料安瓿又不易打碎。适用于注射剂、口服液等液体药剂的盛装，如清开灵注射液、银黄口服液。

(2) Ampoules: There are two kinds of ampoules, glass and plastic. The ampoules have good sealing performance, and the plastic ampoules are not easy to break. It is suitable for containing injections, oral liquids and other liquid medicines, such as Qingkailing Zhusheye, Yinhuang Koufuye.

（3）易拉罐：为铝制的圆柱形筒罐，抗压力较强，质地轻，适用于液体药剂或保健口服液的盛装。

(3) Cans: The cans are cylindrical products made of aluminum with strong pressure resistance and light texture, which are suitable for containing liquid medicines or health oral liquids.

（4）塑料袋：质地轻软，密封性能好，大小规格多，广泛适用于冲剂、片剂、丸剂、散剂等的盛装，是较理想的中、小包装材料。所谓中包装是较大袋内盛装若干小包装，如牛黄解毒片，每一小包装 12 片，每一中包装内盛装 50 个小包装。常用塑料袋盛装的药剂如感冒清热颗粒、小青龙颗粒、牛黄解毒片、银翘解毒丸、参苏丸、如意金黄散等。

(4) Plastic bags: The plastic bags have many sizes and specifications with light and soft texture, good sealing performance, which are widely used in the packaging of granules, tablets, pills, and powders, and the middle size and small size of which are ideal packaging materials. By medium package we mean that contains several small packages in a large bag, take the example of Niuhuang Jiedu Pian to illustrate, each small package contains 12 tablets, and each medium package contains 50 small packages. Commonly used medicinals in plastic bags imclude Ganmao Qingre Keli, Xiaoqinglong Keli, Niuhuang Jiedu Pian, Yinqiao Jiedu Wan, Shensu Wan, and Ruyi Jinhuang San.

（5）小瓷瓶：质地坚厚、抗压力强、密封性能好，适用于小丸剂和丹剂的盛装，如六神丸、速效救心丸、金灵丹等。

(5) Small porcelain bottles: The small porcelain bottles have strong texture, strong pressure resistance, and good sealing performance, which are suitable for the packaging of small-pills and elixirs, such as Liushen Wan, Suxiao Jiuxin Wan, and Jinling Dan.

（6）铝塑板：是近年来开发的新盛装材料，质轻便坚实，封闭性能好，便于包装和携带，适用于片剂、胶囊剂等的盛装，如银翘解毒片、桑姜感冒片、三九胃泰胶囊等。

(6) Aluminum-plastic plates: The aluminum-plastic plates have been developed as new packaging materials for recent years, with light weight and solid texture and good sealing performance, which are easy to package and carry. It is suitable for the containing of tablets and capsules, such as Yinqiao Jiedu Pian, Sangjiang Ganmao Pian, and Sanjiu Weitai Jiaonang.

2. 装潢包装材料

2. Packaging materials for decoration

装潢包装材料多选用精致的软、硬纸片或纸板，套在内包装外面。要求设计一定式样的商标图案，附在装潢包装或外包装上，以美化、宣传中成药商品。宣传的内容一般是药品的名称、功能和适用范围及该药品的科学性、新颖性、特殊性等，以此指导消费、促进销售。装潢包装还有保护内包装，确保药品质量和数量的作用，如六神丸、人参酒、洋参丸、云南田七花粉口服液等。

Most of the packaging materials for decoration are placed outside the inner packaging with delicate soft or hard paper or cardboard. It is required to design a certain trademark and attach it to the decoration packaging or outer packaging to beautify and advertise Chinese patent medicine commodities. The contents of publicity generally include the name of medicinal, function and range of indications, as well as the scientificity, novelty, and particularity of the medicines, aiming at guiding consumption and promoting sales. The decoration packaging also protects the inner packaging to ensure the quality and quantity of medicines, such as Liushen Wan, Renshen Jiu, Yangshen Wan, Yunnan Tianqihuafen Koufuye.

第三节 包装的分类

Section 3 Classifications of the packaging

PPT

包装的分类法有多种，按包装的方式分为直接包装和间接包装两种，药材和饮片商品多属直接包装，中成药商品多属间接包装。按包装程序分内包装和外包装两种，一般药材和饮片商品多属外包装，中成药商品二者兼有。按中药商品流通需要分为运输包装和销售包装两种，现按后者分类简介如下。

There are many types of the classifications of the packaging, which are divided into the direct packaging and the indirect packaging according to the packaging methods. Most of the medicinal materials and decocting pieces are directly packed, and most of the Chinese patent medicine are indirectly packed. According to the packaging process, packages are classified as the inner packaging and the outer packaging. The Packaging of general Chinese medicinal materials and decocting pieces commodities belong to the outer packaging, and Packaging of Chinese patent medicine commodities have both. According to the circulation needs of CMMCs, there are two types involving the transportation packaging and the sale packaging. The classification by the latter is as follows.

一、运输包装

I. Transportation packaging

运输包装属外包装，是选用较坚实或坚韧的包装材料如木箱、纸箱、铁皮、麻袋、布袋、编织袋等进行的包装。其作用是保证中药商品的运输安全、便于运输、装卸、堆码、贮存和计量管理。运输包装要注意：一是根据中药商品的性质，合理选择包装材料，二是包装外面要用绳带、化纤带或铁皮捆紧扎牢，防止在运输中松散。

The transportation packaging is an outer packaging, which is made of relatively solid or tough packaging materials such as the wooden cases, the cartons, the iron sheets, the sacks, the cloth bags, and the woven bags. The role thereof is to ensure the safe transportation of CMMCs, and facilitate transportation, loading and unloading, stacking, storage and measurement management. Notes on the transportation packaging: First, reasonably selecting packaging materials according to the nature of CMMCs. Second, tightly tying the outside of the packaging with ropes, chemical fiber belts or iron sheets to prevent loosening during transportation.

二、销售包装
II. Sale packaging

销售包装多属内包装，是指直接同消费者见面并随同药品一起销售的包装。其作用除保证商品安全外，还有美化、宣传商品，指导消费的作用，便于消费者识别、选购、携带和服用。在销售包装上，一般都要附有装潢。销售包装注意：一是要根据中药商品的性能合理选择包装材料；二是装潢包装的形式要新颖、图案要美观、清晰、便于陈列、展销和识别，对树立企业形象有积极作用。

The sale packaging is mostly the inner packaging, which refers to packaging that meets consumers directly and is sold with medicines. The role thereof is not only to ensure the safety of commodities, but also to beautify and promote them, and to guide consumption as well. It is convenient for consumers to identify, purchase, carry and take. Decoration is usually attached to the sale packaging. Notes on the sale packaging: First, the packaging materials should be reasonably selected according to the performance of CMMCs. Second, the decoration packaging should have novel forms, beautiful and clear patterns for display, exhibition and identification, which has a positive effect on establishing the corporate image.

第四节 包装的标志
Section 4 Marking of the packaging

PPT

中药材商品的包装上要有明显的标志，在每件运输包装上必须注明品名、产地、日期、调出单位，并附有质量合格的标志。

On the packaging of CMMCs shall be indicated obvious marks, the name of the commodity, producing area, production date, the unit of transfer, and attached with the mark of qualified quality on each transport package.

中药饮片商品的标签必须注明品名、规格、产地、生产企业、产品批号、生产日期，实施批准文号管理的中药饮片还必须注明药品批准文号。

On the label of Chinese decocting pieces commodities shall be indicated the name of the commodity, specifications, producing area, manufacturing enterprise, product batch number, and production date. If the said decocting piece is controlled by approval number, the medicinal approval number shall also be indicated.

中成药商品包装必须按照规定印有、贴有标签，并附有说明书。标签或者说明书上必须注明药品的通用名称、成分、规格、生产企业、批准文号、产品批号、生产日期、有效期、适应证或者功能主治、用法、用量、禁忌、不良反应和注意事项。

A label shall be printed on or attached to the package of Chinese patent medicine commodities with an insert sheet attached. On the label or the insert sheet shall be indicated the general name, ingredients, specifications, manufacturer, approval number, product batch number, production date, expiration date, indication or function, usage, dosage, contraindications, adverse reactions and precautions of the medicine.

特别是麻醉药品、精神药品、医疗用毒性药品、放射性药品、外用药品和非处方药的包装上，必须印有规定的标志。

In particular, the package shall be printed in accordance with the provisions of narcotic medicines, psychotropic medicines, medical toxic medicines, radioactive medicines, external medicines and over-the-counter medicines.

重点小结
Summary

中药商品的包装	中药商品包装的含义与作用	包装的含义是："为在流通过程中保护产品，方便贮运、促进销售，按一定技术方法而采用的容器、材料及辅助物等的总体名称"，即是包装的狭义概念。本章所讲的是狭义的包装概念，即盛装商品的容器、材料及辅助物品。药品包装必须适合药品质量的要求，方便储存、运输和医疗使用。中药商品包装作用较多，主要作用有：①确保中药商品的质量；②防止损耗，保持数量；③美化外观，指导消费，促进销售；④方便运输、有利于贮存
	包装材料的分类	中药商品的包装必须与药品性质相适应，直接接触药品的包装材料，必须符合药用要求和保障人体健康、安全的标准，并经国务院药品监督管理部门批准注册。药材及其饮片商品的包装材料有布袋和麻袋，编织袋，筐、篓和苇席，木箱和纸箱，厚型塑料袋，铁器制品和陶瓷制品等。中成药商品的外包装材料有纸箱、塑料桶、塑料盒等。中成药商品的内包装材料分为盛装材料与装潢包装材料两种。盛装包装材料，是指直接盛装药品的包装材料，包括玻璃瓶和塑料瓶，安瓿，易拉罐，塑料袋，小瓷瓶，铝塑板等
	包装的分类	按中药商品流通需要分为运输包装和销售包装两种
	包装的标志	中药商品的包装标志应符合相关规定

Packaging of Chinese Materia Medica Commodities	The meaning and role of packaging of Chinese Materia Medica Commodities	The meaning of packaging is: "the overall name of the container, material, and auxiliary that are used according to a certain technical method, and that are used for protecting the product during circulation, facilitating storage and transportation, and promoting sales", which is the narrow concept of packaging. This chapter is about the narrow concept of packaging, that is, containers, materials and auxiliary items for commodities. The packaging of medicines must be suitable for the quality of medicines, and convenient for storage, transportation and medical use. The packaging of CMMCs has many functions, the main effects are: ① To ensure the quality of CMMCs, ② To prevent loss and maintain quantity, ③ To beautify appearance, guide consumption, and promote sales, ④ To be convenient for transportation and storage

(continued)

	Classifications of the packaging materials	Packaging materials selected for CMMCs shall accommodate to medicinal properties. The immediate packaging materials shall meet the requirements for medicinal use and the standards for ensuring human health and safety, and be subject to registration upon approval by the drug regulatory department under the state council. There are cloth bags and sacks, woven bags, bamboo baskets and reed mats, wooden cases and cartons, thick plastic bags, iron products and ceramic products as the packaging materials for Chinese medicinal materials and decocting pieces thereof. The outer packaging materials for Chinese patent medicine commodities have cartons, plastic buckets and plastic boxes. The inner packaging materials of Chinese patent medicine commodities are divided into two types: the packaging materials for containing and for decoration. The packaging materials for containing which refer to the packaging materials for directly containing medicines, have glass bottles and plastic bottles, ampoules, cans, plastic bags, small porcelain bottles, aluminum-plastic plates
	Classifications of the packaging	According to the circulation needs of CMMCs, there are two types involving the transportation packaging and the sale packaging
	Marking of the packaging	The packaging marks of CMMCs shall comply with relevant regulations

题库

目标检测
Object Detection

一、选择题（Choice question）

（一）单项选择题（One-choice question）

1. 按中药商品流通需要，中药商品的包装可分为运输包装和（　　）

A. 装潢包装　　B. 内包装　　C. 外包装

D. 销售包装　　E. 盛装包装

According to the circulation needs of CMMCs, the packaging of CMMCs can be divided into the transportation packaging and the (　　)

A. decoration packaging　　B. inner packaging　　C. outer packaging

D. sale packaging　　E. packaging for containing

2. 中成药商品的外包装材料主要有塑料桶、塑料盒和（　　）

A. 麻袋　　B. 纸箱　　C. 筐

D. 陶瓷制品　　E. 苇席

There mainly are plastic buckets, plastic boxes and (　　) as the outer packaging materials for Chinese patent medicine commodities

A. sacks　　B. cartons　　C. bamboo baskets

D. ceramic products　　E. reed mats

3. 中成药商品的内包装材料分为盛装材料和（　　）

A. 运输包装材料　　B. 销售包装材料　　C. 间接包装材料

D. 直接包装材料　　E. 装潢包装材料

The inner packaging materials of Chinese patent medicine commodities are divided into packaging materials for containing and (　　)

A. packaging materials for transportation　　B. packaging materials for sale

C. indirect packaging materials　　D. direct packaging materials

E. packaging materials for decoration

（二）多项选择题（Multiple choice question）

1. 中药商品包装的作用主要有（　　）

A. 确保中药商品的质量　　B. 方便运输、有利于贮存

C. 降低中药商品的成本　　D. 美化外观，指导消费，促进销售

E. 防止损耗，保持数量

The packaging of CMMCs has many functions, the main effects are (　　)

A. To ensure the quality of CMMCs.

B. To be convenient for transportation and storage.

C. To reduce the cost of CMMCs.

D. To beautify appearance, guide consumption, and promote sales.

E. To prevent loss and maintain quantity.

2. 药材及其饮片商品的包装材料包括（　　）

A. 木箱　　B. 苇席　　C. 厚型塑料袋

D. 编织袋　　E. 铁器制品

There are (　　) as the packaging materials for Chinese medicinal materials and decocting pieces thereof

A. wooden cases　　B. reed mats　　C. thick plastic bags

D. woven bags　　E. iron products

3. 作为中成药商品的内包装材料之一的盛装包装材料包括（　　）

A. 铝塑板　　B. 塑料袋　　C. 玻璃瓶

D. 安瓿　　E. 塑料瓶

There are (　　) as the packaging materials for containing, which is one of the inner packaging materials of Chinese patent medicine commodities

A. aluminum-plastic plates　　B. plastic bags　　C. glass bottles

D. ampoules　　E. plastic bottles

4. 中药材商品的包装上要有明显的标志，在每件运输包装上必须注明（　　）

A. 品名　　B. 产地　　C. 日期

D. 调出单位　　E. 附有质量合格的标志

On the packaging of CMMCs shall be indicated obvious marks, (　　) on each transport package

A. the name of the commodity　　B. producing areas

C. production date　　D. the unit of transfer

E. attached with the mark of qualified quality

二、思考题（Thinking question）

1. 阐述广义和狭义的中药商品包装的异同。
Explaining the similarities and differences between the broad and narrow the packaging of CMMCs.
2. 为促进中药商品的销量，应如何提升销售包装？
How to improve the sale packaging to promote the sales of CMMCs?
3. 中药商品的包装标志应符合哪些规定？
What are the regulations for the packaging marks of CMMCs?
4. 中药商品的包装有何意义？
What is the significance of the packaging of CMMCs?

第五章 中药市场

Chapter 5 Chinese Materia Medica Market

学习目标 | Learning Target

知识要求：

1. **掌握** 中药市场的概念。

2. **熟悉** 国内外主要中药市场、中药商品进出口概况。

能力要求：

学会区分广义、狭义的中药市场；熟悉国内外主要中药市场的历史和特点。

Knowledge requirements:

1. **Proficiency** The concept of Chinese Materia Medica (CMM) market.

2. **Familiarity** Overview of the major CMM markets in China and at abroad, and the import and export of Chinese Materia Medica Commodities (CMMCs).

Skill requirements:

Learning to distinguish CMM market in a broad and narrow sense. Familiarizing the history and characteristics of major CMM markets in China and at abroad.

市场有广义和狭义之分。广义市场是指在一定的时间和空间条件下，商品交换关系的总和，即把市场看成是商品交换的总体，或者是商品生产、流通、消费的全过程。狭义市场是商品交换的场所。一般设在交通发达，人口稠密的城镇。所以狭义市场是一个有限的区域，但在通讯方式多样化的今天，狭义市场的区域已不断扩大，买卖双方除面对面地进行交易外，还可利用电话、传真、网络等现代通讯方式进行联系或交易，故市场的范围可遍及全国和全世界。

The market has both broad and narrow sense. In broad sense, it refers to the sum of commodity exchange relationship under certain conditions of time and space, which is considered as the whole of commodity exchange, or the whole process of commodity production, circulation, and consumption. In narrow sense, it is a place for commodity exchange, which is generally located in densely populated towns with well-developed transportation. So the narrow market is a limited area, but this area has been expanding with the diversification of communication methods today. In addition to face-to-face transactions between buyers and sellers, modern communication methods such as telephone, fax, and Internet can also be used to make contacts or transactions. Therefore, the market in a narrow sense can cover the whole country and the world.

本章的中药市场属于狭义市场的概念，即是指中药商品交换的场所。中药市场是中药商品生产发展的产物，是扩大社会再生产及其发展的必要条件。

The CMM market in this chapter belongs to the concept of a market in a narrow sense, which refers to the place where CMMCs are exchanged. The CMM market is an outcome of the production development of CMMCs, and is a necessary condition for expanding social reproduction and its development.

中药市场是以中药商品交换为内容的经济联系形式，主要功能是以中药商品为媒介，实现中药商品的流通及其价值的转移，以满足人们用药的需求。同时，中药商品通过市场交换，把药品转变成货币，为我国经济建设积累了一定的资金，因此中药市场在国民经济中占有一定的地位。

The CMM market is an economic link for the exchange of CMMCs, whose main function is to realize the circulation of CMMCs and the transfer of their value to meet people's demand for medicine through the medium-CMMCs. Meanwhile, the market exchange of CMMCs can transform medicines into currency to accumulate a certain amount of funds for Chinese economic construction, thus occupying a certain position in the national economy.

第一节 国内市场

Section 1 Domestic Market

PPT

一、国内市场的形成与发展

I. Formation and development of the domestic market

我国中药市场起源很早，《后汉书》记载了韦彪、张楷等著名采药、卖药之人。东汉恒帝时，霸陵人韩康常采药于名山，在长安市上卖药达 30 多年。同时在我国汉代的《神农本草经》中就提到《范子·计然》一书中论及了药价。这都表明中药作为商品，在市场上进行流通已有几千年的历史。

CMM market has a long history in China. Famous CMM collectors and sellers, such as Wei Biao and Zhang Kai, were recorded in *Hou Han Shu*. During the Heng Emperor of Eastern Han Dynasty, Han Kang, a Baling local, usually collected CMM from famous mountains and sold them in Changan for more than 30 years. Meanwhile, *Shen Nong Ben Cao Jing* in the Han Dynasty mentioned that the price of CMM was discussed in *Fan Zi : Ji Ran*. These show that as commodity CMM have been circulated on the market for thousands of years.

早在三国时期，在江西的"樟树镇"建立了"药圩"，至今已有 1700 多年的历史，号称"药都"。"药圩"是我国早期的中药市场雏形。公元 1076 年，宋政府兴办的"太平卖药所"是我国第一个官办的中药市场；南宋迁都临安后，中药市场又有新的发展，不仅有"生药铺""熟药铺"之分，还建立了"川广生药市"，出现了药材的批发市场。

As early as the Three Kingdoms Period, "Yaoxu" was established in "Zhangshu Town" of Jiangxi, which has a history of more than 1,700 years up to now and is known as "Medicine Capital". "Yaoxu" is an early form of the CMM market in China. The year 1076 witnessed the establishment of "taiping pharmacy" by the Song government, which was the first government-run market for CMM in China. After the relocation of the capital to Linan in the Southern Song Dynasty, the CMM market entered a new stage of development, which was divided into "raw medicine shop" and "processed medicine shop".

Meanwhile, "Chuan Guang raw medicine market" was established and a wholesale market for medicinal materials appeared.

中药市场经过历代的发展，到了明清时期，全国大型的中药市场有著名的四大药市，即河北的"安国"、河南的"禹县"和"百泉"、江西的"樟树"以及安徽的"亳州"。那时经营的规模有大有小，经营的方式各不相同。

After the development of CMM market over the past dynasties, there were four famous national large-scale CMM markets in Ming and Qing Dynasties, namely "Anguo" in Hebei, "Yuxian" and "Baiquan" in Henan, "Zhangshu" in Jiangxi, and "Bozhou" in Anhui. At that time, all markets were run on large or small scales in different ways.

现以河北的"安国"药市为例进行说明。安国市，古称祁州，位于河北省中部，四方水陆交通便利，有水路可达天津，转通于营口、香港等地，为药材商品交换的发展提供了便利条件。安国在历史上因药业发达，在国内外久负盛名而素有"北药都"之称。它不仅在全国各地有极大影响，而且在日本、朝鲜特别是在东南亚各国都有较高的声誉。药都的形成，由来已久。早在北宋太平兴国年间（976–982 年）因药王显灵的传说和药王庙的建立，吸引各地"善男信女"前来朝拜。随之客货云集，名声大振，逐渐发展成为我国大型的中药市场。祁州经营道地药材有著名的"祁州十三邦"，包括关东邦、京通卫邦、口邦、山西邦、怀邦、川汉邦、亳州邦、禹州邦等。药邦是地方药材行业借同乡或同行联合起来的团体，具有明显的竞争和垄断的资本性质。各邦销售当地药材，对当时药材的交流和经济的发展起到了积极的作用。

Now, take the example of "Anguo" CMM market in Hebei to illustrate. Anguo City, known as Qizhou in ancient times, is located in the central part of Hebei province, whose waterway and land transportation are convenient on all sides, having waterway access to Tianjin and connection to Yingkou and Hong Kong by transfer, all of which provide convenient conditions for the development of medicinal material commodities exchange. Anguo has long enjoyed a good reputation for "Northern Medicine Capital" in China and at abroad thanks to its developed pharmaceutical industry. Not only does it have great influence throughout the country, but also has a high reputation in Japan, North Korea, and especially in Southeast Asian countries. It took Anguo a long time to win the title of the medicine capital. As early as in the Taiping Xingguo period (976–982) of Northern Song Dynasty, because of the legend of Yaowang (the king of medicine) making its presence and the establishment of Yaowang Temple, Anguo attracted "devout men and women" from all over the places to worship. Anguo evolved into a large-scale CMM market in China following with the gather of passenger and cargo and the rise to fame. "Qizhou thirteen groups", well-known for the operation of authentic medicinal in Qizhou, including Guandong, Jingtongwei, Kou, Shanxi, Huai, Chuanhan, Bozhou, and Yuzhou groups. "Qizhou thirteen groups" was some groups of local medicinal materials industry united by fellow villagers or peers, having the obvious capital nature of competition and monopoly. These groups sold local medicinal materials and played a positive role in the communication of medicinal materials and economic development at that time.

历代中药市场的建立和发展，都因所在地的药材种植业和加工业发达，交通便利，运价低廉，名医、寺庙的影响以及庙会的群众基础等，使市场从无到有，有小到大，经营的药物品种和市场数量由少至多，同时近十多年来，药材市场规模不断扩大，经营的药材品种日益增多，营业时间也变成常年经营，座商、行商云集市场，交易人群络绎不绝，使市场显得格外繁荣，营业额与日俱增，营业利润成倍增长，上交国家税利逐渐增加。

The establishment and development of CMM market in every dynasty are related to many factors, such as developed medicinal materials plant and processing industry, convenient transportation, low transportation costs, famous doctors, temple and the people's needs at the temple fair. These factors help CMM market grow from small to large, with CMM varieties and total market numbers increasing from few to many. Meanwhile, in the past decade or so, the medicinal materials market scale and variety in operation have increased day by day, and the business hours have become year-round operations. More fixed and mobile merchants gather in the market, and the trading crowd comes in an endless stream, which makes the market particularly prosperous. Therefore, turnover is increasing every day, operating profits are increasing exponentially, and taxes and profits paid to the country are gradually increasing.

我国中药材市场发展很快，数量不断增加，截至1996年，国内市场增至110多家。新老市场的相继发展，对广泛开展中药商品交流，促进中药生产的发展，搞活市场经济，以及在中药企业间引入竞争机制，改善中药生产和经营管理都起到积极作用。但也应该看到，中药市场的无序发展，加上一些地方市场管理混乱，中药市场上产生了一些不容忽视的问题，如严禁药品的违规经营，伪劣药材累查不绝，危害了人民群众的身体健康，甚至威胁到人民群众的生命安全。因此国务院、原卫生部、国家药品监督管理局、国家中医药管理局和国家工商行政管理局不仅联合发出整顿中药材市场的通知，而且多次组织联合检查组到各地中药材市场检查验收整顿的结果。经整顿，1996年国家仅批准保留了17家中药材专业市场：河北安国、安徽亳州、山东鄄城舜王城、哈尔滨三棵树、湖北蕲春、江西樟树、广州清平、广东普宁、成都荷花池、湖南廉桥、河南禹州、西安万寿北路、广西玉林、重庆解放西路、昆明菊花园、湖南岳阳花板桥、兰州黄河。现选有一定代表性的中药材市场简介如下。

The development of CMM market in China is rapid and its number is increasing continually. Up to 1996, the domestic CMM market has increased to more than 110. The development of new and old CMM markets plays a positive role in conducting extensive exchange of CMMCs, promoting the development of CMM production, enlivening market economy, introducing competition mechanism among CMM companies, and improving the production and management of CMM. However, it should also be noted that the disorderly development of CMM market and the nonstandard management of some local markets have created some non-negligible issues, such as illegal operation of illicit drugs and counterfeit medicinal materials, which have endangered the health of the people and even threatened their lives. Therefore, State Council, Ministry of Health, National Medical Products Administration, National Administration of Traditional Chinese Medicine, Administration for Industry and Commerce not only issued notices to rectify the CMM market, but also organized joint inspection teams to inspect and accept the results of the rectification of CMM markets. After rectification, China only approved the retention of 17 specialized CMM markets in 1996: Anguo in Hebei, Bozhou in Anhui, Shunwangcheng in Juancheng, Shandong, Sankeshu in Harbin, Qichun in Hubei, Zhangshu in Jiangxi, Qingping in Guangzhou, Puning in Guangdong, Hehuachi in Chengdu, Lianqiao in Hunan, Yuzhou in Henan, Qanshou North Road in Xi'an, Yulin in Guangxi, Jiefang West Road in Chongqing, Juhua Yuan in Kunming, Huaban Qiao of Yueyang in Hunan, and Huanghe in Lanzhou. A brief introduction to the representative CMM market is as follows.

二、国内主要中药材市场简介

II. Brief introduction to the main domestic CMM markets

1. 河北安国中药材专业市场

1. Professional CMM market in Anguo, Hebei

安国地处京、津、石家庄中心地带，古称祁州，是全国重要的中药材集散地。安国药市历史悠久，源于宋朝，兴于明朝、盛于清朝。素有“天下第一药市”“药都”之称。

Anguo, known as Qizhou in the ancient times, is located in the central zone of Beijing, Tianjin and Shijiazhuang, and is an important center for the distribution of Chinese medicinal materials. Anguo medicine market has a long history, originated from the Song Dynasty and flourished in the Ming and Qing Dynasties, which is known as "the World's First Medicine Market" and "Medicine Capital".

新的安国中药材专业市场兴建于 1993 年，又称“东方药城”，建筑面积 60 万 m^2，总投资 6 亿元，经营 2000 多个品种、日吞吐量超 300 吨、年成交额达 20 亿元。整个药城由 4 条“井”字形大街构成，分为 9 个区，拥有商楼 1100 多座，经营销售已辐射全国各地，远销港澳台、东南亚及欧美等 20 多个国家和地区。中心交易大厅是安国中药材专业市场集中交易场所之一，占地 15 亩，经营面积 12000m^2，拥有固定商位 4000 多个，分为个子货杂药区，企业饮片展销区，精细药材区。

The new Anguo professional CMM market was established in 1993, also known as "Oriental Medicine City", with 600,000m^2 construction area and 600 million yuan investment. Nowadays, it shows a large transaction scale, including operation of more than 2,000 varieties, a daily throughput of over 300 tons, and an annual turnover of 2 billion yuan. The entire medicine city is composed of 4 "Jing (tic-tac-toe)"-shaped streets and divided into 9 districts, with more than 1,100 commercial buildings. Its sales have spread throughout the country and are exported to more than 20 countries and regions including Hong Kong, Macao, Taiwan, Southeast Asia, Europe and the United States. The central trading hall, one of the centralized trading venues of Anguo professional CMM market, covers an area of 15 *mu*, with an operating area of 12,000m^2 and more than 4,000 fixed booths. It is divided into miscellaneous whole medicinal materials area, enterprise decocting pieces exhibition area, and fine medicinal materials area.

2. 江西樟树中药材专业市场

2. Professional CMM market in Zhangshu, Jiangxi

樟树是江西省清远县樟树镇的简称，相传以盛产樟树而得名。素以“药都”著称，享有“药不到樟树不齐，药不过樟树不灵”的美誉，具有 1700 多年的药业史，并以其精湛的饮片炮制技术，形成全国闻名的“樟树邦”。1988 年改为江西省樟树市，地处江西赣中胜地，京九、浙赣铁路、105 国道、赣澳、沪瑞高速公路、赣江等水陆交通便捷。

Zhangshu is the abbreviation of Zhangshu Town of Qingyuan County in Jiangxi Province and is famous for its rich camphor trees. Being known as the "Medicine Capital", it enjoys the reputation of "Compatibility and efficacy of CMM are closely related to the medicinal materials from Zhangshu". With a history of more than 1,700 years in the pharmaceutical industry and with its exquisite decocting pieces processed technology, the nationwide well-known "Zhangshu group" emerged. Zhangshu Town was renamed Zhangshu City of Jiangxi Province in 1988 with convenient waterway transportation, located in central Jiangxi Province, nearby Beijing-Jiujiang and Zhejiang-Jiangxi railways, 105 national highway, Jiangxi-Macao and Shanghai-Ruili freeways, and Gan River.

2001 年竣工的樟树中药材专业市场，占地 500 亩，建筑总面积 25 万平方米，投资 3 亿元，拥有一流的现代网络设施和电子报价系统、物流储运设施，整个市场视野开阔，建筑风格中西合璧，能展现出樟树药业文化的源远流长与博大精深。现有经营药商 2000 余户，年成交量 100 万吨，交易额超 50 亿元，辐射全国 30 个省（市）、港、澳、台以及东南亚地区。

The new Zhangshu professional CMM market was established in 2001 with an area of 500 *mu*, 250,000m^2 construction area and 300 million yuan investment. It has first-class modern network facilities, electronic quotation systems, logistics facilities, storage facilities and transportation facilities.

The entire market has a broad vision and a Chinese-Western mixed architectural style, which can show the long history and profoundness of the Zhangshu medicine culture. Nowadays, there are more than 2,000 merchants, an annual turnover of 1 million tons and a transaction value of over 5 billion yuan in Zhangshu market, the trade of which radiates to 30 provinces (cities), Hong Kong, Macao, Taiwan and Southeast Asia.

3. 安徽亳州中药材专业市场

3. Professional CMM market in Bozhou, Anhui

亳州位于安徽的西北部，三面与苏、鲁、豫毗邻，涡河从西而东贯城而过。由于亳州的地理、气候条件得天独厚，又因这里是华佗故里，神医华佗遗风在亳州经久不衰，所以名医辈出，药师济济。传统的中药材栽培、炮制技艺更是高人一筹，是有名的“药材之乡”。

Bozhou is located in the northwestern part of Anhui and adjacent to Jiangsu, Shandong, and Henan on its three sides. Meanwhile, the Guo River runs through the city from west to east. Thanks to its particularly favorable geographic and climatic conditions and the hometown of Huatuo, along with the enduring legacy left by the miracle doctor Huatuo, a galaxy of famous doctors and pharmacists come forth in Bozhou. As a well-known “hometown of medicinal materials”, the cultivation skills and processing techniques on Chinese medicinal materials are much better.

亳州中药材专业市场交易中心是目前国内规模最大的中药材专业交易市场，该“中心”占地 387 亩，建筑面积 35 万 m^2，拥有 1000 余家中药材经营店面。3.2 万 m^2 的交易大厅有 6000 多个摊位，经营者 2 万多人。中药材日上市量高达 6000 吨，上市品种 2600 余种，中药材成交额达 100 多亿元。

Currently, the Bozhou professional CMM market trade center is the largest professional trading market for CMM in China. The “center” covers an area of 387 *mu*, with a building area of 350,000m^2 and more than 1,000 stores for Chinese medicinal materials trade. There are more than 6,000 booths and 20,000 operators in the 32,000m^2 trading hall. The daily trading volume of Chinese medicinal materials is as high as 6,000 tons, with more than 2,600 kinds of listed varieties, and the turnover is over 10 billion yuan.

2013 年，该中心搬迁到国际现代化的中药材专业市场中国亳州康美中药城，占地面积 106 万 m^2，建筑面积 120 万 m^2，是目前最大的一站式中药材交易中心。

In 2013, the center was relocated to Bozhou Kangmei CMM city in China, an international modernized professional CMM market, covering an area of 1.06 million m^2 and a building area of 1.2 million m^2. It is currently the largest one-stop Chinese medicinal materials trading center.

4. 河南禹州中药材专业市场

4. Professional CMM market in Yuzhou, Henan

禹州位于中原腹地，因帝舜时大禹治水有功，册封于此而得名。禹州被人们公认为我国亘古中药发祥地，是历史上有名的古药都之一。相传唐代孙思邈曾在这里采药行医，著书立说，终老禹州后，当地人厚葬城西关外，为他建庙，尊为药王。禹州的中药材种植历史悠久，素有“中华药城”之称，是我国医药发祥地之一。禹州具有悠久的中药材种植、采集、加工历史，以加工精良、遵古炮制著称于世。历史上就有“药不到禹州不香，医不见药王不妙”之说。

Yuzhou is located in the hinterland of Central Plains. It was named after King Yu who achieved great feats of taming the flood was conferred here during the reign of Emperor Shun. Yuzhou is widely regarded as the birthplace of ancient CMM in China and is one of the famous ancient medicine capitals in history. It is said that Sun Simiao used to collect herbs and practice medicine, wrote books and spread ideas here in Tang Dynasty. After he died in Yuzhou, local people buried outside the west gate of the city, built temples for him and respected him as the king of medicine. Yuzhou has a long history of planting Chinese medicinal materials, known as the "Chinese Medicine City", and is one of the birthplaces of CMM. Yuzhou is famous for its long history of planting, collecting and processing Chinese medicinal materials. There is a saying in history that "the medicine is not fragrant without reaching Yuzhou, the medicine is not miraculous without seeing the king of medicine".

禹州中药材专业市场又称"中华药城"，药城占地面积400余亩，包括建筑面积23000m^2、分上下两层、可容纳2500个摊位的中心交易大厅，以及2000余间三层以上经商楼，市场经营品种上千种，固定从业人员上万人，年交易额达10亿元。

Yuzhou professional CMM market is also known as the "Chinese Medicine City", covering an area of more than 400 *mu*, including a building area of 23,000m^2 and two-storey central trading hall that can accommodate 2,500 booths, and about 2000 three-storey or above commercial buildings. Thousands of CMM are operated in the market, with tens of thousands of permanent employees, and the annual turnover reaches 1 billion yuan.

河南禹州中药材专业市场门店固定，常年经营，商户稳定；药材商品品种较为齐全，且注重经营道地药材，其中冠以"禹"字头的道地品种有禹南星、禹白芷、禹白附、禹余粮等。

In Yuzhou professional CMM market, the stores are in permanent locations, operating all year round with stable merchants; the varieties of medicinal material commodities are relatively complete, focusing on authentic medicinal. Among them, the authentic varieties entitled with "Yu" include Yu Nanxing, Yu Baizhi, Yu Baifu, Yu Yuliang.

5. 成都荷花池中药材专业市场

5. Hehuachi professional CMM market in Chengdu

成都荷花池中药材专业市场建立于20世纪70年代，历经30多年风雨，经过4次产业升级，现整体搬迁到位于成都市北新大道旁的成都国际商贸城，交通极为便利，是西部地区最大的中药材市场。市场占地140余亩，建筑面积20万m^2，拥有4000多个商位，是目前全国体量最大、硬件设施最优秀的中药材专业市场之一。

Chengdu Hehuachi professional CMM market was established in the 1970s. After more than 30 years of ups and downs and 4 industrial upgrades, it is now relocated to Chengdu International Trade City next to Beixin Avenue in Chengdu. Nowadays, with the extremely convenient traffic, it is the largest CMM market in the western region. The market covers an area of more than 140 *mu* and includes a building area of 200,000m^2 and more than 4,000 booths. Currently, it is one of the professional CMM markets in China with the largest volume and best hardware facilities.

市场常年经营户有1700多户，5000余人，经营中药材品种4500余种，常见药材约2000种，其中川产药材1300余种，如道地药材川贝母、川芎、白芷、川乌、麦冬等。也有许多四川草药医生习用的地方药，如大菟丝子、理塘黄芪等，市场日销售额500多万元。

There are more than 1,700 market perennial business users consisting of more than 5,000 people, operating more than 4,500 varieties of Chinese medicinal materials, about 2,000 kinds of common medicinal materials, of which more than 1,300 kinds are from Sichuan, such as authentic medicinal Chuan Beimu, Chuanxiong, Baizhi, Chuangwu, Maidong. There are also many local herbs conventionally used by Sichuan herbalists, namely Da Tusizi, Litang Huangqi, etc. Market turnover is about 5 million yuan every day.

近年来，国家商务部授权发布的中国成都中药材价格指数即是以荷花池中药材专业市场的商户为主要价格采集点。它的制订与发布，将为政府和行业主管部门准确及时了解和掌握中药材贸易动态，为中药材和经营者提供商业信息，同时引领中药材产业发展方向，为广大业内人士提供最有参考价值的市场信息。

In recent years, Chengdu Chinese medicinal materials price index of China was issued by the Ministry of Commerce based on the merchants in Chengdu Hehuachi professional CMM market. The formulation and release of CMM price index will provide the government and the relevant administrative departments with an accurate and timely understanding and command of Chinese medicinal materials trade trends, and provide business information for Chinese medicinal materials and operators. Meanwhile, it can also lead the development direction of the Chinese medicinal materials industry and provide the most valuable market information for the majority of professionals.

6. 哈尔滨三棵树中药材专业市场

6. Professional CMM market in Sankeshu, Harbin

哈尔滨三棵树中药材市场形成于 1991 年，是我国东北、内蒙古自治区唯一的中药材专业市场，位于黑龙江哈尔滨三棵树火车站附近而得名。经多年的建设发展，已成为我国北方中药材经营的集散地。

Harbin Sankeshu professional CMM market formed in 1991 is the only professional CMM market in Northeast China and Inner Mongolia Autonomous Region. The name of this market derives from Sankeshu railway station nearby in Harbin, Heilongjiang. After years of construction and development, it has become a distribution center for Chinese medicinal materials in northern China.

1996 年完成搬迁，占地 6000 多 m^2，建筑面积 23000m^2，可容纳经营户 1000 余个，内设中草药种植科研中心、质检中心、仓储中心。现中药材交易品种已达到 580 余种，其中 107 种量大质优，具地方特色。东北是关药道地药材的主产区，销量居全国之首，如人参、鹿茸、关防风、关龙胆、北五味子等，其中人参 80% 出口到俄罗斯、日本、韩国、东南亚、西欧等国家和地区，药材边境贸易十分活跃。

The relocation of this market was completed in 1996. It covers an area of over 6,000m^2 and includes a building area of 23,000m^2, which can accommodate more than 1,000 merchants. There are CMM planting research center, quality testing center, and storage center in the market. At present, there are more than 580 varieties of Chinese medicinal materials traded in this market, of which 107 are large in quantity and high in quality with local characteristics. Northeast China is the main production area of Guanyao authentic medicinal, and its sales volume ranks first in the country, such as Ginseng, Lurong, Guanfangfeng, Guanlongdan, and Beiwuweizi. The 80% of Ginseng is exported to Russia, Japan, Korea, Southeast Asia, Western Europe and other countries and regions, and the border trade of medicinal materials is very active.

7. 广州清平中药材专业市场

7. Professional CMM market in Qingping, Guangzhou

广州清平中药材专业市场创办于 1979 年，是我国南方重要的药材交易市场之一。经营户来自五湖四海、商品交易活跃，是华南地区最大的中药材特别是贵细滋补中药材和广药的集散地和进出口贸易重地。

Guangzhou Qingping professional CMM market was established in 1979 and is one of the important medicinal materials trade markets in Southern China. Market operators come from all corners of the country and commodity trading is active. This market is the largest distribution center and import and export trade center of Chinese medicinal materials, especially precious and nourishing Chinese medicinal materials and Guangyao, in South China.

2006年完成升级改造，新药市座落于广州清平路和六二三路，是目前唯一建立在大都市中心区域的中药材市场，市场面积达1.1万m^2，有商铺1500多家，年营业额超10亿元。该市场还是全国第一个准许经营范围达5大类别（中药材、中药饮片、中西成药、医疗器械、保健品）的医药展贸平台。药材市场中药材品种齐全，货源充足。

The upgrade of this market was completed in 2006, and the new medicine city is located on Qingping Road and Liu Ersan Road in Guangzhou. Currently, it is the only CMM market established in the downtown area of the metropolis. With a market area about 11,000m^2, there are more than 1,500 shops and an annual turnover over 1 billion yuan. This market is also the first pharmaceutical exhibition and trade platform in China with business scope up to 5 categories (Chinese medicinal materials, Chinese decocting pieces, Chinese and Western patent medicines, medical apparatus and instruments, health products). The medicinal materials market has a full range of Chinese medicinal materials and sufficient supplies.

8. 兰州黄河中药材专业市场

8. Professional CMM market in Huanghe, Lanzhou

兰州黄河中药材专业市场创办于1994年，是甘肃、宁夏、青海、新疆及西藏和内蒙古西部地区唯一的国家级中药材专业市场。经过多年的发展，市场逐步形成了立足甘肃、面向西北、辐射全国的经营格局。2003年，在全国17家中药材专业市场率先实行了公司化管理模式，2008年乔迁至兰州市安宁区高新技术开发区，新建占地约60余亩的现代网络销售物流中心，形成了“前店后厂”的营销模式。市场和公司主要销售甘肃地产药品如党参、黄芪、甘草、当归、生地、板蓝根等优势品种，同时经营全国其他产地常用中药材约800余种，年销售2亿元左右，产品主要销往甘、宁、青、新等地，辐射全国及东南亚等地。

Lanzhou Huanghe professional CMM market was established in 1994 and is the only national-level professional CMM market in Gansu, Ningxia, Qinghai, Xinjiang, Tibet and western Inner Mongolia. After years of development, the market has gradually formed a business structure from Gansu to northwest China and radiated the whole country. In 2003, this market took the lead in implementing a company-based management model in 17 professional CMM markets across the country. In 2008, it was relocated to the High-tech Development Zone in Anning District, Lanzhou City, and the new market includes a modern online sales and logistics center covering an area of about 60 acres and forms a marketing model of “front store and back factory”. The market and the company mainly sell Gansu authentic herbs, such as Dangshen, Huangqi, Gancao, Danggui, Shengdihuang, Banlangen and other dominant varieties. Meanwhile, it operates more than 800 kinds of Chinese medicinal materials commonly used in other regions of the country. The annual turnover of the market is about 200 million yuan, and its products are mainly sold to Gansu, Ningxia, Qinghai, Xinjiang and other places, radiating to the country and Southeast Asia.

9. 中国香港市场

9. Market in Hong Kong, China

历史上中国香港也是我国中药的主要国际市场，中药商品多从香港转口外销，形成了我国中药的重要转口贸易基地。在香港可买到的药材品种约1900多种。在药材铺出售的药材约900种，其中常用的有约400种。药材市场年贸易额约18亿港元左右。出口药材品种中，居前十位的药材品种为：园参、野山参、甘草、当归、党参、黄芪、怀山药、生地黄、菊花、枸杞子，其在港销售约在55%左右，其余则销往中国台湾、东南亚、美国、加拿大等地。香港中医药行业从业人员约 1.2 万，出售中成药已达 3300 种，其中，中成药的 80%、药材和饮片的 90% 是从大陆进口。但近年来随着我国对外开放的发展，中药的转口贸易因日本、韩国、中国台湾等地都直接由大陆发货而大幅度下降，贸易额减少。

In history, Hong Kong is also the main international market for CMM in China. Most CMMCs are re-exported from Hong Kong, forming an important re-export trade base for CMM. There are more than 1,900 varieties of medicinal materials available in Hong Kong, and there are about 900 kinds of medicinal materials sold in the medicinal materials shop, of which about 400 are commonly used. The annual turnover of the medicinal materials market is about 1.8 billion Hong Kong dollars. Among the exported medicinal materials, the top ten medicinal materials are: garden Ginseng, wild Ginseng, Gancao, Danggui, Dangshen, Huangqi, Huaishanyao, Shengdihuang, Juhua, and Gouqizi. Their sales in Hong Kong are about 55%, and the rest are sold to Taiwan (China), Southeast Asia, the United States, Canada and other places. There are about 12,000 employees in the CMM industry in Hong Kong, and 3,300 Chinese patent medicines are available. Among them, 80% of the Chinese patent medicines and 90% of the medicinal materials and decocting pieces are imported from Chinese mainland. However, in recent years, with the development of China's opening to the outside world, the re-export trade of CMM in Hong Kong has fallen sharply because Japan, South Korea, Taiwan (China), and other places have directly shipped goods from Chinese mainland.

10. 中国台湾市场

10. Market in Taiwan, China

中国台湾的中药主要来源为大陆，台湾已成大陆药材出口第 5 大市场。伴随着我国大陆与台湾两岸三通的实现，贸易便利化的增强，海峡两岸在中药贸易领域的合作日益增多，中药进出口贸易保持着持续稳定的增长。全台有 300 多家药商经营中药商品，经营品种总数有 500 余种。近年来多从福建入境，不再从香港转口。

The main source of CMM in Taiwan is Chinese mainland, and Taiwan has become the fifth largest market for mainland medicinal materials exports. With the realization of the three links between mainland and Taiwan, and the enhancement of trade facilitation, the CMM trade is increasing between mainland and Taiwan, and the import and export trade of CMM has maintained a sustained and stable growth. In Taiwan, more than 300 medicine dealers operate more than 500 kinds of CMMCs. In recent years, most CMM have been exported directly from Fujian and no longer re-exported from Hong Kong.

从产品结构来看，我国大陆中药对台出口主要以中药材及饮片、提取物为主，保健品和中成药所占比例很小。市场上的人参、当归、枸杞子、黄芪等品种较为畅销，排名第一为人参类产品，占药材进口总金额的 28.5%。

From the perspective of product structure, CMM exports from mainland to Taiwan are mainly Chinese medicinal materials, decocting pieces, extracts, while health products and Chinese patent medicines account for a small proportion. Ginseng, Danggui, Gouqizi, Huangqi and other varieties are more popular in the market, with Ginseng products ranking first and accounting for 28.5% of the total import value of medicinal materials.

第二节 国际市场
Section 2 International Market

PPT

国际市场是指我国在对外贸易中，中药商品在国外及我国港、澳、台地区进行交换的场所。加强中药商品对外贸易，积极巩固和开辟国际市场，是我国中药商业对外贸易的战略决策。经营的基本原则是在保证国内市场供应的前提下，实行合理组织，分工经营，联合一致，统一对外的购销原则。在坚持这些原则的基础上，积极组织适销对路的中药商品出口和进口，以增加外汇，积累资金，促进我国中医药事业的不断发展。

CMM international market refers to the place where CMMCs are exchanged at abroad and in Hong Kong, Macao and Taiwan regions, China. It is the strategic decisions of foreign trade of CMM business to strengthen the foreign trade of CMMCs and actively consolidate and open up the international market. The basic principle of operation is to implement reasonable organization, division of labor, united collaboration internally, and coordinated actions externally purchase and sales principles on the premise of ensuring the domestic market supply. On the basis of adhering to these principles, the export and import of CMMCs should be encouraged to increase foreign exchange, accumulate funds, and promote the continuous development of CMM industry.

一、中药对外贸易的历史与发展
I. History and development of CMM foreign trade

我国的中药商品对外贸易与交流有着悠久的历史。早在汉武帝时，张骞两次奉命出使西域，开辟了丝绸之路后，中药商品随着医药文化对外交流就开始了初期的对外贸易。当时中药对外贸易主要靠国内外商人之间的商品交换为主，从国外输入的药品有番红花、胡麻等。

CMMCs have a long history of foreign trade and exchange. As early as Emperor Han Wu, Zhang Qian was sent under orders on a diplomatic mission to the Western Regions twice and opened up the Silk Road. CMMCs began their initial foreign trade with the exchange of medical culture. At that time, the foreign trade of CMM was mainly based on the exchange of commodities between domestic and foreign merchants. The imported medicines from abroad included mainly Fanhonghua and Huma.

到了唐代，中药对外贸易与交流有很大发展。那时中药出口的国家主要有朝鲜、日本、印度、越南等。与此同时，从印度、波斯、大秦等国进口的药物有安息香、龙脑香、紫草、血竭、阿魏等。李珣的《海药本草》记载海外进口药材达 124 种，可见中药进出口贸易已经非常发达。

The foreign trade and exchanges of CMM had developed greatly until the Tang Dynasty. At that time, the major export countries of CMM included Korea, Japan, India and Vietnam. Meanwhile, medicines imported from India, Persia, Daqin, and other countries included Anxixiang, Longnaoxiang, Zicao, Xuejie, Awei. Li Xun's *Hai Yao Ben Cao* records 124 kinds of imported medicinal materials overseas, suggesting that the import and export trade of CMM had been very developed.

两宋金元时代，在唐代的基础上，中药对外贸易又有新的发展。公元 971 年，宋政府在广州专门设置“市舶司”，统管对外贸易，更多的中药商品出口到朝鲜、日本、越南、柬埔寨、罗马、阿拉伯等国。据《宋会要》记载，当时出口阿拉伯的中药有朱砂、水银、人参、牛黄、附子、川芎、甘草等58种，并由阿拉伯商人把这些中药运到西方各国。其中牛黄深受国外医家的重视，《伦敦药典》中收载了牛黄，阿拉伯名医阿文左阿记载有“解毒石”（即牛黄）。元代出口的中药也较多，《真腊风土记》（真腊：即柬埔寨）中记载有水银、硫黄、檀香、白芷等中药，说明当时我国与柬埔寨也有频繁的贸易往来。与此同时，当时输入的药物也不少，如乳香、没药、槟榔、丁香等。

During the Northern Song, Southern Song, Jin and Yuan Dynasties, new developments were made in the foreign trade of CMM on the basis of the Tang Dynasty. In 971 AD, the Song government set up a “Shi Bo Si” in Guangzhou to regulate foreign trade. More CMMCs were exported to Korea, Japan, Vietnam, Cambodia, Rome, and Arab countries. According to *Song Hui Yao*, 58 kinds of CMM were exported to Arabia at that time including Zhusha, Shuiyin, Ginseng, Niuhuang, Fuzi, Chuanxiong, and Gancao, and these CMM were shipped to western countries by Arab merchants. Among them, Niuhuang was highly valued by foreign doctors. It is documented in the *London Pharmacopoeia*, and the famous Arab doctor Awenzoa recorded “detoxification stone” (Niuhuang). There were also many CMM exported during the Yuan Dynasty. *Zhen La Feng Tu Ji* (Zhen La: Cambodia) recorded CMM such as Shuiyin, Liuhuang, Tanxiang and Baizhi, indicating that China also had frequent trade with Cambodia at that time. Meanwhile, many medicines were imported at that time, such as Ruxiang, Moyao, Binglang, Dingxiang.

到了明清时代，特别是由于郑和七次奉命下南洋，打通了我国与欧、亚、非三州的海上通道，使明代的中药对外贸易得到了进一步发展。如大黄、当归、鹿茸等出口量不断增加，远销到欧、亚、非三州各国。据《明会要》记载，明代输入的药物有藤黄、乌爹泥（儿茶）、苏木、檀香等50余种，仅暹罗（泰国）输入的药品就达31种之多。公元1606年，西方医生熊三拔来到中国，结合医药的制备方法，编著了《药露说》，从而有了苏合油、丁香油、檀香油、桂花油、冰片油等用于临床。

In the Ming and Qing dynasties, the seaways between China and Europe, Asia, and Africa were available, which attributed to Zheng He’s voyage to the South Seas, and the foreign trade of CMM was further developed in the Ming Dynasty. Dahuang, Danggui and Lurong were exported to countries in Europe, Asia and Africa with larger export volume. According to *Ming Hui Yao*, there were more than 50 kinds of medicines imported in the Ming Dynasty, such as Tenghuang, Wudieni (Ercha), Sumu, and Tanxiang, of which 31 kinds of medicines were from Xianluo (Thailand). In 1606, Xiongsanba, a western doctor, wrote *Yao Lu Shuo* in China by combining the preparation method of medicine, which promoted the clinical application of Suhe oil, Dingxiang oil, Tanxiang oil, Guihua oil, and Bingpian oil.

但清代以后特别是1840年鸦片战争后，中国沦为半殖民地半封建社会，西药充斥国内市场，中药的国内外市场几乎丧失已尽，更无发展可言。但是随着西药的引入，康熙10年，每年有数十箱鸦片输入，给中国人民的健康带来极大的危害。引进的药物也只有《本草纲目拾遗》中有记载，如强水、日精油、西洋参、东洋参、浮大海、洋虫等。

After the Qing Dynasty, especially after the Opium War of 1840, China was relegated to a semi-colonial, semi-feudal country, and western medicine flooded the domestic market, resulting in the loss and stagnant development of the CMM domestic and foreign markets. However, with the introduction of western medicine, dozens of boxes of opium were imported to China every year in the 10 years of Kangxi, which did great harm to the health of the Chinese. The imported medicines are only recorded in *Ben Cao Gang Mu Shi Yi*, such as Qiangshui, Rijingyou, western Ginseng, eastern Ginseng, Fudahai, and Yangchong.

新中国成立后，我国对外贸易的发展使得国际市场逐渐的恢复，并有所发展。近年来，随着我国对外开放的发展和世界各国人民“回归大自然”风潮的高涨，国际市场不断增加。特别是入世后，据相关资料统计我国中药出口覆盖到六大洲、168个国家和地区，规模呈不断扩大的趋势。主要国际市场分为日韩市场、东南亚市场、西方市场、非洲及阿拉伯市场。日韩市场是我国中草药出口稳步发展的市场，但同时也是我国竞争国际草药市场的主要对手，约占世界草药市场的21%；东南亚市场包括东南亚诸国及我国港、澳、台地区，占世界草药市场的26%；西方市场主要包括西欧和北美等国；非洲及阿拉伯市场随着20世纪60年代初我国多批医疗队的派遣，中医药和当地草药治疗的热潮正在形成，是一个正在崛起的中草药国际市场。据2013年国家的统计，亚洲地区我国仍是中药贸易第一大市场，以我国香港地区以及东盟、韩国、日本等亚洲地区为主。2013年1~10月与我国香港地区出售中药8万吨，占45%；对东盟出口3.1万吨，对韩国出口2万吨，对日本出口1.6万吨，对东盟、韩国和日本出口合计占38.4%。

After the founding of New China, the international market has been gradually restored and developed due to the development of Chinese foreign trade. In recent years, with the development of chinese opening to the outside world and the rising tide of "returning to nature" among peoples of all countries in the world, the CMM international market has been increasing. Especially after entering WTO, the CMM export covers six continents, 168 countries and regions, and the scale is expanding according to relevant statistics. The main international markets include Japanese, Korean, Southeast Asian, Western, African and Arab markets. The Japanese and Korean export markets of CMM develop steadily, but they are also Chinese main rivals in the international herbal medicine market, and the scale of their trade accounts for about 21% of the world's herbal medicine market. Southeast Asian market includes Southeast Asian countries and Hong Kong, Macao and Taiwan regions in China, and the scale of their trade accounts for 26% of the world's herbal medicine market. Western market mainly involves the countries in Western Europe and North America. With the dispatch of a number of medical teams from China to African and Arab in the early 1960s, and the boom of CMM and local herbal therapies, African and Arab markets are the rising international markets for CMM exports. According to the national statistics in 2013, China is still the largest market for CMM trade in Asia, and the trade is mainly concentrated in Hong Kong, China and ASEAN, South Korea, Japan and other Asian regions. From January to October 2013, 80,000 tons of CMM were sold to Hong Kong region, which accounted for 45% trade. Meanwhile, CMM exports were 31,000 tons to ASEAN, 20,000 tons to South Korea, 16,000 tons to Japan, and total exports to ASEAN, South Korea and Japan accounted for 38.4% trade.

我国中药出口品种中，2012年所有的中药提取物出口金额是11.3亿美元，占中药出口金额的48.5%。中药材和饮片的出口约7亿美元，占中药出口金额的33%。中成药出口的比例较少。据统计，在中成药出口方面，日本占世界份额的80%，韩国占了15%，而中国只占了3%~5%。我国加大中成药的出口任重道远。

Among the varieties of CMM exports in China, the export value of all CMM extracts in 2012 was 11.3 billion US dollars, accounting for 48.5% of the total value of CMM exports. The export value of Chinese medicinal materials and decocting pieces was about 700 million US dollars, accounting for 33% of the total value of CMM exports. The proportion of Chinese patent medicines export was relatively small. According to statistics, in terms of Chinese patent medicines export, Japan accounts for 80% of the world's share, South Korea accounts for 15%, and China accounts for only 3% to 5%. Therefore, China has a long way to go to increase the export of Chinese patent medicines.

二、中药主要国际市场简介

II. Brief introduction to the main international CMM markets

1. 日本市场

1. Japanese market

我国医药学对日本的影响最大，时间最长。早在秦汉时期我国医药学就开始传入日本，逐渐形成了“汉方医学”。从此以后他们有使用汉方汉药治病的习惯，使之成为我国中药商品的主要国际市场之一。近年来，日本政府对汉方汉药的使用放宽了控制，使药材的需求量大幅增加。据日本汉方生药制剂协会报道，日本国内汉方制剂的年生产总额为 10 亿美元，其生药原料的 70%~80% 从我国进口。中国人参在日本大受欢迎，2006 年对其出口额高达近 1000 万美元。其他出口额超过 100 万美元的产品有：半夏、甘草、茯苓、杜仲、白芍、肉桂、地黄、黄芪、枸杞子、冬虫夏草、白术、黄连等。在日本市场上可见的由我国直接生产、输入或经日方重新包装销售的中成药有 100 余种，补益性药物如三鞭丸、人参鹿茸丸、十全大补丸、首乌延寿片等；治疗常见病药物如华佗膏、鼻渊丸、槐角丸、麻杏止咳片等；特色强、无同类商品的如冠元颗粒、舒筋丸等，但缺少对疑难病症有效的中成药。

Chinese medicine shows the greatest impact on Japan for a very long time. As early as the Qin and Han Dynasties, Chinese medicine was introduced into Japan, and the “Kampo Medicine” were gradually formed. Since then, the Japanese have formed the habit of using CMM to treat diseases, making Japan one of the major international markets for CMMCs. In recent years, the Japanese government has relaxed controls on the usage of CMM, which has increased the demand for medicinal materials. According to the report of Japan Kampo Medicines Manufacturers Association, the total annual production value of Kampo pharmaceutical preparations in Japan is 1 billion US dollars, and 70% to 80% of their raw materials are imported from China. Chinese Ginseng is very popular in Japan, and its export value in 2006 was nearly 10 million US dollars. Other CMM products with an export value of more than 1 million US dollars include Banxia, Gancao, Fuling, Duzhong, Baishao, Rougui, Dihuang, Huangqi, Gouqizi, Dongchongxiacao, Baizhu, Huanglian. There are more than 100 kinds of Chinese patent medicines in the Japanese market, which can be directly produced in China, imported from China, or repackaged by the Japanese company in Japan. The nourishing CMM include Sanbian pill, Ginseng Lurong pill, Shi Quan Da Bu pill, Shouwu Yan Shou tablet. The CMM to treat common diseases include Huatuo extract, Biyuan pill, Huaijiao pill, Ma Xing Zhi Ke tablet. CMMCs with strong characteristics and without similar products are Guan Yuan granula, Shu Jin pill, etc. However, there is a lack of Chinese patent medicines that are effective for difficult and complicated diseases on the market.

2. 韩国市场

2. Korean market

韩国的韩医在历史上也深受中医影响，特别是近年随着制药企业不断研制开发新药的需要，人们生活水平的提高，药材商品数量的需求不断增加。而韩国各版药典所记载 506 种药材中，仅 62 种与中药材同名异物，其余均相同。韩国有中药厂 80 多家，因本土中药资源很少，原料也主要依靠从中国进口。据统计，韩国每年约需中药材 3 万余吨，一直是我国中药材主要市场之一。韩国进口的中药材主要是本地产量少甚至没有的，包括葛根、菊花、甘草、桂枝、藿香、鹿角、鹿茸、桃仁、麻黄、半夏、茯苓、附子、酸枣仁、牛黄、肉桂、猪苓、秦皮、杏仁、黄连、黄柏、厚朴、当归以及抗癌类草药。

Korean medicine in South Korea has also been deeply influenced by Chinese medicine in history. Especially in recent years, with the continuous development of new medicines by pharmaceutical companies and the improvement of people’s living standards, the demand for medicinal material commodities has increased. The names of 62 medicinal materials are the same as Chinese medicinal materials in the 506 medicinal materials listed in Korean Pharmacopoeia, but they represent different medicinal materials, and the rest are the same as CMM. There are more than 80 CMM factories in South Korea, and the raw materials are also mainly imported from China due to the scarcity of local CMM resources. According to statistics, South Korea needs approximately 30,000 tons of Chinese medicinal materials each year, and has been one of the major markets for Chinese medicinal materials exports. The Chinese medicinal materials mainly imported by South Korea includes Gegen, Juhua, Gancao, Guizhi, Huoxiang, Lujiao, Lurong, Taoren, Mahuang, Banxia, Fuling, Fuzi, Suanzaoren, Niuhuang, Rougui, Zhuling, Qinpi, Xingren, Huanglian, Huangbo, Houpo, Danggui, and anti-cancer herbs.

3. 越南市场

3. Vietnam market

自中国和越南关系正常化以来，越南也实行对外开放的政策，放宽了对中药商品贸易的限制，因而进入越南的中药商品品种和数量呈明显上升的趋势，已占越南药品市场的50%以上。出口越南的药材商品主要有人参、黄芪、白术、川芎、党参、桔梗等。

Since the normalization of relations between China and Vietnam, Vietnam has also implemented a policy of opening up to the outside world, which relax restrictions on trade in CMMCs. As a result, the variety and quantity of CMMCs from China to Vietnam have shown a clear upward trend, which has accounted for more than 50% of the Vietnamese medicine market. The medicinal material commodities exported to Vietnam are mainly Ginseng, Huangqi, Baizhu, Chuanxiong, Dangshen, Jiegeng, etc.

4. 北美市场

4. North American market

中药商品很久以来以食品、食品添加剂、土特产等进入北美市场，包括美国、加拿大、墨西哥等。中药如作为药品进入美国市场必须先通过FDA认证，所用资金多且风险大，因此进入难度大。近年美国政府正在放宽对中药进口的限制，专门出台了《植物药在美上市批准法》和《关于植物药品研究指南》，开始接收有复方制剂的植物药作为治疗药物。我国申报的复方丹参滴丸已顺利通过美国FDA的三期临床试验，为进入美国市场提供了较强支撑。新版美国药典收载了一定数量的植物制剂的质量标准。加拿大政府近年来也宣布了对包括中草药在内的天然保健产品的管理方式进行改革。

CMMCs have entered the North American market as food, food additives, and souvenirs for a long time, including the United States, Canada, and Mexico. If CMM enter the United States market as a drug, it must firstly pass FDA certification, which needs a lot of money. Meanwhile, the risks are great, so it is difficult to enter the United States market. In recent years, the United States government is relaxing restrictions on the import of CMM, and has specifically issued *Approval Law for Botanical Drug Product Marketing in USA* and *Guidance for Industry Botonical Drug Products*. Currently, the United States has started to accept plant drugs with CMM as therapeutic drugs. Compound Danshen Dripping Pills have successfully passed the Phase III clinical trial of the United States FDA, which provides strong support for entering the United States market. New United States Pharmacopoeia contains a number of quality standards of plant preparations. The Canadian government has also announced reforms in the management of natural health products including CMM in recent years.

5. 西欧市场

5. Western European market

西欧市场包括德国、法国、英国、比利时、丹麦、希腊、爱尔兰、意大利、卢森堡、荷兰、葡萄牙等国家。欧洲国家对中药进口要求较严，与日韩相比，中药进入欧洲市场难度大。随着对中药认识的转变，近年来西欧各国进口中药的数量也日渐增多，德、法、英、意、西、比、荷七国是进口最多的国家。中药在德国和法国已按欧洲共同体要求注册管理。2012年我国生产的地奥心血康胶囊以治疗性药品通过荷兰药品注册，实现欧盟注册零的突破。

Western European market consists of Germany, France, the United Kingdom, Belgium, Denmark, Greece, Ireland, Italy, Luxembourg, Netherlands, Portugal, etc. European countries have stricter requirements on CMM imports relative to Japan and South Korea, so it is more difficult for CMM to enter the European market. With the change of attitude towards CMM, the number of imported CMM in Western European countries has also increased in recent years. Germany, France, the United Kingdom, Italy, Spain, Belgium, and Netherlands are the most imported countries. CMM has been registered and managed in Germany and France in accordance with European Community requirements. In 2012, Diao Xinxuekang Capsule produced by China passed the Dutch drug registration as a therapeutic drug, which achieved a breakthrough of zero registration in the European Union.

6. 东南亚及其他国际市场

6. Southeast Asia and other international markets

东南亚国家华人较多，各国政府大都承认我国的中药市售药品，中成药得到广泛应用。新加坡每年从我国进口中药材约 2 万吨，马来西亚每年进口中药材 0.8 万吨，泰国每年约需 5000 万美元的中药材，因此该市场最大且相对容易进入。

There are many Chinese in Southeast Asian countries, and governments of various countries have recognized CMM sold in China, so Chinese patent medicines are widely used in these countries. Singapore imports about 20,000 tons of Chinese medicinal materials from China every year, Malaysia imports 80,000 tons of Chinese medicinal materials every year, and Thailand imports about 50 million US dollars of Chinese medicinal materials each year, so this market is the largest market and relatively easy to enter.

其他的国际市场如东欧、澳洲、非洲等随着中药零售企业的增加，需求量也逐渐增加。近年澳大利亚成功实施中医立法，为中医药走向世界迈出了巨大一步。这些市场也是我国今后努力发展的中药商品国际市场。

With the increase of CMM retail enterprises in other international markets such as Eastern Europe, Australia, Africa, the demand for CMM has also gradually increased. In recent years, the successful implementation of Chinese medicine legislation in Australia has taken a huge step for CMM to enter the world. These markets are also the international markets for CMMCs that China will strive to develop in the future. These international markets are also the export markets for CMMCs in the future, which need to be developed by our country.

三、中药商品进出口概况

III. Overview of CMMCs import and export

1. 出口中药商品概况

1. Overview of CMMCs export

我国出口的中药商品主要是药材商品。药材商品大部分属于天然的“草根树皮”，防治疾病的效果安全可靠，副作用小。在世界各国人民“回归大自然”的呼声越来越大的情况下，不少国外厂商都要求从天然的动植物中提取有效成分，代替化学合成的成分研制新药，这是近几年来的一种新的动向和趋势。而中国的药材商品属天然药物，在国际市场上占有绝对优势。但有很多品种，由于长期不能满足国际市场的需要，促使国外开展了试种、引种工作，以获得货源的可靠保障，这对我国增加中药商品出口，开辟新的国际市场极为不利。此外，韩国、印度、越南、缅甸、朝鲜等国家也在出售药材商品，与我国形成了竞争关系，这对我国巩固和扩大国际市场也极为不利。因此我们只有采取有效措施，在大力发展出口中药商品生产，保证出口药品的数量和质量的同时，制订出相应的经营策略与经营计划，才能在激烈的国际市场竞争中取得胜利。

The CMMCs exported by China are mainly medicinal material commodities. Most of the medicinal material commodities belong to the natural "herbs, root, and bark". Their effect on preventing and curing diseases is safe and reliable, and the side effects are small. With the enthusiasm of people from all over the world for "returning to nature", many foreign manufacturers are demanding to extract effective ingredients from natural plants and animals, instead of chemically synthesized ingredients, to develop new medicines. This is a new trend in recent years. Chinese medicinal material commodities are natural medicines, so they have an absolute advantage in the international market. However, there are many varieties of CMM that have not been able to meet the needs of the international market for a long time, which has prompted foreign countries to carry out trial and introduction work to obtain a reliable guarantee of supply. This is extremely detrimental to increasing exports of CMMCs and opening up new international markets. In addition, South Korea, India, Vietnam, Myanmar, North Korea and other countries are also selling medicinal material commodities, and these countries has formed a competitive relationship with China, which is also extremely detrimental to China's consolidation and expansion of international markets. Therefore, we can only take effective measures to vigorously develop CMMCs exports and ensure the quantity and quality of exported medicines. Meanwhile, the corresponding operation strategy and plan should be formulated so that we can win in the fierce international market competition.

我国出口的主要中药商品有甘草、党参、地黄、鹿茸、人参、黄连、当归、川芎、白芍、茯苓、菊花、白术、麦冬、黄芪、云木香、枸杞子、金银花、山药、延胡索、牡丹皮、泽泻、桔梗、川贝母、牛膝、玄参、杜仲、山茱萸、三七、厚朴、黄柏、枳壳、天麻、连翘、柴胡、猪苓等。此外，中成药商品有天麻酒、云南白药、片仔癀等。

The main CMMCs exported by China include Gancao, Dangshen, Dihuang, Lurong, Renshen, Huanglian, Danggui, Chuanxiong, Baishao, Fuling, Juhua, Baizhu, Maidong, Huangqi, Yunmuxiang, Gouqizi, Jinyinhua, Shanyao, Yanhusuo, Mudanpi, Zexie, Jiegeng, Chuanbeimu, Niuxi, Xuanshen, Duzhong, Shanzhuyu, Sanqi, Houpo, Zhiqiao, Tianma, Lianqiao, Chaihu, Zhuling. In addition, Chinese patent medicines include Tianma wine, Yunnan Baiyao, Pianzaihuang.

2. 进口中药商品概况

2. Overview of CMMCs import

我国受各种自然条件的限制，从古至今都需要进口少量的药材，来保证国内人民用药的需要。近几十年来，有些品种在国内发现了新资源或引种成功，减少了进口或不再进口，如血竭、砂仁、木香、西洋参等，为国家节约了外汇。

Due to the limitation of various natural conditions, China needs to import a small amount of medicinal materials in all ages to ensure the domestic people's need for medication. In recent decades, some varieties of CMM have found new resources or been introduced successfully in China, namely Xuejie, Sharen, Muxiang, western Ginseng, etc. These achievements have reduced the import of medicinal materials and saved foreign exchange for the country.

目前，我国主要进口药材品种有儿茶、西洋参、高丽参、西红花、苏合香、安息香、乳香、血竭、沉香、檀香、丁香、母丁香、小茴香、荜茇、豆蔻、肉豆蔻、大风子、西青果、诃子、胖大海、芦荟、猴枣、番泻叶、马钱子、天竺黄、海马、蛤蚧、石斛、砂仁、草果、没食子、木蝴蝶、藤黄、广天仙子、槟榔、胡黄连、石决明、海龙、阿魏、天然冰片（龙脑香）、鸡蛋花、槐花（米）、甘草、伊贝母、穿山龙、肉苁蓉等。

Currently, the main medicinal materials imported by China include Ercha, western Ginseng, Korean Ginseng, Xihonghua, Suhexiang, Anxixiang, Ruxiang, Xuejie, Chenxiang, Tanxiang, Dingxiang, Mudingxiang, Xiaohuixiang, Biba, Doukou, Roudoukou, Dafengzi, Xiqingguo, Hezi, Pangdahai, Luhui, Houzao, Fanxieye, Maqianzi, Tianzhuhuang, Haima, Gejie, Shihu, Sharen, Caoguo, Moshizi, Muhudie, Tenghuang, Guangtianxianzi, Binglang, Huhuanglian, Shijueming, Hailong, Awei, Tianranbingpian (Longnaoxiang), Jidanhua, Huaihua (Mi), Gancao, Yibeimu, Chuanshanlong, Roucongrong.

进口的药材中，近几年来发现质量不稳定、掺杂作伪的现象时有发生，应加强质量管理和检验，严格按照《进口药材质量标准》和《药品管理法》的规定，把好质量关。凡不符合质量规定的药材商品不得进口，以维护我国人民的利益。

In recent years, it has been found that the quality of imported medicinal materials is unstable and adulterated. Therefore, quality management and inspection should be strengthened when importing medicinal materials, and quality must be strictly controlled in accordance with the "Quality Standards for Imported Medicinal Materials" and the "Drug Administration Law". Any medicinal material commodities that do not meet the quality requirements shall not be imported to protect the interests of the people in China.

重点小结
Summary

编号	知识点	阐述
1	市场有广义和狭义之分	广义市场是指在一定的时间和空间条件下，商品交换关系的总和。即把市场看成是商品交换的总体，或者是商品生产、流通、消费的全过程。狭义市场是商品交换的场所。一般都设在交通发达、人口稠密的城镇。所以狭义市场是一个有限的区域，但在通讯方法多样化的今天，狭义市场的区域已不断扩大，买卖双方除面对面地进行交易外，还可利用电话、传真、网络等现代通讯方法进行联系或交易，故市场的范围可遍及全国和全世界
2	1996年国家仅批准保留了17家中药材专业市场	河北安国、安徽亳州、山东鄄城舜王城、哈尔滨三棵树、湖北蕲春、江西樟树、广州清平、广东普宁、成都荷花池、湖南廉桥、河南禹州、西安万寿北路、广西玉林、重庆解放西路、昆明菊花园、湖南岳阳花板桥、兰州黄河。此外，香港、台湾也是我国重要的中药市场
3	中药主要国际市场	日本市场、韩国市场、越南市场、北美市场、西欧市场、东南亚市场及其他国际市场
4	我国进出口的主要中药商品概况	主要进出口药材品种

No.	Knowledge point	Explanation
1	The market has both broad and narrow sense	The broad market refers to the sum of commodity exchange relations under certain time and space conditions. That is to say, the market is considered as the whole of commodity exchange, or the whole process of commodity production, circulation, and consumption. The narrow market is a place for commodity exchange and generally located in densely populated towns with well-developed transportation. So the narrow market is a limited area, but this area has been expanding with the diversification of communication methods today. In addition to face-to-face transactions between buyers and sellers, modern communication methods such as telephone, fax, and Internet can also be used to make contacts or transactions. Therefore, the narrow market can cover the whole country and the world
2	China only approved the retention of 17 professional CMM markets in 1996	Anguo, Hebei; Bozhou, Anhui; Shunwangcheng, Juancheng, Shandong; Sankeshu, Harbin; Qichun, Hubei; Zhangshu, Jiangxi; Qingping, Guangzhou; Puning, Guangdong; Hehuachi, Chengdu; Lianqiao, Hunan; Yuzhou, Henan; Qanshou North Road, Xi'an; Yulin, Guangxi; Jiefang West Road, Chongqing; Juhua Yuan, Kunming; Huaban Qiao,Yueyang, Hunan; Huanghe, Lanzhou. In addition, Hong Kong and Taiwan are also important CMM markets in China
3	The major international markets for CMM	Japanese, Korean, Vietnamese, North American, Western European, Southeast Asian, and other international markets
4	Overview of the main CMMCs import and export in China	The main medicinal materials imported or exported by China

题库

目 标 检 测
Object Detection

一、选择题（Choice question）

（一）单项选择题（One-choice question）

1. 我国中药出口品种中，出口金额占比最高的是（　　）

A. 中药提取物　　B. 中药材　　C. 中药饮片

D. 中成药　　E. 民族药

Among the varieties of CMM exports in China, the highest proportion of export value is (　　)

A. CMM extracts　　B. Chinese medicinal materials

C. Chinese decocting pieces　　D. Chinese patent medicines

E. Ethnic drugs

2. 在中成药出口方面，世界份额占比最高的国家是（　　）

A. 中国　　B. 韩国　　C. 新加坡

D. 日本　　E. 印度

In terms of Chinese patent medicines export, the country with the highest share of the world is (　　)

A. China　B. South Korea　C. Singapore
D. Japan　E. India

3. 早在三国时期，什么地方建立了“药圩”(　　)
A. 江西樟树　B. 山东鄄城舜王城　C. 安徽亳州
D. 河南禹州　E. 广州清平
As early as the Three Kingdoms period, where was the “Yaoxu” established (　　)
A. Zhangshu, Jiangxi
B. Shunwangcheng, Juancheng, Shandong
C. Bozhou, Anhui
D. Yuzhou, Henan
E. Qingping, Guangzhou

（二）多项选择题（Multiple choice question）

1. 经整顿，1996 年国家批准保留的 17 家中药材专业市场有（　　）
A. 河北安国　B. 成都荷花池　C. 中国香港
D. 安徽亳州　E. 广州清平
After rectification, China only approved the retention of 17 professional CMM markets in 1996, and they include (　　)
A. Anguo, Hebei　B. Hehuachi, Chengdu　C. Hong Kong, China
D. Bozhou, Anhui　E. Qingping, Guangzhou

2. 中药主要国际市场包括（　　）
A. 日本市场　B. 北美市场　C. 韩国市场
D. 越南市场　E. 东南亚市场
The main CMM international markets include (　　)
A. Japanese market　B. North American market　C. Korean market
D. Vietnam market　E. Southeast Asian market

3. 下列哪些是我国主要进口药材（　　）
A. 番泻叶　B. 丁香　C. 麦冬
D. 西洋参　E. 三七
Which of the following are the main imported medicinal materials in China (　　)
A. Fanxieye　B. Dingxiang　C. Maidong
D. western Ginseng　E. Sanqi

4. 下列哪些是我国出口的主要中药商品（　　）
A. 人参　B. 地黄　C. 麦冬
D. 西红花　E. 黄连
Which of the following are the main CMMCs exported by China (　　)
A. Ginseng　B. Dihuang　C. Maidong
D. Xihonghua　E. Huanglian

二、解答题（Thinking question）

1. 阐述中药广义和狭义市场的异同。
Explaining the similarities and differences between the broad and narrow CMM markets.

2. 为减少中药商品的进口，我国可以采取哪些措施？
What measures can China take to reduce the imports of CMMCs?
3. 为增加中药商品的出口，我国可以采取那些措施？
What measures can China take to reduce the exports of CMMCs?

第六章　中药商品的经营

Chapter 6　Management of Chinese Materia Medica Commodities

学习目标 | Learning Target

知识要求：

1. **掌握**　中药经营企业分类与特点；中药贮存中主要的养护方法。

2. **熟悉**　药材、饮片与中成药商品收购的特点；中药贮存中常见的变质现象、主要因素。

3. **了解**　中药商品的销售、运输、贮存环节相关事宜。

能力要求：

学会区分广义、狭义的中药商品经营；熟悉中药仓库业务管理的主要环节。

Knowledge requirements:

1. **Proficiency**　The classification and characteristics of Chinese Materia Medica (CMM) enterprises and the main maintenance methods during CMM storage.

2. **Familiarity**　The purchase characteristics of Chinese medicinal material, Chinese decocting pieces and Chinese patent medicine and the common metamorphism phenomena and major factors during CMM storage.

3. **Understanding**　The matters related to sales, transportation and storage of Chinese Materia Medica commodities(CMMCs).

Skill requirements:

Learning to distinguish CMMCs management in a broad and narrow sense. Familiarizing the links of the business management of Chinese medicinal warehouse.

中药商品经营的概念，有广义和狭义两种。广义的概念是指中药经营企业开展中药商品购、销、运、存及其相关经济活动。狭义的概念则仅指中药经营企业开展中药商品的购销活动。本书的中药商品经营的概念是采用广义的概念。

The concept "CMMCs business" has both a broad and a narrow sense. In broad sense, it refers to CMM enterprises that carry out the purchase, sale, transportation, storage and related economic activities of CMMCs. In narrow sense, it refers to CMM enterprises that carry out the purchase and sale of CMMCs. In this book, the broad concept is adopted.

第一节 中药经营企业分类与特点

Section 1 The Classification and Characteristics of CMM Enterprises

PPT

中药经营企业是联系工业与农业，城市与乡村，生产与消费之间的纽带和桥梁，在我国国民经济中占有一定的地位。

CMM enterprises are the links and bridges linking industry and agriculture, cities and villages, production and consumption, and occupy a certain position in China's national economy.

一、中药经营企业的分类

I. Classification of CMM enterprises

按在中药商品流通中的职能不同，中药经营企业可分为批发企业、零售企业。

According to different functions in the circulation of CMMCs, CMM enterprises can be divided into wholesale enterprise and retail enterprise.

（一）批发企业

(I) Wholesale enterprise

是指专门从事收购或调入中药商品，然后转卖给其他中药企业或事业单位为基本业务的中药经营企业。它是组织产销之间、城乡之间、地区之间药品流通的枢纽，既是中药商品流通的起点，又是中药商品流通的中间环节。其经营特点是进行大宗的经营活动，不直接与消费者发生交换关系，在中药商品销售中占有重要地位。

Wholesale enterprise refers to the CMM enterprise which purchases or transfers specially CMMCs and then resell to other CMM enterprise or institutions. It is the pivot of CMM circulation between production and marketing, between urban and rural areas, and between regions. It is not only the starting point of CMMCs circulation, but also the intermediate link. Its operating characteristics are to carry out *bulk* stock transaction, without directly exchanging with consumers, which occupies an important position in the CMMCs sales.

中药批发企业的主要任务是：

The main tasks of CMM wholesale enterprise are as follows:

（1）进行中药商品市场的调查与预测。

(1) To investigate and forecast the market of CMMCs.

（2）根据市场需求，指导和落实中药商品的生产和收购任务，促进中药商品生产的发展。

(2) According to the market demand, guide and carry out the production and purchase tasks of CMMCs, and promote the development of CMMCs production.

（3）根据国家有关方针、政策和计划，组织好中药商品的分配、调拨和供应工作，保证人民用药需要。

(3) Organize related work well about the distribution, allocation and supply of CMMCs in accordance with relevant guidelines, policies and plans to ensure the people's demand for CMM.

（4）根据中药商品的产销情况，合理贮存中药商品，做好养护工作，保证市场供应。

(4) According to the production and marketing situation of CMMCs, store CMMCs reasonably, maintain CMMCs well, and ensure the market supply.

（二）零售企业

(II) Retail enterprise

零售企业是指直接供应消费者或社会团体用药的中药经营企业。它是中药商品流通的最终环节，是直接为广大消费者服务的。它的特点是企业规模小，交易次数多，每次销量小，使中药商品随着从流通领域向消费领域的转移而实现其价值。

Retail enterprise refers to the CMM enterprise that supplies directly CMM to consumers or social organizations. It is the final link of CMMCs circulation and serves the broad consumers directly. It is characterized by the small scale of the enterprise, the large number of transactions, the small sales volume each time, so that realizes its value through transferring the CMMCs from the circulation field to the consumption field.

零售企业的根本任务是根据广大消费者的需要，积极组织适销对路的药品，把好药品质量的最后一关，避免脱销和积压，最大限度地满足人民配方购药的需要，千方百计为他们服务，不断提高服务质量。

The fundamental tasks of CMM retail enterprise are to actively organize marketable CMM according to the needs of the vast number of consumers, control the quality of CMM at the last link, avoid stockouts and a backlog of CMM, provide customers with maximum satisfaction with CMMCs, make every endeavor to serve customers and continuously improve the quality of service.

零售企业按其业务范围的大小又分为综合性零售企业和专营性零售企业，前者业务范围大，一般经营中药、西药、医疗器械等；后者业务范围小，只经营某一类或几类药品，如冬虫夏草专卖店，中成药药店等。

Retail enterprises are divided into comprehensive retail enterprises and franchised retail enterprises according to the business scope. The former has a large business scope, namely CMM, western medicine, medical equipment, etc. The latter has a small one, dealing in only one or a few types of CMM, namely Dongchongxiacao specialty store, Chinese patent medicine Pharmacy, etc.

二、中药经营企业的特点

II. Characteristics of CMM enterprises

中药经营企业的经营除具有一般商业企业的经营特点外，还具自身的经营特点。这些特点主要有以下几方面。

CMM enterprises not only have the operating characteristics of general commercial enterprises, but also have their own ones. These characteristics are as follows.

（一）经营的技术性强、责任重大

(I) Strong technical skills and heavy responsibilities of the management of CMMCs

中药商品主要是治病救人的特殊商品，要求从业人员既要有高尚的职业道德和高度的负责精神，又要有良好的业务素质，即要掌握医药卫生、经营管理和保管养护方面的理论知识和技能，能正确指导消费，否则易发生事故，影响消费者的健康甚至危及生命安全。

CMMCs are mainly special commodities for curing diseases and saving people. The employees are required not only to have high professional ethics and high sense of responsibility, but also to have good professional quality, that is, to master the theoretical knowledge and skills in medicine and health, operation and management, custody and maintenance, to correctly guide consumption, otherwise, accidents may occur, affect the health of consumers or even endanger life safety.

（二）货源和销售量不够稳定

（II）Unstable Supply and sales volume

中药商品特别是药材商品的货源和销量易受自然条件、灾情、疫情等非人为因素的影响，造成经营的复杂性和多变性，因而货源和销售量不稳定。这就要求中药经营企业做好社会调查和市场预测工作，以保证突发灾情、疫情等的药品供应。

The supply and sales volume of CMMCs, especially Chinese medicinal materials, are susceptible to non-human factors such as natural conditions, disasters, and epidemics, which cause the complexity and variability of operations, the supply and sales volume are unstable thereby. This requires the CMM enterprises to do a good job in social investigation and market forecast, to ensure the supply of medicines in case of the sudden disasters or epidemics.

（三）消费者需求弹性小，社会保有量不多

（III）Small demand elasticity and low inventory

中药商品多是消费者在需要治疗疾病的情况下，才被动购买的特殊商品，从整个社会消费的角度来看，少了不够用，多了又没用；不用则不要，要用时则需立即到手，因此必须加强经营中的计划安排与调节，必须有合理的库存，以保证急需时的供应。

CMMCs are mostly special commodities that passively purchased by consumers when they need to treat diseases. From the perspective of the whole social consumption, less is not enough, and more is useless. There is no need without demand, if in need, it must be in one's hands immediately. Therefore, CMM enterprises must strengthen the arrangement and adjustment in operation. It is necessary to have reasonable stock to ensure emergency supplies.

（四）质量第一，优质高效

（IV）Quality first and high efficiency

中药商品具有治病救人，救死愈伤的特殊使用价值，这一特殊的使用价值就决定了经营的药品必须是质量第一、优质高效。因此在经营中必须讲究质量，牢固树立质量第一的观点，严禁销售伪劣药品。

CMMCs have the special use value of curing patients, healing the wounded and rescuing the dying. This special use value determines that quality of CMMCs must come first and CMM in business must be of high quality and high efficiency. Therefore, CMM enterprises must pay attention to the quality, firmly establish the quality first view, strictly prohibit the sale of fake and inferior medicinals in the management.

（五）薄利多销，微利经营

（V）Small profits but high sales

中药经营企业具有两重性，既是经济事业，又是社会福利事业，因而获取利润不是经营中药商品的唯一目的，而经济效益与社会效益同时并重是经营药品的总原则，所以薄利多销，微利经营是中药经营企业自身的经营特点。

CMM enterprises show a dual nature, which is not only economic undertakings, but also social welfare undertakings. Therefore, the profit is not the only purpose. The general principle is that economic benefits and social benefits are equally important. Meager profit but high turnover and small profit management are the special operating characteristics of CMM enterprises.

第二节　中药商品经营的主要环节

Section 2　The Main Links of CMMCs Management

PPT

中药商品经营的主要环节包括购、销、运、存四大环节。其中购销活动是经营的主体和中心，运存活动是开展购销活动的必备条件，是为购销活动服务的。运也是中药商品在空间位置上的实际转移。这四个环节关系密切，缺一不可。必须紧密配合，环环相扣，才能使中药商品从生产领域经过流通领域顺利到达消费领域，以实现其价值的转移。

CMMCs management can be divided into four main links, purchase, sale, transport and storage. The purchase and sale activities are the main body and the center of the operation, and the transport and storage activities are the necessary conditions to carry out the purchase and sale activities, which serve the purchase and sale activities. Transport is also the actual transfer of CMMCs in space. These four links are closely related and indispensable. To realize the value transfer of CMMCs from the production field to the consumption field smoothly, it is necessary to cooperate closely among all link with one another.

一、中药商品的收购

I. Purchase of CMMCs

中药商品的收购是指中药经营企业根据国家的有关规定和市场需要，从生产者手里购买中药商品的一种经济活动。它是中药商品流通的起点，是组织中药商品货源的一种有效手段，也是从事药品经营的物质基础和前提。没有收购就没有货源，经营活动就无法进行。因此，搞好收购对搞好中药商品经营、满足人民用药需求具有十分重要的意义。

Purchase of CMMCs refers to an economic activity in which CMM enterprises buy CMMCs from producers according to the relevant provisions of the state and market needs. It is the starting point of the circulation of CMMCs, an effective means of organizing the supply of CMMCs, as well as the material basis and premise for pharmaceutical business. Without the purchase of CMMCs, business activities can not be carried out. Therefore, it is of great significance for the CMMCs business and meeting the people's demand for medicine.

目前，中药商品的收购，要遵照《药品管理法》规定，坚持按需生产，以销定进的原则，坚持品种、规格、质量、数量和价格并重的原则，处理好国家、集体和个人三者利益的关系，维护好消费者的利益。

At present, the purchase of CMMCs shall comply with the provisions of *Drug Administration Law*, adhere to the principle of production according to demand and purchase according to sale, adhere to the principle of paying equal attention to varieties, specifications, quality, quantity and price, deal with the interests of the state, the collective and the individual, and safeguard the interests of consumers.

中药商品的收购，包括中药材、饮片和中成药的收购，现简介如下。

The purchase of CMMCs, including Chinese medicinal materials, Chinese decocting pieces and Chinese patent medicine is briefly described as follows:

（一）中药材商品的收购

(I) Purchase of Chinese medicinal materials commodities

中药材商品的收购关系重大，国家主管部门积极加强对药材收购工作的全面管理，特别是收购中药材的质量和价格管理，保护中药资源，保护生产者和消费者的利益，依法严厉打击中药材收购中的各种违法行为。为此要充分认识中药材收购的特点，掌握中药材收购的政策、方针和应注意的问题。

It is of great importance to purchase Chinese medicinal materials commodities. National competent department actively strengthen the comprehensive management on the purchase of Chinese medicinal materials, especially the quality and price management thereof, protect the resources of Chinese medicinal materials, protect the interests of producers and consumers, and severely crack down on illegal activities in the purchase of Chinese medicinal materials according to law. Therefore, it is necessary to fully understand the characteristics of the purchase of Chinese medicinal materials, master the policies and guidelines and points to note.

1. 中药材收购的特点

1. Characteristics of the purchase of Chinese medicinal materials

中药材商品是一种特殊商品，生产技术复杂，涉及农、林、牧、副、渔各个方面，所以中药材收购与其他商品收购相比，有自己的特点，主要表现在：

As special commodities, the production technologies of Chinese medicinal materials are complex, involving agriculture, forestry, animal husbandry, sideline and fishery. Therefore, compared with other commodity purchase, the purchase of Chinese medicinal materials commodities has its own characteristics, mainly reflected in the following aspects.

（1）明显的季节性　中药材商品大都来源于药用的动植物，而动植物的种类和药用部位不同，生长周期的长短和各器官成熟时间差异很大，即所谓适时是宝，过时为草。所以中药经营企业应根据不同的生长规律和采收的季节，在采收季节之前提前做好一切准备工作，特别是对大宗中药材商品，更应集中力量，突击收购，从而不失时机把各种中药材商品收好收足。

(1) Obvious seasonality　Chinese medicinal materials commodities are mostly derived from medicinal plants and animals, however, the species, medicinal parts, the length of growth cycle and the maturity time of each organ are very different. That is, the plants or animals harvested at the right time are medicinal materials while the plants or animals missed harvesting time will have no good medicinal value. According to the different growth rule and the harvest season, CMM enterprise should do all the preparations in advance and concentrate on the purchase of bulk of the CMMCs especially, thus lose no time to collect enough all kinds of CMMCs.

（2）复杂的技术性　中药材商品种类繁多，规格复杂，质量要求高。而有的真伪难辨，有的规格等级难分，因此中药材收购业务有复杂的技术性。据此要求收购人员必须熟练掌握中药材商品知识和质量标准与其检定技术，才能准确而快速地分辨真伪，区分规格等级，牢牢把住中药材商品进入流通领域的第一关，从而确保质量和按质论价原则的准确执行。

(2) Complex technicality　Chinese medicinal materials commodities have wide varieties, complex specification and high quality requirement. Some authenticity is difficult to identify, and some specifications are hard to distinguish, so the purchase of Chinese medicinal materials has complex technical requirements. Acquirers must master the relevant knowledge of CMMCs, quality standards and identification technology, so as to accurately and quickly identify the authenticity, distinguish the grades of specifications, firmly grasp the first pass of CMMCs into the circulation field, ensure the commodities

quality and implement the principle of price based on quality.

（3）较强的地区性　中药材生产依赖于自然条件。由于各地自然条件不同以及各种药用动植物对雨量、气候、土壤等的不同要求，按照自然条件的特点形成了药材商品的不同产区；同时药材因产地不同，质量和疗效各有差异，如道地药材比非道地药材的质量好，疗效高。因此中药材商品生产有较强的地区性。据这一特性，中药经营企业应根据主产区与非主产区等的不同，重点抓好主产区、道地产区、集中产区的收购工作，从而保证中药材收购的数量与质量。

(3) Strong zonality　The production of Chinese medicinal materials depends on natural conditions. Due to the different natural conditions in different regions and the different requirements of various medicinal plants and animals on rainfall, climate, soil, etc., different producing areas of medicinal materials were formed according to the characteristics of natural conditions. Meanwhile, due to the origin of the medicinal materials, the quality and curative effect are different. For example, the quality and effect of authentic materials are better than those of non-authentic ones. Therefore, the production of Chinese medicinal material commodities is obvious zonal. According to this characteristic, CMM enterprises should focus on the purchase of major producing areas, authentic producing areas and concentrated producing areas according to the differences between major producing areas and non-major producing areas, so as to ensure the quantity and quality of the purchase of traditional Chinese medicinal materials.

（4）较明显的分散性　我国目前中药材商品的生产，无论是家种家养的还是野生的，主要由中药材种植专业户、个体户进行生产或采集，全国各地均有，因此具有较明显的分散性。根据这一特点，中药商业企业对收购网点的设置，收购人员的安排，产地加工与运输等方面都必须与此相适应，才能保证收购任务的完成。

(4) Obvious dispersion　At present, the production of CMMCs in China, whether domesticated or wild, is mainly produced or collected by professional farmers and self-employed household throughout the country. Therefore, the purchase of Chinese medicinal materials commodities has obvious feature of dispersion. According to this characteristic, CMM enterprises must adapt to the situation of these respects, namely the establishment of purchase sites, the arrangement of purchase personnel, processing in producing areas and transportation etc., so as to ensure the completion of the purchase task.

（5）较强的不稳定性　药材商品的生产受自然条件影响很大，常常出现不同年月，不同地区药材的产量和质量时高时低的情况，因而中药材的品种、数量和质量都不稳定。根据这个特点，中药经营企业在确定收购任务时，既要从市场需要和中药材生产的实际情况出发，又要留有余地，以适应药材生产不稳定的特点。

(5) Strong instability　The production of medicinal materials is greatly affected by natural conditions. The yield and quality of medicinal materials are often high and low in different years and in different areas, the variety, quantity and quality of Chinese medicinal materials are unstable thereby. According to this characteristic, when determining the purchase task, CMM enterprises should not only start from the market demand and the actual situation of Chinese medicinal materials production, but also allow for unforeseen circumstances to adapt to the unstable characteristics.

（6）广泛的群众性　药材商品生产涉及广大农村的千家万户，在收购中除依靠中药经营企业的职工和当地政府外，还要在产区广泛发动和组织群众，取得他们的配合与支持。否则很难完成中药材商品的收购任务。

(6) Extensive mass　The production of medicinal materials involves thousands of families in the rural areas. In addition to relying on the staff of CMM enterprises and the local government, they also

need to mobilize and organize the masses in the producing areas to obtain their cooperation and support. Otherwise, it is difficult to complete the task of purchasing Chinese medicinal materials.

2. 中药材收购的方法

2. Methods of the purchase of Chinese medicinal materials

在中药材收购工作中，除要认真贯彻执行国家的有关经济政策外，还要采用灵活多样的方法，保证收购任务的完成。主要收购方法有：

In the course of Chinese medicinal materials purchase, CMM enterprises not only carry out the national economic policies, but also use flexible methods to ensure the completion of the purchase task. There are several main methods.

（1）突击收购与经常收购相结合　突击收购就是在中药材集中的收购期内，集中力量把中药材收集起来。它适用于产量大、上市集中药材品种的收购。

经常收购是对一些不同产季，分散上市的药材品种，分设若干固定的收购网点，一年四季持续收购，以适应生产者经常交售药材的要求。它适用于产量小，上市分散的小宗药材商品的收购。

(1) Combination of concentrated purchase and frequent purchase　Concentrated purchase is to collect Chinese medicinal materials with concentrated efforts during the purchase period, which is suitable for the purchase of large yield and listed under centralized Chinese medicinal materials.

Frequent purchase is continuous purchase throughout the year aiming at the Chinese medicinal materials of different production season and scattered listing. CMM enterprises set up a number of fixed purchase sites so as to meet the requirements of producers who often sell Chinese medicinal materials. It is suitable for the purchase of minor commodities with small production and scattered distribution.

（2）固定收购与流动收购相结合　固定收购就是在适当的地点设立固定的收购网点，开展药材的收购工作。流动收购派专人到产地进行上门收购，所以流动收购适用于数量零星，用量较小品种的收购。

(2) Combination of fixed purchase and mobile purchase　Fixed purchase means to set up fixed purchasing networks in appropriate locations to carry out the purchase of Chinese medicinal materials. Mobile purchase means to send the person to the producing area to carry out door-to-door purchase. Therefore mobile purchase applies to the varieties whose purchase quantity and consumption are very small.

（3）专业队伍收购与发动群众主动交售相结合　专业队伍收购，就是建立一支专业收购的队伍，负责组织经常性的收购工作，并在突击收购中发挥骨干作用。发动群众交售，就是依靠和广泛发动群众，做好野生药材的采集、加工等工作，然后积极交售。

(3) Combination of professional team purchase and mobilizing the masses to take the initiative to sell　Professional team purchase is to establish a team, which is responsible for the organization of regular purchase work and playing a backbone role in the concentrated purchase. Mobilizing the masses to sell is to rely on and widely mobilize the masses to do a good job in the collection of wild medicinal materials, processing and other works, and then actively sell.

在采用上述各种收购方法的同时，还必须做好收购前的各项准备工作，包括人力、物质、资金、库房、运输、收购网点准备等，以便尽快把应收的药材全部收购起来。

While adopting the above-mentioned acquisition methods, they must also do a good preparation work before the purchase, including manpower, materials, funds, warehouses, transportation, purchase sites, so that they can purchase all the medicinal materials as soon as possible.

（二）饮片与中成药商品的收购

(II) Purchase of Chinese decocting pieces and Chinese patent medicine

饮片与中成药商品的收购是指中药经营企业依据国家的计划指导和市场需要，向中药生产企业收购饮片和中成药的一种经济活动。这与中药材商品收购不同，中药材商品收购是农商之间的经济活动，而饮片与中成药商品的收购是工商之间的经济活动。饮片与中成药商品收购有以下特点。

The purchase of Chinese decocting pieces and Chinese traditional patent medicine refers to an economic activity in which CMM enterprises purchase Chinese decocting pieces and Chinese traditional patent medicine from the manufacturers according to the state's planning and market demand. This is different from the purchase of Chinese medicinal materials, which is an economic activity between agriculture and commerce, while the purchase of Chinese decocting pieces and Chinese patent medicine is an economic activity between industry and commerce. It has the following characteristics.

1. 集中性

1. Concentration

中药工业生产主要集中在城市，有些品种还集中在几个大城市。而饮片与中成药商品的消费则遍及城乡广大地区，它的流向规律是由集中到分散，由城市到乡村，由产地到销地，因此形成集中性的特点。

The industrial production of CMM is mainly concentrated in cities, and some varieties are concentrated in several big cities. However, the consumption of Chinese decocting pieces and Chinese patent medicine is widespread in both urban and rural areas. The flow pattern is from concentration to dispersion, from cities to villages, and from producing areas to marketing sites, thus forming the characteristics of concentration.

2. 均衡性

2. Balance

由于饮片和中成药的工业化生产受自然条件影响比较小，生产的周期也较短，组织生产和收购一年四季比较均匀，形成了均衡性的特点。根据这个特点，中药经营企业必须有计划的合理地安排收购工作，对常年生产、常年使用的药物购后即销，减少库存；对常年生产、季节消费的如防暑药类应有必要的库存，以持续不断地满足市场需要。

Now that the industrial production of Chinese decocting pieces and Chinese patent medicine is less affected by natural conditions, the production cycle is shorter, and the organization of production and purchase is more uniform throughout the year, a balanced characteristic is formed. According to this characteristic, CMM enterprise should arrange the purchase work in a planned and reasonable way. Some medicines that were produced and consumed throughout the year should be sold immediately after being purchased, so as to reduce the inventory. While some medicines that were produced throughout the year and consumed seasonally, such as heatstroke preventive should be necessary in store, so as to consistently meet the demand of the market.

3. 多变性

3. Variability

随着社会生产的发展和人民生活水平的提高，中成药商品特别是滋补保健类品种更新换代较快，同类品种之间市场竞争也很激烈，因而中成药商品品种具有多变性。根据这个特点，中药经营企业应加强市场调查与预测，掌握消费变化的规律，根据这一规律主动做好中成药商品的收购工作，以保证市场需要。

With the development of social production and the improvement of the people's living standards, Chinese patent medicine, especially tonic and health care commodities, are rapidly updated, and the market competition among similar commodities is also very fierce, it has the variable characteristic thereby. According to this characteristic, CMM enterprises should strengthen market investigation and prediction, grasp the law of consumption change and do a good job in purchasing Chinese patent medicine, so as to ensure the market demand.

二、中药商品的销售
II. Sale of CMMCs

中药商品的销售，是指中药经营企业进行中药商品买卖的一种经济活动。它是中药商品流通的主要环节，也是中药经营企业获取社会效益和经济效益的基本手段，因此在中药商品流通中占有十分重要的地位。

Sale of CMMCs refers to an economic activity that CMM enterprises buy and sell CMMCs. It is the main link of the circulation of CMMCs, and also the basic means for CMM enterprises to obtain social and economic benefits. Therefore, it occupies a very important position in the circulation of CMMCs.

（一）中药商品销售的主要方法
(I) Main method of CMMCs sale

中药商品销售的方式方法有多种，根据中药经营企业的性质和其在中药商品流通中的不同地位、作用，主要有如下方法：

There are many methods to sell CMMCs. According to the nature of CMM enterprises and the different positions and functions in the circulation of CMMCs, methods are mainly divided into the following:

1. 批发销售
1. Wholesale

批发销售是指中药经营企业把采购或调入来的中药商品批量供给零售企业、医疗单位、其他批发企业，或供应生产企业的一种经济活动。市场经济体制下，中药经营企业为混合、民营和外资等多种所有制形式。目前全国性的医药流通企业有四家，分别为中国医药、华润医药、上海医药与九州通，其他则是地方性的流通商，这些企业承担着储备、调拨和供应任务，为防病治病、保障人民健康和促进行业发展发挥着重要作用。

Wholesale refers to a kind of economic activity in which CMM enterprises purchase or transfer CMMCs to supply in a bulk mode to retail enterprises, medical units, other wholesale enterprises, or supply production enterprises. Under the market economy system, CMM enterprises consist of mixed, private, foreign investment and other types of ownership. At present, there are four nationwide pharmaceutical circulation enterprises, namely China National Pharmaceutical Group Corporation, China Resources Pharmaceutical Group Limited, Shanghai Pharmaceuticals Holding Company Limited and Jointown Pharmaceutical Group Company Limited, and the others are local pharmaceutical suppliers. These enterprises undertake the tasks of reserve, allocation and supply, and play an important role in preventing and treating diseases, ensuring the people's health and promoting the development of the industry.

此外，会议交易销售也是批发销售的另一种方式。这是指各级中药批发企业主办，其他企业派员参加中药商品交易会或展销会的一种经济活动。会议交易销售与一般批发销售不同的是购销关系不固定，是一种临时集中批发销售的方式。但多能获得好的销售效果，并能收集较多新的市场信息。

In addition, conference trading is another way of wholesale. This refers to an economic activity that the CMM wholesale enterprises at all levels sponsor the fair and delegates of other CMM enterprises take part in. Unlike the general wholesale, the purchase and sale relationship is not fixed. It is a temporary centralized wholesale. But it can obtain good sales effect and collect more new market information.

2. 零售

2. Retail

零售是指中药零售企业把中药商品零星地直接销售给消费者的一种营销活动。零售企业虽然经营的规模小，又多分散在广大农村或城镇居民区，但它们的点多面广，销售方式灵活多样，方便消费者就近配方购药，所以深受广大群众欢迎，总的销售量很大，对中药商品的销售起了辅助的补充作用，是中药商品重要的销售渠道。

Retail refers to a marketing activity in which CMM retail enterprises sell CMMCs to consumers sporadically and directly. Although small, scattered in the vast rural or urban residential areas, retail enterprises are widely distributed. The sales way is more flexible and convenient for consumers to buy medicine, which is very welcomed by the masses. The total sales volume is very big, which plays a supplementary role for CMMCs sale. It is an important sales channel of CMMCs.

（二）中药商品的促销方法

(II) Promotion methods of CMMCs

促销是促进中药商品销售的简称。是指中药经营企业采用各种激励手段，促使消费者购买中药商品的一种方法。其方法是企业派业务人员向消费者宣传所经营药品的有关信息，使消费者认识到购买的益处或利益，从而激发他们的购买欲望，产生购买行为，达到增加销售的目的。

Promotion is short for promoting the sale of CMMCs. It refers to a method whereby CMM enterprises use a variety of incentives to promote consumers to buy CMMCs. The method is to send business personnel to publicize the relevant information of the medicinals to consumers, so that consumers can recognize the benefits or interests of buying, so as to stimulate the strong urge to buy, produce purchasing behavior, and achieve the purpose of increasing sales.

促销的方法有多种，适用于中药经营企业的有人员推销、营业推广和公共关系等。

There are many ways to promote sales. Methods applicable to CMM enterprises are personal selling, sales promotion, public relations, and so on.

（1）人员推销　是通过派出销售人员对消费者作口头宣传或送印刷广告，以促进销售的方法。

(1) Personal selling　Personal selling is a method to promote sales by sending sales personnel to make oral publicity to consumers or to send printed advertisements.

（2）营业推广　是通过中药经营企业主办药品交易会、展销会或赠送价格优惠券、纪念品等给消费者，促使消费者购买药品的一种促销方法。

(2) Sales promotion　Sales promotion is a promotion method that encourages consumers to buy medicinals by holding drug fairs, trade fairs or giving them coupons and souvenirs as gifts.

（3）公共关系　中药经营企业派出专门从事公关的人员到相关单位，专门协调本企业与相关企业或个人之间的关系，树立企业或商品的良好形象，从而达到促销药品的目的。

(3) Public relations　CMM enterprises send public relations practitioners to relevant units to

coordinate the relationship between the enterprise and the relevant enterprises or individuals, establish a good image of the enterprise or commodity, so as to achieve the purpose of promoting medicinals.

三、中药商品的运输
III. Transportation of CMMCs

（一）中药商品运输的分类
(I) Classification of CMMCs transportation

根据中药商品运输环节的先后顺序和业务范围的不同，一般分为发货运输、中转运输和接货运输三类。

According to the sequence of transportation links and business scope of CMMCs transportation, it is generally divided into three categories: shipping transportation, transfer transportation and receiving transportation.

（1）发货运输　发货运输是指由中药商品的生产地或调出地发往消费地的运输。是整个运输环节的开端。发货运输工作的好坏，直接关系到整个运输任务能否圆满完成，所以是整个运输过程中最关键的一环，必须认真抓好。在整个发货运输中，必须做到药品包装牢固、标记明显、凭证齐全、手续清楚、单货同行，否则易发生差错事故。

(1) Shipment transportation　Shipment transportation refers to the transportation from the place of production or transfer out of CMMCs to the place of consumption. It is the beginning of the whole transportation link. The quality of the shipment transportation is directly related to the success of the whole transportation task; therefore it is the most critical link in the whole transportation process, and we must pay close attention to it. During the whole shipment and transportation, CMMCs must be packed firmly, marked clearly, with complete certificates, clear procedures and the delivery order accompanying the commodities. Otherwise errors and accidents are pone to occur.

（2）中转运输　中转运输是指由于受运输条件限制或合理运输需要，中药商品在中途须经中转单位分运或转运的运输。这是整个运输过程的中间环节。中转单位的任务繁重，业务复杂，既要做好接货工作，又要做好发货工作。因此中转单位必须加强收发药品的检查核对和暂时的保管养护工作；必须加强中转的计划安排，缩短药品的待运时间；加强与发货和收货单位的联系，从而节省转运的时间和费用，提高转运效益。

(2) Transfer transportation　Transfer transportation refers to the transportation in which CMMCs have to be shipped or transshipped by the transit unit on the way due to the limitation of transportation conditions or reasonable transportation needs. This is the middle link of the whole transportation process. The task of transfer unit is heavy and the business is complex. Transfer units should do good job in both receiving and shipping commodities. Therefore, the transit units should strengthen the inspection and verification of receiving and shipping medicines and the temporary storage and maintenance work. They should strengthen transit planning and shorten the shipment time of medicines. They also should improve communication with forwarding and receiving units to save time and cost of transshipment and improve transshipment efficiency.

（3）接货运输　接货运输又称收货运输，是指消费地的最终收货单位接收中药商品的运输。这是整个运输过程最后一环，其运输业务的程序是：

①提前做好接货准备，做好有关部门工作的衔接，安排好收货的人力、物力和仓库；②做好接收药品的质量检查和数量的清点查收工作，做到单货相符，准确无误；③做好入仓安排，使药

品及时入库。④发现问题，如药品短缺等，应查明原因，明确责任，公正处理。

(3) Receiving transportation Receiving transportation refers to the transportation of CMMCs are received by the final receiving unit in the place of consumption. This is the last link of the whole transportation process. The procedures for the receiving transportation are: ① To prepare for receiving commodities in advance, to link up the work of related departments, to arrange the manpower, material resources and warehouse for receiving goods well; ② To do a good job of checking the quality and quantity of the received medicinals and ensure that the lists are in conformity with the commodities accurately; ③ To make good warehousing arrangements and keep the medicine in storage in time;④ To find the problem, such as the shortage of medicinals, find out the cause, clarify the responsibility, and deal with it impartially.

（二）中药商品运输的基本要求

(II) Basic requirements for CMMCs transportation

中药经营企业要按照“及时、准确、安全、经济”的要求，协调好与有关部门的关系，合理地组织好中药商品的运输，做到正确编制运输计划，按药品合理的流向，科学地选择运输路线、运输方法和运输工具，加强运输管理，使中药商品以最少的时间，最短的路线，最少的费用从产地运达消费地。

要防止产生对流（同种药品在同条运输线上进行相对方向的运输）、迂回（绕线运输）、倒流（同种药品由产地运到销售地，再由销售地运回原产地），重复（同种药品在同条线上多次运输）等不合理的运输现象。所以在满足生产和市场需要的条件下，应按经济区域组织中药商品的流通。除按近产近销的原则外，还要采用直达、直线运输的手段和“四就直拨”的方法，使中药商品不经中药仓库，就产地、就车站、就发货地点、就码头直拨的办法，直接运到目的地，从而减少中间环节，减少装卸、搬运次数，节省运输时间和费用，降低药品在途中的损耗，获取良好的运输效益。

CMM enterprises should comply with the requirements of “punctuality, accuracy, safety and economy”, coordinate the relationship well with relevant departments, reasonably organize CMMCs transportation, correctly make transportation plan, scientifically select transportation routes, methods and means and strengthen transportation management according to the rational flow direction of CMM, whereby CMMCs can be safely transported from the producing area to the consuming area with the least time, the shortest route, the least cost.

To prevent the occurrence of the opposite flow (the same medicinals are transported in opposite directions on the same transport line), detour (the same medicinals are transported by a longer route), reverse flow (the same medicinals are transported from the producing area to the consuming area and vice versa), repeat (the same medicinals are transported in the same line for many times) and other unreasonable transport phenomenon. Therefore, under the condition of meeting the demands of production and market, CMMCs circulation should be organized according to the economic region. Except for the principle of “close production and close sale”, CMM enterprises should also adopt the means of direct and straight-line transportation and the methods of “four adjacency and direct transfers”, whereby CMMCs can be directly transported to the destination by means of direct transportation close to the place of producing area, the station, ship from location and direct allocation at the wharf without going through the warehouse, so as to reduce the intermediate links, the time of loading and unloading and carrying, save time and transportation cost, reduce the loss of medicinals on the way and obtain good transportation benefits.

四、中药商品的贮存

IV. Storage of CMMCs

（一）中药贮存中常见的变质现象

(Ⅰ) Common deterioration in the storage of CMM

1. 虫蛀

1. Insect damage

虫蛀是指害虫侵入中药内部所引起的破坏作用。药材和饮片经虫蛀后有的形成孔洞，产生蛀粉；有的外形被完全蛀成粉状，失去药用价值。

Insect damage refers to the destructive effect caused by the insect invading the internal of CMM. After insect infestation, some of the medicinal materials and pieces will form holes and produce decaying powder; some external appearance thereof will be completely damaged into powder and lose their medicinal value.

害虫的来源有多种渠道：①药材在采收中受到污染；②在加工炮制过程中未能有效地将害虫或虫卵杀灭；③在贮藏过程中，害虫由外界侵入并繁殖；④储藏的地方和容器本身不清洁，内有害虫生存。害虫的一般生长条件为温度 16℃~35℃，相对湿度 60% 以上，药材和饮片的含水量在 11% 以上。

There are many sources of harmful insects: ① Medicinal materials were hit by insect infestation in the harvest; ② Harmful insects or eggs cannot be effectively killed in the concocted processing course; ③ In the storage process, harmful insects invade from the outside and reproduce; ④ Storage places and containers are not clean and there are harmful insects living inside.The general growth conditions for them are temperature 16℃~35℃, relative humidity above 60%, water content of Chinese medicinal materials and Chinese decocting pieces above 11%.

常见的有害昆虫主要有甲虫类（米象、谷象、药谷盗等）、蛾类（印度谷蛾、地中海粉螟等）、螨类（粉螨、干酪螨等）。

Common harmful insects are mainly beetles (*Sitophilus oryzae*, *Sitophilus granarius*, *Stegobium paniceum*, etc.), moths (*Plodia interpunctella*, *Ephestia kuehniella*, etc.), mites (*Tyroglyphus farinae*, *Tyroglyphus castellani*, etc.).

2. 生霉

2. Mildew

生霉即霉菌在中药表面或内部滋生的现象。大气中存在着大量的霉菌孢子，散落在药材和饮片表面上，在适当的温度（25℃左右），湿度（空气中相对湿度在 85% 以上或药材含水率超过 15%）、适宜的环境（如阴暗不通风的场所）、足够的营养条件下，即萌发为菌丝，分泌酵素，溶蚀药材的内部组织，促使腐败变质，以至药效成分发生变化而失去药效。

Mildew is the phenomenon that mould grows on the surface or inside of CMM. There are a lot of mould spores in the atmosphere. The spores are scattered on the surface of Chinese medicinal materials and Chinese decocting pieces. Under the favourable conditions, including the appropriate temperature (25℃ or so), humidity (air relative humidity above 85% or medicinal material moisture content above 15%), the suitable environment (such as a dark, airless place), adequate nutrition conditions, mould spores will germinate and form mycelium, secrete enzyme, cause the internal organization of CMM to decay. Then CMM became putrefactive and lose its efficacy due to the change of efficacy compositions.

霉菌的种类很多，常见的有根霉属、毛霉属、青霉属、曲霉属等多种霉菌。有些霉菌能产生毒素，属于产毒霉菌，如曲霉属中的黄曲霉菌等。部分黄曲霉菌的代谢产物为黄曲霉毒素，对肝脏有强烈毒性。对中药进行黄曲霉毒素检查是保证其安全性的重要依据。

There are many types of mould, the common types are *Rhizopus*, *Mucor*, *Penicillium*, *Aspergillus* and other kinds of mould. Some mould can produce toxins, belonging to the toxic mould, such as *Aspergillus flavus* aflatus in the *Aspergillus*. Some metabolites of *Aspergillus flavus* are highly toxic to the liver. Aflatoxin examination of CMM is an important basis to ensure its safety.

3. 走油

3. Extensive diffusion of oil

“走油”又称“泛油”，是指某些药材或饮片的挥发油、油脂或者糖类泛出其表面，或因受潮、变色、变质后表面泛出油样物质的变化。走油与贮藏温度过高和贮藏期超时有关。走油时常伴有发霉现象，而且容易发生虫蛀。

Extensive diffusion of oil refers to the volatile oil, lipids or saccharides of some Chinese medicinal materials or Chinese decocting pieces diffuse extensively above the surface, or Chinese medicinal materials or Chinese decocting pieces were affected by damp, change color, metamorphism, the grease-like substance diffuse extensively above the surface thereby. It is related to the high temperature during storage and storage period timeout, which is often accompanied by mildew phenomenon and are prone to insect damage.

4. 变色

4. Discoloration

各种药材和饮片都有固定的色泽，色泽是品质的标志之一。如贮存不当，可使药材或饮片变色。变色与药材和饮片所含成分、烘干时温度、使用某些杀虫剂以及贮藏中温度、湿度、日光、氧气有关。

Various medicinal materials and Chinese decocting pieces have fixed color, which is one of the signs of quality. If storage is not appropriate, the colors of medicinal materials or Chinese decocting pieces will be changed. Discoloration is related to the ingredients in the medicinal materials and Chinese decocting pieces, the temperature during drying, the use of certain pesticides, and the temperature, humidity, sunlight and oxygen during storage.

导致中药仓储变质的现象还有自燃、挥发、自然分解、风化等，要根据情况采用不同的养护措施；药效成分不稳定的中药不能久储。

Spontaneous combustion, volatilization, natural decomposition, weathering and other phenomena can also lead to the deterioration of CMM during storage. Different conservation measures should be adopted according to the different situation. CMM with unstable medicinal components should not be stored for long.

（二）引起中药变质的主要因素

(II) Main factors causing the deterioration of CMM

1. 内在因素 是指中药本身所含的成分因受自然界的影响而引起变异，导致其质量变化。如含淀粉的药材，质地较疏松，易吸收外界水分，受真菌感染，有利于害虫吸取养料赖以生存。含有挥发油的药材，一般气温在20℃左右其油分就会挥发。含有糖类物质的药材，遇水或受潮后即会膨胀发热，引起发酵、霉变；同时糖类物质也是微生物、害虫的最好养料，有利于其繁殖。含有油脂的药材，保管不当，油脂就会发生水解和氧化，其成分受到破坏而产生分解和酸败现象。含有色素的药材，常会受到温度、湿度、日光、空气的影响，导致色素被破坏而引起药材色泽的变化。

1. Internal factors It refers to the variation of ingredients in CMM due to the influence of natural environment, resulting in the quality change.The textures of the starchy Chinese medicinal material is looser, which are easy to absorb external moisture and be infected by fungus. In this case, it is helpful for insect to absorb nourishment to survive. Some medicinal herbs contain volatile oil. The volatile oil will be volatile at about 20℃ generally. Some Chinese medicinal material containing carbohydrate will expand and heat up after being exposed to water or moisture, causing ferment and mildew. Meanwhile, carbohydrate is also the best nutrients for microorganisms and harmful insects, which is conducive to their reproduction. As far as Chinese medicinal material containing grease is concerned, improper storage can lead to the grease undergo hydrolysis and oxidation and the components will be destroyed, then the phenomenon decomposition and rancidity occur. Chinese medicinal material containing pigment is often affected by temperature, humidity, sunlight and air, which leads to the destruction of pigment and the color change of Chinese medicinal material.

此外，各类中药都含有一定的水分，水分对中药的质量起着主导作用。水分过多会使中药腐烂或生霉；水分过少会使中药失润，出现干裂残损。有些中药易发生潮解、风化、软化，都与其本身含水量有关。

In addition, all kinds of CMM contain a certain amount of water, which plays a leading role in the quality. Too much water will make the CMM rot or mildew, while too little water can make CMM lose moist and appear dry and damaged. Some CMM are prone to deliquescence, weathering and softening, all of which are related to the water content.

2. 外在因素 又称“环境因素”，是导致中药变异的自然因素，直接或间接影响其质量。外在因素主要包括日光、空气、湿度、温度和微生物。

2. External factors also known as “environmental factors”. They are the natural factors that lead to the variation and affect the quality of CMM directly or indirectly, including sunlight, air, humidity, temperature and microorganisms.

3. 时间因素 指贮藏期限。在仓储中应做到先进先出，对于贮藏期过长的药物可督促业务部门及时处理。

3. Time factor It refers to the shelf-life. First in, first out during the storage period.For CMM with long storage period, the business department can be urged to deal with them in a timely manner.

（三）中药贮存中主要的养护方法

(III) Main maintenance methods in the storage of CMM

1. 干燥法

1. Drying method

干燥可以除去中药中过多的水分，起到防虫霉的效果。若在库存中发现药材和饮片水分超高时或在梅雨季节，应采用适当的干燥法进行处理。常用的干燥方法有晒、晾、烘、微波、远红外加热干燥法等。其中高温烘燥法适合大多数中药；摊晾法则适用于芳香性叶类、花类、果皮类等；对于颗粒较小的中药粉末状饮片，采用微波干燥或远红外加热干燥。

Drying can remove excessive moisture in CMM and prevent insects and mildew. If it is found that the water content of medicinal materials and pieces is too high in the stock or in the plum-rain season, the appropriate drying method should be adopted for treatment. Common drying methods are air drying, natural draft drying, cabinet drying, microwave drying or far-infrared heating drying, and so on. High temperature drying method is suitable for most CMM. The method of spreading out to dry is applicable to aromatic leaves, flowers and fruit skins. For the powdery Chinese decocting pieces with small particles, microwave drying or far-infrared heating drying are suitable.

2. 冷藏法

2. Low temperature storage method

采用低温贮藏中药，从而有效防止不宜烘、晾中药的生虫、发霉、变色等变质现象的发生。贵重中药饮片多采用冷藏法，例如：蛤士蟆油、人参等贮藏于冷库（2℃~10℃）中。

Low temperature storage method is adopted to effectively prevent the occurrence of insects, mildew, discoloration and other deterioration phenomena of some Chinese medicinal materials that are not suitable for drying and airing. Most of the precious Chinese decocting pieces are are mostly stored in cold storage. For example, Hashimo oil and Renshen are stored in cold storage (2℃~10℃).

3. 密封法

3. Sealed storage method

通过密封使中药与外界的光线、有害气体以及害虫细菌等隔绝，少受或不受各种自然因素的影响，避免虫蛀、霉变等损失。密封时，必须在气温较低，相对湿度不大时进行。

Through sealing, CMM is isolated from the outside light, harmful gas, insects and bacteria, whereby they are less or not affected by a variety of natural factors, to avoid insect damage, mildew and other losses. They must be sealed at low temperature and relative low humidity.

4. 对抗同贮法

4. Antagonistic storage method

对抗同贮法是利用不同品种的中药所散发的特殊气味、吸潮性能或特有驱虫及去霉化学成分的性质来防止另一种中药生虫、霉变等现象的一种贮藏养护方法。这种方法适用于数量不多的中药养护。如牡丹皮与泽泻同贮，泽泻就不易生虫，牡丹皮也不会变色。又如蕲蛇中放花椒，三七内放樟脑，土鳖虫内放大蒜，当归、瓜蒌内放酒等，也都不易生虫。但采用这种方法，最好在生虫发霉前，先把泽泻、蕲蛇、三七、土鳖虫等进行一次杀虫处理，并与密封法结合进行。

Antagonistic storage method refers to a kind of storage and maintenance method, whereby it uses the special smell, moisture absorption performance or the properties of special disinsectization and anti-mold chemical components of different variety of CMM to prevent another variety from growing insects and mildew, and whereby it is suitable for a small amount of CMM maintenance. For example, if store Mudanpi and Zexie together, the latter is not easy to grow insects and the former will not change color. For other examples, store Qishe and Huajiao together, store Sanqi and Zhangnao together, store Tubiechong and Dasuan together, and store Danggui or Gualou together with wine, all of which are not easy to grow insects. However, in this way, it is better to carry out insecticidal treatments for Zezie, Qishe, Sanqi and Tubiechong before they become moldy, in combination with the sealing method.

5. 药物熏蒸法

5. Medicinal fumigation method

此种方法是利用防霉剂和杀虫剂，抑制霉虫的生长和繁殖，以小室密封（熏蒸房）或用熏蒸箱为宜。熏蒸后密闭一定时间须开箱进行适当通风。具体方法包括最早使用的硫黄熏蒸法以及磷化铝熏蒸法、氯化苦熏蒸法、氨水熏蒸法以及醋酸钠喷洒法等。值得注意的是，易变色、变味和质地脆嫩的中药、60多种花类和虫类药材不宜使用硫黄熏蒸法；另外，氯化苦有剧毒，对人体毒性很大，应特别注意不能将氯化苦直接喷洒到中药上。

This method is to use mildew preventive and insecticide to inhibit the growth and reproduction of mildew and insects. It is advisable to seal the room (fumigation room) or use the fumigation box.

After Chinese medicinal materials are sealed for a certain time during fumigation, the box should be opened for proper ventilation. Specific methods include the earliest used sulfur fumigation, aluminum phosphide fumigation, trichloronitromethane fumigation, ammonium hydroxide fumigation and sodium acetate spray method. It is worth noting that sulfur fumigation is not suitable for Chinese medicinal materials that are easy to change color, change flavor and crisp texture, more than 60 kinds of flower and insect Chinese medicinal. In addition, trichloronitromethane is highly toxic to the human body. It should pay special attention that trichloronitromethane cannot be directly sprayed on Chinese medicinal materials.

6. 气调养护方法

6. Gas-regulating storage and maintenance method

气调养护方法即在密闭条件下，人为调整空气的组成，造成低氧的环境，抑制害虫和微生物生长繁殖及中药自身的氧化反应，以保持中药品质的一种方法。该法具有杀虫、防霉的作用，具体形式可采用塑料薄膜罩帐和气调密闭库。

Gas-regulating storage and maintenance is a method of maintaining the quality of CMM by artificially regulating the composition of the air under airtight conditions to create a hypoxic environment, whereby it can inhibit the growth and reproduction of insets and microorganisms as well as the oxidation reaction of CMM. The method has the function of killing insects and preventing mildew, and takes the specific forms such as the plastic film tents and gas-regulating airtight warehouse.

7. 气幕防潮法

7. Repelling moisture using gas curtain method

是于仓库门上装气幕，配合自动门以阻止仓库内外空气对流，减少湿热空气在库内较冷的墙、柱、地面等处形成结露，进而达到防潮的一种方法。

Repelling moisture using gas curtain method refers to install the gas curtain on the door of the warehouse, cooperating with the automatic door to prevent air convection inside and outside the warehouse, to reduce the condensation of hot and humid air in the cold wall, column, the ground etc., and then to repel moisture.

8. 辐射防霉除虫法

8. Radiation anti-mildew and deinsectization method

常用的辐射能为 X 射线、γ 射线等。是利用原子辐射作用杀灭仓虫，或致使仓虫不能完全发育及产生不育成虫。

The commonly used radiation energy is X-ray and γ-ray, etc. It is to use the action of atomic radiation to kill the warehouse insect, or to cause the warehouse insect not to develop completely and produce the sterile adult.

（四）中药商品的仓储

（IV）Storage of CMMCs

1. 仓储的目的和意义

1. Purpose and significance of the storage

中药商品从生产领域到消费领域流通中的停留囤积，叫中药商品的仓储。仓储是中药商品经营的重要环节之一，也是保证中药商品连续流通和市场供应的必备条件。如果没有仓储或仓储方法不当，条件不好，措施不力，就要造成中药商品流通的中断，影响市场供应，因此仓储一定量的中药商品具有重要意义，主要目的如下。

CMMCs staying and hoarding during the circulation from the production field to the consumption field is called the storage of CMMCs. Storage is one of the important links in the operation and also a necessary condition to ensure the continuous circulation and market supply of CMMCs. Without storage or with improper storage method, poor conditions and weak measures, the circulation of CMMCs will be interrupted and the market supply will be affected. Therefore, it is of great significance to store a certain amount of CMMCs, The main objectives are as follows.

（1）贮药备用

(1) Storage of CMM for reserve

贮药备用是贮存的基本目的。中药商品是特殊商品，而生产的特点之一就是产地分散，季节性强。有的是一地生产，供应全国；有的是一季生产，供应全年；有的是全年生产，供应一季。同时药材商品生产受自然条件影响很大，年产量不稳定，有丰有欠，所以必须有一定量的贮备，以满足人民防治疾病的需要。

Storage of CMM for reserve is the basic purpose of storage. As special commodities, one of the production characteristics of CMMCs is the scattered producing area and strong seasonal feature. Some are produced in one place and supplied to the whole country; some are produced in one season and supplied throughout the year; some are produced in one year and supplied in one season. Meanwhile, the production of CMMCs are greatly affected by natural conditions, whose annual output is not stable, abundant or lean. Therefore, there must be a certain amount of reserves to meet the demand of the people to prevent and cure diseases.

（2）保证市场供应，稳定药价

(2) Ensuring market supply and stabilizing medicinal prices

中药商品是特殊商品，是防治疾病，保健强身的有力武器。一旦市场脱销，其价格就要猛涨，为了保证市场供应，稳定药价，维护消费者的利益，就必须有一定量的贮备。

As special commodities, CMMCs are the powerful weapons for disease prevention and health care. Once CMMCs are out of stock, the prices thereof will soar. To guarantee the market supply, stabilize the price of medicine, and protect the interests of consumers, it is necessary to keep a certain amount of storage.

（3）保证中药商品流通的连续性

(3) Ensuring continuity of CMMCs circulation

中药商品从产地到销地，都有一个流通过程和调运时间。为了调节生产与消费之间在时间上和地域上的差异，必然需要有一定量的贮存，以起到“蓄水池”的作用，使之流通连续进行。

There is a circulation process and transportation time for CMMCs from the place of producing to the place of sale. To address the time and regional variance between production and consumption, it is necessary to have a certain amount of storage, thereby playing the role of “reservoir”, to make it circulate continuously.

（4）保证特殊的需要

(4) Ensuring special needs

中药商品是防治疾病，救死扶伤的特殊商品，除了满足国内外正常的药用需要外，还要满足突发事件如地震、涝灾、天旱、传染病大流行等灾情、疫情的需要，因此也必须有一定量的贮备。

CMMCs are special commodities for the prevention and treatment of diseases and the rescue of the dying and the wounded, which can not only meet the normal medical demand in China and at abroad, but also meet the demand of emergencies, such as earthquake, flood, drought and epidemic of infectious diseases. Therefore, there must also be a certain amount of reserve.

（5）保证国际市场的需要

(5) Ensuring demand of international market

中药商品出口销售，有着悠久的历史，随着对外开放，科技文化交流的频繁，中药商品出口的品种和数量不断增加。为了满足国际市场的需要，也必须贮备一定量的中药商品，以不断扩大国际市场，换取更多的外汇，为国民经济的发展积累资金。

The export sales of CMMCs have a long history. With the opening to the outside world and the frequent exchanges of science, technology and culture, the export varieties and quantities of CMMCs are increasing. To meet the demand of the international market, a certain amount of CMMCs must be stored so as to continuously expand the international market and obtain more foreign exchange to accumulate funds for the development of the national economy.

2. 影响仓储量的因素

2. Factors affecting storage volume

影响中药商品仓储量的因素很多，主要有如下几点。

The main factors affecting the storage volume of CMMCs are as follows:

（1）取决于药品销售量的大小

(1) Depending on sales volume of CMMCs

在一般情况下，贮存量与销售量成正比。即销售量越大，贮存量也越多。如常用的大宗药材商品和畅销的名优特新中成药商品销售量大，贮存量也多。

In general, storage is proportional to sales volume. That is, the larger the sales volume, the more the storage. For example, the commonly used bulk Chinese medicinal material commodities and the best-selling famous, optimal, special and new Chinese patent medicine commodities have large sales volume and large storage capacity.

（2）取决于药品生产规模的大小与生产周期的长短

(2) Depending on size of medicinal production scale and length of production cycle

一般说来，药品生产的规模越大，品种越多，贮存也越多；反之，贮存也越少。同时与药品生产周期长短成反比，即生产周期长的药品，贮存多；反之，则少。如皮类药材的生产周期长（10年以上），贮存量要多；紫苏子、山楂等生产周期短（1年），贮存量可少。

Generally speaking, the larger the scale of drug production, the more varieties, the more storage; conversely, the less storage. Meanwhile, it is inversely proportional to the length of medicinal production cycle. That is to say, medicinals with long production cycle and more storage; conversely, the less. For example, the production cycle of plant corks as Chinese medicinal material is long (more than 10 years), the storage quantity should be large thereby; the production cycle of Zisuzi and Shanzha is short (1 year), the storage can be less thereby.

（3）取决于中药商品的性质

(3) Depending on nature of CMMCs

根据中药商品性质包括其物理性质和化学性质是否稳定来确定仓储量的大小。一般药品性质越稳定，仓储量可大，反之，则小。如一般矿物类药品性质稳定，较长期的贮存，不易变质，仓储量可大；而柏子仁等性质不稳，极易泛油变质，仓储量则小。

The storage capacity is determined by the stability of the physical and chemical properties of CMMCs. Generally, the more stable the nature of medicinals, the larger the storage capacity. conversely, the less. For instance, the mineral as Chinese medicinal material in general are stable in nature and can be stored for a long time. It is uneasy to deteriorate and the storage volume can be large. While the nature of Bai Zi Ren is unstable, it is prone to extensive diffusion of oil and deterioration, the storage capacity should be small thereby.

（4）取决于产销的距离和运输条件

(4) Depending on distance between production and marketing, and transportation conditions

药品产销的距离越远，运输条件有限，则仓储量越大，反之越小。药品在途运输的时间越长，在途药品仓储量也会越大；同时在销售地为了保证市场的及时供应，销售地的仓储量要适当增加。

The farther the distance between the production and marketing of medicinals, along with the limited transportation conditions, the larger the storage capacity; conversely, the less. The longer the transportation time of the medicinals on the way, the larger the storage capacity on the way of the medicinals. Meanwhile, to ensure the timely supply to the market, the storage capacity of the place of sale should be increased appropriately.

（5）取决于管理水平的高低

(5) Depending on the level of management

在其他条件不变的情况下，中药经营企业贮存管理的水平越高，药品流通组织越合理，仓储量就可相对减少，反之，则要增加。

Other things being equal, the higher the level of storage management of CMM enterprises and the more reasonable the organization of medicinal circulation, the smaller the storage capacity. If not, increase the storage capacity.

3. 确定贮存量的原则和方法

3. Principles and methods for determining storage capacity

中药商品贮存量的确定，应与正常的销售量的大小相适应。过多会造成药品积压，影响资金周转和药品质量；过少，不能保证市场供应，就会导致药品脱销。所以贮存量应随药品销售量的变化而变化。确定贮存量的一般原则是至少要保证一年内药品的供应，加上适量的贮存损耗。由于贮存药品的主要目的不同，确定的原则和方法有以下 3 种：

The storage capacity of CMMCs should be determined by the normal sales volume. Storing too much will cause medicinal backlog, affect the turnover of funds and drug quality thereby; while storing too little cannot guarantee the market supply, will lead to medicinal out of stock. Therefore, the storage capacity should vary with the change of medicinal sales volume. The general principle for determining storage capacity is to ensure the supply of medicines for at least one year, and add an appropriate amount of storage loss. Now that the main purpose of medicinal storage is different, there are three principles and methods as follows:

（1）药品周转贮存量的确定

(1) Determination of CMM revolving stock capacity

周转性中药商品的贮存目的，是中药经营企业为了保证正常的市场供应而形成的贮存，其贮存量（C），一般是最高贮存量（A）加最低贮存量（B）的平均量，即 $C=(A+B)/2$；周转药品贮存的平均天数（D）等于周转药品平均贮存量（C）除以每日平均的销售量（E），即 $D=C/E$。

The purpose of the revolving storage of CMMCs is that CMM enterprises ensure the normal market supply. The storage amount (C) is generally the average amount of the maximum storage amount (A) plus the minimum storage amount (B), that is, $C = (A+B)/2$. The average number of days of revolving stock (D) is equal to the average amount of revolving stock (C) divided by the average daily sales volume (E), i.e.,

$D = C/E$.

（2）季节性药品贮存量的确定

(2) Determination of seasonal CMM storage capacity

季节性中药商品的贮存目的是为了保证季节性市场供应。其贮存量的确定是根据中药商品不同的生产周期、药品性质、消费规律和交通运输条件等多种因素来决定的。其原则是既要保证当令药品、重大节日的季节性供应，又不要贮存过多而造成浪费。如银花露是夏季的当令药品，贮存过少不能保证夏季市场的需要，过多则过了夏季销售量大减，又不能久贮，易失效报废，造成损失。所以只能根据其性质、正常的生产周期、消费规律等来确定夏季到来之前的贮存量。

The storage purpose of seasonal CMMCs is to ensure the seasonal market supply. The determination of its storage capacity is determined by various factors such as different production cycles, medicinal properties, consumption law and traffic condition. Its principle is to ensure the seasonal medicinals and seasonal supplies for major festivals, but not to store too much and cause waste. For example, Yin Hua Dew is a seasonal medicinal in summer. Storing too little can not ensure the needs of the summer market. However, too much storage can be a problem in that sales volume of Yin Hua Dew slumps over the summer. In addition, it is not good for a long time storage and easy to invalidate, resulting in losses. So CMC enterprise only determine the amount of storage before the arrival of summer according to its nature, normal production cycle, consumption law.

（3）专用药品贮存量的确定

(3) Determination of special CMM storage capacity

专用药品贮存目的，是中药经营企业为了保证突发病情、灾情等市场的特殊需要，形成的机动性贮存。其贮存量多少由国家主管部门决定和控制。

The purpose of special CMM storage is to guarantee the special needs of the market, such as sudden illness, disaster, CMM enterprise store medicinals flexibly. The storage capacity is determined and controlled by national competent authorities.

4. 仓储中的业务管理

4. Business management in storage

中药商品仓储的主要场所是中药仓库，仓储中的业务管理就是中药仓库的业务管理。业务管理的主要任务是做好仓储中药商品的收发和保管养护工作。要求做到贮存多、进出快、养护好、费用省、损耗小、保安全。中药仓库业务管理的环节主要有：

The main place of CMMCs storage is Chinese medicinal warehouse. The business management in storage is the business management of Chinese medicinal warehouse. The main task of business management is to do a good job of CMMCs receiving and shipping, storage and maintenance in the storage. Requirements for storage are storage more, fast in and out, good maintenance, cost saving, small loss, security. The links of the business management of Chinese medicinal warehouse mainly include the following aspects.

（1）收货　是中药仓库业务管理的第一个环节，做好中药收货工作，是做好其他环节的基础。基本要求是保证入库中药商品的品种、数量准确，规格质量符合要求，包装完整牢固，手续清楚，入库迅速，发现问题要查明原因，分清责任。其业务程序有：

(1) Receiving　Receiving is the first step in the business management of Chinese medicinal warehouse. To do a good job in receiving CMM is the basis for other steps. The basic requirements are to ensure that the type and quantity of CMMs in storage are accurate, the specifications and quality meet the

requirements, the packaging is complete and firm, the procedures are clear, the storage is fast. If problems are found, find out the cause and the responsibility. Its business procedures are:

① 接货验收：接货验收又叫入库验收，是指保管人员根据入库凭证，对将要入库药品的名称、品种、数量、质量、规格、等级、产地（厂家）、包装等逐一核对、清点，检查有无单货不符或漏收、错发等问题。验收的重点是质量验收，检查药品规格、等级、色泽、气味、干燥程度、有无变质现象和掺杂作伪等。验收要从实际出发，应根据供货单位的信誉、运输方法、路程远近、包装好坏、季节气候、价值大小等，区别情况，确定全验、抽验或免验，一般以抽验为主。

① Receiving inspection: It is also called warehouse entry inspection, which means that the custodian checks and counts the name, varieties, quantity, quality, specifications, grades, producing areas (manufacturers), packaging etc. of the medicinials one by one to be put into storage according to the storage vouchers, and checks whether there is any inconsistency, missed receipt, wrong delivery and other issues. The key point of check is the quality acceptance, checking the medicinal specification, grade, color, smell, degree of dryness and whether there is deterioration and adulteration. Check shall be based on the actual situation and determine the full inspection, sampling or exemption from inspection based on the supplier's reputation, transportation method, distance, packaging, seasonal climate and value. In general, sampling is the main form.

② 分类堆垛：经过验收合格的中药商品，按照不同的品名、规格、等级和产地、性质等选定库房和仓位进行分类堆垛，并保持适当的墙距、货距、柜距、顶距、灯距，垛底要垫货架，垛脚要牢固、整齐，以便通风排潮，保管养护。垛堆的形状和高度，按各种药品的性质、特点与包装，结合气候情况，按照小压大，轻压重，不倒放等原则进行堆码成垛。对贵重和剧毒药材及易燃药品要专人、专库（柜）加锁保管，并建立专用收发账册。分类堆垛要在安全和方便管理的前提下，精打细算地安排垛位，改进堆垛技术，努力提高库房的利用率。

② Classification of stacking: CMMCs that have passed the receiving inspection will be sorted and stacked according to the different name, specification, grade, producing area and property. In the process of stacking, it is necessary to maintain the appropriate distance between the goods and the wall, cargo, ark, zenith, lamp. The stacking bottom shall be padded with shelves, and the stacking feet shall be firm and tidy, so as to facilitate ventilation, moisture discharge,storage and maintenance. The shape and height of the stacks are determined by the nature, characteristics and packaging of a variety of medicinals, combined with the climate. The medicinals should be stacked according to the principle of the small putting on the top of the big, the light putting on the top of the heavy, and no inversion. For valuable and highly toxic Chinese medicinal material and flammable medicinals, it is necessary to custody by special person, special storehouse (cabinet) with locks, and set up special receipt and delivery account books. On the premise of safety and convenient management, classified stacking should be carefully arranged to improve stacking technology and the utilization rate of the warehouse.

③ 签证记账：签证记账就是在药品堆垛完成后，要及时点准数量，做好分层标量，在货垛明显处悬挂货卡。同时，照凭证所列内容，记好中药商品的保管账，盖上“货已收讫”的印章，与随货同行的单据一起及时交业务部门。

③ Visa bookkeeping: It refers to count the quantity in time, make a good layered scalar and hang cargo card on the obvious location of goods stack after medicinals stacking is completed. Meanwhile, according to the contents listed in the voucher, keep a good record of the custody account of CMMCs, stamp the seal of "customer acknowledging delivery of goods", and timely submit to the business department together with the documents accompanying the commodities.

(2) 发货　发货即药品出库，这是中药贮存管理的最终环节。中药商品一经出库，就结束了它的贮存过程，继续进行流通。因此加强中药商品的发货管理，对于加强药品流通，满足社会用药需要，降低贮存费用等都有重要意义。

(2) Shipping　Shipping means the medicinal is delivered from storage, which is the final link of Chinese medicinal storage and management. Once delivered from storage, CMMCs end its storage process and continue to circulate. Therefore, strengthening the shipping management of CMMCs is of great significance for strengthening the circulation of medicinals, meeting the needs of social medication and reducing the storage cost.

发货的基本要求是：①要认真核对所配发药品名称、品种、数量、规格、等级、件数、到货地点等是否与票据相符；②发出药品的包装是否完整牢固，在药品卡上要写明药名、收货单位、到站名称、重量等；③对变质药品或伪劣药品，一律不准出库；④出口药品必须由专人验发；⑤坚持先进先出，单货同行，手续简便，发货及时和迅速的原则，做到出库的药品质量高、数量足、批次不乱、不出差错。

The basic requirements for shipping are:① To check carefully whether the name, variety, quantity, specification, grade, number of pieces, place of arrival, etc. of the dispensed medicinals are consistent with the bill; ② To check whether the package of the medicinals is complete and firm and indicate clearly the name, the consignee, the name of the station, weight, etc. of the medicinals; ③ The deteriorated or fake medicinals are not allowed to deliver from the storage; ④ medicinals for export must be inspected and distributed by responsible persons; ⑤ Adhere to the principle of "first in, first out", the delivery order accompanying the commodities, simple procedures, timely and rapid delivery, so as to ensure high quality, sufficient quantity, batch without mess nor mistakes.

发货的基本程序是：①细心核对。发货必须依据正式的提货单、出库单等凭证，经细心核对，准确无误后，才能交保管人员配货；②配货。保管员按出库凭证的要求，根据先进先出的原则配齐药品，做到数量准确，质量优良，包装完好，堆放有序；③复核。为防止差错，必须进行单、货详细复核，核查无误后，在出库凭证上签字；④出库。凡由买方直接提货的，应出具提货证明，由门卫点验无误后收证放行；凡由仓库发货的，保管人员要填写磅码单，通过运输部门按规定发运；⑤记账。药品出库后，保管人员根据出库凭证所列内容，在保管账册上做发货记录，同时在发货卡上注销已发药品。

The basic procedure of shipping is: ① Careful check. The shipping must be based on the formal bill of loading, outbound delivery order and other vouchers, after careful check without any errors, it can be delivered to the custodian for distribution; ② Distribution. According to the requirements of the certificate of delivery and the principle of "first in, first out", the custodian shall prepare the medicinals in an accurate quantity, good quality, intact packaging and orderly stacking. ③ Review. To prevent errors, it is necessary to conduct a detailed review of the order and commodities. After verification, the custodian will sign on the outgoing list. ④ Delivery from storage. If the buyers take delivery of the goods directly, they shall show the delivery certification. After checking the accuracy of procedures, the guard collects the certification and releases the buyers. While the commodities are shipped from the warehouse, the custodian shall fill in the weight list and ship the commodities through the transportation department as required. ⑤ Accounting. After the medicinals are delivered from the storage, the custodian shall make shipping records in the custody account book and cancel the medicinals already delivered on the shipping card.

重点小结
Summary

中药商品的经营	中药经营企业分类与特点	分类	批发企业、零售企业	
		特点	①经营的技术性强、责任重大；②货源和销售量不够稳定；③消费者需求弹性小，社会保有量不多；④质量第一，优质高效；⑤薄利多销，微利经营	
	中药商品经营的主要环节	收购	中药材收购特点	①明显的季节性；②复杂的技术性；③较强的地区性；④较明显的分散性；⑤较强的不稳定性；⑥广泛的群众性
		销售	主要方法	批发销售、零售
		运输	分类	发货运输、中转运输和接货运输
		贮存	常见的变质现象	虫蛀、生霉、走油、变色
			引起的变质的主要因素	内在因素、外在因素和时间因素
			主要养护方法	干燥法、冷藏法、密封法、对抗同贮法、药物熏蒸法、气调养护法、气幕防潮法、辐射防霉除虫法

Management of Chinese Materia Medica Commodities	The Classification and Characteristics of CMM Enterprises	Classification	Wholesale enterprise and retail enterprise	
		Characteristics	① Strong technical skills and heavy responsibilities of the management of CMMCs ② Unstable supply and sales volume ③ Small demand elasticity and low inventory ④ Quality first and high efficiency ⑤ Small profits but quick turnover	
	The Main Links of CMMCs Management	Purchase	Characteristics of purchase of Chinese medicinal materials	① Obvious seasonality; ② Complicated technicality; ③ Strongly zonal; ④ Obvious dispersion; ⑤ Strong instability; ⑥ Extensive mass
		Sale	The main method	Wholesale and retail
		Transport	Classification	Shipment transportation, transfer transportation and receiving transportation
		Storage	Common deterioration	insect damage, mildew, extensive diffusion of oil and discoloration
			The main factors causing deterioration	Internal factors, external factors and time factor
			The main maintenance methods	Drying method, low temperature storage method, sealed storage method, antagonistic storage method, medicinal fumigation method, gas-regulating storage and maintenance method, repelling moisture using gas curtain method, radiation anti-mildew and deinsectization method

题库

目标检测
Object Detection

一、选择题（Choice question）

（一）单项选择题（One-choice question）

1. 哪项不是中药批发企业的主要任务（　　）
   A. 进行中药商品市场的调查与预测
   B. 根据市场需求，指导和落实中药商品的生产和收购任务，促进中药商品生产的发展
   C. 根据国家有关的方针、政策和计划，组织好中药商品的分配、调拨和供应工作，保证人民用药需要
   D. 根据中药商品的产销情况，合理贮存中药商品，做好养护工作，保证市场供应
   E. 最大限度地满足人民配方购药的需要
   Which of the following is not the main task of CMM wholesale enterprises (　　)
   A. To investigate and forecast the market of CMMCs
   B. According to the market demand, guide and carry out the production and purchase tasks of CMMCs, and promote the development of CMMCs production
   C. Organize related work well about the distribution, allocation and supply of CMMCs in accordance with relevant guidelines, policies and plans to ensure the people's demand for CMM
   D. According to the production and marketing situation of CMMCs, store the CMMCs reasonably, maintain CMMCs well, and ensure the market supply
   E. Provide customers with maximum satisfaction with CMMCs
2. 下列为饮片与中成药商品收购的特点是（　　）
   A. 分散性　B. 均衡性　C. 群众性　D. 技术性　E. 季节性
   Which of the following is the characteristic of the purchase of Chinese decocting pieces and Chinese patent medicine (　　)
   A. Dispersion　B. Balance　C. Mass
   D. Technicality　E. Seasonality
3. 下列哪项不是中药商品经营的主要环节（　　）
   A. 采收加工　B. 收购　C. 销售　D. 运输　E. 贮存
   Which of the following is not the main links of CMMCs management (　　)
   A. Harvest and process　B. Purchase　C. Sale
   D. Transport　E. Storage
4. 下列不是中药材收购特点的是（　　）
   A. 明显的季节性　B. 复杂的技术性
   C. 较强的地区性和较明显的集中性　D. 较强的不稳定性
   E. 广泛的群众性
   Which of the following is not the characteristics of Chinese medicinal materials acquisition (　　)
   A. Obvious seasonality

B. Complex technicality
C. Strong zonality and obvious concentricity
D. Strong instability
E. Extensive mass

5. 下列不是中药贮存中常见的变质现象的是（　　）
A. 虫蛀　　B. 生霉　　C. 走油
D. 变色　　E. 干燥

Which of the following is not the common deterioration in the storage of CMM (　　)
A. insect damage　　B. Mildew　　C. extensive diffusion of oil
D. Discoloration　　E. Drying

（二）多项选择题（Multiple choice question）

1. 中药经营企业的特点是（　　）
A. 经营的技术性强、责任重大
B. 货源和销售量不够稳定
C. 消费者需求弹性小，社会保有量不多
D. 质量第一，优质高效
E. 薄利多销，微利经营

The characteristics of CMM enterprises are (　　)
A. Strong technical skills and heavy responsibilities of the management of CMMCs
B. Unstable supply and sales volume
C. Small demand elasticity and low inventory
D. Quality first and high efficiency
E. Small profits but quick turnover

2. 中药商品运输的分类包括有（　　）
A. 产地运输　　B. 发货运输　　C. 中转运输
D. 接货运输　　E. 库内运输

Classification of CMMCs transportation include (　　)
A. Transportation of producing area
B. Shipping transportation
C. Transfer transportation
D. Receiving transportation
E. Warehouse transport

3. 关于中药材收购工作叙述正确的是（　　）
A. 是农商之间的经济活动，需认真贯彻执行国家的有关经济政策
B. 突击收购与经常收购相结合是主要收购方法之一
C. 固定收购与流动收购相结合是主要收购方法之一
D. 专业队伍收购与发动群众主动交售相结合是主要收购方法之一
E. 要做好收购前人力、物质、资金、库房、运输、收购网点准备工作

Which of the following are true about the purchase of Chinese medicinal materials commodities (　　)
A. It is an economic activity between industry and commerce and should carry out the national economic policies

B. combination of concentrated purchase and frequent purchase is one of the main purchase methods

C. Combination of fixed purchase and mobile purchase is one of the main purchase methods

D. Combination of professional team purchase and mobilizing the masses to sell is one of the main purchase methods

E. A lot of preparation needs to be done including manpower, materials, funds, warehouses, transportation, purchase sites before the purchase

4. 关于中药商品运输叙述正确的是（　　）

A. 按近产近销的原则

B. 采用直达、直线运输的手段

C. 采用就产地、就车站、就发货地点、就码头直拨的办法

D. 减少中间环节，减少装卸、搬运次数

E. 降低在途中的损耗

Which of the following are true about the transportation of CMMCs (　　)

A. According to the principle of "close to production and close to sale"

B. To adopt the means of direct and straight-line transportation

C. To transport to the destination by means of direct transportation close to the place of producing area, the station, the delivery location

D. To reduce the intermediate links, the time of loading, unloading and carrying

E. To reduce the loss of medicinals on the way

二、解答题（Thinking question）

中药贮存中主要的养护方法有哪些?

What are the main maintenance methods in CMM storage?

第七章　中药商品的管理

Chapter 7　Management of Chinese Materia Medica Commodities

学习目标 ┆ Learning Target

知识要求：

1. **掌握**　影响中药商品的质量的主要因素；划分药材商品规格等级的依据与方法。
2. **熟悉**　中药商品的价格体系及分类。

能力要求：

学会中药商品的整体质量管理体系内容；如何划分中药商品的规格和等级。

Knowledge requirements:

1. **Proficiency**　Main factors affecting the quality of Chinese Materia Medica Commodities (CMMCs). Basis and method for classifying medicinal material commodities specifications.
2. **Familiarity**　The Price System and Classification of CMMCs.

Skill requirements:

Learning the contents of the comprehensive quality management system of CMMCs. How to divide the specifications and grades of CMMCs.

中药商品的管理是以中药商品购销活动为主体的经济活动，是以指挥、控制中药商品经营为根本任务的管理活动。管理的主要职能是对中药商品经营的各个环节进行决策、计划、组织、指挥、协调和控制，以最低的消耗换取最佳的经济效益。

The management of CMMCs is an economic activity whose main activity is the purchase and sale of CMMCs. It is a management activity that directs and controls the operation of CMMCs. The main function of management is to make decisions, plan, organize, direct, coordinate and control all aspects of the operation of CMMCs, in exchange for the best economic benefits with the lowest consumption.

中药商品的管理涉及面十分广泛，中药商品流通领域及其相关工作都要涉及管理。如中药商品的收购、销售、运输、贮存；中药商品的品种、质量、市场、价格以及计划、财务、劳动工资、信息等诸多方面都离不开管理。

The management of CMMCs is very extensive, and every major link in the field of CMMCs circulation and its related work must involve management. For example, the purchase, sale, transportation, and storage of CMMCs; the variety, quality, market, price, and planning, finance, labor wages and information of CMMCs are inseparable from management.

第一节 中药经营与质量管理

Section 1 Chinese Materia Medica Management and Quality Management

PPT

一、中药经营

I. Chinese Materia Medica Management

我国中药经营企业的管理机构是从中央到地方的各级药品监督管理机构。

The management agencies of CMM material enterprises in China are drug supervision and management agencies at all levels from the central to the local governments.

（一）监督管理机构

(I) Supervision and Management Agencies

国家食品药品监督管理局主管全国食品药品监督管理工作。国务院有关部门在各自的职责范围内负责与药品有关的监督管理工作。省、自治区、直辖市人民政府药品监督管理部门负责本行政区域内的药品监督管理工作。

China Food and Drug Administration(CFDA) is in charge of national drug supervision and administration. Relevant departments of the State Council are responsible for drug-related supervision and management within their respective responsibilities. The drug supervision and administration departments of the people's governments of provinces, autonomous regions, and municipalities directly under the Central Government are responsible for drug supervision and management in their respective administrative areas.

（二）质量监测机构

(II) Quality Monitoring Agency

中国食品药品检定研究院是药品监督管理部门设置的药品检验机构，承担依法实施药品审批和药品质量监督检查所需的药品检验工作，是国家检验药品生物制品质量的法定机构和最高技术仲裁机构。

China Food and Drug Inspection and Research Institute is a drug inspection agency set up by the drug supervision and administration department. It is responsible for the drug inspection work required to implement drug approval and drug quality supervision in accordance with law. It is the national statutory agency and the highest technical arbitration agency for testing the quality of pharmaceutical and biological products.

（三）经营管理法规

(III) Management Regulations

我国中药经营企业的主要管理法规有：

The main management regulations of CMM enterprises in China include:

1.《中华人民共和国药品管理法》（简称《药品管理法》）

1. *Law of the People's Republic of China on the Administration of Drugs* (abbreviated as *The Drug Administration Law*)

《药品管理法》是国家强制执行，具有普遍效力的行为规范，是我国药品生产、经营、使用和药品管理部门必须共同遵守的国家法律。同时，《药品管理法》是制订药品监督管理法规和行政规章的"基本法"。

The Drug Administration Law is a nationally enforced, universally valid code of conduct, and a national law that must be complied with by the drug production, operation, use, and drug administration departments in China. At the same time, the *The Drug Administration Law* is the "Basic Law" for the formulation of pharmaceutical supervision and management regulations and administrative regulations.

2.《药品经营质量管理规范》(简称 GSP)

2. *Good Supply Practice for Pharmaceutical Products* (abbreviated as GSP)

要求药品经营企业在药品购进、贮运和销售等环节实行质量管理，建立包括组织结构、职责制度、过程管理和设施设备等方面的质量体系，并使之有效运行。对药品批发的质量管理主要从管理职责、人员与培训、设施与设备、进货、验收与检验、储存与养护、出库与运输、销售与售后服务等方面明确要求，确保药品经营过程中的质量。对药品零售的质量管理主要从管理职责、人员与培训、设施和设备、进货与验收、陈列与储存、销售与服务六个方面明确了要求，确保药品服务质量。

GSP requires drug supply enterprises to implement quality management in the purchase, storage, transportation, and sales of medicines, establish a quality system including organizational structure, responsibility systems, process management, and facilities and equipment, and make it operate effectively. The quality management of pharmaceutical wholesale mainly includes management responsibilities, personnel and training, facilities and equipment, purchase, acceptance and inspection, storage and maintenance, warehouse delivery and transportation, sales and after-sales service and so on. This is to ensure the quality during the pharmaceutical business process. The quality management of medicine retail mainly defines management requirements, personnel and training, facilities and equipment, purchase and acceptance, display and storage, sales and service in order to ensure the quality of drug service.

此外，还有《药品经营许可证管理办法》《处方与非处方药分类管理办法》《医疗用毒性药品管理办法》等法规。

In addition, there are *Measures for the Administration of Business Licenses of Drugs*, *Measures for the Classification of Administration of the Prescription and Non-Prescription Drugs*, and *Measures for the Control of Medicinal Toxic Drugs* and other regulations.

二、中药商品的质量管理

II. Quality Management of Chinese Materia Medica Commodities

(一) 中药商品全面质量管理

(I) Comprehensive Quality Management of CMMCs

中药商品全面质量管理是指中药经营企业对中药商品的全部质量和整个流通过程的工作质量都进行全面的管理。

The comprehensive quality management of CMMCs refers to the comprehensive management of the overall quality of the CMMCs and the work quality during the entire distribution process by CMM enterprises.

1. 中药商品全面质量管理包含的内容 中药商品是药品，其质量包含的内容较多，主要内容包括有效性、安全性、稳定性、均一性、经济性及其包装和便于服用等特性。此外，药品的包装要美观大方，便于养护、运输、贮存和使用，这是药品质量的组成部分，不能忽视。

1. Contents of CMMCs Comprehensive Quality Management CMMCs are medicines, and their quality contains a lot of content such as effectiveness, safety, stability, uniformity, economy, and their packaging and ease of taking. In addition, the packaging of medicines must be beautiful and easy to maintain, transport, store and use. This is an integral part of the quality of medicines and cannot be ignored.

2. 对中药商品实行全面质量管理的意义 对中药商品实行全面质量管理与以前的质量管理要求不同，它不仅要求对中药商品的全部质量进行管理，而且要求对其流通全过程的工作质量和企业全体职工都要参加系统的质量管理工作。这就扩大了质量管理的范围和提高了对质量管理工作的要求，对提高药品质量和中药商业企业的经济效益具有重要意义。

2. Significance of Implementing Comprehensive Quality Management for CMMCs The comprehensive quality management of CMMCs is different from the previous quality management requirements. It not only requires the management of the overall quality of CMMCs, but also requires the quality of the entire process of its circulation and all employees of the company to participate in systematic quality management. This expands the scope of quality management and raises the requirements for quality management work, which is of great significance for improving the quality of medicines and the economic benefits of Chinese medicine commercial enterprises.

（1）能最大限度地满足人民安全有效的用药需要　人们对药品的基本要求是其有效性和安全性，旨在防治疾病和保健强身，以恢复和保持自身的健康为目的。中药商业企业的天职就是通过对药品质量的全面管理，保证药品优质、高效、安全的质量，从而最大限度地满足人民安全有效的用药需要。

(1) Meeting the needs of people's safe and effective medication utmostly　The basic requirements for medicines are their effectiveness and safety. They are designed to prevent diseases and maintain health, and to restore and maintain their own health. The bounden duty of Chinese medicine commercial enterprises is to ensure the high-quality, efficiency and safe quality of medicines through the comprehensive management of the quality of medicines, so as to meet the needs of people's safe and effective medication utmostly.

（2）能促进生产企业提高药品质量　中药商业企业实行药品的全面质量管理，择优选购生产企业生产的优质药品，直接影响生产企业的生产效益，加上目前同类药品激烈的竞争，只有质量优良，价格合理的药品才能在竞争中取胜。从而促进生产企业提高产品质量，以增加销售量，提高经济效益。

(2) Promoting manufacturers to improve medicines quality　CMM commercial enterprises implement comprehensive quality management of medicines. Selecting and purchasing high-quality medicines produced by production enterprises directly affects their efficiency of production enterprises. In addition to the current fierce competition of similar medicines, only medicines with good quality and reasonable prices can win the competition, thus promoting production enterprises to improve product quality, increase sales and improve economic efficiency.

（3）能提高中药商业企业的经济效益　中药商品的质量与中药商业企业的经济效益是统一的。药品质量优，销售量大，企业的经济效益就好。中药商业企业实行全面质量管理后，不仅可以杜绝伪劣药品进入消费领域，全面提高了药品质量，而且由于加强了流通全过程和全体职工参加质量管理，加速了药品流通，减少了药品损耗和积压，也加速了资金周转，因而又可提高企业的经济效益。

(3) Improving the economic benefits of CMM commercial enterprises The quality of CMMCs is consistent with the economic benefits of CMM commercial enterprises. The quality of the medicine is good, and the sales volume is large, then the economic benefits of the company are good. After the CMM commercial enterprises implement comprehensive quality management, not only can they prevent fake and inferior medicines from entering the consumer field and comprehensively improve the quality of medicines, but also strengthen the entire distribution process and the participation of all employees in quality management, which speeds up medicine distribution and reduces medicinal loss and backlog. It also accelerates capital turnover, which in turn can improve the economic efficiency of the enterprise.

3. 对中药商品实行全面质量管理的要求 中药商品具有来源广泛、产地分散、品种多、数量大、规格等级复杂、性质各异等特点，所以实行全面质量管理的任务重，难度大。为了克服全面质量管理中的困难，完成繁重的管理任务，特提出以下要求。

3. Requirements for comprehensive quality management of CMMCs CMMCs have a wide range of sources, scattered origins, many varieties, large numbers, complex specifications and grades, and different characteristics. Therefore, the task of implementing comprehensive quality management is heavy and difficult. To overcome the difficulties in total quality management and complete the burdensome management tasks, the following requirements are proposed.

（1）树立“质量第一”的思想，全体职工参加质量管理 中药商业企业牢固树立“质量第一”“质量出效益”的思想。并按质量管理的要求，严格遵守全面质量管理工作制度，运用PDCA 循环工作法，把全面质量管理工作搞好。

(1) Establish the “Quality First” concept, and all employees participate in quality management CMM commercial enterprises firmly establish the “Quality First” and “Quality Yields Benefits” ideas. To do a good job in comprehensive quality management invloves compliance with the requirements of quality management, strict abidance by the comprehensive quality management work system, and using the PDCA cycle work method.

（2）建立健全质量管理工作机构 除了各级药品监督管理部门等的质量管理、监督检查机构外，各省、市、自治区和地（市）的中药商业企业，也应建立健全由经理直接领导的质量管理和质量监督检验机构（处、科或室）；县级药材公司及其批发、零售企业应有专职或兼职的质量管理和质量检验人员。只有机构健全，组织落实，权责分明，才能保证全面质量管理任务的完成。

(2) Establishing and improving quality management institutions In addition to the quality management, supervision and inspection institutions at all levels of medicines supervision and administration departments, CMM commercial enterprises in all provinces, municipalities, autonomous regions and prefectures (cities) should also establish the quality management and quality supervision and inspection institutions (Country, department or office) that directly led by the manager. County-level medicinal materials companies, their wholesale and retail enterprises should have full-time or part-time quality management and quality inspection personnel. Only when the organization is sound and implemented, the powers and responsibilities are clearly defined, can the comprehensive quality management tasks be completed.

（3）严格把好各流通环节的质量关 中药商品流通环节主要有购，销、运、存。把好这四大环节的质量关，是搞好全面质量管理工作的关键。

(3) Strictly controlling the quality of each circulation link The circulation of CMMCs mainly includes purchase, sale, transportation and storage. Improving the quality of these four links is the key to

improving overall quality management.

（4）培养技术管理人才　中药经营企业要有专职或兼职的专业技术人员把好质量关，技术要熟练，责任心要强，办事要公正。同时要保持专业队伍的相对稳定，这是搞好全面质量管理工作的关键。技术力量不足或技术水平低的企业，要通过"以老带新"或举办培训班或送出进修等办法培训技术管理人才，以适应全面质量管理工作的需要。

(4) Cultivating technical management talents　CMM enterprises must have full-time or part-time professional and technical personnel to ensure good quality, with skilled technology, strong sense of responsibility, and fairness. At the same time, it is necessary to maintain the relative stability of the professional team, which is the key to good comprehensive quality management. Enterprises with insufficient technical strength or low technical level shall train technical management talents by "Professionals Teach Newcomers" or holding training courses or sending out for further studies to meet the needs of comprehensive quality management.

（5）建立健全奖惩制度　为了搞好质量管理和质量检验工作，严格把好质量关，企业要对有关人员进行定期或不定期的考核。对工作中有显著成绩的单位和个人要给予表扬和物质奖励；对不按规定办事，徇私舞弊者，要予以批评教育或行政的、经济的惩罚，造成重大事故，后果严重，影响恶劣的，应追究刑事责任。

(5) Establishing and improving the reward and punishment system　In order to do a good job of quality management and quality inspection, and strictly control the quality, the enterprise must conduct regular or irregular inspections of relevant personnel. Units and individuals with outstanding achievements in work must be given praise and material rewards; those who do not act in accordance with the regulations and engage in malpractices for personal gain must be criticized for education or administrative and economic punishment, causing major accidents with serious consequences and bad influence. Criminal responsibility should be investigated.

4. 中药商品全面质量管理的制度　为了保证中药商品的质量，国家主管部门制订了全面质量管理的工作制度。

4. Comprehensive quality management systems of CMMCs　In order to ensure the quality of CMMCs, the competent national authorities have formulated a comprehensive quality management work system.

（1）药品质量档案制　生产企业和经营企业都要建立商品质量档案。中药经营企业对所经营药品质量档案的内容包括药名、产地或厂家生产批号、药品质量标准、购进药品检验的记录、质量变动情况、药品质量问题的处理情况和用户查询意见等。

(1) Medicine quality file system　Both manufacturing and operating enterprises must establish commodity quality files. The contents of the quality files of the medicines handled by the CMM enterprises include the names of the medicines, the place of origin or the manufacturer's production number, the quality standards of the medicines, the records of the purchased medicines inspection, the situation of quality changes, the treatment of the medicines quality problems, and the user's query opinions.

（2）药品质量分析制　生产企业和经营企业的各级领导都要定期召开药品质量分析会，讨论药品质量问题，实行 PDCA 工作法管理。

(2) Medicine quality analysis system　Leaders at all levels of manufacturing enterprises and operating enterprises must regularly hold medicine quality analysis meetings to discuss medicine quality issues and implement PDCA work method management.

（3）药品留样观察制　生产企业和经营企业要认真开展药品留样观察工作。要专人负责，定期复查质量，观察质量变化情况，并作好观察记录，归入留样观察档案。通过留样，观察药品的稳定性。

(3) Observation system for medicine retained samples　Manufacturers and operating enterprises should seriously carry out observation of pharmaceutical samples. Special persons should be responsible for regularly reviewing the quality, observing the quality changes, making observation records, and putting them into the retained sample observation file. By retaining samples, observe the stability of the medicine.

（4）药品保管养护制　中药经营企业按规定的条件，如避光、通风、干燥、隔热等保管条件进行药品贮存，观察其质量变化情况，做好记录，归入保管养护档案。同时实行药品“先进先出，易变勤查”等办法，严格把好入库、在库养护和出库的质量关，严禁伪劣和变质失效药品进入消费领域。

(4) Medicine storage and maintenance system　CMM enterprises store medicines in accordance with prescribed conditions, such as protection from light, ventilation, dryness, heat insulation, etc., observe changes in their quality, make records, and put them into storage and maintenance archives. At the same time, the implementation of “First in, First out” and “Variable Inspection” methods of medicines, strictly put good storage, maintenance and delivery of quality, and strictly prohibit the fake and inferior medicines from entering the consumer field.

（5）药品质量统计报告制　中药生产企业要定期向上级主管部门报送药品质量情况统计表，并逐级上报至国家主管部门。报表中要有文字说明和原因分析。

(5) Statistical reporting system for medicine quality　CMM manufacturers should submit statistical reports on medicine quality to their competent authorities on a regular basis, and report to the competent authorities on a level-by-level basis. There should be text description and cause analysis in the report.

（6）药品质量事故报告制　药品质量事故分为一般事故和重大事故两类。除一般事故要及时向上级主管部门或人员报告外，重大事故要按规定及时逐级上报。

(6) Medicine quality accident reporting system　Medicine quality accidents are classified into general accidents and major accidents. Except for general accidents, which should be reported to the competent department or personnel in a timely manner, major accidents should be reported without delay and level-by-level.

（7）用户访问制　中药企业要树立“一切为了用户”的思想，全心全意为用户服务。要定期走访用户，征求对药品（产品）的意见；对来信来访，要热情接待，认真核实，及时妥善处理。

(7) User access system　CMM companies should establish the “All for the Users” ideology and serve the users wholeheartedly. It is necessary to visit users regularly to solicit opinions on medicines (products), to receive letters and visits. Meanwhile, we must give a warm reception to letters and visits, verify them carefully, and handle them promptly and properly.

5. 在流通中出现中药商品质量问题的处理办法　中药商品在流通过程中，由于受到药品本身性质和外界诸多因素的影响，常常出现一些质量问题。对出现的药品质量问题，除按中药商品质量管理制度处理外，买卖双方（或甲乙双方）都应本着保证药用安全有效和尽量避免或减少损失的原则，坚持法制观念，采取实事求是和认真负责的态度，分清情况，辨明责任，双方平等协商，妥善处理。常见的有以下三种情况：

5. Measures to deal with quality problems of CMMCs in circulation　Due to the nature of the medicine itself and many external factors, some quality problems often occur in the process of circulation of CMMCs. For the quality problems of medicines, in addition to the quality management system of CMMCs, buyers and sellers (or A and B) should adhere to the principles of ensuring the safety and effectiveness of medicines, and avoiding or minimizing losses. Furthermore, we should adhere to the concept of the legal system, adopt a realistic and responsible attitude, to clarify the situation and identify responsibilities. Both buyers and sellers negotiate on an equal basis, and properly handle. There are three common situations:

（1）验收中发现药品质量问题的处理办法　验收中发现药品质量问题，应按合同或上级主管部门的有关规定，及时向供货方写出查询信件，提出切实可行的处理意见，并要求对方尽快答复解决。在问题未解决之前，进货方仍应认真负责地作好药品的保管养护工作，以减少损失。

(1) Measures for medicine quality problems found during acceptance　If a quality problem is found during the inspection, a letter of inquiry should be written to the supplier in a timely manner in accordance with the relevant provisions of the contract or the competent department in charge. Then we should put forward some pieces of practical advice. Before the problem is resolved, the purchaser should still do a good job in the storage and maintenance of the medicine to reduce losses.

（2）售出中发现药品质量问题的处理办法　对已售出中药商品的质量问题，无论单位或个人来信来访，售出方必须热情接待，认真答复处理。凡属重大的用药事故应按有关规定，逐级上报，并通知有关进货单位就地封存，停止销售和使用，听候处理。

(2) Treatment methods for quality problems found during the sale　Regarding the quality of the CMMCs sold, no matter what letters and visits from units or individuals, the seller must receive them warmly and reply earnestly. All major medicine accidents shall be reported step by step in accordance with relevant regulations, and the relevant purchase units shall be notified to be sealed in situ, cease sales and use, and wait for disposal.

（3）库存药品质量问题的处理办法　库存药品在检查中发现质量问题，应根据变质情况和程度，认真寻找原因。针对变质原因，采取相应的有效措施，防止变质现象漫延，尽量减少损失。如确系变质严重，经检查不能药用的，要逐级上报，请求报废。

(3) How to deal with the quality problems of stock medicines　When quality problems of stock medicines are found during inspection, the cause should be carefully searched according to the deterioration and degree of deterioration. According to the cause of deterioration, effective measures shall be taken to prevent the deterioration and minimize losses. If it is indeed severely deteriorated and cannot be used for medicine after inspection, it shall be reported to be scrapped level-by-level.

（二）影响中药商品质量的主要因素

(II) Main factors affecting the quality of CMMCs

影响中药商品质量的因素很多，从品种、产地、种植、采收、加工、运输、贮藏、养护到使用过程，要经过很多环节。由于药品要受自身和外界诸多因素的影响，容易产生质量变化。其主要因素如下。

There are many factors that affect the quality of CMMCs, from varieties, producing areas, planting, harvesting, processing, transportation, storage, conservation to the use process, through many links. Medicines are affected by many factors of themselves and the outside world, quality changes are easy to occur. The main factors are as follows.

1. 品种

1. Variety

品种是影响中药商品质量非常重要的因素。中药有效成分多来源于次生代谢产物，不同品种的植（动）物，由于遗传特性不同，合成与积累次生代谢产物的种类和量存在很大的差异。中药商品中，一药多基原的情况较多，有的来源于不同属不同种，有的来源于同科不同属。如黄芪，在全国各地有多种黄芪属和崖黄芪属植物的根作黄芪药用；虽然来源于同科或同属，但品种不同，各种品种所含的活性成分不同，其药物的性、味、功效不同。所以品种对中药商品质量非常重要。

Variety is a very important factor affecting the quality of CMMCs. The active ingredients of CMM are mostly derived from secondary metabolites. Plants (animals) of different varieties have different types and amounts of secondary metabolites due to different genetic characteristics. There are many cases of one medicinal with multiple origins in CMMCs. Some medicinals are from different genera and different species, and some from different genera of the same family. Such as *Astragali Radix*, there are a variety of *astragalus* and *Cliff astragalus* roots used as *Astragali Radix* medicinal plants throughout the country. Although they are derived from the same family or the same genus, but they have different varieties. Different active ingredients cause different effects. Therefore, the variety is very important to the quality of CMMCs.

2. 产地

2. Producing areas

中药商品的质量与品种密切相关外，其药效成分在药用动植物体内的形成和积累与其道地产地关系亦很密切，对其质量优劣影响很大。我国疆域辽阔，中药材产地广布，但因产地不同，地理、气候、土壤不同，水质、生态各异，造成不同产地的同种药材质量上的差异。

In addition to the quality of CMMCs, which are closely related to the variety, the formation and accumulation of medicinal ingredients in medicinal plants and animals are also closely related to their local real estate, which greatly affects their quality. China has a vast territory and widely-produced Chinese medicinal materials. However, due to the different producing areas, the geographies, climates, soils, water and ecology are different. The quality of the same medicinal materials of different producing areas varies.

3. 栽培养殖

3. Cultivation

中药材生产、栽培（养殖）技术的规范与中药商品质量密切相关。我国目前经营的大宗商品药材主要为栽培（养殖）品种，如人参、鹿茸、三七、川芎等。有的品种栽培技术粗放，不规范，造成种质不佳，品种混杂，种质特性退化。如川牛膝的种质退化导致川牛膝的根越种越小。此外，在栽培中滥施农药、化肥，会造成药材农残残存、重金属含量超标，严重影响了中药商品的质量。对中药实施规范化栽培（养殖），是提高药材质量和保证中药商品质量稳定的基础。

The specifications of the production and cultivation (cultivation) technology of Chinese medicinal materials are closely related to the quality of CMMCs. The bulk commodity medicinal materials currently operated in China are mainly cultivated (breeding) species, such as *Ginseng Radix et Rhizoma*, *Cervi Cornu Pantotrichum*, *Notoginseng Radix et Rhizoma*, *Chuanxiong Rhizoma* and so on. Some varieties have extensive cultivation techniques which are not standardized, resulting in poor germplasm, mixed varieties, and degradation of germplasm characteristics. For example, the germplasm degradation of *Cyathulae Radix* causes its roots grow smaller and smaller. In addition, excessive application of pesticides and fertilizers in cultivation cause residues of medicinal materials and residues of heavy metals, which will seriously affect the quality of CMMCs. The standardized cultivation (breeding) of CMM is the basis for improving the quality of medicinal materials and ensuring the stability of the quality of CMMCs.

4. 采收

4. Harvest

中药商品的采收年限、季节、方法等也直接影响中药商品的质量和产量。故谓之“凡诸草、木、昆虫，产之有地；根、叶、花、实采之有时。失其地，则性味少异；失其时，则气味不全”。如槐花在花蕾期芦丁含量达28%，而在花盛期芦丁含量急剧下降。中药材的适宜采收是影响中药商品质量的重要环节。

The harvest time, season and method of CMMCs also directly affect the quality and output of CMMCs. Therefore, it is said that “Every herb, wood, insect has its own land; every root, leaf, flower, fruit, and occasional harvest. Without its place of origin and its harvest season, its efficacy is incomplete.” For example, the content of rutin in the flower bud stage of the *Sophoraeflos* reached 28%, while the content of rutin dropped sharply during the flowering period. Proper harvesting of CMM is an important link that affects the quality of CMMCs.

5. 加工

5. Processing

中药商品加工多在原产地进行，属原药材生产范围，又称中药商品产地加工，是为提供中药商品药材所进行的独特技术，主要按中药商品规格、等级要求进行加工。中药商品产地加工的规范与否，是保证中药商品质量的重要环节之一。如五倍子在产地加工时，将采收的鲜五倍子投入沸水中杀青，边煮边搅拌，3~5分钟后，待五倍子表面由黄褐色变为灰色，取出晾干、阴干或烘干。如不通过杀青处理，直接晒干，易出现爆裂、霉烂，色泽灰暗，质差，对中药材实施规范的加工是保证中药商品质量的重要环节。

CMMCs commodity processing is mostly carried out in the place of origin, which belongs to the scope of the original medicinal materials production, also known as CMMCs origin processing, which is a unique technology for providing CMMCs materials. It is mainly processed according to the specifications and grade requirements of CMMCs. It is one of the important links to ensure the quality of CMMCs whether the processing of TCM products is standardized or not. For example, when processing *Galla Chinensis* is processed in the producing area, put the collected fresh *Galla Chinensis* into boiling water, stirring while blanching. After 3 to 5 minutes, when the surface of the *Galla Chinensis* change from yellow-brown to gray, take them out to dry in the air, in the shade or by baking. If it is not processed with blanching and dried in the sun directly, it is easy to burst and mildew, showing dark gray color and poor quality. So, the standardized processing of Chinese medicinal material is an important link to ensure the quality of CMMCs.

6. 贮藏

6. Storage

中药商品的贮藏是中药商品从生产到消费流通中的停当囤积，贮藏是中药商品经营中的重要环节之一，是保证中药商品连续流通和供应的必备条件。如果贮藏方法不当，措施不力，就会造成虫蛀、霉变等，导致中药商品质量下降，造成中药资源浪费，甚至市场流通中断。

The storage of CMMCs is the stagnant accumulation of the CMMCs from production to consumption. Storage is one of the important links in the operation of CMMCs, and it is an indispensable condition to ensure the continuous circulation and supply of CMMCs. If the storage method is improper and the measures are inadequate, it will cause maggots, mildew, etc., which bring about the quality of CMMCs to decline, waste of Chinese medicine resources, and even interrupt market circulation.

第二节 药材商品规格与等级制订

Section 2 Formulation of Medicinal Material Commodities Specifications and Grades

PPT

药材商品的品质、规格及等级，是衡量药材商品质量好坏的准则。品质是对药材品种与质量的原则要求；规格是划分药材商品质量，分等分级的具体标准。药材商品的品质与规格、等级标准，也是进行其质量管理的依据。

The quality, specifications and grades of medicinal material commodities are the criteria for measuring the quality thereof. Quality is the principle requirement for the variety and quality of medicinal materials; specifications are specific standards for classifying and grading them. The quality, specifications and grade standards of medicinal material commodities are also the basis for quality management.

药材质量必须优良，才能保证人民用药的安全有效；同时药材又是一种特殊商品，必须符合商品按质论价的要求。因此药材既具有药用性，又具有商品性。

Medicinal materials are special items used to prevent and treat diseases and strengthen health. The quality must be excellent to ensure the safety and effectiveness of the people's medication. At the same time, medicinal materials are a special commodity and must meet the requirements of commodity valuation. Therefore, the medicinal materials are both medicinal and commercial.

一、制订药材商品规格与等级的原则

I. Principles for Formulating the Specifications and Grades of Medicinal Materials

制订药材商品规格、等级的标准，仍以外观和性状特征为主，制订的原则有：国家药品标准和《七十六种药材商品规格标准》，中华中医药学会标准化办公室发布的 2018 年修订《中药材商品规格等级 226 种》的行业标准。制订的原则有：

The formulation of commodity specifications and grades of medicinal materials is still mainly based on appearance quality and characteristics. The principles are as follows: National Drug Standard and *The Standard for the Specifications of 76 kinds of Medicinal Materials*, and the industry standard of *The Commodity Specification Grade of Chinese Medicinal materials* (*226 kinds*), revised and released by Standardization Office of China Association of Traditional Chinese Medicine and Pharmacy in 2018. The principles formulated are:

（一）按质论价的原则

(I) The principle of valuing by quality

为了达到中药商品按质论价的要求，保证药材的质量与疗效，按质论价原则是制订药材商品规格与等级的基本原则。

To achieve the requirements of CMMCs pricing, and to ensure the quality and efficacy of medicinal materials, the principle of pricing based on quality is the basic principle for formulating the specifications and grades of pharmaceutical products.

（二）有利于生产发展原则

（II）Conduciveness to the principle of production development

为了保证市场供应，满足人民用药要求，必须不断发展药材生产。为了促进药材生产质量的提高，采用划分药材规格与等级的手段，以优价收购优质药材的办法，来促进高质量药材生产的发展。

In order to ensure market supply and meet the people's requirements for medicinal use, we must continue to develop the production of medicinal materials. In order to promote the improvement of the quality of medicinal materials, we adopt the method of dividing the specifications and grades of medicinal materials and purchasing high-quality medicinal materials at high prices to promote the development of high-quality medicinal materials.

（三）不断改革的原则

（III）The Principle of Continuous Reform

在不影响药材商品质量和产、供、销、用的前提下，改革那些不合理的或过于繁杂的、不便掌握的规格与等级标准及其相应的加工方法，以减少加工环节，降低成本，提高生产效益。

Without affecting the quality of medicinal material commodities and the production, supply, sales, use, and reform those unreasonable or too complicated, inconvenient to master grade standards and specifications and corresponding processing methods to reduce processing sectors, reduce costs, and improve production efficiency.

（四）便于量化原则

（IV）The Principle of Convenience for Quantification

在药材商品中的同种药材，因产地采收期、生产方式（家种与野生）或加工方法不同，质量和疗效确有明显差异，应划分规格，适当区分等级。但各规格、等级之间要有明显的量化指标，如大小（长短、厚薄、直径）、重量（单个重或每千克或半公斤的个数）或有效成分含量的差异等，以便统一掌握实施。

The same kind of medicinal materials in medicinal material commodities are obviously different in quality and curative effect due to different harvesting time, production methods (domestic and wild), or processing methods. Therefore, the specifications should be divided into grades. However, there must be obvious quantitative indicators between the specifications and grades, such as size (length, thickness, diameter), weight (individual weight or the number per kilogram or half kilogram), or the difference in the content of active ingredients, etc., so as to uniformly grasp the implementation.

（五）试用原则

（V）Probation Principle

对新制订的或改革后的规格、等级标准，要通过一段时间的试用，在试用中不断修订补充，使之合理、完善，再正式实行。

The newly formulated or reformed specifications and grade standards should be tested for a period of time, and continuously revised and supplemented during the trial to make them reasonable and complete, and then formally implemented.

二、划分药材商品规格等级的方法

II. Method for Classifying Medicinal Material Commodities Specification Grade

药材商品质量优劣的客观标准取决于有效成分含量的多少和疗效的显著性。划分药材规格与等级使用常用的方法有：

The objective criterion for the quality of medicinal material commodities depends on the amount of active ingredients and the significance of the efficacy. Common methods for classifying medicinal material commodities specification grade are:

（一）按产地不同来划分

（I）Classification According to Producing Areas

同种药材，其产地是否道地，外在和内在质量是不同的，划分的规格与等级就不一样。如广藿香，按产地不同划分为石牌广藿香与海南广藿香两种规格。前者含广藿香酮，香气浓郁，质量好，为道地药材；后者不含广藿香酮，香气较弱，质量较次。

Whether the origin of the same medicinal material is authentic, the external and internal quality is different, and the specifications and grades are different. For example, *Pogostemonis Herba* is divided into two types: Shipai Guanghuoxiang and Hainan Guanghuoxiang. The former contains patchoulenone, with strong aroma and good quality, which is an authentic medicinal; the latter does not contain patchoulenone, which has a weaker aroma and a lower quality.

（二）按采收季节不同来划分

（II）Classification According to Different Harvest Seasons

一般药材的采收期只有一个，但有的药材有几个。采收的季节不同，质量差异较大，在中药商品学上常据此划分成不同的规格。如三七，按采收期不同划分为“春三七”和“冬三七”两种规格。“春三七”于花前期采收，体重质坚，质优；“冬三七”于果期采收，体较轻，质较次。两种规格的三七又按每 500g 的个数再划分成一至十一个等级。

Generally, there is only one harvesting period for medicinal materials, but some medicinal materials have several harvesting periods. The harvest season is different, and the quality varies greatly. According to the CMMC, it is often divided into different specifications. For example, *Notoginseng Radix et Rhizoma* can be divided into two specifications: “Chun Sanqi” and “Dong Sanqi” according to different harvest periods. “Chun Sanqi ” was harvested in the early flowering period, with firm weight and high quality; “Dong Sanqi” was harvested in the fruit period, with lighter body and lower quality. The two specifications of *Notoginseng Radix et Rhizoma* are divided into one to eleven grades according to the number of per 500g.

（三）按产地加工方法不同来划分

（III）Classification According to Processing Methods of Producing Areas

因产地加工方法不同引起性状上的差异，据此可划分出不同的规格。如肉桂，按产地加工法不同可划分成“板桂”“企边桂”“桂通”“桂碎”和“桂心”。

Due to the differences in properties caused by different processing methods of origin, different specifications can be divided according to that. For example, *Cinnamomi Cortex* can be divided into “Bangui” “Qibiangui” “Guitong” “Guisui” and “Guixin” according to the origin of processing methods.

（四）按药材的外部形态来划分

（IV）Classification According to the External Form of Medicinal Materials

有些药材的外部形态或完整程度不同，其商品质量亦不同。如浙贝母，依据外形和完整程度不一可分为“元宝贝”和“珠贝”。元宝贝为单一的外层鳞片，呈“元宝”状，质优；后者为较小的完整鳞茎，大小不一，呈扁圆形，质较次。

Some medicinal materials have different external shapes or completeness, and their product quality is also different. Such as *Fritillariae Thunbergii Bulbus*, can be divided into “Yuanbaobei” and “Zhubei” based on different shapes and completeness. The Yuanbaobei is a single outer scale with a "Yuanbao" shape and good quality; the latter is a small complete bulb with different sizes and a flat round shape, which is inferior in quality.

（五）按药材大小或重量不同来划分

(V) Classification According to the Size or Weight of Medicinal Materials

单个药材的大小或轻重与其质量有密切的关系。通常个大体重者质优，个小体轻者质次。如天麻，首先按采收季节不同分为"春天麻"和"冬天麻"两种规格。每种规格又依据单个的大小和重量不同分为四个等级。如每千克 26 只以内为一等，40 只以内的为二等。

The size or weight of a single medicinal material is closely related to its quality. Usually the medicinal materials with large volume and weight are superior in quality, while those with small volume and light weight are of inferior quality. For example, *Gastrodiae Rhizoma* is divided into two types: "Chuntianma" and "Dongtianma" according to different harvest seasons. Each specification is divided into four levels according to the individual size and weight. For example, if the number is less than 26 per kilogram, it is the first grade, and if it is less than 40, it is the second grade.

（六）按药材的老嫩程度不同来划分

(VI) Classification According to Maturity of the Medicinal Materials

药材的老嫩程度（生长期长，开始衰老的习称为"老"；生长期短，生长旺盛的习称为"嫩"）不同，其质量也不同，甚至不能药用。所以常据此来划分规格与等级。如花鹿茸，按茸角的老嫩，分叉的多少不一划分成"二杠"和"三岔"等规格；每一规格又按茸体粗细长短、色泽、骨化程度不同分成 1~3 个等级。

The maturity level of medicinal materials (the habit of growing long and starting to age is called "old"; the habit of growing short and growing vigorously is called "tender"), the quality is different, and even it is not medicinal. Therefore, the specifications and grades are often divided according to this. Such as Hualurong, according to the old and tender horn of the Hualurong, the number of forks is divided into "Ergang" and "Sancha" and other specifications; each specification is divided according to the thickness of the Hualurong slender and short, color, ossification degree is divided into 1~3 grades.

（七）按药用部位的不同来划分

(VII) Classification According to Different Medicinal Parts

有的药材的药用部位不同，疗效有别，据此划分规格。如当归，按药用部位疗效的差异分为"全归"和"归头"两种规格。每种规格又按其每千克的支头数再分别划成 1~4 个等级和 1~5 个等级。

Some medicinal materials have different medicinal parts and different curative effects, so the specifications are divided accordingly. Such as *Angelicae Sinensis Radix*, according to the difference in efficacy of medicinal parts they are divided into "Quangui" and "Guitou" two specifications. Each specification is further divided into 1 to 4 grades and 1 to 5 grades according to the number of supports per kilogram.

（八）按药材的来源不同来划分

(VIII) Classification According to the Source of Medicinal Materials

同一药材因药用植物来源不同，内在质量或外形不一，可据此划分规格。如麻黄，按其来源的种不同分为"草麻黄""中麻黄"和"木贼麻黄"三种规格。

Due to the different sources of medicinal plants, the same medicinal materials have different internal quality or appearance, and the specifications can be divided accordingly. Such as *Ephedrae*

Herba, according to the species of its origin, it is divided into three specifications: "Cao mahuang" "Zhongmahuang" and "Muzeimahuang".

第三节 中药商品的价格管理

Section 3 Price Management of Chinese Materia Medica Commodities

PPT

药品是与人民生活关系重大的商品。目前我国的物价按"统一领导，分级管理"的原则，由各级物价管理部门分别进行管理。随着我国市场经济体制和现代企业制度的建立，从中央到地方，从地方到企业，都把过分集中的物价管理权限逐层下放。因此国家对中药商品价格管理的原则也与其他商品一样，实行宏观管理，微观放开的原则，以适应市场经济发展的需要。我国对药品价格实行政府调控和市场调节相结合的管理方式。

Medicines are commodities that have a great bearing on the people's lives. At present, prices in China are managed by price management departments at all levels according to the principle of "Unified Leadership and Hierarchical Management". With the establishment of China's market economy system and modern enterprise system, from the central to the local, from the local to the enterprise, overly centralized price management authority has been decentralized layer by layer. Therefore, the principle of price management of CMMCs is the same as that of other commodities. The principle of macro management and micro liberalization is implemented to meet the needs of the development of market economy. China implements a combination of government regulation and market regulation on medicinal prices.

一、中药商品价格组成

I. Composition of CMMCs Price

中药商品价值是由在生产过程中已经消耗的物化劳动转移到产品中的价值，表现在货币形式上就是生产成本、流通费用、税金和利润。这就是组成商品价格的四个要素。这四个要素是制订和调整价格的最基本的依据。

The value of CMMCs is the value transferred from the materialized labor that has been consumed in the production process to the product, which is expressed in the form of money as production costs, circulation costs, taxes and profits. These are four elements that make up the price of a commodity. These four elements are the most basic basis for setting and adjusting prices.

二、中药商品的价格体系及其分类

II. The Price System and Classification of CMMCs

中药商品的价格体系是由相互联系，相互制约的不同类的价格组成。一般根据不同的分类标准，有以下两种不同的分类方法。

The price system of CMMCs is composed of different types of prices that are interrelated and mutually restricted. Generally according to different classification standards, there are the following two different classification methods.

（一）按照价格管理的形式分类

(I) Classification According to the Form of Price Management

根据各类中药商品对国计民生影响的大小和管理权限不同，分为政府定价、政府指导价和市场调节价三种。

According to the impact of various types of CMMCs on the national economy and the people's livelihood, and their management authority, they are divided into three types: government pricing, government guidance prices, and market adjustment prices.

1. 政府定价 政府定价是指按照物价管理权限，对列入国家基本医疗保险用药目录的药品，以及生产经营具有垄断性的药品由政府制定价格。根据《价格法》规定，对列入政府定价的药品价格，生产经营企业必须严格执行。

1. Government Pricing Government pricing refers to prices set by the government for medicines listed in the National Basic Medical Insurance Drug Catalogue and medicines that have a monopoly in production and operation in accordance with price management authority. According to the *Price Law*, production and operation of enterprises must be strictly implemented medicinal prices for the inclusion of government pricing.

2. 政府指导价 是国家依据中药产品的不同特点，在国家物价政策的指导下，由各级政府采用不同的方法制订的指导性价格，并由各级政府的物价主管部门分级负责。列入政府指导价的药品，药品经营者必须在政府规定的指导价范围内制定具体价格。

2. Government-guided Prices Depending on the characteristics of the national Chinese medicine products, under the guidance of national price policy, adopted by the governments at all levels to guide pricing different methods developed by all levels of government pricing authorities' levels of responsibility. The inclusion of government guidance medicinal, medicinal operators are required to develop specific price within a specified government guidance.

3. 市场调节价 市场调节价是由中药商品的生产企业、经营企业和医疗机构的生产者和经营者在国家物价政策规定的范围内按照公平、合理和诚实信用、质价相符的原则自行制订的价格。其特点是随行就市，自由涨落，具有自发性和不稳定性。但在价格大起大落时，各级物价部门和业务主管部门应及时加强管理，以保护生产者、经营者和消费者的利益。

3. Market-adjusted Price CMMCs price is regulated by the market commodity producers, distributors and medical institutions of the producers and operators within the limits of national price policy in accordance with the credit, the quality and price consistent with the principle of fair, reasonable and honest to formulate their own prices. Its features reflect market conditions, fluctuations freedom, spontaneity and instability. However, when price fluctuations, the price departments at all levels and departments in charge of business management should be strengthened, so as to protect the interests of producers, operators and consumers.

按照目前建立市场经济体制和现代企业制度的要求，在中药商品价格体系中，属于国家定价和国家指导价的品种会不断减少，属于市场调节价的品种会不断增多，以充分发挥市场的调节作用和价格的杠杆作用。但对国计民生影响大的，药材资源濒于枯竭的药材如麝香等和进口药材的价格实行国家定价或国家指导价也是必要的。这对于保护药源，有计划的进口药材和保证人民用药需要都有重要意义。

According to the current requirements of the market economy and the establishment of modern enterprise system, commodity prices in the Chinese system, belonging to the State and State guided pricing will continue to reduce the variety, species belonging to the market adjustment will continue to increase, so as to give full play to the role of market regulation and leverage prices. But the impact on the national economy and large, medicinal herbs such as depletion of resources on the brink of musk and the price of imported medicines subject to state pricing or national guidance is necessary. It is of great significance for the protection of medicine sources, the planned import of medicinal materials and the guarantee of the people's need for medicine.

（二）按照价格形成的阶段分类

(II) Classification According to the Stage of Price Formation

中药商品从生产领域进入流通领域要经过收购调拨销售、批发销售、零售等不同环节，因而形成了收购价、出厂价、调拨价、批发价和零售价组成的价格体系。

CMMCs are allocated through the acquisition of different segments of sales, wholesale sales, retail from producing areas to circulation, creating a price system purchase price, ex-factory price, transfer price, consisting of wholesale and retail prices.

1. 收购价 是指药材的经营者向生产者收购药材的价格，由生产成本、税金、生产纯收益构成。收购价格涉及工农之间、国家与农民之间的经济利益和生产与消费的关系，有的药材品种还关系到药源保护问题，因此，在制订和调整中药材收购价格，必须十分慎重。

1. The purchase price Refers to the price of the acquisition of medicinal herbs operators to producers, consists of the cost of production, taxes and net income production. The purchase price related to economic relations between the workers and peasants, between the State and the interests of farmers and production and consumption, and some medicinal species also related to the drug source protection, it should be very careful in the development and adjustment of the purchase price of Chinese herbal medicines thereby.

2. 出厂价 是指中药生产企业出售产品的价格。中成药出厂价格一般由生产成本、税金和工业利润构成；中药饮片出厂价格一般由生产成本、税金、加工损耗费，加工费和工业利润构成。中药工业产品出厂价也是中药商业企业的收购价格。它涉及工商双方的利润分配，反映工商企业之间的经济关系。同时中药工业产品出厂价格是其进入流通领域第一个环节的价格，是其他环节价格的基础，决定着零售价格水平。

2. Ex-factory price Ex-factory price is the price of products sold by Chinese medicine manufacturers. The ex-factory price of proprietary Chinese patent medicines generally consists of production costs, taxes, and industrial profits. The ex-factory prices of Chinese decocting pieces generally consist of production costs, taxes, processing losses, processing fees and industrial profits. The ex-factory price of CMM industrial products is also the purchase price of CMM commercial enterprises. It involves the distribution of profits between industry and commerce, and reflect the economic relations between the industrial and commercial enterprises. Meanwhile, CMM industrial product prices into circulation is the first part of the price. The price is the basis for other sectors, determine the retail price level.

3. 调拨价 是指中药商业企业内部调拨销售中药商品的价格。也是企业之间调拨销售药品后结算的价格，一般是依据主产地或中转地的市场批发价格，按规定的计算方法及倒扣率制订的，有的也由上级业务部门制订，主要涉及中药批发企业间的经济利益。合理制订或调整调拨价，有利于各批发企业之间的密切协作，促进各地区之间的药品交流，保证中药市场的正常供应。

3. Transfer Price It refers to the price allocated for the sale of CMMCs by Chinese medicine commercial enterprises. It is also the price settled after the sale of medicines between enterprises. Generally, it is based on the market wholesale price of the main place of production or transit, and is calculated according to the prescribed calculation method and kickback rate. Economic benefits between enterprises. Reasonably formulating or adjusting the transfer price is conducive to close cooperation between wholesale enterprises, promoting medicinal exchange between regions, and ensuring the normal supply of the Chinese medicine market.

4. 批发价格 是指中药批发企业销售给零售企业或医疗单位的价格；也是零售企业或医疗单位的购进价格。一般由购进价、流通费用和批发利润构成。批发价格反映了批发者与零售者之间的经济关系，又是零售价格计算的基础，直接影响中药商品市场零售价格的水平。

4. Wholesale Price It refers to the price sold by a Chinese medicine wholesale enterprise to a retail enterprise or medical unit; it is also the purchase price of a retail enterprise or medical unit. Generally consists of purchase price, circulation costs and wholesale profits. The wholesale price reflects the economic relationship between the wholesaler and the retailer, and is the basis of the retail price calculation, which directly affects the level of the retail price of CMMCs market.

5. 零售价 是指中药零售企业或医疗单位向城乡人民群众或社会集团销售中药商品的价格，由当地的批发价格、零售的流通费用、税金、零售利润构成。中药商品的零售价格是其流通领域中最后一个环节的价格，与消费者有直接联系，同时体现了国家与广大消费者的利益关系，积累与消费的关系，是中药商品价格体系中政策性最强的一种价格。

5. Retail Price Retail price refers to the price at which CMM retail enterprises or medical units sell CMMCs to urban and rural people or social groups. It is composed of local wholesale prices, retail circulation costs, taxes, and retail profits. The retail price of CMMCs is the price of the last link in its circulation field. It has direct links with consumers. Meanwhile, it reflects the interest relationship between the country and consumers, and the relationship between accumulation and consumption. The retail price of CMMCs is the most policy-oriented price in the CMMCs price system.

三、影响药材商品价格的主要因素

III. The Main Factors Affecting the Price of Medicinal Material Commodities

药材商品是生产中成药、中药提取物和饮片的原材料，药材商品价格的变化是引起中成药、中药提取物和饮片商品价格变化的基本因素。所以我们着重介绍影响药材商品价格的主要因素。

Medicinal material commodities are the raw material of the production of Chinese patent medicines, CMM extracts and Chinese decoction pieces. Changes in the price of medicinal material commodities are an essential factor in causing Chinese patent medicines, CMM extracts and Chinese decoction pieces price changes. So, we highlight the main factors affecting the price of medicinal material commodities.

药材商品的价格（元/kg，下同）是其药用价值的货币表现，由于药材商品生产的特殊性和经营管理的复杂性，其价格除受价值规律制约外，还受到药材商品生产、经营外部和内部诸多因素的影响，使其价格变化大。因此每种药材商品的价格在一定时期内难以稳定。只能根据市场调查和预测结果的分析，粗略估计一定时期内价格变化的范围。故本书在各论具体药材商品项下，不便标明具体的价格。影响药材商品价格的因素有外部因素和内部因素两种：

Medicinal material commodities prices (yuan/kg, the same below) are the monetary expression of its medicinal value. Due to the particularity of medicinal material commodities and the complexity of management, the price not only being subject to the law of value constraints, but also being affected by the production of medicinal material commodities, impact of external and internal operations of many factors, making it big price changes. Therefore, the prices of each medicinal material commodities are difficult to stabilize within a certain period. We can only roughly estimate the range of price changes in a certain period based on the analysis of market surveys and forecast results. In this book, it is inconvenient to indicate the specific price under the monograph specific medicine products. Factors affecting the prices of medicinal material commodities have external and internal factors in two ways:

（一）影响药材商品价格的外部因素

(I) External Factors Affecting the Price of Medicinal Material Commodities

影响药材商品价格的主要外部因素有：与其他农副产品的比价失调、药源的减少和天灾人祸的出现等三个因素。

The main external factors that affect the price of medicinal materials include three factors: the imbalance of the price ratio with other agricultural and sideline products, the reduction of medicine sources, and the emergence of natural disasters and human disasters.

1. 与其他农副产品的比价失调

1. Imbalanced Parity with Other Agricultural and Sideline Products

与其他农副产品的比价是制订或调整药材商品价格的依据之一。若其价格与其他农副产品的比价失调，将直接影响药农种植药材的积极性，造成药材产量的增加或减少。产量增加，供大于求，价格下降；产量减少，供不应求，价格上升。

The price comparison with other agricultural and sideline products is one of the basis for formulating or adjusting the prices of medicinal materials. If the price is out of balance with other agricultural and sideline products, it will directly affect the enthusiasm of medicinal farmers to grow medicinal materials, resulting in an increase or decrease in the output of medicinal materials. Increased production, supply exceeds demand, prices fall; reduce production, demand, prices rise.

2. 中药资源的减少

2. Decrease in Chinese Medicine Resources

药材商品中，有 60% 左右的药材品种都靠采集野生药源。经过长期乱挖乱采，造成药材资源枯竭，产量逐渐下降，产不足销，价格上升。

About 60% of the medicinal product varieties are collected from wild sources. After a long period of random digging and mining, the resources of medicinal materials dried up, the output gradually decreased, the output was insufficient, and the price increased.

3. 自然灾害或重大疫情出现

3. Natural Disaster or Major Outbreaks

药材商品生产特别是野生药材生产目前还处于“靠天吃饭”的境地，一旦受旱涝灾害或病虫害的影响，产量减少，产不足销而价格上升。

The production of medicinal materials, especially wild medicinal materials, is still in a “reliance on the heaven” situation. Once affected by droughts, floods, or diseases and insect pests, the output will decrease, the production will be insufficient and the price will rise。

此外，突发性传染病流行，需求量的增加也引起价格上涨。在以上影响药材商品价格的外部因素中，除天灾人祸难以预料和控制外，其余两种因素是可采取及时调整比价和保护药源的措施加以控制，以消除对药材商品的影响。

In addition, the sudden infectious disease epidemic, increasing demand has also caused prices to rise. Among the above external factors affecting the price of medicinal materials, in addition to the unpredictability and control of natural disasters and human calamities, the remaining two factors can be controlled by timely adjusting the price comparison and protecting the source of medicine to eliminate the impact on medicinal material commodities.

（二）影响药材商品价格的主要内部因素

(II) Main internal factors affecting the price of medicinal materials

影响药材商品价格的内部因素很多，但起决定作用的是货源、销售量、库存量和质量。这些因素又常相互联系和制约，其结果都可影响药材商品的价格。

There are many internal factors affecting the prices of medicinal material commodities, but those play a decisive role including the supply, sales, inventory and quality. These factors often interrelate and constrains, the result can affect the price of medicinal material commodities.

1. 货源 在药材商品销售量和库存量基本不变的情况下，货源的多少是影响价格的主要因素。而货源的多少取决于产量的大小。货源多，供大于求，则价格下降；货源少，供不应求，则价格上升；供求平衡，价格稳定。

1. Supply In the case that the sales volume and inventory of medicinal materials are basically unchanged, the amount of supply is the main factor affecting the price. The amount of supply depends on the size of the output. Multi-sourcing, supply exceeds demand, the price dropped; less supply, demand, then prices rise; supply and demand balance and price stability.

2. 销售量 在货源和存量基本不变的条件下，销售量多少也是影响价格的主要因素。销量增加，价格上升；销量减少，价格下降。

2. Sales Volume In the supply and stock of essentially the same conditions, the number of sales is the main factor affecting the price. Sales increase and prices rise; sales decrease and prices fall.

3. 库存量 调节市场供应，保证中药商品流通的连续性和满足人民用药需要，中药商品都有一定量的库存。在产销平衡时，库存量的大小对价格影响不大，但如出现产不足销时，库存量的大小对价格就会产生明显的影响。

3. Inventory Regulate the market supply to ensure the continuity of the circulation of CMMCs and meet the needs of the people's medication. CMMCs have a certain amount of inventory. In the balance of production and sales, the size of the inventory has little effect on the price, but if there is insufficient sales, the size of the inventory will have a significant impact on the price.

4. 质量 中药商品是治病救人的特殊商品，其质量的优劣不仅关系到人民生命的安全，而且是生产、经营和使用单位生存与发展的关键。在其他条件相同的情况下，质量的优劣是决定价格高低的主要因素。质优则价高，质差则价低。因而，药品质量的高低自然是影响药材商品价格的主要因素之一。

4. Quality CMMCs are special products for treating diseases and saving people. Their quality is not only related to the safety of the people's lives, but also the key to the survival and development of production, management and use units. Under other conditions being equal, the pros and cons of quality is the main factor in determining price level. Good quality leads to high prices; poor quality leads to low prices. Therefore, the quality of medicine is naturally one of the main factors affecting the price of medicinal materials.

在影响中药商品价格的四个内部因素中，都可通过价值规律制约和发挥市场的调节作用加以控制或消除。即可通过按需生产、以销定购、以优促销、合理库存的办法来控制或消除这些因素对中药商品价格的影响，达到宏观调控，微观搞活，保证供应，稳定药价的目的。

In the four internal factors affecting commodity prices in CMMCs, can be restricted by the law of value and play a regulatory role of the market be controlled or eliminated. It can control or eliminate the influence of these factors on the prices of CMMCs through production on demand, ordering with sales, promotion with reasonable prices, and reasonable inventory, and achieve the objectives of macro-control, micro-activation, guaranteed supply, and stable medicinal prices.

第四节 中药商品的商标与广告管理

Section 4 Trademark and Advertising Management of Chinese Materia Medica Commodities

PPT

药品是一种不同于一般商品的特殊商品。每一种药品都有自己特定的功能主治和特定的使用对象，药品广告的内容对指导合理用药、安全用药起着至关重要的作用。所以，对其广告内容的审核发布和监督管理较之其他产品更为严格，药品广告必须经过药品主管部门的审核批准后才能发布。

Medicine is a special commodity different from general commodities. Each medicinal has its own specific functions and users, and the content of medicinal advertisements plays a vital role in guiding the rational and safe use of medicinal. Therefore, the review, release and supervision of its advertising content are more stringent than those of other products, and pharmaceutical advertisements must be reviewed and approved by the medicinal authority before they can be released.

一、中药商品广告审批管理

I. Administration of Approval of CMMCs Advertising

1. 为保证人民用药安全、有效，防止和杜绝某些药品广告夸大疗效、误导患者的宣传，药品广告须经企业所在地省、自治区、直辖市人民政府药品监督管理部门批准，并发给药品广告批准文号；未取得药品广告批准文号的，不得发布。

1. To ensure that the people's medication is safe and effective, and to prevent and eliminate certain drug advertisements from exaggerating the effects and misleading patient's publicity, drug advertisements must be approved by the drug regulatory department of the people's government of the province, autonomous region, and municipality where the enterprise is located, and a drug advertisement approval document is issued number. No drug advertisement approval number can be issued.

2. 处方药可以在国务院卫生行政部门和国务院药品监督管理部门共同指定的医学、药学专业刊物上介绍，但不得在大众传播媒介发布广告或者以其他方式进行以公众为对象的广告宣传。

2. Prescription drugs can be introduced in medical and pharmaceutical professional publications jointly designated by the health administrative department of the State Council and the drug supervision and administration department of the State Council. However, it is not allowed to publish advertisements in the mass media or otherwise use public advertisements.

3. 省、自治区、直辖市人民政府药品监督管理部门应当对其批准的药品广告进行检查，对于违反《中华人民共和国广告法》的广告，应当向广告监督管理机关通报并提出处理建议，广告监督管理机关应当依法做出处理。

3. The drug regulatory department of the people's government of the province, autonomous region, or municipality directly under the Central Government shall check the drug advertisements approved by them. For advertisements that violate *Advertising Law of the People's Republic of China*, they shall notify the advertising supervision and administration department and make suggestions for handling them. The advertising supervision and management authority shall handle the matter according to law.

4. 经国务院或者省、自治区、直辖市人民政府的药品监督管理部门决定，责令暂停生产、销售和使用的药品，在暂停期间不得发布该品种药品广告；已经发布广告的，必须立即停止。

4. After the State Council or the drug regulatory department of the people's government of the province, autonomous region, or municipality directly under the Central Government has decided to suspend the production, sale, and use of drugs, advertisements for the drug of that variety must not be issued during the suspension period; if advertisements have been issued, they must stop immediately.

二、中药商品广告内容管理

II. Content Management of CMMCs Advertising

中药商品广告的内容是否真实，对正确指导患者合理用药、安全用药十分重要，与患者的生命安全和身体健康关系极大，故中药商品广告内容必须实行严格管理，主要规定如下：

The authenticity of CMMCs advertisements is very important to correctly guide patients to use medicines reasonably and safely. It has a great relationship with patients' life safety and physical health. Therefore, the contents of CMMCs advertisements must be strictly managed. The main rules are as follows:

1. 药品广告的内容必须真实、合法，以国务院药品监督管理部门批准的说明书为准，不得含有虚假的内容。

1. The contents of drug advertisements must be true and legal. The instructions that are approved by the drug regulatory department of the State Council shall prevail. They shall not contain false content.

2. 药品广告不得含有不科学的表示功效的断言或者保证；不得利用国家机关、医药科研单位、学术机构或者专家、学者、医师、患者的名义和形象作证明。

2. Drug advertisements must not contain unscientific assertions or guarantees of efficacy; the names and images of state agencies, medical research units, academic institutions or experts, scholars, physicians, and patients must not be used as proof.

3. 非药品广告不得有涉及药品的宣传。

3. Non-drug advertisements must not include publicity related to drugs.

重 点 小 结
Summary

<table>
<tr><td rowspan="6">影响中药商品质量主要因素</td><td colspan="2">品种</td><td>品种所含的活性成分不同，其药物的性、味、功效不同</td></tr>
<tr><td colspan="2">产地</td><td>产地生态环境各异，造成药材质量有差异</td></tr>
<tr><td colspan="2">栽培养殖</td><td>栽培技术不规范，造成种质不佳，同时影响中药商品的质量</td></tr>
<tr><td colspan="2">采收</td><td>采收失时，则功效有异</td></tr>
<tr><td colspan="2">加工</td><td>中药商品产地加工的规范与否，是保证中药商品质量的重要环节之一</td></tr>
<tr><td colspan="2">贮藏</td><td>贮藏方法不当，导致中药商品质量下降</td></tr>
<tr><td rowspan="8">划分药材商品规格等级的依据和方法</td><td colspan="2">产地</td><td>广藿香可分为“石牌广藿香”与“海南广藿香”</td></tr>
<tr><td colspan="2">采收季节</td><td>三七可分为“春三七”和“冬三七”</td></tr>
<tr><td colspan="2">产地加工方法</td><td>肉桂可分为“板桂”“企边桂”“桂通”“桂碎”和“桂心”</td></tr>
<tr><td colspan="2">药材的外部形态</td><td>浙贝母可分为“元宝贝”和“珠贝”</td></tr>
<tr><td colspan="2">药材大小或重量</td><td>天麻可分为“春天麻”和“冬天麻”</td></tr>
<tr><td colspan="2">药材的老嫩程度</td><td>花鹿茸可分为“二杠”和“三岔”等规格</td></tr>
<tr><td colspan="2">药用部位</td><td>当归“全归”和“归头”</td></tr>
<tr><td colspan="2">药材的来源</td><td>麻黄可分为“草麻黄”“中麻黄”和“木贼麻黄”</td></tr>
<tr><td rowspan="8">中药商品的价格体系及分类</td><td rowspan="3">价格管理的形式分类</td><td>政府定价</td><td>生产经营企业必须严格执行</td></tr>
<tr><td>政府指导价</td><td>药品经营者必须在政府规定的指导价范围内制定具体价格</td></tr>
<tr><td>市场调节价</td><td>随行就市，具有自发性和不稳定性</td></tr>
<tr><td rowspan="5">价格形成的阶段分类</td><td>收购价</td><td>收购价格涉及范围广，须慎重制订和调整收购价</td></tr>
<tr><td>出厂价</td><td>是其他环节价格的基础，决定着零售价格水平</td></tr>
<tr><td>调拨价</td><td>涉及中药批发企业间的经济利益</td></tr>
<tr><td>批发价格</td><td>直接影响中药商品市场零售价格的水平</td></tr>
<tr><td>零售价</td><td>是中药商品价格体系中政策性最强的一种价格</td></tr>
</table>

<table>
<tr><td rowspan="6">Main factors affecting the quality of CMMCs</td><td>Variety</td><td>Different active ingredients contained in the varieties cause different effects</td></tr>
<tr><td>Origin</td><td>The ecological environment of the place of origin is different, resulting in differences in the quality of medicinal materials</td></tr>
<tr><td>Cultivation</td><td>Cultivation techniques are not standardized, resulting in poor germplasm, while affecting the quality of CMMCs</td></tr>
<tr><td>Harvest</td><td>Missing the harvest time will affect the effect</td></tr>
<tr><td>Processing</td><td>Whether the standardization of the processing place of CMMCs is one of the important links to ensure the quality of CMMCs</td></tr>
<tr><td>Storage</td><td>Due to improper storage methods, the quality of CMMCs has declined</td></tr>
</table>

continued

<table>
<tr><td rowspan="8">Basis and Method for Classifying Medicinal Material Commodities Specifications</td><td>The Place of Origin</td><td colspan="2">Pogostemonis Herba can be divided into “Shipai Huoxiang” and “Hainan Huoxiang”</td></tr>
<tr><td>Harvest seasons</td><td colspan="2">Notoginseng Radix et Rhizoma can be divided into “Chun Sanqi” and “Dong Sanqi”</td></tr>
<tr><td>Processing methods of origin</td><td colspan="2">Cinnamomi Cortex can be divided into “Bangui” “Qibian Gui” “Guitong” “Guisui” and “Guixin”</td></tr>
<tr><td>The external form of medicinal materials</td><td colspan="2">Fritillariae Thunbergii Bulbuscan be divided into “Yuanbaobei” and “Zhubei”</td></tr>
<tr><td>The Size or Weight of medicinal materials</td><td colspan="2">Gastrodiae Rhizoma can be divided into “Chun Tianma” and “Dong Tianma”</td></tr>
<tr><td>The age of the medicinal materials</td><td colspan="2">Hualurong can be divided into “Er Gang” and “San Cha”</td></tr>
<tr><td>Medicinal parts</td><td colspan="2">Angelicae Sinensis Radixcan be divided into “Quangui” and “Guitou”</td></tr>
<tr><td>The Source of medicinal materials</td><td colspan="2">Ephedrae Herba can be divided into “Caomahuang” “Zhongmahuang” and “Muzeimahuang”</td></tr>
<tr><td rowspan="8">The Price System and Classification of CMMCs</td><td rowspan="3">The form of price management</td><td>Government Pricing</td><td>Production and operation enterprises must strictly implement</td></tr>
<tr><td>Government-guided Prices</td><td>Drug operators are required to develop specific price within a specified government guidance</td></tr>
<tr><td>Market-adjusted Price</td><td>Its features reflect market conditions, spontaneity and instability</td></tr>
<tr><td rowspan="5">The stage of price formation</td><td>The purchase price</td><td>The purchase price involves a wide range, and the purchase price must be carefully set and adjusted</td></tr>
<tr><td>Ex-factory price</td><td>It is the basis of prices in other links and determines the level of retail prices</td></tr>
<tr><td>Transfer Price</td><td>Economic benefits between enterprises</td></tr>
<tr><td>Wholesale Price</td><td>Directly affects the level of the retail price of CMMCs market</td></tr>
<tr><td>Retail Price</td><td>The retail price is the most policy-oriented price in the CMMCs price system</td></tr>
</table>

题库

目 标 检 测
Object Detection

一、选择题（Choice question）

（一）单项选择题（One-choice question）

1.《药品经营质量管理规范》的简称是（　　）

A. GAP　　B. GSP　　C. GDP　　D. GCP　　E. GLP

The abbreviation of “Management Standards for Drug Operation Quality” is (　　)

A. GAP　　B. GSP　　C. GDP　　D. GCP　　E. GLP

2. 决定药材商品价格高低最主要的因素是（ ）
   A. 货源
   B. 库存量
   C. 质量
   D. 中药资源的减少
   E. 与其他农副产品的比价失调
   The main factor that determines the price of medicinal products is ( )
   A. Supply
   B. Inventory
   C. Quality
   D. Decrease in Chinese Medicine Resources
   E. Imbalanced parity with other agricultural and sideline products

（二）多项选择题（Multiple choice question）

1. 对中药商品实行全面质量管理的意义是（ ）
   A. 能最大限度地满足人民安全有效的用药需要
   B. 能促进生产企业提高药品质量
   C. 能提高中药商业企业的经济效益
   D. 能促进中药经营企业的发展
   E. 能提高中药材的产量
   The significance of comprehensive quality management of Chinese medicine products is ( )
   A. Meeting the needs of the people's safe and effective medication utmostly
   B. Promoting manufacturers to improve medicines quality
   C. Improving the economic benefits of CMM commercial enterprises
   D. Promote the development of Chinese medicine business enterprises
   E. Increase the output of Chinese medicinal materials
2. 药材商品质量优劣的客观标准取决于（ ）
   A. 药材的重量　　B. 疗效的显著性
   C. 药材的完整性　　D. 有效成分含量
   E. 药材的药用部位
   Objective criteria for the quality of medicinal products depend on ( )
   A. Weight of medicinal materials
   B. The significance of the efficacy
   C. Integrity of medicinal materials
   D. Active ingredient content
   E. Medicinal parts of medicinal materials
3. 中药商品价格组成的因素有哪些（ ）
   A. 利润　　B. 税金　　C. 药效
   D. 流通费用　　E. 生产成本
   What are the factors that make up the price of CMMCs ( )
   A. Profits　　B. Taxes
   C. Medicinal materials effect　　D. Circulation costs
   E. Production costs

4. 零售价的组成有（　　）

A. 当地的批发价格　　B. 零售的流通费用　　C. 税金

D. 零售利润　　E. 货源

The retail price consists of (　　)

A. Local wholesale prices　　B. Retail circulation costs　　C. Taxes

D. Retail profits　　E. Supply

5. 中药商品的价格按照价格管理的形式分类有哪些（　　）

A. 政府定价　　B. 调拨价　　C. 政府指导价

D. 市场调节价　　E. 收购价

What are the prices of Chinese medicine commodities classified according to the form of price management (　　)

A. Government Pricing　　B. Transfer Price

C. Government-guided Prices　　D. Market-adjusted Price

E. The purchase price

二、判断题（Judgment question）

1.《中华人民共和国药品管理法》是国家强制执行，具有普遍效力的行为规范，是我国药品生产、经营、使用和药品管理部门必须共同遵守的国家法律。

Law of the People's Republic of China on the Administration of Drugs is a nationally enforced and universally valid code of conduct. It is a national law that must be jointly observed by China's pharmaceutical production, operation, use, and pharmaceutical administrations.

2. 未取得药品广告批准文号的中药商品不得发布。

Without obtaining a medicinal advertisement approval number of Chinese goods should not be released.

3. 保健品可以使用药品的宣传。

Promotion of the use of medicines in health products.

各论
Monograph

中药材，是中药的重要组成部分，同时又是生产中药饮片和中成药的主要原料，在中药商品的经营管理和应用中占有重要地位。中药商品学以传统道地药材分类为基础，根据近代药材商品主产地或集散地变迁的实际情况，结合市场经营管理的需求，将药材商品主要分为川药类、广药类、云药类、贵药类、怀药类、浙药类、关药类、北药类、西药类、南药类和进口药类等。各类药材因其所在产区的不同地理位置、生态环境和气候条件，形成了不同的道地特性。以下分列专章介绍。

Chinese medicinal materials, an important constituent part of Chinese Materia Medica and the main production materials of Chinese medicinal decoction pieces and Chinese patent medicines, take a significant position in management, administration and application of Chinese Materia Medica commodity. In Commodity Science of Chinese Materia Medica, the commodities of Chinese medicinal materials are classified as Chuan, Guang, Yun, Gui, Huai, Zhe, Guan, Bei, Xi, Nan, imported medicinal materials, etc. on the basis of their traditional classifications, according to actual changes of main producing areas and distribution regions in modern times, and the demand of market management and administration. Chinese medicinal materials in different classifications form their own authentic characteristics due to different geographic locations, ecological environments and climate conditions of their producing areas. Detailed knowledge on these classifications will be introduced respectively in the following specialized chapters.

PPT

第八章 川 药
Chapter 8 Chuan Medicinal Materials

学习目标 | Learning Target

知识要求：

1. 掌握 川药的含义及其主要道地药材品种。川芎、川贝母、附子的道地产地、规格等级及贮藏方法。

2. 熟悉 冬虫夏草、白芷、黄连的道地产地、规格等级及贮藏方法。

3. 了解 川药产区的自然环境条件。

能力要求：

1. 掌握 川芎、川贝母、附子药材的商品规格等级辨识能力。

2. 学会 川芎、川贝母、附子、冬虫夏草、白芷、黄连商品的贮藏方法。

Knowledge requirements:

1. Proficiency The meaning and major varieties of Chuan Medicinal Materials. The authentic producing areas, specifications and grades, and storage methods of Chuanxiong Rhizoma, Fritillariae Cirrhosae Bulbus and Aconiti Lateralis Radix Praeparata.

2. Familiarity The producing areas, specifications and grades, and storage methods of Cordyceps, Angelicae Dahuricae Radix and Coptidis Rhizoma.

3. Understanding The natural environment in producing areas of Chuan Medicinal Materials.

Skill requirements:

1. To acquire identification capacity of the specifications and grades of Chuanxiong Rhizoma, Fritillariae Cirrhosae Bulbus and Aconiti Lateralis Radix Praeparata.

2. To know how to storage Chuanxiong Rhizoma, Fritillariae Cirrhosae Bulbus, Aconiti Lateralis Radix Praeparata, Cordyceps, Angelicae Dahuricae Radix and Coptidis Rhizoma.

一、川药概述
I. Overview of Chuan Medicinal Materials

以四川、重庆为主要产区或集散地的大宗商品药材称为川药。其产区地处中国西南，位于东经 97° 22′ 至 110° 10′，北纬 26° 03′ 至 34° 20′ 之间。川药产区地形复杂，水利资源非常丰富。美丽富饶的四川盆地，为我国著名的四大盆地之一，海拔跨度极大，100~7000m。西部属青藏高原，山高谷深，地势崎岖，平均海拔为3000~4000m。川药产区气候复杂多样。东部属亚热带湿润东南季风气候，冬暖、春早、夏长、气温高；西南山地属亚热带干湿交替的西南季风气候，冬无严寒，夏无酷暑；四川高原气候寒冷，长冬无夏。全川年降雨量多数地区约1000mm，西北高原约400~700mm。四川盆地由于秦岭大巴山阻挡了寒流，夏季南方热的气流越过大娄山下沉，使四川盆地冬暖夏热，霜日极少，几乎全年皆为动植物的生长期。年均气温16℃~17℃，无霜期长达300天左右。

Chuan Medicinal Materials are known as the bulk commodities of medicinal materials, mainly produced or collected and distributed in Sichuan Province and Chongqing Municipality. This area is located in southwest of China, between longitude 97° 22′ to 110° 10′ east and latitude 26° 03′ to 34° 20′ north, with complex terrain and rich water resources. The beautiful and fertile Sichuan basin, with a large elevation span from 100m to 7000m above sea level, is one of the four famous basins in China. The western part is the Qinghai-Tibet Plateau, with high mountains and deep valleys, at an average elevation of 3000~4000m. The climate of Chuan Medicinal Materials producing area is complicated. The eastern area belongs to humid subtropical southeast monsoon climate characterized by warm winters, early springs, long summers and high temperature. The southwestern mountainous area belongs to subtropical southwest monsoon climate, wet-dry cycling characterized by no severe hot in summer and no severe cold in winter. Sichuan plateau is characterized by coldness, long winters without summer. The annual rainfall is 1,000mm in most areas and about 400-700mm in the northwest plateau. As the cold current is stopped by Daba Mountain in Qinling and the hot airflow from south in summer drops after passing over Dalou Mountain, it is warm in winter and cold in summer in Sichan Basin, with few frost days and year-round growing period of animals and plants. The average temperature in Sichan Basin is 16℃~17℃ and nearly 300 days in the year are frost-free.

川药产区生态环境和气候多样，药材资源极为丰富，并呈明显的区域性和地域性分布。如高山的冬虫夏草、川贝母、麝香等；岷江流域的干姜、郁金等。其他如江油的附子，绵阳的麦冬，都江堰、彭州的川芎，遂宁的川白芷，中江的丹参、白芍，汉源的花椒，天全、金口河的川牛膝，石柱的黄连，合川的使君子、补骨脂等，均在国内外久负盛名。

Producing areas of Chuan Medicinal Materials are extremely rich in the resources of Chinese medicinal materials (CMMs) because of diverse ecological environment and climate. The distribution of CMMs resources in this producing areas shows obvious regionality and locality, such as Cordyceps, Fritillariae Cirrhosae Bulbus and Moschus in high mountain, Zingiberis Rhizoma and Curcumae Radix in Minjing river, Aconiti Lateralis Radix Praeparata produced from Jiangyou, Ophiopogonis Radix produced from Mianyang, Chuanxiong Rhizoma produced from Dujiangyan and Pengzhou, Angelicae Dahuricae Radix produced from Suining, Salviae Miltiorrhizae Radix et Rizoma and Paeoniae Radix Alba produced from Zhongjiang, Zanthoxyli Pericarpium produced from Hanyuan, Cyathulae Radix produced from Tianquan and Jinkouhe, Coptidis Rhizoma produced from Shizhu, Quisqualis Fructus and Psoraleae Fructus produced from Hechuan, etc. These CMMs have enjoyed a good reputation for a long time in the world.

二、药材品种
II. Varieties of Medicinal Materials

川芎 (Chuanxiong) | Chuanxiong Rhizoma (Szechwan Lovage Rhizome)

【基原 / Origin】

为伞形科植物川芎 *Ligusticum chuanxiong* Hort. 的干燥根茎。

Szechwan Lovage Rhizome is the dried rhizome of *Ligusticum chuanxiong* Hort. (Fam. Umbelliferae).

【产地 / Producing area】

主产于四川都江堰市、彭州、什邡、新都、崇州、彭山等地，江西武宁、瑞昌及湖北阳新、崇阳等地。其他地区如湖南、甘肃、云南等省亦产，但产量较小，多自销。

Mostly produced in Dujiangyan, Pengzhou, Shifang, Xindu, Chongzhou, Pengshan of Sichuan Province, Wuning, Ruichang of Jiangxi Province, and Yangxin, Chongyang of Hubei Province; also produced in other provinces and regions such as Hunan, Gansu and Yunnan, less output, more local sale.

【采制 / Collection and preparation】

川芎　平坝栽种者于 5~6 月（小满前后）采挖；山地栽种者于 7~8 月，当茎部在节盘处显著膨大，并略带紫色时采挖。挖出全株，除去茎苗，去净泥土，晒 4~5 天再用小火炕干，撞去须根即成。

Szechwan Lovage Rhizome　The rhizome cultivated in flat ground is collected from May to June (before and after Lesser Fullness of Grain); the rhizome cultivated in mountains is collected from July to August when the node of stem becomes obviously swollen and purplish. Dig out the whole plants, remove the stems and soil, then bake gently after sun-drying for 4 to 5 days, finally collide to remove the rootlets.

川芎片　取药材，除去杂质，分开大小，洗净，润透，切厚片，晒干或低温干燥。

Szechwan Lovage Rhizome slices　Take the rhizome, eliminate foreign matter, grade the rhizomes by size, wash clean, soak thoroughly, cut into thick slices, and dry in the sun or at low temperature.

【商品特征 / Commodity characteristics】

川芎　呈不规则的结节状团块，表面灰褐色，有突起的平行节纹。质坚实，气芳香，味苦辛、微甜带麻。

Szechwan Lovage Rhizome　Irregular knotty and fist-like, externally greyish-brown, with parallel and raised annulations. Texture, compact. Odour, strongly aromatic. Taste bitter, pungent and slight numb, and with a sweet after taste.

川芎片　呈不规则厚片，外表皮灰褐色，具皱缩纹。切面黄白色或灰黄色，具有明显波状环纹或多角形纹理，散生黄棕色油点。

Szechwan Lovage Rhizome slices　Irregular thick slices. Externally greyish-brown with wrinkles. Cut surface, yellowish-white or greyish-yellow, showing obvious undulate ring or polygonal striation, scattering yellowish-brown oil dots.

【商品特征 / Specification and grade】

商品中分川芎（四川产者）和抚芎（又称茶芎，江西、湖北、湖南等产者）两种。二者气味稍有不同。川芎优于抚芎。川芎分家川芎和山川芎，家川芎又分为三等。其规格等级标准为：

As commodity, two commercial specifications of Szechwan Lovage Rhizome are "Chuanxiong" (produced in Sichuan Province) and "Fuxiong" (also called Chaxiong, produced in Jiangxi, Hubei and Hunan Provinces). There is slightly difference in smell and taste between the two of them. The quality of "Chuanxiong" is better than that of Fuxiong. The former is further divided into garden Chuangxiong and mountain Chuanxiong. The garden Chuanxiong is marketed by three grades.

The specification and grade criteria are as follows:

家川芎 一等：呈结节状，质坚实。表面黄褐色，断面灰黄色或黄白色，有特异香气，味苦辛，麻舌。每 kg 44 个以内，单个重量不低于 20g。

Garden Chuanxiong First grade: Irregular knotty and texture compact. Externally yellowish-brown; cut surface, greyish-yellow or yellowish-white. Odour, strongly and distinctively aromatic; taste bitter, pungent, and numb tongue. There are less than 44 rhizomes in per kg and the weight of single rhizome is not less than 20g.

二等：每 kg 70 个以内，余同一等。

Second grade: There are less than 70 rhizomes in per kg. Other criteria in this grade are in accordance with those in First grade.

三等：每 kg 70 个以上，个大空心的也属此等。余同一等。

Third grade: There are more than 70 rhizomes in per kg, including large hollow ones. Other criteria in this grade are in accordance with those in First grade.

山川芎 统货。呈结节状，体枯质瘦。表面褐色，断面灰白色。有特异香气，味苦辛，麻舌。大小不分。

Mountain Chuanxiong Unified grade. Irregular knotty, withered and thin. Externally brown; cut surface, greyish-white. Odour, strongly and distinctively aromatic. Taste bitter, pungent and numb tongue. Small and big rhizomes mixed.

【化学成分 / Chemical constituent】

主含挥发油、生物碱、酚酸类成分。包括藁本内酯、欧当归内酯 A、二氢藁本内酯、川芎嗪、川芎哚、阿魏酸等。

It mainly contains volatile oil, alkaloids and phenolic acids, including ligustilide, levistilide A, dihydroligustilide, ligustrazine, perlolyrine, ferulic acid, etc.

【检查 / Examination】

水分不得过 12.0%；总灰分不得过 6.0%，酸不溶性灰分不得过 2.0%。

Water, not more than 12.0%. Total ash, not more than 6.0%. Acid-insoluble-ash, not more than 2.0%.

【质量要求 / Quality requirement】

外观质量 以个大、肉多、外皮黄褐而内有黄白色菊花心者为佳。

Appearance quality Good quality for big, full, externally yellowish-brown, cut surface with yellowish-white chrysanthemum-flower-like radial lines (Juhuaxin).

内在质量 浸出物含量：醇溶性浸出物（热）不得少于 12.0%。含量测定：按高效液相色谱法测定，含阿魏酸不得少于 0.10%。

Intrinsic quality Extract content: not less than 12.0% of ethanol-soluble extractives (hot).

Assay: It contains not less than 0.10% of ferulic acid according to the determination method of HPLC.

【功能主治 / Function and indication】

温，辛。活血行气，祛风止痛。用于胸痹心痛，胸肋刺痛，跌扑肿痛，月经不调，经闭痛经，癥瘕腹痛，头痛，风湿痹痛。

Warm, pungent. To activate blood, move *qi*, dispel wind and relieve pain. For chest *bi* disorder with heart pain, stabbing pain in the chest and hypochondrium, swelling and pain caused by traumatic injuries, menstrual irregularities, amenorrhea and dysmenorrhea, abdominal pain and masses, headache, painful *bi* disorders caused by wind-dampness.

【贮藏养护 / Storage and maintenance】

用麻袋或编织袋包装。本品极易虫蛀、发霉、泛油。应在原商品产地日晒或微火炕干，以免受潮生虫。在贮存中，特别是梅雨季节，应经常检查，必须置于阴凉干燥处保存，切忌受潮、受热。

Packed in jute or woven bags. Moth damaging, mildewing and extensive diffusion of oil usually happen in the storage of Szechwan Lovage Rhizome. Dried in the sun or by low fire in case of dampness and insects. Usually checked during storage, especially in rain season. Stored in a cool and dry place, protected from moisture and heat.

【用法用量 / Administration and dosage】

3~10g。

3~10g.

川贝母 (Chuanbeimu) ⁝ Fritillariae Cirrhosae Bulbus (Tendrilleaf Fritillary Bulb)

【基原 / Origin】

为百合科植物川贝母 *Fritillaria cirrhosa* D. Don、暗紫贝母 *Fritillaria unibracteata* Hsiao et K. C. Hsia、甘肃贝母 *Fritillaria przewalskii* Maxim.、梭砂贝母 *Fritillaria delavayi* Franch.、太白贝母 *Fritillaria taipaiensis* P. Y. Li 或瓦布贝母 *Fritillaria unibracteata* Hsiao et K. C. Hsia var. *wabuensis*（S. Y. Tang et S. C. Yue）Z. D. Liu, S. Wang et S. C. Chen 的干燥鳞茎。按性状不同分别称为“松贝”“青贝”“炉贝”和“栽培品”。

Tendrilleaf Fritillary Bulb is the dried bulb of *Fritillaria cirrhosa* D. Don, *Fritillaria unibracteata* Hsiao et K.C. Hsia, *Fritillaria przewalskii* Maxim, *Fritillaria delavayi* Franch, *Fritillaria taipaiensis* P. Y. Li or *Fritillaria unibracteata* Hsiao et K. C. Hsia var. *wabuensis* (S. Y. Tang et S. C. Yue) Z. D. Liu, S. Wang et S. C. Chen (Fam. Liliaceae). According to the different characters, the bulbs derived from the former three are known as “Songbei” and “Qingbei”, respectively, derived from the fourth are known as “Lubei”, and derived from the last two are known as “Zaipeipin” (cultivated).

【产地 / Producing area】

我国西南、西北地区多有生产：松贝，主产于四川北部的松潘、马尔康等阿坝一带；青贝，主产于青海玉树，云南德钦，新疆木叠河，四川西部及甘肃岷县等地；炉贝，主产于四川康定、青海、云南一带。历史上四川产品多集散在打箭炉，故名炉贝；太白贝母主要分布在湖北、陕西、甘肃、四川等地；瓦布贝母主要分布在四川西北部的北川、黑水、茂县、松潘、重庆城口等地。

Southwest and Northwest of China are the major producing regions of Fritillariae Cirrhosae Bulbus. “Songbei” is mostly produced in Songpan and Ma’erkang of Aba Autonomous Prefecture, the northern Sichuan; “Qingbei” is mainly from Yushu of Qinghai Province, Deqin of Yunnan Province, Mudiehe of the Xinjiang Uygur Autonomous Region, western Sichuan and Minxian of Gansu Province. The production of “Lubei” is primarily around the area of Kangding, Sichuan Province, Qinghai Province and Yunnan Province. Historically, it was often collected and distributed in the place of Dajianlu (Sichuan

Province), so named "Lubei"; *Fritillaria taipaiensis* mainly grows in Hubei, Shaanxi, Gansu and Sichuan Provinces; *Fritillaria unibracteata* var. *wabuensis* mainly distributes in Beichuan, Heishui, Maoxian, Songpan, the northwest of Sichuan Province and Chengkou of Chongqing Municipality.

【采制 / Collection and preparation】

因各地气候条件不同，采收时间不一，多在茎叶枯萎前进行采挖，过晚茎叶枯萎不易寻找。栽培者多于下种 3 年后秋季茎叶枯萎时采收，此时浆汁多，产品质量好。四川、云南大约在 6~7 月为盛采期；青藏高原则约在 8 月；甘肃省在 5~6 月。采挖后除去须根、粗皮及泥沙，晒干或低温干燥。

The harvesting time varies according to the climatic conditions in different regions. The bulbs are usually collected before the withering of stems and leaves, otherwise they are difficult to be found. Cultivated bulbs are often harvested with the abundant juice and good quality when the stems and leaves die away in the autumn after the third year of planting. The harvesting season is about June to July in Sichuan and Yunnan Province, August in Tibetan Plateau, May to June in Gansu Province. After being dug out, the bulbs are dried in the sun or at low temperature with fibrous roots, raw bark and soil removed.

【商品特征 / Commodity characteristics】

呈圆锥形、扁圆形或卵圆形，大小不一。类白色，外层两枚鳞叶相互抱合形似怀中抱月，顶端不开口（松贝），或对合形似观音合掌（青贝），或错合，形大，表皮有斑纹（炉贝），顶端尖或钝，一般顶端有开口。栽培品呈类扁球形或短圆柱形，颗粒大，表面稍粗糙，有的具浅黄色斑点，鳞叶大小相近，顶部多开裂而较平。质坚实，富粉性，对剖后内有鳞叶和心芽。

Conical, oblate or oval, in various size. Being off-white, two outer scale leaves embrace each other like "HuaizhongBaoyue" (holding the moon in the arms), with apex closed (*Songbei*), or like "GuanyinHezhang" (the Goddess Guanyin presses her palms together) with apex opened (*Qingbei*). Or two outer scale leaves are big and mismatch with some patches on their epidermis (*Lubei*), top acute or obtuse, apex usually open. Zaipeipin (cultivated), flattened subglobal or short cylindrical, big size, slightly coarse in surface, some with pale yellow patches. Outer scale leaves almost uniform in size, apex mostly open and obtuse. Texture solid, starchy, with scale leaves and buds inside after cut in half.

【商品特征 / Specification and grade】

商品上分松贝、青贝、炉贝（知贝）和栽培品四种规格。松贝分为二等；青贝分为四等；炉贝分为二等；栽培品为统货。其规格等级标准为：

As commodity, four commercial specifications of Fritillariae Cirrhosae Bulbus are Songbei, Qingbei, Lubei (Zhibei) and Zaipeipin. Songbei and Lubei are marketed by two grades respectively; Qingbei, by four grades; Zaipeipin, marketed by unified grade. The specifications and grading criteria thereof are as follows:

松贝 一等：呈类圆锥形或近球形，鳞瓣两枚，大瓣紧抱小瓣，未抱合部分呈新月形，顶端闭口，底部圆平。表面白色，体坚实，质细腻。断面粉白色。味甘微苦。每 50g 在 240 粒以外，无黄贝、油子、破碎。

Songbei First grade: Subconical or subglobose; two scale leaves, the large scale leave closely embracing the small one; the uncovered part appearing crescent. Apex closed, base even and round. Externally whitish, hard, texture delicate. Fracture, white, starchy. Taste, sweet and slightly bitter. There are more than 240 bulbs in per 50g. No yellow bulb, nor diffused sap bulb, nor broken pieces.

二等：顶端闭口或开口，基部平或略平，每 50g 在 240 粒之内。间有黄贝、油子、破碎，余同一等。

Second grade: Apex closed or open, base even or slightly even. There are less than 240 bulbs in per 50g. Occasionally yellow bulbs, diffused sap bulbs and broken pieces. Other critieria in this grade are the same as those in First grade.

青贝 一等：扁球形或类圆形，两枚鳞瓣大小相似。顶端闭口或微开口，基部较平或圆形，表面白色、细腻，体结实。断面粉白色。味淡微苦。每 50g 在 190 粒以外。对开瓣不超过 20%。无黄贝、油子和破碎。

Qingbei First grade: Suboblate or subround, two scale leaves, almost uniform in size. Apex closed or slightly open, base slightly even or round. Externally whitish, delicate, hard. Fracture white, starchy. Taste, light and slightly bitter. There are more than 190 bulbs in per 50g. The numbers of single scale leaves not more than 20%. No yellow bulb, nor diffused sap bulb, nor broken pieces.

二等：顶端闭口或开口，每 50g 在 130 粒以外。对开瓣不超过 25%。间有花子，但不超过 5%，无黄贝、油子、碎贝。余同一等。

Second grade: Apex closed or open. There are more than 130 bulbs per 50g. The numbers of single scale leaves are not more than 25%. Occasionally blighted bulbs, but not more than 5%. No yellow bulb, nor diffused sap bulb, nor broken pieces. Other criteria in this grade are the same as those in First grade.

三等：每 50g 在 100 粒以外。对开瓣不超过 30%，间有油子、碎贝、黄贝，但不超过 5%。余同二等。

Third grade: There are more than 100 bulbs in per 50g. The numbers of single scale leaves are not more than 30%. Occasionally with diffused sap bulbs, broken pieces and yellow bulbs, but not more than 5%. Other criteria in this grade are the same as in Second grade.

四等：顶端闭口或开口较多，表面牙白色或黄白色。大小粒不分。兼有油子、碎贝、黄贝，余同三等。

Fourth grade: Apex closed or mostly open. Externally cream-white or yellowish-white. Small and big bulbs mixed, with some diffused sap bulbs, broken pieces and yellow bulbs. Other criteria in this grade are the same as those in Third grade.

炉贝 一等：呈长圆锥形，贝瓣略似马牙。表面白色，体结实，断面粉白色，味苦。大小粒不分，间有油子和白色破瓣。

Lubei First grade: Long conical, scale leaves as horse teeth. Externally whitish, hard, fracture white, starchy. Taste, bitter. Small and big bulbs mixed, occasionally with diffused oil bulbs and white broken scale leaves.

二等：表面黄白色或淡黄棕色，有的具棕色斑点。大小粒不分。间有油子、破瓣，余同一等。

Second grade: Externally yellowish-white or pale yellowish-brown, some with brown patches. Small and big bulbs mixed, occasionally with diffused sap bulbs and broken scale leaves. Other criteria in this grade are the same as those in First grade.

【化学成分 / Chemical constituent】

主含甾体生物碱，如贝母辛、西贝母碱、贝母素甲、贝母素乙等。

It mainly contains steroidal alkaloids, such as peimisine, sipeimine, peimine, peiminine, etc.

【检查 / Examination】

水分不得过 15.0%；总灰分不得过 5.0%。

Water, not more than 15.0%. Total ash, not more than 5.0%.

【质量要求 / Quality requirement】

外观质量 均以质坚实，色白、粉性足，个完整不碎者为佳。

Appearance quality Good quality for being hard, white, sufficiently starchy, intact and not broken.

内在质量 浸出物含量：稀乙醇溶性浸出物（热）不得少于 9.0%。含量测定：按高效液相色谱法测定，含总生物碱以西贝母碱计，不得少于 0.050%。

Intrinsic quality Extract content: not less than 9.0% of dilute ethanol-soluble extractives (hot). Assay: It contains not less than 0.050% of total alkaloids, calculated as sipeimine according to HPLC method.

【功能主治 / Function and indication】

微寒，苦、甘。清热润肺，化痰止咳，散结消痈。用于肺热燥咳，干咳少痰，阴虚劳嗽，痰中带血，瘰疬，乳痈，肺痈。

Mild cold; bitter, sweet. To clear heat, moisten the lung, resolve phlegm, suppress cough, dissipate binds and disperse abscesses. For the treatment of lung heat, dryness cough, dry cough with scanty phlegm, cough caused by yin consumptive disease, blood in sputum, scrofula, acute mastitis, and lung abscess.

【贮藏养护 / Storage and maintenance】

麻袋或塑料袋包装。本品在贮存中易虫蛀、发霉、变色。应防潮，置干燥处保存。

Packed in sacks or plastic bags. Moth damaging, mildewing and discolouring usually happen in the storage of Fritillariae Cirrhosae Bulbus. Preserved in dry place, and protected from moisture.

【用法用量 / Administration and dosage】

3~10g；研粉冲服，一次 1~2g。

3~10g, ground into powder for oral administration (taking the drug after mixing it with water), 1~2g per time.

白芷 (Baizhi) ⋮ Angelicae Dahuricae Radix (Dahurian Angelica Root)

【基原 / Origin】

为伞形科植物白芷 *Angelica dahurica* (Fisch. ex Hoffm.) Benth. et Hook. f. 或杭白芷 *Angelica dahurica* (Fisch. ex Hoffm.) Benth. et Hook. f. var. *formosana* (Boiss.) Shan et Yuan 的干燥根。

Dahurian Angelica Root is the dried root of *Angelica dahurica* (Fisch. ex Hoffm.) Benth. et Hook. f. or *Angelica dahurica* (Fisch. ex Hoffm.) Benth. et Hook. f. var. *formosana* (Boiss.) Shan et Yuan (Fam. Umbelliferae).

【产地 / Producing area】

产于四川遂宁者习称“川白芷”；产于安徽亳州者习称“亳白芷”；产于河南长葛、禹州者习称“禹白芷”；产于河北安国者习称“祁白芷”；产于浙江、福建者习称“杭白芷”。

Angelicae Dahuricae Radix produced in Suining of Sichuan Province, is called *Chuan baizhi;* The one produced in Bozhou of Anhui Province, is called *Bo baizhi;* The one produced in Yuzhou of Henan Province, is called *Yu baizhi*; The one produced in Anguo of Hebei Province, is called *Qi baizhi*; The one produced in Zhejiang Province and Fujian Province, is called *Hang baizhi*.

【采制 / Collection and preparation】

夏、秋间叶黄时采收，除去地上部分及须根，洗净泥土，晒干或烘干。

The drug is collected in summer or autumn when leaves turn yellow, removed from rootlet and soil, and dried in sun or at a lower temperature.

【商品特征 / Commodity characteristics】

圆锥形，灰黄皮上疙瘩疔，断面粉质心纹显，香气浓烈，味苦、辛。

Conical, externally greyish-yellow with rootlet scars and lenticel-like transverse protrusions. Fracture starchy, obvious cambium ring. Odour, aromatic; taste, pungent and bitterish.

【商品特征 / Specification and grade】

商品按产地不同分为川白芷、亳白芷、禹白芷、祁白芷、杭白芷，均分为三等。规格等级标准为：

As commodity, five commercial specifications of Angelicae Dahuricae Radix are *Chuan baizhi*, *Bo baizhi*, *Yu baizhi*, *Qi baizhi* and *Hang baizhi* according to their producing areas, marketed by three grades respectively. The specifications and grading criteria are as follows:

一等：呈圆锥形。表面灰白色或黄白色，体坚。断面白色或黄白色，具粉性。有香气，味辛微苦。每 kg 36 支以内。无空心、黑心、芦头、细条。

First grade: Conical. Externally greyish-white or yellowish-white, hard. Fracture white or yellowish-white, starchy. Odour aromatic, taste pungent and bitterish. There are less than 36 roots in per kg. No hollow, nor black core, nor rhizome, nor thin root.

二等：每 kg 60 支以内，余同一等。

Second grade: More than 60 roots in per kg. Other criteria in this grade are the same as those in First grade.

三等：每 kg 60 支以外，顶端直径不得小于 0.7cm。间有白芷尾、黑心、异状、油条，但总数不能超过 20%。余同一等。

Third grade: Less than 60 roots in per kg. The diameter of root top shall not be smaller than 0.7cm. Sometimes there are thin roots, black cener roots, abnormal shape roots and oil-spilling roots, but the total amount is less than 20%. Other criteria in this grade are the same as those in First grade.

【化学成分 / Chemical constituent】

主含欧前胡素、异欧前胡素、珊瑚菜素等香豆精衍生物。另含挥发油。

It mainly contains coumarin derivatives such as imperatorin, isoimperatorin, and phellopterin. Besides, volatile oil.

【检查 / Examination】

水分不得过 14.0%；总灰分不得过 6.0%。

Water, not more than 14.0%. Total ash, not more than 6.0%.

【质量要求 / Quality requirement】

外观质量 均以支条粗壮、体重、质硬、粉性足、香气浓者为佳；条瘦小、体轻泡、粉性小、香气淡薄者次。

Appearance quality Good quality for the roots with thick, heavy, hard, strong starchy and aromatic characteristics. The thin, light, weak starchy and aromatic roots are inferior.

内在质量 浸出物含量：稀乙醇醇溶性浸出物（热）不得少于 15.0%。

Intrinsic quality Extract content: not less than 15.0% of dilute ethanol-soluble extractives (hot).

含量测定：按高效液相色谱法测定，含欧前胡素不得少于 0.080%。

Assay: It contains not less than 0.080% of imperatorin according to HPLC method.

【功能主治 / Function and indication】

温，辛。解表散寒，祛风止痛，宣通鼻窍，燥湿止带，消肿排脓。用于感冒头痛，眉棱骨痛，鼻塞流涕，鼻鼽，鼻渊，牙痛，带下，疮疡肿痛。

Warm, pungent. To release the exterior, dissipate cold, dispel wind, relieve pain, open nose orifices, dry dampness and relieve abnormal vaginal discharge, disperse swelling and expel pus. For the treatment of common cold, headache, supra-orbital bone pain, nasal congestion, nasal discharge, allergic rhinitis, sinusitis, toothache, vaginal discharge, sore, ulcer, swelling and pain.

【贮藏养护 / Storage and maintenance】

麻袋包装，置干燥通风处。本品为芳香粉性药材，极易虫蛀、发霉、变色，必须保持通风干燥。大批贮存应先对仓库彻底消毒，将潜伏在壁缝里的虫及卵杀死，密封仓库。如量小，经炕或晒，热退后置于密封容器内。

Packed in jute bags, stored in dry and ventilated place. Aromatic and starchy, easily damaged by moth, mildew and discolour during storage. The warehouse should be thoroughly disinfected to kill the insects and eggs hiding inside the wall before bulk storage, then seal the warehouse. If the amount is small, bake or dry it first, then cool and store it in an airtight container.

【用法用量 / Administration and dosage】

3~10g。

3~10g.

附子 (Fuzi) ¦ Aconiti Lateralis Radix Praeparata (Prepared Common Monkshood Daughter Root)

【基原 / Origin】

为毛茛科植物乌头 *Aconitum carmichaeli* Debx. 子根的加工品。

Prepared Common Monkshood Daughter Root is the processed daughter root of *Aconitum carmichaeli* Debx. (Fam. Ranunculaceae).

【产地 / Producing area】

主产于四川江油、安县、平武、青川、布拖，陕西汉中、城固，目前全国大部地区已引种栽培。

Mainly produced in Jiangyou, Anxian, Pingwu, Qingchuan and Butuo of Sichuan Province, and Hanzhong and Chenggu of Shaanxi Province. At present, the herb has been introduced and cultivated in the most areas in China.

【采制 / Collection and preparation】

夏至到小暑间采收。挖取后，除去母根、须根及泥沙，称为“泥附子”或“生附子”。一般要及时加工，以免腐烂。按照不同的加工方法加工成不同的规格。

The roots are collected in the Summer solstice to Slight heat, removed from the parent root, rootlet and soil. It is known as “Nifuzi” or “Shengfuzi” (no processing), which should be processed into the following commercial varieties in time to avoid rot.

选择个大、均匀的泥附子，洗净，浸入胆巴的水溶液中过夜，再加食盐，继续浸泡，每日取出晒晾，并逐渐延长晒晾时间，直至附子表面出现大量结晶盐粒（盐霜）、质地变硬为止，习称“盐附子”。

Select the big and uniform Nifuzi, wash clean and soak over night in mother liquor of mineral salt preparation. Add salt, soak and take it out to sun-dry and air-dry every day. Gradually prolong the time for dryness until a lot of salt is crystallized on the surface of the drug and its texture becomes hard. It is known as “Yanfuzi”.

取泥附子，按大小分别洗净，浸入胆巴的水溶液中数日，连同浸液煮至透心，捞出，水漂，纵切成厚约 0.5cm 的片，再用水浸漂，用调色液使附片染成浓茶色，取出，蒸至出现油面、光泽后，烘至半干，再晒干或继续烘干，习称“黑顺片”。

Grade Nifuzi according to size, wash clean and soak in mother liquor of mineral salt preparation for several days. Boil in the infusion thoroughly. Take out, rinse in water, cut longitudinally into slices about 0.5cm in thickness. Soak and rinse in water once again. Stain the slices dark brown and steam them until the slices turn to be oily and lustrous. Bake the slices to half-dryness, and then sun-dry or bake to complete dryness. It is known as “Heishunpian”.

选择大小均匀的泥附子，洗净，浸入胆巴的水溶液中数日，连同浸液煮至透心，捞出，剥去外皮，纵切成厚约 0.3cm 的片，用水浸漂，取出，蒸透，晒干，习称“白附片”。

Select the Nifuzi of uniform size, wash clean and soak in mother liquor of mineral salt preparation for several days. Boil in the infusion thoroughly. Take out, peel the bark and cut longitudinally into slices about 0.3cm in thickness. After soaking and rinsing in water, take out, steam thoroughly, sun-dry to dryness. It is known as “Baifupian”.

【商品特征 / Commodity characteristics】

盐附子 呈圆锥形，长 4~7cm，直径 3~5cm。表面灰黑色，被盐霜，顶端有凹陷的芽痕，周围有瘤状突起的支根或支根痕。体重，横切面灰褐色，可见充满盐霜的小空隙和多角形形成层环纹，环纹内侧导管束排列不整齐。气微，味咸而麻，刺舌。

Yanfuzi (salted conite daughter root) Conical, 4~7cm long, 3~5cm in diameter. Externally greyish-black, covered with fine powder of salt, topped with depressed bud scars and encircled with tubercled short rootlets or rootlet scars. Texture heavy. Transversely cut surface greyish-brown, showing small clefts filled with fine powder of salt and a polyangular cambium ring, and vascular bundles arranged irregularly inside the ring. Odour, slight; taste, salty, numb and pungent.

黑顺片 为纵切片，上宽下窄，长 1.7~5.0cm，宽 0.9~3.0cm，厚 0.2~0.5cm。外皮黑褐色，切面暗黄色，油润具光泽，半透明状，并有纵向导管束。质硬而脆，断面角质样。气微，味淡。

Heishunpian (black slice) Longitudinal slices, the upper portion wide and the lower portion narrow, 1.7~5.0cm long, 0.9~3.0cm wide, 0.2~0.5cm thick. The outer bark blackish-brown, cut surface dark yellow, oily and lustrous, translucent and showing longitudinal vascular bundles. Texture hard and fragile. Fracture horny. Odour, slight; taste, plain.

白附片 无外皮，黄白色，半透明，厚约 3mm。

Baifupian (white slice) Without outer bark, yellowish-white, translucent, about 3mm thick.

【规格等级 / Specification and grade】

目前，附子主要有盐附子、黑顺片、白附片等商品规格。其规格等级标准为：

As commodity, three commercial specifications of Prepared Common Monkshood Daughter Root are Yanfuzi, Heishunpian, Baifupian, which are marketed by different grades in each. The specifications and grading criteria are as follows:

盐附子 一等：呈圆锥形，上部肥圆有芽痕，下部有支根痕，表面灰褐色或黑褐色，附有食盐结晶。体重，断面黄褐色。味咸而麻，刺舌。每 kg 16 个以内。

Yanfuzi (salted root) First grade: Conical, the upper part of the root is round with bud marks, root marks in the lower part of root; externally greyish-brown or blackish-brown, with salt crystals. Texture heavy, fracture yellowish-brown. Taste, salty, numb and pungent. There are less than 16 roots in per kg.

二等：每 kg 24 个以内，余同一等。

Second grade: There are not more than 24 roots in per kg, other characteristics are the same as those in First grade.

三等：每 kg 80 个以内，间有小药扒耳，但直径不小于 2.5cm。余同一等。

Third grade: There are not more than 80 roots in per kg, the sublateral roots mixed occasionally, but not less than 2.5cm in diameter. Other criteria in this grade are the same as those in First grade.

黑顺片 为二、三等附子不去外皮，纵切成 0.2~0.3cm 的薄片。边缘黑褐色，片面暗黄色。片面光滑油润。片张大小不一，厚薄均匀。

Heishunpian (processed slice of black colour) For the Second and Third grades of aconite with the outer skin, longitudinally cut into 0.2-0.3cm thin slices. The edge colour is dark brown and the section is dark yellow. The slice surface is smooth and oily. The slices are uneven in size, but uniform in thickness.

白附片 一等：为一等的附子去净外皮，纵切成厚 0.2~0.3cm 的薄片。片面白色，半透明，片大而均匀。

Baifupian (processed slice of white colour) First grade: Select the First grade Fuzi to peel off its bark and cut longitudinally into slices about 0.2-0.3cm in thickness. The slices are white, translucent, large and uniform.

二等：为二等附子去净外皮，纵切而成厚 0.2~0.3cm 的薄片，片张较小。余同一等。

Second grade: Select the Second grade Fuzi to peel off its bark and cut longitudinally into slices about 0.2~0.3cm in thickness. The slices are smaller than the First grade. Other criteria in this grade are the same as those in First grade.

三等：为三等附子去净外皮，纵切成厚 0.2~0.3cm 的薄片，片张小。余同一等。

Third grade: Select the Third grade Fuzi to peel off its bark and cut longitudinally into slices about 0.2~0.3cm in thickness. The slices are smaller than the Second grade. Other criteria in this grade are the same as those in First grade.

【化学成分 / Chemical constituent】

生附子含剧毒的乌头碱、新乌头碱、次乌头碱等双酯型生物碱，经炮制后生成毒性较小的苯甲酰乌头原碱、苯甲酰新乌头原碱和苯甲酰次乌头原碱等单酯型生物碱，甚至毒性更小的乌头胺、新乌头胺、次乌头胺等胺醇型生物碱。盐附子及附片生物碱成分主要为单酯型和胺醇型生物碱。

Raw Aconiti Lateralis Radix Praeparata contains highly toxic aconitine, mesaconitine, hypaconitine and other diester alkaloids. After processing, lower toxic benzoylaconitine, benzoylmesaconitine, benzoylhypoaconitine and other monoester alkaloids are formed, which further produce even less toxic aconine, mesaconine, hypaconine and other aminoalcohol alkaloids. Yanfuzi and processed slices mainly contain monoester alkaloids and aminoalcohol alkaloids.

【检查 / Examination】

水分不得过 15.0%。按高效液相色谱法测定，含双酯型生物碱以新乌头碱、次乌头碱和乌头碱的总量计，不得过 0.020%。

Water, not more than 15.0%. It contains not more than 0.020% of the total amount of mesaconine, hypaconitine and aconitine according to HPLC method.

【质量要求 / Quality requirement】

外观质量 均以身干、肥大、坚实，无须根，无空心者为佳。盐附子以表面色灰黑，起盐霜者为佳；黑顺片以片大，均匀，表面具油润光泽者为佳；白附片以片大、色白、半透明者为佳。

Appearance quality

Yanfuzi: Finest quality with the characteristics of dry, big, hard, without rootlets, no hollow, greyish-black color and salt rust on the surface.

Heishunpian: Good quality for big and uniform slice, surface with oily lustrous.

Baifupian: Good quality for big, white and translucent slice.

内在质量 含量测定：按高效液相色谱法测定，含苯甲酰新乌头原碱、苯甲酰乌头原碱和苯甲酰次乌头原碱的总量不得少于 0.010%。

Intrinsic quality Assay: It contains not less than 0.010%, of the total amount of which includes benzoylmesaconine, benzoylaconitine and benzoylhypaconitine according to HPLC method.

【功能主治 / Function and indication】

大热，辛，甘；有毒。回阳救逆，补火助阳，散寒止痛。用于亡阳虚脱，肢冷脉微，心阳不足，胸痹心痛，虚寒吐泻，脘腹冷痛，肾阳虚衰，阳痿宫冷，阴寒水肿，寒湿痹痛。

Highly hot; pungent and sweet; toxic. To restore yang, induce resuscitation tonify fire assist yang, dissipate cold and relieve pain. For the treatment of Yang collapse, coldness of limbs and faint pulse, deficiency of heart yang with chest *bi* disorder and heart pain, deficiency cold vomiting and diarrhea, cold pain in the epigastrium and abdomen, debilitation of kidney *yang*, impotence and uterine coldness, *yin*-cold edema, external contraction with yang deficiency, and cold-dampness arthralgia.

【贮藏养护 / Storage and maintenance】

麻袋或木箱装。本品易虫蛀、发霉，应置干燥处保存。为保持附片完好，应防压碎。加工干燥时应控制其温度不超过 70℃，以免脆裂。盐附子因用盐加工，宜密闭，置阴凉干燥处保存，注意防潮。

Packed in jute bag or wooden case. Preserved in a dry place because it is easily damaged by moth and mildew. In order to keep intact, the slices should be prevented from crushing. The processing and drying temperature should not exceed 70℃, so as to avoid brittle cracking. Yanfuzi should be packed in a well closed container because of processing with salt, and stored in a cool and dry place, protected from moisture.

【用法用量 / Administration and dosage】

3~15g，先煎，久煎。

3~15g. It should be decocted first and for a long time.

【注意 / Precaution and Warning】

孕妇慎用；不宜与半夏、瓜蒌、瓜蒌子、瓜蒌皮、天花粉、川贝母、浙贝母、平贝母、伊贝母、湖北贝母、白蔹、白及同用。

Used cautiously for pregnant woman. Incompatible with Pinelliae Rhizoma, Trichosanthis Fructus, Trichosanthis Semen, Trichosanthis Pericarpium, Trichosanthis Radix, Fritillariae Cirrhosae Bulbus, Fritillariae Thunbergii Bulbus, Fritillariae Ussuriensis Bulbus, Fritillariae Pallidiflorae Bulbus, Fritillariae Hupehensis Bulbus, Ampelopsis Radix and Bletillae Rhizoma.

【附注 / Annotation】

生附子是毒性中药品种，需按医疗用毒性药品进行特殊管理。

Raw Aconiti Lateralis Radix Praeparata is a toxic Chinese medicinal material, which needs special management according to the toxic drugs for medical use.

冬虫夏草 (Dongchongxiacao) | Cordyceps (Chinese Caterpillar Fungus)

【基原 / Origin】

为麦角菌科真菌冬虫夏草菌 *Cordyceps sinensis* (Berk.) Sacc. 寄生在蝙蝠蛾科昆虫幼虫上的子

座和幼虫尸体的干燥复合体。

Chinese Caterpillar Fungus is a composite consisting of the stroma of the fungus, *Cordyceps sinensis* (Berk.) Sacc. (Fam. Hypocreaceae), parasitized on the larva of some species of insects (Fam. Hepialidea), and the dead caterpillar.

【产地 / Producing area】

主产于四川甘孜州和阿坝州，如松潘、理县、壤塘等；西藏的那曲、昌都、林芝；青海玉树、果洛、同德、同仁等；云南香格里拉、德钦、丽江等地。此外甘肃、新疆亦产。以四川的产量大。

Mainly produced in Songpan, Lixian and Rangtang of Ganzi Tibetan Autonomous Prefecture or Aba Tibetan and Qiang Autonomous Prefecture of Sichuan Province, Naqu, Changdu and Linzhi of Tibet Autonomous Region, and Yushu, Guoluo, Tongde, Tongren of Qinghai Province; Xianggelila, Deqin, Lijiang, and other places of Yunnan Province. Also produced in other provinces and regions such as Gansu and Xinjiang. A large output in Sichuan.

【采制 / Collection and preparation】

夏初子实体出土、孢子未发散时挖取。晒至 6~7 成干，除去似纤维状附着物及杂质，晒干或低温干燥。

Chinese Caterpillar Fungus is often collected in early Summer while the stromata have come up out of the ground but the spores have not ejected, partially dried in the sun, removed from the attached fibrous matter and other foreign matters, and dried in the sun or at low temperature.

【商品特征 / Commodity characteristics】

虫体似蚕，头部红棕色，体表深黄色至黄棕色，具环纹 20~30 条，全体 8 对足，腹面中部 4 对足明显。子座如草，表面深褐色至褐色，气微腥。

The caterpillar resembling a silkworm, head reddish-brown, externally deep yellow to yellowish-brown, with 20~30 annulations, feet 8 pairs, the 4 pairs in the middle relatively obvious; stromata slenderly cylindrical, externally dark brown to brown. Odour, slightly fishy.

【规格等级 / Specification and grade】

目前市场上冬虫夏草商品根据包装不同，分散装和扎把分装两种规格。等级以每 kg 的条数分为若干个等级。

As commodity, there are two commercial specifications of Chinese Caterpillar Fungus according to the packing, loose packing and bundled packing. Chinese Caterpillar Fungus are marketed by several grades according to the number in per kg.

【化学成分 / Chemical constituent】

主含粗蛋白、氨基酸、脂肪、虫草酸、腺苷、虫草多糖、虫草素等。

It mainly contains crude protein, amino acid, fat, cordycepic acid, adenosine, cordyceps polysaccharide, cordycepin, etc.

【质量要求 / Quality requirement】

外观质量　均以条丰满肥大、外形完整、无碎节、色泽黄亮、断面黄白色、子座深棕色者为佳。

Appearance quality　Good quality for a full and fat strip, complete appearance, no broken parts, yellow color, yellowish-white section, externally dark brown stromata.

内在质量　含量测定：按高效液相色谱法测定，含腺苷不得少于 0.010%。

Intrinsic quality　Assay: It contains not less than 0.010% of adenosine according to HPLC analysis method.

【功能主治 / Function and indication】

甘，平。补肾益肺，止血化痰。用于肾虚精亏，阳痿遗精，腰膝酸痛，久咳虚喘，劳嗽咯血。

Sweet, neutral. Supplement the lung and boost the kidney, stanch bleeding and dissolve phlegm. For the treatment of deficiency of kidney essence, impotence and seminal emission, limp aching in the lower back and knees, chronic cough and dyspnea of deficiency type, cough caused by consumptive disease, and hemoptysis.

【贮藏养护 / Storage and maintenance】

以纸包装，再装于纸箱内。本品易虫蛀、发霉、变色，应密封后，置阴凉干燥处保存。为防虫蛀，在装箱时可同时放入一些牡丹皮碎块。

Packed in paper first, and then stored in cartons. Because moth damaging, mildewing and discolouring usually happen in the storage of Chinese Caterpillar Fungus, store it in a cool and dry place after sealing, with some pieces of Moutan bark to avoid moth damaging.

【用法用量 / Administration and dosage】

3~9g。

3~9g.

黄连 (Huanglian) ┊ Coptidis Rhizoma (Golden Thread)

【基原 / Origin】

为毛茛科植物黄连 *Coptis chinensis* Franch、三角叶黄连 *Coptis deltoidea* C. Y. Cheng et Hsiao 或云连 *Coptis teeta* Wall. 的干燥根茎。商品依次称为"味连""雅连"和"云连"。

Golden Thread is the dried rhizome of *Coptis chinensis* Franch., *Coptis deltoidea* C. Y. Cheng et Hsiao or *Coptis teeta* Wall. (Fam. Ranunculaceae), commonly known as "Wei-lian" "Ya-lian" or "Yun-lian" respectively.

【产地 / Producing area】

味连主产于重庆石柱、南川，湖北利川、来凤等地者名"南岸连"，产量较大；主产于重庆城口、巫山、巫溪，湖北房县、巴东、竹溪等地者习称"北岸连"，产量不如南岸连，但质量好。雅连主产于四川峨眉、洪雅等地。云连主产于云南德钦、维西、腾冲等地。

"Wei-lian" mainly produced in Shizhu and Nanchuan of Chongqing Municipality. Produced in Lichuan, Laifeng of Hubei Province, commonly known as "Nan, an-lian", whose output is large. Mainly produced in Chengkou, Wushan and Wuxi of Chongqing Municipality, Fangxian, Badong and Zhuxi of Hubei Province, commonly known as "Beian-lian", whose output is less, but quality is better. "Ya-lian" mainly produced in Emei and Hongya of Sichuan Province, while "Yun-lian" mainly in Deqin, Weixi, Tengchong of Yunnan Province.

【采制 / Collection and preparation】

黄连 栽培 5~6 年后即可采收，一般在 10~11 月下雪前采挖根茎。除去茎叶和泥土，干燥，再撞去残留须根。

Coptidis Rhizoma It is often collected after the five to six years of plantation. The harvest season is about October to November before snows. Remove its stems, leaves and soil, and dry, then strike off residual fibrous roots.

黄连片 取黄连，润透后切薄片，晾干或用时捣碎。

Coptidis Rhizoma slices Take the rhizome, soften thoroughly, cut into thin slices, dry in air, or break to pieces before use.

酒黄连 取黄连片，用黄酒拌匀，润透后置锅内，以文火炒干。

Coptidis Rhizoma processed by **wine (Jiu huanglian)** Take the Coptidis Rhizoma slices, mix well with yellow rice wine, soften thoroughly in a pan, and dry with small fire.

姜黄连 取黄连片，用姜汁拌匀，润透后置锅内，以文火炒干。

Coptidis Rhizoma processed by **ginger (Jiang huanglian)** Take the Coptidis Rhizoma slices, mix well with ginger juice, soften thoroughly in a pan, and dry with small fire.

萸黄连 取吴茱萸加适量水煎煮，煎液与黄连片拌匀，润透后置锅内，以文火炒干。

Coptidis Rhizoma processed by **Evodiae Fructus (Yu huanglian)** Take the Coptidis Rhizoma slices, mix well with appropriate amount of Evodia Fructus decoction, soften thoroughly in a pan, and dry with small fire.

【商品特征 / Commodity characteristics】

黄连 呈鸡爪形（味连）或鼓锤状（雅连）或弯曲的细柱形（云连）。表面黄褐色，粗糙，有过桥。质硬，断面深黄色或黄棕色，味极苦。

Coptidis Rhizoma Mostly gathered to a cluster, curved, like “chicken’s feet” (Wei-lian), or cylindrical (Ya-lian), or curved hook-like (Yun-lian). Externally yellowish-brown, rough, some internodes smooth as stem, commonly known as “Guoqiao” (bridge piece). Texture hard, fracture dark yellow or yellowish-brown; taste, extremely bitter.

黄连片 呈不规则的薄片，外表皮灰黄色或黄褐色，粗糙，有细小的须根。切面鲜黄色或红黄色，具放射状纹理。气微，味极苦。

Coptidis Rhizoma slices Irregular thin slices. Externally greyish-yellow or yellowish-brown, rough and with fine rootlets. Cut or broken surface fresh yellow or reddish-yellow, with radiate striations. Odour, slightly; taste, extremely bitter.

酒黄连 形如黄连片，色泽加深，略有酒香气。

Coptidis Rhizoma processed by wine (Jiu huanglian) In the shape of Coptidis Rhizoma slices, dark colour, slight odour of wine.

姜黄连 形如黄连片，表面棕黄色，有姜的辛辣味。

Coptidis Rhizoma processed by ginger (Jiang huanglian) In the shape of Coptidis Rhizoma slice, externally brownish-yellow, pungent odour of ginger.

萸黄连 形如黄连片，表面棕黄色，有吴茱萸的辛辣香气。

Coptidis Rhizoma processed by Evodiae Fructus (Yu huanglian) In the shape of Coptidis Rhizoma slice, externally brownish-yellow, pungent and spicy odour of Evodiae Fructus.

【规格等级 / Specification and grade】

商品因产地和来源不同，分为味连（鸡爪连）、雅连、云连三类。各分 1~2 等。其规格等级标准为：

As commodity, according to the producing area and origin, three commercial specifications of Coptidis Rhizoma are Wei-lian, Ya-lian and Yun-lian which are marketed by one or two grades respectively. The specifications and grading criteria are as follows:

味连 一等：多成簇聚成鸡爪形，少有单枝，表面黄褐色，间有过桥，长不超 2cm。体肥壮坚实，易折断，断面金黄色或黄色。味极苦。无短于 1.5cm 的碎节、碎渣、焦枯、残茎。

Wei-lian First grade: Mostly gathered to a cluster, curved, like “chicken’s feet”, less single, externally yellowish brown, some internodes smooth as stem, commonly known as “Guoqiao” (bridge piece), not longer than 2cm. The rhizome is fat and sturdy, easy to break, fracture golden yellow or yellow, taste, extremely bitter. There are no broken nodes of shorter than 1.5cm, nor slag, nor scorched product, nor the remains of stems.

二等：条较一等瘦小，有过桥，但长不超过 2cm，间有碎节、碎渣、焦枯。余同一等。

Second grade: The rhizome is smaller than the First grade, with bridge piece, not longer than 2cm. Occasionally, there are some broken knots, slag and scorched product. Other criteria in this grade are in accordance with those in First grade.

雅连 一等：单枝，圆柱形，略弯曲，条粗壮，过桥少，长不得超过 2.5cm，质坚硬，表面黄褐色，断面金黄色，味极苦。无碎节、碎渣、焦枯、残茎。

Ya-lian First grade: Mostly single, cylindrical, slightly curved, strong rhizome, less bridge piece, not longer than 2.5cm. Texture sturdy, surface yellowish-brown, fracture, golden yellow, taste, extremely bitter. There are no broken nodes, nor slag, nor scorched product, nor the remains of stems.

二等：条较一等瘦小，过桥较多，间有碎节、毛须、焦枯。余同一等。

Second grade: The rhizome is smaller than the First grade, more bridge piece. Occasionally, there are some broken knots, hairy fibrous and scorch product. Other criteria in this grade are in accordance with those in First grade.

云连 一等：单枝，圆柱形，微弯曲，顶端有褐绿色鳞片，有残叶。条粗壮，质坚实，直径在 0.3cm 以上。表面黄棕色，断面金黄色，味极苦。无碎节、碎渣、焦枯、残茎。

Yun-lian First grade: Mostly single, cylindrical, slightly curved, brown-green scales and dry leaves at the top of rhizome. The rhizome strong, texture sturdy, more than 0.3cm in diameter. Surface, yellowish-brown, fracture, golden-yellow, taste, extremely bitter. No broken nodes, nor slag, nor scorched product, nor the remains of stems.

二等：条较瘦小，间有过桥。表面深黄色。直径在 0.3cm 以下。余同一等。

Second grade: The rhizome is smaller than the First grade, occasionally with bridge piece. Externally dark yellow. The diameter is less than 0.3cm. Other criteria in this grade are in accordance with those in First grade.

【化学成分 / Chemical constituent】

主含小檗碱、黄连碱、表小檗碱、巴马汀、药根碱等多种生物碱。此外，尚含阿魏酸、绿原酸等多种酚性成分。

It mainly contains a variety of alkaloids such as berberine, coptisine, epiberberine, palmatine, jatrorrhizine etc. In addition, it also contains ferulic acid, chlorogenic acid and other phenolic components.

【检查 / Examination】

水分不得过 14.0%；总灰分不得过 5.0%。

Water, not more than 14.0%. Total ash, not more than 5.0%.

【质量要求 / Quality requirement】

外观质量 味连和雅连以身干、粗壮、连珠形，无残茎毛须，体重质坚，断面色红黄者为佳；云连以身干、条细坚实，曲节多，须根少，色黄绿者为佳。

Appearance quality Good quality of “Wei-lian” and “Ya-lian” for the characteristics of dry, strong, bearing irregular nodular protruding, no rootlets and the remains of stems, texture hard, red-yellow section. Good quality of “Yun-lian” for dry, fine and texture hard, more curved nodes, less rootlets, yellow-green colour.

内在质量 浸出物含量：稀乙醇醇溶性浸出物（热）不得少于 15.0%。

Intrinsic quality Extract content: not less than 15.0% of dilute ethanol-soluble extractives (hot).

含量测定：按高效液相色谱法测定，以盐酸小檗碱计，味连含小檗碱不得少于5.5%，表小檗碱不得少于0.80%，黄连碱不得少于1.6%，巴马汀不得少于1.5%。雅连含小檗碱不得少于4.5%，云连含小檗碱不得少于7.0%。饮片含小檗碱不得少于5.0%，表小檗碱、黄连碱和巴马汀的总量不得少于3.3%。

Assay: Wei-lian contains not less than 5.5% of berberine, 0.80% of epiberberine, 1.6% of coptisine, 1.5% of palmatine. Ya-lian and Yun-lian contain not less than 4.5% and 7.0% of berberine, respectively. Slices contains not less than 5.0% of berberine, 3.3% of the total amount of epiberberine, coptisine, and palmatine according to HPLC analysis method.

【功能主治 / Function and indication】

寒、苦。清热燥湿，泻火解毒。用于湿热痞满，呕吐吞酸，泻痢，黄疸，高热神昏，心火亢盛，心烦不寐，心悸不宁，血热吐衄，目赤，牙痛，消渴，痈肿疔疮；外治湿疹，湿疮，耳道流脓。酒黄连善清上焦火热。用于目赤，口疮。姜黄连清胃和胃止呕。用于寒热互结，湿热中阻，痞满呕吐。萸黄连舒肝和胃止呕。用于肝胃不和，呕吐吞酸。

Cold, Bitter. To clear heat, dry dampness; purge fire and remove toxin. For the treatment of dampness-heat stuffiness and fullness, vomiting, acid reflux, diarrhea and dysentery, jaundice, high fever with loss of consciousness, intense heart fire, insomnia caused by vexation, palpitations, blood heat with hematemesis, red eyes, toothache, consumptive disease, swelling abscess, deep-rooted boil and sore. Topical application: eczema, dampness sore, purulent discharge from the ear. Coptidis Rhizoma processed with wine is good at clearing fire-heat in the upper energizer, and can be used for red eyes and aphtha. Coptidis Rhizoma processed with ginger can clear the stomach and harmonize the stomach and check vomiting, and can be used for cold-heat binds, dampness-heat obstruction in the middle, stuffiness and fullness, and vomiting. Coptidis Rhizoma processed with Evodiae Fructus can soothe the liver, harmonize the stomach, stop vomiting, and can be used for vomiting and acid reflux.

【贮藏养护 / Storage and maintenance】

以篾篓或麻袋盛放，置干燥通风处保存。本品不易虫蛀，但易发霉，故贮存时应保持干燥。

Packed in bamboo baskets or woven bags, and stored in a ventilated and dry place. Not easily damaged by moth, but easily damaged by mildew, so stored in a dry place.

【用法用量 / Administration and dosage】

2~5g，外用适量。

2~5g. A proper amount is used externally.

重点小结
Summary

药材	主产地	商品规格	等级标准
川贝母	松贝主产于松潘等，青贝主产于玉树等，炉贝主产于马尔康等，栽培品主产于茂县等	按性状分为松贝、青贝、炉贝及栽培品	松贝、青贝按每50g的粒数分别分二、四等；炉贝按颜色分二等；栽培品为统货

续表

药材	主产地	商品规格	等级标准
川芎	四川都江堰、彭州	按产地分川芎和抚芎；按采收分家川芎、山川芎	家川芎按每 kg 的个数分三等
冬虫夏草	四川阿坝、甘孜等，西藏那曲、昌都等，青海玉树、云南香格里拉		以每 kg 的条数分等
白芷	四川遂宁、安徽亳州、河南禹州、河北安国、浙江磐安、福建等	按产地分川白芷、禹白芷、杭白芷、祁白芷、亳白芷	均按大小分三等
附子	四川江油、安县、布拖等	按加工方法分：盐附子、黑顺片、白附片等	盐附子和白附片按大小分三等，其他一般为统货
黄连	重庆石柱县等	按来源分为味连、雅连、云连	均按大小分二等

Medicinal material	Main Producing area	Specification	Grade
Fritillariae Cirrhosae Bulbus	Songbei: Songpan of Sichuan Province. Qingbei: Yushu of Qinghai Province. Lubei: Malerkang of Sichuan Province. Cultivar: Mao county of Sichuan Province	Four specifications of Songbei, Qingbei, Lubei, and cultivar according to the difference of their characteristics	Songbei, two grades. Qingbei, four grades according to the number of Bulbs in per 50g; Lubei, two grades according to its colour. Cultivar, unified grade with the same price
Chuanxiong Rhizoma	Dujiangyan, Pengzhou of Sichuan Province	Two specifications of Chuanxiong and Fuxiong according to producing area "Chuan xiong" is divided into garden Chuangxiong and mountain Chuanxiong	Garden Chuangxiong is divided into three grades according to the number of rhizomes per kg
Cordyceps	Ganzi Tibetan Autonomous Prefecture and Aba Tibetan and Qiang Autonomous Prefecture of Sichuan Province Naqu, Changdu of Tibet Autonomous Region Yushu of Qinghai Province; Xianggelila of Yunnan Province		The number of Cordyceps in per kg
Angelicae Dahuricae Radix	Suining of Sichuan Province Bozhou of Anhui Province Yuzhou of Henan Province Anguo of Hebei Province Panan of Zhejiang Province; Fujian Province	Chuan baizhi, Bo baizhi, Yu baizhi, Qi baizhi and Hang baizhi according to producing areas	Three grades according to their root size
Aconiti Lateralis Radix Praeparata	Jiangyou, Anxian and Butuo of Sichuan Province	Yanfuzi, Heishunpian, and Baifupian according to processing methods	Yanfuzi and Baifupian are divided into three grades according to size others, unified grade with the same price
Coptidis Rhizoma	Shizhu of Chongqing Municipality	Three commercial specifications are Wei-lian, Ya-lian and Yun-lian according to their origins	Two grades according to the rhizome size

题库

目标检测
Object Detection

一、选择题（Choice question）

（一）单项选择题（One-choice question）

1. 以下为川产道地药材的是（　　）

A. 人参　　B. 黄芪　　C. 五味子
D. 牛膝　　E. 附子

Which authentic medicinal material is produced in Chuanyao producing area (　　)

A. Ginseng　　B. Astragali Radix
C. Schisandrae Chinensis Fructus　　D. Achyranthis Bidentata Radix
E. Aconiti Lateralis Radix Praeparata

2. 川贝母中呈"怀中抱月"的商品规格是（　　）

A. 松贝　　B. 青贝　　C. 炉贝
D. 大贝　　E. 元宝贝

Which commercial specification is that two outer scale leaves embrace each other like HuaizhongBaoyue (holding the moon in the arms) (　　)

A. Songbei　　B. Qingbei　　C. Lubei
D. Dabei　　E. Yuanbaobei

3. 附子最著名的道地产区是（　　）

A. 江油　　B. 遂宁　　C. 都江堰
D. 平武　　E. 彭州

Where is the famous authentic production area of Aconiti Lateralis Radix Praeparata (　　)

A. Jiangyou　　B. Suining　　C. Dujiangyan
D. Pingwu　　E. Pengzhou

4. 黄连最著名的道地产区是（　　）

A. 重庆合川　　B. 重庆石柱　　C. 四川大足
D. 四川北川　　E. 重庆万县

Where is the famous authentic production area of Coptidis Rhizoma (　　)

A. Hechuan of Chongqing Municipality
B. Shizhu of Chongqing Municipality
C. Dazu of Sichuan Province
D. Beichuan of Sichuan Province
E. Wanxian of Chongqing Municipality

5. 冬虫夏草目前在市场分等级的标准为（　　）

A. 每 kg 条数　　B. 每 500g 条数　　C. 颜色
D. 长短　　E. 产地

What's the grading criteria of Cordyceps (　　)

A. Number of Cordyceps in per kg　　B. Number of Cordyceps in per 500g

C. Colour　　D. Length
E. Production area

6. 松贝划分等级的标准是(　)
A. 长度　B. 重量　C. 直径　D. 宽度　E. 颜色
What's the grading criteria of Songbei (　)
A. Length　B. Weight　C. Diameter
D. Width　E. Colour

7. 炉贝划分等级的标准是(　)
A. 长度　B. 重量　C. 直径　D. 宽度　E. 颜色
What's the grading criteria of Lubei (　)
A. Length　B. Weight　C. Diameter
D. Width　E. Colour

(二)多项选择题(Multiple choice question)

1. 以下是川药产区道地药材的是(　)
A. 川贝母　B. 川牛膝　C. 川乌
D. 黄连　E. 补骨脂
Which authentic medicinal are produced in materials producing areas of Chuan Medicinal Materials (　)
A. Fritillariae Cirrhosae Bulbus　B. Cyathulae Radix
C. Aconiti Radix　D. Coptidis Rhizoma
E. Psoraleae Fructus

2. 白芷药材按产地分(　)
A. 川白芷　B. 禹白芷　C. 杭白芷
D. 祁白芷　E. 亳白芷
What are the commercial specifications of Angelicae Dahuricae Radix according to producing area (　)
A. Chuan baizhi　B. Yu baizhi　C. Hang baizhi
D. Qi baizhi　E. Bo baizhi

3. 川芎的商品规格有(　)
A. 川芎　B. 抚芎　C. 家川芎
D. 山川芎　E. 芎藭
What are the commercial specifications of Chuanxiong Rhizoma (　)
A. Chuanxiong　B. Fuxiong　C. Garden Chuanxiong
D. mountain Chuanxiong　E. Xiongqiong

4. 白芷药材商品在贮藏中极易(　)
A. 虫蛀　B. 发霉　C. 变色
D. 化苗　E. 风化
Which phenomena usually happen in the storage of Angelicae Dahuricae Radix (　)
A. Moth damaging　B. Mildewing　C. Discolouring
D. Diminution　E. air-slake

二、思考题（Thinking question）

1. 冬虫夏草商品为何在流通过程中易化苗？

Why are Cordyceps commodities prone to be diminution in trade flows?

2. 为何川产道地药材品种多，产量大？

Why do authentic medicinal materials produced from Sichuan have many varieties and large output?

3. 川芎药材在贮藏中易发生哪些质量变异现象？为什么？

What quality variation phenomena are prone to happen on Chuanxiong Rhizoma during the storage? Why?

PPT

第九章　广　　药
Chapter 9　Guang Medicinal Materials

学习目标 | Learning Target

知识要求：

1. **掌握**　广药的含义及其主要道地药材品种；肉桂、陈皮、金钱白花蛇、砂仁的道地产地、采制、规格等级、商品特征、质量要求。

2. **熟悉**　肉桂、陈皮、金钱白花蛇、砂仁的化学成分、检查和贮藏方法。

3. **了解**　广药产区的自然环境条件。

能力要求：

会运用所学规格等级、商品特征、检查、质量要求等知识和方法鉴别市场上肉桂、陈皮、金钱白花蛇和砂仁的真伪优劣。

Knowledge requirements:

1. **Proficiency**　The meaning and main varieties of Guang Medicinal Materials. The authentic producing areas, collection and preparation, specifications and grades, commodity characteristics and quality requirements of Cassia Bark, Dried Tangerine Peel, Bungarus Parvus and Villous Amomum Fruit.

2. **Familiarity**　The chemical constituents, examination and storage methods of Cassia Bark, Dried Tangerine Peel, Bungarus Parvus and Villous Amomum Fruit.

3. **Understanding**　Natural environment in the producing areas of Guang Medicinal Materials.

Skill requirements:

Learn to identify the authenticity and evaluate the quality of Cassia Bark, Dried Tangerine Peel, Bungarus Parvus and Villous Amomum Fruit on the market by applying the knowledge and methods of specification and grade, commodity characteristics, examination and quality requirement, etc.

一、广药概述
I. Overview of Guang Medicinal Materials

以广东、广西及海南为主要产区或集散地的大宗商品药材称为广药。其产区位于东经104° 29′ ~119° 59′，北纬3° 28′ ~26° 23′，该地区气候温暖，雨量充沛，年均温度在20℃以上，年均降水量 1500~3000mm，土壤为强酸性，植被覆盖良好，适宜热带、亚热带药用动植物的生长。本区生物种类丰富，高等植物有 7000 种以上，药用植物 5000 种，药用动物近 300 种。主要的广药有：阳春的砂仁，石牌的广藿香，高要、德庆的巴戟天，玉林的肉桂，新会的广陈皮，海南的槟榔，合浦的珍珠，徐闻的高良姜，百色的金钱白花蛇，化州的化橘红，龙津、大新的蛤蚧等。

The bulk commodities of medicinal materials, mainly produced or distributed in Guangdong, Guangxi and Hainan provinces, are known as Guang Medicinal Materials. The producing area is located at 104° 29′ ~119° 59′ E and 3° 28′ ~26° 23′ N. The climate in this area is warm and the rainfall is abundant. The average annual temperature is above 20℃, and the average annual precipitation is about 1500-3000mm. The strong acid soil and good vegetation coverage are suitable for the growth of tropical and subtropical medicinal animals and plants. This area is rich in biological species. There are more than 7000 species of higher plants, 5000 species of medicinal plants and nearly 300 species of medicinal animals. The main Guang Medicinal Materials include Amomi Fructus in Yangchun, Pogostemonis Herba in Shipai, Morindae Officinalis Radix in Gaoyao and Deqing, Cinnamomi Cortex in Yulin, Guang Dried Tangerine Peel in Xinhui, Arecae Semen in Hainan, Margarita in Hepu, Alpiniae Officinarum Rhizoma in Xuwen, Bungarus Parvus in Baise, Citri Grandis Exocarpium in Huazhou, Gecko in Longjin and Daxin, etc.

二、药材品种
II. Varieties of Medicinal Materials

肉桂 (Rougui) ¦ Cinnamomi Cortex (Cassia Bark)

【基原 / Origin】

为樟科植物肉桂 *Cinnamomum cassia* Presl 的干燥树皮。

Cassia Bark is the dried stem bark of *Cinnamomum cassia* Presl (Fam. Lauraceae).

【产地 / Producing area】

主产于广西桂平、平南、容县、防城港、玉林，广东德庆、信宜、肇庆等地。国外主产于越南、印度、老挝、印度尼西亚等国。以广西产量最大。

Mainly produced in Guiping, Pingnan, Rongxian, Fangchenggang and Yulin of Guangxi Province; Deqing, Xinyi and Zhaoqing of Guangdong Province. Also produced in Vietnam, India, Laos, Indonesia, etc. The most amount of Cassia Bark is produced in Guangxi Province.

【采制 / Collection and preparation】

每年分两期采收，第一期于 4~5 月间，第二期于 9~10 月间，以第二期产量大、香气浓、质量佳。根据采收加工方法不同，有如下加工品。

Collect in two stages every year, the first one from April to May and the second one from September to October. The herbs collected at the latter stage are better for the high yield, strong aroma and superior quality. According to different harvesting and processing methods, there are the following processed products.

桂通 剥取栽培 5~6 年生幼树的干皮和粗枝皮，或老树枝皮，不经压制，自然卷曲成筒状，长 30cm，直径 2~3cm。

Guitong Dried bark and rough branch bark from cultivated trees about 5~6 years old, or branch bark from older trees, not compressed, naturally curly to tubular shape, about 30cm in length and 2~3cm in diameter.

企边桂 剥取 10 年生以上树的干皮，将两端削成斜面，突出桂心，夹在木制的凹凸板之间，压成两侧向内卷曲的浅槽状。长 40cm，宽 6~10cm。

Qibiangui Dried bark from the trees more than ten years old, sliced obliquely at both ends to expose the interior ("Guixin"), stuck in a special concave-convex wooden board, compressed to shallow-slot shape with two ends curly inwards, about 40cm in length, 6~10cm in width.

板桂 剥取老树最下部近地面的干皮，夹在木制的桂夹内，晒至九成干，经纵横堆叠，加压，约 1 月完全干燥，成为扁平板状。

Bangui Dried bark was stripped from the bottom parts of old trees, stuck in wooden clamps, dried in the sun to almost 90% of dry, stacked up vertically and horizontally, pressured, and continually dried for one month to be flat-plate shape.

桂碎 在桂皮加工过程中的碎块，多供香料用。

Guisui fragments during processing, usually used for flavoring.

桂心 即刮去外皮者。

Guixin Cinnamomi Cortex peeled off outer bark.

【商品特征 / Commodity characteristics】

形状因加工规格不一。外表面灰棕色，厚者有地衣斑；内表面红棕色，划之有油痕；断面不平坦，显颗粒性，中有黄棕色线纹；香气浓，味甜、辣。

Processed specifications vary in shape. Outer surface greyish-brown, with thicker ones showing greyish-white lichen spots; inner surface reddish-brown, with exhibiting oily trace on scratching. Fracture uneven, granular, showing a yellowish-brown line between inner and outer layers. Odor, strongly aromatic; taste, sweet and pungent.

【规格等级 / Specification and grade】

根据采收加工方法不同，分为企边桂、桂通、板桂、桂碎和桂心等规格，暂无全国统一的等级标准。

According to the methods of collection and preparation, it is mainly divided into four specifications of Qibiangui, Guitong, Bangui, Guisui and Guixin. Temporarily there is no nationally unified grade criteria.

企边桂 呈两侧向内卷曲的浅槽状，两端成斜面而露出桂心。外表面灰棕色，有细皱纹及横向突起的皮孔；内表面红棕色，略平坦，有细纵纹，划之有油痕。质硬脆，断面外侧呈棕色较粗糙，内侧红棕色而油润，中间有一条黄棕色的线纹。

Qibiangui Shallowly channeled, with two sides curled inwards. Both ends with bevels to expose Guixin. Outer surface grayish-brown, with fine wrinkles and transverse protruding lenticels; inner surface reddish-brown, somewhat even, with fine longitudinal striations and exhibiting oily trace on scratching. Texture hard and fragile, outer layer of fracture brown and relatively rough, inner layer reddish-brown and oily, showing a yellowish-brown line between two layers.

桂通 呈双卷筒或单卷筒状。

Guitong Double or single tubular shape.

板桂 呈扁平的板状。外表面灰褐色，略粗糙，有的可见灰白色地衣斑；内表面稍显凹凸不平。质坚硬，油性少。

Bangui In flat shape. Outer surface greyish-brown, relatively rough, some showing greyish-white lichen spots; inner surface slightly uneven. Texture hard, less oily.

桂碎 呈大小不规则的片块状或短卷筒状。

Guisui Slice-shaped or lump-shaped with irregular size, or short tubular shape.

桂心 为刮去外皮者，表面红棕色。

Guixin The bark of which the cork is stripped off, with reddish-brown surface.

【化学成分 / Chemical constituent】

主含挥发油，油中主要成分为桂皮醛和醋酸桂皮酯，另含少量的苯甲醛、肉桂酸和水杨酸等；还含鞣质及黏液质等。

It mainly contains volatile oil with the dominant components of cinnamic aldehyde and cinnamyl acetate, and a small amount of benzonic aldehyde, cinnamic acid and salicylic acid. It also contains tannins and mucilage, etc.

【检查 / Examination】

水分不得过 15.0%。总灰分不得过 5.0%。

Water, not more than 15.0%. Total ash, not more than 5.0%.

【质量要求 / Quality requirement】

外观质量 以大小整齐、不破碎、皮细而质坚实、质厚而沉重、断面紫红色、油性足、香气浓厚、味甜辣、嚼之无渣者为佳。

Appearance quality Good quality for regular size, no broken pieces, fine surface, hard and thick texture, heavy weight, reddish-brown section, sufficient oil, strong aroma, sweet and pungent taste, and no residue when chewing.

内在质量 含量测定：按挥发油测定法测定，含挥发油不得少于 1.2%（ml/g）；按高效液相色谱法测定，含桂皮醛不得少于 1.5%。

Intrinsic quality Assay: It contains not less than 1.2% (ml/g) of volatile oil according to volatile oil determination method, and not less than 1.5% of cinnamic aldehyde according to HPLC analysis method.

【功能主治 / Function and indication】

大热，辛、甘。补火助阳，引火归元，散寒止痛，温经通脉。用于阳痿宫冷，腰膝冷痛，肾虚作喘，虚阳上浮，眩晕目赤，心腹冷痛，虚寒吐泻，寒疝腹痛，痛经经闭。

Highly hot, pungent and sweet. To tonify fire, assist yang, conduct fire back to its origin, dissipate cold, relieve pain, warm and unblock the meridians. For the treatment of impotence and uterine coldness, cold pain in the lower back and knees, wheezing caused by kidney deficiency, upfloating of deficiency yang, dizziness and red eyes, cold pain in the heart and abdomen, deficiency cold vomiting and diarrhea, abdominal pain caused by cold abdominal colic, dysmenorrhea and amenorrhea.

【贮藏养护 / Storage and maintenance】

用麻袋包装。本药材易失油润、干枯，应密封置阴凉处保存。

Packed in sacks. Easy to lose grease and be withered. Sealed and preserved in cool place.

【用法用量 / Administration and dosage】

1~5g。有出血倾向者及孕妇慎用；不宜与赤石脂同用。

1~5g. Use with caution during pregnancy and for patients prone to bleeding. Incompatible with Halloysitum Rubrum.

陈皮（Chenpi）| Citri Reticulatae Pericarpium（Dried Tangerine Peel）

【基原 / Origin】

为芸香科植物橘 *Citrus reticulata* Blanco 及其栽培变种的干燥成熟果皮。

Dried Tangerine Peel is the dried pericarp of the ripe fruit of *Citrus reticulata* Blanco or its cultivars (Fam. Rutaceae).

【产地 / Producing area】

主产于广东新会、四会、江门等地，习称“广陈皮”，质佳，产量小；主产于重庆江津、綦江，四川简阳等地，习称“陈皮”，产量较大。

It is mainly produced in Xinhui, Sihui and Jiangmen of Guangdong Province, which is known as “Guang Chenpi” with low yield and better quality. It is also mainly produced in Jiangjin and Qijiang of Chongqing Municipality, Jianyang of Sichuan Province, which is known as “Chenpi” with high yield.

【采制 / Collection and preparation】

陈皮 9~11 月果实成熟，剥取果皮，晒干或低温干燥，根据产地不同分为广陈皮和陈皮。

Dried Tangerine Peel The pericarp is peeled off when the fruit ripe in September to November, and dried in the sun or at a low temperature. The drug is subdivided into “Chenpi” and “Guang Chenpi”, according to producing area.

陈皮丝 取陈皮净药材，除去杂质，喷淋水，润透，切丝，干燥。

Slivers of Dried Tangerine Peel It is prepared from Dried Tangerine Peel by being removed from foreign matter, sprayed with water, softened thoroughly, cut into slivers and dried in shade.

【商品特征 / Commodity characteristics】

陈皮 剥成数瓣，基部相连，有的呈不规则块片状。外表面橙红色或红棕色，久贮颜色变深，有细皱纹及凹下的点状油室；内表面浅黄白色，粗糙，附黄白色或黄棕色筋络状维管束。对光照视之，油室大小不均，靠内侧。质稍硬而脆。气香，味辛、苦。

Chenpi Often peeled in several lobes connecting at base, or in irregular slices. Outer surface orange-red to reddish-brown, or deep color during long time storage, with fine wrinkles and concave and dotted oil cavity; inner surface pale yellowish-white, rough, bearing yellowish-white or yellowish-brown vein-like vascular bundles. The oil cavity irregular in size and near inner surface when observed against light. Texture slightly hard and fragile. Odor, aromatic; taste, pungent and bitter.

广陈皮 常三瓣相连（三花），翻卷，形状整齐，厚度均匀。外表面橙红色或红棕色，久贮颜色变深，内表面白色。点状油室大，对光照视，透明清晰，靠表层。质较柔软。气香，味辛、苦。

Guang Chenpi Often peeled in three lobes connecting at base, regular in shape and even in thickness. Outer surface orange-red or reddish-brown, or deep color during long time storage; inner surface whitish. The oil cavity relatively large, transparent and near outer surface when observed against light. Texture slightly soft. Odor, aromatic; taste, pungent and bitter.

陈皮丝 呈不规则条状或丝状。外表面橙红色或红棕色，有细皱纹和凹下的点状油室。内表面浅黄白色，粗糙，附黄白色或黄棕色筋络状维管束。气香，味辛、苦。

Slivers of Citri Reticulatae Pericarpium Irregular strips or slivers. Outer surface orange-red to reddish-brown, with fine wrinkles and concave and dotted oil cavity; inner surface pale yellowish-white, rough, bearing yellowish-white or yellowish-brown vein-like vascular bundles. Odor, aromatic; taste, pungent and bitter.

【规格等级 / Specification and grade】

商品上广陈皮分为三个等级，陈皮分为二个等级。其规格等级标准如下：

As commodity, Guang Chenpi is marketed by three grades and Chenpi is marketed by two grades. The specifications and grading criteria are as follows.

广陈皮 一等：剖成三至四瓣，裂瓣多向外反卷。表面橙红色或棕紫色，显皱缩，有无数大而凹入的油室。内表面白色、略呈海绵状。片张较厚。质柔，断面不齐。气清香浓郁，味微辛。无杂质、虫蛀、霉变、病斑。

Guang Chenpi First grade: Peeled in three to four lobes which usually roll outwards. Outer surface orange-red to brownish-purple, wrinkled, with numerous big and concave oil cavity. Inner surface whitish, slightly spongy. Peel thicker. Texture soft, fracture irregular. Odor, strongly aromatic; taste, slightly pungent. No foreign matter, nor moth, nor mildew, nor disease spot.

二等：剖成三至四瓣或不规则片张，裂瓣多向外反卷。表面橙红色或红棕色，有无数大而凹入的油室。内表面白色、较光洁。片张较薄。质较柔，断面不齐。气清香，味微苦辛。无杂质、虫蛀、霉变、病斑。

Second grade: Peeled in three to four lobes which usually roll outwards, or in irregular slices. Outer surface orange-red to reddish-brown, with numerous big and concave oil cavity. Inner surface whitish, smoother. Peel slightly thinner. Texture slightly soft, section irregular. Odor, aromatic; taste, slightly bitter, pungent. No foreign matter, nor moth, nor mildew, nor disease spot.

三等：剖成三至四瓣，裂瓣多向外反卷。表面红色或带有青色，有无数凹入的油室。内表面类白色。皮薄而片小。质坚而脆。有香气，味微辛、不甚苦。无杂质、虫蛀、霉变。

Third grade: Peeled in three to four lobes which usually roll outwards. Outer surface reddish or greenish, with numerous concave oil cavity. Inner surface off-white. Peel thin and small. Texture hard and fragile. Odor, aromatic; taste, slightly pungent, slightly bitter. No foreign matter, nor moth, nor mildew.

陈皮 一等：呈不规则片状，片张较大。表面橙红色或红黄色，有无数凹入的油点（鬃眼），对光照视清晰。内表面白黄色。质稍硬而脆，易折断。气香，味辛苦。无杂质、虫蛀、霉变、病斑。

Chenpi First grade: Irregular slices, relatively bigger. Outer surface orange-red or reddish-yellow, with numerous concave oil cavity (called "Zongyan") that is clear when observed against light. Inner surface yellowish-white. Texture slightly hard and fragile, easily broken. Odor, aromatic; taste, pungent and bitter. No foreign matter, nor moth, nor mildew, nor disease spot.

二等：呈不规则片状，片张较小，间有破块。表面黄褐色或黄红色。内表面类黄白色或灰黄色，较松泡。质硬而脆，易折断。气香，味微苦。无杂质、虫蛀、霉变、病斑。

Second grade: Irregular slices, relatively smaller or occasionally broken pieces. Outer surface yellowish-brown or yellowish-red. Inner surface yellowish-white or greyish-yellow, slightly loose. Texture hard and fragile, easily broken. Odor, aromatic; taste, slightly bitter. No foreign matter, nor moth, nor mildew, nor disease spot.

【化学成分 / Chemical constituent】

主含黄酮类，如橙皮苷、橘皮素、新橙皮苷等；还含挥发油，油中主要成分有右旋柠檬烯、柠檬醛、β- 月桂烯等；尚含辛弗林、β- 谷甾醇、肌醇等。

It mainly contains flavonoids, namely hesperidin, tangeretin, neohesperidin, etc. It also contains volatile oils, in which the main components are (+)-cinene, citral, β-myrcene, etc. It contains synephrine,

β-sitosterol, inositol, etc. as well.

【检查 / Examination】

水分不得过 13.0%。每 1kg 含黄曲霉毒素 B_1 不得过 5μg，含黄曲霉毒素 G_2、黄曲霉毒素 G_1、黄曲霉毒素 B_2 和黄曲霉毒素 B_1 总量不得过 10μg。

Water, not more than 13.0%. Aflatoxin B_1, not more than 5μg/kg; the sum of aflatoxin G_2, aflatoxin G_1, aflatoxin B_2 and aflatoxin B_1: not more than 10μg/kg.

【质量要求 / Quality requirement】

外观质量 以瓣大、完整、外皮色深红、内表面白色、肉厚油性大、香气浓郁者为佳。

Appearance quality Good quality for being big and unbroken, outer surface dark red, inner surface whitish, peel thick, oil sufficient and aroma strong.

内在质量 含量测定：按高效液相色谱法测定，陈皮药材含橙皮苷不得少于 3.5%，陈皮丝含橙皮苷不得少于 2.5%。

Intrinsic quality Assay: Dried Tangerine Peel contains not less than 3.5% of hesperidin and slivers of Dried Tangerine Peel contains not less than 2.5% of hesperidin, according to HPLC analysis method.

【功能主治 / Function and indication】

温，苦、辛。理气健脾，燥湿化痰。用于脘腹胀满，食少吐泻，咳嗽痰多。

Warm, bitter and pungent. To regulate *qi*, fortify the spleen, dry dampness and resolve phlegm. For the treatment of distention and fullness in the epigastrium and abdomen, reduced food intake with vomiting and diarrhea, cough and profuse sputum.

【贮藏养护 / Storage and maintenance】

用麻袋包装。应防潮、防热，置阴凉干燥处保存。如发现包内发热，应摊晾，忌暴晒，以免有损香气。

Packed in sacks. Preserved in cool and dry place, and protected from moisture and heat. If it is found that the sack is hot inside, the medicinal material should be spread and dried in the air, and avoiding exposure to the sun, so as not to damage the fragrance.

【用法用量 / Administration and dosage】

3~10g。

3~10g.

金钱白花蛇 (Jinqianbaihuashe) ¦ Bungarus Parvus (Coin-like White-banded Snake)

【基原 / Origin】

为眼镜蛇科动物银环蛇 *Bungarus multicinctus* Blyth 的幼蛇干燥体。

Coin-like White-banded Snake is the dried body of *Bungarus multicinctus* Blyth. (Fam. Elapidae).

【产地 / Producing area】

主产于广西百色、田东、都安、龙津及广东揭阳、普宁等地。现江西、河南等地有家养。以广东、广西产者著名。

It is mainly produced in Baise, Tiandong, Du'an and Longjin of Guangxi Province; Jieyang and Puning of Guangdong Province. Nowadays it is domesticated in Jiangxi Province and Henan Province. Those produced in Guangdong and Guangxi are famous.

【采制 / Collection and preparation】

夏、秋两季捕捉后，剖腹去内脏，洗净，放入乙醇中浸 3 天，以头为中心盘成圆形，尾含于口中，用竹签横穿固定，晒干或烘干。

Collected in summer or autumn, opened in the abdomen, removed from the viscera, cleaned, immersed in ethanol for three days, coiled up in disc shape with tail in mouth, fixed with a bamboo slip, and dried.

【商品特征 / Commodity characteristics】

呈圆盘状。头盘在中间，尾细，常纳口内，口腔内上颌骨前端有毒沟牙一对，鼻间鳞2片，无颊鳞，上下唇鳞通常各7片。背部黑色或灰黑色，具白色环纹；白环纹在背部宽1~2行鳞片，向腹部增宽；黑环纹宽3~5行鳞片；背正中明显突起一条脊棱，脊鳞扩大呈六角形，背鳞细密；尾下鳞单行。气微腥，味微咸。

Disc-shaped. Head located in the center of disc; tail slender, usually inserted into the mouth; 1 pair of poisonous grooved fangs on the anterior end of maxilla in mouth, 2 internasals, loreal absent, upper and lower labials usually 7 respectively. Dorsum black or greyish-black, with white annulations; the white rings 1~2 scales wide on the back, gradually widened towards the venter, and the black rings 3-5 scales wide. A median vertebral ridge raising distinctly. Scales on the vertebral ridge enlarged into hexagonal; dorsal scales small and dense; subcaudals single row. Odor, slightly stinking; taste, slightly salty.

【规格等级 / Specification and grade】

商品分为大条（盘径为10~15cm）、中条（盘径6~7cm）、小条（盘径3~3.5cm）三种规格。

As commodity, it is marketed by three specifications of big disc (10~15cm in disc diameter), middle disc (6~7cm in disc diameter) and small disc (3~3.5cm in disc diameter).

【化学成分 / Chemical constituent】

主含蛋白质，脂肪，鸟嘌呤核苷。头部毒腺含三磷酸腺苷酶等酶类、蛇毒及神经生长因子等。

It mainly contains proteins, fats and guanosine hydrates. Poison gland in the head includes enzymes such as adenosine triphosphatase, ophidic toxin and nerve growth factor.

【质量要求 / Quality requirement】

外观质量 以身干、头尾俱全，花纹明亮、鳞片有光泽、肉黄白色、盘径小、不臭者为佳。

Appearance quality Good quality for being dry and intact with head and tail, annulations clear and bright, scales lustrous, meat yellowish-white, disc small and not smelly.

内在质量 浸出物含量：醇溶性浸出物（热）不得少于15.0%。

Intrinsic quality Extract content: not less than 15.0% of ethanol-soluble extractives (hot).

【功能主治 / Function and indication】

温，甘、咸；有毒。祛风，通络，止痉。用于风湿麻痹，麻木拘挛，中风口眼㖞斜，半身不遂，抽搐痉挛，破伤风，麻风，疥癣。

Warm, sweet and salty; toxic. To dispel wind, unblock the collaterals, and arrest convulsions. For the treatment of wind-dampness protracted *bi* disorder, numbness and spasm, deviated eye and mouth caused by wind-stroke, hemiplegia, convulsions, tetanus, leprosy, scabies and tinea.

【贮藏养护 / Storage and maintenance】

本品置石灰缸内，宜在30℃以下保存。与花椒同放以防虫蛀。

Preserved in crock with calcium lime inner at the temperature of under 30 ℃. Or preserved together with pepper to prevent moth.

【用法用量 / Administration and dosage】

2~5g。研末吞服1~1.5g。

2~5g. It can be ground into powder for oral administration, 1~1.5g.

砂仁 (Sharen) ¦ Amomi Fructus (Villous Amomum Fruit)

【基原 / Origin】

为姜科植物阳春砂 *Amomum villosum* Lour.、绿壳砂 *Amomum villosum* Lour. var. *xanthioides* T. L. Wu et Senjen 或海南砂 *Amomum longiligulare* T. L. Wu 的干燥成熟果实。

Villous Amomum Fruit is the dried ripe fruit of *Amomum villosum* Lour., *Amomum villosum* Lour. var. *xanthioides* T. L. Wu et Senjen or *Amomum longiligulare* T. L. Wu. (Fam. Zingiberaceae).

【产地 / Producing area】

阳春砂主产于广东省，以阳春、阳江出产者最为有名；绿壳砂主产于云南南部临沧、文山、景洪等地；海南砂主产于海南澄迈、崖县等地。习惯认为产于广东阳春县的阳春砂品质最优。

Amomum villosum grows mainly in Guangdong Province, with those produced in Yangchun and Yangjiang best known; *Amomum villosum* var. *xanthioides* grows chiefly in south of Yunnan Province, such as Lincang, Wenshan, Jinghong, etc.; *Amomum longiligulare* grows primarily in Chengmai and Yaxian of Hainan Province. *Amomum villosum* produced in Yangchun usually has the best quality.

【采制 / Collection and preparation】

砂仁 8~9 月果实成熟时采收，将果穗放于筛中或竹席上用微火烘至半干时，趁热喷冷水 1 次，令其骤然收缩，使果皮和种子紧密结合，保存时不易发霉。也可将果实直接晒干而成。

Villous Amomum Fruit The drug is collected when the fruits ripe in August to September, the infructescence is put in sieve or on bamboo mat, heated with low flame until semi-dry, immediately sprayed with cold water once to make the fruit contracted suddenly with the pericarp and seeds clinging closely, and seldom mildewing during preservation. Or the fruit is dried directly in the sun.

净砂 为砂仁除去果皮的种子团。

Villous Amomum Seeds masses Derived from Villous Amomum Fruit by removed from the pericarp.

【商品特征 / Commodity characteristics】

阳春砂、绿壳砂 呈椭圆形或卵圆形，有不明显的三棱。表面棕褐色，密生刺状突起，顶端有花被残基，基部常带果梗。果皮薄而软。种子集结成团，具三钝棱，中有白色隔膜，将种子团分为 3 瓣。种子为不规则多面体；表面棕红色或暗褐色，有细皱纹，外被淡棕色膜质假种皮；质硬，胚乳灰白色。气芳香而浓烈，味辛凉、微苦。

Fruit of *Amomum villosum* and *Amomum villosum* var. *xanthioides* Ellipsoidal or ovoid, indistinctly 3-ridged. Externally dark brown, densely covered with spiny protrudings, apex with remains of perianth, and base often bearing a fruit stalk. Pericarp thin and soft. Seeds agglutinated into a mass, 3-ridged obtusely, divided into 3 groups by white septa. Seeds irregularly polyhedral; externally brownish-red or dark brown, finely wrinkled, covered with pale brown membranous aril; texture hard, endosperm greyish-white. Odour, strongly aromatic; taste, pungent, cool and slightly bitter.

海南砂 呈长椭圆形或卵圆形，有明显的三棱。表面被片状、分枝状软刺，基部具果梗痕。果皮厚而硬。种子团较小。气味稍淡。

Fruit of *Amomum longiligulare* Long ellipsoidal or ovoid, distinctly 3-ridged. Surface with flaky and branched soft spines, base showing a scar of fruit stalk. Pericarp thickened and hard. Masses of seeds relatively small. Odour and taste slightly weak.

净砂 种子团呈钝三棱状的椭圆形或卵形，分成 3 瓣。每瓣约有种子 10 数粒，籽粒饱满，表面灰褐色，破开后，内部灰白色。味辛凉微辣。

Villous Amomum Seeds masses Obtusely and triangularly ellipsoidal or ovoid, divided into 3 groups, and each group containing about more than 10 seeds. Seeds full, externally greyish-brown, internally greyish-white when broken. Taste, pungent, cool and slightly spicy.

砂壳 为砂仁剥下的果皮。呈瓢形或压缩成片状。表面红棕色、棕褐色或绿褐色，有许多短柔刺；内表面光洁，色泽较淡。气微、味淡。

Villous Amomum Pericarp It is the pericarp of Villous Amomum Fruit. Ellipsoidal halves or compressed flaky slices. Outer surface reddish-brown, dark brown or greenish-brown, with numerous short and soft spines; inner surface smooth and clean, palely colored. Odour, slight; taste, weak.

【规格等级 / Specification and grade】

按来源将砂仁分为阳春砂、绿壳砂和海南砂三种规格，绿壳砂和海南砂因除去果皮的加工方法又可分为砂壳和净砂。阳春砂、绿壳砂、海南砂及砂壳均为统货，净砂的等级标准如下。

Villous Amomum Fruit is divided into three specifications of Fruit of *Amomum villosum*, Fruit of *Amomum villosum* var. *xanthioides* and Fruit of *Amomum longiligulare*, according to its origin. Fruit of *Amomum villosum* var. *xanthioides* and Fruit of *Amomum longiligulare* are marketed by two more specifications of Villous Amomum Pericarp and Villous Amomum seeds masses, due to the processing of removing pericarp. The former four specifications are marketed by unified grade with the same price. The grading criteria of Villous Amomum seeds masses is as following.

一等：种子团完整。每 50g 150 粒以内。无糖子、果壳、杂质、霉变。

First grade: Seeds masses intact. There are less than 150 seeds in per 50g. No spoiled seeds masses, nor pericarp, nor foreign matter, nor mildew.

二等：形状气味与一等相同，唯种子团较小而瘪瘦。每 50g 150 粒以外，间有糖子。无果壳、杂质、霉变。

Second grade: Identical with First grade in shape, odour and taste, the seeds masses are smaller and shrunken. There are more than 150 seeds in per 50g, occasionally spoiled seeds masses. No pericarp, nor foreign matter, nor mildew.

【化学成分 / Chemical constituent】

主含挥发油，油中主要有乙酸龙脑酯、龙脑、芳樟醇等；还含皂苷及锌、铁、锰、铜等。

It mainly contains volatile oil, the chief components thereof are bornyl acetate, borneol and linalool, etc. It also contains saponins, Zn, Fe, Mn and Cu, etc.

【检查 / Examination】

水分不得过 15.0%。

Water, not more than 15.0%.

【质量要求 / Quality requirement】

外观质量 以个大、坚实、仁饱满、香气浓者为佳。

Appearance quality Good quality for big size, compact texture, full seeds, and strong aroma.

内在质量 含量测定：按挥发油测定法测定，阳春砂、绿壳砂种子团含挥发油不得少于 3.0%（ml/g）；海南砂种子团含挥发油不得少于 1.0%（ml/g）。按气相色谱法测定，含乙酸龙脑酯不得少于 0.90%。

Intrinsic quality Assay: The seeds masses of *Amomum villosum* and *Amomum villosum* var. *Xanthioides* contain not less than 3.0% (ml/g) of volatile oil, while the seeds masses of *Amomum longiligulare* contain not less than 1.0% (ml/g), according to volatile oil determination method. Amomi

Fructus contains not less than 0.90% of bornyl acetate according to GC analysis method.

【功能主治 / Function and indication】

温，辛。化湿开胃，温脾止泻，理气安胎。用于湿浊中阻，脘痞不饥，脾胃虚寒，呕吐泄泻，妊娠恶阻，胎动不安。

Warm; pungent. To resolve dampness, increase the appetite, warm the spleen, stop diarrhea, regulate *qi*, and prevent miscarriage. For the treatment of dampness-turbidity obstruction in the middle energizer, epigastric stuffiness, spleen-stomach deficiency cold, vomiting, diarrhea, morning sickness, and threatened miscarriage.

【贮藏养护 / Storage and maintenance】

用纸箱包装。密闭，置阴凉干燥处保存。忌暴晒和受热，以免泛油、散粒和走失香气。

Packed in cartons. Sealed and preserved in a cool and dry place. To avoid overexposure to the sun and heat, in case of external diffusion of oil, scattering of seeds and loss of fragrance.

【用法用量 / Administration and dosage】

3~6g。后下。

3~6g, added when the decoction is nearly done.

重点小结
Summary

药材	主产地	规格等级	质量要求
肉桂	主产于广东、广西等地	根据采收加工方法不同，分为企边桂、桂通、板桂、桂碎和桂心等规格，企边桂质佳。暂无全国统一的等级标准	以大小整齐、不破碎、皮细而质坚实、质厚而沉重、断面紫红色、油性足、香气浓厚、味甜辣、嚼之无渣者为佳。含挥发油不得少于1.2%（ml/g）；含桂皮醛不得少于1.5%
陈皮	主产于广东新会、四会、江门等地，习称"广陈皮"；主产于重庆江津、綦江，四川简阳等地，习称"陈皮"	广陈皮和陈皮均依据表面颜色、片张的厚薄、片张的大小、质地是否柔软等方面分别分为三个等级和两个等级	以瓣大、完整、外皮色深红、内表面白色、肉厚油性大、香气浓郁者为佳。陈皮药材含橙皮苷不得少于3.5%，陈皮丝含橙皮苷不得少于2.5%
金钱白花蛇	主产于广西百色、田东、都安、龙津及广东揭阳、普宁等地	根据盘径大小分为大条、中条、小条三种规格	以身干、头尾俱全，花纹明亮、鳞片有光泽、肉黄白色、盘径小、不臭者为佳。醇溶性浸出物（热）不得少于15.0%
砂仁	阳春砂主产于广东阳春、阳江；绿壳砂主产于云南临沧、文山、景洪等地；海南砂主产于海南澄迈、崖县等地。习惯认为产于广东阳春县的阳春砂品质最优	按来源将砂仁分为阳春砂、绿壳砂和海南砂三种规格，绿壳砂和海南砂因除去果皮的加工方法又可分为砂壳和净砂。阳春砂、绿壳砂、海南砂及砂壳均为统货，净砂根据50g的粒数分为2个等级	以个大、坚实、仁饱满、香气浓者为佳。阳春砂、绿壳砂种子团含挥发油不得少于3.0%（ml/g）；海南砂种子团含挥发油不得少于1.0%（ml/g）。含乙酸龙脑酯不得少于0.90%

Medicinal material	Main producing area	Specification and grade	Quality requirement
Cassia Bark	Main producing areas are Guangdong Province and Guangxi Province, etc.	According to the methods of collection and preparation, it is mainly divided into four specifications of Qibiangui, Guitong, Bangui, Guisui and Guixin. Qibiangui is of the best quality. Temporarily there is no nationally unified grade criteria	Good quality for regular size, no broken pieces, fine surface, hard and thick texture, heavy weight, reddish-brown section, sufficient oil, strong aroma, sweet and pungent taste, and no residue when chewing. It contains not less than 1.2% (ml/g) of volatile oil and not less than 1.5% of cinnamic aldehyde
Dried Tangerine Peel	Mainly produced in Xinhui, Sihui and Jiangmen of Guangdong Province, which is known as "Guang Chenpi". Also mainly produced in Jiangjin and Qijiang of Chongqing Municipality, Jianyang of Sichuan Province, which is known as "Chenpi"	Guang Chenpi and Chenpi are respectively marketed by three and two grades, according to surface color, slice thickness, slice size, texture soft or not, etc.	Good quality for being big and unbroken, outer surface dark red, inner surface whitish, peel thick, oil sufficient and aroma strong. Dried Tangerine Peel contains not less than 3.5% of hesperidin and Slivers of Dried Tangerine Peel not less than 2.5%
Coin-like White-banded Snake	Mainly produced in Baise, Tiandong, Du'an and Longjin of Guangxi Province; Jieyang and Puning of Guangdong Province	Marketed by three specifications of big disc, middle disc and small disc, according to the disc diameter	Good quality for being dry and intact, annulations clear and bright, scales lustrous, meat yellowish-white, disc small and not smelly. It contains not less than 15.0% of ethanol-soluble extractives (hot)
Villous Amomum Fruit	*Amomum villosum* grows mainly in Yangchun and Yangjiang of Guangdong Province; *Amomum villosum* var. *xanthioides* grows chiefly in south of Yunnan Province, such as Lincang, Wenshan, Jinghong; *Amomum longiligulare* grows primarily in Chengmai and Yaxian of Hainan Province. *Amomum villosum* produced in Yangchun is usually known to be of the best quality	According to origin, three specifications of Fruit of *Amomum villosum*, Fruit of *Amomum villosum* var. *xanthioides* and Fruit of *Amomum longiligulare* are divided. Fruit of *Amomum villosum* var. *xanthioides* and Fruit of *Amomum longiligulare* are marketed by two more specifications of Villous Amomum Pericarp and Villous Amomum seeds masses, due to the processing of removing pericarp. The former four specifications are marketed by unified grade with the same price. Villous Amomum seeds masses is marketed by two grades, according to the number of seeds masses in per 50g	Good quality for size big, texture compact, seeds full, and aroma strong. Seeds masses of *Amomum villosum* and *Amomum villosum* var. *Xanthioides* contain not less than 3.0% (ml/g) of volatile oil, and seeds masses of *Amomum longiligulare* contain not less than 1.0% (ml/g) of volatile oil. Amomi Fructus contains not less than 0.90% of bornyl acetate

题库

目标检测
Object Detection

一、选择题（Choice question）

（一）单项选择题（One-choice question）

1. 药典记载肉桂的商品来源为（　　）

A. 肉桂　树皮　　B. 肉桂　枝皮　　C. 肉桂　根皮

D. 肉桂　嫩枝　　E. 肉桂　根

Which choice is the origin of Cassia Bark, as recorded in Chinese Pharmacopeia (　　)

A. *Cinnamomum cassia*, Stem bark

B. *Cinnamomum cassia*, Branch bark

C. *Cinnamomum cassia*, Root bark

D. *Cinnamomum cassia*, Young branch

E. *Cinnamomum cassia*, root

2. 下列为剥取栽培 5~6 年后幼树的干皮和粗枝皮，或老树枝皮加工而成的是（　　）

A. 桂通　　B. 企边桂　　C. 板桂

D. 桂心　　E. 桂碎

Which commercial specification is removed from the bark and rough branch bark of cultivated trees about 5-6 years old, or from the branch bark of older trees (　　)

A. Guitong　　B. Qibiangui　　C. Bangui

D. Guixin　　E. Guisui

3. 下列为剥取老树最下部近地面的干皮加工而成的是（　　）

A. 桂通　　B. 企边桂　　C. 板桂

D. 桂心　　E. 桂碎

Which commercial specification is processed from the bark of the bottom parts of older trees (　　)

A. Guitong　　B. Qibiangui　　C. Bangui

D. Guixin　　E. Guisui

4. 下列为剥取 10 年生以上的干皮，将两端削成斜面，突出桂心加工而成的是（　　）

A. 桂通　　B. 企边桂　　C. 板桂

D. 桂心　　E. 桂碎

Which commercial specification is obtained from the bark of the trees more than ten years old and sliced obliquely at both ends to expose the “Guixin” (　　)

A. Guitong　　B. Qibiangui　　C. Bangui

D. Guixin　　E. Guisui

5. 陈皮为芸香科植物（　　）

A. 橘及其栽培变种的干燥未成熟果实

B. 橘及其栽培变种的干燥未成熟果皮

C. 橘及其栽培变种的干燥成熟果皮

D. 酸橙及其栽培变种的干燥成熟果皮
E. 酸橙及其栽培变种的干燥未成熟果实
Which choice correctly describes the origin of Dried Tangerine Peel ( )
A. The dried unripe fruit of *Citrus reticulata* Blanco or its cultivars
B. The dried pericarp of unripe fruit of *Citrus reticulata* Blanco or its cultivars
C. The dried pericarp of the ripe fruit of *Citrus reticulata* Blanco or its cultivars
D. The dried pericarp of ripe fruit of *Citrus aurantium* L. or its cultivars
E. The dried unripe fruit of *Citrus aurantium* L. or its cultivars

6. 关于广陈皮商品特征下面说法错误的是( )
A. 三瓣相连，裂瓣常翻卷 B. 外表橙红，内色白 C. 油室大而清晰，靠内侧
D. 质地柔软，香气浓郁 E. 味辛、苦
Which choice is wrong about the Commodity characteristics of Guang Chenpi ( )
A. Peeled in three to four lobes which usually roll outwards.
B. Outer surface orange-red, inner surface whitish.
C. The oil cavity relatively large, transparent and near inner surface.
D. Texture soft. Odor, strongly aromatic.
E. Taste, pungent and bitter.

7. 药材金钱白花蛇的原动物是( )
A. 五步蛇 B. 乌梢蛇 C. 银环蛇
D. 金环蛇 E. 赤链蛇
Which animal is the origin of Coin-like White-banded Snake ( )
A. *Agkistrodon acutus* B. *Zaocys dhumnades* C. *Bungarus multicinctus*
D. *Bungarus fasciatus* E. *Dinodon rufozonatum*

8. 金钱白花蛇以下列哪项划分规格等级( )
A. 外表颜色 B. 盘径大小 C. 每千克条数
D. 蛇体的粗细 E. 环纹的数量
Which choice is the grading criteria of Coin-like White-banded Snake ( )
A. Surface color of the drug
B. Disc size of the drug
C. The number of snake per kilogram
D. Diameter of the snake
E. The quantity of annulations

9. 金钱白花蛇宜与下列哪项共贮( )
A. 牡丹皮 B. 生姜 C. 花椒 D. 大蒜 E. 陈皮
Coin-like White-banded Snake is suitable to be preserved together with ( )
A. Tree Peony Bark (Moutan Cortex)
B. Ginger
C. Pepper
D. Garlic
E. Dried Tangerine Peel (Citri Reticulatae Pericarpium)

10. 习惯认为砂仁中品质最优的是( )
A. 阳春砂 B. 绿壳砂 C. 海南砂

D. 缩砂　　E. 红壳砂

With regard to Villosum Amomum Fruit, which is usually known to be of the best quality (　　)

A. Fruit of *Amomum villosum*

B. Fruit of *Amomum villosum* var. *xanthioides*

C. Fruit of *Amomum longiligulare*

D. Fruit of *Amomum villosum* var. *xanthioides produced aboard*

E. Fruit of *Amomum aurantiacum*

11. 以下为除去果皮的商品是(　　)

A. 阳春砂　　B. 绿壳砂　　C. 海南砂

D. 净砂　　E. 砂壳

Which commodity below is derived by removing from the pericarp (　　)

A. Fruit of *Amomum villosum*

B. Fruit of *Amomum villosum* var. *xanthioides*

C. Fruit of *Amomum longiligulare*

D. Villous Amomum Seeds masses

E. Villous Amomum Pericarp

(二)多项选择题(Multiple choice question)

1. 广药产区的道地药材有(　　)

A. 砂仁　　B. 广藿香　　C. 巴戟天

D. 肉桂　　E. 槟榔

Which are the Guang Authentic Medicinal Materials below (　　)

A. Villous Amomum Fruit　　B. Pogostemon Cablin Herb

C. Morinda Officinalis Root　　D. Cassia Bark

E. Areca Nut

2. 肉桂的商品规格有(　　)

A. 桂通　　B. 企边桂　　C. 板桂

D. 桂碎　　E. 桂枝

Which are the commercial specifications of Cassia Bark (　　)

A. Guitong　　B. Qibiangui　　C. Bangui

D. Guisui　　E. Cassia Twig

3. 肉桂主要含有哪些化学成分(　　)

A. 挥发油　　B. 桂皮醛　　C. 肉桂酸

D. 鞣质类　　E. 黏液质

Which are the main constituents of Cassia Bark (　　)

A. Volatile oil　　B. Cinnamic aldehyde　　C. Cinnamic acid

D. Tannis　　E. Mucilage

4. 以下哪些方面为陈皮与广陈皮商品特征的区别(　　)

A. 外表面的颜色　　B. 质地是否柔软　　C. 油室的位置

D. 气味是否浓郁　　E. 油室的大小

Which choices are the differences between the commodity characteristics of Chenpi and Guang Chenpi (　　)

A. Surface color　　B. Texture soft or not

C. Position of the oil cavity
D. Odour and taste strong or not
E. Size of the oil cavity

5. 关于金钱白花蛇的商品特征描述正确的是（　　）
A. 幼蛇盘成饼状
B. 尾下鳞单行
C. 黑体白环
D. 白环在背部宽只有 1~2 行鳞片
E. 背鳞呈五角形
Which choices correctly describe the commodity characteristics of Coin-like White-banded Snake (　　)
A. Derived from young snake and disc-shaped
B. Subcaudals single row
C. Dorsum black or greyish-black, with white annulations
D. the white rings 1-2 scales wide on the black
E. Scales on the vertebral ridge pentagonal

6. 药典中记载，砂仁的商品来源有（　　）
A. 阳春砂
B. 绿壳砂
C. 海南砂
D. 细砂仁
E. 红壳砂仁
Which choices are the origin of Villous Amomum Fruit, as recorded in Chinese Pharmacopeia (　　)
A. *Amomum villosum*
B. *Amomum villosum* var. *xanthioides*
C. *Amomum longiligulare*
D. *Amomum microcarpum*
E. *Amomum aurantiacum*

7. 砂仁的商品规格有（　　）
A. 阳春砂
B. 绿壳砂
C. 海南砂
D. 净砂
E. 砂壳
Which are the commercial specifications of Villous Amomum Fruit (　　)
A. Fruit of *Amomum villosum*
B. Fruit of *Amomum villosum* var. *xanthioides*
C. Fruit of *Amomum longiligulare*
D. Villous Amomum Seeds masses
E. Villous Amomum Pericarp

二、思考题（Thinking question）

1. 广药产区的气候环境特点如何？
How about the climate and environment characteristics of producing areas of Guang Medicinal Materials?
2. 如何评价肉桂的质量？
How to evaluate the quality of Cassia Bark?
3. 如何评价陈皮的质量？
How to evaluate the quality of Dried Tangerine Peel?
4. 如何评价金钱白花蛇的质量？
How to evaluate the quality of Coin-like White-banded Snake?
5. 如何评价砂仁的质量？
How to evaluate the quality of Villous Amomum Fruit?

PPT

第十章 云 药

Chapter 10 Yun Medicinal Materials

学习目标 | Learning Target

知识要求：

1．**掌握** 云药的含义及其主要道地药材品种；三七、木香、茯苓的道地产地、规格等级、商品特征、贮藏方法等内容。

2．**熟悉** 三七、木香、茯苓的化学成分、质量要求、检查等内容。

3．**了解** 云药产区的自然环境条件。

能力要求：

学会依据规格等级、商品特征、检查、质量要求等知识和方法鉴别市场上三七、木香、茯苓的真伪优劣。

Knowledge requirements:

1. **Proficiency** The meaning and major varieties of Yun Medicinal Materials. The authentic producing areas, specifications and grades, commodity characteristics and storage methods of Notoginseng Radix et Rhizoma, Aucklandiae Radix and Poria.

2. **Familiarity** The chemical constituents, quality requirements and examinations of Notoginseng Radix et Rhizoma, Aucklandiae Radix and Poria.

3. **Understanding** Natural environment in producing area of Yun Medicinal Materials.

Skill requirements:

Learn to identify the authenticity and evaluate the quality of Notoginseng Radix et Rhizoma, Aucklandiae Radix and Poria on the market according to the knowledge and methods of specification and grade, commodity characteristics, examination and quality requirement, etc.

一、云药概述

I. Overview of Yun Medicinal Materials

以云南及西藏南部为主要产区或集散地的大宗商品药材，称为云药。其产区位于东经97° 32′~106° 12′，北纬21° 8′~29° 15′之间，年均降水量600~2300mm，年平均气温4℃~24℃。地理及气候条件十分复杂，气候类型有北热带、南亚热带、中亚热带、北亚热带、南温带、中温带和高原气候区共7个气候类型，因此，有"一山分四季，十里不同天"的"立体气候"特点。形成了丰富的天然药物资源产区，主要包括滇南和滇北两大区。滇西北为横断山区，适宜云茯苓、云木香等生长。雪线以上地区亦盛产冬虫夏草等药材。滇南是我国少有的静风区，出产诃子、槟榔、儿茶等。最南端的勐腊县，适宜胡椒、肉桂等的栽培。处于滇南、滇北之间的文山、思茅地区以盛产三七闻名于世。藏南谷地是藏药的主要产地。主要道地药材有冬虫夏草、灵芝、滇重楼、雪莲花等。

The bulk commodity of medicinal materials with Yunnan and southern Tibet as the main production areas or distribution centers are called Yun Medicinal Materials. The production areas are located between 97° 32′~106° 12′ E and 21° 8′~29° 15′ N, with an average annual precipitation of 600-2300mm and an average temperature of 4~24℃. The geographical and climatic conditions are very complex including 7 climatic types: the north tropics, south subtropics, middle subtropics, north subtropics, south temperate zone, middle temperate zone and plateau. Therefore, it features in a "three-dimensional climate" of "one mountain with four seasons, different weathers within ten miles". Producing areas with abundant natural drug resource have been formed, mainly including two large districts: Southern and Northern Yunnan. Northwestern Yunnan, the Hengduan Mountain area, is suitable for the growth of Yun Aucklandiae Radix and Yun Poria. Cordyceps and other medicinal materials are also abundant in areas above the snow line. Southern Yunnan is a rare quiet-wind area in China, where Myrobalan, Areca, Catechu, etc. are produced. Mengla county, the end of southern Yunnan, is suitable for the cultivation of Piperis Fructus, Cinnamomic Cortex, etc. Areas of Wenshan and Simao, which are located between the Southern and the Northern of Yunnan, are famous for high quality production of Notoginseng Radix at Rhizoma. Zangnangudi is the main producing area of Tibetan medicines. The major authentic medicinal materials are Cordyceps, Ganoderma, Paridis Rhizoma, Saussureae Medusae Herba, etc.

二、药材品种
II. Varieties of Medicinal Materials

三七 (Sanqi) ¦ Notoginseng Radix et Rhizoma (Sanchi)

【基原 / Origin】

为五加科植物三七 *Panax notoginseng*（Burk.）F. H. Chen 的干燥根和根茎。

Sanchi is the dried root and rhizome of *Panax notoginseng* (Burk.) F. H. Chen (Fam. Araliaceae).

【产地 / Producing area】

主产于云南文山、砚山、广南、马关、西畴、邱北、富宁，广西靖西、睦边、百色等地。

Main producing areas are Wenshan, Yanshan, Guangnan, Maguan, Xichou, Qiubei, Funing of Yunnan Province, Jingxi, Mubian, Baise, etc. in Guangxi Province.

【采制 / Collection and preparation】

种植三年后即可采收，开花前挖取的习称"春三七"，摘除果实后采收的习称"冬三七"，采收后除茎叶、杂质，剪下芦头、侧根及须根，曝晒至半干，反复揉搓以后，边晒边搓，直至全干，放入麻袋内撞至表面光滑即得。剪下的芦头称"剪口"，较粗支根称"筋条"，细小支根及须根称"绒根"。取三七药材，洗净，干燥，碾成细粉，为三七粉。

Sanchi is collected after three-year planting. The ones, collected before flowering, are commonly known as "Chunsanqi"; the ones, collected after removing fruits, are commonly known as "Dongsanqi". It is obtained by removing stems, leaves and foreign matter, cutting off rhizomes, branch roots and fibrous roots, drying partly, and rubbing repeatedly as dried in the sun until fully drying. Strike to smooth surface in jute bag. The rhizome is known as "Jiankou", the branch root is known as "Jintiao" and the fibrous root is known as "Ronggen". Take Sanchi, wash clean and dry it, grind it into fine powder, which is Sanchi Powder.

【商品特征 / Commodity characteristics】

春三七 有瘤头，身短，铜皮，铁心，体重质坚，击碎后皮部与木部常分离，先苦后甜。

Chunsanqi Bearing knot-like tubercles, short main root, copper-like skin, iron-like core, texture hard and heavy. After being crushed, the bark and xylem mostly separated, taste first bitter and then sweet.

冬三七 主根与春三七类似，唯表面灰黄色，有皱纹或抽沟。断面黄绿色。不饱满，体稍轻。

Dongsanqi The main root is similar to Chunsanqi, and the surface is greyish-yellow, wrinkled or grooved. Fracture is yellowish-green, not plump, slightly light.

剪口 不规则皱缩小块或条状，表面灰黄色或暗棕色。有数个明显的茎痕和环纹。断面中心灰绿色或灰白色，边缘深绿色或灰色。

Jiankou Irregularly shrunken lump-shaped or slat-shaped, surface greyish-yellow or dark brown, externally with several conspicuous stem scars and annulations; fracture is greyish-green or greyish-white in the center and deep green or grey at the margin.

筋条 为圆柱形或圆锥形，上粗下细。表面灰黄色，断面灰绿色或黄绿色。

Jintiao Cylindrical or conical, thick in the upper part and thin in lower part. The surface is greyish-yellow, and fracture is greyish-green or yellowish-green.

绒根 细小圆柱形，弯曲，常缠绕成团。

Ronggen It is thin, cylindrical, bent and often twined into a mass.

三七粉 为灰白色或黄色粉末。气微，味微苦而后甜。

Sanqi Powder The powder is greyish-white or yellow colour. With tiny odor, the taste is bitter and sweet.

【规格等级 / Specification and grade】

按采收时间不同分为春三七、冬三七两种规格，再按每 kg 的头数分等。

According to the different harvest time, it can be divided into two specifications, Chunsanqi and Dongsanqi, and then graded according to the numbers of roots in per kg.

春三七等级标准为：

The grade criteria of Chunsanqi are as follows:

一等：呈圆锥形或类圆柱形。表面灰黄色或黄褐色。质坚实、体重。断面灰褐色。味苦微甜。每 kg 在 40 头以内。长不超过 6cm。

First Grade: Conical or cylindrical. The surface is greyish-yellow or yellowish-brown, with hard texture and heavy weight. The fracture is greyish-brown. The taste is bitter and slightly sweet. Less than 40 main roots in per kg, not more than 6cm in length.

二等：每 kg 在 60 头以内。其余同一等。

Second Grade: Less than 60 main roots in per kg. Other characteristics are the same to those of First grade.

三等：每 kg 在 80 头以内，长不超过 5cm。其余同一等。

Third Grade: Less than 80 main roots in per kg, not more than 5cm in length. Other characteristics are the same to those of First grade.

四等：每 kg 在 120 头以内，长不超过 4cm。其余同一等。

Fourth Grade: Less than 120 main roots in per kg, not more than 4cm in length. Other characteristics are the same to those of First grade.

五等：每 kg 在 160 头以内，长不超过 3cm。其余同一等。

Fifth Grade: Less than 160 main roots in per kg, not more than 3cm in length. Other characteristics are the same to those of First grade.

六等：每 kg 在 240 头以内，长不超过 2.5cm。其余同一等。

Sixth Grade: Less than 240 main roots in per kg, not more than 2.5cm in length. Other characteristics are the same to those of First grade.

七等：每 kg 在 320 头以内，长不超过 2cm。其余同一等。

Seventh Grade: Less than 320 main roots in per kg, not more than 2cm in length. Other characteristics are the same to those of First grade.

八等：每 kg 在 400 头以内，其余同七等。

Eighth Grade: Less than 400 main roots in per kg. Other characteristics are the same to those of Seventh grade.

九等：每 kg 在 500 头以内，长不超过 1.5cm。其余同一等。

Ninth Grade: Less than 500 main roots in per kg, not more than 1.5cm in length. Other characteristics are the same to those of First grade.

十等：每 kg 在 600 头以内，其余同九等。

Tenth Grade: Less than 600 main roots in per kg, the other characteristics are the same to those of Ninth grade.

十一等：每 kg 在 900 头以内，其余同十等。

Eleventh Grade: Less than 900 main roots in per kg, the other characteristics are the same to those of Tenth grade.

十二等（筋条）：间有从主根上剪下的细支根（筋条）。不分春、冬七。每 kg 在 900~1200 头以内，支根上端直径不低于 0.8cm，下端直径不低于 0.5cm。其余同十一等。

Twelfth Grade (Jintiao): Occasionally thin branch roots (Jintiao) cut from the main root. Indiscrimination of Chunsanqi or Dongsanqi. Less than 900-1200 roots in per kg with the diameter of the upper end of the branch root is not less than 0.8cm, and the diameter of the lower end is not less than 0.5cm. Other characteristics are the same to those of Eleventh grade.

十三等（剪口）：不分春、冬七。主要是三七的芦头（羊肠头）及糊七（内部未烤焦的）。

Thirteenth Grade (Jiankou): Indiscrimination of Chunsanqi or Dongsanqi. It is mainly composed of the rhizome (Yangchangtou) and Huqi (the internal part not burnt).

此外，三七细小的支根及须根，商品上称绒根。

In addition, small branch roots and fibrous roots of sanchi are known as Ronggen.

冬三七　各等头数与春三七相同。

The Dongsanqi: main root of mumbers different grades are the same to those of Chunsanqi.

【化学成分 / Chemical constituent】

含多种皂苷，主要为达玛脂烷型皂苷，有人参皂苷 Rb_1、Rb_2、Rc、Rd、Re、Rg_1、Rg_2、Rh_1 及三七皂苷 R_1、R_2、R_3、R_4、R_6、Fa、K。另含田七氨酸、三七黄酮 B 及槲皮素等成分。尚含挥发油、微量元素及氨基酸。

It contains a variety of saponins, mainly dammarane type saponins, including ginsenoside Rb_1, Rb_2, Rc, Rd, Re, Rg_1, Rg_2, Rh_1 and notoginsenoside R_1, R_2, R_3, R_4, R_6, Fa, K. In addition, it contains dencichine, notoginseng flavone B and quercetin. It also contains volatile oil, trace elements and amino acids.

【检查 / Examination】

水分不得过 14.0%。总灰分不得过 6.0%；酸不溶性灰分不得过 3.0%。

Water, not more than 14.0 %. Total ash, not more than 6.0 %. Acid-insoluble ash, not more than 3.0 %.

【质量要求 / Quality requirement】

外观质量　均以个大、体重、质坚、表面光滑、断面灰绿色或黄绿色者为佳。

Appearance Quality　Good quality for big and heavy body, hard texture, smooth surface and grey-green or yellowish-green fracture.

内在质量　浸出物含量：甲醇浸出物（热）不到少于 16.0%。含量测定：按高效液相色谱法测定，人参皂苷 Rg_1、人参皂苷 Rb_1 及三七皂苷 R_1 的总量不得少于 5.0%。

Intrinsic Quality　Extract content: not less than 16.0% of methanol-soluble extractives (hot).

Assay: It contains not less than 5.0% of the total amount of Ginsenoside Rg_1, ginsenoside Rb_1 and notoginsenoside R_1 according to HPLC analysis method.

【功能主治 / Function and indication】

温，甘、微苦。散瘀止血，消肿定痛。用于咯血，吐血，衄血，便血，崩漏。外伤出血，胸腹刺痛，跌扑肿痛。

Warm, sweet and mild bitter. Disperse stasis, stanch bleeding, disperse swelling and relieve pain. It is used for hemoptysis, hematemesis, epistaxis, hematochezia, menstrual flooding and spotting, traumatic bleeding, stabbing pain in chest and abdomen, and swelling and pain caused by traumatic injuries.

【贮藏养护 / Storage and maintenance】

用硬纸盒或木箱包装，内衬防潮纸。置于阴凉干燥处密封保存。

Packed in cardboard box or wooden case, internally lined with moisture-proof paper. Stored in a cool and dry place and sealed.

【用法用量 / Administration and dosage】

3~9g；研粉吞服 1~3g。外用适量。

3~9g; Ground into powder for oral administration, 1~3g. Appropriate amount for topical application.

木香 (Muxiang) ⋮ Aucklandiae Radix (Common Aucklandia Root)

【基原 / Origin】

为菊科植物木香 *Aucklandia lappa* Decne. 的干燥根。

Common *Aucklandia* Root is the dried root of *Aucklandia lappa* Decne. (Fam. Compositae).

【产地 / Producing area】

木香过去由印度、缅甸等地经广州进口，故称“广木香”。现主产云南丽江地区和迪庆州，又称“云木香”。此外，四川、湖北、湖南、广东、广西、陕西、甘肃、西藏等省区亦有产。

Aucklandiae Radix was previously imported from India and Burma through Guangzhou, known as “Guangmuxiang”. Now it is mainly produced in Lijiang region and Diqing Prefecture of Yunnan Province, and known as “Yunmuxiang”. In addition, it is also produced in Sichuan, Hubei, Hunan, Guangdong, Guangxi, Shaanxi, Gansu Provinces and Tibet Autonomous Region, etc.

【采制 / Collection and preparation】

一般于霜降前采挖种植 2~3 年的根，除去茎叶、须根及泥土。根切成 6~12cm 长的短条，粗大者剖为 2~4 块，晒干或阴干。猛火烘易出油而影响质量。

Aucklandiae Radix　Roots, planted for 2~3 years, are usually collected before Frost’s Descent, removed from stems, leaves, fibrous roots and soil; cut into 6~12cm short strips or 2~4 lumps for the thick ones, dried in the sun or in the shade. It is easy to exudate oil and affect the quality when baked with high fire.

经切制或煨制可制成木香片和煨木香。

Aucklandiae Radix is processed to slices by cutting, or to roasted slices by heating the slices wraped with oil-absorbing paper.

【商品特征 / Commodity characteristics】

木香 圆柱形或半圆柱形，灰棕色，表面可见菱形网纹，体重质坚，断面菊花心，油性大、香气浓，味苦辛。

Aucklandiae Radix Cylindrical or semicylindrical, externally greyish-brown, with rhombic reticular veins. Heavy weight and hard texture, cross-section obvious radiate striations and fissures (like the radiate center of chrysanthemum), oily. Odour, strongly aromatic, taste, bitter and pungent.

木香片 类圆形或不规则的厚片。周边外皮显黄棕色至灰褐色，有纵皱纹。切面显灰褐色或棕黄色，中部有明显菊花心状的放射纹理，间有暗褐色或灰褐色环纹，褐色油点（油室）散在，质坚。有特异香气，味苦。

Aucklandiae Radix slice In Subrounded or irregular thick slices. Externally yellowish-brown to greyish-brown with longitudinal wrinkles. Cut surface greyish-brown or brownish-yellow, the center marked with obvious chrysanthemum-like radial lines, occasionally cambium ring in dark-brown or greyish-brown colour, and brown oil spots (oil cavities) scattered, texture hard. Odour, characteristic aromatic; taste, bitter.

煨木香 如木香片。气微香，味微苦。

***Aucklandiae Radix* Roasted** Similar to *Aucklandiae Radix slice*. Odour, slightly aromatic; taste, slightly bitter.

【规格等级 / Specification and grade】

按大小将木香药材商品分为两等，其等级标准为：

According to the size, Aucklandiae Radix is divided into two grades, and the grade criteria are as follows:

一等：干货，呈圆柱形或半圆柱形。表面棕黄色或灰棕色。体实。断面黄棕色或黄绿色，具油性。气香浓，味苦而辣。根条均匀，长 8~12cm，最细的一端直径在 2cm 以上。不空、不泡、不朽。无芦头、根尾、焦枯、油条、杂质、虫蛀、霉变。

First grade: Dry roots, cylindrical or semi-cylindrical. Surface brownish-yellow or greyish-brown. Texture hard. Fracture yellowish-brown or yellowish-green, oily. Odour, strong aromatic. Taste, bitter and spicy. The roots are uniform, 8~12cm long, and the diameter of the thinnest end is more than 2cm. No hollow, nor loose, nor decayed. No rhizome, nor rootlets, nor scorched and oily roots. No foreign matter, nor moth, nor mildew.

二等：干货，呈不规则的条状或块状。表面棕黄色或灰棕色。体实。断面黄棕色或黄绿色。具油性。气香浓，味苦而辣。长 3~10cm，最细的一端直径在 0.8cm 以上。间有根头根尾、碎节、破块。无须根、枯焦、杂质、虫蛀、霉变。

Second grade: Dry roots, in irregular strips or lumps. Externally brownish-yellow or greyish-brown. Texture hard. Section yellowish-brown or yellowish-green, oily. Odour, aromatic; taste, bitter and spicy. The length is 3~10cm, and the diameter of the thinnest end is more than 0.8cm. Occasionally there are rhizomes, rootlets, broken knots and broken pieces. No fibrous roots, nor scorch, nor foreign matter, nor moth, nor mildew.

【化学成分 / Chemical constituent】

含挥发油，油中主要成分为去氢木香内酯、木香烃内酯、木香内酯、二氢木香内酯等。尚含 α- 及 β- 环木香烯内酯、豆甾醇、棕榈酸、天台乌药酸等。另含木香碱、菊糖和氨基酸。

It contains volatile oil, and the main constituents of the oil are dehydrocostuslactone, costunolide, costuslactone, dihydrocostuslactone, etc. It also contains α- and β- cycloxylene lactone, stigmasterol, palmitic acid, linderic acid, etc. In addition, it contains saussurine, inulin and amino acids.

【检查 / Examination】

水分不得过 14.0%。总灰分不得过 4.0%。

Water, not more than 14.0%. Total ash, not more than 4.0%.

【质量要求 / Quality requirement】

外观质量　均以根粗壮均匀，体重坚实，香气浓郁、油性足、无须根者为佳。

Appearance Quality　Good quality for thick and even roots, heavy weight, hard texture, strong aromatic, adequate oil, and no fibrous root.

内在质量　浸出物含量：木香片的乙醇浸出物（热）不得少于 12.0%。含量测定：按高效液相色谱法测定，木香含木香烃内酯和去氢木香内酯的总量不得少于 1.8%；木香片含木香烃内酯和去氢木香内酯的总量不得少于 1.5%。

Intrinsic Quality　Extract content: not less than 12.0% of ethanol-soluble extractives (hot). Assay: Aucklandiae Radix contains not less than 1.8% of the total amount of costunolide and dehydrocostuslactone according to HPLC analysis method.

Aucklandiae Radix slices contains not less than 1.5% of the total amount of costunolide and dehydrocostuslactone according to HPLC analysis method.

【功能主治 / Function and indication】

温，辛、苦。行气止痛，健脾消食。用于胸胁、腹脘胀痛，泻痢后重，食积不消，不思饮食。煨木香实肠止泻。用于泄泻腹痛。

Warm, pungent and bitter. To move *qi*, relieve pain, fortify the spleen and promote digestion. Used for distending pain in the chest, hypochondrium, epigastrium and abdomen, tenesmus in diarrhea and dysentery, food retention, no desire for food and drink. Rosted Aucklandiae Radix can strengthen intestine and stop diarrhea, and can be used for abdominal pain in diarrhea.

【贮藏养护 / Storage and maintenance】

用麻袋、编织袋或竹篓装，内衬笋壳包装；或用纸包好放木箱内密封。本品易虫蛀、发霉、泛油，应置阴凉干燥处保存，防潮，防霉及香气散失。若受潮，应马上晾晒。因本品含挥发油成分，不宜切片保存。

Packed in sacks, woven bags or bamboo baskets, internally lined with bamboo shell, or wrapped in paper and sealed in wooden cases. This product is prone to be damaged by worms, go moldy and be oily. Stored in a cool and dry place, kept from moisture, mildew and aroma loss. If damped, dry it immediately. Avoid being stored in slices for its volatile oil.

【用法用量 / Administration and dosage】

3~6g。调剂时捣碎，另包，后下。

3~6g. When making up a prescription, mash it, pack it separately, and put it when the decoction is nearly finished.

茯苓 (Fuling) ¦ Poria (Indian Bread)

【基原 / Origin】

为多孔菌科真菌茯苓 *Poria cocos* (Schw.) Wolf 的干燥菌核。

Indian bread is the dried sclerotium of the fungus, *Poria cocos* (Schw.) Wolf (Fam. Polyporaceae).

【产地 / Producing area】

野生品主产于云南丽江、维西、中甸、福贡等地；家种品主产于云南普洱市和楚雄州。安徽、河南、四川等地亦有种植。野生者以云南产质量最优，称“云苓”。栽培者以湖北、安徽产量大。

Wild Poria is mainly produced in Lijiang, Weixi, Zhongdian, Fugong and other places in Yunnan Province. Cultivated Poria is mainly produced in Pu'er City and Chuxiong Prefecture in Yunnan Province. It is also planted in Anhui, Henan, Sichuan Provinces and other places. For wild products, those produced in Yunnan are of the best quality, which are called “Yunling”. Cultivated varieties in Hubei and Anhui Provinces have large output.

【采制 / Collection and preparation】

野生茯苓常在 7 月至次年 3 月于松林中采挖。人工栽培茯苓于接种后第二年 7~9 月采挖。

Wild Poria is collected in pine forest mostly from July to next March. Artificial planting Poria is collected mostly in next July to September.

茯苓个　鲜茯苓去净泥沙，堆置“发汗”，摊晾，再“发汗”3~4 次，阴干。

Fulingge (dried sclerotium)　Fresh Poria is removed from soil, piled up to the surface wetted (sweating), then spread to the surface dried. Repeat this operation for 3 to 4 times, dried in the shade.

茯苓皮　取茯苓个，浸泡，洗净，润透，稍蒸后趁热扒取外皮，干燥。

Fulingpi　Fulingge is soaked, washed clean, moistened thoroughly, then steamed and removed off outer skin immediately, dried.

茯苓片　鲜茯苓削去外皮，或茯苓个稍蒸后趁热扒取外皮后切片。

Fulingpian (Poria slices)　Peel off the scarfskin of fresh Poria or slightly steam Fulingge, then cut into slices.

茯苓块　鲜茯苓削去外皮，或茯苓个稍蒸后趁热扒取外皮后切成方形或长方形块者。

Fulingkuai (Poria cubics)　Peel off the scarfskin of fresh Poria or slightly steam Fulingge, then cut into square or rectangular blocks.

茯神　茯苓中有松根者。

Fushen　Poria with pine root inside.

赤茯苓　切去茯苓皮后显淡红色者。

Chifuling (red Poria)　Those who show light red after peeling off Poria scarfskins.

白茯苓　切去赤茯苓后的白色部分。

Baifuling (white Poria)　White portions left after peeling off Poria scarfskin.

【商品特征 / Commodity characteristics】

茯苓个　类球形、椭圆形、扁圆形或不规则团块，表面棕褐色，粗糙。体重、质坚。断面颗粒性，有的具裂隙，外层淡棕色，内部白色。味淡。嚼之粘牙。遇碘试液不变黑。

Fulingge　Subglobose, ellipsoid, oblate or irregular-shaped masses or lumps. Externally brown and rough, texture heavy and hard. Fracture granular, some cracked, the outer layer pale brown, inner part white. Taste, weak and sticky when chewed. Iodine test solution, not becoming black.

茯苓片 呈不规则厚片，厚薄不一。白色、淡红色或淡棕色。

Fulingpian (Poria slices) Irregular thick slices, variable in thickness. White, pale red or pale brown colour.

茯苓块 呈立方块状或方块状厚片，大小不一。白色、淡红色或淡棕色。

Fulingkuai (Poria blocks) Cubic pieces or cubic thick slices, variable in size. White, pale red or pale brown colour.

茯神 多为不规则片状，外表面棕褐色或黑褐色，内表面白色或淡棕色。

Fushen (Poria with pine root inside) Irregular-shape slices, externally brown or black brown colour, internally white or pale-brown colour.

赤茯苓 块状或片状，棕红色或淡红色。

Chi fuling (red Poria) lumps or slice, brownish-red or pale-red colour.

白茯苓 块状或片状，白色。

Bai fuling (white Poria) lumps or slices, white colour.

【规格等级 / Specification and grade】

按药用部位和加工形状，将茯苓药材分为九种规格，其中茯苓个和白苓片均分为二等；白苓块、赤苓块、茯神块、骰方、白碎苓、赤碎苓和茯神木均为统货。其规格等级标准为：

According to the medicinal parts and processing shapes, Poria is divided into nine specifications, among which Fulingge and Bailingpian are divided into two grades; Bailingkuai, Chilingkuai, Fushenkuai, Shaifang, Baisuiling, Chisuiling and Fushenmu are all unified grade with the same price. The specifications and grade criteria are as follows:

茯苓个 一等：呈不规则圆球形或块状。表面黑褐色或棕褐色。体坚实、皮细。断面白色。味淡。大小圆扁不分。无杂质、霉变。

Fulingge First Grade: Irregular globose or lumps. Externally dark brown or brown, texture hard and compact, skin fine. Fracture white. Taste, plain. Indiscrimination of size and shape. No foreign matter, nor mildew.

二等：呈不规则圆球形或块状。表面黑褐色或棕色。体轻泡、皮粗、质松。断面白色至黄赤色。味淡。间有皮沙、水锈、破伤。无杂质、霉变。

Second Grade: Irregular globose or lumps. Externally dark-brown or brown. Weight light, skin rough, texture loose. Section white to yellow-red. Taste, plain. Occasionally there are surface roughness, incrustation and broken parts. No foreign matter, nor mildew.

白苓片 一等：为茯苓去净外皮，切成薄片。白色或灰白色。质细。厚度每厘米 7 片，片面长宽不得小于 3cm。无杂质、霉变。

Bailingpian First Grade: Remove off the outer skin of Poria and cut into thin slices. White or greyish-white, Texture fine. Thickness, 7 pieces in per cm, and the length or width of a piece shall not be less than 3cm. No foreign matter, nor mildew.

二等：为茯苓去净外皮，切成薄片。白色或灰白色。质细。厚度每厘米 5 片，片面长宽不得小于 3cm。无杂质、霉变。

Second Grade: Remove off the outer skin of Poria and cut into thin slices. White or greyish-white. Texture fine. Thickness, 5 pieces in per cm, and the length or width of a piece shall not be less than 3cm. No foreign matter, nor mildew.

白苓块 统货：为茯苓去净外皮切成扁平方块。白色或灰白色。厚度 0.4~0.6cm 之间，长度 4~5cm，边缘苓块，可不成方形。间有 1.5cm 以上的碎块。无杂质、霉变。

Bailingkuai Unified grade with the same price. Remove off the outer skin of Poria and cut into flat square blocks. White or greyish-white. Thickness between 0.4~0.6cm, 4~5cm in length. The shape of edge parts can not be square. Occasionally there are more than 1.5cm pieces. No foreign matter, nor mildew.

赤苓块 统货：为茯苓去净外皮切成扁平方块。赤黄色。厚度 0.4~0.6cm 之间，长度 4~5cm，边缘苓块，可不成方形。间有 1.5cm 以上的碎块。无杂质、霉变。

Chilingkuai Unified grade with the same price. Remove off the outer skin of Poria and cut into flat square blocks. Reddish-yellow. The thickness between 0.4~0.6cm, length 4~5cm. The shape of edge parts can not be square. Occasionally there are more than 1.5cm blocks. No foreign matter, nor mildew.

茯神块 统货：为茯苓去净外皮切成扁平方形块。色泽不分，每块含有松木心。厚度 0.4~0.6cm，长宽 4~5cm。木心直径不超过 1.5cm。边缘苓块，可不成方形。间有 1.5cm 以上的碎块，无杂质、霉变。

Fushenkuai Unified grade with the same price. Remove off the outer skin of Poria and cut into flat square blocks. Variable colour. Each block with pine wood core inside. Thickness 0.4~0.6cm, length and width are 4~5cm. The diameter of wood core is not more than 1.5cm. The shape of edge parts can not be square. Occasionally there are more than 1.5cm blocks. No foreign matter, nor mildew.

骰方 统货：干货。为茯苓去净外皮切成立方形块。白色。质坚实。长、宽、厚在 1cm 以内，均匀整齐。间有不规则的碎块，但不超过 10%。无粉末、杂质、霉变。

Shaifang Unified grade with the same price, dry goods. Remove off the outer skin of Poria and cut into cubes. White with hard texture. The length, width and thickness are not more than 1cm, even and uniform. Occasionally there are irregular fragments, but not more than 10%. No powder, nor foreign matter, nor mildew.

白碎苓 统货：干货。为加工茯苓时的白色或灰白色的大小碎块或碎屑，均属此等。无粉末、杂质、虫蛀、霉变。

Baisuiling Unified grade with the same price, dry goods. White or greyish-white pieces or debris in processing Poria are all in this grade. No powder, nor foreign matter, nor moth, nor mildew.

赤碎苓 统货：干货。为加工茯苓时的赤黄色大小碎块或碎屑，均属此等。无粉末、杂质、虫蛀、霉变。

Chisuiling Unified grade with the same price, dry goods. Redish-yellow pieces or debris in processing Poria are all in this grade. No powder, nor foreign matter, nor moth, nor mildew.

茯神木 统货：干货。为茯苓中间生长的松木，多为弯曲不直的松根，似朽木状。色泽不分，毛松体轻。每根周围必须带有三分之二的茯苓肉。木杆直径最大不超过 2.5cm。无杂质、霉变。

Fushenmu Unified grade with the same price, dry goods. It is the pine wood growing inside of Poria, most of which are crooked and not straight pine roots, like rotten wood. Variable colour, texture loose and light. Each root must be surrounded by two-thirds of Poria. The wooden pole is not more than 2.5cm in diameter. No foreign matter, nor mildew.

【化学成分 / Chemical constituent】

菌核含 β- 茯苓聚糖，含量可达约 75%。还含茯苓酸、齿孔酸、块苓酸、松苓酸等，以及麦角甾醇、胆碱、腺嘌呤、卵磷脂、蛋白质、氨基酸等。茯苓聚糖无抗肿瘤活性。但经切断支链，成为 β-(1→3) 葡萄糖聚糖（称茯苓次聚糖），具有抗肿瘤活性。

The content of β- pachyman in sclerotia is about 75%. It also contains pachymic acid, eburicoic acid, tumulosic acid, pinicolic acid, ergosterol, choline, adenine, lecithin, protein, amino acid, etc. Pachyman has no antitumor activity. However, it is cut off the branched chain and becomes β-(1→3) glucose glycan (known as pachymaran), the later possesses antitumor activity.

【检查 / Examination】

茯苓个、茯苓块及茯苓片水分不得过18.0%；总灰分不得过2.0%。茯苓皮水分不得过15.0%，总灰分不得过5.5%，酸不溶性灰分不得过4.0%。

Fulingge, Fulingkuai and Fulingpian: Water, not more than 18%; Total ash, not more than 2.0%.

Fulingpi: Water, not more than 15.0%. Total ash, not more than 5.5%; Acid-insoluble ash, not more than 4.0%.

【质量要求 / Quality requirement】

外观质量 茯苓个以体重、坚实、外皮棕褐、无裂隙、断面色白细腻，嚼之粘性强者为佳，茯苓块以块状不碎，色洁白者为佳。

Appearance Quality Fulingge Good quality for heavy weight, hard texture, brownish skin, no crack, white and fine section, strong chewing viscosity.

Fulingkuai Good quality for blocks without being broken, and white colour.

内在质量 浸出物含量：茯苓个、茯苓块及茯苓片稀乙醇浸出物（热）不得少于2.5%。茯苓皮稀乙醇浸出物（热）不得少于6.0%。

Intrinsic Quality Extract content: not less than 2.5% of ethanol-soluble extractives (hot) for Fulingge, Fulingkuai and Fulingpian, and not less than 6.0% of ethanol-soluble extractives (hot) for Fulingpi.

【功能主治 / Function and indication】

平，甘、淡。利水渗湿，健脾，宁心。用于水肿尿少，痰饮眩悸，脾虚食少，便溏泄泻，心神不安，惊悸失眠。

Neutral, sweet and bland. To promote urination to drain dampness, fortify the spleen, and calm the heart. It is used for edema, small quantity of urination, dizziness, and palpitations caused by phlegm-fluid retention, spleen deficiency, reduced food intake, sloppy stool, diarrhea, disquieted heart spirit, fright palpitation and insomnia.

茯苓皮利水消肿，用于水肿、小便不利。茯神宁心安神，用于心虚惊悸，失眠健忘。

Fulingpi Promote urination to alleviate edema. It is used for edema, and dysuria.

Fushen Calming the heart and tranquilizing the mind. It is used for heart deficiency, palpitation, insomnia and forgetfulness.

【贮藏养护 / Storage and maintenance】

茯苓个一般用麻袋或编织袋装。茯苓块用纸箱装；茯神块用纸箱内衬防潮纸包装。本品易虫蛀、发霉、变色，应密闭，置于阴凉干燥处保存。不宜暴晒，以免变色和起裂纹，为防虫蛀可用药物熏蒸或以气调养护。

Fulingge is usually packed in sacks or woven bags. Fulingkuai is packed in cartons; Fushenkuai is packed in cartons internally lined with moisture-proof paper. Poria is prone to be damaged by worms, go mouldy and change colour. Sealed and stored in a cool and dry place. Avoid being exposed to the sun in case of discoloration and cracking. Fumigated with drugs or conserved by air conditioning to prevent moth damage.

【用法用量 / Administration and dosage】

茯苓个、茯苓块及茯苓片10~15g。

Fulingge, Fulingkuai and Fulingpian 10~15g.

重点小结
Summary

药材	主产地	商品规格	等级标准
三七	云南文山、砚山、广南、马关、西畴、邱北、富宁，广西靖西、睦边、百色等地	主根按采收时间分春三七和冬三七。另有剪口、筋条、绒根	春三七和冬三七各分为十一个等级
木香	云南丽江地区和迪庆州	不分规格	按根的长度和直径将木香分为二个等级
茯苓	野生品主产于云南丽江、维西、香格里拉等地；家种品主产于云南普洱市、楚雄州	按药用部位和加工方法分为茯苓个、白苓片、白苓块、赤苓块、茯神块、骰方、白碎苓、赤碎苓和茯神木九种规格	茯苓个和白苓片均分为二个等级；其余七种规格均统货

Medicinal material	Main producing area	Commodity specification	Grade standard
Notoginseng Radix et Rhizoma	Wenshan, Yanshan, Guangnan, Maguan, Xichou, Qiubei, Funing of Yunnan Province, Jingxi, Mubian, Baise and other areas in Guangxi Province	According to the different harvesting time, the main root can be divided into two specifications of Chunsanqi and Dongsanqi. By different portions, whole root can be divided into Jiankou, Jintiao and Ronggen	Chunsanqi and Dongsanqi are divided into eleven grades, respectively
Aucklandiae Radix	Lijiang and Diqing in Yunnan Province	No specification	According to the length and diameter, the roots are divided into two grades
Poria	Wild products are mainly produced in Lijiang, Weixi, Zhongdian, Fugong and other places in Yunnan Province; cultivated products are mainly produced in Pu'er City and Chuxiong Prefecture in Yunnan Province	According to the different portions and processing methods, Poria are divided into nine specifications of Fulingge, Bailingpian, Bailingkuai, Chilingkuai, Fushenkuai, Shaifang, Baisuiling, Chisuiling and Fushenmu	Fulingge and Bailingpian are divided into two grades, respectively. Others are unified grade with the same price

目标检测
Object Detection

一、选择题（Choice question）

（一）单项选择题（One-choice question）

1. 以（　　）为主产区或集散地的大宗商品药材，称为云药
   A. 云南及广西东部　　B. 云南及西藏南部　　C. 云南及贵州南部
   D. 云南及四川南部　　E. 贵州及四川南部

题库

Where are the main production areas or distribution center for the bulk commodity of Yun medicinal materials (　　)

A. Yunnan and Eastern Guangxi　　B. Yunnan and southern Tibet

C. Yunnan and Southern Guizhou　　D. Yunan and southern Sichuan

E. Guizhou and southern Sichuan

2. 三七的根茎药材商品习称（　　）

A. 芦头　B. 剪口　C. 筋条　D. 绒根　E. 三七

What is known for the medicinal commodity of Sanchi rhizome (　　)

A. Lutou　B. Jiankou　C. Jintiao

D. Ronggen　E. Sanchi

3. 春三七的等级划分标准为（　　）

A. 按每 kg 的头数分等　B. 按每 500g 的头数分等　C. 按主根的直径分等

D. 按主根的长度分等　E. 按主根的宽度分等

What is the grade criteria for Chunsanqi (　　)

A. The number of main root in per kg

B. The number of main root in per 500g

C. Diameter of the main root

D. Length of the main root

E. Width of the main root

4. 木香药材商品等级划分标准为（　　）

A. 按每 kg 的头数分等　B. 按每 500g 的头数分等

C. 按主根的长度和直径分等　D. 按主根的长度分等

E. 按主根的直径分等

What is the grade criteria for Aucklandiae Radix (　　)

A. The number of main root in per kg　B. The number of main root in per 500g

C. Length and diameter of main root　D. Length of main root

E. Diameter of main root

5. 云木香的主要产区为（　　）

A. 普洱市和楚雄州　B. 丽江地区和迪庆州　C. 丽江和香格里拉

D. 昆明市和普洱市　E. 楚雄州和昆明市

The main producing areas of Aucklandiae Radix are in (　　)

A. Pu'er and Chuxiong　B. Lijiang and Diqing　C. Lijiang and Xianggelila

D. Kunming and Pu'er　E. Chuxiong and Kunming

（二）多项选择题（Multiple choice question）

1. 下列药材中属于云南道地药材的为（　　）

A. 三七　B. 重楼　C. 木香

D. 茯苓　E. 草果

The authentic medicinal materials of Yunnan are (　　)

A. Notoginseng Radix et Rhizoma　B. Paridis Rhizoma

C. Aucklandiae Radix　D. Poria

E. Tsaoko Frutus

2. 三七的商品种类有（ ）

A. 春七 B. 剪口 C. 筋条

D. 绒根 E. 三七粉

The commodity types of Notoginseng Radix et Rhizoma are ( )

A. Chunsanqi B. Jiankou C. Jintiao

D. Ronggen E. Sanqifen

3. 茯苓的商品规格有（ ）

A. 茯苓个 B. 白苓片 C. 白苓块

D. 茯神块 E. 白碎苓

The commercial specifications of Poria are ( )

A. Fulingge B. Bailingpian C. Bailingkuai

D. Fushenkuai E. Baisuiling

4. 在云南，茯苓家种品主产于（ ）

A. 丽江 B. 普洱市 C. 维西

D. 香格里拉 E. 楚雄州

The main producing areas of cultivated Poria in Yunnan Province are ( )

A. Lijiang B. Pu'er C. Weixi

D. Xianggelila E. Chuxiong

二、解答题

II. Thinking question

1. 如何划分三七的商品规格和等级？

How to divide the specification and grade of Notoginseng Radix et Rhizoma?

2. 木香药材在贮藏中易发生哪些质量变异现象？应如何贮藏？

What are the qualitative variation in the storage of Aucklandiae Radix? How to store it?

3. 云南有何地理气候特征？请例举 5 种道地药材。

What are the geographical and climatic conditions in Yunnan Province? List five authentic medicinal materials there.

PPT

第十一章　贵　　药
Chapter 11　Gui Medicinal Materials

学习目标 | Learning Target

知识要求：

1．**掌握**　贵药的含义及其主要道地药材品种。天麻、杜仲的道地产地、规格等级及贮藏方法。

2．**熟悉**　天麻、杜仲的采制方法和质量要求。

3．**了解**　贵药产区的自然环境条件。

能力要求：

1．**掌握**　天麻、杜仲药材的商品规格等级辨识能力。

2．**掌握**　天麻、杜仲商品的包装及贮藏方法。

Knowledge requirements:

1. **Proficiency**　The meaning and major varieties of Gui Medicinal Materials. The authentic producing areas, specifications, grades and storage methods of Gastrodiae Rhizoma and Eucommiae Cortex.

2. **Familiarity**　Collection and preparation methods, quality requirements of Gastrodiae Rhizoma and Eucommiae Cortex.

3. **Understanding**　The natural environment in the producing areas of Gui Medicinal Materials.

Skill requirements:

To acquire identification capacity of the specifications and grades of Gastrodiae Rhizoma and Eucommiae Cortex.

To master the packing and storage methods of Gastrodiae Rhizoma and Eucommiae Cortex.

一、贵药概述
I. Overview of Gui Medicinal Materials

以贵州为主要产区或集散地的大宗商品药材，称为贵药。其产区地处云贵高原东南部，位于东经 103° 36′~109° 35′，北纬 24° 37′~29° 13′，属于中亚热带东部湿润季风气候区，年均气温 12℃~18℃，夏季平均气温 22℃~25℃，年均降水量为 1000~1400mm。贵州道地药材产区面积的 90% 以上为山地和丘陵，主要有黔西北高原山地、黔东北武陵山脉一带、黔西南河谷丘陵地区、黔北大娄山山地及河谷地区、雷公山及茂兰自然保护区、贵阳市及安顺地区等。尤以苗岭、梵净山、大娄山区为多。主要道地药材有天麻、杜仲、吴茱萸、五倍子、石斛、白及、朱砂、冰片（艾片）、南沙参（轮叶沙参）、淫羊藿、黔党参、金果榄等。

Gui Medicinal Materials are known as the bulk commodities of medicinal materials, mainly produced or collected and distributed in Guizhou Province. The area is located in the southeast of Yunnan-Guizhou Plateau, between longitude 103° 36′ to 109° 35′ east and latitude 24° 37′ to 29° 13′ north. It belongs to the humid monsoon climate zone in the eastern part of the central subtropical region, with the average annual temperature of 12℃~18℃, the average summer temperature of 22℃~25℃, and the average annual precipitation of 1000~1400mm. More than 90% production areas of Gui medicinal materials are mountains and hills, mainly including the plateau mountains in the northwest of Guizhou, the Wuling mountains in the northeast of Guizhou, the river valleys and hills in the southwest of Guizhou, the Dalou mountains and valleys in the north of Guizhou, the Leigong mountains and Maolan nature reserve, Guiyang city and Anshun area, especially in Miaoling, Fanjing mountain, Dalou mountain area. Main authentic medicinal materials are Gastrodiae Rhizoma, Eucommiae Cortex, Euodiae Fructus, Galla Chinensis, Dendrobii Caulis, Bletillae Rhizoma, Cinnabaris, *l*-Borneolum, Adenophorae Radix, Epimedii Folium, Codonopsis Tubulosae Radix, Tinosporae Radix.

二、药材品种
II. Varieties of Medicinal Materials

天麻 (Tianma) ¦ Gastrodiae Rhizoma (Tall Gastrodia Tuber)

【基原 / Origin】

为兰科植物天麻 *Gastrodia elata* Bl. 的干燥块茎。

Tall Gastrodia Tuber is the dried rhizome of *Gastrodia elata* Bl. (Fam. Orchidaceae).

【产地 / Producing area】

近代野生天麻的道地产区在西南，尤以云南昭通地区和贵州毕节地区所产的天麻质优而驰名。四川宜宾、乐山、峨眉，溯岷江而上至雅安地区亦为野生天麻的著名产区。栽培天麻以陕西、湖北、湖南、安徽、河南产量大。此外，甘肃、吉林等地亦产。

Since modern times, the authentic producing area of wild Gastrodiae Rhizoma has been the southwest of China. Zhaotong of Yunnan Province and Bijie of Guizhou Province are especially famous for its superior quality. And Yibin, Leshan and Emei in Sichuan Province, along Min River up to Ya'an are also well-known for the production areas of wild Gastrodiae Rhizoma. Shaanxi, Hubei, Hunan, Anhui, Henan Provinces yield the most quantity of cultivated Gastrodiae Rhizoma. Besides, Gansu Province, Jilin Province, etc. are the producing areas as well.

【采制 / Collection and preparation】

一般在立冬后至次年清明前挖取地下茎，洗净泥土，除去地上茎，及时擦去粗皮，浸入明矾水中，半小时后捞出，蒸至无白心为度，取出晾至半干，再晒干或烘干。

Gastrodiae Rhizoma is generally collected from winter to next spring, washed and removed the stems, wiped off the rough bark, immersed in alum water for half an hour, then steamed until no white colour in the center of rhizome, dried to half-dryness, and then sun-dry or bake to complete dryness.

冬麻 冬末或春初初出芽时采挖者，习称“冬麻”，体重饱满，质优。

Dongma (harvested in winter) Collected in the early budding at the end of winter or the beginning of spring, called "Dongma". Texture heavy, plump, with higher quality.

春麻 春季或夏季地上茎已长时采挖者，习称"春麻"，皮多皱缩，体轻质次。

Chunma (harvested in spring) Collected at the spring or summer when stems grow, called "Chunma". Skin wrinkled, texture light with lower quality.

天麻片 取块茎洗净，润透或蒸软，切薄片，干燥。

Gastrodiae Rhizoma Slices Take the tuber, wash clean, moistened thorough or steamed soft, cut into thin slices and baked or dried.

【商品特征 / Commodity characteristics】

冬麻 长扁圆形或椭圆形，顶端有的具"鹦哥嘴"或"红小辫"，底端有"肚脐眼"，体表有点状横环纹。质坚实沉重，断面角质样，色明亮。

Dongma (harvested in winter) Long oblate or elliptic, apex with reddish-brown to deep brown parrot-beat-like buds ("Yinggezui" or "Hongxiaobian"), bottom end with a round scar ("*Duqiyan*"), and surface with transverse annulations arranged by dots. Texture hard and heavy, fracture horny, bright.

春麻 长扁圆形或椭圆形，顶端具残留茎基，质轻泡，断面色晦暗，空心。

Chunma (harvested in spring) Long oblate or elliptic, apex with residual stem base, texture light and loose, fracture dull, hollow.

天麻片 不规则薄片。外表皮淡黄色至淡黄棕色，有时可见点状排列的横环纹。切面黄白色至淡棕色。角质样，半透明。气微，味甘。

Tianma Pian (Slices) Irregular thin slices. Externally pale yellow to pale yellowish-brown, sometimes transverse annulations arranged by visible dots. Cut surface yellowish-white to pale brown, horny, semitransparent. Odour light, taste sweet.

【规格等级 / Specification and grade】

按采收时间分为冬麻、春麻。按大小分为四个等级。其等级标准为：

As commodity, two commercial specifications of Gastrodiae Rhizoma are Dongma (winter) and Chunma (spring) according to the harvesting time. The commercial specification is marketed by four grades according to the size of the tuber. The specifications and grading criteria are as follows:

一等：干货。呈长椭圆形。扁缩弯曲，去净粗栓皮，表面黄白色，有横环纹，顶端有残留茎基（春麻）或红黄色的枯芽（冬麻），末端有圆盘状的凹脐形疤痕。质坚实、半透明。断面角质，牙白色。味甘微辛。每 kg 26 支以内，无空心、杂质、虫蛀、霉变。

First grade: Dry tuber. Long elliptic, compressed and curved. Surface yellowish-white, transverse annulations when removed the rough cork. Apex with remains of stem base (Chunma) or reddish-yellow withered buds (Dongma), bottom end with a round scar. Texture hard and uneasily broken, semitransparent. Fracture horny, white. Taste sweet and slightly acrid. There are less than 26 tubers in per kg, no hollow, nor foreign matter, nor moth, nor mildew.

二等：每 kg 46 支以内，余同一等。

Second grade: There are less than 46 tubers in per kg. Other criteria in this grade are in accordance with those in First grade.

三等：断面牙白色或棕黄色稍有空心。每 kg 90 支以内，大小均匀。余同二等。

Third grade: Fracture, cream white or brownish-yellow color, slightly hollow. There are less than 90 tubers in per kg, uniform size. Other criteria in this grade are in accordance with those in Second grade.

四等：每 kg 90 支以外。凡不符合一、二、三等的碎块、空心及未去皮者均属此等。

Fourth grade: There are more than 90 tubers in per kg. Fragments, hollow and unpeeled parts which are not up to First, Second and Third grades belong to this grade.

【化学成分 / Chemical constituent】

含天麻素，另含赤箭苷、对羟苄基甲醚、双（4- 羟苄基）醚，以及对羟基苯甲醛、对羟基苯甲醇（天麻苷元）、派立辛、β- 谷甾醇等。

It mainly contains gastrodin, gastrodioside, p-hydroxybenzyl methyl ether, 4-hydroxybenzyl ether, 4-hydroxybenzaldehyde, p-hydroxybenzyl alcohol (gastrodigenin), parishin, β-sitosterol, etc.

【检查 / Examination】

水分不得过 15.0%。总灰分不得过 4.5%。二氧化硫残留量不得过 400mg/kg。

Water, not more than 15.0%. Total ash, not more than 4.5%. Residue of sulfur dioxide, not more than 400mg/kg.

【质量要求 / Quality requirement】

外观质量 以个大、色黄白、质坚实体重、断面半透明、有光泽、无空心者为佳。

Appearance quality Good quality for big and yellowish-white colour, hard and heavy texture, semitransparen fracture, luster, no hollow.

内在质量 浸出物含量：稀乙醇浸出物（热）不得少于 15.0%。

Intrinsic quality Extract content: not less than 15.0% of dilute ethanol-soluble extractives (hot).

含量测定：按高效液相色谱法测定，天麻素和对羟基苯甲醇的总量不得少于 0.25%。

Assay: It contains not less than 0.25% of the total amount of gastrodin and p-hydroxybenzyl alcohol according to HPLC method.

【功能主治 / Function and indication】

平，甘。息风止痉，平抑肝阳，祛风通络。用于小儿惊风，癫痫抽搐，破伤风，头痛眩晕，手足不遂，肢体麻木，风湿痹痛。

Neutral, sweet. To extinguish wind, arrest convulsions, pacify and repress the liver yang, dispel wind and dredge the collaterals. Be indicated for infantile convulsion, epilepsy, convulsion, tetanus, headache, dizziness, paralyzed limbs, numbness of the limbs, arthralgia caused by wind-dampness.

【贮藏养护 / Storage and maintenance】

可用塑料编织袋内衬聚乙烯薄膜的复合包装袋，或瓦楞纸箱内衬防潮纸包装。本品易虫蛀、发霉，应置干燥、通风处保存，注意避光，防潮，防霉及防虫蛀，不宜久贮。在夏季应经常检查并翻晒。

Packed in composite packaging bags of plastic woven bags lined with polythene film, or packed in corrugated cartons lined with moisture-proof paper. Gastrodiae Rhizoma is prone to be moth-eaten and moldy, kept in dry and ventilated place, avoiding light, moisture, mildew and moth. Not stored for a long time. Checked frequently and tedded in summer.

【用法用量 / Administration and dosage】

3~10g。

3~10g.

杜仲 (Duzhong) ¦ Eucommiae Cortex (Eucommia Bark)

【基原 / Origin】

为杜仲科植物杜仲 *Eucommia ulmoides* Oliv. 的干燥树皮。

Eucommia Bark is the dried bark of the *Eucommia ulmoides* Oliv. (Fam.Eucommiaceae).

【产地 / Producing area】

主产于贵州遵义、正安、湄潭，四川广元、青川、平武，陕西镇坪、安康、西乡，湖北兴山、鹤峰、恩施，云南水善、镇雄等地。此外，湖南、河南、江西等省亦产。贵州产者最佳。

Mainly produced in Zunyi, Zheng'an, Meitan of Guizhou Province; Guangyuan, Qingchuan, Pingwu of Sichuan Province; Zhenping, Ankang, Xixiang of Shaanxi Province; Xingshan, Hefeng, Enshi of Hubei Province; Shuishan, Zhenxiong of Yunnan Province. Besides, Hunan, Henan, Jiangxi Provinces are also the producing area. The best quality is produced in Guizhou Province.

【采制 / Collection and preparation】

杜仲 春季清明至夏至采收，以年久皮厚者为佳。选取生长 10 年以上的植株，剥取树皮，刮去粗皮，堆置“发汗”至内皮呈紫褐色，晒干。

Eucommiae Cortex The cork is collected from Qingming Festival to the Summer Solstice. Good quality is for thick bark of long-year growth. Plants of more than 10-year-growth are selected, picked off bark and removed from the coarse skin. Piled up to inner surface purplish-brown, then dried in the sun.

杜仲经炮制加工成杜仲块、杜仲丝、盐杜仲。

Eucommia Bark can be processed into Eucommiae Cortex pieces, Eucommiae Cortex slivers and salted Eucommiae Cortex (processed with salt).

【商品特征 / Commodity characteristics】

杜仲 呈板片状或两边稍向内卷，外表面粗糙，淡棕色或灰褐色，内表面暗紫色，光滑。质脆，易折断，断面有细密、银白色、富弹性的橡胶丝相连，一般可拉至 1cm 左右或以上才断。气微，味稍苦。

Eucommia Bark Flat pieces, or two edges somewhat curving inwards, outer surface rough, light brown or greyish-brown, inner surface dark purple, smooth. Texture fragile, easily broken, fracture linked up by fine, dense, silvery and elastic rubber threads pulled to 1cm or more before breaking. Odour, slight; taste, slightly bitter.

杜仲块 呈小方块状。余同杜仲。

Eucommia Bark Pieces Small square blocks. Other characteristics are the same to those of Eucommia Bark.

杜仲丝 呈丝状。余同杜仲块。

Eucommia Bark Slivers Shredded. Other characteristics are the same to those of Eucommia Bark pieces.

盐杜仲 形如杜仲块或丝。表面黑褐色，内表面褐色，折断时橡胶丝弹性差。味微咸。

Eucommia Bark processed by salt Shaped like pieces or slivers of Eucommia Bark. Surface dark brown, inner surface brown, rubber threads with poor elasticity when broken. Taste, slightly salty.

【规格等级 / Specification and grade】

以宽度和厚度为确定等级的主要标准，长度只作参考。商品分特等、一等、二等、三等四个等级，等级标准为：

Eucommiae Cortex are marketed by four grades according to its width and thickness. Its length is for reference of dividing grade. The grading criteria are as follows:

特等：呈平板状，两端平齐，去净粗皮。表面呈灰褐色，内表面紫褐色，质脆。折断处有银白色胶丝相连，味微苦。整张长 70~80cm，宽 50cm 以上，厚 7mm 以上。碎块不超过 10%。无卷形、杂质、霉变。

Top grade: Flat, blunt at both ends, removed from rough skin. Surface grey-brown, inner surface purplish-brown, texture fragile. Fracture linked by argenteous rubber threads. Taste, slightly bitter. The whole bark is 70~80cm long, more than 50cm wide and more than 7mm thick. Broken pieces, not more than 10%. No roll shape, nor foreign matter, nor mildew.

一等：整张长 40cm 以上，宽 40cm 以上，厚 5mm 以上。碎块不超过 10%，余同特等。

First grade: The whole bark is more than 40cm long, 40cm wide and 5mm thick. Broken pieces, not more than 10%. Other criteria in this grade are the same as those in Top grade.

二等：呈板片状或卷筒状，内表皮青紫色。整张长 40cm 以上，宽 30cm 以上，厚 3mm 以上。碎片不超过 10%，余同一等。

Second grade: Plate-like or roll-shaped with bluish-purple inner surface. The whole bark is more than 40cm long, 30cm wide and 3mm thick. Broken pieces, not more than 10%. Other criteria in this grade are the same as those in First grade.

三等：凡不符合特等及一、二等标准，厚度最薄不得小于 2mm，包括枝皮、根皮、碎块，均属此等。

Third grade: All drugs are not up to Top, First and Second grades belong to this grade, including branch barks, root barks and fragments. However, the thinnest bark shall not be less than 2mm.

【化学成分 / Chemical constituent】

含木脂素类，如松酯醇二葡萄糖苷、杜仲素 A、松脂素等；环烯醚萜苷类，如桃叶珊瑚苷、京尼平苷、杜仲苷等；甾醇类，如 β- 谷甾醇等；三萜类，如白桦脂醇等；橡胶类，如杜仲胶，为一种硬质橡胶，其含量因树龄和皮片厚度不同而异。

Lignans, for example pinoresinol diglucoside, eucommin A, pinoresinol, etc. Iridoid glycosides, such as aucubin, geniposide, ulmoside, etc. Sterol, β-sitosterol. Triterpenes, betulin. Rubber (Eucommea rubber) is a sort of solid rubber whose content varies according to tree age and bark thickness.

【检查 / Examination】

水分不得过 13.0%。总灰分不得过 10.0%。

Water, not more than 13.0%. Total ash, not more than 10.0%.

【质量要求 / Quality requirement】

外观质量 以皮厚、块大、去净粗皮、内表面暗紫色、断面银白色橡胶丝多者为佳。

Appearance quality Good quality for thick and large bark, rough surface removed, the inner surface dark purple, broken section with more silver-white rubber silk.

内在质量 浸出物含量：乙醇（75%）浸出物（热）不得少于 11.0%。

Intrinsic quality Extract content: not less than 11.0% of 75% ethanol-soluble extractives (hot).

含量测定：按高效液相色谱法测定，含松脂醇二葡萄糖苷不得少于 0.10%。

Assay: It contains not less than 0.10% of pinoresinol diglucoside according to HPLC method.

【功能主治 / Function and indication】

温，甘。补肝肾，强筋骨，安胎。用于肝肾不足，腰膝酸痛，筋骨无力，头晕目眩，妊娠漏血，胎动不安。

Warm and sweet. To tonify liver-kidney, strengthen sinew and bone, prevent miscarriage. Be indicated for deficiency of liver-kidney, limp aching in the lower back and knees, lack of strength of sinew and bone, dizziness and vertigo, vaginal bleeding during pregnancy, threatened abortion.

【贮藏养护 / Storage and maintenance】

打捆，一般为压缩打包件，每件 50kg。本品易发霉，应置干燥通风处保存。

Bundled, generally package compressed, 50kg for each. This product is prone to mildew, preserved in a dry and ventilated place.

【用法用量 / Administration and dosage】

6~10g。

6~10g.

重点小结

Summary

药材	主产地	商品规格	等级标准
天麻	野生天麻主产于贵州毕节、云南昭通，四川宜宾、乐山、峨眉、平武。栽培品天麻以陕西、湖北、湖南、安徽、河南产量大	按采收时间分为冬麻和春麻	均按照每 kg 的个数分为 1~4 个等级
杜仲	贵州遵义等，四川广元等，陕西镇坪等，湖北襄阳等，云南水善等地	不分规格	以宽度和厚度为标准，商品分特等、一等、二等、三等

Medicinal material	Main producing area	Specification	Grade
Gastrodiae Rhizoma	Wild Gastrodiae Rhizoma in Bijie of Guizhou Province, Zhaotong of Yunnan Province, and Yibin, Leshan, Emei, Pingwu of Sichuan Province. Cultivated Gastrodiae Rhizoma in quantity in Shaanxi, Hubei, Hunan, Anhui, Henan Provinces	Dongma (winter) and Chunma(spring) according to harvesting time	Four grades, according to the number of tubers in per kg
Eucommiae Cortex	Zunyi of Guizhou Province. Guangyuan of Sichuan Province. Zhenping of Shaanxi Province. Xingshan of Hubei Province. Shuishan of Yunnan Province	Unified specification	Four grades, according to the width and thickness of bark. (top, first, second, third grades)

题库

目标检测

Object Detection

一、选择题（Choice question）

（一）单项选择题（One-choice question）

1. 主产于贵州的药材为（　　）

A. 附子　　B. 龙胆　　C. 南沙参

D. 天麻　　E. 砂仁

Which Chinese medicinal materials is mainly produced in Guizhou（　　）

A. Aconm Lateralis Radix Praeparaia

B. Gentianae Radix et Rhizoma
C. Adenophorae Radix
D. Gastrodiae Rhizoma
E. Amomi Fructus

2. 天麻的道地产区在（ ）
A. 华北　B. 西北　C. 东北
D. 西南　E. 东南
Where is the authentic production area of Gastrodiae Rhizoma（ ）
A. North of China　B. Northwest of China　C. Northeast of China
D. Southwest of China　E. Southeast of China

3. 天麻的规格等级分类中，每千克 46 支属于（ ）
A. 特等　B. 一等　C. 二等
D. 三等　E. 四等
According to the classification of Gastrodiae Rhizoma, it can be defined with（ ）if there are 46 pieces of Gastrodiae Rhizoma in per kg.
A. Top grade　B. First grade　C. Second grade
D. Third grade　E. Fourth grade

4. 天麻药材划分等级的标准是（ ）
A. 长度　B. 重量　C. 直径
D. 色泽　E. 厚度
What's the grading criteria of Gastrodiae Rhizoma（ ）
A. Length　B. Weight　C. Diameter
D. Colour　E. Thickness

5. 下列属于贵州的道地药材是（ ）
A. 天南星　B. 北沙参　C. 杜仲
D. 浙贝母　E. 姜黄
Which authentic medicinal materials is mainly produced in Guizhou（ ）
A. Arisaematis Rhizoma　B. Glehniae Radix
C. Eucommiae Cortex　D. Fritillariae Thunbergii Bulbus
E. Curcumae Longae Rhizoma

（二）多项选择题（Multiple choice question）

1. 杜仲药材划分等级的标准是（ ）
A. 长度　B. 重量　C. 直径
D. 宽度　E. 厚度
The grading criteria of Eucommiae Cortex are（ ）
A. Length　B. Weight　C. Diameter
D. Width　E. Thickness

2. 天麻药材的商品特征包括（ ）
A. 鹦哥嘴　B. 红小辫　C. 肚脐痕
D. 横环纹　E. 残留茎基
The commodity characteristics of Gastrodiae Rhizoma are（ ）
A. Yinggezui　B. Hongxiaobian　C. Duqiyan

D. Transverse annulations　　E. Residual stem base

3. 规格等级分类中具有特等级别的药材为 (　　)

A. 人参　　B. 地黄　　C. 天麻

D. 三七　　E. 杜仲

Which Chinese medicinal materials are divided into Top grade (　　)

A. Ginseng Radix et Rhizoma　　B. Rehmanniae Radix

C. Gastrodiae Rhizoma　　D. Notoginseng Radix et Rhizoma

E. Eucommiae Cortex

4. 天麻药材商品在市场上按采收时间不同分为 (　　)

A. 春麻　　B. 夏麻　　C. 秋麻

D. 冬麻　　E. 野天麻

What are the commercial specifications of Gastrodiae Rhizoma according to harvesting time in market (　　)

A. Chunma (spring)　　B. Xiama (summer)　　C. Qiuma (autumn)

D. Dongma (winter)　　E. Wild Gastrodiae Rhizoma

二、思考题（Thinking question）

1. 为何冬麻药材质量优于春麻药材?

Why is the quality of Dongma (winter) better than Chunma (spring)?

2. 为何杜仲药材商品的等级划分标准为宽度和厚度，而不是长度?

Why is the grading criteria of Eucommiae Cortex based on bark width and thickness, instead of length?

第十二章　怀　　药
Chapter 12　Huai Medicinal Materials

PPT

学习目标 | Learning Target

知识要求：

1. **掌握**　怀药的含义及其主要道地药材品种。

2. **熟悉**　主要怀药的采制、规格等级、商品特征、检查及贮藏方法。

能力要求：

会运用所学规格等级、商品特征、检查、质量要求等知识和方法鉴别市场上山药、牛膝和地黄的真伪优劣。

Knowledge requirements:

1. **Proficiency**　The concept and major varieties of Huai Medicinal Materials.

2. **Familiarity**　The knowledge for collection, preparation, specification, grade, commodity characteristics, examination, and storage method of main Huai Medicinal Materials.

Skill requirements:

Learn to identify the authenticity and evaluate the quality of Dioscoreae Rhizoma, Achyranthis Bidentatae Radix, and Rehmanniae Radix on the market by applying the knowledge and methods of specification and grade, commodity characteristics, examination and quality requirement, etc.

一、怀药概述
I. Overview of Huai Medicinal Materials

以古怀庆境内或现以河南省为主要产区或集散地的大宗商品药材均称为怀药。其产区位于东经 110°~116°，北纬 31°~36°之间。北、西、南三面有太行山、伏牛山、桐柏山、大别山四大山脉环绕，东部是广阔的黄淮海冲积平原，大部分地处暖温带，南部跨亚热带，属北亚热带向暖温带过渡的大陆性季风气候。境内有黄河、淮河、卫河、汉水四大水系，大小河道 1500 多条。河南地理环境优越，气候多样，为众多药材生长提供了适宜的地理生态环境。著名的怀药有怀地黄、怀牛膝、怀山药、怀菊花、山茱萸、金银花、禹白芷、猫爪草、银杏等。

The bulk commodity of medicinal materials, mainly produced or distributed in ancient Huaiqing region or now Henan Province, are called Huai Medicinal Materials. Its producing area is located between 110°~116° east longitude and 31°~36° north latitude. The north, west, and south are surrounded by the four major mountains, including Taihang, Funiu, Tongbai, and Dabie Mountains. The east is the vast Huanghuaihai alluvial plain, most of which are within the warm temperate zone, and the south spans the subtropics, belonging to continental monsoon climate from northern subtropics to warm temperate. There are four major river systems: the Yellow River, Huai River, Wei River, and Hanshui River, with more than 1500 river channels. Henan's superior geographical environment and diverse climate provide a suitable geographical and ecological environment for the growth of many medicinal plants. The well-known Huai medicinal materials include Huai Rehmanniae Radix, Huai Achyranthis Bidentatae Radix, Huai Dioscoreae Rhizoma, Huai Chrysanthemi Flos, Dogwood, Honeysuckle, Yu Angelicae Dahuricae Radix, Cat's Claw, Ginkgo, etc.

二、药材品种
II. Varieties of Medicinal Materials

山药 (Shanyao) ¦ Dioscoreae Rhizoma (Common Yam Rhizome)

【基原 / Origin】

为薯蓣科植物薯蓣 *Dioscorea opposita* Thunb. 的干燥根茎。

Common Yam Rhizome is the dried rhizome of *Dioscorea opposita* Thunb. (Fam. Dioscoreaceae).

【产地 / Producing area】

主产于河南。湖南、湖北、山西、云南、河北、陕西、江苏、浙江、江西、贵州、四川等地亦产。以河南博爱、沁阳、武陟、温县等地（古怀庆所属）所产质量最佳，习称"怀山药""铁棍山药"，为著名的"四大怀药"之一。

Dioscoreae Rhizoma is mainly produced in Henan Province. It is also produced in Hunan, Hubei, Shanxi, Yunnan, Hebei, Shaanxi, Jiangsu, Zhejiang, Jiangxi, Guizhou, and Sichuan Provinces, etc. Dioscoreae Rhizoma with the best quality is produced in Bo'ai, Qinyang, Wuzhi, Wenxian and other places (belonging to ancient Huaiqing) of Henan Province, commonly known as "Huai Dioscoreae Rhizoma" or "Iron stick Dioscoreae Rhizoma", which is one of the famous "four major Huai Medicinal Materials".

【采制 / Collection and preparation】

毛山药　冬季茎叶枯萎后采挖植物，切去根头，洗净，除去外皮和须根，干燥。

Mao Shanyao　The rhizome is collected in winter when the stem and leaves are withered, washed and cleaned after cutting off the root stock, then dried after peeling the outer bark and fibrous roots.

光山药　选择肥大顺直的毛山药，置清水中，浸至无干心，闷透，切齐两端，用木板搓成圆柱状，晒干，打光。

Guang Shanyao　The large fleshy, straight and dried Mao Shanyao is sorted and soaked in clean water until no dry core visible and then softened thoroughly. Two ends are cut to smooth plane and rubbed on a board to become cylindrical in shape, then dried in the sun and finally polished.

山药片　新鲜山药除去外皮，趁鲜切厚片，干燥。亦可取毛山药或光山药，除去杂质，分开大小个，泡润至透，切厚片，干燥。

Shanyao Pian　The rhizome is peeled outer bark and cut into thick slices while fresh, and dried. Or take Mao Shanyao or Guang Shanyao, remove the foreign matter, separate large and small rhizomes and soak thoroughly. Cut into thick slices and dried.

山药分别经麸炒、土炒炮制成麸炒山药和土炒山药。

Dioscoreae Rhizoma is processed to Bran Shanyao Pian and Loess Shanyao Pian by fried with bran and loess.

【商品特征 / Commodity characteristics】

毛山药 略呈圆柱状，弯曲而稍扁。表面黄白色或淡黄色，有纵沟、纵皱纹及须根痕，偶有浅棕色外皮残留。体重，质坚实，断面白色，粉性。气微，味淡、微酸，嚼之发黏。

Mao Shanyao It is subcylindrical, curved or somewhat flattened. Externally yellowish-white or pale yellow with longitudinal furrows and wrinkles, fibrous root scars and light-brown skin left occasionally. Body heavy, texture compact and tough, fracture white and starchy. Odour slight, taste plain, mildly sour and sticky when chewed.

光山药 呈圆柱状，两端平齐，粗细均匀。表面光滑，白色或黄白色。

Guang Shanyao It is cylindrical with two flat ends and even thickness. Externally smooth, white or yellowish-white.

山药片 呈类圆形的厚片，表面类白色或淡黄白色，质脆，易折断，切面类白色，富粉性。

Shanyao Pian Sub-round thick slice. Surface off-white or light yellowish-white; texture fragile, easily broken; fracture off-white and starchy.

麸炒山药 形如山药片，切面黄白色或微黄色，偶见焦斑，略有焦香气。

Bran Shanyao Pian Its shape is similar to that of Shanyao Pian; fracture yellowish-white or light yellow, occasionally with focal spot and slightly scorched aroma.

土炒山药 形如山药片，切面土红色，粘有土粉，略具焦香气。

Loess Shanyao Pian Its shape is similar to that of Shanyao Pian. Fracture, red soil colour with bentonite, odor lightly scorched aroma.

【规格等级 / Specification and grade】

本品按加工方法将山药分为光山药和毛山药两种规格。光山药分为四个等级，毛山药分为三个等级。其等级标准如下：

Dioscoreae Rhizoma is divided into two specifications, i.e. Guang Shanyao and Mao Shanyao, according to the processing methods. Guang Shanyao is subclassified into four grades, and Mao Shanyao is subclassified into three grades. The grading criteria are as follows:

光山药 一等：呈圆柱形，条均挺直，光滑圆润，两头平齐。内外均匀为白色。质坚实，粉性足。味淡。长 15cm 以上，直径 2.3cm 以上。无裂痕、空心、炸头、杂质、虫蛀、霉变。

Guang Shanyao First grade: It is cylindrical, straight and smooth with two even ends. It is both externally and internally white. Texture compact and tough, fracture sufficiently starchy. Taste weak. Its size is more than 15cm in length and more than 2.3cm in diameter. There are no crack, nor hollow, nor xerochastic head, nor foreign matter, nor moth, and nor mildew.

二等：长 13cm 以上，直径 1.7cm 以上。其余同一等。

Second grade: More than 13cm in length and 1.7cm in diameter. Other criteria in this grade are the same as those in First grade.

三等：长 10cm 以上，直径 1cm 以上。其余同一等。

Third grade: More than 10cm in length and 1cm in diameter. Other criteria in this grade are the same as those in First grade.

四等：直径 0.8cm 以上，长短不分，间有碎块。无杂质、虫蛀、霉变。其余同一等。

Fourth grade: More than 0.8cm in diameter, regardless of length, occasionally fragments. There are no foreign matter, nor moth, and nor mildew. Other criteria in this grade are the same as those in First grade.

毛山药 一等：呈长条形，弯曲稍扁，有顺皱纹或抽沟，去净外皮。内外均为白色或黄白色，有粉性。味淡。长 15cm 以上，中部围粗 10cm 以上。无破裂、空心、黄筋、杂质、虫蛀、霉变。

Mao Shanyao

First grade: Long strip, curved or somewhat flattened. Externally longitudinally furrowed and wrinkled, white or yellowish-white without outer scarfskin. Texture starchy, and taste weak. Its size is more than 15cm in length and 10cm in diameter of the middle part. No crack, nor hollow, nor yellow tendon, nor foreign matter, nor moth and mildew.

二等：长 10cm 以上，中部围粗 6cm 以上。其余同一等。

Second grade: More than 10cm in length and 6cm in diameter of the middle part. Other criteria in this grade are the same as those in First grade.

三等：长 10cm 以上，中部围粗 3cm 以上。间有碎块。无杂质、虫蛀、霉变。其余同一等。

Third grade: More than 10cm in length and 3cm in diameter of the middle part. Occasionally fragments. No foreign matter, nor moth, nor mildew. Other criteria in this grade are the same as those in First grade.

【化学成分 / Chemical constituent】

主含薯蓣皂苷元、薯蓣皂苷，另含多种甾醇、山药多糖、3，4- 二羟基苯乙胺、植酸、尿囊素、多种氨基酸等。

It mainly contains diosgenins, dioscins, various sterols, yam polysaccharides, 3,4-dihydroxyphenethylamine, phytic acid, allantoin, various amino acids, etc.

【检查 / Examination】

毛山药、光山药水分均不得过 16.0%；山药片、麸炒山药水分不得过 12.0%。毛山药、光山药、麸炒山药总灰分不得过 4.0%；山药片（鲜切）总灰分不得过 5.0%；山药片（干切）总灰分不得过 2.0%。毛山药、光山药、麸炒山药二氧化硫残留量不得过 400mg/kg，山药片不得过 10mg/kg。

Water, not more than 16.0% for Mao Shanyao and Guang Shanyao, not more than 12.0% for Shanyao Pian and Bran Shanyao Pian.

Total ash, not more than 4.0% for Mao Shanyao, Guang Shanyao and Bran Shanyao Pian, not more than 5.0% and 2.0% for Shanyao Pian prepared from fresh and dry Shanyao, respectively.

Sulfur dioxide residue, not more than 400mg/kg for Mao Shanyao, Guang Shanyao and Bran Shanyao Pian, not more than 10mg/kg for Shanyao Pian.

【质量要求 / Quality requirement】

外观质量 以条粗、质坚实、粉性足、色洁白者为佳。

Appearance quality Good quality for thick strip, compact and tough texture, sufficient starchiness and whitish color.

内在质量 浸出物测定：水溶性浸出物（冷）毛山药、光山药不得少于 7.0%，山药片（鲜切）不得少于 10.0%，山药片（干切）、麸炒山药不得少于 4.0%。

Intrinsic quality Extract content: not less than 7.0%, 10.0% and 4.0% of water-soluble extractives (cold) for Mao Shanyao and Guang Shanyao, Shanyao Pian processed from fresh Shanyao, Shanyao Pian processed from dry Shanyao and Bran Shanyao, respectively.

【功能主治 / Function and indication】

平、甘。补脾养胃，生津益肺，补肾涩精。用于脾虚食少，久泻不止，肺虚喘咳，肾虚遗精，带下，尿频，虚热消渴。麸炒山药补脾健胃。用于脾虚食少，泄泻便溏，白带过多。

Neutral and sweet. To tonify spleen and stomach, engender fluids, nourish lung, tonify kidney and astringe essence. The indications are spleen deficiency and reduced food intake, chronic diarrhea, dyspnea and cough caused by lung deficiency, seminal emission caused by kidney deficiency, abnormal vaginal discharge, frequent urination, deficiency heat and wasting-thirst. Bran-fried Dioscoreae Rhizoma can tonify spleen and invigorate the stomach to treat spleen deficiency and reduced food intake, diarrhea, sloppy stool, and profuse white vaginal discharge.

【贮藏养护 / Storage and maintenance】

用纸箱包装，箱内用牛皮纸铺垫，密封。本品由于含有多量的黏液和淀粉，易受潮变软发黏发霉，置通风干燥处，防蛀。

It is packed in a carton, padded with kraft paper on the bottom and sealed. Prone to dampness to become soft, sticky and moldy due to the large amount of mucus and starch. Preserved in a ventilated and dry place, and protected from moth.

【用法用量 / Administration and dosage】

15~30g。

15~30g.

牛膝 (Niuxi) ¦ Achyranthis Bidentatae Radix (Twotoothed Achyranthes Root)

【基原 / Origin】

为苋科植物牛膝 *Achyranthes bidentata* Bl. 的干燥根。

Twotoothed Achyranthes Root is the dried root of *Achyranthes bidentata* Bl. (Fam. Amaranthaceae).

【产地 / Producing area】

主产于河南武陟、沁阳、温县、博爱等地（古怀庆所属），质量最佳，习称“怀牛膝”，为著名的“四大怀药”之一。

The best quality of Achyranthis Bidentatae Radix is mainly produced in Wuzhi, Qinyang, Wenxian, Bo’ai and other places of Henan Province (belonging to ancient Huaiqing), commonly known as “Huai Achyranthes Bidentatae Radix”, which is one of the famous “four major Huai Medicinal Materials”.

【采制 / Collection and preparation】

牛膝 冬季茎叶枯萎时采挖，除去须根和泥沙，捆成小把，晒至干皱后，将顶端切齐，晒干。

Achyranthes Bidentatae Radix It is collected in winter when the aerial part is withered, removed from rootlets and soil, tied up in a small bundle, dried in the sun to be externally wrinkled. Then dried thoroughly after being cut the ends flat.

牛膝段 药材除去杂质，洗净，润透，除去残留芦头，切段，干燥。

Achyranthes Bidentatae Radix segments It is obtained by removing the foreign matter, washed, soaked thoroughly, remains of rhizomes removed, cut into segments, and dried.

牛膝分别经黄酒、食盐炮制成酒牛膝和盐牛膝。

Achyranthes Bidentatae Radix is processed to Wine Achyranthes Bidentatae Radix and Salted Achyranthes Bidentatae Radix by dealing with yellow rice wine and salt, respectively.

【商品特征 / Commodity characteristics】

牛膝 呈细长圆柱形，挺直或稍弯曲。表面灰黄色或淡棕色，有微扭曲的细纵皱纹、排列稀疏的侧根痕和横长皮孔样的突起。质硬脆，断面平坦，淡棕色，略呈角质样而油润，中心维管束木质部较大，黄白色，其外周散有多数黄白点状维管束，断续排列成 2~4 轮。气微，味微甜而稍苦涩。

Achyranthes Bidentatae Radix It is slender, cylindrical, straight or slightly curved. Externally greyish-yellow or pale brown, with slightly twisted and fine longitudinal wrinkles, transverse lenticel-like protrusions and sparse rootlet scars. Texture hard and fragile, fracture even, pale brown, slightly horny and oily. Xylem of vascular bundles in the center is relatively large, yellowish-white. The outside is scattered with many spotted vascular bundles arranged in 2~4 whorls. Odour, slight; taste, slightly sweet, somewhat bitter and astringent.

牛膝段 呈圆柱形的段。外表皮灰黄色或淡棕色，有微细的纵皱纹及横长皮孔。质硬脆，易折断，受潮变软。切面平坦，淡棕色或棕色，略具角质样而油润，中心维管束木部较大，黄白色，其外围散有多数黄白色点状维管束，断续排列成 2~4 轮。气微，味微甜而稍苦涩。

Achyranthes Bidentatae Radix segments Cylindrical segments. Externally greyish-yellow or pale brown, with fine longitudinal wrinkles and transverse lenticel-like protrusions. Texture hard and fragile, easily broken, softened when moistened; cut surface even, pale brown or brown, slightly horny and oily; central vascular bundles with larger xylem in yellowish white, scattered many yellowish-white dotted vascular bundles in 2~4 whorls in outer part. Odour, slight; taste, sweet and slightly bitter and astringent.

酒牛膝 形如牛膝段，表面色略深，偶见焦斑，微有酒香气。

Wine Achyranthes Bidentatae Radix Its shape is similar to that of Achyranthes Bidentatae Radix segment. Externally somewhat deeper in color, burned spots occasionally visible. Odour, slightly wine aromatic.

盐牛膝 形同牛膝段，表面色略深，带黄斑，略带咸味。

Salt Achyranthes Bidentatae Radix Its shape is similar to that of Achyranthes Bidentatae Radix segment. Externally somewhat deeper in colour, yellow spots visible. It tastes slightly salty.

【规格等级 / Specification and grade】

本品按大小分成三等。其等级标准如下：

As commodity, Achyranthes Bidentatae Radix is divided into three grades according to the size. The grading criteria are as follows:

一等（头肥）：呈长条圆柱形。内外黄白色或浅棕色。味淡微甜。中部直径 0.6cm 以上，长 50cm 以上。根条均匀。无冻条、油条、破条、杂质、虫蛀、霉变。

First grade (tou fei): It is slender and cylindrical, externally yellowish-white or light brown. It tastes slightly sweet, more than 0.6cm in diameter of the middle part and 50cm in length with even roots. No frozen stick, nor oily root, nor broken root, nor foreign matter, nor moth, and nor mildew.

二等（二肥）：中部直径 0.4cm 以上，长 35cm 以上。其余同一等。

Second grade (er fei): The root diameter of the middle part is larger than 0.4cm, and the length is longer than 35cm. Other criteria in this grade are the same as those in First grade.

三等（平条）：中部直径 0.4cm 以下，但不小于 0.2cm，长短不分，间有冻条、油条、破条。无杂质、虫蛀、霉变。其余同一等。

Third grade (ping tiao): The root diameter of the middle part is shorter than 0.4cm, but not shorter than 0.2cm, regardless of the root length, occasionally with frozen sticks, oily roots, and broken roots. No foreign matter, nor moth, nor mildew. Other criteria in this grade are the same as those in First grade.

【化学成分 / Chemical constituent】

含有三萜皂苷类化合物，苷元为齐墩果烷型五环三萜。另含有甾酮类化合物，包括牛膝甾酮、β- 蜕皮甾酮、旌节花甾酮 D、红苋甾酮等。

It contains triterpenoid saponins, and the aglycones are oleanolane pentacyclic triterpenes. It also contains sterones, including achyrantosterone, β-ecdysterone, stigmatonone D, and erythrosterone.

【检查 / Examination】

水分不得过 15.0%。总灰分不得过 9.0%。二氧化硫残留量不得过 400mg/kg。

Water, not more than 15.0%. Total ash, not more than 9.0%. Sulfur dioxide residue, not more than 400mg/kg.

【质量要求 / Quality requirement】

外观质量 以根长、肉肥、皮细、黄白、味甘者为佳。

Appearance quality Good quality for long, plump and fine surface of roots, yellowish-white colour and sweet taste.

内在质量 浸出物测定：醇溶性浸出物（热）牛膝不得少于 6.5%；牛膝段不得少于 5.0%；酒牛膝不得少于 4.0%。含量测定：按高效液相色谱法测定，β- 蜕皮甾酮不得少于 0.030%。

Intrinsic quality Extract content: Alcohol-soluble extractives (hot) of Achyranthes Bidentatae Radix, not less than 6.5%; Achyranthes Bidentatae Radix segment, not less than 5.0%; Wine Achyranthes Bidentatae Radix, not less than 4.0%.

Assay: It contains not less than 0.030% of β-ecdysterone according to HPLC analysis method.

【功能主治 / Function and indication】

平，苦、甘、酸。逐瘀通经，补肝肾、强筋骨，利尿通淋，引血下行。用于经闭，痛经，腰膝酸痛，筋骨无力，淋证，水肿，头痛，眩晕，牙痛，口疮，吐血，衄血。

Neutral, bitter, sweet and sour. To expel stasis, unblock the meridian, tonify liver and kidney, strengthen sinew and bone, promote unration, relieve stranguria, and conduct blood and downward. It is also used for the treatments of amenorrhea, dysmenorrhea, limp aching in the lower back and knees, lack of strength of sinew and bone, stranguria, edema, headache, dizziness, toothache, mouth sore, hematemesis, and epistaxis.

【贮藏养护 / Storage and maintenance】

多装纸箱，内衬防潮纸，固封。酒牛膝、盐牛膝密闭。本品高温易走油变黑，宜置阴凉干燥处，防潮。

It is mostly packed in cartons, covered with moisture-proof paper inside and sealed. Wine Achyranthes Bidentatae Radix and Salted Achyranthes Bidentatae Radix are also sealed. It is preserved in a cool and dry place, and protected from moisture in order to avoid becoming oily and blackening at high temperature.

【用法用量 / Administration and dosage】

5~12g。

5~12g.

【注意 / Caution】

孕妇慎用。

Use with caution for women during pregnancy.

地黄 (Dihuang) ¦ Rehmanniae Radix (Rehmannia Root)

【基原 / Origin】

为玄参科植物地黄 *Rehmannia glutinosa* Libosch. 的新鲜或干燥块根。

Rehmannia Root is the fresh or dried root tuber of *Rehmannia glutinosa* Libosch. (Fam. Scrophulariaceae).

【产地 / Producing area】

主产于河南焦作地区的温县、武陟、博爱、沁阳、孟州，山东菏泽、成武，河北安国、定州，山西临汾、运城、长治，陕西蒲城、渭南，安徽亳州、阜阳等地亦产。以河南焦作产量大，质量优，习称"怀地黄"，为著名的"四大怀药"之一。

Rehmanniae Radix is mainly produced in Wenxian, Wuzhi, Bo'ai, Qinyang and Mengzhou of Jiaozuo region, Henan Province. It is also produced in Heze and Chengwu of Shandong Province; Anguo and Dingzhou of Hebei Province; Linfen, Yuncheng and Changzhi of Shanxi Province; Pucheng and Weinan of Shaanxi Province; Bozhou and Fuyang of Anhui Province, etc. Jiaozuo in Henan Province has a large output with excellent quality, known as "Huai Rehmanniae Radix" and is one of the famous "four major Huai Medicinal Materials".

【采制 / Collection and preparation】

鲜地黄 秋季采挖，除去芦头、须根及泥沙。

Xian Dihuang (Fresh Rehmannia Radix) It is collected in autumn with root stock, rootlets and soil removed.

生地黄 鲜地黄缓缓烘焙至八成干，即得生地黄。

Sheng Dihuang (Unprocessed Rehmanniae Radix) It is obtained by baking Fresh Rehmanniae Radix slowly to 80% dryness.

生地黄片 生地黄除去杂质，洗净，闷润，切厚片，干燥。

Sheng Dihuang slice After foreign matter is removed, Sheng Dihuang are washed, cleaned, soaked, cut into thick slices, and dried.

生地黄炭 取生地黄片武火炒至发泡鼓起，外表焦黑色，内显焦褐色，喷水少许灭尽火星，取出，凉透。

Sheng Dihuang Tan (Unprocessed Rehmanniae Radix Carbonization) The Rehmanniae Radix pieces are fried with strong fire until it foams and swells. The outer surface is black, and the inner is brown. Small amount of water is sprayed to crush out sparks. Then take it out and cool it thoroughly.

熟地黄 炮制方法有酒炖和蒸制两种。

Shu Dihuang (Processed Rehmanniae Radix) It is processed with two methods: stewing with wine and steaming.

（1）取净生地黄，用黄酒拌匀，置蒸制容器内，密闭隔水炖至酒吸尽，取出，晾晒至外皮黏液稍干时，切厚片或块，干燥。

(1) The Rehmanniae Radix is mixed with yellow rice wine and stewed until the wine is absorbed entirely, and then taken out, dried under the sun until the mucilage on surface is slightly dried, cut into thick slices or pieces, and dried thoroughly.

（2）取净生地黄，置蒸制容器内，用蒸汽加热蒸至黑润，取出，晒至八成干时，切厚片或块，干燥。

(2) The Rehmanniae Radix is steamed until it becomes blackish and shiny, and taken out, dried

under the sun to be 80% dried, cut into thick slices or pieces, and dried thoroughly.

熟地黄炭　取熟地黄片置锅内，文火炒至干燥，炒动有响声，再用武火炒至表面焦黑色，取出，晾凉。

Shu Dihuang Tan (Processed Rehmanniae Radix Carbonization)　Rehmanniae Radix is stir-frying processed with gentle heat until it is dried, then strongly fried until the surface is black, taken out, and cooled.

【商品特征 / Commodity characteristics】

鲜地黄　呈纺锤状或条状。表面浅红黄色，具弯曲的纵皱纹、芽痕、横长皮孔样突起及不规则疤痕。肉质，断面皮部淡黄白色，可见橘红色油点，木部黄白色，导管呈放射状排列。气微，味微甜、微苦。

Xian Dihuang　It exhibits spindle-like form or bar form and is externally pale reddish-yellow with curved longitudinal wrinkles, bud scars, elongated transverse lenticel-like protrusions and irregular scars. Its texture is fleshy, and its fracture, showing a pale yellowish-white bark with orange-red oil spots, and a yellowish-white wood, vessels arranged radially. Odour, slight; taste, slightly sweet and slightly bitter.

生地黄　多呈不规则的团块状或长圆形。表面棕黑色或棕灰色，具不规则的横曲纹。体重，质较软而韧，断面棕黑色或乌黑色，有光泽，具黏性。气微，味微甜。

Sheng Dihuang　It exhibits mostly in irregular masses or oblong and is externally brownish-black or brownish-grey, with irregular transverse wavy lines. Its texture is heavy, soft and tenacious, fracture brownish-black or black, lustrous, viscous. Odour, slight; taste, slightly sweet.

生地黄片　为类圆形或不规则的厚片。外表皮棕黑色或棕灰色，具不规则的横曲纹。切面棕黑色或乌黑色，有光泽，具黏性。气微，味微甜。

Sheng Dihuang Pian　It is in subrounded or irregular thick slices and externally brownish-black or brownish-grey with irregular transverse wavy lines. Its cut section is brownish-black or jet-black, lustrous, and viscous. Odour, slight; taste, a little bit sweet.

生地黄炭　为不规则块片，表面焦黑色，体轻质松泡，外皮焦脆，中心呈棕黑色并有蜂窝状间隙。有焦苦味。

Sheng Dihuang Tan　It occurs in irregular slices and is externally burnt black. Its texture is bulged and loose, body light; and the center is brown black with honeycomb-shaped gaps. Taste, burnt bitter.

熟地黄　为不规则的块片或碎块，表面乌黑色，有光泽，黏性大。质柔软而带韧性，断面乌黑色，有光泽。气微，味甜。

Shu Dihuang　It occurs in irregular slices and pieces, broken lumps, varying in size and thickness. It is externally black, lustrous, and more sticky. Its texture is soft and flexible, fracture black, and lustrous. Odour, slight; taste, sweet.

熟地黄炭　为不规则块片，表面焦黑色而光亮，质脆，味甜，微苦涩。

Shu Dihuang Tan　It occurs in irregular slices and is externally burnt black and lustrous. The texture, fragile; taste, sweet and slightly bitter and astringent.

【规格等级 / Specification and grade】

生地黄按 kg 支头数分为五等，熟地黄为统货。

生地黄，其等级标准如下：

Unprocessed Rehmanniae Radix is divided into five grades according to the numbers in per kg. Shu Dihuang is unified grade with the same price. The grading criteria of Unprocessed Rehmanniae Radix are as follows:

一等：呈纺锤形或条形圆根。体重质柔润。表面棕灰色或灰褐色。断面黑褐色或黄褐色，具有油性。味微甜。每 kg 16 支以内。无芦头、老母、生心、焦枯、杂质、虫蛀、霉变。

First grade: It is a round root in spindle or bar form. Its texture is heavy and soft and is externally brownish-grey or greyish-brown, fracture blackish-brown or yellowish-brown, lustrous. It tastes slightly sweet. Less than 16 root tubers in per kg. No rhizome, nor old root, nor semi-dry center of the root, nor scorched parts, nor foreign matter, nor moth, and nor mildew.

二等：每 kg 32 支以内。其余同一等。

Second grade: Less than 32 in per kg. Other criteria in this grade are the same as those in First grade.

三等：每 kg 60 支以内。其余同一等。

Third grade: Less than 60 in per kg. Other criteria in this grade are the same as those in First grade.

四等：每 kg 100 支以内。其余同一等。

Fourth grade: Less than 100 in per kg. Other criteria in this grade are the same as those in First grade.

五等：油性少，支根瘦小。每 kg 100 支以外，最小货直径 1cm 以上。其余同一等。

Fifth grade: There are less oil and thinner roots. More than 100 in per kg. The smallest root is more than 1cm in diameter. Other criteria in this grade are the same as those in First grade.

【化学成分 / Chemical constituent】

主含梓醇、二氢梓醇、乙酰梓醇、益母草苷、桃叶珊瑚苷、单蜜力特苷、蜜力特苷等环烯醚萜苷类化合物，其中以梓醇含量最高。苯乙醇苷类化合物有毛蕊花糖苷等。多糖类成分主要有水苏糖、棉子糖、甘露三糖、毛蕊花糖、半乳糖及地黄多糖 a、b 等。腺苷、麦角甾苷也是地黄主要有效成分。另外还含有多种微量元素、氨基酸。

It mainly contains cycloalkenyl terpenoids, such as catalpol, dihydrocatalol, acetyl catalpol, leonuride, aucubin, monomelitin, melitin, among which content of catalpol is the highest. Phenylglycosides include verbascoside, etc. The polysaccharides are mainly stachyose, raffinose, mannose, verbascose, galactose, and digiton polysaccharides a and b. Adenosine and ergostatin are also the main active ingredients of Rehmanniae Radix. It also contains various trace elements and amino acids.

【检查 / Examination】

生地黄、生地黄片及熟地黄水分不得过 15.0%，总灰分不得过 8.0%，酸不溶性灰分不得过 3.0%。

Unprocessed Rehmanniae Radix, unprocessed Rehmanniae Radix slices and processed Rehmanniae Radix Water, not more than 15.0%. Total ash, not more than 8.0%. Acid-insoluble ash, not more than 3.0%.

【质量要求 / Quality requirement】

外观质量 鲜地黄以粗壮、色红黄者为佳。生地黄以块大、体重、断面乌黑者为佳。熟地黄以块根肥大，软润、内外乌黑有光泽者为佳。

Appearance quality Good quality of Xian Dihuang for the sturdy and redish-yellow; Good quality of Unprocessed Rehmanniae Radix for large size, heavy weight, black fracture; Good quality of Processed Rehmanniae Radix for plump roots, soft texture, black and lustrous color inside and outside.

内在质量 浸出物测定：生地黄、生地黄片及熟地黄水溶液浸出物（冷）不得少于 65.0%。含量测定：按高效液相色谱法测定，生地黄及生地黄片含梓醇不得少于 0.20%，含毛蕊花糖苷不得少于 0.020%；熟地黄含毛蕊花糖苷不得少于 0.020%。

Intrinsic quality Extract content: not less than 65.0% of water-soluble extractives (cold) for unprocessed Rehmanniae Radix, unprocessed Rehmanniae Radix slices and processed Rehmanniae Radix.

Assay: It contains not less than 0.20% of catalpol and 0.020% of verbascoside calculated with reference to the dried medicinal material of unprocessed Rehmanniae Radix or unprocessed Rehmanniae Radix slice according to HPLC analysis method. And It contains not less than 0.020 % of verbascoside calculated with reference to the dried medicinal material of Processed Rehmanniae Radix according to HPLC analysis method.

【功能主治 / Function and indication】

鲜地黄 寒，甘、苦。清热生津，凉血，止血。用于热病伤阴，舌绛烦渴，温毒发斑，吐血，衄血，咽喉肿痛。

Xian Dihuang It is cold, sweet and bitter, and used to clear heat, engender fluid, cool the blood, and stop bleeding. It is also used for the treatment of febrile disease damaging yin, crimson tongue, vexation, thirst, macula and papule caused by warm toxin, hematemesis, epistaxls, and swelling and sore throat.

生地黄 寒，甘。清热凉血，养阴生津。用于热入营血，温毒发斑，吐血衄血，热病伤阴，舌绛烦渴，津伤便秘，阴虚发热，骨蒸劳热，内热消渴。

Sheng Dihuang It is cold and sweet, and used to clear heat, cool the blood, nourish yin and engender fluids, and for the treatment of heat entering nutrient-blood aspects, macula and papule caused by warm toxin, hematemesis damaging yin, crimson tongue, vexation, thirst, fluid consumption, yin deficiency fever, steaming, bone, consumptive fever, interior heat, and wasting-thirst.

熟地黄 微温，甘。补血滋阴，益精填髓。用于血虚萎黄，心悸怔忡，月经不调，崩漏下血，肝肾阴虚，腰膝酸软，骨蒸潮热，盗汗遗精，内热消渴，眩晕，耳鸣，须发早白。

Shu Dihuang It is slightly warm and sweet, and used for tonifying blood and nourishing yin, and enriching essence and filling marrow. It is also used for the treatment of blood deficiency and chlorosis, heart palpitations, irregular menstruation, metrorrhagia embolism in blood, liver and kidney yin deficiency, waist and knee weakness, bone steaming and fever, night sweats and nocturnal emission, internal heat and thirst, dizziness, tinnitus and hair mustache early whitening.

【贮藏养护 / Storage and maintenance】

鲜地黄一般采用竹筐、蒲包或荆条筐包装，易腐烂，不宜久藏，埋在沙土中。生地黄多用篓装或麻袋装，置于干燥通风处，谨防潮湿，防霉，防蛀。熟地黄可装入内衬防潮油纸的纸箱内密封，置通风干燥处。饮片应入瓮内密闭。

Xian Dihuang is often packaged in bamboo baskets, tarpaulins or vitex baskets, which are perishable and should not be stored for long periods of time. It can be buried in sand.

Sheng Dihuang is usually packed in baskets or sacks and placed in dry and ventilated condition to prevent moisture, mildew and moth.

Shu Dihuang should be sealed in a cardboard box lined with moisture-proof oiled paper inside, and kept in ventilated and dried place. The pieces should be sealed inside the urn.

【用法用量 / Administration and dosage】

鲜地黄：12~30g；生地黄：10~15g；熟地黄：9~15g。

Xian Dihuang: 12~30g;

Unprocessed Rehmanniae Radix: 10~15g;

Processed Rehmanniae Radix: 9~15g.

重点小结
Summary

药材	主产地	商品规格	等级标准
山药	主产于河南。湖南、湖北、山西、云南、河北、陕西、江苏、浙江、江西、贵州、四川等地亦产。以河南博爱，沁阳、武陟、温县等地（古怀庆所属）所产质量最佳	按加工方法将山药分为光山药和毛山药	光山药分为四个等级，毛山药分为三个等级
牛膝	主产于河南武陟、沁阳、温县、博爱等地（古怀庆所属）	不分规格	按大小分成三等
地黄	主产于河南焦作地区的温县、武陟、博爱、沁阳、孟州，山东菏泽、成武，河北安国、定州，山西临汾、运城、长治，陕西蒲城、渭南，安徽亳州、阜阳等地亦产	按加工方法将地黄分为生地黄和熟地黄	生地黄按 kg 支头数分为五等，熟地黄为统货

Medicinal material	Main producing area	Specification	Grade
Dioscoreae Rhizoma	Dioscoreae Rhizoma is mainly produced in Henan Province. It is also produced in Hunan, Hubei, Shanxi, Yunnan, Hebei, Shaanxi, Jiangsu, Zhejiang, Jiangxi, Guizhou, and Sichuan Provinces etc. Dioscoreae Rhizoma with the best quality is produced in Bo'ai, Qinyang, Wuzhi, Wenxian and other places (belonging to ancient Huaiqing) of Henan Province	Dioscoreae Rhizoma is divided into two specifications, i.e. Guangshanyao and Maoshanyao, according to processing methods	Guangshanyao is subclassified into four grades, and Maoshanyao is subclassified into three grades
Achyranthis Bidentatae Radix	The herb is mainly produced in Wuzhi, Qinyang, Wenxian, Bo'ai and other places (belonging to ancient Huaiqing) of Henan Province	Unified specification	This product is divided into three grades according to size
Rehmanniae Radix	Rehmanniae Radix is mainly produced in Wenxian, Wuzhi, Bo'ai, Qinyang, Mengzhou of Jiaozuo region, Henan Province. It is also produced in Heze, Chengwu of Shandong Province; Anguo, Dingzhou of Hebei Province; Linfen, Yuncheng, Changzhi of Shanxi Province; Pucheng, Weinan of Shaanxi Province; Bozhou, Fuyang of Anhui Province; and so on	Rehmanniae Radix is divided into Unprocessed Rehmanniae Radix and Processed Rehmanniae Radix according to processing methods	Unprocessed Rehmanniae Radix is divided into five grades according to the numbers of per kilogram. Processed Rehmanniae is unified grade

题库

目 标 检 测
Object Detection

一、选择题（Choice question）

（一）单项选择题（One-choice question）

1. 怀药的产地是（　　）

A. 河南省　　B. 安徽省　　C. 湖南省

D. 湖北省　　E. 山东省

The producing area of Huai Medicinal Materials is (　　)

A. Henan Province　　B. Anhui Province　　C. Hunan Province

D. Hubei Province　　E. Shandong Province

2. 山药的来源是（　　）

A. 山药科植物山药的干燥根茎　　B. 山药科植物山药的成熟果实

C. 薯蓣科植物山药的干燥根茎　　D. 薯蓣科植物薯蓣的成熟果实

E. 薯蓣科植物薯蓣的干燥根茎

The origin of Dioscoreae Rhizoma is (　　)

A. Dry rhizomes of Dioscoreae Rhizoma

B. Ripe fruits of Dioscoreae Rhizoma

C. Dried rhizomes of Dioscorea yam

D. Ripe fruits of Dioscorea yam

E. Dried rhizome of *Dioscorea opposita* Thunb.

3. 牛膝来源于苋科植物牛膝的干燥（　　）

A. 茎　　B. 根　　C. 成熟果实

D. 根茎　　E. 地上部分

Achyranthes Bidentatae Radix is derived from the dried (　　) of *Achyranthes bidentata* Bl.

A. stem　　B. root　　C. mature fruit

D. rhizome/shoot　　E. The parts above ground

4. 地黄的来源是（　　）

A. 地黄科植物的成熟果实　　B. 玄参科植物的新鲜或干燥块根

C. 地黄科植物的新鲜或干燥块根　　D. 玄参科植物成熟果实

E. 苋科植物的新鲜或干燥的根及根茎

The origin of Rehmanniae Radix is (　　)

A. Ripen fruits of Fam. Rehmanniae

B. Fresh or dried root tuber of Fam. Scrophulariaceae

C. Fresh or dried root tuber of Fam. Rehmanniae

D. Ripen fruits of Fam. Scrophulariaceae

E. Fresh or dried root tuber of Fam. Amaranthaceae

5. 下列哪个药材不宜久藏，宜埋在沙土中（　　）

A. 鲜地黄　　B. 生地黄　　C. 熟地黄

D. 地黄炭　　E. 熟地炭

Which of the following medicinal materials should not be stored for a long time, but can be buried in sand (　　)

A. Fresh Rehmannia Radix
B. Unprocessed Rehmanniae Radix
C. Processed Rehmanniae Radix
D. Unprocessed Rehmanniae Radix Carbonization
E. Processed Rehmanniae Radix Carbonization

（二）多项选择题（Multiple choice questions）

1. 四大怀药指的是（　　）

A. 怀山药　　B. 怀菊花　　C. 怀地黄
D. 怀牛膝　　E. 怀桔梗

The "four major Huai Medicinal Materials" are (　　)

A. Huai shanyao　　B. Huai juhua　　C. Huai Dihuang
D. Huai niuxi　　E. Huai jiegeng

2. 山药的习称有（　　）

A. 铁山药　　B. 怀山药　　C. 铁棍山药
D. 棍山药　　E. 温山药

Dioscoreae Rhizoma is traditionally called (　　)

A. Iron yam　　B. Huai Dioscoreae Rhizoma
C. Iron Stick Dioscoreae Rhizoma　　D. Stick Dioscoreae Rhizoma
E. Wen Dioscoreae Rhizoma

3. 山药药材按照采制可分为（　　）

A. 毛山药　　B. 光山药　　C. 山药片
D. 蜜炒山药　　E. 醋炒山药

According to collection and preparation method, Dioscoreae Rhizoma can be divided into (　　)

A. Mao Shanyao　　B. Guang Shanyao　　C. Shanyao pills
D. Honey Shanyao　　E. Vinegar Shanyao

4. 牛膝的商品种类有（　　）

A. 牛膝段　　B. 牛膝　　C. 盐牛膝
D. 醋牛膝　　E. 土牛膝

Commodity types of Achyranthes are (　　)

A. Achyranthes Bidentatae Radix segment
B. Achyranthes Bidentatae Radix
C. Salt Achyranthes Bidentatae Radix
D. Vinegar Achyranthes Bidentatae Radix
E. Loess Achyranthes Bidentatae Radix

5. 下列药材需要检查二氧化硫残留量的是（　　）

A. 生地　　B. 山药　　C. 熟地　　D. 牛膝　　E. 菊花

In the following medicinal materials, (　　) are required to be checked the residual amount of sulfur dioxide.

A. Unprocessed Rehmanniae Radix　　B. Dioscoreae Rhizoma

C. Processed Rehmanniae Radix
D. Achyranthis Bidentatae Radix
E. chrysanthemum

二、思考题（Thinking questions）

1. 毛山药、光山药以及山药片在采制方法上有哪些差别？

What are the differences in the collection and preparation methods of Maoshanyao, Guangshanyao, and Shanyaopian?

2. 如何评价山药的质量？

How to evaluate the quality of Dioscoreae Rhizoma?

3. 牛膝按照采制方法分为哪些种类？

What types of Achyranthes Bidentatae Radix are classified according to the methods of collection and processing?

4. 如何评价牛膝的药材质量？

How to evaluate the quality of Achyranthes Bidentatae Radix?

5. 牛膝的贮藏养护应注意什么？

What should we pay attention to during storage and conservation of Achyranthes Bidentatae Radix?

6. 地黄的商品种类有哪些？

What are the commodity types of Rehmanniae Radix?

7. 如何评价鲜地黄、生地黄以及熟地黄的质量？

How to evaluate the quality of Fresh Rehmannia Radix, Unprocessed Rehmanniae Radix and Processed Rehmanniae Radix?

PPT

第十三章 浙 药
Chapter 13 Zhe Medicinal Materials

学习目标 | Learning Target

知识要求：

1．**掌握** 浙药的含义及其主要道地药材品种。

2．**熟悉** 主要浙药的采制、规格等级、商品特征、检查、贮藏方法。

能力要求：

会运用所学规格等级、商品特征、检查、质量要求等知识和方法鉴别市场上白术、麦冬和浙贝母的真伪优劣。

Knowledge requirements:

1. **Proficiency** The concept and major varieties of Zhe Medicinal Materials.

2. **Familiarity** The knowledge for the collection, specification, grade, commodity characteristics, examination, and storage method of main Zhe Medicinal Materials.

Skill requirements:

Learn to identify the authenticity and evaluate the quality of Atractylodis Macrocephalae Rhizoma, Ophiopogonis Radix and Fritillariae Thunbergii Bulbus on the market by applying the knowledge and methods of specification and grade, commodity characteristics, examination and quality requirement, etc.

一、浙药概述
I. Overview of Zhe Medicinal Materials

以浙江为主要产区或集散地的大宗商品药材称为浙药。也有称杭药、温药。产区位于中国东南沿海，地处亚热带，气候温和湿润，四季分明，光照充足。年平均气温15℃~18℃，无霜期东南沿海达270天。年降水量1000~2200mm。河流水源充足，地表水平均年径流总量900多亿立方米。植被资源在3000种以上，森林覆盖率达45.8%。本产区的道地中药材较多，最为著名的当属“浙八味”，指杭白术、杭白芍、浙贝母、杭白菊、延胡索、玄参、浙麦冬、温郁金这八味中药材。

The bulk commodities of medicinal materials, mainly produced and distributed in Zhejiang Province, are called Zhe Medicinal Materials, also known as Hang Medicinal Materials or Wen Medicinal Materials. Its producing area is located in south-east coastal region in subtropical zone, with a mild and humid climate, four distinct seasons, and sufficient solar light. The average annual temperature is 15℃~18℃ and there are 270 days of frost-free period on the southeast coast. The annual precipitation is 1000~2200mm. Rivers supply sufficient water sources, and the average annual surface runoff totals are over 90 billion cubic meters. There are more than 3000 species of the vegetation resources and the forest coverage rate reaches 45.8% in this producing area, where many authentic medicinal materials are produced. The most famous varieties are "Zhebawei" "Zhebawei" refers to the eight Chinese herbs that are mainly produced in Zhejiang Province, including Hangbaizhu, Hangbaishao, Zhebeimu, Hangbaiju, Yanhusuo, Xuanshen, Zhemaidong and Wenyujin.

二、药材品种
II. Varieties of Medicinal Materials

白术 (Baizhu) ¦ Atractylodis Macrocephalae Rhizoma (Largehead Atractylodes Rhizome)

【基原 / Origin】

为菊科植物白术 *Atractylodes macrocephala* Koidz. 的干燥根茎。

Largehead Atractylodes Rhizome is the dried rhizome of *Atractylodes macrocephala* Koidz. (Fam. Compositae).

【产地 / Producing area】

主产于浙江新昌、嵊县、磐安、东阳、天台，安徽亳州，湖南平江，河北安国，四川宝兴、天全等地。

Main producing areas are Xinchang, Shengxian, Pan'an, Dongyang, Tiantai of Zhejiang Province; Bozhou of Anhui Province; Pingjiang of Hunan Province; Anguo of Hebei Province; Baoxing and Tianquan of Sichuan Province.

【采制 / Collection and preparation】

白术 冬季下部叶枯黄、上部叶变脆时采挖，除去泥沙，烘干或晒干，再除去须根。

Atractylodis Macrocephalae Rhizoma It is collected in winter when the leaves at the lower part of the plant turn yellow and the leaves at the upper part become fragile. After the soil is removed, it is baked or dried in the sun, and then fibrous root is removed.

白术分别经切制和炒制而成白术片、麸炒白术、土炒白术。

Atractylodis Macrocephalae Rhizoma is processed to Atractylodis Macrocephalae Rhizoma slices, Bran-fried Atractylodis Macrocephalae Rhizoma and Soil-fried Atractylodis Macrocephalae Rhizoma with the preparation ways of cutting and frying, respectively.

【商品特征 / Commodity characteristics】

白术 呈不规则肥厚团块状。表面灰黄色、黄棕至灰棕色，一端常有一短段木质中空的地上茎或渐细，俗称"术腿"或"鸡腿"；从"术腿"一端至另一端，逐渐粗大，有不规则瘤状突起及断续的纵皱纹和沟纹，并有须根痕，至底部明显膨大，形似"如意头"，俗称为"云头"。质坚硬，不易折断。断面不平坦，黄白色至淡棕色，棕色的点状油室散在；烘干者断面角质样，色较深，有裂隙。气清香，味甜、微辛，口嚼之略带黏性。

Atractylodis Macrocephalae Rhizoma In irregularly plump masses. It is externally greyish-yellow or yellowish-brown to greyish-brown. A short stem on the one end, wooden, hollow, and gradually thin, is commonly known as "Zhutui" or "Jitui". From one end of "Zhutui" to the other end, the rhizome is gradually thicker and larger, with irregularly warty protrusions, interrupted longitudinal wrinkles and grooves, and scars of fibrous rootlets, shaped like "Ruyitou", it is known as "Yuntou". Texture is hard and not easy to be broken; fracture uneven, yellowish-white to pale brown, scattered with brown dotted oil cavities; the fractures of the baking-dried rhizomes are horny, relatively dark colored or cracked. Odour aromatic; taste, sweet, slightly pungent and viscous on chewing.

白术片 呈不规则的厚片。外表皮灰黄色或灰棕色。切面黄白色至淡棕色，散生棕黄色的点状油室，木部具放射状纹理；烘干者切面角质样，色较深或有裂隙。气清香，味甘、微辛，嚼之略带黏性。

Atractylodis Macrocephalae Rhizoma Slices In irregular thick slices, it is externally greyish-yellow or greyish-brown. Fracture is yellowish-white to pale brown, scattered with brownish-yellow dotted oil cavities, xylem with radial striations; the fractures of baking-dried materials are horny with deeper color and clefts. Odour, aromatic; taste, sweet, slightly pungent and somewhat viscous when chewed.

麸炒白术 形如白术片，表面黄棕色，偶见焦斑。略有焦香气。

Bran Atractylodis Macrocephalae Rhizoma The shape is similar to Atractylodis Macrocephalae Rhizoma slices. It is externally yellowish-brown, burned spots occasionally visible and odour, slightly burned aromatic.

土炒白术 形如白术片，表面杏黄土色，附有细土末，有土香气。

Loess Atractylodis Macrocephalae Rhizoma The shape is similar to Atractylodis Macrocephalae Rhizoma slices. Its surface is apricot-loess-colored, with fine soil power and slight loess aroma.

【规格等级 / Specification and grade】

本品按大小分为四个等级。其等级标准如下：

It is divided into four grades according to the size. The grading criteria are as follows:

一等：呈不规则团块，体形完整。表面灰棕色或黄褐色。断面黄白色或灰白色。味甘微苦。每 kg 40 只以内。无焦枯、油个、虚泡、杂质、虫蛀、霉变。

First grade: It is in irregular masses, intact. Externally greyish-brown or yellowish-brown. Cut surface is yellowish-white to greyish-white, odour aromatic and taste bitter. Less than 40 pieces in per kg. No scorch, nor oil diffused ones, nor hollow, nor foreign matter, nor moth, and nor mildew.

二等：每 kg 100 只以内。其余同一等。

Second grade: Less than 100 pieces in per kg. Other criteria in this grade are the same as those in First grade.

三等：每 kg 200 只以内。其余同一等。

Third grade: Less than 200 pieces in per kg. Other criteria in this grade are the same as those in First grade.

四等：每 kg 200 只以外、间有程度不严重的碎块、油个、焦枯、虚泡。无杂质、霉变。

Fourth grade: More than 200 pieces in per kg, with less seriously broken sections, oily, scorched, and hollow. No foreign matter, nor mildew.

【化学成分 / Chemical constituent】

含挥发油，油中主要成分为苍术酮、桉叶醇、茅术醇，以及白术内酯Ⅰ、Ⅱ、Ⅲ等倍半萜内酯类化合物等多种成分。另外还含有苷类成分，由半乳糖、鼠李糖等组成的 PSAM-1 多糖和由木糖等组成的 PSAM-2 多糖等成分。

It mainly contains volatile oil, of which the main components are atractylone, eucalyptol, aristolochiol, sesquiterpene lactone compounds namely atractylolides I, II, and III, etc. In addition, it also contains glycosides, PSAM-1 polysaccharide composed of galactose and rhamnose, and PSAM-2 polysaccharide composed of xylose, etc.

【检查 / Examination】

水分不得过 15.0%。总灰分不得过 5.0%。二氧化硫残留量不得过 400mg/kg。

Water, not more than 15.0%. Total ash, not more than 5.0%. Sulfur dioxide residue, not more than 400mg/kg.

【质量要求 / Quality requirement】

外观质量 以个大、体重、表面灰黄色、断面黄白色、有黄色放射纹理、质坚实、无空心、香气浓，甜味浓而辣味少者为佳。

Appearance quality Good quality for large size, heavy body, externally greyish-yellow, cut surface yellowish-white, with yellow radial venations, compact and hard texture, no hollows, strong aroma, more sweet and less spicy taste.

内在质量 浸出物测定：醇溶性浸出物（热），不得少于 35.0%。

Intrinsic quality Extract content: not less than 35.0% of ethanol-soluble extractives (hot).

【功能主治 / Function and indication】

温，苦、甘。健脾益气，燥湿利水，止汗，安胎。用于脾虚食少，腹胀泄泻，痰饮眩悸，水肿，自汗，胎动不安。

It is warm, bitter and sweet. To fortify the spleen and replenish qi, dry dampness and promote unhation, stop sweating, and prevent miscarriage. It is used for the treatment of spleen deficiency with reduced food intake, abdominal distension and diarrhea, dizziness and palpitations caused by phlegm-fluid retention, edema, spontaneous sweating, and threatened miscarriage.

【贮藏养护 / Storage and maintenance】

多用麻袋和竹篓包装或方竹篓外套麻袋包装，最好内衬防潮纸等。置阴凉干燥处，防蛀。避光。饮片须晒干、放冷后装入坛内闷紧，梅雨季节宜入石灰缸存放。

It is usually packed in sacks and bamboo baskets or square bamboo baskets coated by sacks, better with moisture-proof paper inside, preserved in cool and dry place, and protected from moth and sunlight. The pieces should be dried, sealed in jar after cooling, and stored in crock together with calcium lime during the rainy season.

【用法用量 / Administration and dosage】

6~12g。

6~12g.

麦冬 (Maidong) ¦ Ophiopogonis Radix (Dwarf Lilyturf Tuber)

【基原 / Origin】

为百合科植物麦冬 *Ophiopogon japonicus* (L. f) Ker-Gawl. 的干燥块根。

Dwarf Lilyturf Tuber is the dried root tuber of *Ophiopogon japonicus* (L.f) Ker-Gawl (Fam. Liliaceae).

【产地 / Producing area】

主产于浙江省慈溪、余姚、肖山、杭州、笕桥，称为“浙麦冬”“笕麦冬”或“杭麦冬”，为浙江著名的道地药材“浙八味”之一；主产于四川绵阳地区三台县者，称为“川麦冬”。

“Zhe Maidong” “Jian Maidong” or “Hang Maidong” are mainly produced in Cixi, Yuyao, Xiaoshan,

Hangzhou, and Jianqiao of Zhejiang Province, known as one of Zhejiang's famous authentic medicinal materials "Zhebawei" "Chuan Maidong" is mainly produced in Santai County of Mianyang, Sichuan Province.

【采制 / Collection and preparation】

浙麦冬　于栽培后第三年小满至夏至采挖。洗净，反复暴晒、堆置，至七八成干，除去须根，干燥。

Zhe Maidong　It is collected in the period from Xiaoman to the summer solstice in the third year after cultivation, washed, cleaned, sun-dried and piled up repeatedly to 70%~80% dryness, removed from rootlets, and dried.

川麦冬　于栽培第二年清明至谷雨采挖，剪取块根，洗净，反复暴晒、堆置，至七八成干，除去须根，干燥。

Chuan Maidong　It is collected during the period from Fresh Green to Grain Rain in the second year after cultivation, washed clean, sun-dried and piled up repeatedly to 70%~80% dryness, removed from rootlets, and dried.

麦冬片　取麦冬，除去杂质，洗净，润透，轧扁，干燥。

Maidong Pian　Ophiopogon Radix, foreign matter removed, is washed, cleaned, soaked thoroughly, pressed to be flattened, and dried.

朱麦冬　取去心麦冬，置盆内喷水少许，微润，加朱砂细粉，撒布均匀，并随时翻动，至麦冬外面匀被朱砂为度，取出，晾干。

Zhu Maidong　Ophiopogon Radix, core removed, is put in the basin with a little water spayed in, slightly moisturized, fine powder of cinnabar added and spread evenly, turned over at any time until the outside of Ophiopogon Radix is all coated with cinnabar, then taken out and dried.

【商品特征 / Commodity characteristics】

浙麦冬　呈纺锤形，两头钝尖，中部肥满，微弯曲。表面黄白色，半透明，有不规则的纵皱纹。折断面黄白色，角质状。横断面中央有细小的木质部。气微香，味微甘、微苦。

Zhe Maidong　It shows a slightly curved spindle-like shape with two blunt ends and a plump middle part, externally yellowish-white and translucent, with irregularly longitudinal wrinkles. Fracture is yellowish-white and horny with a tiny xylem on the centor of the section. Odour, slightly aromatic; taste, sweetish and slightly bitter.

川麦冬　形状与杭麦冬相似而较短粗。表面乳白色，有光泽。质较坚硬；香气较小；味较淡，少黏性。

Chuan Maidong　It is similar to Zhe Maidong in shape but is shorter and thicker. It is externally milky and lustrous, with hard texture, less aroma, plain taste and less stickiness.

麦冬片　呈厚片状或碎段，切面角质半透明状，中央有白色木心。

Maidong Pian　It is in thick slices or broken sections. Cut surface is translucent and horny, with a white xylem in the center.

朱麦冬　形如麦冬。表面被朱砂细粉，呈淡红色。

Zhu Maidong　It is similar to Maidong in shape. Its surface is pale red with cinnabar fine powder.

【规格等级 / Specification and grade】

本品按产地分为浙麦冬、川麦冬两个规格，各分为三等。其规格等级标准如下：

Ophiopogonis Radix is divided into Zhe Maidong and Chuan Maidong according to the producing areas, each of which is also subdivided into three grades. The specifications and grading criteria are as follows:

浙麦冬 一等：呈纺锤形半透明体，表面黄白色。质柔韧。断面牙白色，有木质心。味微甜，嚼之有黏性。每 50g 150 只以内。无须根、油粒、烂头、杂质、霉变。

Zhe Maidong First grade: spindle-shaped and semitransparent. Externally yellowish-white. Texture pliable, fracture cream-white, with small stele. Taste, slightly sweet and sticky on chewing. Less than 150 pieces in per 50g. No rootlets, nor oily particles, nor rotten root tuber, nor foreign matter, and nor mildew.

二等：每 50g 280 只以内。其余同一等。

Second grade: Less than 280 pieces in per 50g. Other criteria in this grade are the same as those in First grade.

三等：每 50g 280 只以外，最小不低于麦粒大。油粒、烂头不超过 10%。无须根、杂质、霉变。其余同一等。

Third grade: More than 280 pieces in per 50g, the minimum size is not smaller than that of wheat grains. Oil particles and bad heads should not exceed 10%. No rootlets, nor foreign matter, and nor mildew. Other criteria in this grade are the same as those in First grade.

川麦冬 一等：呈纺锤形半透明体。表面淡白色，木质心细软。味微甜，嚼之少黏性。每 50g 190 粒以内，无须根、乌花、油粒、杂质、霉变。

Chuan Maidong First grades: it is spindle-shaped and semitransparent. Externally pale white with soft stele. Taste is slightly sweet and sticky on chewing. Less than 190 pieces per 50g. No rootlets, nor broken surface, nor oily particles, nor foreign matter and nor mildew.

二等：每 50g 300 粒以内。其余同一等。

Second class: Less than 300 pieces in per 50g. Other criteria in this grade are the same as those in First grade.

三等：每 50g 300 粒以外，最小不低于麦粒大。间有乌花、油粒不超过 10%，无须根、杂质、霉变。其余同一等。

Third class: More than 300 pieces in per 50g, the minimum size is not smaller than that of wheat grains. The number of broken surface and oily particles should not exceed 10%. No rootlets, nor foreign matter, and nor mildew. Other criteria in this grade are the same as those in First grade.

【化学成分 / Chemical constituent】

主含麦冬皂苷 A、B、B′、C、C′、D、D′等甾体皂苷类化合物，麦冬高异黄酮类化合物，另含多糖、氨基酸等。

It mainly contains steroidal saponins, such as Ophiopogosides A, B, B′, C, C′, D, and D′, as well as other homoisoflavonoids. It also contains polysaccharides, amino acids, etc.

【检查 / Examination】

水分不得过 18.0%。总灰分不得过 5.0%。

Water, not more than 18.0%. Total ash, not more than 5.0%.

【质量要求 / Quality requirement】

外观质量 以表面淡黄白色、肥大、质柔、气香、味甜、嚼之发黏者为佳。以瘦小、色棕黄、嚼之黏性小者为次。

Appearance quality Good quality for pale yellowish-white surface, plump and large body, soft texture, fragrant odour, sweet taste and stickiness on chewing. Inferior quality for small size, brownish-yellow color, and less stickiness on chewing.

内在质量 浸出物测定：水溶性浸出物（冷）不得少于 60.0%。含量测定：按高效液相色谱法测定，麦冬总皂苷以鲁斯可皂苷元计，不得少于 0.12%。

Intrinsic quality Extract content: not less than 60.0% of water-soluble extractive (cold).

Assay: It contains not less than 0.12% of ruscogenin, calculated with reference to the dried medicinal material according to HPLC analysis method.

【功能主治 / Function and indication】

微寒，甘、微苦。养阴生津，润肺清心。用于肺燥干咳，阴虚痨嗽，喉痹咽痛，津伤口渴，内热消渴，心烦失眠，肠燥便秘。

It is mild cold, sweet and slightly bitter. To nourish yin, engender fluid, moisten the lung, and clear the heart. For the treatment of dry cough caused by lung dryness, cough caused by yin consumptive disease, throat *bi* disorder, sore throat, thirst caused by fluid comsumption, interior heat dianhea, insomnia caused by vexation, and constipation caused by intestinal dryness.

【贮藏养护 / Storage and maintenance】

用纸箱盛装，箱内衬防潮纸，盛满，压紧，密闭。本品含糖分，易虫蛀，宜密封。置阴凉干燥处，防潮。

It is packed in cardboard boxes covered with moisture-proof paper inside, filled, compacted and sealed. Containing sugar, easy to be moth-eaten, it should be sealed and preserved in a cool and dry place, and protected from moisture.

【用法用量 / Administration and dosage】

6~12g。

6~12g.

浙贝母 (Zhebeimu) ¦ Fritillariae Thunbergii Bulbus (Thunberg Fritillary Bulb)

【基原 / Origin】

为百合科植物浙贝母 *Fritillaria thunbergii* Miq. 的干燥鳞茎。

Thunberg Fritillary Bulb is the dried bulb of *Fritillaria thunbergii* Miq. (Fam. Liliaceae).

【产地 / Producing area】

主产于浙江宁波、磐安、东阳、缙云等，为浙江著名的道地药材“浙八味”之一；江苏海门、南通，安徽广德、宁国，湖北板桥等地也产。

It is mainly produced in Ningbo, Pan’an, Dongyang, Jinyun of Zhejiang Province and is one of Zhejiang’s famous authentic medicinal materials, “Zhebawei”. It is also produced in Haimen and Nantong of Jiangsu Province; Guangde and Ningguo of Anhui Province; Banqiao of Hubei Province.

【采制 / Collection and preparation】

大贝 初夏植株枯萎时采挖，洗净。取大者（直径在 2.5cm 以上者），分成两瓣，除去芯芽。撞擦除去外皮，拌以煅过的贝壳粉，吸去擦出的浆汁，干燥。

Dabei It is collected in early summer when the plant is withered, washed and cleaned. The larger one (with more than 2.5cm in diameter), is divided into two scale leaves with the central bud removed. It is struck and rubbed to remove outer skin, mixed with calcined shell powder, sucked off the wiped slurry, and dried.

珠贝 初夏植株枯萎时采挖，洗净。取小者（直径在 2.5cm 以下者），不去芯芽。同上加工。

Zhubei It is collected in early summer when the plant is withered, washed and cleaned. The smaller ones (with less than 2.5cm in diameter) are used with central buds retained. The processing method is the same as that used for Dabei.

浙贝片　取鳞茎，大小分开，洗净，除去芯芽，趁鲜切成厚片，洗净，干燥。

Zhebei Pian　Bulbs are divided according to size, washed, with central buds removed, cut into thick slices while fresh, washed, cleaned, and dried.

【商品特征 / Commodity characteristics】

大贝　为鳞茎外层的单瓣鳞叶，略呈新月形，习称元宝贝。外表面类白色至淡黄色，内表面白色或淡棕色，被有白色粉末。质硬而脆，断面白色至黄白色，富粉性。气微，味微苦。

Dabei　Outer single scale leaf of bulb, slightly in crescent shape, traditionally called Yuanbaobei. The outer surface, off-white to pale yellow; the inner surface, white or pale brown, covered with white powder. Texture, hard and fragile; fracture, white to yellowish-white, highly starchy. Odour, slight; taste, slightly bitter.

珠贝　为完整的鳞茎，呈扁圆形。表面类白色，外层鳞叶 2 瓣，肥厚，略似肾形，互相抱合，内有小鳞叶 2~3 枚和干缩的残茎。

Zhubei　Intact bulb, oblate. Externally off-white; scale leaves on outer layer 2, plump and fleshy, slightly reniform, holding to each other, 2-3 small scale leaves inside and stem remains dried and shrunken.

浙贝片　为鳞茎外层的单瓣鳞叶切成的片。椭圆形或类圆形。边缘表面淡黄色，切面平坦，粉白色。质脆，易折断，断面粉白色，富粉性。

Zhebei Pian　Slices cut from the single scale leaves on outer layers of bulbs, elliptical or subrounded. Surface of edge, pale yellow; cut section, flat and white; texture, fragile and easily broken; fracture, white and highly starchy.

【规格等级 / Specification and grade】

本品分为大贝和珠贝两种商品规格。均为统货。

It is divided into two kinds of specifications: Dabei and Zhubei. Both are unified grade.

【化学成分 / Chemical constituent】

主含生物碱和皂苷，生物碱类成分有贝母素甲、贝母素乙、浙贝酮、贝母辛、异浙贝母碱、浙贝母碱苷、浙贝宁苷等。

It mainly contains alkaloids and saponins. The components of alkaloids include peimine, peiminime, zhebeinone, peimisine, isoverticine, peiminoside, zhebeininoside, etc.

【检查 / Examination】

水分不得过 18.0%。总灰分不得过 6.0%。

Water, not more than 18.0%. Total ash, not more than 6.0%.

【质量要求 / Quality requirement】

外观质量　以鳞叶肥厚、质坚实、粉性足、断面色白、不松泡、无僵子者为佳。

Appearance quality　Good quality for plump and fleshy scale leaves, compact and tough texture, sufficient starchiness, white fracture, no loose, swell, immature bulb.

内在质量　浸出物测定：醇溶性浸出物（热）不得少于 8.0%。含量测定：按高效液相色谱法测定，含贝母素甲和贝母素乙的总量，不得少于 0.080%。

Intrinsic quality　Extract content: not less than 8.0% of ethanol-soluble extractives (hot).

Assay: It contains not less than 0.080% of the total amount of peimine and peiminime according to HPLC analysis method.

【功能主治 / Function and indication】

寒，苦。清热化痰止咳，解毒散结消痈。用于风热咳嗽，痰火咳嗽，肺痈，乳痈，瘰疬，疮毒。不宜与川乌、制川乌、草乌、制草乌、附子同用。

It is cold and bitter. To clear away heat, resolve phlegm and suppress cough; remove toxin, dissipate binds and disperse abscesses. For the treatment of wind-heat cough, phlegm-fire cough, lung abscess, acute mastitis, scrofula, sore and skin infections. It is incompatible with Aconiti Radix, processed Aconiti Radix, Aconiti Kusnezoffii Radix, processed Aconiti Kusnezoffii Radix and Aconiti Lateralis Radix.

【贮藏养护 / Storage and maintenance】

一般用麻袋或木箱包装，置干燥处，防蛀。

It is usually packed in sacks or wooden boxes, preserved in a dry place and protected from moth.

【用法用量 / Administration and dosage】

5~10g。

5-10g.

重点小结
Summary

药材	主产地	商品规格	等级标准
白术	主产于浙江新昌、嵊县、磐安、东阳、天台，安徽亳州，湖南平江，河北安国，四川宝兴、天全等地	不分规格	均按照大小分为1~4个等级
麦冬	主产于浙江省慈溪、余姚、肖山、杭州、笕桥，称为“浙麦冬”、“笕麦冬”或“杭麦冬”，为浙江著名的道地药材“浙八味”之一；主产于四川绵阳地区三台县者，称为“川麦冬”	按产地分为浙麦冬、川麦冬两个规格	均按大小分为1~3等
浙贝母	主产于浙江宁波、磐安、东阳、缙云等；江苏海门、南通，安徽广德、宁国，湖北板桥等地也产	分为大贝和珠贝两种商品规格	均为统货

Medicinal material	Main producing area	Specification	Grade
Atractylodis Macrocephalae Rhizoma	Main producing areas are Xinchang, Shengzhou, Pan'an, Dongyang, Tiantai of Zhejiang Province; Bozhou of Anhui Province; Pingjiang of Hunan Province; Anguo of Hebei Province; Baoxing and Tianquan of Sichuan Province	Unified specification	It is divided into four grades according to the size

continued

Medicinal material	Main producing area	Specification	Grade
Ophiopogonis Radix	"Zhe Maidong", "Jian Maidong" or "Hang Maidong" are mainly produced in Cixi, Yuyao, Xiaoshan, Hangzhou, and Jianqiao of Zhejiang Province; "Chuan Maidong" is mainly produced in Santai County of Mianyang region, Sichuan province	Ophiopogonis Radix is divided into Zhe Maidong and Chuan Maidong according to the producing area	Each of them is divided into three grades according to weight
Fritillariae Thunbergii Bulbus	It is mainly produced in Ningbo, Pan'an, Dongyang, Jinyun of Zhejiang Province and also produced in Haimen, Nantong of Jiangsu Province; Guangde, Ningguo of Anhui Province, and Banqiao of Hubei Province	The product is divided into two specifications of Dabei and Zhubei	Unified grade

题库

目标检测
Object Detection

一、选择题（Choice question）

（一）单项选择题（One-choice question）

1. 浙药的产地是（　　）

A. 浙江省　　B. 安徽省　　C. 湖南省

D. 湖北省　　E. 山东省

The producing area of Zhe Medicinal Materials is (　　)

A. Zhejiang Province　　B. Anhui Province　　C. Hunan Province

D. Hubei Province　　E. Shandong Province

2. 白术来源于菊科植物白术的干燥（　　）

A. 根茎　　B. 成熟果实　　C. 地上部分

D. 全草　　E. 块茎

Atractylodis Macrocephalae Rhizoma is derived from the dried (　　) of *Atractylodes macrocephala* Koidz (Fam. Compositae).

A. Rhizome　　B. Mature fruit　　C. Parts above ground

D. whole plant　　E. Tuber

3. 麦冬来源于百合科植物麦冬的干燥（　　）

A. 茎　　B. 块根　　C. 成熟果实

D. 全草　　E. 地上部分

Ophiopogonis Radix is derived from the dried (　　) of *Ophiopogon japonicus* (Thunb.) Ker Gawl (Fam. Liliaceae).

A. Stem B. Root tuber C. Mature fruit
D. whole plant E. Parts above ground

4. 浙贝母来源于百合科植物浙贝母的干燥（　　）
A. 成熟果实 B. 块根 C. 鳞茎
D. 根及根茎 E. 地上部分
Fritillariae Thunbergii Bulbus is derived from the dried (　　) of *Fritillaria thunbergii* Miq (Fam. Liliaceae).
A. Mature fruit B. Tuber C. Bulb
D. Root and rhizome E. Parts Above ground

5. "如意头"是下列哪个药材的鉴别术语（　　）
A. 白术 B. 白芍 C. 地黄
D. 麦冬 E. 贝母
"Ruyitou" is the identification term for which of the following medicinal materials (　　)
A. Atractylodis Macrocephalae Rhizoma B. Paeoniae Radix Alba
C. Rehmanniae Radix D. Ophiopogonis Radix
E. Fritillariae Thunbergii Bulbus

（二）多项选择题（Multiple choice questions）

1. 下列属于"浙八味"的是（　　）
A. 杭白术 B. 杭白芍 C. 浙贝母
D. 浙麦冬 E. 川麦冬
Which authentic medicinal materials are "zhebawei" (　　)
A. Hangbaizhu B. Hangbaishao C. Zhebeimu
D. Zhemaidong E. Chuanmaidong

2. 按产地不同，麦冬可称为（　　）
A. 浙麦冬 B. 川麦冬 C. 杭麦冬
D. 笕麦冬 E. 温麦冬
According to the producing area, Ophiopogonis Radix can be called (　　)
A. Zhe maidong B. Chuan maidong C. Hang maidong
D. Jian maidong E. Wen maidong

3. 浙贝母的商品种类包括（　　）
A. 大贝 B. 珠贝 C. 浙贝片
D. 中贝 E. 小贝
What are the commercial specifications of Fritillariae Thunbergii Bulbus (　　)
A. Dabei B. Zhubei C. Zhebei
D. Zhongbei E. Xiaobei

4. 麦冬的商品种类有（　　）
A. 浙麦冬 B. 川麦冬 C. 朱麦冬
D. 醋麦冬 E. 土麦冬
Commodity types of Ophiopogonis Radix are (　　)
A. Zhe maidong B. Chuan maidong C. Zhu maidong
D. Vinegar maidong E. Loess maidong

5. 下列不需要检查二氧化硫残留量的是（　　）

A. 山药　B. 麦冬　C. 贝母　D. 白芍　E. 白术

In the following medicinal materials, (　　) do not need to be checked the residual amount of sulfur dioxide.

A. Dioscoreae Rhizoma

B. Ophiopogonis Radix

C. Fritillariae Thunbergii Bulbus

D. Paeoniae Radix Alba

E. Atractylodis Macrocephalae Rhizoma

二、思考题（Thinking questions）

1. 如何评价白术药材的质量？

How to evaluate the quality of Atractylodis Macrocephalae Rhizoma?

2. 白术贮藏养护时应注意什么？

What should you pay attention to when you store and conserve Atractylodis Macrocephalae Rhizoma ?

3. 浙麦冬和川麦冬采制有哪些差别？

What are the differences in harvesting and processing between the Zhejiang Dwarf lilyturf and Sichuan Dwarf lilyturf?

4. 浙麦冬和川麦冬商品特征有哪些差别？

What are the differences in product characteristics between Zhejiang Dwarf lilyturf and Sichuan Dwarf lilyturf?

5. 浙贝母分为哪些种类？

How many types is Fritillariae Thunbergii Bulbus divided into? What are they?

6. 大贝和珠贝商品特征有哪些差别？

What are the differences in the commodity characteristics of Dabei and Zhubei?

7. 贝母使用时应注意什么？

What should we pay attention to when using Fritillariae Thunbergii Bulbus?

PPT

第十四章　南　药
Chapter 14　Nan Medicinal Materials

学习目标 | Learning Target

知识要求：

1．**掌握**　南药的含义及其主要道地药材品种；牡丹皮、薄荷、蟾酥的道地产地、采制、规格等级、商品特征、质量要求。

2．**熟悉**　牡丹皮、薄荷、蟾酥的化学成分、检查和贮藏方法。

3．**了解**　南药产区的自然环境条件。

能力要求：

会运用所学规格等级、商品特征、检查、质量要求等知识和方法鉴别市场上牡丹皮、薄荷和蟾酥的真伪优劣。

Knowledge requirements:

1. **Proficiency**　The concept and main varieties of Nan Medicinal Materials. The authentic producing areas, collections and preparations, specifications and grades, commodity characteristics, identifications and quality requirements of Tree Peony Bark, Peppermint, and Toad Venom.

2. **Familiarity**　The chemical constituents, examinations and storage methods of Tree Peony Bark, Peppermint, and Toad Venom.

3. **Understanding**　Natural environment in the producing areas of Nan Medicinal Materials.

Skill requirements:

Learn to identify the authenticity and evaluate the quality of Tree Peony Bark, Peppermint, and Toad Venom on the market by applying the knowledge and methods of specification and grade, commodity characteristics, examination and quality requirement, etc.

一、南药概述
I. Overview of Nan Medicinal Materials

以长江中下游以南、南岭以北大部分地区为主要产区或集散地的大宗商品药材，称为南药。南药产区主要包括华东、华中的广大亚热带东部地区，涵盖了湖南、湖北、江苏、安徽、福建、江西、台湾等省区。本地区位于我国三大阶梯中的最低一级，以低山丘陵为主，平均海拔 500m

左右；气候温暖而湿润，冬温夏热，四季分明。年均降水量在800~1600mm，由东南沿海向西北递减。本区湖泊星罗棋布，水生药用植物丰富，有莲、芡实、菖蒲等；丘陵地区的野生药用植物有丹参、玄参、牛膝、百部、海金沙、何首乌等；作为冲积平原的耕作区，气候适宜、土质好，适用于多种药材的栽培。主要的南药有：安徽的凤丹皮、宣木瓜，江苏的苏薄荷、茅苍术、太子参、蟾酥等，福建的建泽泻、蕲蛇；江西新干、樟树的江枳壳，宜春香薷，丰城鸡血藤，泰和乌骨鸡等；江汉平原的龟甲、鳖甲；湖南平江白术、沅江枳壳、邵东湘玉竹等。

The bulk commodities of medicinal materials, which mainly produced or marketed in the most regions between south of the middle and lower reaches of the Yangtze River and north of Nanling Mountains, are known as Nan Medicinal Materials. The production areas mainly include the vast subtropical eastern region of eastern and central China, consisting of Hunan, Hubei, Jiangsu, Anhui, Fujian, Jiangxi, Taiwan, etc. The region is located in the lowest of China's three ladders, and is dominated by low mountains hills. The average altitude is about 500m; the climate is warm and humid, warm in winter and hot in summer, with four distinctive seasons. The average annual precipitation is 800-1600mm, decreasing from the southeast coast to the northwest. In this area, there are abundant aquatic plants along with the scattered lakes, namely Nelumbinis, Euryales Semen, Acorus calamus, etc.; and wild medicinal plants in the hilly areas, such as *Salvia miltiorrhiza*, *Scrophularia ningpoensis*, *Achyranthes bidentata*, *Stemona japonica*, *Lygodium japonicum*, *Fallopia multiflora*, etc.; and as a farming area on the alluvial plain with suitable climate and high quality soil, it is suitable for the cultivation of many kinds of medicinal herbs. The main Nan Medicinal Materials are as follows: "Fengdanpi"(Moutan Cortex) and "Xuanmugua"(Chaenomelis Fructus) from Anhui Province; "Subohe"(Menthae Haplocalycis Herba), "Maocangzhu"(Atractylodis Rhizoma), Pseudostellariae Radix, Bufonis Venenum, etc. from Jiangsu Province; "Jianzexie"(Alismatis Rhizoma) and Agkistrodon from Fujian Province; "Jiangzhiqiao"(Aurantii Fructus) of Xin'gan and Zhangshu, Moslae Herba of Yichun, Spatholobi Caulis of Fengcheng, and Taihe black-bone chicken, etc. from Jiangxi Province; Testudinis Carapax et Plastrumt, and Trionycis Carapax from Jianghan Plain; Atractylodis Macrocephalae Rhizoma of Pingjiang, Aurantii Fructus of Yuanjiang, Polygonati Odorati Rhizoma of shaodong, etc. from Hunan Province.

二、药材品种
II. Varieties of Medicinal Materials

牡丹皮 (Mudanpi) ¦ Moutan Cortex (Tree Peony Bark)

【基原 / Origin】

为毛茛科植物牡丹 *Paeonia suffruticosa* Andr. 的干燥根皮。

Tree Peony Bark is the dried root bark of *Paeonia suffruticosa* Andr. (Fam. Ranunculaceae).

【产地 / Producing area】

主产于安徽铜陵、南陵、青阳、泾县；重庆垫江；四川都江堰、康定；湖南邵阳、长沙、衡阳；湖北、河南、陕西、山东、甘肃、贵州等地亦产。安徽铜陵产者习称“凤丹皮”；重庆、四川产者习称“川丹皮”；甘肃、陕西产者习称“西丹皮”。

The main producing areas are Tongling, Nanling, Qingyang and Jingxian of Anhui Province; Dianjiang of Chongqing Municipality; Dujiangyan and Kangding of Sichuan Province; Shaoyang, Changsha and Hengyang of Hunan Province; and the provinces of Hubei, Henan, Shaanxi, Shandong,

Gansu and Guizhou, etc. Those produced in Tongling, Anhui Province are traditionally called "Fengdanpi"; those produced in Chongqing Municipality and Sichuan Province are traditionally called "Chuandanpi"; those produced in Gansu and Shaanxi Province are traditionally called "Xidanpi".

【采制 / Collection and preparation】

牡丹皮 栽培3~5年后采收，于秋季采挖根部，除去细根和泥沙，剥取根皮，晒干或刮去粗皮，除去木心，晒干。前者习称连丹皮，后者习称刮丹皮。

Tree Peony Bark The root is collected in autumn after 3~5 years of cultivation, removed from rootlets and soil. The root bark is peeled off, and dried in the sun; or coarse bark is scraped off, removed from woody part, and dried in the sun. The former is known as Liandanpi and the latter as Guadanpi.

牡丹皮片 取牡丹皮，迅速洗净，润后切薄片，晒干。

Slices of Tree Peony Bark The Tree Peony Bark is washed clean rapidly, softened, cut into thin slices, and dried in the sun.

【商品特征 / Commodity characteristics】

连丹皮 呈筒状或半筒状，有纵剖开的裂缝，略向内卷曲或张开。外表面灰褐色或黄褐色，有多数横长皮孔样突起及细根痕，栓皮脱落处粉红色；内表面淡灰黄色或浅棕色，有明显的细纵纹，常见发亮的结晶。质硬而脆，易折断，断面较平坦，淡粉红色，粉性。气芳香，味微苦而涩。

Liandanpi Quilled or semiquilled, with longitudinal cut fissures, somewhat rolling inwards or open. Outer surface greyish-brown or yellowish-brown, showing numerous transverse lenticel-like protuberances and rootlet scars, the exposed surface where cork falls off appearing pink; inner surface pale greyish-yellow or pale brown, with obvious fine longitudinal striations, usually showing bright crystals. Texture, hard and fragile, easily broken; section, relatively even, mealy, pale pink. Odour, aromatic; taste, slightly bitter and astringent.

刮丹皮 外表面有刮刀削痕，外表面红棕色或淡灰黄色，有时可见灰褐色斑点状残存外皮。

Guadanpi Outer surface exhibiting the scraping traces, reddish-brown or pale greyish-yellow, sometimes greyish-brown spotted remains of outer bark visible.

牡丹皮片 呈圆形或卷曲形的薄片。连丹皮外表面灰褐色或黄褐色，栓皮脱落呈粉红色；刮丹皮外表面红棕色或淡灰黄色，内表面有时可见发亮的结晶，切面淡粉红色，粉性。气芳香，味微苦而涩。

Slices of Tree Peony Bark In rounded or curled thin slices. Outer surface of Liandanpi greyish-brown or yellowish-brown, the exposed surface where cork falls off appearing pink; outer surface of Guadanpi reddish-brown or pale greyish-yellow. Inner surface sometimes showing bright crystals. Cut surface pale pink, mealy. Odour, aromatic; taste, slightly bitter and astringent.

【规格等级 / Specification and grade】

商品按加工不同分为连丹（原丹）、刮丹、丹须三种。按产区分为安徽丹皮（凤丹、瑶丹、西山丹）、川丹皮、山东丹皮、湖南丹皮、西丹皮、统杂丹（各地）。其规格等级标准如下。

According to different processing, the commodity includes three specifications: Liandanpi (Yuandanpi), Guadanpi and Danxu. According to the producing areas, it includes Anhui Danpi (Fengdan, Yaodan, Xishandan), Chuandanpi, Shandong Danpi, Hunan Danpi, Xi Danpi, Mixed Dan (various producing areas). The specifications and grading criteria are as follows:

凤丹皮 一等：呈圆筒状，条均匀，微弯，两端剪平，纵形隙口紧闭。皮细肉厚，表面褐色。质硬而脆，断面粉白色，粉质足，有亮银星。香气浓，味微苦涩。长6cm以上，中部直径2.5cm以上。无木心、青丹、杂质、霉变。

Fengdanpi First grade: cylindric, strip even and slightly curved, both ends flat, longitudinal fissures closed, surface fine and pulp full, surface brown, texture hard and fragile. Section pink white, mealy, with bright crystals. Odour, strongly aromatic; taste, slightly bitter and astringent. The length is more than 6cm, and the diameter of the middle part is more than 2.5cm. No woody part, nor green root bark, nor foreign matter, nor mildew.

二等：长 5cm 以上，中部直径 1.8cm 以上，余同一等。

Second grade: More than 5cm in length, and more than 1.8cm in diameter of the middle Part. Other criteria in this grade are the same as those in First grade.

三等：长 4cm 以上，中部直径 1cm 以上，余同一等。

Third grade: More than 4cm in length, and more than 1cm in diameter of the middle Part. Other criteria in this grade are the same as those in First grade.

四等：凡不符合一、二、三等的细条、断支、碎片，均属此等。但最小直径不低于 0.6cm，无木心、杂质、霉变。

Fourth grade: All the thin strips, broken strips and fragments, not up to the first three grades, belong to this grade. But the minimum diameter is not less than 0.6cm, and no woody part, nor foreign matter, nor mildew.

连丹皮 一等：呈圆筒状，条均匀，微弯曲。表面灰褐色或棕褐色，栓皮脱落处呈粉褐色。质硬而脆，断面粉白色或淡褐色，有粉性。香气浓，味微苦涩。长 6cm 以上，中部直径 2.5cm 以上，碎节不超过 5%。去净木心，无杂质、霉变。

Liandanpi First grade: cylindric, strip even and slightly curved. Outer surface greyish-brown or brown, the exposed surface where cork falls off appearing pinkish-brown. Texture hard and fragile. Fracture pink white or pale brown, mealy. Odour, strongly aromatic; taste, slightly bitter and astringent. The length is more than 6cm; the diameter of the middle part is more than 2.5cm; and broken parts are not more than 5%. No woody part, nor foreign matter, nor mildew.

二等：长 5cm 以上，中部直径 1.8cm 以上，余同一等。

Second grade: More than 5cm in length, and more than 1.8cm in diameter of the middle Part. Other criteria in this grade are the same as those in First grade.

三等：长 4cm 以上，中部直径 0.9cm 以上，余同一等。

Third grade: More than 4cm in length, and more than 0.9cm in diameter of the middle Part. Other criteria in this grade are the same as those in First grade.

四等：凡不符合一、二、三等的细条及断支碎片，均属此等。但最小直径不低于 0.6cm，无木心、杂质、霉变。

Fourth grade: All the thin strips, broken strips and fragments, not up to first three grades belong to this grade. But the minimum diameter is not less than 0.6cm, and no woody part, nor foreign matter, nor mildew.

刮丹皮 一等：呈圆筒状，条均匀。刮去外皮，表面粉红色，在节疤、皮孔、根痕处偶有未去净的栓皮，形成棕褐色的花斑。质坚硬，断面粉白色，有粉性。气香浓，味微苦涩。长 6cm 以上，中部直径 2.4cm 以上，碎节不超过 5%，无木心、杂质、霉变。

Guadanpi First grade: cylindric, strip even. Coarse bark scraped off, surface pink. Occasionally, there are unremoved cork at the knots, lenticels and root scars, forming brown spots. Texture hard, fracture pink white, mealy. Odour, strongly aromatic; taste, slightly bitter and astringent. The length is more than 6cm; the diameter of the middle part is more than 2.4cm, and broken parts are not more than 5%. No woody part, nor foreign matter, nor mildew.

二等：长 5cm 以上，中部直径 1.7cm 以上，余同一等。

Second grade: More than 5cm in length, and more than 1.7cm in diameter of the middle Part. Other criteria in this grade are the same as those in First grade.

三等：长 4cm 以上，中部直径 0.9cm 以上，余同一等。

Third grade: More than 4cm in length, and more than 0.9cm in diameter of the middle Part. Other criteria in this grade are the same as those in First grade.

四等：凡不符合一、二、三等的断支、碎片均属此等，无木心、碎片、杂质、霉变。

Fourth grade: All the broken strips and fragments, not up to first three grades, belong to this grade. No woody part, nor fragment, nor foreign matter, nor mildew.

【化学成分 / Chemical constituent】

含丹皮酚、牡丹酚苷等酚类化合物，芍药苷、羟基芍药苷、苯甲酰芍药苷等萜类化合物。

It contains phenolic compounds, namely paeonol, paeonoside, etc.; also contains terpenoids namely paeoniflorin, hydroxypaeoniflorin, benzoylpaeoniflorin, etc.

【检查 / Examination】

水分不得过 13.0%。总灰分不得过 5.0%。

Water, not more than 13.0%. Total ash, not more than 5.0%.

【质量要求 / Quality requirement】

外观质量 以条粗长、皮厚、无木心、断面白色、粉性足、内表面结晶多、香气浓者为佳。

Appearance quality Good quality for thick and long strip, thick bark, no woody part, whitish section, mealy texture, with more crystals on the inner surface and strong aroma.

内在质量 浸出物含量：醇溶性浸出物（热）不得少于 15.0%。含量测定：按高效液相色谱法测定，含丹皮酚不得少于 1.2%。

Intrinsic quality Extract content: not less than 15.0% of ethanol-soluble extractives (hot). Assay: not less than 1.2% of paeonol according to HPLC analysis method.

【功能主治 / Function and indication】

微寒，苦、辛。清热凉血，活血化瘀。用于热入营血，温毒发斑，吐血衄血，夜热早凉，无汗骨蒸，经闭痛经，跌扑伤痛，痈肿疮毒。

Mild cold; bitter and pungent. To clear heat and cool the blood, activate the blood and resolve stasis. For the treatment of heat entering nutrient-blood aspect, macula and papule caused by warm toxin, hematermesis, epistaxis, fever at night and cool in the morning, steaming bone fever without sweating, amenorrhea, dysmenorrhea, pain caused by traumatic injuries, swelling abscess, sore and skin infections.

【贮藏养护 / Storage and maintenance】

用纸箱或麻袋装。本品易发霉、变色，应贮于阴凉干燥处。

Packed in cartons or sacks. Prone to mildew and discolor. Preserved in a cool and dry place.

【用法用量 / Administration and dosage】

6~12g。孕妇慎用。

6~12g. Use with caution during pregnancy.

薄荷 (Bohe) ⋮ Menthae Haplocalycis Herba (Peppermint)

【基原 / Origin】

为唇形科植物薄荷 *Mentha haplocalyx* Briq. 的干燥地上部分。

Peppermint is the dried aerial part of *Mentha haplocalyx* Briq. (Fam. Labiatae).

【产地 / Producing area】

主产于江苏的太仓、南通、海门及浙江、安徽、江西、湖南等地。江苏太仓出产的薄荷最佳，江苏所产者称为“苏薄荷”。

Main producing areas are Taicang, Nantong and Haimen of Jiangsu Province, and Provinces of Zhejiang, Anhui, Jiangxi, Hunan, etc. Peppermint produced in Taicang is of the best quality, and those produced in Jiangsu Provinces are often called “Subohe”.

【采制 / Collection and preparation】

薄荷　夏、秋二季茎叶茂盛或花开至三轮时，选晴天，分次采割，晒干或阴干。

Peppermint　The drug is collected in summer and autumn when foliage branch growing luxuriantly or in the third round of flowering, several times on fine days, and dried in the sun or in the shade.

薄荷段　取薄荷，除去老茎和杂质，略喷清水，稍润，切短段，及时低温干燥。

Peppermint segments　Peppermint, removed the old stems and foreign matter, sprayed with a small quantity of water, moistened briefly, cut into short sections, and dried at a lower temperature in time.

【商品特征 / Commodity characteristics】

薄荷　茎呈方柱形，有对生分枝；表面紫棕色或淡绿色，棱角处具茸毛；质脆，断面白色，髓部中空。叶对生，有短柄；叶片皱缩卷曲，完整者展平后呈宽披针形、长椭圆形或卵形；上表面深绿色，下表面灰绿色，稀被茸毛，有凹点状腺鳞。轮伞花序腋生，花萼钟状，先端5齿裂，花冠淡紫色。揉搓后有特殊清凉香气，味辛凉。

Peppermint　Stems square, with opposite branches; externally purplish-brown or pale green, the angular regions pubescent; texture fragile, section white, pith hollowed; leaves opposite, short petioled, lamina crumpled and rolled, when whole, broadly lanceolate, long-elliptical or ovate; the upper surface dark green and the lower surface greyish-green, sparsely pubescent, bearing concavely dotted glandular scales. Verticillaster axillary, calyx campanulate, with five terminal teeth, corolla pale purple. Odour, characteristic and aromatic after rubbing; taste, pungent and cool.

薄荷段　呈不规则的段，余同薄荷。

Peppermint segments　In irregular segments. Other characteristics are the same to those of Peppermint.

【规格等级 / Specification and grade】

商品按产区分为太仓薄荷、杭薄荷等规格；按采收季节分为“头刀薄荷”和“二刀薄荷”，头刀薄荷分枝较多，茎多紫褐色，较长，品质优，二刀薄荷分枝较少，茎多黄绿色，较短，偶有开花者，质次；按生境分野生薄荷、栽培薄荷等规格。一般为统货。

According to the producing areas, the commodity includes Taicang peppermint, Hang peppermint and other specifications. According to the harvest season, it includes “First cut peppermint” and “Second cut peppermint”; First cut peppermint, with many branches, the stem long and mostly purplish-brown, is of best quality; Second cut peppermint, with few branches, the stem short and mostly yellow-green, occasionally flowering, is of inferior quality. And according to the habitat, it contains Wild peppermint, Cultivated peppermint and other specifications. It is marketed by unified grade with the same price.

【化学成分 / Chemical constituent】

含挥发油，油中主要成分为1- 薄荷醇，其次为1- 薄荷酮。另含醋酸薄荷酯，莰烯、柠檬烯、异薄荷酮、蒎烯、薄荷烯酮、树脂及少量鞣质、迷迭香酸等。

It contains volatile oil, of which the chief is 1-menthol and the second is 1-menthone. It also contains menthol acetate, camphene, limonene, isomenthone, pinene, piperitone, resins and a small amount of tannins and rosmarinic acid, etc.

【检查 / Examination】

叶不得少于30%。薄荷水分不得过15.0%，薄荷段水分不得过13.0%。总灰分不得过11.0%，酸不溶性灰分不得过3.0%。

Leaves, not less than 30%. Water, in Peppermint, not more than 15.0%; in Peppermint segments, not more than 13.0%. Total ash, not more than 11.0%. Acid-insoluble ash, not more than 3.0%.

【质量要求 / Quality requirement】

外观质量 以叶多、色深绿、味清凉、香气浓者为佳。

Appearance quality Good quality for more leaves, dark green color, cool taste and strong aroma.

内在质量 含量测定：薄荷含挥发油不得少于0.80%（ml/g），薄荷段挥发油不得少于0.40%（ml/g）。

Intrinsic quality Assay: not less than 0.80% (ml/g) of volatile oil in Peppermint; not less than 0.40% (ml/g) of volatile oil in Peppermint segments.

【功能主治 / Function and indication】

凉，辛。疏散风热，清利头目，利咽，透疹，疏肝行气。用于风热感冒，风温初起，头痛，目赤，喉痹，口疮，风疹，麻疹，胸胁胀闷。

Cool; pungent. To disperse wind-heat, clear and sooth head and eyes, soothe the throat, promote eruption, soothe the liver, and move qi. For the treatment of common cold caused by wind-heat, early onset of wind-warmth disease, headache, red eyes, throat *bi* disorder, mouth sore, rubella, measles, distention and oppression in the chest, and the hypochondrium.

【贮藏养护 / Storage and maintenance】

一般为压缩打包件，每件45kg。本品不耐热，应贮于阴凉干燥避光处。

Usually packed in compression, 45kg per pack. This product is not heat resistant, and should be preserved in a cool and dry place.

【用法用量 / Administration and dosage】

3~6g，后下。

3~6g, added when the decoction is nearly done.

蟾酥 (Chansu) ⁞ Bufonis Venenum (Toad Venom)

【基原 / Origin】

为蟾蜍科动物中华大蟾蜍 *Bufo bufo gargarizans* Cantor 或黑眶蟾蜍 *Bufo melanostictus* Schneider 的干燥分泌物。

Toad Venom is the dried secretion of *Bufo bufo gargarizans* Cantor or *Bufo melanostictus* Schneider (Fam. Bufonidae).

【产地 / Producing area】

主产于江苏镇江、泰兴、苏州，河北遵化、玉田、蓟县，山东莒南、临沂，四川，湖南，浙江等地。

Main producing areas are Zhenjiang, Taixing and Suzhou of Jiangsu Province; Zunhua, Yutian and Jixian of Hebei Province; Ju'nan and Linyi of Shandong Province; and the provinces of Sichuan, Hunan, Zhejiang, etc.

【采制 / Collection and preparation】

蟾酥 夏、秋二季捕捉蟾蜍，洗净，用铜镊子挤取耳后腺和皮肤腺的白色浆液，置于瓷器中（忌铁器），干燥。

Toad Venom The toad is collected in summer or autumn, washed clean. The white serous fluid of the parotid glands and skin glands is squeezed out with copper tweezers, placed in porcelain (avoid iron), and dried.

蟾酥粉 取蟾酥，捣碎，加白酒浸渍，时常搅动至呈稠膏状，干燥，粉碎。

Toad Venom powder Bufonis Venenum is broken to pieces, macerated in white rice wine, frequently stirred to concentrated paste, dried and pulverized.

【商品特征 / Commodity characteristics】

蟾酥 呈扁圆形团块或片状，棕褐色或红棕色。团块状者质坚，不易折断，断面棕褐色，角质样，微有光泽；片状者质脆，易碎，断面红棕色，半透明。气微腥，味初甜而后有持久的麻辣感，粉末嗅之作嚏。

Toad Venom In flattened and rounded masses or slices, brown or reddish-brown. Texture of the mass hard, uneasily broken, section brown, cuticuloid, slightly lustrous. Texture of the slice fragile, easily broken; section, reddish-brown, translucent. Odour, slightly stinking; taste, sweet at first, persistently tingling and pungent latter. Sneeze on smelling the powder.

蟾酥粉 呈棕褐色粉末状，略有酒气。

Toad Venom powder Brown powder; odour, slightly alcoholic.

【规格等级 / Specification and grade】

分东酥、片酥和棋子酥等规格，一般均为统货。

The specifications include Dongsu, Piansu and Qizisu, etc. In general, it marketed by unified grade with the same price.

东酥（团酥、光东酥） 呈扁圆形、团块状或饼状，直径 4~8cm，厚 4~10mm，重 60~100g。

Dongsu (mass Dongsu, smooth Dongsu) In flattened and rounded masses or pancake shape, 4-8mm in diameter, 4-10mm in thickness and 60-100g in weight.

片酥（片子酥、盘酥） 呈圆形浅盘状或长方形片状，厚约 2mm，重约 15g。

Piansu (Pianzisu, Pansu) In rounded shallow plate shape or rectangular slice, 2mm in thickness, about 15g in weight each.

棋子酥（杜酥） 呈扁圆形，似围棋子状，重约 15g。

Qizisu (Dusu) In flattened and rounded masses like weiqi chess pieces, about 15g in weight each.

【化学成分 / Chemical constituent】

主要含强心甾类化合物，包括蟾毒配基类，如华蟾酥毒基（约 5%）、脂蟾毒配基（约 3.4%）、蟾毒灵（约 1.8%）、羟基华蟾毒基（约 1.6%）、蟾毒配基（约 1.5%）、远华蟾毒基（约 1.4%）等；以及上述蟾毒配基类与酸形成的酯类，即蟾毒类。另一类主要成分为吲哚生物碱，主要有蟾酥碱、蟾酥甲碱、蟾酥硫碱及 5- 羟色胺等。另含甾醇类及多种氨基酸等。

It mainly contains cardenolides, including bufogeinins, namely approximately 5% cinobufagin, 3.4% resibufogenin, 1.8% bufalin, 1.6% hydroxyl-cinobufogenin, 1.5% bufotalin, 1.4% telocinobufagin, etc; and the esters named bufotoxins formed by the above mentioned bufogeinins and acids. Another major components are indole alkaloids, including bufotenine, bufotenidine, bufothionine and 5-HT, etc. It also contains sterols and many kinds of amino acids.

【检查 / Examination】

水分不得过 13.0%。总灰分不得过 5.0%，酸不溶性灰分不得过 2.0%。

Water, not more than 13.0%. Total ash, not more than 5.0%; acid-insoluble ash, not more than 2.0%.

【质量要求 / Quality requirement】

外观质量 以红棕色或紫黑色、半透明、断面光亮如胶（角质状）、有光泽者为佳。

Appearance quality Good quality for being reddish-brown or purple-black, translucent, section lustrous like glue (cuticuloid) and glossy.

内在质量 含量测定：按高效液相色谱法测定，含华蟾酥毒基和脂蟾毒配基的总量不得少于6.0%。

Intrinsic quality Assay: The total amount of cinobufagin and resibufogenin is not less than 6.0% according to HPLC analysis method.

【功能主治 / Function and indication】

温，辛。有毒。解毒，止痛，开窍醒神。用于痈疽疔疮，咽喉肿痛，中暑神昏，痧胀腹痛吐泻。

Warm; pungent, toxic. To remove toxin, relieve pain, open the orifices and lighten the spirit. For the treatment of abscesses and cellulitis, deep-rooted boil and sore, swollen sore throat, loss of consciousness caused by summer heat stroke, vomiting and diarrhea with abdominal pain in Shazhang (acute gastrointestinal infection).

【贮藏养护 / Storage and maintenance】

以纸包装，装硬纸盒或小木盒内。本品易发霉、黏结，应密封贮于干燥处。

Packed in paper, and kept in a cardboard box or small wooden box. Prone to mildew and bond together. Sealed and preserved in a dry place.

【用法用量 / Administration and dosage】

0.015~0.03g，多入丸散用。外用适量。孕妇慎用。

0.015~0.03g, usually used in pills or powder. Appropriate amount for topical application. Used with caution during pregnancy.

重点小结
Summary

药材	主产地	规格等级	质量要求
牡丹皮	主产于安徽、重庆、四川、湖南、湖北、河南、陕西、山东、甘肃、贵州等地	商品规格：按加工不同分为连丹、刮丹、丹须三种；按照产区分，分为安徽丹皮（凤丹、瑶丹、西山丹）、山东丹皮、湖南丹皮、西丹皮、川丹皮、统杂丹（各地）。各规格下根据品质及粗细长短分1~4等	以条粗长、皮厚、无木心、断面白色、粉性足、内表面结晶多、香气浓者为佳。含丹皮酚不得少于1.2%
薄荷	主产于江苏、浙江、安徽、江西、湖南等地。江苏所产者称为“苏薄荷”	商品按产区分为太仓薄荷、杭薄荷等规格；按采收季节分为“头刀薄荷”和“二刀薄荷”，头刀薄荷品质优；二刀薄荷质次；按生境分野生薄荷、栽培薄荷等规格。一般为统货	以叶多、色深绿、味清凉、香气浓者为佳。薄荷含挥发油不得少于0.80%（ml/g），薄荷段挥发油不得少于0.40%（ml/g）
蟾酥	主产于江苏、河北、山东等地	分东酥、片酥和棋子酥等规格	以红棕色或紫黑色、半透明、断面光亮如胶（角质状）、有光泽者为佳。含华蟾酥毒基和脂蟾毒配基的总量不得少于6.0%

Medicinal material	Main producing area	Specification and grade	Quality requirement
Tree Peony Bark	Main producing areas are Anhui Province, Chongqing Municipality, Sichuan Province; Hunan Province, and Provinces of Hubei, Henan, Shaanxi, Shandong, Gansu and Guizhou, etc.	Specifications for Moutan Cortex: According to different processing, there are three specifications: Original Dan, Scraping Dan and Fibrous Dan. According to the origin, there are Anhui Danpi (Fengdan, Yaodan, Xishan Dan), Shandong Danpi, Hunan Danpi, Xidanpi, Chuandanpi, Mixed Dan (various origin). For each specification, there are 1~4 grades according to quality, diameter and length	Good quality for thick and long strip, thick bark, no woody part, whitish fracture, mealy texture, with more crystals on the inner surface and strong aroma. Not less than 1.2% of paeonol
Peppermint	Main producing areas are Provinces of Jiangsu, Zhejiang, Anhui, Jiangxi, Hunan, etc. Those produced in Jiangsu Province are often called "Subohe"	According to the producing area, there are Taicang peppermint, Hang peppermint. According to the harvest season, there are "First cut peppermint" and "Second cut peppermint"; the former has better quality than that of the latter. And according to the habitat, there are Wild peppermint, Cultivated peppermint. It is marketed by unified grade with the same price	Good quality for more leaves, dark green color, cool taste and strong aroma. Not less than 0.80% (ml/g) of volatile oil in Peppermint, not less than 0.40% (ml/g) of volatile oil in Peppermint segments
Toad Venom	Main producing areas are Jiangsu Province, Hebei Province, Shandong Province, etc.	The specifications include Dongsu, Piansu and Qizisu, etc.	Good quality for being reddish-brown or purple-black, translucent, section lustrous like glue (cuticuloid) and glossy. Not less than 6.0% of the total amount of cinobufagin and resibufogenin

目标检测
Object Detection

题库

一、选择题（Choice question）

（一）单项选择题（One-choice question）

1. 凤丹皮药材商品的主产地是（　　）

A. 重庆垫江　B. 湖北恩施　C. 安徽铜陵

D. 四川都江堰　E. 湖南长沙

The main producing area of "Feng Danpi "(Moutan Cortex) is (　　)

A. Dianjiang, Chongqing　B. Enshi, Hubei　C. Tongling, Anhui

D. Dujiangyan, Sichuan　E. Changsha, Hunan

2. 牡丹皮的来源是(　　)
   A. 为毛茛科植物牡丹的干燥根
   B. 为毛茛科植物牡丹的干燥根茎
   C. 为毛茛科植物芍药的干燥果皮
   D. 为毛茛科植物芍药的干燥根皮
   E. 为毛茛科植物牡丹的干燥根皮
   The origin of Moutan Cortex is (　　)
   A. the dried root of *Paeonia suffruticosa* Andr. (Fam. Ranunculaceae).
   B. the dried rhizome of *Paeonia suffruticosa* Andr. (Fam. Ranunculaceae).
   C. the dried pericarp of ripe fruit of *Paeonia lactiflora* PalL (Fam. Ranunculaceae).
   D. the dried root bark of *Paeonia lactiflora* PalL (Fam. Ranunculaceae).
   E. the dried root bark of *Paeonia suffruticosa* Andr. (Fam. Ranunculaceae).
3. 薄荷药材叶的比例应不少于(　　)
   A. 35%　B. 30%　C. 25%　D. 20%　E. 15%
   The proportion of leaves in peppermint should be not less than (　　)
   A. 35%　B. 30%　C. 25%　D. 20%　E. 15%
4. 牡丹皮刮去粗皮，除去木心，晒干，习称(　　)
   A. 连丹皮　B. 刮丹皮　C. 亳丹皮
   D. 凤丹皮　E. 川丹皮
   During the collection and preparation of Moutan Cortex, which specification is it, when the root bark is scraped coarse bark off, woody part removed, and dried in the sun? (　　)
   A. Liandanpi　B. Guadanpi　C. Bodanpi
   D. Fengdanpi　E. Chuandanpi
5. 按高效液相色谱法测定，蟾酥含华蟾酥毒基和脂蟾毒配基的总量不得少于(　　)
   A. 4.0%　B. 5.0%　C. 6.0%　D. 7.0%　E. 8.0%
   The total amount of cinobufagin and resibufogenin in Toad Venom according to HPLC analysis method should be not less than (　　)
   A. 4.0%　B. 5.0%　C. 6.0%　D. 7.0%　E. 8.0%

（二）多项选择题（Multiple choice question）

1. 牡丹皮按照产地可分为(　　)
   A. 安徽丹皮　B. 山东丹皮　C. 湖南丹皮
   D. 西丹皮　E. 川丹皮
   According to the producing areas, the specifications of Moutan Cortex include (　　)
   A. Anhui Danpi　B. Shandong Danpi　C. Hunan Danpi
   D. Xidanpi　E. Chuandanpi
2. 薄荷药材商品特征有(　　)
   A. 茎呈方柱形　B. 叶对生　C. 轮伞花序腋生
   D. 揉搓后有特殊清凉香气　E. 味辛凉
   The commodity characteristics of Menthae Haplocalycis Herba are (　　)
   A. stems square
   B. leaves opposite
   C. verticillaster axillary

D. odour, characteristic and aromatic after rubbing
E. taste, pungent and cool

3. 薄荷药材按照采收季节可分为（ ）
A. 头刀薄荷 B. 二刀薄荷 C. 三刀薄荷
D. 四刀薄荷 E. 五刀薄荷
According to the harvest season, the specifications of Menthae Haplocalycis Herba include ( )
A. First cut Peppermint B. Second cut Peppermint C. Third cut Peppermint
D. Fourth cut Peppermint E. Fifth cut Peppermint

4. 蟾酥的商品规格有（ ）
A. 东酥 B. 片酥 C. 棋子酥
D. 统货 E. 条酥
The commodity specifications of Bufonis Venenum include ( )
A. Dongsu B. Piansu C. Qizisu
D. Unified grade E. Tiaosu

5. 下列属于南药的有（ ）
A. 甘草 B. 枳壳 C. 鳖甲
D. 玉竹 E. 防风
In the following, which belong to Nan Medicinal Materials ( )
A. *Nardostachyos Radix et Rhizoma*
B. *Aurantii Fructus*
C. *Trionycis Carapax*
D. *Polygonati Odorati Rhizoma*
E. *Saposhnikoviae Radix*

二、解答题（Thinking question）

1. 本章南药产区的范围包括哪些？
What are the production areas of Nan Medicinal Materials in this chapter?
2. 牡丹皮的商品按加工不同包括哪些种类？
What commercial specifications does the Tree Peony Bark include according to different processing method?
3. 优质的薄荷应该是怎样的？
What are the characteristics of Peppermint with good quality?
4. 蟾酥的质量如何评价？
How to evaluate the quality of Toad Venom?

第十五章　关　药
Chapter 15　Guan Medicinal Materials

PPT

学习目标 ¦ Learning Target

知识要求：

1．**掌握**　关药的含义及其主要道地药材品种；人参、五味子、鹿茸的道地产地、规格等级、商品特征、贮藏方法等内容。

2．**熟悉**　人参、五味子、鹿茸的化学成分、质量要求、检查等内容。

3．**了解**　关药产区的自然环境条件。

能力要求：

学会依据规格等级、商品特征、检查、质量要求等知识和方法鉴别市场上人参、五味子、鹿茸的真伪优劣。

Knowledge requirements:

1. **Proficiency**　The meaning and major varieties of Guan Medicinal Materials. The authentic producing areas, specifications, grades, commodity characteristics, storage methods of Ginseng Radix et Rhizoma, Schisandrae Chinensis Fructus and Cervi Cornu Pantotrichum.

2. **Familiarity**　Chemical constituents, quality requirements, examinations of Ginseng Radix et Rhizoma, Schisandrae Chinensis Fructus and Cervi Cornu Pantotrichum.

3. **Understanding**　The natural environment in the producing areas of Guan Medicinal Materials.

Skill requirements:

Learn to identify the authenticity and evaluate the quality of Ginseng Radix et Rhizoma, Schisandrae Chinensis Fructus and Cervi Cornu pantotrichum on the market according to the knowledge and methods of specification and grade, commodity characteristics, examination and quality requirement, etc.

一、关药概述
I. Overview of Guan Medicinal Materials

以山海关以北的辽宁、吉林、黑龙江省和内蒙古东部为主产区或集散地的大宗商品药材，称为关药。其产区位于约东经 120°~135°，北纬 40°~55°之间，属于寒温带、温带的湿润和半湿润地区。年均降水量 400~700mm。区内森林茂密、气候凉爽湿润。东南侧的长白山地区大部分为山岭与丘陵，北段为大、小兴安岭，东北角为低陷的三江源平原，是北方重要的药材产区。关药产区药用植物达 1600 多种，药用动物 300 多种，药用矿物 50 多种。著名的关药有人参、鹿茸、关防风、关黄柏、关龙胆、北五味子、蛤蟆油等。

"Guan Medicinal Materials" is the bulk commodity of medicinal materials whose main producing area or distributing center are north to Shanhaiguan including Liaoning, Jilin, Heilongjiang Provinces and eastern Inner Mongolia. This area belongs to humid and subhumid regions in cold temperate zone or temperate zone for eastern longitude 120~135 degree, and northern latitude 40~55 degree. The annual mean precipitation is between 400~700mm. Forests there are dense, and the climate is cool and humid. The area is an important producing place of Guan Medicinal Materials, Changbai Mountain located in the southeast with mountains and hills, Daxing'an and Xiaoxing'an mountains in the north, and sunken Sanjiangyuan plain in the northeast. There are more than 1600 species for medicinal plants, 300 species for medicinal animals, and more than 50 types of medicinal minerals in the area. The famous Guan Medicinal Materials are Ginseng Radix et Rhizoma, Cervi Cornu Pantotrichum, Saposhnikoviae Radix, Phellodendri Amurensis Cortex, Guan Gentianae Radix et Rhizoma, Schisandrae Chinensis Fructus, Ranae Oviductus, etc.

二、药材品种
II. Varieties of Medicinal Materials

人参 (Renshen) ¦ Ginseng Radix et Rhizoma (Ginseng)

【基原 / Origin】

为五加科植物人参 *Panax ginseng* C. A. Mey. 的干燥根和根茎。栽培者为"园参"，野生者为"山参"。

Ginseng is the dried root and rhizome of *Panax ginseng* C. A. Mey. (fam. Araliaceae). The drug derived from the cultivated form is known as "Yuanshen" (garden ginseng) and the drug derived from the wild origin is known as "Shanshen" (mountain ginseng).

【产地 / Producing area】

主产于吉林抚松、集安，辽宁恒仁、宽甸，黑龙江五常、尚志等地区。主为栽培品，习称"园参"。野生品产量甚少，习称"野山参（或山参）"。

Main producing areas are Fusong, Ji'an of Jilin Province, Hengren, Kuandian of Liaoning Province, Wuchang, Shangzhi of Heilongjiang Province, etc. The majority of Ginseng Radix et Rhizoma (known as Garden ginseng) are cultivated. Wild Ginseng Radix et Rhizoma, commonly known as Wild mountain ginseng (or Wild ginseng), has very low output.

【采制 / Collection and preparation】

1. 园参　多于秋季采挖，洗净，除去支根或保留支根后晒干或烘干，称"生晒参"或"全须生晒参"。鲜园参除去支根及根茎部的不定根，或仅除去细支根及须根，蒸制后晒干或烘干，称"红参"。经真空冷冻干燥法加工得到的为"活性参"。人参栽培品根据其根的形态分为"大马牙""二马牙""长脖""圆膀圆芦"等品种。

1. Garden ginseng　Mostly dug out and collected in autumn, washed and removed from rootlets or maintained rootlets, dried in the sun or hot air, is known as "Shengshaishen" or "Quanxu shengshaishen". Fresh garden ginseng by removing its rootlets and adventitious roots on rhizomes, or thin rootlets and fibrous roots only, steamed and dried in the sun or hot air, is known as "Red ginseng". "Huoxingshen" is processed by vacuum freeze-drying method. Cultivated ginseng is classified in different varieties as "Damaya" "Ermaya" "Changbo" "Yuanbangyuanlu", etc. according to the root shapes.

2. 野山参 在7月下旬至9月间果熟变红时易于发现、采挖。挖取时保持支根、须根完整，晒干，称"全须生晒参"。此外还包括"艼变山参""籽种山参"（籽海、野籽）、"池底参""趴货参""移山参"及"林下参"（籽海）。

2. Wild ginseng Easily found and collected from late July to September when fruits ripe and turn red. Rootlets and fibrous roots, kept integrated, dried, known as "Quanxushengshaishen". In addition, varieties of wild ginseng include "Dingbianshanshen" "Zizhongshanshen" (Zihai or Yezi), "Chidishen" "Pahuoshen" "Yishanshen" and "Linxiashen" (Zihai).

生晒参片 生晒参润透，切薄片，干燥。

Shengshaishen slice Shengshaishen, soaked thoroughly, cut into thin slices and dried.

红参片 红参润透，切薄片，干燥。

Red ginseng slice Red ginseng, soaked thoroughly, cut into thin slices and dried.

【商品特征 / Commodity characteristics】

1. 药材

1. Crude materials

（1）山参类

(1) Wild ginseng

生晒山参 主根与根茎等长或较短，呈人字形、菱形或圆柱形。表面灰黄色，具纵纹，上端有紧密而深陷的环状横纹。下部多具2条主要支根，形似人体。根茎细长，上部扭曲，茎痕密生，下部常无芦碗而光滑，不定根较粗。须根稀疏，长约为主根的1~2倍，柔韧不易折断，有明显的疣状突起（习称"珍珠疙瘩"）。气香浓厚，味甜微苦，口嚼之有清香感。山参的性状较为特殊，鉴别时注意其根茎（芦头）、不定根（艼）、主根（体）、支根（腿）、须根（须）、表面等部位。芦头：长而弯曲，习称"雁脖芦"。一般分为3段，分别是"马牙芦""对花芦""圆芦"（灯草心）。芦头细长如线，至上端变粗呈"对花芦"形式，习称"线芦"。艼：按形状一般分为枣核艼、蒜瓣艼、顺体艼3种。体：有横灵体、顺笨体2种。纹：紧密的环形纹，纹深而细，皱纹略显得向上兜皱，纹紧密，沟色较深，习称"螺旋纹""黑兜纹"或"铁线纹"。环纹延伸到参体的中部或下部，这种纹叫"一纹到底"。皮：呈淡黄白色，结实光润，皮质老，细而不粗糙，习称"皮细如绵"或"细结皮"，光泽显著。腿：一般为1~2条，最多3条。腿短，上粗下细，分裆处多呈八字形，两腿斜叉而不并拢。须：疏生而不散乱，犹如鞭子的皮条，柔韧，故有"皮条须"之称。须的表面生长着疣状突起（小疙瘩），呈长圆形、方圆形不等，习称"珍珠须"或"珍珠尾"。

Shenshaishanshen Main roots, as long as or shorter than rhizome, V-shaped, rhomboid or cylindrical. Externally greyish-yellow, longitudinally wrinkled, the upper part exhibiting compact, deep transverse striations. The lower part bearing 2 branch roots, similar to the human body. Rhizomes slender, the upper part exhibiting twisty, stem scar in dense; the lower part is smooth without stem scars usually, adventitious roots relatively thick. Slender rootlets sparse with obvious minute warts (commonly known as Zhenzhugeda), approximately 1 to 2 times the length of the main roots, flexible and uneasy to be broken. Odour, strong fragrant; taste, sweet and slightly bitter, fragrant when chewing on it. The characters of wild ginseng are special, and attention should be paid to identify the features of rhizome (Lutou), adventitious roots (Ding), main root (Ti), branching root (Tui), rootlets (Xu), surface, etc. Lutou: long and curve, commonly known as Yanbolu, usually divided into three sections as Mayalu (upper section, rhizome with remnant stem scars, like the horse tooth), Duihualu (middle section, rhizomes stagger and overlap with compact stem scars) and Yuanlu (also named Dengcaoxin, lower section, cylindrical rhizomes with unconspicuous stem scars). Lutou, slender like a thread, thicker on the upper part like a Duihualu, is known as Xianlu. Ding is generally divided into three types as Zaoheding (adventitious root of date pit shape, sturdy, tapering at both ends), Suanbanding (adventitious root of garlic clove shape, blunt at one end and tapering at the other end) and Shuntiding (adventitious root, thicker at the upper part, and more slender downward). Ti, including Henglingti (taproot, sturdy, mostly in the shape of short block or water chestnut) and Shunbenti (taproot, fusiform or cylindrical). Wrinkles, annular, dense, deep and fine, raised and pursy upward, ditch with deeper colour, commonly known as Luoxuanwen, Heidouwen and Tiexianwen. Annular wrinkles extend to the middle or lower part of root, commonly known as Yiwendaodi. Skin, pale yellowish-white, burly and luster, tough epidermis, fine and not coarse, obvious gloss, commonly known as Pixirumian or Xijiepi. Tui, 1~2 branches, at most 3; short, tapering, fork in a figure of up-side-down "V" mostly, two legs skew and not close. Xu, sparse and not scattered, like thong, pliable, commonly known as Pitiaoxu. Surface with minute warts, long circular, squircle, commonly known as Zhenzhuxu or Zhenzhuwei.

艼变山参 参形特异。芦头大，多数偏斜不正。由多条艼组成，无主体。艼多为顺体，大艼上可生有横纹，其纹粗浅不连续。只有 1 条参腿（艼之尾部）。皮嫩而有光泽。须有少量的珍珠疙瘩。

Dingbianshanshen Specific shape. Lutou big and mostly skew. The root is composed of several Dings and with no main root. Ding mostly straight, and the big one with transverse wrinkles, coarse and shallow, discontinuous. Only one Tui (the tail of Ding). Skin tender and glossy. Slender rootlets sparse with few Zhenzhugeda.

籽种山参 芦头多为线芦、竹节芦，芦头较长，也偶有马牙芦或圆芦。艼少，多为顺体，不旁斜，上翘者少，均为互生，下部呈尖尾形。参体形状不定，参腿 2~3 条，略呈"八"字分裆。皮黄白色，较细嫩，有光泽，横纹不明显。参须柔软细嫩而短，珍珠点小，口嚼则出现碎末及少量纤维。味苦，有清香气。

Zizhongshanshen Lutou is longer, mostly Xianlu or Zhujielu, a few Mayalu or Yuanlu. Few Ding, mostly straight and not warp, few upward, all alternate, the lower part appears sharp tail. Main root shows irregular shape. Tui, 2~3, fork in a figure of up-side-down "V". Skin, yellowish-white, tender and glossy, with less obvious transverse striations. Rootlets, soft, tender and short, small Zhenzhudian. Dregs and few fiber when chewed. Taste, bitter; odour, fragrant.

池底参和趴货参 芦头基部为圆芦，圆芦以上为"马牙芦"，而芦碗沿着芦头旋转生长，芦碗较大，芦碗边有芦棱。艼粗大，齐头，常为 3~5 枚，生 2 枚者，多对生（掐脖子艼）。艼大于并重于参体。参体多为顺体，腿粗细不一，2~3 条或更多，有"八"字分裆的体形。皮黄白色，粗糙而疏松。横纹浅或断续，无螺旋纹，有的一纹到底，也有半环纹者，状似园参。参须较嫩，易折断，蓬乱不清疏，珍珠疙瘩少而小。

Chidishen and Pahuoshen The base of Lutou is Yuanlu, Mayalu above the Yuanlu; Luwans are big with ridge on the edge, and distribute on Lutou and spiral upward. Ding, large, verticillate, 3-5 usually; the one with 2 Ding, mostly distichous, is namely Qiaboziding. Ding is bigger and heavier than root. Root, mostly straight, Tui, 2~3 or more with different diameters, fork in a figure of up-side-down "V". Skin, yellowish-white, coarse and loose. Transverse striations shallow or interrupted, no spiricle, ring or half ring, shape like garden ginseng. Rootlets, tender, easy to broken, in a mess, Zhenzhugeda, few and small.

移山参 芦碗略显长而稀疏。芦头常骤然变细或变粗，不呈对花芦而呈转芦，常出现线芦或竹节芦。芦多为顺长体，但生长年久者也有的为枣核艼。参体以顺笨体为多见，腿较顺长，1~3条或多条。皮质略泡而嫩，粗糙，不光润。有稀疏不紧密的横纹，常到底。参须细嫩而短，下端分枝较多，珍珠疙瘩稀疏而小。

Yishanshen Luwan is slightly longer, few and scattered. Lutou often shows abruptly thick or thin, with the form of Zhuanlu (rhizome with the stem scars appearing sharp turn) but not Duihualu, usually exhibits Xianlu or Zhujielu. Lu, mostly straight and long, but the older of long-time growth with Zaoheding. Roots, mostly straight and clumsy, Tui, straight and long, 1~3 or more. Skin, loose and tender, coarse, not glossy with sparse transverse-striations to the end. Rootlets, slender, tender and short, many ramifications at the end, Zhenzhugeda, sparse and small.

（2）园参类　主根上部有断续的粗横纹。根茎上部一面或二面生有芦碗，上生 1 条至数条不定根。支根 2~6 条，末端多分枝。须根形似扫帚，短而脆，易折断，珍珠点小而极少。

(2) Garden ginseng　Wide transverse striations discontinuously show on the upper part of main roots. Luwans distribute on one side or two sides of rhizome which grows one or more adventitious roots. Branch roots, 2~6, multi-branch at the end. Rootlets, shape broom-like, short and crisp, easily broken, Zhenzhudian, small and few.

生晒参 主根纺锤形或圆柱形。表面灰黄色，上部或全体有疏浅断续的粗横纹及纵皱纹，下部有侧根 2~3 条，有多数细长的须根，须根上偶有不明显的细小疣状突起。根茎（芦头）多拘挛而弯曲，具不定根（艼）和稀疏的凹窝状茎痕（芦碗）。质较硬，断面淡黄白色，显粉性，有棕黄色环纹，皮部有黄棕色的油点及放射状裂隙。气特异，味微苦、甜。

Shengshaishen Main root, fusiform or cylindrical; externally greyish-yellow; the upper part or entire root exhibiting sparse, shallow, interrupted and coarse transverse striations and distinct longitudinal wrinkles; the lower part bearing 2~3 branch roots and numerous slender rootlets with inconspicuously minute tubercles. Rhizome (Lutou) mostly constricted and curved, bearing adventitious roots (Ding) and showing sparse depressed-circular stem scars (Luwan). Texture relatively hard, fracture yellowish-white, starchy, cambium ring brownish-yellow, bark exhibiting yellow-brown dotted resin canals and radial clefts. Odour, characteristic; taste, slightly bitter and sweet.

林下参 主根呈圆柱形、菱角形或人字形，与根茎等长或较短，长 1~6cm。表面灰黄色，具纵皱纹，上部或中上部有环纹，支根多为 2~3 条，须根少而细长，清晰不乱，有较明显的疣状突起，习称“珍珠点”。根茎细长少数粗短，中上部具稀疏或密集而深陷的茎痕。

Linxiashen Main root as long as or shorter than rhizome, cylindrical, rhomboid or herringbone, 1~6cm in length. Externally greyish-yellow, longitudinally wrinkled, the upper or middle-upper part with annulations, branch roots mostly 2~3, rootlets less and slender, orderly arranged and showing some distinct warts, commonly known as Zhenzhudian. Rhizomes slender, seldomly stout, the upper part exhibiting sparse or dense deep depressed stem scars.

红参 主根纺锤形、圆柱形或扁方柱形。表面红棕色，半透明，偶有不透明的暗黄褐色斑块，习称“黄马褂”；上部具断续的不明显环纹，下部支根 2~3 条。根茎长 1~2cm，有茎痕及 1~2 条不定根。质硬脆，断面平坦，角质样。气微香而特异，味甜、微苦。

Red ginseng Main roots fusiform, cylindrical or flat squared columnar. Externally reddish-brown, translucent, occasionally exhibiting a few dark yellowish-brown patches, commonly known as Huangmagua; the upper part exhibiting interrupted indistinct annulations, the lower part bearing 2~3 branch roots. Rhizome 1~2cm long, showing stem scars and 1~2 adventitious roots. Texture, hard and fragile; fracture, even, horny. Odour, delicate fragrant and characteristic; taste, sweet and slightly bitter.

边条红参　主根长圆柱形。芦黄色略柴质，芦碗稍大而凹陷。具有“3 长”特点，即身长体圆、芦长有碗、腿长多 2~3 分枝。

Biantiao red ginseng　Main roots long cylindrical. Lutou yellow, a little hard and dry. Luwan slightly big and sunken. “Three long” characteristics, long and round body, long Lutou with Luwan, long Tui with mostly 2~3 branch roots.

白干参　形似生晒参，栓皮已刮去，表面淡黄色或类白色，环纹不明显，横纵皱少或无，质较坚实，断面白色，显菊花心。味甜、微苦。

Baiganshen　Shape like Shengshaishen, cork scraped; externally faint yellow or sub-whitish, indistinct annulations, few or no transverse striations and longitudinal wrinkles. Texture quite solid, fracture white, showing chrysanthemum-flower-like radial lines (Juhuaxin). Taste, sweet and slightly bitter.

皮尾参　不定根呈长条圆柱形，上端有茎痕而无芦，下部不带须根。表面土黄色，常有褐色环纹及纵向抽皱。质较轻泡，断面白色，显菊花心。

Piweishen　Adventitious roots strip cylindrical; the upper part exhibiting stem scars but no Lutou, the lower part bearing no rootlets. Externally khaki, mostly brown annulations and longitudinal furrows and wrinkles. Texture, light and loose; fracture, white, showing hrysanthemum-flower-like radial lines (Juhuaxin).

白参须　分为直须、弯须、混须 3 种。直须上端直径约 0.3cm，中、下端渐细，长短不一，最长可达 20cm。弯须则弯曲而细乱。

Baishenxu　Three types of rootlets, including straight rootlets, curving rootlets and mixing rootlets. Straight rootlets, about 0.3cm for the diameter of upper part, the middle and lower part thin gradually, variable in length, 20cm at most. Curving rootlets, curly and thin in a mess.

2. 饮片

2. Prepared slices

（1）生晒参片　为圆形或椭圆形薄片，周边灰黄色，有纵皱纹。切面黄白色或类白色，环纹棕黄色，皮部有黄棕色树脂道小点和放射状裂隙，木部淡黄色，显菊花纹。体轻质脆，粉性。香气特异，味甜、微苦。

(1) Slices of Shengshaishen　Rounded or subrounded thin slices; externally greyish-yellow, exhibiting longitudinal wrinkles. Cut surface yellowish-white or sub-whitish; cambium ring brownish-yellow; yellowish-brown dotted resin canals and radical clefts in cortex; xylem faint yellow, showing hrysanthemum-flower-like radial lines (Juhuaxin). Texture light, fragile, starchy. Odour, specific fragrant; taste, sweet and slightly bitter.

（2）红参片　为圆形或长椭圆形斜片，周边红棕色，有纵横皱纹。切面红棕色或棕色，环纹和树脂道小点不明显，致密无裂隙，显菊花纹。半透明，角质样。质硬而脆，粉性。香气特异，味甜、微苦。

(2) Slices of red ginseng　Rounded or long elliptical oblique slices. Externally reddish-brown, exhibiting transverse striations and longitudinal wrinkles. Cut surface reddish-brown or brown, indistinct annular wrinkles and dotted resin canals; compact and no clefts, showing hrysanthemum-flower-like radial lines (Juhuaxin). Translucent, horny. Texture hard and fragile, starchy. Odour, specific fragrant;

taste, sweet and slightly bitter.

（3）白参片　为横切片或斜切片，外皮松泡，白色，质嫩而薄，断面黄白色。气微香味甜，嚼之能溶化。

(3) Slices of Baishen　Slices of transverse or oblique section, loose shuck, white; texture tender, thin; cut surface yellowish-white. Odour, slightly fragrant; taste, sweet, dissolved when chewed.

【规格等级 / Specification and grade】

商品分山参和园参两大类，以山参质优。其规格等级标准为：

Commodities are divided into two types of wild ginseng and garden ginseng. Wild ginseng possesses super quality. The grading criteria are as follows:

山参　一等：主根粗短呈横灵体，支根八字分开，五形全美。有圆芦。艼中间丰满，形似枣核。皮紧细。主根上部纹紧密而深。须根清疏而长，质坚韧，有明显的珍珠疙瘩。表面牙白色或黄白色，断面白色。味甜、微苦。每支重 100g 以上，艼帽不超过主根重量的 25%。无疤痕、杂质、虫蛀、霉变。

Wild ginseng　First grade: Main roots, thick and short, exhibiting Henglingti; branch roots fork as a figure of up-side-down "V"; Lutou, Ding, Ti, Tui and Xu are all perfect. Rhizome, showing Yuanlu; Ding, plump in the middle, shape like date pit; skin tight and fine. The upper part of main roots exhibiting compact, deep wrinkles. Slender rootlets sparse and long with obvious Zhenzhugeda, texture tough. Externally cream white or yellowish-white, fraction white. Taste, sweet and slightly bitter. More than 100g per ginseng root, the weight of Dingmao (rhizome and adventitious roots) is not more than 25% of the main root. No scar, nor foreign matter, nor moth, nor mildew.

二等：每支重 55g 以上，余同一等。

Second grade: More than 55g per ginseng root, other characteristics are the same to those of First grade.

三等：每支重 32.5g 以上，余同一等。

Third grade: More than 32.5g per ginseng root, other characteristics are the same to those of First grade.

四等：每支重 20g 以上，余同一等。

Fourth grade: More than 20g per ginseng root, other characteristics are the same to those of First grade.

五等：每支重 12.5g 以上，艼帽不超过主根重量的 40%。余同一等。

Fifth grade: More than 12.5g per ginseng root, the weight of Dingmao is not more than 40% of the main root, other characteristics are the same to those of First grade.

六等：根部呈横灵体、顺体、畸形体（笨体）。每支重 6.5g 以上，艼帽不大，无杂质、虫蛀、霉变。余同一等。

Sixth grade: Main roots exhibiting Henglingti, Shunti, Jixingti (Benti). More than 6.5g per ginseng root, no big Dingmao. No foreign matter, nor moth, nor mildew. Other characteristics are the same to those of First grade.

七等：根部呈横灵体、顺体、畸形体。有圆芦。皮紧细。主根上部横纹紧密而深。须根清疏而长，有珍珠疙瘩。表面牙白色或黄白色，断面白色。味甜、微苦。每支重 48g 以上，无杂质，虫蛀、霉变。

Seventh grade: Main roots exhibiting Henglingti, Shunti, Jixingti. Lutou showing Yuanlu; Skin tight and fine. The upper part of main root exhibiting compact, deep transverse wrinkles. Slender rootlets sparse and long with Zhenzhugeda. Externally cream white or yellowish-white, fraction white. Taste, sweet and slightly bitter. More than 48g per root. No foreign matter, nor moth, nor mildew.

八等：每支重 28g 以上。间有芦须不全的残次品。余同七等。

Eighth grade: More than 28g per ginseng root. Occasionally defective ginseng with incomplete rhizome or rootlets. Other characteristics are the same to those of Seventh grade.

艼变山参、籽种山参、趴货参、池底参、移山参，一般按山参八或九等收购。

Dingbianshanshen, Zizhongshanshen, Pahuoshen, Chidishen and Yishanshen are usually purchased according to the Eighth grade or Ninth grade of wild ginseng.

园参　商品根据加工方法以及大小等的不同，分为边条鲜参、普通鲜参、边条红参、普通红参、生晒参、白参须、红参须等规格。各规格再分为不同的等级。

Garden ginseng　Commodities are divided into the specifications of Biantiaoxianshen, Putongxianshen, Biantiao red ginseng, common red ginseng, Shengshaishen, Baishenxu, Hongshenxu, etc., according to processing method and root size. Each specification is divided into different grades.

边条鲜参　一等：鲜货。根呈长圆柱形，芦长、身长、腿长，有 2~3 个分枝。须芦齐全，体长不短于 20cm。浆足，丰满。每支重 125g 以上，艼帽不超过 15%。不烂，无疤痕、水锈、泥土、杂质。

Biantiaoxianshen　First grade: Fresh ginseng. Root, long cylindrical. Rhizome, main root and branch roots are all long, branch root 2~3; integrate rhizome and rootlets, whole root no less than 20cm; succulence, plump. More than 125g per root, the weight of Dingmao is not more than 15% of the main roots. No rot, nor scar, nor speckle, nor soil, nor foreign matter.

二等：体长不短于 18.3cm。每支重 85g 以上。余同一等。

Second grade: Whole root not less than 18.3cm in length; more than 85g per root in weight. Other characteristics are the same to those of First grade.

三等：体长不短于 16.7cm。每支重 60g 以上。余同一等。

Third grade: Whole root not less than 16.7cm in length; more than 60g per root in weight. Other characteristics are the same to those of First grade.

四等：体长不短于 15cm。每支重 45g 以上。余同一等。

Fourth grade: Whole root not less than 15cm in length; more than 45g per root in weight. Other characteristics are the same to those of First grade.

五等：体长不短干 13.3cm。每支重 35g 以上。余同一等。

Fifth grade: Whole root not less than 13.3cm in length; more than 35g per root in weight. Other characteristics are the same to those of First grade.

六等：每支重 25g 以上。余同一等。

Sixth grade: More than 25g per root in weight. Other characteristics are the same to those of First grade.

七等：须芦齐全。浆足，丰满。每支重 12.5g 以上。

Seventh grade: Complete rhizome and rootlets; succulence, plump. More than 12.5g per root in weight.

八等：根呈长圆柱形，凡不符合以上规格和缺须少芦、破断根条者。每支重 5g 以上。

Eighth grade: Root long cylindrical. There are no rhizome and rootlets, inconformity to the grades above and with broken roots. More than 5g per root in weight.

普通鲜参　特等：鲜货。根呈圆柱形，有分枝，须芦齐全，浆足。每支重 100~150g。不烂，无疤痕、水锈、泥土、杂质。

Common fresh ginseng Top grade: Fresh ginseng. Roots cylindrical with branches; complete rhizome and rootlets, succulence; 100~150g per root. No rot, nor scar, nor speckle, nor soil, nor foreign matter.

一等：每支重 62.5g 以上。余同特等。

First grade: More than 62.5g per root in weight. Other characteristics are the same to those of Top grade.

二等：每支重 41.5g 以上。余同特等。

Second grade: More than 41.5g per root in weight. Other characteristics are the same to those of Top grade.

三等：每支重 31.5g 以上。余同特等。

Third grade: More than 31.5g per root in weight. Other characteristics are the same to those of Top grade.

四等：每支重 25g 以上。不烂，无泥土、杂质。余同特等。

Fourth grade: More than 25g per root in weight. No rot, nor soil, nor foreign matter. Other characteristics are the same to those of Top grade.

五等：每支重 12.5g 以上。余同四等。

Fifth grade: More than 12.5g per root in weight. Other characteristics are the same to those of Fourth grade.

六等：鲜货。根呈圆柱形，每支重 5g 以上，不合以上规格和缺须少芦折断者。

Sixth grade: Fresh ginseng. Roots cylindrical, more than 5g per root in weight. There are no rhizome and rootlets. Inconformity to grades above and with broken roots.

16 支边条红参 一等：根呈长圆柱形，芦长、身长、腿长，体长 18.3cm 以上，有 2~3 个分枝。表面棕红或淡棕色，有光泽，上部色较淡，有皮有肉。质坚实，断面角质样。气香，味苦。每 500g16 支以内，每支重 31.3g 以上。无中尾、黄皮、破疤、虫蛀、霉变、杂质。

Sixteen Biantiaohongshen First grade: Main roots long cylindrical. Rhizome, main root and branch root are all long; main root is longer than 18.3cm with 2~3 branches. Externally brownish-red or maple, gloss; the upper part pale colour, bearing epidermis and tissue. Texture hard and compacted, fracture horny. Odour, fragrant; taste, bitter. Less than 16 roots in per 500g, more than 31.3g of per root. No medial rootlet, nor yellow patch, nor scar, nor moth, nor mildew, nor foreign matter.

二等：表面棕红色或棕色，稍有黄皮，抽沟，干痕。余同一等。

Second grade: Externally brownish-red or brown; exhibiting yellow patches, furrow, scar occasionally. Other characteristics are the same to those of First grade.

三等：色泽较差。有黄皮、抽沟、破痕。腿红。余同一等。

Third grade: Poor colour and lustre. Exhibiting yellow patches, furrow, scar and red branch. Other characteristics are the same to those of First grade.

25 支边条红参 一等：根呈长圆柱形，芦长、身长、腿长，体长 16.7cm 以上，有 2~3 个分枝。表面棕红色或淡棕色，有光泽，上部色较浅，有皮有肉。质坚实，断面角质样。气香，味苦。每 500g 25 支以内，每支重 20g 以上。无中尾、黄皮、破疤、虫蛀、霉变、杂质。

Twenty-five Biantiaohongshen First grade: Main root long cylindrical. Rhizome, main root and branch root are all long; Main root, longer than 16.7cm, with 2~3 branches. Externally brownish-red or maple, gloss; the upper part pale colour, bearing epidermis and tissue. Texture hard and compacted;

fracture horny. Odour, fragrant; taste, bitter. Less than 25 roots in per 500g, more than 20g of per root. No medial rootlet, nor yellow patches, nor scar, nor moth, nor mildew, nor foreign matter.

二等：表面稍有黄皮、抽沟、干疤。余同一等。

Second grade: Externally exhibiting few yellow patches, furrow, scar. Other characteristics are the same to those of First grade.

三等：色泽较差。有黄皮、抽沟、破疤，腿红。余同一等。

Third grade: Poor colour and lustre. Exhibiting yellow patches, furrow, scar and red branch. Other characteristics are the same to those of First grade.

35 支条边红参　一等：根呈长圆柱形，芦长、身长、腿长，体长 15cm 以上，有 2~3 个分枝。表面棕红色或淡棕色，有光泽，上部色较浅，有皮有肉。质坚实，断面角质样。气香，味苦。每 500g 35 支以内，每支重 14.3g 以上。无中尾、黄皮、破疤、虫蛀、霉变、杂质。

Thirty-five Biantiaohongshen　First grade: Main roots long cylindrical. Rhizome, main root and branch root are all long; main root, longer than 15cm, with 2~3 branches. Externally brownish-red or maple, gloss; the upper part pale colour, bearing epidermis and tissue. Texture hard and compacted; fracture horny. Odour, fragrant; taste, bitter. Less than 35 roots in per 500g, more than 14.3g per root. No medial rootlet, nor yellow patches, nor scar, nor moth, nor mildew, nor foreign matter.

二等：表面稍有黄皮、抽沟、干疤。余同一等。

Second grade: Externally exhibiting yellow patches, furrow, scar occasionally. Other characteristics are the same to those of First grade.

三等：色泽较差。有黄皮、抽沟、破疤，腿红。余同一等。

Third grade: Poor colour and lustre. Exhibiting yellow patches, furrow, scar and red branch. Other characteristics are the same to those of First grade.

45 支边条红参　一等：根呈长圆柱形，芦大、身长、腿长，体长 11.7cm 以上，有 2~3 个分枝。表面棕红色或淡棕色，有光泽，上部色较淡，有皮有肉。质坚实，断面角质样。气香，味苦。每 500g 45 支以内，支头均匀。无中尾、黄皮、破疤、虫蛀、霉变、杂质。

Forty-five Biantiaohongshen　First grade: Main roots long cylindrical. Rhizome, main root and branch root are all long; main root, longer than 11.7cm, with 2~3 branches. Externally brownish-red or maple, gloss; the upper part pale colour, bearing epidermis and tissue. Texture hard and compacted; fracture horny. Odour, fragrant; taste, bitter. Less than 45 roots in per 500g, uniform roots. No medial rootlet, nor yellow patch, nor scar, nor moth, nor mildew, nor foreign matter.

二等：稍有黄皮、抽沟、干疤。余同一等。

Second grade: Externally yellow patches, furrow, scar occasionally. Other characteristics are the same to those of First grade.

三等：色泽较差。有黄皮、抽沟、破痕，腿红。余同一等。

Third grade: Poor colour and lustre. Exhibiting yellow patches, furrow, scar and red branch. Other characteristics are the same to those of First grade.

55 支边条红参　一等：根呈长圆柱形，芦长、身长、腿长，体长 11.7cm 以上，有 2~3 个分枝。表面棕红色或淡棕色，有光泽，上部色较淡，有皮有肉。质坚实，断面角质样。气香，味苦。每 500g 55 支以内，支头均匀。无中尾、黄皮、破疤、虫蛀、霉变、杂质。

Fifty-five Biantiaohongshen　First grade: Main root long cylindrical. Rhizome, main root and branch root are all long; main root, longer than 11.7cm, with 2~3 branches. Externally brownish-red or maple, gloss; the upper part pale colour, bearing epidermis and tissue. Texture hard and compacted;

fracture horny. Odour, fragrant; taste, bitter. Less than 55 roots in per 500g, uniform roots. No medial rootlet, nor yellow patch, nor scar, nor moth, nor mildew, nor foreign matter.

二等：稍有黄皮、抽沟、干疤。余同一等。

Second grade: Externally exhibiting yellow patches, furrow, scar occasionally. Other characteristics are the same to those of First grade.

三等：色泽较差。有黄皮、抽沟、破疤，腿红。余同一等。

Third grade: Poor colour and lustre. Exhibiting yellow patches, furrow, scar and red branch. Other characteristics are the same to those of First grade.

80 **支边条红参** 一等：根呈长圆柱形，芦长、身长、腿长，体长 11.7cm 以上。表面棕红或淡棕色，有光泽，上部色较淡，有皮有肉。质坚实，断面角质样。气香，味苦。每 500g 80 支以内，支头均匀。无中尾、黄皮、破疤、虫蛀、霉变、杂质。

Eighty Biantiaohongshen First grade: Main roots long cylindrical. Rhizome, main root and branch root are all long; main root, longer than 11.7cm, with 2~3 branches. Externally brownish-red or maple, gloss; the upper part pale colour, bearing epidermis and tissue. Texture hard and compacted; fracture horny. Odour, fragrant; taste, bitter. Less than 80 roots in per 500g, uniform roots. No medial rootlet, nor yellow patch, nor scar, nor moth, nor mildew, nor foreign matter.

二等：稍有黄皮、抽沟、干疤。余同一等。

Second grade: Externally exhibiting yellow patches, furrow, scar occasionally. Other characteristics are the same to those of First grade.

三等：色泽较差。有黄皮、抽沟、破疤，腿红。余同一等。

Third grade: Poor colour and lustre. Exhibiting yellow patch, furrow, scar and red branch. Other characteristics are the same to those of First grade.

小货边条红参 一等：根呈长圆柱形。表面棕红或淡棕色，有光泽，上部色较淡，有皮有肉。断面角质样。气香，味苦。支头均匀。无中尾、黄皮、破疤、虫蛀、霉变、杂质。

Xiaohuo Biantiaohongshen First grade: Main roots long cylindrical; externally brownish-red or maple, gloss; the upper part pale colour, bearing epidermis and tissue. Fracture horny. Odour, fragrant; taste, bitter. Uniform roots. No medial rootlet, nor yellow patch, nor scar, nor moth, nor mildew, nor foreign matter.

二等：有黄皮，但不超过身长的 1/2。稍有抽沟、干疤。余同一等。

Second grade: Yellow patches, not more than half length of roots. Externally exhibiting furrow, scar occasionally. Other characteristics are the same to those of First grade.

三等：色泽较差。有黄皮、抽沟、破疤，腿红。余同一等。

Third grade: Poor colour and lustre. Exhibiting yellow patch, furrow, scar and red branch. Other characteristics are the same to those of First grade.

20 **支普通红参** 一等：根呈圆柱形。表面棕红或淡棕色，有光泽。质坚实，断面角质样。无细腿、破痕、黄皮、虫蛀。气香，味苦。每 500g 20 支以内，每支重 25g 以上。

Twenty common red ginseng First grade: Main roots cylindrical; externally brownish-red or maple, gloss. Texture hard and compacted; fracture horny. No thin branch, nor scar, nor yellow patch, nor moth. Odour, fragrant; taste, bitter. Less than 20 roots in per 500g, more than 25g per root.

二等：稍有干疤、黄皮、抽沟。余同一等。

Second grade: Externally exhibiting scar, yellow patch, furrow occasionally. Other characteristics are the same to those of First grade.

三等：色泽较差。有黄皮、干疤、抽沟，腿红。余同一等。

Third grade: Poor colour and lustre. Exhibiting yellow patch, scar, furrow, and red branch. Other characteristics are the same to those of First grade.

32 **支普通红参** 一等：根呈圆柱形。表面棕红或淡棕色，有光泽。质坚实，断面角质样。每500g 32 支以内，每支重 15.6g 以上。无细腿、破痕、黄皮、虫蛀。

Thirty-two common red ginseng First grade: Main roots cylindrical; externally brownish-red or maple, gloss. Texture hard and compacted; fracture horny. Less than 32 roots in per 500g, more than 15.6g per root. No thin branch, nor scar, nor yellow patch, nor moth.

二等：稍有干疤、黄皮、抽沟，腿红。余同一等。

Second grade: Externally exhibiting scar, yellow patch, furrow, red branch occasionally. Other characteristics are the same to those of First grade.

三等：色泽较差。有黄皮、干疤、抽沟，腿红。余同一等。

Third grade: Poor colour and lustre. Exhibiting yellow patch, scar, furrow, and red branch. Other characteristics are the same to those of First grade.

48 **支普通红参** 一等：根呈圆柱形。表面棕红或淡棕色，有光泽。质坚实，断面角质样。气香，味苦。每 500g 48 支以内，支头均匀。无细腿、破痕、黄皮、虫蛀。

Forty-eight common red ginseng First grade: Main roots cylindrical; externally brownish-red or maple, gloss. Texture hard and compacted; fracture horny. Odour, fragrant; taste, bitter. Less than 48 roots in per 500g, uniform roots. No thin branch, nor scar, nor yellow patch, nor moth.

二等：稍有干疤、黄皮、抽沟。余同一等。

Second grade: Externally exhibiting scar, yellow patch, furrow occasionally. Other characteristics are the same to those of First grade.

三等：色泽较差。有黄皮、干疤、抽沟，腿红。余同一等。

Third grade: Poor colour and lustre. Exhibiting yellow patch, scar, furrow, and red branch. Other characteristics are the same to those of First grade.

64 **支普通红参** 一等：根呈圆柱形。表面棕红或淡棕色，有光泽。质坚实。气香，味苦。每500g 64 支以内，支头均匀。无细腿、破痕、黄皮、虫蛀。

Sixty-four common red ginseng First grade: Main roots cylindrical; externally brownish-red or maple, gloss. Texture hard and compacted. Odour, fragrant; taste, bitter. Less than 64 roots in per 500g, uniform roots. No thin branch, nor scar, nor yellow patch, nor moth.

二等：有干疤、黄皮、抽沟。无细腿、虫蛀。余同一等。

Second grade: Externally exhibiting scar, yellow patch, furrow. No thin branch, nor moth. Other characteristics are the same to those of First grade.

三等：色泽较差。有黄皮，抽沟，腿红。余同一等。

Third grade: Poor colour and lustre. Exhibiting yellow patch, furrow, and red branch. Other characteristics are the same to those of First grade.

80 **支普通红参** 一等：根呈圆柱形。表面棕红或淡棕色，有光泽。质坚实，断面角质样。每500g 80 支以内，支头均匀。无细腿、破疤、黄皮、虫蛀。

Eighty common red ginseng First grade: Main roots cylindrical; externally brownish-red or maple, gloss. Texture hard and compacted; fracture horny. Less than 80 roots in per 500g, uniform roots. No thin branch, nor scar, nor yellow patch, nor moth.

二等：稍有干疤、黄皮、抽沟。余同一等。

Second grade: Externally exhibiting scar, yellow patch, furrow occasionally. Other characteristics are the same to those of First grade.

三等：色泽较差。有黄皮、干疤、抽沟，腿红。余同一等。

Third grade: Poor colour and lustre. Exhibiting yellow patch, scar, furrow, and red branch. Other characteristics are the same to those of First grade.

小货普通红参 一等：根呈圆柱形。表面棕红或淡红色，有光泽。质坚实，断面角质样。气香，味苦。支头均匀。无细腿、破疤、黄皮、虫蛀。

Xiaohuo common red ginseng First grade: Main roots cylindrical; externally brownish-red or maple, gloss; texture hard and compacted; fracture horny. Odour, fragrant; taste, bitter. Uniform roots. No thin branch, nor scar, nor yellow patch, nor moth.

二等：稍有干疤、黄皮、抽沟。余同一等。

Second grade: Externally exhibiting scar, yellow patch, furrow occasionally. Other characteristics are the same to those of First grade.

三等：色泽较差。有黄皮、干疤、抽沟，腿红。余同一等。

Third grade: Poor colour and lustre. Exhibiting yellow patch, scar, furrow, and red branch. Other characteristics are the same to those of First grade.

红混须 统货。根须呈长条形或弯曲状。棕红色或橙红色，有光泽，半透明。断面角质样。气香，味苦。须条长短不分，其中直须50%以上。无碎末、杂质、虫蛀、霉变。

Honghunxu Unified grade. Slender rootlets straight or curving. Externally brownish-red or orange-red, glossy, translucent. Fracture horny. Odour, fragrant; taste, bitter. Rootlet irregular length, and the straight rootlets are more than half of all. No fragments, nor foreign matter, nor moth, nor mildew.

红直须 一等：根须呈长条形，粗壮均匀。棕红色或橙色，有光泽，半透明状。断面角质样。气香，味苦。长13.3cm以上。无干浆、毛须、杂质、虫蛀、霉变。

Hongzhixu First grade: Slender rootlets strip, uniform thickness. Externally brownish-red or orange, gloss, translucent. Fracture horny. Odour, fragrant; taste, bitter. More than 13.3cm in length. No waterless pulp, nor fibril, nor foreign matter, nor moth, nor mildew.

二等：长13.3cm以下，最短不低于8.3cm。余同一等。

Second grade: Less than 13.3cm, at least not less than 8.3cm in length. Other characteristics are the same to those of First grade.

红弯须 统货。根须呈条形弯曲状，粗细不均。橙红色或棕黄色，有光泽，呈半透明状。气香，味苦。无碎末、杂质、虫蛀、霉变。

Hongwanxu Unified grade. Slender rootlets strip-curve, irregular thickness. Externally orange-red or brownish-yellow, glossy, translucent. Odour, fragrant; taste, bitter. No powder, nor foreign matter, nor moth, nor mildew.

干浆参 统货。根呈圆柱形，体质轻泡，瘪瘦或多抽沟。表面棕黄色或黄白色。味苦。无杂质、虫蛀、霉变。

Ganjiangshen Unified grade. Roots cylindrical; texture light, loose, shrivelled, and mostly furrow. Externally brownish-yellow or yellowish-white. Taste, bitter. No foreign matter, nor moth, nor mildew.

全须生晒参 一等：根呈圆柱形，有分枝。体轻有抽沟，有艼帽，芦须全。表面黄白色或较深，断面黄白色。气香，味苦。每支重10g以上，绑尾或不绑尾。无破疤、杂质、虫蛀、霉变。

Quanxu shengshaishen First grade: Roots cylindrical with branches; texture light, exhibiting furrow. There are Dingmao, Lutou and Xu. Externally yellowish-white or darker; fracture yellowish-white. Odour, fragrant; taste, bitter. More than 10g per root; fibrous roots bound or not. No scar, nor foreign matter, nor moth, nor mildew.

二等：每支重 7.5g 以上。余同一等。

Second grade: More than 7.5g per root. Other characteristics are the same to those of First grade.

三等：每支重 5g 以上。余同一等。

Third grade: More than 5g per root. Other characteristics are the same to those of First grade.

四等：大小支不分，绑尾或不绑尾。芦须不全，间有折断。余同一等。

Fourth grade: Different sizes mixed, fibrous roots bound or not. Rhizome and rootlets incomplete, broken occasionally. Other characteristics are the same to those of First grade.

生晒参 一等：根呈圆柱形，体轻有抽沟，去净艼须。表面黄白色。气香，味苦。每 500g 60 支以内。无破疤、杂质、虫蛀、霉变。

Shengshaishen First grade: Roots cylindrical; texture light, exhibiting furrow; removed off adventitious roots (Ding) and rootlets (Xu). Externally yellowish-white. Odour, fragrant; taste, bitter. Less than 60 roots in per 500g. No scar, nor foreign matter, nor moth, nor mildew.

二等：每 500g 80 支以内。余同一等。

Second grade: Less than 80 roots in per 500g. Other characteristics are the same to those of First grade.

三等：每 500g 100 支以内。余同一等。

Third grade: Less than 100 roots in per 500g. Other characteristics are the same to those of First grade.

四等：体轻有抽沟、死皮。每 500g 130 支以内。余同一等。

Fourth grade: Texture light, exhibiting furrow, dried epidermis. Less than 130 roots in per 500g. Other characteristics are the same to those of First grade.

五等：每 500g 130 支以外。余同四等。

Fifth grade: More than 130 roots in per 500g. Other characteristics are the same to those of Fourth grade.

白干参 一等：根呈圆柱形，去净支根。皮细，色白，芦小，质充实。断面白色。气香，味苦。每 500g 60 支以内，支条均匀。无抽沟、皱皮、水锈、杂质、虫蛀、霉变。

Baiganshen First grade: Roots cylindrical, removed off branch roots. Skin fine, white, small rhizome; texture stout. Fracture white. Odour, fragrant; taste, bitter. Less than 60 roots in per 500g, uniform roots. No furrow, nor wizened epidermis, nor speckle, nor foreign matter, nor moth, nor mildew.

二等：每 500g 80 支以内。余同一等。

Second grade: Less than 80 roots in per 500g. Other characteristics are the same to those of First grade.

三等：表面稍有抽沟、水锈。每 500g100 支以内。余同一等。

Third grade: Externally furrow, and speckle occasionally. Less than 100 roots in per 500g. Other characteristics are the same to those of First grade.

四等：表面有抽沟、水锈。每 500g100 支以外。余同一等。

Fourth grade: Externally furrow, and speckle. More than 100 roots in per 500g. Other characteristics are the same to those of First grade.

皮尾参 统货。根呈圆柱形，条状，无分枝。表面灰棕色，断面黄白色，气香，味苦。无杂质、虫蛀、霉变。

Piweishen Unified grade. Roots cylindrical, strip, with no branch. Externally greyish-brown; fracture yellowish-white. Odour, fragrant; taste, bitter. No foreign matter, nor moth, nor mildew.

白混须 统货。根须呈长条形或弯曲状。黄白色。气香，味苦。长短不分，其中直须占 50% 以上。无碎末、杂质、虫蛀、霉变。

Baihunxu Unified grade. Slender rootlets strip or curving. Externally yellowish-white. Odour, fragrant; taste, bitter. Rootlet irregular length, and the straight rootlets are more than half of all. No powder, nor foreign matter, nor moth, nor mildew.

白直须 一等：根须呈条状，有光泽。表面、断面均呈黄白色。气香，味苦。长 13.3cm 以上，条大小均匀，无水锈、破皮、杂质、虫蛀、霉变。

Baizhixu First grade: Slender rootlets strip, glossy. Surface and fracture, yellowish-white. Odour, fragrant; taste, bitter. More than 13.3cm in length, uniform roots. No speckle, nor broken epidermis, nor foreign matter, nor moth, nor mildew.

二等：长 13.3cm 以下，最短不低于 8.3cm。余同一等。

Second grade: Less than 13.3cm, at least not less than 8.3cm in length. Other characteristics are the same to those of First grade.

进口品 朝鲜人参 系人参栽培品（大马牙、二马牙）。参体粗壮顺长，芦粗短且多为双芦（习称“双马蹄芦”）。

Imported gingseng Korean ginseng Cultivated ginseng (Damaya, taproot, stout shape; Ermaya, taproot, slightly thick and long shape). Main root sturdy, straight and long; rhizome thick, short, mostly double (commonly known as Shuangmatilu).

① 朝鲜红参：又称“高丽参”、“别直参”。呈圆柱形或方圆柱形，长 13~15cm，粗细不一。芦短粗，长 1.5~2cm，直径几乎和主根同。主根顺长，多单支。棕红色，半透明。气无，味甜、微苦。余同国产品。商品尚有原形朝鲜红参（全须），用支根和须根做成的大尾、大中尾、中尾、小尾、细尾等规格。品质按优次分等。以皮细质坚、无破皮、无疤痕者为优，皮粗、皮黄者次之，有疤、有破皮者更次一等，内心空泡者最次。优者称天字，中等者称地字、人字，最次者称翁字。又按每 500g 或 600g 所含片（支）的数量，划分为 10、15、20、30、40、50、60、70、80、小片 10 个等级，一般 10 支者虚 2 支、15 支者虚 3 支、20 支以上者虚 8 支。

① Korean red ginseng: Commonly known as “Gaolishen”, “Biezhishen”. Cylindrical or quadrate cylindrical, 13-15cm long, irregular thickness. Rhizome short and thick, 1.5-2cm long, the diameter is almost as long as the main root. Main root straight and long, mostly single. Externally brownish-red, translucent. Odourless; taste, sweet and slightly bitter. Other characteristics are the same to those of ginseng cultivated in China. Commodities also include original Korean red ginseng (Quanxu), different specifications of Dawei, Dazhongwei, Zhongwei, Xiaowei and Xiwei made of branch roots and rootlets. Grades are divided according to quality. The best grade, exhibiting fine skin, tough texture, no broken epidermis and scar. The second grade, exhibiting coarse or yellow skin. The third grade, bearing scar and broken epidermis. The worst grade, empty and loose in center. The best quality is Tianzi; the worst is Wengzi; and medium are Dizi and Renzi. Ginseng are divided into ten grades of ten, fifteen, twenty, thirty, forty, fifty, sixty, seventy, eighty and small slice according to the numbers of pieces (roots) in per 500 or 600g, generally two pieces subtracted in Ten grade, three pieces subtraced in Fifteen grade, eight pieces subtracted in beyond Twenty grade.

② 朝鲜白参：直接干燥品。呈圆锥形或圆柱形，全长约 10cm，粗细不一。芦体较朝鲜红参略细，直径稍细于主根。主根略粗短有分支。全体白色，具不规则纵抽皱，体轻泡。气无，味微

甜、苦。分为一、二、三、四等，重量分等同红参。亦有用支根和须根做成的大尾、中尾、细尾、皮尾等规格。

② Korean ginseng: directly dried ginseng. Conical or cylindrical, about 10cm long, irregular thickness. Rhizome is thinner than Korean red ginseng. The diameter is slightly thinner than main roots. Main roots slightly short and thick, branches. Externally white, irregular longitudinal wrinkles. Texture light and loose. Odourless; taste, slightly sweet and bitter. Korean ginseng is divided into four grades, and the criteria is the same to those of Korean red ginseng. Besides, branch roots and slender rootlets are processed to specifications of Dawei, Zhongwei, Xiwei and Piwei.

日本红参：又称“东洋参”。为人参的栽培品。成品形色介于朝鲜红参和国产红参之间，但芦较朝鲜红参稍细。主根上部常有黄皮，中下端比上端略显粗大，分枝短、急剧变细。分天字、地字 2 种规格和 10~40 支 5 个等级，尚有驳枝、比枝等规格。

Japanese red ginseng: also known as “Dongyangshen”, is the cultivated ginseng. The shape and colour are between Korean red ginseng and Chinese red ginseng, however the rhizome is thinner than Korean red ginseng. The upper part of main roots, often bearing yellow patches; the middle and lower parts thicker and bigger than the upper part; short branches, quick diminution. Japanese red ginseng are divided into two specifications of Tianzi and Dizi, five grades of ten to forty roots. In addition, there are specifications of Bozhi and Bizhi.

【化学成分 / Chemical constituent】

主含皂苷类化合物，根含总皂苷约 4%，须根中含量较主根高。主要皂苷种类约 14 种以上分别称为人参皂苷 R_0、R_a、R_{b1}、R_{b2}、R_{b3}、R_c、R_d、R_e、R_{g1} 等，以及丙二酰基人参皂苷 mR_{b1}、mR_{b2}、mR_c、mR_d，均为三萜皂苷。其中以四环三萜的达玛脂烷系皂苷为主要活性成分。其次为五环三萜的齐墩果烷系皂苷，其苷元为齐墩果酸。挥发油约含 0.12%，油中主要成分有 β- 榄香烯、人参炔醇及多炔环氧物人参醇等。人参多糖包括水溶性多糖 38.7%，碱溶性多糖 7.8%~10%。

Ginseng mainly contains ginsenosides, about 4% total ginsenosides in roots, and the content in fibrous roots is higher than that in main roots. There are approximately more than fourteen types of primary ginsenosides, including ginsenoside R_0, R_a, R_{b1}, R_{b2}, R_{b3}, R_c, R_d, R_e, R_{g1}, etc., and malonyl ginsenoside mR_{b1}, mR_{b2}, mR_c, mR_d which are all triterpenoid ginsenosides. Ginsenosides of dammarane tetracyclic triterpenoids are its main active constituents. In addition, other important constituents are the ginsenosides of oleanane pentacyclic triterpenes whose aglycone is cleanolic acid. Ginseng contains about 0.12% volatile oil, mainly consisting of β-elemene, panaxynol, panaxynol epoxide, etc. Ginseng polysaccharides contain 38.7% water-soluble polysaccharides and 7.8%~10% alkali-soluble polysaccharides.

【检查 / Examination】

水分不得过 12.0%。总灰分不得过 5.0%，酸不溶性灰分不得过 1.0%。

Water, not more than 12.0%. Total ash, not more than 5.0%. Acid-insoluble ash, not more than 1.0%.

【质量要求 / Quality requirement】

外观质量 生晒参以根大饱满、表面色黄白、皮细纹深、质硬、气味浓者为佳。红参以身长、芦长、腿长、色棕红、皮细光泽、半透明、无黄皮者为佳。

Appearance quality Good quality of Shengshaishen for big roots, plumpness, yellowish-white surface, fine skin, deep wrinkles, hard texture, strong odour and taste. Good quality of red ginseng for long body, rhizome and branch, brownish-red, glossy fine skin, translucent, and without yellow patch.

内在质量 含量测定：按高效液相色谱法测定，含人参皂苷 Rg_1 和人参皂苷 R_e 的总量不得少于 0.30%，人参皂苷 R_{b1} 不得少于 0.20%。

Intrinsic quality Assay: It contains not less than 0.30% of ginsenoside Rg_1 and R_e, and not less than 0.20% of ginsenoside R_{b1} according to HPLC analysis method.

【功能主治 / Function and indication】

温，甘、微苦。大补元气，复脉固脱，补脾益肺，生津养血，安神益智。用于体虚欲脱、肢冷脉微、脾虚食少、肺虚喘咳、津伤口渴、内热消渴、气血亏虚，久病虚羸、惊悸失眠、阳痿宫冷。

Mild warm; sweet and mild bitter. To tonify the original qi greatly, resume pulse, secure collapse, tonify spleen, replenish lung, engender fluid, nourish the blood, tranquilize the mind, and replenish wisdom. For the treatment of coming essence exhaustion caused by body deficiency, cold limbs, faint pulse, low appetite caused by spleen deficiency, dyspnea and cough caused by lung deficiency, thirsty caused by fluid damage, interior heat, wasting-thirst, deficiency of qi and blood, frail caused by long-term illness, fright palpitations, insomnia, impotence, and uterine coldness.

【贮藏养护 / Storage and maintenance】

人参为名贵药材，一般用较精制的容器包装并密封，置干燥处贮存。对拆零散装待用的参类药物，按常法多贮于石灰缸中保存。

Ginseng is famous and precious medicinal material, usually packed and sealed in more delicate containers which are kept in dry place. Standby separate ginseng roots are conventionally kept in the vat with lime inside for storage.

【用法用量 / Administration and dosage】

3~9g，另煎兑入汤剂服。山参若研粉吞服，1 次 2g，1 日 2 次。不宜与藜芦同用。

3~9g, ginseng is decocted separately, added into prescription decoction before taking. Shanshen is ground into powder for swallowing, 2g once, twice a day. Not suitable for administration with *Veratrum nigrum*.

五味子 (Wuweizi) ⁝ Schisandrae Chinensis Fructus (Chinese Magnoliavine Fruit)

【基原 / Origin】

为木兰科植物五味子 *Schisandra chinensis* (Turcz.) Baill. 的干燥成熟果实。习称“北五味子”。

Chinese Magnoliavine Fruit is the dried ripe fruit of *Schisandra chinensis* (turcz.) Baill. (Fam. Magnoliaceae). The fruit is known as “Bei Wuweizi” (Northern Magnoliavine Fruit).

【产地 / Producing area】

主产于吉林桦甸、蛟河，辽宁本溪，凤城，黑龙江阿城，宁安等地。

Main producing areas are Huadian, Jiaohe of Jilin Province, Benxi, Fengcheng of Liaoning Province, Acheng, Ning’an of Heilongjiang Province.

【采制 / Collection and preparation】

北五味子 在 8 月下旬至 10 月上旬，果实呈紫红色时，随熟随收，拣出果梗等杂质，晒干或阴干。

Northern Magnoliavine Fruit The purplish-red fruits are collected when ripen from late August to early October, dried in the sun or in the shade, and purified by removing stalk and foreign matter.

五味子分别经米醋、黄酒、蜂蜜炮制成醋五味子、酒五味子、蜜五味子。

Northern Magnoliavine Fruit is processed into vinegar Schisandrae Fructus, wine Schisandrae Fructus, and honey Schisandrae Fructus with vinegar, Chinese rice wine, honey, respectively.

【商品特征 / Commodity characteristics】

北五味子 果实呈不规则的圆球形或扁球形。表面红色、紫红色或暗红色，皱缩，显油性；有的呈黑红色或出现“白霜”。果肉柔软。种子 1~2 粒，呈肾形，表面棕黄色，有光泽，种皮硬而脆，较易破碎；种仁呈钩状，黄白色，半透明，富油性。果肉气弱，味酸；种子破碎后有香气，味辛、微苦。

Northern Magnoliavine Fruit Irregularly spheroidal or flattened spheroidal; externally red, purplish-red or dark red, shrunken, oily, with soft pulp, sometimes externally blackish-red or covered with “white frost”. Seeds 1~2, reniform, externally brownish-yellow, lustrous; testa hard, crisp and fragile. Seed kernels, hook-like, yellowish-white, translucent, oily. Odour of pulp, slight; taste, sour. Odour of seeds, aromatic on crushing; taste, pungent and slightly bitter.

醋五味子 表面黑色，质柔润或显油润，微具醋气。

Vinegar Schisandrae Chinensis Fructus Externally black, soft or oily, slight odour of vinegar.

酒五味子 表面紫黑色或黑褐色，质柔润或显油润，微具酒气。

Wine Schisandrae Chinensis Fructus Externally purplish-black or blackish-brown, soft or oily, slight odour of wine.

蜜五味子 色泽加深，略具光泽，味酸、甜。

Honey Schisandrae Chinensis Fructus Colour deepened, slightly glossy, taste sour and sweet.

【规格等级 / Specification and grade】

北五味子按照果实表面颜色和干瘪粒数的比例分为两等，其等级标准如下。

Northern Magnoliavine Fruit is divided into two grades according to the proportion of surface color and the withered fruits. The grading criteria are as follows:

一等：呈不规则球形或椭圆形。表面红色、紫红色或红褐色，皱缩，肉厚，质柔润。果肉味酸，种子有香气。干瘪粒不超过 2%，无枝梗、杂质、虫蛀、霉变。

First grade: Irregularly spheroidal or oval, externally red, purplish-red or reddish-brown, shrunken, with thick and soft pulp. Pulp tastes sour, seed smells aromatic. The number of withered fruits is not more than 2%. No stalk, nor foreign matter, nor moth, nor mildew.

二等：表面黑色、暗红或淡红色，皱缩，肉较薄。干瘪粒不超过 20%。余同一等。

Second grade: Externally black, dark red or light red, shrunken, with thin pulp. The number of withered fruits is not more than 20%. Other characteristics are the same to those of First grade.

【化学成分 / Chemical constituent】

果实含挥发油 0.89%，油中含倍半萜烯、β_2- 没药烯、β- 花柏烯及 α- 衣兰烯。含木脂素约 5%，包括五味子甲素、乙素、五味子醇甲等，为本品的有效成分。

Fruit contains 0.89% volatile oil, mainly composed of sesquiterpene, β_2-bisabolene, β-chamigrene, α-ylangene; 5% lignins, including schisandrin A, schisandrin B, schizandrol A etc., which are the effective constituents.

【检查 / Examination】

杂质不得过 1.0%。水分不得过 16.0%。总灰分不得过 7.0%。

Foreign matter, not more than 1.0%. Water, not more than 16.0%. Total ash, not more than 7.0%.

【质量要求 / Quality requirement】

外观质量 以粒大、紫红、肉厚、柔润光泽、气味浓者为佳。

Appearance quality Good quality for big fruit, purplish-red colour, thick pulp, softness, gloss and strong odour and taste.

内在质量　含量测定：按高效液相色谱法测定，含五味子醇甲不得少于 0.40%。

Intrinsic quality　Assay: it contains not less than 0.40% of schisandrin according to HPLC analysis method.

【功能主治 / Function and indication】

温，酸、甘。收敛固涩，益气生津，补肾宁心。用于久嗽虚喘、梦遗滑精、遗尿尿频、久泻不止、自汗盗汗、津伤口渴、内热消渴、心悸失眠等。

Warm, sour and sweet. To astringe and secure, tonify qi, engender fluid, tonify the kidney and calm the heart. For the treatment of chronic cough, dyspnea of deficiency type, dream emission, spermatorrhea, enuresis, frequent urination, chronic diarrhea, spontaneous sweating, night sweating, thirst caused by fluid comsumption, interior heat wasting-thirst, palpitations and insomnia.

【贮藏养护 / Storage and maintenance】

多以麻袋包装或席包。贮存于干燥，通风、凉爽处。少量五味子宜置瓮内密封存放。

Usually packed in sack or mat bag. Preserved in ventilated, dry and cool place. Small amount of fruits are stored in sealed urn.

【用法用量 / Administration and dosage】

2~6g。

2~6g.

鹿茸 (Lurong) ¦ Cervi Cornu Pantotrichum (Pilose Antler)

【基原 / Origin】

为鹿科动物梅花鹿 *Cervus nippon* Temminck 或马鹿 *Cervus elaphus* Linnaeus 的雄鹿未骨化密生茸毛的幼角。前者习称“花鹿茸”，后者习称“马鹿茸”。

Pilose Antler is the young unossified hairy antler of male *Cervus nippon* Temminck or *Cervus elaphus* Linnaeus (Fam. Cervidae). The former is known as “Hualurong” (sika deer pilose antler), the latter known as “Malurong” (red deer pilose antler).

【产地 / Producing area】

花鹿茸主产于吉林、辽宁、河北等地。马鹿茸主产于黑龙江、吉林、内蒙古、新疆、青海、云南、四川、甘肃等地，其中东北产者称“东马鹿茸”，品质较优；西北产者称“西马鹿茸”，品质较次。现多为饲养。

Main producing areas of “Hualurong” are the provinces of Jilin, Liaoning, Hebei, etc. “Malurong” is mainly produced in the provinces of Heilongjiang, Jilin, Inner Mongolia, Xinjiang, Qinghai, Yunnan, Sichuan, Gansu, etc. Eastern “Malurong” (Dong-malurong) produced in Northeast of China, is considered to be high quality. Western “Malurong” (Xi-malurong) produced in Northwest of China, is thought as inferior quality. Both of them are artificially fed now.

【采制 / Collection and preparation】

一般分锯茸和砍茸 2 种方法。

Two collection methods of sawing and chopping pilose antler.

1. 采收

1. Collection

锯茸　育成公鹿第一次长出的圆柱形茸，锯下称“初生茸”或“初角茸”。梅花鹿 3~4 岁进入正常产茸期，应以采收“二杠茸”为主。5 岁以上可采收“三岔茸”。一年之中第二次采收的茸称“再生茸”或“二茬茸”。马鹿锯茸一般采收“莲花”“三岔茸”和“四岔茸”。

Sawing pilose antler Cylindrical pilose antler grown firstly by mature male deer, is sawed-off and named Chushengrong or Chujiaorong (nascent pilose antler). Ergangrong (double-branched pilose antler) is mainly collected when *Cervus nippon* grows up to the common period of producing antler at 3~4 years old. Sancharong (triple-branched pilose antler) can be collected from the deer over 5 years old. The antler collected for the second time in one year, namely Zaishengrong or Ercharong (regenerative pilose antler). Lianhua (lotus shaped pilose antler), Sancharong (triple-branched pilose antler) and Sicharong (quadruple-branched pilose antler) are collected from *Cervus elaphus*.

砍茸 砍头采收带脑骨和皮的鹿茸称“砍茸”，通常是在需要淘汰的鹿身上进行。

Chopping pilose antler The antler collected with skull and fur when obsolete deer is chopped off the head, namely “Kanrong”.

采收时间 根据鹿的种类及茸生长情况，确定个体公鹿采茸时间，一般在5月末至8月下旬。成年公鹿生长“二杠茸”，如主干与眉枝肥壮，长势良好，可适时晚收：采收“三岔茸”时，如主干较细者应早收，如主干和眉枝粗壮，茸型好，上嘴头肥嫩的“三岔茸”可适当晚收。砍茸采收时间应比同规格锯茸适当提前。正常生长的“初生茸”应于6月中旬锯尖（平槎），在8月下旬分期分批采收。“再生茸”可于配种前适时采收。采收马鹿锯茸时，如“三岔茸”嘴头肥壮，可延至顶端拉沟未扭嘴前采收。纤细瘦条茸适时采收。“四岔茸”应在第五侧枝分生前嘴头粗壮时适当采收。“马砍茸”采收期同锯茸。

Collecting time The collecting time of individual male deer is decided according to the types of deer and growing state of antler, generally between the end of May and the end of August. Ergangrong of adult male deer can be collected appropriate late if its main branch and lateral branch are stout, strong, and grow well. Sancharong needs to be collected earlier if its main branch is thinner. Otherwise, it can be collected appropriate late if Sancharong appears stout and strong main branch and lateral branch, good shape of antler, plump and tender. The collecting time of Chopping pilose antler should be earlier than that of the same specification of sawing pilose antler. Chushengrong growing normally should be sawed tine (Pingcha) in the middle of June, and collected group by group at different periods in the late of August. Zaishengrong can be collected before the deer breed. Sancharong can be collected before the top of the Lagou not twisty if the sawing pilose antler from *Cervus elaphus* is stout and strong. Slender antler should be collected timely. Sicharong should be collected timely before the fifth lateral branch generates and the antler is stout and strong. The collecting time of chopping pilose antler from *Cervus elaphus* is the same to that of sawing pilose antler.

收茸方法 先将取茸鹿由鹿舍拨到小圈里，再由小圈逐头经通道推入保定器内保定，以限制其自由活动，便于锯（砍）茸。保定器分夹板式、抬杆式和吊索式，或用麻醉法保定。固定后开始锯茸，用锯（消毒）从角盘上2~3cm处快速锯下鹿茸，立即将止血药粉敷到锯口创面上并包扎好。然后将鹿从保定器中放出来，完成锯茸。收取砍茸，即在保定器内将鹿杀死，解下头部，再将茸连头盖骨取下。收茸后应立即加工处理。

Collecting method of pilose antler Drive deer that will be collected antlers from deer shed to little fold. Fix the deer in fixing implement after driving them one by one by passageway, then limit its movement in order to saw (chop) pilose antler. Fixing implements are divided into types as splint, lifting pole and sling, and anaesthetization is also used to fasten deer. After fixing the deer, cut the antler quickly with disinfected saw from 2~3cm above the antler plate. Apply hemostatic powder on the surface of the wound immediately, then bound it up. Set the deer free from fixing implements after sawing. To collect chopping pilose antler, kill the deer in fixing implements and dissect the head. Take off the antler with skull. After collection, pilose antler should be processed immediately.

2. 加工 鹿茸的加工是鹿茸生产中一个关键环节，主要有三种方法。

2. Processing Processing is a key step in the production of pilose antler, mainly including three methods.

（1）排血茸 首先用真空泵从茸的锯口处将茸体内的血液抽出，然后把茸固定在操作架上进行煮炸。煮炸时间：第一天煮炸加工称为第一水，之后为第二水、第三水和第四水（即第二天、第三天和第四天煮炸），连续若干次入水煮后有一间隔冷凉过程，把冷凉过程间隔的诸次合称作排，分一排、二排……，每次入水煮炸时间为10~60秒不等，冷凉时间为10~35分钟，煮炸次数及时间长短可视茸的种类、重量酌情掌握。煮炸方法：第一水常为两排，先将茸体放入沸水中（只露锯口）烫5~10秒，取出检查，发现茸皮有损伤可敷上蛋清面，以防煮炸时破裂。第一排煮炸经连续数次下水后，茸内大量血液排完，出现血沫，茸毛直立，茸头富有弹性，散出熟蛋黄香气时，取出冷凉。等茸不烫手时开始第二排煮炸，当茸熟透，茸内血液基本排净，结束第一水煮炸。以后2~4日的煮炸统称回水。第二水煮炸称为“二排”，煮炸次数和时间酌减，以煮透为原则，等锯口出现气泡为止。然后卸架后凉透，置烘箱内，在65℃~70℃下烘烤30~50分钟，取出后风干。第三水煮炸一般只一排，煮炸时可不上架，当茸尖由硬变软，再由软变为有弹性为止，然后如前法进行烘烤，风干。第四水主要煮炸茸尖、嘴头和主干上半部，每次入水时间可稍长，煮至茸头富有弹性为止，在70℃烘烤30分钟，风干。四水后的5~6天里每隔1天煮1次茸头，烘烤20~30分钟。以后可根据茸的干燥程度和气候情况不定期煮头烘烤。

(1) Paixuerong (pilose antler excluded blood) Blood in antler is pumped from cut surface with vacuum pump, then the antler is boiled after fixed on a handling frame. Boiling time: Boiling on first day is called “first boiling”, later “second boiling” “third boiling” and “fourth boiling” (namely boiling on the second, third, and fourth day). There is an interval cooling procedure after a number of continuous boiling, the interval number of times in the course of cooling are called Pai, namely one Pai, two Pai, etc. Time period per boiling is between 10~60 seconds, and the cooling time is between 10~35 minutes. The number of boiling times and boiling duration are taken into consideration of type and weight of antler. Boiling method: First boiling is mostly two Pai, the antlers (showing cut surface only) are put into boiling water for 5~10 seconds. After examination, the antlers might be applied the mixture of flour and albumen if there is any damaged skin in case of break in course of boiling. A lot of blood in antlers is discharged after several times of entering boiling water in one Pai. The antlers are taken out and cooled when its fragrance of cooked yolk released, while hairs of the antler is up-right and the top of antler own high resilience. Two Pai can start when antlers are not hot. First boiling is over when antlers cooked completely and blood in antlers mostly discharged. Boiling of 2~4 days later is called Huishui. Second boiling is called two Pai in which time and duration are reduced discretionarily for the aim of thoroughly boiling. Two Pai is over when bubbles appear on the cut surface of antlers. The antlers are discharged from shelf and cooled thoroughly. Then antlers are taken out and air-dried after roasted under 65℃~70℃ for 30~50 minutes in oven. Third boiling is only one Pai, and does not need to be done on shelf. Toasting and air-drying are proceeded as former method after the top of antler changes from hard to soft, then to elastic. Fourth boiling is for the top of antler, crotch and the top half of main branch, and the time of boiling may be longer until the top of antler is elastic. Then antlers are air-dried after roasted under 70℃ for 30 minutes. For 5~6 days after fourth boiling, the top of antler is boiled every other day, then roasted for 20~30 minutes. The antlers can be boiled and roasted non-scheduled according to their drying degree and climatic conditions.

（2）带血茸　收茸后迅速将锯口向上立放，不使茸内血液流失，马上封闭锯口进行加工处理、经过多次连续水煮和烘烤，通过茸皮渗透作用，散掉茸内水分，把茸血中的色素及干物质保留在茸体内。主要加工马鹿锯茸，其产品多供应出口。

(2) Pilose antler with blood　The antlers are collected and placed erectly with cut surface upward, so blood can be kept. Cut surface is sealed immediately, and the antlers are processed after several times of boiling and roast. Moisture in antler is got rid by permeation. Pigment and dry matter are kept in the antlers. Sawing pilose antlers from *Cervus elaphus* are mainly processed by this method, and the products are mostly for export.

（3）砍茸　其方法与锯茸加工基本相似，由于砍茸重量较大，并且连带部分头骨和头皮，加工操作要细致。此外可采用微波远红外线烘干和冷冻干燥法等新工艺进行加工。

(3) Chopping pilose antler　The processing method is the same to that of sawing pilose antler. Owing to heavy weight and connecting with part skull and scalp, operation should be carefully. In addition, microwave heating, far-infrared ray heating and freeze-drying methods can be applied to the processing of Chopping pilose antlers.

（4）鹿茸片及鹿茸粉　取原药材，燎去茸毛，刮净，以布带缠绕茸体，自锯口面小孔不断灌入热白酒至满，浸润至透。稍蒸，横切薄片，压平，干燥后制得鹿茸片。取原药材，燎去茸毛，刮净，劈成碎块，研成细粉后制得鹿茸粉。

(4) Slices and powder of pilose antler　Pilose antler is burnt away the soft hairs, scrape clean, wrap with a clothing band, add hot white rice wine into the small holes on the cut surface until it is moistened thoroughly. Steamed briefly, cut into thin slices, pressed to be flat, and dry. Pilose antler is burnt away the soft hairs, scrape clean, split into pieces and pulverize to powder.

【商品特征 / Commodity characteristics】

1. 药材

1. crude material

（1）花鹿茸

(1) Hualurong

锯茸　呈圆柱状分枝，具1个分枝者习称“二杠”茸，主枝习称“大挺”，长17~20cm，锯口直径4~5cm，离锯口约1cm处分出侧枝，习称“门桩”或“眉枝”，长9~15cm，直径较大挺略细。外皮红棕色或棕色，多光润，表面密生红黄色或棕黄色细茸毛，上端较密，下端较疏；分岔间具1条灰黑色筋脉，皮茸紧贴，习称“扈口封口线”。锯口黄白色，外围无骨质，中部密布细孔。体轻，气微腥，味微咸。具2个分枝者，习称“三岔茸”，大挺长23~33cm，直径较二杠茸细，略呈弓形，微扁，枝端略尖，下部多有纵棱筋及突起疙瘩，习称“起筋”或“骨钉”，皮红黄色，茸毛较稀而粗。二茬茸与头茬茸相似，但主枝长而不圆或下粗上细，下部有纵棱筋，皮灰黄色，茸毛较粗糙，锯口外围多已骨化，体较重。

Sawing pilose antler　Branched, cylindrical. The antler with one side branch commonly known as “Ergang” (double branches); the main branch as “Dating” (big branch), 17~20cm long, cut surface 4~5cm in diameter; the side branch separating at about 1cm from the cut surface known as “Menzhuang” (side branch) or “Meizhi”, 9~15cm long, slightly smaller than “Dating” in diameter. The outer skin reddish-brown or brown, usually lustrous, densely covered with reddish-yellow or brownish-yellow soft hairs, relatively dense at the upper end, and sparse at the lower end; a greyish-black vein at the base between the main and side branches, the skin and hairs nestled closely each other, commonly known as “Hukoufengkouxian”. The cut surface yellowish-white, without bony element in the outer part, small pores densely distributed in the central portion. Texture light. Odour, slightly stinking; taste, slightly salty. The antler with two side branches commonly known as "Sancha" (triple branches), Dating 23-33cm long and smaller than that of "Ergang" in diameter, slightly bow-shaped and flattened, the tip slightly pointed, the lower part usually bearing longitudinal ridged veins and lumps commonly known as "Qijin" or "Guding". Skin reddish-yellow, the soft hairs relatively sparse and thick. The Toucha similar to the Ercha, but Dating is long and not round, or lower part thicker than upper part, the lower part with longitudinal ridged veins. Skin greyish-yellow, the soft hairs relatively coarse. The outer part of the cut surface usually ossified. Rather heavy.

砍茸 为带脑骨的茸，茸形与锯茸同，二茸相距约 7cm，脑骨前端平齐，后端有 1 对弧形骨分列两旁，习称"虎牙"。外附脑皮，皮上密生毛。

Chopping pilose antler The antler with skull, same shape to sawing pilose antler. Two antler branches bearing 7cm in distance. Skull, flush in the front, a pair of arc-shaped bone distributed both sides in the back, commonly known as "huya" (tiger tooth). Adherent skin on skull, densely hairs on skin.

（2）马鹿茸 较花鹿茸粗大，分枝较多，具有 1 个分枝者习称"单门"，2 个分枝者习称"莲花"，3 个分枝者习称"三岔"，4 个分枝者习称"四岔"或更多。其中以莲花、三岔为主。

(2) Malurong Larger and thicker than Hualurong, more branched. The antler with one, two, three, four or more side branches commonly known as "Danmen" (single side branch), "Lianhua" (lotus), "Sancha" (triple side brsnches) and "Sicha" (quadruple side branches), respectively. Mostly Lianhua and Sancha.

东马鹿茸 单门的大挺长 25~27cm，直径约 3cm。外皮灰黑色，茸毛灰褐色或灰黄色，锯口面外皮较厚，灰黑色，中部密布蜂窝状细孔，质嫩；莲花的大挺长可达 33cm，下部有棱筋，锯口面蜂窝状小孔稍大；三岔皮色深，质较老；四岔茸毛粗而稀，大挺下部具棱筋及疙瘩，分枝顶端多无毛，习称"捻头"。

Dongmalurong Dating of Danmen 25~27cm long, about 3cm in diameter. The outer skin greyish-black, soft hairs greyish-brown or greyish-yellow. The outer skin of the cut surface rather thick, greyish-black. The central portion of the cut surface dense with small pores. Texture tender. Dating of Lianhua up to 33cm long, with ridged veins at the lower part, the cut surface with relatively larger honeycomb-like pores. The skin of Sancha dark, texture rather tough. Sicha with sparse and thick soft hairs; the lower part of Dating with ridged veins and lumps, tip usually without soft hairs, commonly known as "Niantou" (hairless tip).

西马鹿茸（新疆马鹿茸） 多为血茸，锯茸大挺更长，可至 1m，直径达 7~8cm，大挺多不圆而带纵棱或抽缩扁斜，分枝较长且弯曲，皮深灰色，茸毛粗长，灰色或黑灰色。锯口色较深，常见骨质。气腥，味咸。

Ximalurong (Xinjiang malurong) Mostly Xuerong, Dating of sawing pilose antler more longer to 1m, diameter, 7~8cm. Dating usually not round, with ridges or shrunken and shriveled. The branches rather long and curved; the skin dark grey; the soft hairs thick and long, grey or greyish-black. The cut surface in a relative dark colour and usually bony. Odour, stinking; taste, salty.

马鹿茸砍茸一般较梅花鹿砍茸大，也有因需淘汰而未等茸生长充分就砍杀的，此时加工的茸形小，头皮及毛为淡褐棕色至褐灰色。

Chopping pilose antler of *Cervus elaphus* is generally bigger than that of *Cervus nippon*. Sometimes processed antlers are smaller owing to obsolete deer with under-grown antler. Skin on the skull and the soft hairs show light brown to brownish-gray colour.

2. 饮片

2. Decocting slices

（1）花鹿茸片 角尖部切片习称“嘴片”或“蜡片”，为圆形薄片，表面浅棕色或黄白色，半透明，微显光泽，外围红棕色或棕色，质坚韧。在“蜡片”之后切制的依次习称“粉片”“纱片”“老角片”或“骨片”。为圆形或类圆形厚片，表面粉白色或浅棕色，中间有蜂窝状细孔，外围无骨质或略具骨质，周边粗糙，红棕色或棕色，质坚脆。气微腥，味微咸。

(1) Hualurong slices Slices of the tip, commonly known as “Zuipian” or “Lapian”; round thin slices, surface light brown or yellowish-white, translucent, slightly glossy; periphery reddish-brown or brown, texture hard and tenacious. Slices after Lapian are “Fenpian”, “Shapian”, “Laojiaopian” or “Gupian” consecutively. Thick slices circle or quasi-circle, externally pinkish-white or light brown, bearing honeycomb-like pores intermediately; the outer part of the cut surface no or slightly ossified; rim coarse, reddish-brown or brown, texture hard and crisp. Odour, slightly stinking; taste, slightly salty.

（2）马鹿茸片 蜡片为类圆形薄片，中央为米黄色，半透明，微显光泽，外围皮较厚，周边灰黑色，质坚韧。粉片、纱片、老角片为圆形或类圆形厚片，粉片切面有致密的细蜂窝状小孔，纱片与骨片中央有稀疏的蜂窝状孔眼。外皮较厚，无骨质或略具骨质。周边灰黑色，质坚脆。气微腥，味微咸。

(2) Malurong slices Lapian, quasi-circle slices; the center beige, translucent, slightly glossy; periphery skin thick, rim greyish-black, texture hard and tenacious. Fenpian, Shapian and Laojiaopian, thick circle or quasi-circle slices. The cut surface of Fenpian, bearing densely honeycomb-like pores; the center of Shapian and Gupian, bearing sparse honeycomb-like pores. Scarf skin rather thick, no or slightly ossified; rim greyish-black, texture hard and crisp. Odour, slightly stinking; taste, slightly salty.

（3）鹿茸粉 为灰白色或米黄色粉末。气微腥，味微咸。

(3) Lurong powder Greyish-white or beige powder. Odour, slightly stinking; taste, slightly salty.

【规格等级 / Specification and grade】

分梅花鹿茸和马鹿茸两大类。其规格等级标准为以下几种。

Pilose antler is divided into two types of Hualurong and Malurong, whose grading criteria are as follows.

1. 梅花鹿茸

1. Hualurong

二杠锯茸 分为四个等级。一等：干品不臭，无虫蛀，加工不乌皮，主干不存折，眉枝存折不超过一处，不悬皮，不破皮，不拧嘴，锯口有正常的孔隙结构，有正常典型分岔，主干与眉枝相称，圆粗嫩壮，茸皮、锯口有正常色调。每支重 85g 以上。

Sawing Ergang Divided into four grades. First grade: Dried antler no foul smell, nor moth, nor dark skin, nor crack on main branch, nor more than one crack on lateral branch, nor Xuanpi (skin upheaval), nor broken skin, nor Ningzui; normal pores in the cut surface, normal side branches; symmetric main branch and lateral branch, round, tender, thick, normal colour of skin and the cut surface. More than 85g per antler.

二等：主干破皮不显露结缔组织，虎口以下稍有突起棱纹，每支重 65g 以上。余同一等。

Second grade: Main branch with broken skin, but not bearing connective tissue inside. There are ridge and wrinkle below Hukou (forfication of two branches). More than 65g per antler. Other characteristics are the same to those of First grade.

三等：不显露皮下结缔组织，主干存折不超过一处，具有分枝，枝岔较瘦，不拧嘴，不抽沟，锯口有蜂窝状细孔，虎口以下有棱纹，每支重45g以上。余同一等。

Third grade: Not bearing connective tissue inside; not more than one crack on main branch; side branches, relatively thin branches, no Ningzui, nor furrow. Honeycomb-like pores on the cut surface; ridge and wrinkle below Hukou. More than 45g per antler. Other characteristics are the same to those of First grade.

四等：干品不臭，无虫蛀，不拧嘴，不抽沟。具独挺，畸形者和不符合一、二、三等者均属此等。

Fourth grade: Dried antler no foul smell, nor moth, nor Ningzui, nor furrow. Bearing sole Dating, malformation and inconformity to First, Second and Third grades belong to Fourth grade.

三岔锯茸 分为四个等级。一等：干品不臭，无虫蛀，加工不乌皮，不悬皮，不破皮，嘴头丰满，锯口有蜂窝状细孔，不拧嘴，主干嘴头不存折。有正常典型分岔和匀称结构，短粗嫩壮，下部稍有纵棱筋。骨豆不超过茸长的30%。每支重250g以上。

Sawing Sancha Divided into four grades. First grade: Dried antler no foul smell, nor moth, nor dark skin, nor Xunpi, nor broken skin; plump Zuitou, honeycomb-like pores on the cut surface, no Ningzui; no crack on Zuitou of main branch. Normal side branches and symmetric structure, short, tender, thick; the lower part occasionally bearing longitudinal ridged veins. Gudou (also named Guding, minute tubercles at the antler base), no more than 30% of the antler length. More than 250g per antler.

二等：不乌皮（黑皮茸除外），不抽沟，不破皮，存折不超过一处，突起纵棱长不超过2cm，骨豆不超过茸长的40%。每支重200g以上。余同一等。

Second grade: No dark skin (except Heipirong), nor furrow, nor broken skin; no more than one crack. Raised longitudinal ridged veins, no longer than 2cm; Gudou, no more than 40% of the antler length. More than 200g per antler. Other characteristics are the same to those of First grade.

三等：条杆稍瘦，稍有破皮不露茸，不悬皮，存折不超过二处，纵棱筋，骨豆较多。嘴头不破皮（一、二等因嘴头破皮按三等收购），有正常分岔（但三岔无眉枝的按三等收购），枝干较瘦，茸、皮或锯口色调正常，无再生茸骨化现象。有蜂窝状细孔。每支150g以上。余同一等。

Third grade: The antler slightly thin, slightly broken skin not showing inside. No more than two cracks; more longitudinal ridged veins and Gudou. No broken skin on Zuitou (broken skin on Zuitou of First and Second grades purchased as Third grade); normal side branches (Sancha without Meizhi purchased as Third grade). Branches slightly thin; normal colour of antler, skin and the cut surface; Zaishengrong, no ossification; bearing honeycomb-like pores. More than 150g per antler. Other characteristics are the same to those of First grade.

四等：体畸形成怪角，顶端不窜尖，皮毛色灰暗。不符合一、二、三等者均属此等。

Fourth grade: Malformed antler of strange shape, tip no Cuanjian, skin and the soft hairs, murky grey. Inconformity to First, Second and Third grades belongs to Fourth grade.

二杠砍茸 分为四个等级。特等：肥圆粗壮，眉枝与主干匀称。主干顶端不扁头，嘴头肥满。不拉沟，左右对称，不空头，不破皮，无存折，不底漏、不底老和无黑根，不臭，无腮骨残肉。头骨坚实、洁白，后脑皮与后脑骨平齐，眶骨留50%。每架茸估重为2500g。

Chopping Ergang Divided into four grades. Top grade: The antler fat, round, thick; symmetric main branch and lateral branch. The top of main branch, no oblate; Zuitou, plump. Left and right side symmetric, no empty tip, nor broken skin, nor crack, nor leaked bottom, nor Dilao (broken skin at the bottom of antler), nor Heigen (black colour at the botton of antler), nor smelly, nor jawbone, nor residual meat. Skull hard, pure white; skin, flush with back skull; retaining 50% of orbital bone. About 2500g per antler.

一等：短圆粗壮，嘴头丰满。每架 1200g 以上的干品。

First grade: The antler short, round, thick; Zuitou, plump. More than 1200g per dried antler.

二等：每架 1kg 以上的干品，其余同一等。

Second grade: More than 1000g per dried antler. Other characteristics are the same to those of First grade.

三等：重量要求每架茸重 350g 至 1kg。稍瘦条、色调乌暗、畸形怪角、顶端不穿尖以及其它不符合特、一、二等者均属此等。

Third grade: Weight from 350g to 1000g per antler. Slightly thin, dark colour, malformed antler of strange shape, tip no Cuanjian (no broken, nor exposure of bone at the top of antler). Inconformity to Top, First and Second grades belongs to Third grade.

三岔砍茸　分为三个等级。特等：细毛红地，粗嫩肥壮，无拉沟、底老、存折、底漏、破皮、空皮、黑根，不臭，无虫蛀。有疙状突起，不超过主干长的 30%，头骨坚实、洁白。无腮骨残肉，后头皮与后头骨平齐，眶骨留 50%，每架 1750g 以上的干成品。

Chopping Sancha　Divided into three grades. Top grade: The soft hairs thin; skin red; antler thick, tender, plump; No furrow, nor Dilao, nor crack, nor leaked bottom, nor broken skin, nor Kongpi, nor Heigen, nor foul smell, nor moth. Minute tubercles, no more than 30% of the antler length. Skull hard, pure white. No jawbone, nor residual meat; skin, flush with back skull; retaining 50% of orbital bone. More than 1750g per dried antler.

一等：主干圆，疙状突起不超过主干长的 40%，每架重 1200g 以上的成品。余同特等。

First grade: Main branch round. Minute tubercles, not more than 40% of the main antler length. More than 1200g per dried antler. Other characteristics are the same to those of Top grade.

二等：疙状突起，不超过主干长的 50%，每架重 1kg 以上。余同特等。

Second grade: Minute tubercles, not more than 50% of the main antler length. More than 1000g per dried antler. Other characteristics are the same to those of Top grade.

2. 马鹿茸　分东马鹿茸和西马鹿茸，等级标准基本相同。

2. Malurong　Divided into Dong-malurong and Xi-malurong, the grading criteria are almost the same.

带血锯茸：分为三个等级。一等：主干圆嫩的三岔，肥嫩上冲的莲花，不拉沟，不破皮，不畸形，主干及嘴头无折伤。水工足，不生干，不空头，不瘪头。茸内含血充分，分布均匀，呈深红色，无臭味，无虫蛀，每支重不低于 500g 以上。

Sawing pilose antler with blood: Divided into three grades. First grade: Sancha with round and tender main branch, fat and tender Lianhua, no furrow, nor broken skin, nor malformation, nor crack on main branch and Zuitou. Sufficient Shuigong, no dry, nor empty tip, nor flat tip. The antler, sufficient blood inside, dark red. No foul smell, nor moth. Not less than 500g per antler.

二等：三岔、主干圆嫩的四岔，人字角，茸顶端丰满，不破皮，不生干，无存折，不空头，不瘪头，无臭味，无虫蛀，茸内含血充分，呈深红色的干晶，每支重 300g 以上。

Second grade: Sancha, Sicha with round and tender main branch, Renzijiao, plump tip, no broken skin, nor dry, nor crack, nor empty tip, nor flat tip, nor foul smell, nor moth. The antler, sufficient blood inside, bearing dark red crystal. More than 300g per antler.

三等：不足一、二等的莲花、三岔、四岔和肥嫩的畸形茸，无破皮，不生干，不存折。无臭味，无虫蛀。茸内充分含血，每支重 225g 以上。

Third grade: Lianhua, Sancha and Sicha unmatched with First and Second grades, and fat and tender malformed antler, no broken skin, nor dry, nor crack, nor foul smell, nor moth. The antler, sufficient blood inside. More than 225g per antler.

排血锯茸：除茸内不含血外，一、二、三等要求与带血马鹿锯茸相同。

Sawing pilose antler discharged blood: The grading criteria of First, Second and Third grades are same to those of sawing pilose antler with blood except for blood in antler.

【化学成分 / Chemical constituent】

含脑素、雌酮、雌二醇、硫酸软骨素 A、神经鞘磷脂等多糖类物质、氨基酸、甾体类、尿嘧啶、尿素、尿嘧啶核苷、烟酸、肌酐、脂肪酸、多种前列腺素及无机元素等。

The antler contains polysaccharides including cerebrin, oestrone, estradiol, chondroitin sulfate A, sphingomyelin. It also contains amino acids, sterides, uracil, urea, uridine, niacin, creatinine, fatty acid, prostaglandins, and multiple mineral elements, etc.

【质量要求 / Quality requirement】

外观质量 花鹿茸一般以茸粗壮、主枝圆、顶端丰满、质嫩、毛细、皮色红棕、有油润光泽者为佳。马鹿茸以饱满、体轻、毛色灰褐、下部无棱线者为佳。

Appearance quality Good quality of Hualurong for thickness, round main branch, plump tip, tender texture, thin soft hairs, reddish-brown and lustrous skin. Good quality of Malurong for plumpness, low weight, greyish-brown soft hairs, no ridge at the lower end.

【功能主治 / Function and indication】

温，甘、咸。壮肾阳，益精血，强筋骨，调冲任，托疮毒。用于肾阳不足，精血亏虚，阳痿滑精、宫冷不孕、羸瘦、神疲、畏寒、眩晕、耳鸣耳聋、腰脊冷痛、筋骨痿软、崩漏带下，阴疽不敛等。

Warm; sweet, salty. To invigorate kidney yang, replenish essence and blood, strengthen sinew and bone, harmonize thoroughfare and conception vessels, expel sore and toxin. For the treatment of deficiency of kidney yang, deficiency of essence and blood, impotence and spermatorrhea, infertility caused by uterine coldness, emaciation, lassitude, intolerance to cold, dizziness, tinnitus, deafness, cold pain in the low back and spine, limp wilting sinew and bone, menstrual flooding and spotting, vaginal discharge, and unhealing yin flat-abscesses.

【贮藏养护 / Storage and maintenance】

可用木箱、铁箱或新陶器装外用木器套框，先将茸用纸包好，箱内铺软草，用纸塞紧，勿使动摇，以免损伤。本品最易遭受虫蛀、变色，箱内可放樟脑、花椒或冰片，然后将箱封固严密，或箱内放入白酒密封贮存。在产地加工时用盐水浸渍或在涂敷的泥中加盐防臭。

Wooden boxes, iron boxes or wooden frames for new pottery can be used to store the antlers. The antlers are packed well with paper and boxes are paved in with grasses and tightly filled paper. Keep the antlers unmoved in case they are damaged. The antlers easily suffer from moth and discoloration, so seal the boxes after putting camphor, Zanthoxyli Pericarpium, borneol or white rice wine in them. The antlers can be deodorized by dipping in saline or applying salty mud during processing.

【用法用量 / Administration and dosage】

1~2g，研末冲服。

1-2g, ground into powder and administered after mixing with water.

重点小结
Summary

药材	主产地	商品规格	等级标准
人参	主产于吉林抚松、集安，辽宁恒仁、宽甸，黑龙江五常、尚志	分为山参和园参。园参根据加工方法以及大小的不同，分为边条鲜参、普通鲜参、边条红参、普通红参、生晒参、白参须、红参须等规格	山参依据形体、芦头、艼、皮、须根、重量及艼帽占主根比例等标准分为八等，园参的边条鲜参分为八等，普通鲜参六等，边条红参及普通红参商品均为三等。此外，全须生晒参分为四等，生晒参分为五等，白干参也为四等
五味子	吉林桦甸、蛟河，辽宁本溪，凤城，黑龙江阿城，宁安	不分规格	按表面颜色和干瘪粒比例分为二个等级
级鹿茸	花鹿茸主产于吉林、辽宁、河北。马鹿茸主产于黑龙江、吉林、内蒙古、新疆、青海、云南、四川、甘肃	按来源分为花鹿茸和马鹿茸，按采茸方法分为锯茸和砍茸	花鹿茸中二杠锯茸、三岔锯茸、二杠砍茸均分为四个等级，三岔砍茸包括三个等级；马鹿茸包括带血锯茸、排血锯茸，均为三等

medicinal material	Main producing area	Commodity specification	Grade standard
Ginseng Radix et Rhizoma	Main producing areas are Fusong, Ji'an of Jilin Province, Hengren, Kuandian of Liaoning Province, Wuchang, Shangzhi of Heilongjiang Province	Two main types of Garden ginseng and wild ginseng. Garden ginseng is divided into seven specifications of Biantiaoxianshen, Putongxianshen, Biantiaohongshen, Putonghongshen, Shengshaishen, Baishenxu, Hongshenxu according to processing method and root weight	Wild ginseng is divided into eight grades according to Xing, Ti, Lutou, Ding, Pi, fibrous root, weight and ratio of Dingmao to main roots; Among garden ginseng, Biantiaoxianshen is divided into eight grades, Putonghongshen is seven grades. Biantiaohongshen and Putonghongshen are three grades. In addition, Quanxushengshaishen, Shengshaishen and Baiganshen are divided into four, five and four grades, respectively
Schisandrae Chinensis Fructus	Main producing areas are Huadian, Jiaohe of Jilin Province, Benxi, Fengcheng of Liaoning Province, Acheng, Ning'an of Heilongjiang Province	Unified specification	Northern Magnoliavine Fruit is divided into two grades according to fruit colour and the proportion of withered fruits
Cervi Cornu Pantotrichum	Main producing areas of "Hualurong" are the provinces of Jilin, Liaoning, Hebei. Main producing areas of "Malurong" are the provinces of Heilongjiang, Jilin, Inner Mongolia, Xinjiang, Qinghai, Yunnan, Sichuan, Gansu, etc.	Pilose antler is divided into "Hualurong", "Malurong" according to the origin, and sawing and chopping pilose antler according to collecting method	Hualurong: Sawing Ergang, sawing Sancha and chopping Ergang are divided into four grades, and chopping Sancha is divided into three grades. Malurong: Sawing pilose antler with blood and discharged blood are both divided into three grades

题库

目标检测
Object Detection

一、选择题（Choice question）

（一）单项选择题（One-choice question）

1. 以下为关药产区道地药材的是（　　）

A. 冬虫夏草　B. 菊花　C. 人参
D. 牛膝　E. 附子

Which one is the authentic medicinal materials in the producing areas of Guan Medicinal Materials (　　)

A. Cordyceps　B. Chrysanthemi Flos
C. Ginseng Radix et Rhizoma　D. Achyranthis Bidentatae Radix
E. Aconiti Lateralis Radix Praeparata

2. 人参最著名的道地产区是（　　）

A. 桦甸　B. 抚松　C. 本溪　D. 宽甸　E. 宁安

The most famous producing area of authentic Ginseng Radix et Rhizoma is (　　)

A. Huadian　B. Fusong　C. Benxi　D. Kuandian　E. Ningan

3. 生晒参目前在市场分等的标准为（　　）

A. 大小　B. 质地　C. 颜色　D. 长短　E. 产地

The grade criterion for Shengshaishen in market is (　　)

A. size　B. texture　C. colour
D. fracture　E. producing area

4. 花鹿茸药材的主流商品是（　　）

A. 莲花　B. 三岔茸　C. 四岔茸　D. 二杠茸　E. 再生茸

The mainstream commodity of Hualurong is (　　)

A. Lianhua　B. Sancharong　C. Sicharong
D. Ergangrong　E. Zaishengrong

5. 五味子药材商品主产省区是（　　）

A. 贵州　B. 云南　C. 黑龙江　D. 河北　E. 河南

The main producing area of Schisandrae Chinensis Fructus is in (　　)

A. Guizhou Province　B. Yunnan Province　C. Heilongjiang Province
D. Hebei Province　E. Henan Province

（二）多项选择题（Multiple choice question）

1. 山参商品包括（　　）

A. 艼变山参　B. 籽种山参　C. 池底参
D. 趴货参　E. 移山参

Commodities of wild ginseng include (　　)

A. Dingbianshanshen　B. Zizhongshanshen　C. Chidishen
D. Pahuoshen　E. Yishanshen

2. 边条鲜参划分等级的标准是（ ）

A. 颜色 B. 长度 C. 每支重量

D. 宽度 E. 直径

The grade criteria for Biantiaoxianshen are ( )

A. colour B. length C. weight

D. width E. diameter

3. 五味子药材商品划分等级的标准是（ ）

A. 直径 B. 颜色 C. 重量

D. 宽度 E. 干瘪粒数的比例

The grade criteria for Schisandrae Chinensis Fructus are ( )

A. diameter B. colour C. weight

D. width E. proportion of withered fruits

4. 鹿茸药材商品在贮藏中极易发生的变质现象是（ ）

A. 虫蛀 B. 发霉 C. 变色

D. 化苗 E. 风化

Metamorphic phenomena that easily happen in the storage of Cervi Cornu Pantotrichum are ( )

A. moth B. mildew C. discoloration

D. Huamiao E. weathering

二、解答题（Thinking question）

1. 朝鲜红参、国产红参及日本红参在商品特征和规格等级上有哪些不同？

What are the differences in commodity characteristics, specification and grade among Japanese red ginseng, Korean red ginseng and Chinese red ginseng?

2. 花鹿茸与马鹿茸在规格等级划分上为何具有较多不同？

Why are there many differences in specification and grade between Hualurong and Malurong?

PPT

第十六章 北 药
Chapter 16 Bei Medicinal Materials

学习目标 | Learning Target

知识要求：

1. **掌握** 北药的含义及其主要道地药材品种。金银花、黄芪、党参的道地产地、规格等级及贮藏方法。

2. **熟悉** 金银花、黄芪、党参的采制方法和质量要求。

3. **了解** 北药产区的自然环境条件。

能力要求：

1. **学会** 区分金银花、黄芪、党参的规格等级。

2. **学会** 判别金银花、黄芪、党参的质量优劣。

Knowledge requirements:

1. **Proficiency** The meaning and main varieties of Bei Medicinal Materials. The authentic producing areas, specifications, grades and storage methods of Japanese Honeysuckle Flower, Milkvetch Root and Tangshen.

2. **Familiarity** Collection and preparation methods, quality requirements of Japanese Honeysuckle Flower, Milkvetch Root and Tangshen.

3. **Understanding** The natural environment in the producing areas of Bei Medicinal Materials.

Skill requirements:

1. Learn to distinguish different specifications and grades of Japanese Honeysuckle Flower, Milkvetch Root and Tangshen.

2. Learn to distinguish between high quality and poor quality of Japanese Honeysuckle Flower, Milkvetch Root and Tangshen.

一、北药概述
I. Overview of Bei Medicinal Materials

以河北、山东、山西省，北京、天津市以及内蒙古中部为主要产区或者集散地的大宗商品药材，称为北药。其产区位于东经 110°~120°，北纬 35°~42°之间。该地区自然环境复杂，其中，山东半岛和北京地区的年平均气温 11.8℃~14℃，年降水量 500~640mm，属于暖温带的半湿润、半干旱气候；内蒙古中部地区气温偏低，降水量少，年平均气温 3℃~8℃，年降水量 200~400mm，为温带大陆性季风气候。区域内夏热多雨，冬季晴朗干燥，春季多风沙，是我国道地药材“北药”的主产区。北药产区药用植物达 1500 多种，药用动物 250 多种，药用矿物 30 多种。著名的北药有金银花、黄芪、党参、山楂、沙参、板蓝根、阿胶等。

The bulk commercial medicinal materials with Hebei, Shandong, Shanxi, Beijing, Tianjin and the central part of Inner Mongolia as the main producing areas or distribution centers are called Bei Medicinal Materials. The region is located in east longitude 110°~120°, north latitude 35°~42°. The natural environment of this area is complex. The annual average temperature of Shandong Peninsula and Beijing is 11.8℃~14℃, and the annual precipitation is 500~640mm, which belongs to the warm temperate semi-humid and semi-arid climate. The temperature in the central part of Inner Mongolia is relatively low, with little precipitation. The annual average temperature is 3℃~8℃, and the annual precipitation is 200~400mm, which is a temperate continental monsoon climate. The area is hot and rainy in summer, sunny and dry in winter, windy and sandy in spring. It is the main producing area of Bei Medicinal Materials. There are more than 1,500 medicinal plants, 250 medicinal animals and 30 medicinal minerals in the producing area of Bei Medicinal Materials. The famous Bei Medicinal Materials include Japanese Honeysuckle Flower, Milkvetch Root, Tangshen, hawthorn, root of straight ladybell, isatis root, donkey-hide gelatin, etc.

二、药材品种
II. Varieties of Medicinal Materials

金银花 (Jinyinhua) ¦ Lonicerae Japonicae Flos (Japanese Honeysuckle Flower)

【基原 / Origin】

为忍冬科植物忍冬 *Lonicera japonica* Thunb. 的干燥花蕾或带初开的花。

Honeysuckle Flower is the dried flower bud or flowers in bloom of *Lonicera japonica* Thunb. (Fam. Caprifoliaceae).

【产地 / Producing area】

主产于河南、山东及河北等省。产于河南，称为“密银花”；产于山东，称为“东银花”。

It is mainly produced in the provinces of Henan, Shandong, Hebei, etc. Produced in Henan, it is called “Miyinhua”. Produced in Shandong, it is called “Dongyinhua”.

【采制 / Collection and preparation】

夏初于花开放前采收。河南于花蕾呈棒状，青绿色时采收，烘干；山东于花蕾呈棒状，绿白色时采收，晒干。

The drug is collected before flowering in early summer. In Henan Province, the flower buds are collected and dried, when clavate and green. In Shandong Province, the flower buds are collected and dried, when greenish-white.

金银花分别经炒黄、蜜炙、炒炭炮制成炒金银花、蜜银花、金银花炭。

Japanese Honeysuckle Flower can be processed into stir-bake Lonicerae Japonicae Flos, honeyed Lonicerae Japonicae Flos, Lonicerae Japonicae Flos scorch by stir-frying, stir-frying with honey, carbonizing, respectively.

【商品特征 / Commodity characteristics】

密银花　花蕾为细长棒状，上粗下细，略弯曲。表面呈黄白色或绿白色，密被短柔毛。偶见叶状苞片。花萼绿色，先端5裂，裂片有毛。开放者花冠为筒状，先端呈二唇形；雄蕊5，附于筒壁，黄色；雌蕊1，子房无毛。气清香，味淡、微苦。

Miyinhua Clavate, stout in upper part and tapered downwards, slightly curved. Externally yellowish-white or greenish-white, densely pubescent. Folisceous bracts occasionally visible. Calyx green, 5-lobed at the apex, lobes pubescent. Corolla tubular when open, apex 2-lipped; stamens 5, epipetalous, yellow; pistil 1, ovary glabrous. Odour, delicately aromatic; taste, weak and slightly bitter.

东银花 外观性状与密银花近似，但花稍短。表面呈黄色或浅黄色，密被短柔毛。香气较密银花稍淡。

Dongyinhua The appearance is similar to Miyinhua, but the buds are shorter. Externally yellow or slightly yellow, densely pubescent. The aroma is lighter than Miyinhua.

炒金银花 表面为黄色。质轻脆，易碎。

Stir-bake Lonicerae Japonicae Flos Externally yellow. Light, crisp; fragile.

蜜银花 表面为黄色。有蜜糖焦香气。

Honeyed Lonicerae Japonicae Flos Externally yellow. Odour of honey.

金银花炭 表面为焦褐色。质轻脆，易碎。

Lonicerae Japonicae Flos scorch Externally burnt brown. Light, crisp; fragile.

【规格等级 / Specification and grade】

按照产地、来源将金银花分为密银花、东银花两种商品规格。密银花、东银花均按开放花的数目、色泽、杂质含量等分为四个等级。规格等级标准为：

Lonicerae Japonicae Flos is divided into two commercial specifications, Miyinhua and Dongyinhua, according to the origin and producing areas. Miyinhua and Dongyinhua consist of four grades respectively, according to the number of flowers in bloom, color, foreign matter content, etc. The specifications and grading criteria are as follows:

密银花 一等：花蕾呈棒状，上粗下细，略弯曲。表面绿白色，质稍硬。气清香，味甘微苦。无开放的花朵，破裂花蕾及黄条不超过5%。无黑条、黑头、枝叶、杂质、虫蛀及霉变。

Miyinhua First grade: Clavate, stout in upper part and tapered downwards, slightly curved. Externally greenish-white. Slightly hard texture. Odour, delicately aromatic; taste, sweet and slightly bitter. No flowers in bloom. The number of broken or yellow buds is not more than 5%. No black bud, nor black head bud, nor branches and leaves, nor foreign matter, nor moth and mildew.

二等：开放的花朵不超过5%，花冠厚，质地硬，黑头、破裂花蕾及黄条不超过10%。余同一等。

Second grade: The number of flowers in bloom is not more than 5%. Corolla thick, texture hard. The number of black buds, broken and yellow bud is not more than 10%. Other criteria in this grade are the same as those in First grade.

三等：表面为白色或黄白色，花冠厚，质地硬，开放的花朵、黑条不超过30%。余同一等。

Third grade: Externally white or yellowish-white. Corolla thick, texture hard. The number of flowers in bloom and black buds is not more than 30%. Other criteria in this grade are the same as those in First grade.

四等：花蕾或开放的花朵兼有，色泽不分，枝叶不超过3%。余同一等。

Fourth grade: Buds and flowers in bloom both exist. Irrespective of colour and lustre. The number of branches and leaves is not more than 3%. Other criteria in this grade are the same as those in First grade.

东银花 一等：花蕾呈棒状、肥壮。上粗下细，略弯曲。表面为黄白色、青色。气清香，味甘微苦。开放的花朵不超过 5%。无嫩蕾、黑头、枝叶、杂质、虫蛀及霉变。

Dongyinhua　First grade: Clavate, fullness. Stout in upper part and tapered downwards, slightly curved. Externally yellowish-white and cyan. Odour, delicately aromatic; taste, sweet and slightly bitter. The number of flowers in bloom is not more than 5%. No tender buds, nor black head buds, nor branches and leaves, nor foreign matter, nor moth and mildew.

二等：开放的花朵不超过 15%，黑头不超过 3%。余同一等。

Second grade: The number of flowers in bloom is not more than 15%. The number of black head buds is not more than 3%. Other criteria in this grade are the same as those in First grade.

三等：花蕾瘦小，开放的花朵不超过 25%，黑头不超过 15%，枝叶不超过 1%。余同一等。

Third grade: Bud is thin. The number of flowers in bloom is not more than 25%.　The number of black head buds is not more than 15%. The number of branches and leaves is not more than 1%. Other criteria in this grade are the same as those in First grade.

四等：花蕾或开放的花朵兼有，色泽不分，枝叶不超过 3%。余同一等。

Fourth grade: Buds and flowers in bloom both exist. Irrespective of colour and lustre. The number of branches and leaves is not more than 3%. Other criteria in this grade are the same as those in First grade.

【化学成分 / Chemical constituent】

花蕾主要含有酚酸类成分，包括绿原酸、3,5- 二 -O- 咖啡酰基奎宁酸、4,5- 二 -O- 咖啡酰基奎宁酸等。还含有黄酮类成分，包括木犀草素、木犀草苷等。另外，尚含挥发油类成分，包括双花醇、芳樟醇等。

The flower bud mainly contains phenolic acids, including chlorogenic acid, 3,5-di-O-caffeoylquinic acid, 4,5-di-O-caffeoylquinic acid, etc. It also contains flavonoids, including luteolin, luteolin glycoside, etc. In addition, it also contains volatile oil components, including bisanthol, linalool, etc.

【检查 / Examination】

水分不得过 12.0%。总灰分不得过 10.0%；酸不溶性灰分不得过 3.0%。铅不得过 5mg/kg；镉不得过 1mg/kg；砷不得过 2mg/kg；汞不得过 0.2mg/kg；铜不得过 20mg/kg。

Water, not more than 12.0%. Total ash, not more than 10.0%. Acid-insoluble ash, not more than 3.0%. The contents of Lead, Cadmium, Arsenic, Mercury and Copper are not more than 5mg/kg, 1mg/kg, 2mg/kg, 0.2mg/kg and 20mg/kg, respectively.

【质量要求 / Quality requirement】

外观质量　以花蕾多、肥壮、色青绿微白，气清香者为佳。

Appearance quality　Good quality for more flower buds, fullness, green and slightly white and delicately aromatic ordour.

内在质量　含量测定：按高效液相色谱法测定，含绿原酸不得少于 1.5%；含酚酸类以绿原酸、3,5- 二 -O- 咖啡酰基奎宁酸和 4,5- 二 -O- 咖啡酰基奎宁酸的总量计，不得少于 3.8%；含木犀草苷不得少于 0.050%。

Intrinsic quality　Assay: It contains not less than 1.5% of chlorogenic acid according to HPLC analysis method. It contains not less than 3.8% of phenolic acids, calculated by the total amount of chlorogenic acid, 3,5-di-o-caffeoylquinic acid and 4,5-di-o-caffeoylquinic acid. It contains not less than 0.050% of luteolin-7-O-glucoside.

【功能主治 / Function and indication】

甘，寒。清热解毒，疏散风热。用于痈肿疔疮，喉痹，丹毒，热毒血痢，风热感冒，温病发热。

Cold, sweet. To clear heat, remove toxin, and disperse wind-heat. For the treatment of swelling abscess, deep-rooted boil, sore, throat bi disorder, erysipelas, heat-toxin blood dysentery, common cold caused by wind-heat, and fever in warm disease.

【贮藏养护 / Storage and maintenance】

置阴凉干燥处，防潮，防蛀。

Preserved in a cool and dry place, and protected from moisture and moth.

【用法用量 / Administration and dosage】

6~15g。

6~15g.

黄芪 (Huangqi) ¦ Astragali Radix (Milkvetch Root)

【基原 / Origin】

为豆科植物蒙古黄芪 *Astragalus membranaceus* (Fisch.) Bge. var. *Mongholicus* (Bge.) Hsiao 或膜荚黄芪 *Astragalus membranaceus* (Fisch.) Bge. 的干燥根。

Milkvetch Root is the dried root of *Astragalus membranaceus* (Fisch.) Bge. var. *mongholicus* (Bge.) Hsiao or *Astragalus membranaceus* (Fisch.) Bge. (Fam. Leguminosae).

【产地 / Producing area】

蒙古黄芪主产于山西、内蒙古、河北等省区。产于山西者为道地药材，习称"西黄芪"或者"绵芪"；产于内蒙古习称"蒙芪"。膜荚黄芪主产于黑龙江、吉林、辽宁、内蒙古、山西等省区，习称"北芪""关芪"。

Mongolian Astragalus is mainly produced in Shanxi, Inner Mongolia, Hebei and other provinces. Those produced in Shanxi are authentic medicinal materials, which are often called "Xihuangqi" or "Mianqi"; those produced in Inner Mongolia are often called "Mengqi". *Astragalus membranaceus* is mainly produced in Heilongjiang, Jilin, Liaoning, Inner Mongolia, Shanxi and other provinces, which are often called "Beiqi" or "Guanqi".

【采制 / Collection and preparation】

膜荚黄芪 野生品于春、秋二季采挖，以秋季采挖者质佳。东北地区雪期比较长，春采货多于四五月间入山采挖。挖取后，除净泥土、须根，晒至六、七成干，分大小，理直，扎成小捆，晒干。

Astragalus membranaceus Wild products are collected in spring and autumn, and those collected in autumn are of good quality. In Northeast China, the snow period is relatively long, and more goods are collected in spring in April and May. After digging, with the soil and fibrous roots removed first, they are dried to 60% or 70% dry, tied straightly into small bundles according to size, and dried in the sun.

栽培品 河北安国、山东等地于播种当年秋季茎叶枯萎时采收，割去地上部分，在畦的一侧挖深沟，将根依次挖出，除净泥土，剪掉芦头，晒至七、八成干，剪去支根、须根，分大小，扎成小捆，堆积 1~2 天，晒干。

Cultivated products They are harvested in the autumn of the year of sowing when the stems and leaves wither, in Anguo, Hebei Province, Shandong Province and other places. Cut off the parts on the ground, dug deep ditches on one side of the border, dug out the roots in turn, remove the soil, cut off the rhizome, dry them to 70%~80% dry and removed from the branch roots and fibrous roots. Then they are tied into small bundles according to size, piled up for 1~2 days, and dried in the sun.

蒙古黄芪（原生芪） 野生品于秋后采挖，栽培品于播种 4~5 年，秋季茎叶枯萎后或春季萌芽前采挖。采挖后除去须根、泥土，晒干即可。山西产者多为栽培品，内蒙古武川产者多为野生品。

***Astragalus mongholicus* (Yuanshengqi)** Wild products are dug after autumn. Cultivated products planted for 4-5 years, with withered stems and leaves in autumn, are dug before sprouting in spring. After excavation, with fibrous roots and soil removed, they are dried in the sun. Most of the products produced in Shanxi are cultivated products, and those produced in Wuchuan, Inner Mongolia are wild products.

黄芪分别经切制、蜜炙炮制成生黄芪片、蜜黄芪片。

Astragali Radix is processed into raw Astragali Radix slices and honey Astragali Radix slices by cutting and honey, respectively.

【商品特征 / Commodity characteristics】

蒙古黄芪 野生品为长圆柱形，单枝，芦头稍扁，略岔开，常有茎基残留，中央枯空较深，老根可达 15cm 以上。表面为灰黄色或黄白色。质地较柔软而韧，断面纤维性，略显疏松，皮部松软，淡黄白色，木部为黄色，菊花心明显。气香，味微甜，嚼之有较浓的生豆腥味。

Root of Astragalus mongholicus The wild product is long-cylindrical, no branch, rhizome slightly flat, slightly bifurcated, often with residual stem base and deep rotten hollow in the center, and old root of more than 15cm. Externally greyish-yellow or yellow-white. Texture soft and tough, fracture fibrous, slightly loose, bark soft and yellowish-white, wood yellow, showing obvious chrysanthemum-flower-like radial lines (Juhuaxin). Odour, fragrant; taste, slightly sweet and bean-like on chewing.

栽培品 根为细长圆柱形，分枝较少。质地较绵软。断面皮部、木部均较紧密。

Cultivated products The roots are slender and cylindrical with few branches. The texture is soft. The bark part and wood part of the section are relatively tight.

膜荚黄芪 根为圆柱形，有的有分枝，上端较粗，长 30~90cm，直径 1~3.5cm。平直或略扭曲，芦头和幼根除去，芦头切口为正圆形。表面为淡棕黄色或淡棕褐色，有不整齐的纵皱纹或纵沟。质硬而韧，不易折断，断面纤维性强，并显粉性。皮部稍松，呈黄白色，木部紧密，为淡黄色，放射状纹理和裂隙明显（菊花心），习称“皮松肉紧”。老根中央偶呈枯朽状，黑褐色或呈黑洞，习称“空头”。气微，味微甜，嚼之微有豆腥味。

Root of Astragalus membranaceus Root cylindrical, some branched, upper part relatively thick, 30~90cm in length, 1~3.5cm in diameter. Straight or slightly twisted, rhizome and tender roots are removed. The incision of rhizome is round. Externally pale brownish-yellow or pale brown, with irregular, longitudinal wrinkles or furrows. Texture hard and tenacious, uneasily broken, fracture highly fibrous and starchy. Bark is slightly loose, yellowish-white. Wood is dense, pale yellow, with obvious radiate striations and fissures (showing chrysanthemum-flower-like radial lines), which are often called “loose cortex and tight wood”. The center part of old root occasionally rotten-wood-shaped, blackish-brown or hollowed, which are often called “hollowed head”. Odour, weak; taste, slightly sweet and slightly bean-like on chewing.

黄芪饮片 呈类圆形或椭圆形的厚片，外表皮黄白色至淡棕褐色，可见纵皱纹或纵沟。切面黄白色，皮部有裂隙，木部淡黄色，有放射状纹理及裂隙，有的中心偶有枯朽状，黑褐色或呈空洞。气微，味微甜，嚼之有豆腥味。

Prepared slices In subrounded or elliptical thick slices. Externally yellowish-white or pale brown, with longitudinal wrinkles or furrows. Cut surface yellowish-white in bark part and pale yellow in wood part, with radiated striations and fissures (chrysanthemum-flower-like radial lines, Juhuaxin), some center parts rotten-wood-shaped, blackish-brown or hollowed. Odour, slight; taste, slightly sweet, bean-like on chewing.

炙黄芪 形如黄芪片。切面为金黄色。质地较脆。略有黏性，味甜。

Honey Astragali Radix slices It is similar to raw Astragali Radix slices. The section, golden; texture, crisp, slightly sticky and sweet.

【规格等级 / Specification and grade】

商品黄芪按照条长、中上部直径分为四个等级。等级标准为：

Commodity Milkvetch Root consists of four grades according to the root length and the diameter of middle and upper part. The grading criteria are as follows:

黄芪 特等：呈圆柱形单条，斩去疙瘩头或喇叭头，顶端无或间有空心。表面为灰白色或淡褐色，质地硬而韧，断面外层为白色，中间为淡黄色或黄色，有粉性，味甘，有生豆气。无须根或老皮。长为 70cm 以上，上中部直径约 2cm 以上，末端粗不小于 0.6cm。

Milkvetch Root Top grade: Cylindrical with no branch, knots or trumpet shaped head cut off, and the top has or has no hollow space. Externally grey-white or light brown; texture, hard and tough; outer layer of the section, white; middle part, light yellow or yellow, starchy; taste, sweet; odour, raw bean-like. No fibrous roots or old bark. The length is more than 70cm; the diameter of the upper and middle part is more than 2cm and the thickness of the end is more than 0.6cm.

一等：长为 50cm 以上，上中部直径 1.5cm 以上，末端粗不小于 0.5cm，余同特等。

First grade: The length is more than 50cm; the diameter of the upper and middle part is more than 1.5cm; the end thickness is not less than 0.5cm. Other criteria in this grade are the same as those in top grade.

二等：长为 40cm 以上，上中部直径 1cm 以上，末端粗不小于 0.4cm，间有老皮。余同特等。

Second grade: The length is more than 40cm, the diameter of the upper and middle part is more than 1cm. The end thickness is not less than 0.4cm, occasionally with old bark. Other criteria in this grade are the same as those in Top grade.

三等：不分长短，上中部直径为 0.7cm 以上，末端粗不小于 0.3cm，间有破短节子，余同特等。

Third grade: Regardless of length, the diameter of the upper and middle part is more than 0.7cm; the end thickness is not less than 0.3cm, occasionally with broken short root segments. Other criteria in this grade are the same as those in Top grade.

【化学成分 / Chemical constituent】

根含皂苷、黄酮、多糖、氨基酸等成分。其中黄芪甲苷、毛蕊异黄酮葡萄糖苷成分常作为质量控制指标。

Roots contain saponins, flavonoids, polysaccharides, amino acids and other components. Astragaloside A and maorui isoflavone glucoside are often used as quality control indicators.

【检查 / Examination】

水分不得过 10.0%。总灰分不得过 5.0%。六六六（总 BHC）不得过 0.2mg/kg；滴滴涕（总 DDT）不得过 0.2mg/kg；五氯硝基苯（PCNB）不得过 0.1mg/kg。铅不得过 5mg/kg；镉不得过 0.3mg/kg；砷不得过 2mg/kg；汞不得过 0.2mg/kg；铜不得过 20mg/kg。

Water, not more than 10.0%. Total ash, not more than 5.0%. Benzene hexachloride (BHC) (sum of α, β, γ and δ-BHC), not more than 0.2mg/kg. Dichloro diphenyl trichloroethane (DDT) (sum of pp′-DDE, pp′-DDD, op′-DDT and pp′-DDT), not more than 0.2mg/kg. Pentachloronitrobenzene (PCNB), not more than 0.1mg/kg. The contents of Lead, Cadmium, Arsenic, Mercury and Copper are not more than 5mg/kg,

0.3mg/kg, 2mg/kg, 0.2mg/kg and 20mg/kg, respectively.

【质量要求 / Quality requirement】

外观质量　以单枝粗长、质坚而绵、断面色黄白、粉性足、味甜且豆腥味浓者为佳。

Appearance quality　Good quality for long and thick single branch, hard and mealy texture, yellowish-white cross section, rich starchiness, sweet taste and strong beany flavor.

内在质量　浸出物含量：水溶性浸出物（冷）含量不得少于17.0%。含量测定：按高效液相色谱法测定，药材及饮片含黄芪甲苷不得少于0.040%；含毛蕊异黄酮葡萄糖苷不得少于0.020%。

Intrinsic quality　Extract content: not less than 17.0% of water-soluble extractives (cold).

Assay: It contains not less than 0.040% of astagarloside IV and 0.020% of calycos in-7-O-*β*-D-glycoside, according to HPLC analysis method.

【功能主治 / Function and indication】

微温，甘。补气升阳，固表止汗，利水消肿，生津养血，行滞通痹，托毒排脓，敛疮生肌。用于气虚乏力，食少便溏，中气下陷，久泻脱肛，便血崩漏，表虚自汗，气虚水肿，内热消渴，血虚萎黄，半身不遂，痹痛麻木，痈疽难溃，久溃不敛。

Mild warm, sweet. To tonify qi, upraise yang, secure the exterior, stop sweating, promote urination, alleviate edema, engender fluids, nourish blood, move stagnation, relieve impediment, expel toxin and pus, promote wound healing and promote tissue regeneration. For the treatment of qi deficiency and lack of strength, reduced food intake, sloppy stool, sunken middle qi, chronic diarrhea, prolapse of the rectum, bloody stool, menstrual flooding and spotting, exterior deficiency with spontaneous sweating, qi deficiency edema, interior heat wasting-thirst, blood deficiency and sallow complexion, hemiplegia, arthralgin, numbness, abscesses and cellulitis difficult to suppurate and perforate, or difficult to heal.

【贮藏养护 / Storage and maintenance】

置通风、干燥处，防潮，防蛀。

Preserved in a ventilated and dry place, and protected from moisture and moth.

【用法用量 / Administration and dosage】

9~30g。

9-30g.

党参 (Dangshen) ¦ Codonopsis Radix (Tangshen)

【基原 / Origin】

为桔梗科植物党参 *Codonopsis pilosula*（Franch.）Nannf.、素花党参 *Codonopsis pilosula* Nannf. var. *modesta*（Nannf.）L. T. Shen 或川党参 *Codonopsis tangshen* Oliv. 的干燥根。

Tangshen is the dried root of *Codonopsis pilosula* (Franch.) Nannf., *Codonopsis pilosula* Nannf. var. *modesta* (Nannf.) L. T. Shen or *Codonopsis tangshen* Oliv. (Fam. Campanulaceae).

【产地 / Producing area】

党参（又称潞党参或白条党、白皮党）主产于山西、甘肃、陕西、辽宁等省，其中东北地区所产又称东党或辽党，山西五台山区野生品称台党。

Root of *Codonopsis Pilosula* (also known as Ludangshen or Baitiaodang, Baipidang)　Mainly produced in Shanxi, Gansu, Shaanxi, Liaoning and other provinces, among which the Northeast region is also called Dongdang or Liaodang, and the wild products in the area of Wutaishan in Shanxi Province are known as Taidang.

素花党参（又称西党、纹党、晶党） 主产于甘肃、四川、陕西等省。

Root of *Codonopsis Pilosula* var. *modesta* (also known as Xidang, Wendang and Jingdang) Mainly produced in Gansu, Sichuan, Shaanxi and other provinces.

川党参（又称条党、单枝党、板桥党） 主产于湖北、重庆、陕西等省。

Root of *Codonopsis tangshen* (also known as Tiaodang, Danzhidang and Banqiaodang) Mainly produced in Hubei, Chongqing, Shaanxi and other provinces.

【采制 / Collection and preparation】

党参 秋末采挖栽培3年以上的党参，去净泥土与残茎，按粗细分级，晒至半干，揉搓使皮部与木部紧贴，反复搓晒3~4次，最后晒干。

Codonopsis Radix At the end of autumn, those cultivated for more than 3 years are collected, with soil and residual stems removed, graded according to thickness and thinness, half dried in the sun, rubbed to make the skin clingy to the wood, rubbed repeatedly for 3~4 times, and finally dried in the sun.

党参分别经切制、米炒、蜂蜜炮制成党参片、米党参、蜜党参。

Codonopsis Radix can be processed into Codonopsis Radix slice, rice Codonopsis Radix and honey Codonopsis Radix by cutting, stir-baking with rice, honey, respectively.

【商品特征 / Commodity characteristics】

党参 呈长圆柱形，稍弯曲。表面灰黄色、黄棕色至灰棕色，根头部有多数疣状突起的茎痕及芽（习称“狮子盘头”），每个茎痕的顶端呈凹下的圆点状；根头下有致密的环状横纹，向下渐稀疏，有的达全长的一半，栽培品环状横纹少或无；全体有纵皱纹和散在的横长皮孔样突起，支根断落处常有黑褐色胶状物。质稍柔软或稍硬而略带韧性，断面稍平坦，有裂隙或放射状纹理，皮部淡棕黄色至黄棕色，木部淡黄色至黄色。有特殊香气，味微甜。

Root of *Codonopsis Pilosula* Long cylindrical, slightly curved. Externally greyish-yellow, yellowish-brown to greyish-brown, with numerous warty prominent stem scars and buds on the root stock (commonly known as “Shizipantou”), and the apex of each stem scar sunkenly dotted; dense transverse annulations occurring below the root stock, gradually sparse downwards, some up to half length of the root while the transverse annulations rare or absent in some cultivars; whole root showing longitudinal wrinkles and scattered transverse lenticel-like protrudings, frequently with blackish-brown gelatinous substances at the fractured area of the rootlet. Texture slightly soft or hard with a little toughness, fracture somewhat even, cleft or striated radially, bark pale brownish-yellow to yellowish-brown, wood pale yellow to yellow. Odour, characteristic and aromatic; taste, sweetish.

素花党参（西党参） 表面黄白色至灰黄色，根头下致密的环状横纹常达全长的一半以上。断面裂隙较多，皮部灰白色至淡棕色。

Root of *Codonopsis Pilosula* var. *modesta* (Xidangshen) Externally greyish-white to pale yellow, dense transverse annulations occurring below the root stock, frequently up to over half length of the root. Fracture more cleft, bark greyish-white to pale brown.

川党参 表面灰黄色至黄棕色，有明显不规则的纵沟。质较软而结实，断面裂隙较少，皮部黄白色。

Root of *Codonopsis tangshen* Externally greyish-white to yellowish-brown, with distinctly irregular longitudinal wrinkles. Texture slightly soft and compact, fracture less cleft, bark yellowish-white.

党参片 呈类圆形的厚片。外表皮灰黄色、黄棕色至灰棕色，有时可见根头部有多数疣状突起的茎痕和芽。切面皮部淡棕黄色至黄棕色，木部淡黄色至黄色，有裂隙或放射状纹理。有特殊香气，味微甜。

Codonopsis Radix slice　In subrounded thick slices. Externally greyish-yellow, yellowish-brown to greyish-brown, sometimes with plentiful warty prominent stem scars and buds on the root stock. Cut surface pale brownish-yellow to yellowish-brown in bark part and pale yellow to yellow in wood part, with clefts or radial striations. Odour, characteristic and aromatic; taste, sweetish.

米党参　形同党参片，表面深黄色，偶有焦斑。

Rice Codonopsis Radix　The shape similar to Codonopsis Radix slices, externally dark yellow, occasionally with burnt stains.

蜜党参　形同党参片，表面黄棕色，显光泽，味甜。

Honey Codonopsis Radix　The shape similar to the Codonopsis Radix slices, externally yellowish-brown, lustrous; taste, sweet.

【规格等级 / Specification and grade】

依据产地和来源分为潞党、西党、东党、条党（川党）、白党等规格，西党、潞党、条党分为 3 个等级，东党、白党分为 2 个等级。其等级标准为：

According to the producing area and origin, the specifications of Codonopsis Radix are divided into Ludang, Xidang, Dongdang, Tiaodang (Chuandang), Baidang. Xidang. Ludang and Tiaodang are divided into three grades; Dongdang and Baidang are divided into two grades. The grading criteria are as follows.

潞党　一等：呈圆柱形，芦头较小。表面黄褐色或灰黄色。质柔韧，断面黄白色，糖质多，味甜。芦下直径 1cm 以上。无油条、杂质、虫蛀、霉变。

Ludang　First grade: Cylindrical, with smaller rhizome (Lutou). Externally yellowish-brown or greyish-yellow. Texture flexible, fracture yellowish-white, taste sweet with more sugariness. The diameter below the rhizome is more than 1cm. No oily root, nor foreign matter, nor moth, nor mildew.

二等：芦下直径 0.8cm 以上，余同一等。

Second grade: The diameter below the rhizome is more than 0.8cm. Other criteria in this grade are in accordance with those in First grade.

三等：芦下直径 0.4cm 以上，油条不超过 10%，余同一等。

Third grade: The diameter below the rhizome is more than 0.4cm. The oily roots are not more than 10%. Other criteria in this grade are in accordance with those in First grade.

西党　一等：干货。呈圆锥形，头大尾小，上端多横纹。外皮粗松，表面米黄色或灰褐色。断面黄白色，有放射状纹理。糖质多，味甜。芦下直径 1.5cm 以上。无油条、杂质、虫蛀、霉变。

Xidang　First grade: Dried roots. Conical, with big head and small tail. The upper shows many transverse annulations. Outer cortex is coarse and loose. Externally maize-yellow or greyish-brown. Fracture yellowish-white, with radial striations. Taste sweet with more sugariness. The diameter below the rhizome is more than 1.5cm. No oily root, nor foreign matter, nor moth, nor mildew.

二等：芦下直径 1cm 以上，余同一等。

Second grade: The diameter below the rhizome is more than 1cm. Other criteria in this grade are in accordance with those in First grade.

三等：芦下直径 0.6cm 以上，油条不超过 15%，余同二等。

Third grade: The diameter below the rhizome is more than 0.6cm. The oily roots are not more than 15%. Other criteria in this grade are in accordance with those in Second grade.

条党　一等：干货。呈圆锥形，头上茎痕较少而小，条较长，上端有横纹或无，下端有纵皱纹。表面糙米色。断面白色或黄白色，有放射状纹理。有糖质，味甜。芦下直径 1.2cm 以上，无油条、杂质、虫蛀、霉变。

Tiaodang First grade: Dried roots. Conical, with fewer and smaller stem scars on the top, longer root. The upper part has or has no transverse annulations, and the lower part has longitudinal wrinkles. Externally, coarse-rice-colored. Fracture white or yellowish-white, with radial striations. Taste sweet with sugariness. The diameter below the rhizome is more than 1.2cm. No oily root, nor foreign matter, nor moth, nor mildew.

二等：芦下直径 0.8cm 以上，余同一等。

Second grade: The diameter below the rhizome is more than 0.8cm. Other criteria in this grade are in accordance with those in First grade.

三等：芦下直径 0.5cm 以上，油条不超过 10%，余同二等。

Third grade: The diameter below the rhizome is more than 0.5cm. The oily roots are not more than 10%. Other criteria in this grade are in accordance with those in Second grade.

东党 一等：干货。呈圆锥形，芦头较大，芦下有横纹。体较松，质硬。表面土黄色或灰黄色，粗糙。断面黄白色，中心淡黄色，显裂隙，味甜。长 20cm 以上，芦下直径 1cm 以上。无毛须、杂质、虫蛀、霉变。

Dongdang First grade: Dried roots. Conical, with bigger rhizome, transverse annulations occurring below the rhizome. Looser root, hard texture. Externally earthy yellow or greyish-yellow, coarse. Fracture yellowish-white, pale yellow center with cleft, taste sweet. The length is more than 20cm, and the diameter below the rhizome is more than 1cm. No fibrilla, nor foreign matter, nor moth, nor mildew.

二等：长 20cm 以下，芦下直径 0.5cm 以上，余同一等。

Second grade: The length is less than 20cm, and the diameter below the rhizome is more than 0.5cm. Other criteria in this grade are in accordance with those in First grade.

白党 一等：干货。呈圆锥形，具芦头。表面黄褐色或灰褐色。体较硬。断面黄白色，糖质少，味微甜。芦下直径 1 cm 以上。无杂质、虫蛀、霉变。

Baidang First grade: Dried roots. Conical with rhizome. Externally yellowish-brown or greyish-brown. Texture harder, fracture yellowish-white, taste slightly sweet with less sugariness. The diameter below the rhizome is more than 1cm. No foreign matter, nor moth, nor mildew.

二等：芦下直径 0.5cm 以上。间有油条、短节，余同一等。

Second grade: The diameter below the rhizome is more than 0.5cm. Occasionally oily roots and short sections. Other criteria in this grade are in accordance with those in First grade.

【化学成分 / Chemical constituent】

含无羁萜、蒲公英萜醇乙酸酯、党参炔苷、党参苷 I 等。

Friedelin, taraxeryl acetate, lobetyolin, tangshenoside I, etc.

【检查 / Examination】

水分不得过 16.0%。总灰分不得过 5.0%。二氧化硫残留量不得过 400mg/kg。

Water, not more than 16.0%. Total ash, not more than 5.0%. Residue of sulfur dioxide, not more than 400mg/kg.

【质量要求 / Quality requirement】

外观质量 以根条粗长、质地柔润、气味浓甜、嚼之无渣者为佳。

Appearance quality Good quality for thick and long roots, soft and moist texture, strong sweet smell and odour, no residue on chewing.

内在质量 浸出物含量：45%乙醇浸出物（热）含量不得少于 55.0%。

Intrinsic quality Extract content: not less than 55.0% of 45% ethanol-soluble extractives (hot).

【功能主治 / Function and indication】

平，甘。健脾益肺，养血生津。用于脾肺气虚，食少倦怠，咳嗽虚喘，气血不足，面色萎黄，心悸气短，津伤口渴，内热消渴。

Neutral; sweet. To fortify the spleen, replenish lung, nourish blood and engender fluids. For the treatment of spleen-lung qi deficiency, reduced food intake, fatigue, cough and dyspnea of deficiency type, deficiency of qi and blood, sallow complexion, palpitations and shortness of breath, thirst caused by fluid consumption, and wasting thirst internal heat.

【贮藏养护 / Storage and maintenance】

置通风干燥处，防蛀。

Preserved in a ventilated and dry place, and protected from moth.

【用法用量 / Administration and dosage】

9~30g。

9~30g.

重点小结 Summary

药材	主产地	商品规格	等级标准
金银花	主产于河南、山东及河北等省	按照产地、来源分为密银花、东银花	按照开放花的数目、色泽、杂质含量等分为1~4等
黄芪	蒙古黄芪主产于山西、内蒙古、河北等省区 膜荚黄芪主产于黑龙江、吉林、辽宁、内蒙古、山西等省区	不分规格	按照条长、中上部直径分为特等、一等、二等、三等
党参	党参主产于山西、甘肃、陕西、辽宁等省，山西五台山区野生品称台党 素花党参主产于甘肃、四川、陕西等省 川党参主产于湖北、重庆、陕西等省	按产地和来源分为潞党、西党、东党、条党（川党）、白党等规格	西党、潞党、条党分为3个等级，东党、白党分为2个等级

medicinal material	Main producing area	Commodity specification	Grade standard
Lonicerae Japonicae Flos	It is mainly produced in Henan, Shandong, Hebei Provinces	Lonicerae Japonicae Flos is divided into two commercial specifications, Miyinhua and Dongyinhua, according to the origin and producing area	Miyinhua and Dongyinhua consists of four grades respectively, according to the number of flowers in bloom, color, foreign matter content, etc
Astragali Radix	Mongolian Astragalus is mainly produced in Shanxi, Inner Mongolia, Gansu, Hebei and other provinces. Astragalus membranaceus is mainly produced in Heilongjiang, Jilin, Liaoning, Inner Mongolia, Shanxi and other provinces	Unified specification	Commodity Milkvetch Root consists of four grades according to the length of root and the diameter of middle and upper part

(continued)

medicinal material	Main producing area	Commodity specification	Grade standard
Codonopsis Radix	Root of *Codonopsis Pilosula* mainly produced in Shanxi, Gansu, Shaanxi, Liaoning and other provinces, and the wild products in the area of Wutaishan in Shanxi are known as Taidang Root of *Codonopsis Pilosula* var. *modesta* mainly produced in Gansu, Sichuan, Shaanxi and other provinces Root of *Codonopsis tangshen* mainly produced in Hubei, Chongqing, Shaanxi and other provinces	According to the producing area and origin, the specification of Codonopsis radix is divided into Ludang, Xidang, Dongdang, Tiaodang (Chuandang), Baidang	Xidang, Ludang and Tiaodang are divided into three grades; Dongdang and Baidang are divided into two grades

题库

目 标 检 测
Object Detection

一、选择题（Choice question）

（一）单项选择题（One-choice question）

1. 北药主要产区或者集散地为（　　）

A. 东北大部分省区　B. 华北大部分省区　C. 西北大部分省区
D. 北京　E. 内蒙古

Where is the main producing area or distribution center of Bei Medicinal Materials (　　)

A. Most provinces and regions in Northeast China
B. Most provinces and regions in North China
C. Most provinces and regions in Northwest China
D. Beijing
E. Inner Mongolia

2. "密银花" 产于（　　）

A. 河北　B. 广西　C. 山东　D. 河南　E. 山西

Where is "Miyinhua" produced in (　　)

A. Hebei　B. Guangxi　C. Shandong
D. Henan　E. Shanxi

3. 密银花、东银花均按开放花的数目、色泽、杂质含量等分为（　　）等

A. 四　B. 二　C. 三　D. 五　E. 六

How many grades are Miyinhua and Dongyinhua divided into respectively, according to the number of flowers in bloom, color, foreign matter content, etc. (　　)

A. Four　B. Two　C. Three　D. Five　E. Six

4. 下列哪一项不是密银花的商品特征（　　）

A. 花蕾为细长棒状，上细下粗，略弯曲

B. 表面呈黄白色或绿白色，密被短柔毛

C. 开放者花冠为筒状，先端呈二唇形

D. 花萼绿色，先端 5 裂，裂片有毛

E. 气清香，味淡、微苦

Which of the following is not the commodity characteristics of Miyinhua (　　)

A. Clavate, tapered in upper part and stout downwards, slighly curved

B. Externally yellowish-white or greenish-white, densely pubescent

C. Corolla tubular when open, apex 2-lipped

D. Calyx green, 5-lobed at the apex, lobes pubescent

E. Odour, delicately aromatic; taste, weak and slightly bitter

5. 密银花一等为（　　）

A. 无开放的花朵，破裂花蕾及黄条不超过 15%

B. 无开放的花朵，破裂花蕾及黄条不超过 10%

C. 无开放的花朵，破裂花蕾及黄条不超过 5%

D. 无开放的花朵，破裂花蕾及黄条不超过 20%

E. 无开放的花朵，破裂花蕾及黄条不超过 25%

Which of the following belongs to the First Grade of Miyinhua (　　)

A. No flowers in bloom. The number of broken and yellow buds is not more than 15%

B. No flowers in bloom. The number of broken and yellow buds is not more than 10%

C. No flowers in bloom. The number of broken and yellow buds is not more than 5%

D. No flowers in bloom. The number of broken and yellow buds is not more than 20%

E. No flowers in bloom. The number of broken and yellow buds is not more than 25%

6. “绵芪”产于（　　）

A. 河北　B. 广西　C. 山东　D. 河南　E. 山西

Where is “Mianqi” produced in (　　)

A. Hebei　B. Guangxi　C. Shandong

D. Henan　E. Shanxi

7. 膜荚黄芪的“空头”是指（　　）

A. 幼根中央偶呈枯朽状，黑褐色或呈黑洞

B. 老根中央偶呈枯朽状，黑褐色或呈黑洞

C. 老根表面偶呈枯朽状，黑褐色或呈黑洞

D. 老根上部偶呈枯朽状，黑褐色或呈黑洞

E. 幼根表面偶呈枯朽状，黑褐色或呈黑洞

What does “hollowed head”of Astragalus membranaceus refer to (　　)

A. The centre part of young root occasionally rotten-wood-shaped, blackish-brown or hollowed

B. The centre part of old root occasionally rotten-wood-shaped, blackish-brown or hollowed

C. External of old root occasionally rotten-wood-shaped, blackish-brown or hollowed

D. The upper part of old root occasionally rotten-wood-shaped, blackish-brown or hollowed

E. External of young root occasionally rotten-wood-shaped, blackish-brown or hollowed

8. 中药材党参的原植物属于（　　）
A. 五加科　　B. 桔梗科　　C. 菊科
D. 蓼科　　E. 萝藦科
The original plant of Codonopsis Radix belongs to (　　)
A. Araliaceae　　B. Campanulaceae　　C. Compositae
D. Polygonaceae　　E. Asclepiadaceae

（二）多项选择题

(II) Multiple choice question

1. 金银花外观质量要求包括（　　）
A. 花蕾多　　B. 肥壮　　C. 色青绿、微白
D. 气清香　　E. 上细下粗
What are the appearance quality requirements of Lonicerae Japonicae Flos (　　)
A. more flower buds
B. fullness
C. green and slightly white
D. odour delicately aromatic
E. tapered in upper part and stout downwards
2. 关于特等黄芪下列选项正确的为（　　）
A. 圆柱形单条，斩去疙瘩头或喇叭头，顶端无或间有空心
B. 表面为灰白色或淡褐色
C. 质地硬而韧，断面外层为白色，中间为淡黄色或黄色，有粉性
D. 味甘
E. 无生豆气
Which of the following are correct for Top grade Astragali Radix (　　)
A. It has a cylindrical single root, with the knots or trumpet shaped head cut off, and the top has or has no hollow space
B. Externally gray white or light brown
C. The texture is hard and tough; the outer layer of the section is white and the middle part is light yellow or yellow. It is starchy
D. It tastes sweet
E. It doesn't have the smell of raw beans
3. 黄芪外观质量要求包括（　　）
A. 单枝粗长　　B. 质坚而绵　　C. 断面色黄白
D. 粉性足　　E. 味甜且豆腥味浓
Which of the following are Appearance quality Requirement of Astragali Radix (　　)
A. Long and thick single root
B. Texture hard and soft
C. Cross section yellowish-white
D. Starchy enough
E. Sweet taste and strong beany flavor
4. 著名的北药有（　　）
A. 金银花　　B. 黄芪　　C. 党参

D. 山楂　　E. 沙参

Which of the followings are the famous Bei Medicinal Materials (　　)

A. Japanese Honeysuckle Flower　　B. Astragali Radix

C. Codonopsis Radix　　D. hawthorn

E. root of straight ladybell

5. 按照产地、来源将金银花划分的规格包括 (　　)

A. 密银花　　B. 双花　　C. 东银花

D. 山银花　　E. 二花

What are the commercial specifications of Lonicerae Japonicae Flos divided into according to the origin and producing area (　　)

A. Miyinhua　　B. Shuanghua　　C. Dongyinhua

D. Shanyinhua　　E. Erhua

6. 中药材党参商品规格的划分依据是 (　　)

A. 产地　　B. 来源　　C. 采收

D. 加工　　E. 体重

The commodity specification of Codonopsis Radix is divided according to (　　)

A. producing area　　B. origin　　C. collection

D. preparation　　E. weight

7. 中药材党参的商品规格有 (　　)

A. 潞党　　B. 西党　　C. 东党

D. 条党　　E. 白党

The commodity specifications of Codonopsis Radix are (　　)

A. Ludang　　B. Xidang　　C. Dongdang

D. Tiaodang　　E. Baidang

二、思考题 (Thinking question)

1. 请思考总结密银花、东银花的商品特征。

Please think over and summarize the commodity characteristics of Miyinhua and Dongyinhua.

2. 请思考总结蒙古黄芪、膜荚黄芪的商品特征。

Please think over and summarize the commodity characteristics of Astragalus mongholicus and Astragalus membranaceus.

3. 简述中药材党参商品规格等级的划分依据。

Briefly describe the basis for the classification of commodity specifications and grades of Codonopsis Radix.

第十七章　西　　药
Chapter 17　Xi Medicinal Materials

PPT

学习目标 | Learning Target

知识要求：

掌握：①西药的含义及其主要道地药材品种；②大黄、当归、甘草、枸杞子的道地产地、采制、规格等级、商品特征、鉴别与检查、贮藏方法。

能力要求：

通过本章节的学习，学生具有对主要西药进行采制、规格等级划分、商品鉴定、贮藏养护的能力。

Knowledge requirements:

Proficiency: 1. The meaning and major varieties of Xi Medicinal Materials.

2. The knowledge for authentic producing area, collection, preparation, specification, grade, product characteristics, identification and examination, and storage and maintenance methods of Rhei Radix et Rhizoma, Angelicae Sinensis Radix, Glycyrrhizae Radix et Rhizoma, and Lycii Fructus.

Skill requirements:

Through the study of this chapter, students have the ability to collect, classify, identify, store and maintain the main Xi Medicinal Materials.

一、西药概述
I. Overview of Xi Medicinal Materials

以陕西以西广大地区为主要产区或集散地的大宗商品药材均称为西药。西药产区位于东经74°~111° 15′，北纬31° 41′~48°，主要包括陕西、新疆、青海、甘肃、宁夏、内蒙古西部。本地区春秋战国时大部分为秦国治地，古称为秦地，西药亦称为秦药（如秦皮、秦归、秦艽等）。西药的地理范围广泛，地形、气候复杂，海拔高，山脉纵横，多高山峻岭，地势复杂，但高原占绝大部分，沙漠及戈壁也有较大面积。大部分地区冬季干燥寒冷，而夏季凉爽，日照时间长，气温日差较大，干旱少雨，年降雨量为150~660mm，海拔155~8000m以上。本区主产的中药材种类多、产量大，道地药材有大黄、当归、甘草、枸杞子、党参（西党或纹党）、阿魏、银柴胡、秦艽、秦皮、牛黄、羚羊角、甘遂、伊贝母、沙苑子、茜草、茵陈、独一味、淫羊藿、紫草、硼砂等。

All of the bulk commercial medicinal materials whose main producing area or distribution center is the vast area to the west of Shaanxi are called Xi Medicinal Materials. Producing area is located at 74°-111° 15′ E, 31° 41′-48° N, mainly includes provinces of Shaanxi, Xinjiang, Qinghai, Gansu, Ningxia and Western Inner Mongolia. During the period of Spring and Autumn and the Warring States, most regions were governed by the state of Qin, which was called Qin land in ancient times, so Xi Medicinal Materials are also called Qin Medicinal Materials (namely Qinpi, Qingui, Qinjiao, etc.). The geographical scope of Xi Medicinal Materials is wide. The terrain and climate are complex. There are high altitude, vertical and horizontal mountains, many high mountains and complex terrain, but the plateau accounts for the vast majority, and the desert and Gobi also have a large area. Most regions are dry and cold in winter and cool in summer; the duration of sunshine is long; the daily temperature difference is large; and there is little rain and drought. The annual rainfall is 150-660mm, 155-8000m above sea level. There are numerous varieties and large output of medicinal materials in this area. The main authentic medicinal materials produced in this area are Rhei Radix et Rhizoma, Angelicae Sinensis Radix, Glycyrrhizae Radix et Rhizoma, Lycii Fructus, Codonopsis Radix (Xidang or Wendang), Ferulae Rerina, Stellariae Radix, Gentianae Macrophyllae Radix, Fraxini cortex, Bovis Calculus, Saigae Tataricae Cornu, Kansui Radix, Fritillariae Pallidiflorae Bulbus, Astragali Complanati Semen, Rubiae Radix et Rhizoma, Artemisiae Scopariae Herba, Lamiophlomis Herba, Epimedii Folium, Arnebiae Radix, Borax, etc.

二、药材品种
II. Varieties of Medicinal Materials

大黄 (Dahuang) ¦ Rhei Radix et Rhizoma (Rhubarb)

【基原 / Origin】

为蓼科植物掌叶大黄 *Rheum palmatum* L.、唐古特大黄 *Rheum tanguticum* Maxim. et Balf. 和药用大黄 *Rheum officinale* Baill. 的干燥根及根茎。

Rhubarb is the dried root and rhizome of *Rheum palmatum* L., *Rheum tanguticum* Maxim. ex Balf. or *Rheum officinale* Baill.(Fam. Polygonaceae).

【产地 / Producing area】

掌叶大黄主产甘肃、青海、四川等省。唐古特大黄主产于青海、甘肃、西藏、四川等省。药用大黄主产于四川、河南、湖北、陕西、贵州、云南等省。

Main producing areas of *Rheum palmatum* are the provinces of Gansu, Qinghai and Sichuan. Main producing areas of *Rheum tanguticum* are the provinces of Qinghai, Gansu, Xizang and Sichuan. Main producing areas of *Rheum officinale* are the provinces of Sichuan, Henan, Hubei, Shaanxi, Guizhou and Yunnan.

【采制 / Collection and preparation】

秋末茎叶枯萎或次春发芽前采挖。除去细根，刮去外皮，切瓣或段，绳穿成串干燥或直接干燥。取块大者撞光，加工成卵圆形，习称“蛋吉”；成为瓣状半圆形块者，称为“蛋片吉”。较大块横切成段者，按大小分等，分别称为“中吉”“苏吉”“小吉”。支根撞去外皮，称“水根”。

The drug is collected in late autumn when stem and leaves are withered or in next spring just before budding, removed from rootlet and the outer bark, cut into segments or sections, either stringed together to be dried, or dried directly. Crash the big to be surface-smooth, and process them into oval shape (It is known as Danji); the shaped semicircle (It is known as Danpianji). The larger crosscut segments are divided according to size into Zhongji, Suji, Xiaoji. The branches crashed skin (It is known as Shuigen in Province of Gansu).

西大黄　来源为掌叶大黄及唐古特大黄的根及根茎，产于青海、甘肃、西藏，习称“西大黄”。

West Rhei Radix et Rhizoma　It is the dried root and rhizome of *Rheum palmatum* L. and *Rheum tanguticum* Maxim. ex Balf. Main places of origin are the provinces of Qinghai, Gansu and Xizang. (It is known as West Rhei Radix et Rhizoma).

南大黄　来源为药用大黄的根及根茎，产于四川东部、湖北、云南、贵州者，习称“南大黄”。

South Rhei Radix et Rhizoma　It is the dried root and rhizome of *Rheum officinale* Baill. Main producing areas are the provinces of Sichuan (Eastern), Hubei, Yunnan and Guizhou. (It is known as *South Rhei Radix et Rhizoma*)

雅大黄　来源为药用大黄的根及根茎，产于甘孜、阿坝、凉山州、青海（德格）者，习称“雅大黄”。

Ya Rhei Radix et Rhizoma　It is the dried root and rhizome of *Rheum officinale* Baill. Main producing areas are in Prefecture Ganzi, Aba and Liangshanzhou, Sichuan Province, Prefecture Dege (Qinghai Province) (It is known as Yaan Rhei Radix et Rhizoma)

大黄分别经切制、蒸制、酒制、醋制、炒制而成大黄片、熟大黄、酒大黄、醋大黄、大黄炭。

Rhei Radix et Rhizoma is processed into Rhei Radix et Rhizoma slice, processed Rhei Radix et Rhizoma (steamed), wine Rhei Radix et Rhizoma (Processed with wine), vinegar Rhei Radix et Rhizoma (Processed with vinegar) or carbonized Rhei Radix et Rhizoma (processed by carbonization) by cutting, steaming or frying with wine, vinegar, respectively.

【商品特征 / Commodity characteristics】

西大黄　根茎圆柱形、圆锥形或不规则块片状。除去外皮者黄棕色至红棕色，有的可见类白色网状纹理，习称“锦纹”；残留外皮者棕褐色，多具绳孔及粗皱纹。质坚实，有的中心稍松软，断面淡红棕色或黄棕色，颗粒性，习称“高粱碴”；根茎髓部宽广，有星点环列或散在。根木部发达，具有放射性纹理，形成层环明显，无星点。气清香，味苦而微涩，嚼之粘牙，有砂粒感。

West Rhei Radix et Rhizoma　In subcylindrical, conical, ovoid or irregular pieces. Externally yellowish-brown to reddish-brown when peeled outer skin, sometimes whitish reticulation visible (known as *Jingwen*), occasionally with brown patches of cork, mostly with a hole through which the string passed, and coarse wrinkles. Texture compact, sometimes rather loose and soft in the center, fracture pale reddish-brown or yellowish-brown, granular, known as “Gaoliangcha”. Pith of the rhizome broad, with star spots arranged in a ring or irregularly scattered. Wood of the root well developed, lined radially, cambium ring distinct, without star spots. Odour, delicately aromatic; taste bitter and lightly astringent, sticky and gritty on chewing.

南大黄　类圆柱形似马蹄。表面黄褐色或黄棕色。质坚实或较疏松，易折断，断面黄褐色，多孔隙。髓部星点较大，散在。

South Rhei Radix et Rhizoma　In subcylindrical, like a Horse's hoof. Externally tawny or yellowish-brown. Texture compact or rather loose, easy to break, fracture yellowish-brown, porous. Big star spots irregularly scattered.

雅大黄　商品特征同南大黄。

Ya Rhei Radix et Rhizoma　The characteristics are the same as those of South Rhubarb.

大黄片　为不规则类圆形厚片或块，大小不等。外表面黄棕色或黄褐色，有纵皱纹及疙瘩状隆起，切面黄棕色至淡红棕色，较平坦，有明显散在或排列成环的星点，有空隙。

Rhei Radix et Rhizoma slice　Irregularly subrounded thick slices or pieces, varying in size. Externally yellowish-brown or brown, with longitudinal wrinkles and tuberculate. Fracture yellowish-brown to pale reddish-brown, relatively even, with distinct star spots scattered or arranged in a ring, showing some fissures.

酒大黄　形如大黄片，表面深棕黄色，偶有焦斑。微有酒香气。

Wine Rhei Radix et Rhizoma　Similar to Rhei Radix et Rhizoma slices, externally dark brownish-yellow, occasionally bearing burnt patches. Odour, slightly wine-like aromatic.

熟大黄　本品呈不规则的块片，表面黑色。断面中间隐约可见放射状纹理，质坚硬，气微香。

Prepared Rhei Radix et Rhizoma　Irrigularly pieces, externally black, radical striations indistinct in the center of fracture. Texture hard. Odour, slightly aromatic.

醋大黄　形如大黄片，表面深棕色至棕褐色，偶有焦斑。微有醋香气。

Vinegar Rhei Radix et Rhizoma　Similar to Rhei Radix et Rhizoma slices, externally dark brownish to brown, occasionally bearing burnt patches. Odour, slightly vinegar-like aromatic.

大黄炭　形如大黄片，表面焦黑色，断面焦褐色。质轻脆，易折断。无臭，味微苦。

Carbonized Rhei Radix et Rhizoma　Similar to Rhei Radix et Rhizoma slices, externally charred-black, fracture parched brown. Texture light and fragile. Odourless. taste, slightly bitter.

【规格等级 / Specification and grade】

西大黄　依据色泽、大小、重量、切制方法等，划分四个规格。

West Rhei Radix et Rhizoma　It is divided into four specifications of Danjipian, Suji, Shuigeng and Yuandahuang according to colour, size, weight and processing method.

1. 蛋片吉　一等：无粗皮，纵切成瓣。表面黄棕色，体重质坚，断面淡红棕或黄棕色，具放射状纹理及明显环纹，红肉白筋。髓部有星点环列或散在。无虫蛀、霉变、杂质。每 kg 8 个以内，糠心者不超过 15%。

Danpianji　First grade: No coarse cortex, longitudinally cut into segments or sections. Externally yellowish-brown. Texture heavy and compact, fracture reddish-brown or yellowish-brown, lined radially, cambium ring and whitish reticulation distinct. Pith of the rhizome, with star spots arranged in a ring or irregularly scattered. No worms, nor moldy, nor foreign matter. Not more than 8 roots in per kg. Not more than 15% of the drugs with texture loose and soft in the center.

二等：每千克 12 个以内，其余同一等。

Second grade: Not more than 12 roots in per kg. Other characteristics are the same to those of First grade.

三等：每千克 18 个以内，其余同一等。

Third grade: Not more than 18 roots in per kg. Other characteristics are the same to those of First grade.

2. 苏吉　一等：无粗皮，圆柱形、圆锥形或卵形。表面黄棕色，体重质坚，断面淡红棕色或黄棕色，具放射状纹理及明显环纹，红肉白筋，髓部有星点环列或散在。无虫蛀、霉变、杂质。每 kg 20 个以内，糠心者不超过 15%。

2. Suji　First grade: No coarse cortex, cylindrical, conical or ovoid. Externally yellowish-brown. Texture heavy and compact, fracture reddish-brown or yellowish-brown. Lined radially, cambium ring and whitish reticulation distinct. Pith of the rhizome, with star spots arranged in a ring or irregularly scattered. No moth, nor moldy, nor foreign matter. Not more than 20 roots in per kg. Not more than 15% of the drugs with texture loose and soft in the center.

二等：每 kg 30 个以内。其余同一等。

Second grade: Not more than 30 roots in per kg. Other characteristics are the same to those of First grade.

三等：每 kg 40 个以内，其余同一等。

Third grade: Not more than 40 roots in per kg. Other characteristics are the same to those of First grade.

3. 水根 为掌叶大黄或唐古特大黄的主根尾部及支根的加工品，呈长柱状，除去栓皮。表面棕色或黄褐色。长短不限，间有闷茬，小头直径不小于 1.3cm。无杂质、虫蛀、霉变。

Shuigen Taproot tail and lateral root of *Rheum palmatum* and *Rheum tanguticum*. Long cylindrical, removed cork. Externally brown or yellowish-brown, nonuniform in length. Occasionally, there's a loose center. Not less than 1.3cm in diameter. No foreign matter, nor worms, nor mold.

4. 原大黄（统货） 无粗皮，切成瓣、段、块片，大小不分。表面黄褐色，断面具放射状纹理及明显环纹。髓部有星点或散在颗粒，中部直径在 2cm 以上，糠心者不超过 15%。气清香，味苦微涩。无虫蛀、霉变、杂质。

Yuandahuang Unified grade. No coarse cortex, segments or pieces, regardless of size. Externally yellowish-brown, lined radially and cambium ring distinct. Pith of the rhizome, with star spots arranged in a ring or irregularly scattered. More than 2cm in diameter of the middle part. Not more than 15% of the drugs with texture loose and soft in the center. Odour, delicately aromatic; taste bitter and lightly astringent. No worms, nor mold, nor foreign matter.

雅大黄（马蹄大黄） 按照大小和重量划分为三个等级。

Yaan Rhei Radix et Rhizoma It is divided into three grades according to root size and weight.

一等：切成不规则块状，似马蹄形，无粗皮。表面黄色或黄褐色，体重质坚，断面黄色或棕褐色，无杂质、枯糖、焦糊、虫蛀、霉变。气微香，味苦。每只重 150~250g。

First grade: Irregular pieces, like a Horse's hoof, no coarse cortex. Externally yellow or yellowish-brown, texture heavy and compact, fracture yellow or brown. No foreign matter, nor kutang, nor jiaohu, nor worms, nor mold. Odour, slightly aromatic; taste bitter. 150~250g per root.

二等：断面黄褐色，每只重 100~200g，其余同一等。

Second grade: Fracture yellowish-brown, 100~200g per root. Other characteristics are the same to those of First grade.

三等：未去粗皮，体轻泡。大小不分，间有直径 3.5cm 以上。其余同二等。

Third grade: Coarse cortex retained, texture loose and light. Regardless of root size. Occasionally more than 3.5cm in diameter. Other characteristics are the same to those of Second grade.

南大黄（南川大黄） 按照大小和重量划分为两个等级。

South Rhei Radix et Rhizoma It is divided into two grades according to size and weight.

一等：横切成段，类圆柱形似马蹄，无粗皮。表面黄褐色，体坚实。断面黄色或黄绿色，长 7cm 以上，直径 5cm 以上。气微香，味苦涩。无杂质、枯糖、焦糊、水根、虫蛀、霉变。

First grade: In subcylindrical, like a Horse's hoof. No coarse cortex. Externally yellowish-brown, texture compact, fracture yellow or yellowish-green. More than 7cm in length, 5cm in diameter. Odour, slightly aromatic, taste, bitter, astringent. No foreign matter, nor kutang, nor jiaohu, nor Shuigen, nor worms, nor moldy.

二等：较一等轻泡，大小不分，间有水根，最小头直径不低于 1.2cm。其余同一等。

Second grade: Texture looser than those of First grade, regardless of size, occasionally Shuigen, not less than 1.2cm in diameter. Other characteristics are the same to those of First grade.

大黄出口品 出口有片子、吉子、糠心、粗渣等，其中以片子为最佳，中吉次之。以内茬红度所占比例分等级，有九成、八成、七成、六成四种。小吉、糠心、粗渣无红度之分。

Exported Rhei Radix et Rhizoma It is divided into the specifications of *Pianzi, Jizi, Kangxin and Cuzha* according to processing method. Among them, the *Pianzi* is the best quality, followed by *Zhongji*. Four grades are divided into *Jiuchengji, Bachengji, Qichengji, Liuchengji* according to red degree. No difference of red degree for *Xiaoji*, *Kangxin* and *Cucha*.

【化学成分 / Chemical constituent】

主含蒽醌类衍生物。游离蒽醌类有大黄酸、大黄素、大黄酚、芦荟大黄素、大黄素甲醚。结合性蒽醌系双蒽酮苷类，为大黄的泻下成分：番泻苷 A、B、C、D、E、F。

Mainly contains anthraquinone derivative. Free anthraquinones include rhein, emodin, chrysophanol, aloe-emodin and physcion. The conjugated anthraquinone is also a dianthranone glycoside including rheinoside (A, B, C, D, E, F) with laxative effect.

【检查 / Examination】

水分不超过 15.0%。总灰分不得过 10.0%。

Water, not more than 15.0%. Total ash, not more than 10.0%.

【质量要求 / Quality requirement】

外观质量 以个大、色黄棕、体重、质坚实、锦纹星点明显、气清香、味苦而不涩、嚼之发黏、无糠心者为佳。

Appearance quality Good quality for being big, yellowish brown, weight heavy, texture compact, whitish reticulations and scattered star spot more visible, odour delicately aromatic, taste bitter and no astringent, sticky on chewing, no loose and soft in the center.

内在质量 浸出物含量：水溶性浸出物（热）不得少于 25.0%。含量测定：按高效液相色谱法测定，含总蒽醌以芦荟大黄素、大黄酸、大黄素、大黄酚、大黄素甲醚的总量不得少于 1.5%；含游离蒽醌以芦荟大黄素、大黄酸、大黄素、大黄酚和大黄素甲醚的总量计，不得少于 0.20%。

Intrinsic quality Extract content: not less than 25.0% of water-soluble extractives (hot).

Assay: Total anthraquinone It contains not less than 1.5% of the total amount of aloe-emodin, rhein, emodin, chrysophanol and physcion according to HPLC method.

Free anthraquinone It contains not less than 0.20% of the total amount of aloe-emodin, rhein, emodin, chrysophanol and physcion according to HPLC method.

【功能主治 / Function and indication】

寒，苦。泻下攻积，清热泻火，凉血解毒，逐瘀通经，利湿退黄。用于实热积滞便秘，血热吐衄，目赤咽肿，痈肿疔疮，肠痈腹痛，瘀血经闭，产后瘀阻，跌打损伤，湿热痢疾，黄疸尿赤，淋证，水肿；外治烧烫伤。酒大黄善清上焦血分热毒，用于目赤咽肿、齿龈肿痛。熟大黄泻下力缓、泻火解毒，用于火毒疮疡。大黄炭凉血化瘀止血，用于血热有瘀出血症。

Cold, bitter. To remove accumulation with purgation, clear heat, purge fire, cool the blood, remove toxin, expel stasis, unblock the meridians, and drain dampness to abate jaundice. For the treatment of accumulation stagnation and constipation caused by excess heat, hematemesis caused by blood heat, red eyes, swollen throat, swelling abscess, deep-rooted boil and sore, abdominal pain caused by intestinal abscess, blood-stasis, amenorrhea, postpartum stasis and obstruction, traumatic injuries, dampness-heat dysentery, jaundice, red urine, stranguria, and edema; topical application for burn and scald. Wine-fried Rhei Radix et Rhizoma is good at clearing heat toxin in the upper energizer blood aspect, which can be applied for red eyes, swollen throat, and painful swollen gum. The purgation power of prepared Rhei Radix et Rhizoma is mild, and it can purge fire and remove toxin to treat sore and ulcer caused by fire-toxin. Charred Rhei Radix et Rhizoma can cool the blood, resolve stasis and stop bleeding which can be applied to bleeding symptoms caused by blood heat and stasis.

【贮藏养护 / Storage and maintenance】

贮于通风干燥避光处，防蛀。

Preserved in a ventilated, dry place, and protected from light and moth.

【用法用量 / Administration and dosage】

3~15g；用于泻下不宜久煎。外用适量，研末敷于患处。

3~15g. It should not be decocted long for purgation. Appropriate amount for topical application, ground into powder and applied to the locations of injury.

甘草 (Gancao) ¦ Glycyrrhizae Radix et Rhizoma (Liquorice Root)

【基原 / Origin】

为豆科植物甘草 *Glycyrrhiza uralensis* Fisch.、胀果甘草 *Glycyrrhiza inflata* Bat. 或光果甘草 *Glycyrrhiza glabra* L. 的干燥根及根茎。

Liquorice Root is the dried root and rhizome of *Glycyrrhiza uralensis* Fisch., *Glycyrrhiza inflata* Bat. or *Glycyrrhiza glabra* L. (Fam. Leguminosae).

【产地 / Producing area】

甘草主产于内蒙古、甘肃、宁夏等省。光果甘草主产于新疆。胀果甘草主产于新疆、甘肃等省。

The main producing areas of *Glycyrrhiza uralensis* are the provinces of Inner Mongolia, Gansu and Ningxia, etc. *Glycyrrhiza inflata* is mainly produced in the Xinjiang Uygur Autonomous Region. *Glycyrrhiza glabra* is mainly produced in the Xinjiang Uygur Autonomous Region and Gansu Province.

西草　主产于内蒙古西部及甘肃、陕西、宁夏、青海、新疆等地者，习称“西草”。

Xicao　Main producing areas are western Inner Mongolia, the provinces of Gansu, Shaanxi, Ningxia, Qinghai and Xinjiang Uygur Autonomous Region. It is known as “Xicao” (Western Liquorice Root).

东草　产于内蒙古东部及东北三省、河北、山西等地者，习称“东草”。

Dongcao　Main producing areas are eastern Inner Mongolia, the provinces of Jilin, Liaoning, Heilongjiang, Hebei, Shaanxi, etc. It is known as “*Dongcao*” (Eastern Liquorice Root).

新疆草　产于新疆，来源为胀果甘草，习称“新疆草”。

Xinjiangcao　Main producing area is Xinjiang Uygur Autonomous Region. It is the dried root and rhizome of *Glycyrrhiza inflata,* and known as “*Xinjiangcao*” (Xinjiang Liquorice Root).

洋甘草　产于新疆或欧洲，来源为光果甘草，习称“洋甘草”或“欧甘草”。

Yanggancao　Main producing areas are Xinjiang Uygur Autonomous Region and Europe. It is the dried root and rhizome of *Glycyrrhiza glabra*, and known as “*Yanggancao*” or “*Ougancao*” (Foreign or Europe Liquorice Root).

【采制 / Collection and preparation】

甘草　春秋二季采挖，除去须根及茎基，切成适当的段，晒干。亦有刮去外皮，切成段晒干者，习称“粉甘草”。

甘草分别经切制、蜜制而成甘草片、炙甘草。

Liquorice root is collected in spring or autumn, removed from rootlet and caulis base, cut into sections and dried in the sun. Sometimes the roots are scraped off the skin, cut into sections and dried in the sun, called “Fengancao” (starchy Liquorice Root).

Licorice is processed by cutting or frying with honey into *Gancaopian* (Liquorice Root slices) or Zhigancao (honey Liquorice Root).

【商品特征 / Commodity characteristics】

甘草　根呈圆柱形，长 25~100cm，直径 0.6~3.5cm。外皮松紧不一。表面红棕色或灰棕色，具显著的纵皱纹、沟纹、皮孔及稀疏的细根痕。质坚实，断面略显纤维性，黄白色，粉性，形成层环明显，射线放射状，有的有裂隙。根茎呈圆柱形，表面有芽痕，断面中部有髓。气微，味甜而特殊。

Root of *Glycyrrhiza uralensis*　Roots cylindrical, 25~100cm long, 0.6~3.5cm in diameter. The outer bark loose or tight. Externally reddish-brown or greyish-brown, obviously longitudinally wrinkled, furrowed, lenticel-like protruded, and with sparse rootlet scars. Texture compact, fracture slightly fibrous, yellowish-white, starchy, cambium ring distinct, rays radiate, some with clefts. Rhizomes cylindrical, externally with bud scars, pith present in the centre of fracture. Odour, slight; taste, sweet and characteristic.

胀果甘草　根和根茎木质粗壮，有的分枝，外皮粗糙，多灰棕色或灰褐色。质坚硬，木质纤维多，粉性小。根茎不定芽多而粗大。

Root of *Glycyrrhiza inflate*　Root and rhizomes woody and stout, some branched, the outer bark rough, mostly greyish-brown. Texture compact, lignified fibres abundant, and less starchy. Rhizomes with more and large adventitious buds.

光果甘草　根和根茎质地较坚实，有的分枝，外皮不粗糙，多灰棕色，皮孔细而不明显。

Root of *Glycyrrhiza glabra*　Texture of root and rhizomes relatively compact, some branched, the outer bark not rough, mostly greyish-brown. Lenticels small and indistinct.

甘草片　本品呈类圆形或椭圆形切片。外表皮红棕色或灰棕色。切面略显纤维性，中心黄白色，有明显射线放射状纹理及形成层环，质坚实，有粉性。气微，味甜而特殊。

Gancaopian　Subrounded or elliptical thick slices. Externally reddish-brown or greyish-brown with longitudinal wrinkles. Cut surface showing slightly fibrous, center yellowish-white, with distinctly radial striations and cambium ring. Texture compact, starchy. Odour, slight, taste sweet and characteristic.

炙甘草　外表微有光泽，切面黄色至深黄色，略有黏性，具焦香气，味甜。其它特征与甘草片相同。

Prepared Glycyrrhizae Radix et Rhizoma　Externally slightly lustrous, cut surface yellow to deep yellow, texture sticky. Odour, with agreeable burnt smelling; taste, sweet. Other characteristics are the same to Those of Gancaopian.

【规格等级 / Specification and grade】

商品甘草分西草和东草两种规格。按照甘草加工方法和大小分为大草、条草、毛草、草节和疙瘩头等规格。各规格下有按照药材的长度大小、顶端直径分等级。

Two commodities are divided according to the producing areas, Xicao and Dongcao. Five specifications are divided according to the processing method and size, Dacao, Tiaocao, Maocao, Caojie and Gedatou. Grades are divided according to the root length and diameter of root upper part.

1. 西草

Western Liquorice Root

大草（统货） 呈圆柱形。表面红棕色、棕黄色或灰棕色，皮细紧，有纵纹。斩去头尾，切口整齐。质坚实。断面黄白色，粉性足。味甜。长 25~50cm，顶端直径 2.5~4cm，黑心草不超过总重量的 5%。无须根、杂质、虫蛀、霉变。

Dacao (Unified grade) Roots cylindrical, externally reddish-brown, brownish-yellow or greyish-brown. Skin tight, longitudinally wrinkled. Cut off the head and tail, and cut surfaces neatly. Texture compact, fracture yellowish-white, starchy, taste sweet. 25~50cm long, 2.5~4cm in diameter of root upper part. Not more than 5% of the roots with black center in total root weight. No rootlet, nor foreign matter, nor worms, nor mold.

条草 一等：呈圆柱形，单枝顺直。长 25~50cm，顶端直径 1.5cm 以上，余同大草。

Tiaocao

First grade: Roots cylindrical, straight single branch. 25~50cm long, more than 1.5cm in diameter of root upper part. Other characteristics are the same to those of Dacao.

二等：长 25~50cm，顶端直径 1cm 以上，余同大草。

Second grade: 25~50cm long, more than 1cm in diameter of root upper part. Other characteristics are the same to those of Dacao.

三等：长 25~50cm，顶端直径 0.7cm 以上。余同大草。

Third grade: 25~50cm long, more than 0.7cm in diameter of root upper part. Other characteristics are the same to those of Dacao.

毛草（统货） 呈圆柱形弯曲的小草，去净残茎，不分长短。表面红棕色、棕黄色或灰棕色。断面黄白色，味甜。项端直径 0.5cm 以上。无须根、杂质、虫蛀、霉变。

Maocao (Unified grade) Small roots, cylindrical curved, stem removed, regardless of length. Externally reddish-brown, brownish-yellow or greyish-brown. Fracture yellowish-white, taste sweet. More than 0.5cm in diameter of root upper part. No rootlet, nor foreign matter, nor worms, nor mold.

草节 一等：呈圆柱形，单枝条。长 6cm 以上，顶端直径 1.5cm 以上。无须根、疙瘩头、杂质、虫蛀、霉变。

Caojie

First grade: Cylindrical, single root. more than 6cm long, 1.5cm in diameter of root upper part. No rootlet, nor Gedatou, nor foreign matter, nor worms, nor moldy.

二等：顶端直径 0.7cm 以上。余同一等。

Second grade: 0.7cm in diameter of root upper part. Other characteristics are same to those of First grade.

疙瘩头 系加工条草砍下之根头，呈疙瘩头状。去净残茎及须根。表面黄白色。味甜。大小长短不分，间有黑心。无杂质、虫蛀、霉变。

Gedatou (Head of liquorice root, Lumpy) Root head with some knots. Stump and rootlet removed. Fracture yellowish-white, taste sweet. Regardless of size, some roots with black center. No foreign matter, nor worms, nor mold.

2. 东草

Eastern Liquorice Root

条草 一等：呈圆柱形，上粗下细。表面紫红色或灰褐色，皮粗糙。不斩头尾。质松体轻。断面黄白色，有粉性。味甜。长 60cm 以上，芦下 3cm 处直径 1.5cm 以上。无杂质、虫蛀、霉变。

Tiaocao

First grade: Roots cylindrical, thick upper part and thin down part. Externally fuchsia or Taupe. Rough skin. Root head and tail remained. Texture light and loose, fracture yellowish-white, starchy, taste sweet. More than 60cm long, 1.5cm in diameter of root upper part. No foreign matter, nor worms, nor mold.

二等：长 50cm 以上，芦下 3cm 处直径 1cm 以上，余同一等。

Second grade: More than 50cm long, 1cm in diameter of root upper part. Other characteristics are the same to those of First grade.

三等：长 40cm 以上，芦下 3cm 处直径 0.5cm 以上。无细小须根，余同一等。

Third grade: More than 40cm long, 0.5cm in diameter of root upper part. No rootlet. Other characteristics are the same to those of First grade.

【化学成分 / Chemical constituent】

主含甘草甜素、甘草苷、甘草苷元、异甘草苷、异甘草苷元、芒柄花黄素等。

Mainly contains glycyrrhizin, liquiritin, liquiritingenin, iso-liquiritin, iso-liquritingenin, formononetin, etc.

【检查 / Examination】

水分不得过 12.0%。总灰分不得过 7.0%。酸不溶性灰分不得过 2.0%。重金属及有害元素：铅不得过 5mg/kg；镉不得过 0.3mg/kg；砷不得过 2mg/kg；汞不得过 0.2mg/kg；铜不得过 20mg/kg。有机氯农药残留量：总六六六不得过 0.2mg/kg；总滴滴涕不得过 0.2mg/kg；五氯硝基苯不得过 0.1mg/kg。

Water, not more than 12.0%. Total ash, not more than 7.0%. Acid-insoluble ash, not more than 2.0%. Heavy metals and harmful elements: not more than 5mg/kg of lead, 0.3mg/kg of cadmium, 2mg/kg of arsenic, 0.2mg/kg of mercury and 20mg/kg of copper.

Residual organochlorine pesticides: not more than 0.2mg/kg of total hexachlorocyclohexane (the total amount of α-BHC, β-BHC, γ-BHC, δ-BHC), 0.2mg/kg of total chlorophenothane (the total amount of pp′-DDE, pp′-DDD, op′-DDT, pp′-DDT), and 0.1mg/kg of pentachloride nitrobenzene (PCNB).

【质量要求 / Quality requirement】

外观质量 以外皮细紧、色红棕、质坚实、体重、断面黄白色、粉性足、味甜者为佳。

Appearance quality Good quality for the outer bark tight, externally reddish-brown, texture compact, fracture yellowish-white, sufficient starchy, taste sweet.

内在质量 含量测定：按高效液相色谱法测定，含甘草苷不得少于 0.50%；含甘草酸不得少于 2.0%。

Intrinsic quality Assay: it contains not less than 0.50% of liquiritin and 2.0% of glycyrrhizic acid according to HPLC method.

【功能主治 / Function and indication】

平，甘。补脾益气，清热解毒，祛痰止咳，缓急止痛，调和诸药。用于脾胃虚弱，倦怠乏力，心悸气短，咳嗽痰多，脘腹、四肢挛急疼痛，痈肿疮毒，缓解药物毒性、烈性。炙甘草具有补脾和胃，益气复脉的功能。

Neutral and sweet. To tonify spleen, tonify qi, clear heat, remove toxin, dispel phlegm, suppress cough, relax spasm, relieve pain, and moderate drug actions. For the treatment of spleen-stomach weakness, fatigue, lack of strength, palpitations, shortness of breath, cough and profuse sputum, painful spasm in the stomach duct, abdomen and limbs, swelling abscess, sore, skin infections, and reducing the other drugs'toxin and drastic action. Zhigancao (honey Liquorice root) to tonify spleen, harmonize the stomach, tonify qi, and restore pulse.

【贮藏养护 / Storage and maintenance】

用麻袋或纸箱包装。贮存于阴凉、通风干燥处，防蛀。

Usually packed in sack or carton. Preserved in a ventilated, dry and cool place, and protected from moth.

【用法用量 / Administration and dosage】

2~10g。

2~10g.

当归 (Danggui) ┆ Angelicae Sinensis Radix (Chinese Angelica)

【基原 / Origin】

为伞形科植物当归 *Angelica sinensis* (Oliv.) Diels 的干燥根。

Chinese Angelica is the dried root of *Angelica sinensis* (Oliv.) Diels (Fam. Umbelliferae).

【产地 / Producing area】

主要产于甘肃、云南，四川。产于甘肃岷县者称为“岷归”。

Main producing areas are the provinces of Gansu, Yunnan and Sichuan. Produced in Minxian, Gansu Province, known as Mingui.

【采制 / Collection and preparation】

当归一般栽培至第二年秋后采挖，除去叶、须根及泥土，待水分稍蒸发后，捆成小把，上棚，以烟火慢慢熏干。当归按不同部位加工成全归、归头、归身、归尾。

The roots are collected in late autumn of the second year of cultivation. Removed from leaves, rootlet and soil, slightly dried and tied up in small bundles, placed on a shelf and smoke-dried. Chinese Angelica is processed into Quangui (whole root), Guitou (root head and main root), Guishen (main root), Guiwei (branch root) according to different root parts.

当归分别经切制、酒制（黄酒）成当归片、酒当归。

Angelicae Sinensis Radix is processed to Angelicae Sinensis Radix slice or wine Angelicae Sinensis Radix by cutting or frying with Chinese rice wine.

【商品特征 / Commodity characteristics】

全归 本品略呈圆柱形，下部有支根 3~5 条或更多，长 15~25cm。表面黄棕色至棕褐色，具纵皱纹和横长皮孔样突起。根头（归头）直径 1.5~4cm，具环纹，上端圆钝，或具数个明显突出的根茎痕，有紫色或黄绿色的茎和叶鞘的残基；主根（归身）表面凹凸不平；支根（归尾）上粗下细，多扭曲，直径 0.3~1cm，有少数须根痕。质柔韧，断面黄白色或淡黄棕色。皮部厚、有裂隙和多数棕色点状分泌腔，木部色较淡，形成层环黄棕色。有浓郁的香气，味甘、辛、微苦。柴性大、干枯无油或断面呈绿褐色者不可供药用。

Quangui Somewhat cylindrical, 3-5 or more branched at the lower part, 15~25cm in length. Externally pale brown to brown, longitudinally wrinkled and transversely lenticels-like protruded. Root stock (Guitou) 1.5~4cm in diameter, annulated, apex and rounded or with several obvious protrudent rhizome scars, showing purple or yellowish-green remains of stems and leaf sheaths; main root (Guishen) lumpy on the surface; branching root (Guiwei) 0.3~1cm in diameter, the upper portion thick and the lower portion thin, mostly twisted and exhibiting a few rootlet scars. Texture flexible, fracture yellowish-white or pale yellowish-brown, bark thick, showing some clefts and numerous brown dotted secretory cavities, wood paler in colour, cambium ring yellowish-brown. Odour, strongly aromatic; taste, sweet, pungent and slightly bitter. It can not be used medicinally if the roots become woody, withered and not oily, or greenish-brown on the fracture.

当归片 类圆形、椭圆形或不规则薄片。外表皮浅棕色至棕褐色。切面浅棕黄色或黄白色，平坦，有裂隙，中间有浅棕色的形成层环，并有多数棕色的油点。香气浓郁，味甘、辛、微苦。

Angelicae Sinensis Radix slice In subrounded, elliptical or irregular thin slices. Externally pale brown to brown. Cut surface yellowish-white or pale brownish-yellow, even, with clefts, a pale brown cambium ring in the middle, numerous brown oily dots visible. Odour, strongly aromatic; taste, sweet, pungent and slightly bitter.

酒当归 本品形如当归片。切面深黄色或浅棕黄色，略有焦斑。香气浓郁，并略有酒香气。

Wine Angelicae Sinensis Radix (stir-baked with wine) The shape similar to the slices of Angelicae Sinensis Radix. Cut surface dark yellow or pale brownish-yellow, somewhat with burnt specks. Odour strongly aromatic, and slightly with wine aromatic odour.

【规格等级 / Specification and grade】

按加工方法常常分为全归、归头两个规格。另外，市场商品还有归身，归尾，箱归等规格。

Two specifications are divided according to the processing method, Quangui and Guitou. In addition, there are Guishen, Guiwei, carton Angelicae Sinensis Radix and other commodities.

全归 一等：干货。主根圆柱形，下部有多条支根，根梢不细于 0.2cm。表面浅棕色或棕褐色。断面黄白或淡黄色，具油性。每千克 30 支以下。气芳香，味甘、辛、微苦。无须根、杂质、虫蛀、霉变。

Quangui First grade: Dry root, cylindrical, more branched at the lower part. The tip is not less than 0.2cm in diameter. Externally pale brown to brown. Fracture yellowish-white or pale yellow, oily. Not more than 30 roots in per kg. Odour, strongly aromatic; taste, sweet, pungent and slightly bitter. No rootlet, nor foreign matter, nor worms, nor mold.

二等：每千克 30~50 支，余同一等。

Second grade: Not more than 30~50 roots in per kg. Other characteristics are the same to those of First grade.

三等：每千克 50 支以上，余同一等。

Third grade: Not less than 50 roots in per kg. Other characteristics are the same to those of First grade.

统货：大小不分。余同一等。

Unified grade Mixture of different size roots. Other characteristics are the same to those of First grade.

归头 一等：干货。纯主根，呈长圆形或拳状。直径 1.5~4cm。刮去外皮，表面黄白色。断面黄白或淡黄色，具油性。每千克 40 支以下。气芳香，味甘、辛、微苦。无油个、枯干、杂质、虫蛀、霉变。

Guitou First grade: Dry roots. All taproot, oblong or fist shaped, diameter 1.5-4cm. Scrape off the skin, externally yellowish-white. Fracture yellowish-white or pale yellow, oily. Not more than 40 roots in per kg. Odour, strongly aromatic; taste, sweet, pungent and slightly bitter. No diffused oil, nor withering, nor foreign matter, nor worms, nor mildew.

二等：每千克 40~60 支，余同一等。

Second grade: 40~60 roots in per kg. Other characteristics are the same to those of First grade.

三等：每千克 60 支以上。余同一等。

Third grade: more than 60 roots in per kg. Other characteristics are the same to those of First grade.

【化学成分 / Chemical constituent】

主含挥发油（藁本内酯、正丁烯基酞内酯）、水溶性成分（阿魏酸）、倍半萜烯及微量元素等。

Mainly contains volatile oil (ligustilide, *n*-butenyllactone), water-soluble ingredients (ferulic acid), sesquiterpene, and microminerals, etc.

【检查 / Examination】

水分不得过 15.0%。总灰分不得过 7.0%。酸不溶性灰分不得过 2.0%。

Water, not more than 15.0%. Total ash, not more than 7.0%. Acid-insoluble ash, not more than 2.0%.

【质量要求 / Quality requirement】

外观质量 以主根粗长、油润、外皮色棕褐色、断面色黄白、气味浓郁，味甘、辛、微苦者为佳。

Appearance quality Good quality for main roots thick and long, oily, externally brown, fracture yellowish-white, odour strongly aromatic, taste sweet, pungent and slightly bitter.

内在质量 浸出物含量：醇溶性（70% 乙醇）浸出物（热）不得少于 45.0%。含量测定：按挥发油测定法（乙法）测定，含挥发油不得少于 0.4%(ml/g)。按高效液相色谱法测定，含阿魏酸不得少于 0.050%。

Intrinsic quality Extract content: not less than 45.0% of ethanol (70%)-soluble extractives (hot).

Assay: It contains not less than 0.4% (ml/g) of volatile oil. It contains not less than 0.050% of ferulic acid according to HPLC method.

【功能主治 / Function and indication】

温，甘、辛。补血活血，调经止痛，润肠通便。用于血虚萎黄，眩晕心悸，月经不调，经闭痛经，虚寒腹痛，风湿痹痛，跌扑损伤，痈疽疮疡，肠燥便秘。酒当归活血通经。用于经闭痛经，风湿痹痛，跌扑损伤。

Warm, sweet and pungent. To nourish blood, activate blood, regulate menstruation, relieve pain, moisten the intestines and relax the bowels. For the treatment of blood deficiency with sallow complexion, dizziness, palpitations, menstrual irregularities, amenorrhea and dysmenorrheal, deficiency cold abdominal pain, painful bi disorder caused by wind-dampness, traumatic injuries, abscesses and cellulitis, sore and ulcer, and constipation caused by intestinal dryness. Angelicae Sinensis Radix (processed with wine) could activate blood and unblock the meridian, and could be used for amenorrhea and dysmenorrhea, painful bi disorder caused by wind-dampness, and traumatic injuries.

【贮藏养护 / Storage and maintenance】

用麻袋或纸箱包装。置阴凉干燥处，防潮，防蛀。

Usually packed in sack or carton. Preserved in a dry and cool place, and protected from moisture and moth.

【用法用量 / Administration and dosage】

6~12g。

6~12g.

枸杞子 (Gouqizi) ¦ Lycii Fructus (Barbary Wolfberry Fruit)

【基原 / Origin】

为茄科植物宁夏枸杞 *Lycium barbarum* L. 的干燥成熟果实。

Barbary Wolfberry Fruit is the dried ripe fruit of *Lycium barbarum* L. (Fam. Solanaceae).

【产地 / Producing area】

主产于宁夏的中宁和中卫，量大质优。产于宁夏、甘肃、青海、新疆、内蒙古等省的习称"西枸杞"，产于河北、山西等地的习称"血枸杞"。

Main Producing areas are Zhongning and Zhongwei, Ningxia Province, with high quality and large quantity. It is also produced in the provinces of Ningxia, Gansu, Qinghai, Xinjiang and Inner Mongolia, known as Xi gouqi (Western Barbary Wolfberry Fruit). Barbary Wolfberry Fruit produced in the provinces of Hebei and Shanxi is known as Xue gouqi (Blood Barbary Wolfberry Fruit).

【采制 / Collection and preparation】

夏、秋二季果实呈红色时采收，热风烘干，除去果梗。或晾至皮皱后，晒干，除去果梗和宿萼。晾晒时，不宜用手翻动，以免变黑。

It is collected in summer and autumn when the fruit turns red, hot-air dried and removed from the fruit stalk and calyx; or dried in the shade to the exocarp shrunk, and dried in the sun to dryness, removed from the fruit stalk and calyx. Attention, when dried in the shade, unfavorable turned over with the hand, lest turning black.

【商品特征 / Commodity characteristics】

西枸杞 本品呈类纺锤形或椭圆形。表面红色或暗红色，顶端有小突起状的花柱痕，基部有白色的果梗痕。果皮柔韧，皱缩；果肉肉质，柔润。种子类肾形，扁而翘，表面浅黄色或棕黄色。气微，味甜。

Western Barbary Wolfberry Fruit Subfusiform or ellipsoid. Externally red or dark red, with a protrudent style scar at the apex, and a white fruit stalk scar at the base. Pericarp pliable and shrunken, sarcocarp fleshy, soft and viscous. Seeds subreniform, flat and bent upwards, pale yellow or brownish-yellow on surface. Odour, slight; taste, sweet.

血枸杞 颗粒均匀，皮薄、籽多、糖质较少、色泽鲜红、味甜微酸。

Blood Barbary Wolfberry Fruit Fruit uniformity, thin skin, more seeds, less saccharic, bright red, taste sweet and slight sour.

【规格等级 / Specification and grade】

按产地分为西枸杞和血枸杞两种规格，各规格下分等级。其规格等级标准为：

Two specifications are divided according to producing areas, Western Barbary Wolfberry Fruit and Blood Barbary Wolfberry Fruit. Each of them is divided into different grades. The criteria of their specification and grade are as follows:

西枸杞 按每 50g 的粒数划分为 5 个等级。

West Barbary Wolfberry Fruit Five grades are divided according to the fruit numbers in per 50g.

一等：果实椭圆形或长卵形，色泽鲜红或红色、暗红色，质柔软，多糖质，滋润，味甜。每 50g 370 粒以内。大小均匀，无油粒、破粒、杂质、虫蛀、霉变。

First grade: Fruit ellipsoid or long-ovate; bright red, red or dark red, soft texture and moisten, more saccharic and taste sweet. Not more than 370 fruits in per 50g. Uniform in size. No decay fruits, nor broken parts, nor foreign matter, nor worms, nor mildew.

二等：每 50g 580 粒以内。其余同一等。

Second grade: Not more than 580 fruits in per 50g. Other characteristics are the same to those of First grade.

三等：每 50g 900 粒以内。果实暗红或橙红色，糖质较少，其余同一等。

Third grade: Not more than 900 fruits in per 50g. Fruits dark red or orange-red, less saccharic. Other characteristics are the same to those of First grade.

四等：每 50g 1120 粒以内。果实暗红或橙红色，糖质少，无油粒。其余同一等。

Fourth grade: Not more than 1120 fruits in per 50g. Fruits dark red or orange-red, less saccharic. No decay fruit. Other characteristics are the same to those of First grade.

五等：每 50g 1120 粒以外。大小不分，破粒，油粒不超过 30%。余同四等。

Fifth grade: More than 1120 fruits in per 50g. Mixed fruits in difference sizes, not more than 30% of broken and decay fruits. Other characteristics are the same to those of Fourth grade.

血枸杞 按每 50g 的粒数划分等级。

Blood Barbary Wolfberry Fruit Divided into Three grades according to the fruit numbers in per 50g.

一等：果实类纺锤形，鲜红或深红色。每 50g 600 粒以内。无油粒、黑果、破粒、杂质、虫蛀、霉变。

First grade: Fusiform, bright red or dark red. Not more than 600 fruits in per 50g. No decay fruit, nor black fruit, nor broken parts, nor foreign matter, nor worms, nor mildew.

二等：每 50g 800 粒以内。油果不过 10%。其余同一等。

Second grade: Not more than 800 fruits in per 50g. Not more than 10% of decay fruit. Other characteristics are the same to those of First grade.

三等：每 50g 800 粒以外。紫红色或淡红色，含有少量油果。其余同一等。

Third grade: Not more than 800 fruits in per 50g. Purplish-red or light red, containing a small amount of decay fruits. Other characteristics are the same to those of First grade.

目前市场上有以具体产地分为宁夏枸杞、新疆枸杞、内蒙枸杞、河北枸杞等。

Other specifications There are Ningxia, Xinjiang, Neimeng and Hebei Barbary Wolfberry Fruit, according to the producing areas.

出口商品：分特级（贡果面）、甲级（贡果面）、乙级（贡果）、丙级（超王级）4 个规格。

Exported Barbary Wolfberry Fruit There are Top, A, B and C grades according to the producing areas.

【化学成分 / Chemical constituent】

主含甜菜碱、枸杞多糖、胡萝卜素、烟酸、维生素 B_1、维生素 B_2、维生素 C、硫胺素、玉蜀黍黄素等。

Fruit contains betaine, lycium barbarum polysaccharide, renieratene, nicotinic acid, Vitamin B_1,Vitamin B_2, Vitamin C, zeaxanthin, thiamine, etc.

【检查 / Examination】

杂质不得过 0.5%。水分不得过 13.0%。总灰分不得过 5.0%。重金属及有害元素：铅不得过 5mg/kg；镉不得过 0.3mg/kg；砷不得过 2mg/kg；汞不得过 0.2mg/kg；铜不得过 20mg/kg。

Foreign matter, not more than 0.5%. Water, not more than 13.0%. Total ash, not more than 5.0%. Heavy metals and harmful elements: Not more than 5mg/kg of lead, 0.3mg/kg of cadmium, 2mg/kg of arsenic, 0.2mg/kg of mercury and 20mg/kg of copper.

【质量要求 / Quality requirement】

外观质量　以粒大、肉厚、籽小、色红、质柔、味甜者为佳。

Appearance quality　Good quality for big fruits, thick pulp, small seed, red colour, soft texture and sweet taste.

内在质量　浸出物含量：水溶性浸出物（热）不得少于 55.0%。含量测定：按紫外 - 可见分光光度法测定，含枸杞多糖以葡萄糖计，不得少于 1.8%。按薄层色谱扫描法测定，含甜菜碱不得少于 0.30%。

Intrinsic quality　Extract content: not less than 55.0% of water-soluble extractives (hot). Assay: It contains not less than 1.8% of polysaccharides according to UV-vis method. It contains not less than 0.30% of betaine according to TLCS method.

【功能主治 / Function and indication】

平，甘。滋补肝肾，益精明目。用于虚劳精亏，腰膝酸痛，眩晕耳鸣，阳痿遗精，内热消渴，血虚萎黄，目昏不明。

Neutral, sweet. To nourish the liver and kidney, replenish essence, and improve vision. For the treatment of consumptive disease with deficiency of essence, limbs aching in the lower back and knees, dizziness, tinnitus, impotence, seminal emission, interior heat diarrhea, blood deficiency, sallow complexion, and blurred vision.

【贮藏养护 / Storage and maintenance】

贮于阴凉干燥处，防闷热、防潮，防虫蛀。

Preserved in a dry and cool place, and protected from heat, moisture and moth.

【用法用量 / Administration and dosage】

6~12g。

6~12g.

重点小结
Summary

药材	主产地	商品规格	等级标准
大黄	掌叶大黄主产甘肃，唐古特大黄主产于青海与甘肃，药用大黄主产四川北部等	西大黄、南大黄、雅黄	蛋片吉、苏吉按每 kg 个数分三个等级；雅大黄按照大小和重量分三个等级 南大黄按大小和重量分二个等级
甘草	甘草主产于内蒙古、甘肃、宁夏等省。光果甘草主产于新疆。胀果甘草主产于新疆、甘肃等省	西草（大草、条草、毛草、草节、疙瘩头）、东草（条草、毛草）、新疆草	各规格下有按照根顶端直径、根长的大小分等级
当归	产于甘肃岷县者称为“岷归”	全归、归头、归身、归尾、箱归	全归、归头按每 kg 支数分三个等级
枸杞子	主产于宁夏中宁和中卫，甘肃、青海、新疆、内蒙古等	按产地分为宁夏枸杞（西枸杞）、血枸杞	按每 50g 中果实的粒数分等

Medicinal material	Main producing area	Specification	Grade
Rhei Radix et Rhizoma	Main producing area of *Rheum palmatum* is Gansu Province. Main producing area of *Rheum tanguticum* is provinces of Qinghai and Gansu. Main producing area of *Rheum officinale* is Sichuan Province	West Rhei Radix et Rhizoma, South Rhei Radix et Rhizoma and Ya Rhei Radix et Rhizoma	Danpianji and Suji: divided into three grades according to root numbers in per kg Ya Rhei Radix et Rhizoma: divided into three grades according to size and weight. South Rhei Radix et Rhizoma: divided into two grades according to size and weight
Glycyrrhizae Radix et Rhizoma	Main producing areas of *Glycyrrhiza uralensis* are provinces of Inner Mongolia, Gansu and Ningxia. Main producing area of *Glycyrrhiza inflata* is Xinjiang Uygur Autonomous Region. Main producing areas of *Glycyrrhiza glabra* are Xinjiang Uygur Autonomous Region and Gansu Province	Western Liquorice Root (Dacao, Tiaocao, Maocao, Caojie and Gedatou), Eastern Liquorice Root (Tiaocao and Maocao), Xinjiang-cao	Grades are divided according to the root length and diameter of root tip
Angelicae Sinensis Radix	Mingui is produced in Gansu Province	Quangui, Root stock (Guitou), main root (Guishen), branching root (Guiwei) and Xianggui	Quangui and Guitou: divided into three grades according to root numbers in per kg
Lycii Fructus	Main producing areas are in Zhongning and Zhongwei, Ningxia Province, and also in provinces of Gansu, Qinghai, Xinjiang and Inner Mongolia	Two specifications are Ningxia Barbary Wolfberry Fruit (Western Barbary Wolfberry Fruit) and Blood Barbary Wolfberry Fruit divided according to producing area	Grades are divided according to fruit numbers in per 50g

题库

目标检测
Object Detection

一、选择题（Choice question）

（一）单项选择题（One-choice question）

1. “锦纹”属于下列哪种药材的鉴别特征（　　）

A. 大黄　　B. 当归　　C. 甘草　　D. 枸杞子　　E. 牛膝

“Jinwen” belongs to which of the following identification characteristics of Chinese medicinal materials (　　)

A. *Rhei Radix et Rhizoma*　　B. *Angelicae Sinensis Radix*

C. *Glycyrrhizae Radix et Rhizoma*　　D. *Lycii Fructus*

E. *Achyranthis Bidentatae Radix*

2. 大黄药材断面星点分布于（ ）
   A. 根髓部 B. 根茎皮层 C. 根茎髓部
   D. 根茎韧皮部 E. 木质部
   Where are the star-spots on the Rhubarb cross-section ( )
   A. pith of root B. rhizome cortex C. pith of rhizome
   D. rhizome phloem E. Xylem
3. 甘草的商品等级是如何划分的（ ）
   A. 仅根据直径 B. 仅根据长短
   C. 根据直径和长短 D. 根据每支重量
   E. 根据每 kg 中甘草的数量
   How is the commodity grade of licorice root divided ( )
   A. based only on diameter
   B. based only on length
   C. based only on diameter and length
   D. Based on the weight of each root
   E. based on the root numbers of per kg
4. 当归一般栽培至第几年秋后采挖（ ）
   A. 1 年 B. 2 年 C. 3 年 D. 4 年 E. 5 年
   How many years have the root of *Angelicae Sinensis* been cultivated before collected in late autumn ( )
   A. first year B. second year C. third year
   D. fourth year E. fifth year
5. 按每多少克重量单位中果实的粒数来划分枸杞子等级（ ）
   A. 50g B. 100g C. 500g D. 1000g E. 2000g
   What is the weight unit that Lycii Fructus is divided into grades according to ( )
   A. 50g B. 100g C. 500g D. 1000g E. 2000g

（二）多项选择题（Multiple choice question）

1. 大黄的商品来源是（ ）
   A. 掌叶大黄 B. 唐古特大黄 C. 药用大黄
   D. 华北大黄 E. 波叶大黄
   What is the origin of Rhubarb? ( )
   A. root and rhizome of *Rheum palmatum* L
   B. root and rhizome of *Rheum tanguticum* Maxim. ex Balf
   C. root and rhizome of *Rheum officinale* Baill
   D. root and rhizome of *Rheum franzenbachii* Munt
   E. root and rhizome of *Rheum undulatum* L
2. 甘草的主要功效是（ ）
   A. 补脾益气 B. 清热解毒 C. 祛痰止咳
   D. 缓急止痛 E. 调和诸药
   What are the functions of Glycyrrhizae Radix et Rhizoma ( )
   A. To tonify spleen, tonify qi
   B. clear heat, remove toxin

C. dispel phlegm, suppress cough

D. relax spasm, relieve pain

E. moderate drug actions

3. 当归的功能包括下列哪些（　　）

A. 补血活血　　B. 调经止痛　　C. 润肠通便

D. 祛痰止咳　　E. 调和诸药

What are the functions of Angelicae Sinensis Radix (　　)

A. nourish blood, activate blood

B. regulate menstruation

C. relieve pain, moisten the intestines and relax the bowels

D. dispel phlegm, suppress cough

E. moderate drug actions

4. 枸杞子的性状描述下列哪些正确（　　）

A. 类纺锤形　　B. 表面红色或暗红色　　C. 果皮柔韧，皱缩

D. 种子类肾形　　E. 气微，味甜

Which of the following is true about the character descriptions of Western Barbary Wolfberry Fruit (　　)

A. subfusiform　　B. extermally red or dark red

C. pericarp pliable and shrunken　　D. seeds subreniform

E. odour slight, taste sweet

二、解答题（Thinking question）

1. 简述大黄的规格是如何划分的?

Briefly describe how the grades of Rhubarb are divided?

2. 简述全归的等级是如何划分的?

Briefly describe how the specifications of Quangui are divided?

第十八章　进　口　药

Chapter 18　Imported Medicinal Materials

PPT

学习目标 ¦ Learning Target

知识要求：

掌握　进口药的含义及其主要的药材品种。

能力要求：

会运用所学规格等级、商品特征、检查、质量要求等知识和方法鉴别与评价市场上沉香、血竭等药材的真伪和质量。

Knowledge requirements:

Proficiency　The meaning and varieties of Imported Medicinal Materials.

Skill requirements:

Learn to identify the authenticity and evaluate the quality of Aquilariae Lignum Resinatum and Draxonis Sanguis on the market by applying the knowledge and methods of specification and grade, commodity characteristics, examination and quality requirement, etc.

一、进口药概述

I. Overview of Imported Medicinal Materials

以全部或大部分从国外进口的大宗商品药材，称为进口药。中药是我国的传统药物，品种多，用量大，除了我国自主生产的中药之外，也从国外进口一部分药物。中药在国际市场上进行商品交换已有悠久的历史。早在汉代张骞出使西域时，就引进了石榴、苏合香等外来药。唐代药物的交流兴盛，引进了胡椒、阿魏、胖大海、番木鳖、诃黎勒、豆蔻等药材。宋元时期，在我国与日本的物资交流中，中药贸易是重要的一项。当时我国输出日本的中药主要是“香药”，而日本输入的大宗中药则是硫黄。之后，我国政府又派医官去朝鲜教学，朝鲜栽培的人参、关白附等药材亦输入中国。

Imported Medicinal Materials are all or most of the bulk commercial medicinal materials imported from abroad. CMM is the traditional medicine in China, which owes many types and large amounts in use. In addition to the self-sufficient Traditional Chinese medicines, some are imported from abroad. CMM owes a long history of commodity exchange in the international market. As early as Zhang Qian's mission to the western regions in the Han Dynasty, he introduced foreign medicinal materials such as

Granati Pericarpium, Styrax, etc. The exchange of CMMs in the Tang Dynasty was prosperous, and Piperis Fructus, Ferulae Resina, Sterculiae Lychnophorae Semen, Strychni Semen, Chebulae Fructus, Alpiniae Katsumadai Semen and other medicinal materials were introduced. During the Song and Yuan Dynasties, CMMs trade was an important part in the material exchange between China and Japan. At that time, CMMs exported to Japan was mainly "aromatic medicines", while the bulk CMMs imported from Japan was Sulfur. After that, medical officials were sent by the government then to Korea for teaching, and Ginseng Radix et Rhizoma, Aconiti Coreani Radix and other medicinal materials cultivated in Korea were also imported into China.

公元 1132 年前后，中外进行贸易的中药品种逐渐增多，如犀角、象牙、龙脑、玳瑁、乳香、丁香、豆蔻、茴香、沉香、檀香、麝香、安息香、龙涎香、木香、荜澄茄、胡椒、胡黄连等，既推动了世界药学的发展，又从其他国家的药学中汲取了学术精华。明代，郑和率领庞大船队 7 次下西洋，不仅带去了中药，还有医生偕同前往，与 30 多个国家建立了外交贸易关系，促进了经济、文化、医药的交流，外国药物的输入也丰富了本草学的内容。清代，更多的外国药物传入我国。

Around 1132 AD, the varieties of CMMs that traded between China and foreign countries gradually increased, such as Rhinoceros Horn, Ivory, Berneolum, Carapax Eretmochelydis, Olibanum, Caryophylli Flos, Amomi Fructus Rotundus, Foeniculum Vulgare, Aquilariae Lignum Resinatum, Santali Albi Lignum, Moschus, Benzoinum, Ambergris, Aucklandiae Radix, Litseae Fructus, Piperis Fructus, Picrorhizae Rhizoma, etc., which not only promoted the development of the world's pharmacy, but also absorbed the essence of pharmacy from other countries. In the Ming Dynasty, Zheng He led large fleets to the western seas for seven times with CMMs and doctors. He established diplomatic and trade relations with more than 30 countries, and promoted economic, cultural, and medical communications. Simultaneously, the import of foreign medicines also enriched the content of Materia Medica. More Western medicines were introduced to China in the Qing Dynasty.

近年来中药进口有了较大的增长。我国进口中药的主要品种有：西洋参（美国、加拿大），高丽参（韩国、朝鲜），沉香（印度尼西亚、马来西亚、越南、柬埔寨），肉桂（越南、柬埔寨、斯里兰卡），海马（马来西亚、新加坡、日本），蛤蚧（越南、泰国），丁香（斯里兰卡、桑给巴尔地区），肉豆蔻（泰国、印度尼西亚、马来西亚、印度、缅甸），草果（越南），荜茇（印度、越南、菲律宾），胖大海（泰国、印度尼西亚、缅甸），西红花（西班牙、伊朗、希腊），番泻叶（印度），乳香、没药（索马里、埃塞俄比亚），阿魏（阿富汗、伊朗、印度），血竭（印度尼西亚、马来西亚），苏合香（土耳其、伊朗、索马里、印度），豆蔻（泰国、印度尼西亚），羚羊角（俄罗斯、蒙古），儿茶（马来西亚、印度尼西亚）等。

The import of CMMs has increased greatly in recent years. The major imported CMMs include Panacis Quinquefolii Radix (USA, Canada), Korean ginseng (Korea, North Korea), Aquilariae Lignum Resinatum (Indonesia, Malaysia, Vietnam, Cambodia), Cinnamomi Cortex (Vietnam, Cambodia, Sri Lanka), Hippocampus (Malaysia, Singapore, Japan), Gecko (Vietnam, Thailand), Caryophylli Flos (Sri Lanka, Zanzibar region), Myristicae Semen (Thailand, Indonesia, Malaysia, India, Myanmar), Tsaoko Fructus (Vietnam), Piperis Longi Fructus (India, Vietnam, Philippines), Sterculiae Lychnophorae Semen (Thailand, Indonesia, Myanmar), Croci Stigma (Spain, Iran, Greece), Sennae Folium (India), Olibanum, Myrrha (Somalia, Ethiopia), Ferulae Resina (Afghanistan, Iran, India), Draconis Sanguis (Indonesia, Malaysia), Styrax (Turkey, Iran, Somalia, India), Amomi Fructus Rotundus (Thailand, Indonesia), Saigae Tataricae Cornu (Russia, Mongolia), Catechu (Malaysia, Indonesia), etc.

二、药材品种
II. Varieties of Medicinal Materials

血竭 (Xuejie) ¦ Draxonis Sanguis (Dragon's Blood)

【基原 / Origin】

为棕榈科植物麒麟血竭 *Daemonorops draco* Bl. 果实渗出的树脂经加工制成。

Dragon's blood is the prepared resin of the fruit of *Daemonorops draco* Bl. (Fam. Palmae)

【产地 / Producing area】

主产于印度尼西亚及马来西亚，土尔其、叙利亚、埃及、索马里和波斯湾附近各国亦产。

Main producing areas are Indonesia, Malaysia, Turkey, Syria, Egypt, Somalia and countries near the Persian Gulf.

【采制 / Collection and preparation】

原装血竭　采集成熟果实，充分晒干，加贝壳一起放入容器内用力振动，松脆的红色树脂即脱落，筛去杂质，用布包裹树脂，放入热水中使树脂软化挤成团块状，取出放冷，即得原装血竭。

Original Dragon's Blood　The ripe fruits are collected and dried fully in the sun, put into container with shells to vibrate vigorously. After the crisp red resins drop off, screen the foreign matter. The resins are wrapped in cloth, put into hot water to be squeezed into block mass, taken out and cooled, thus Original Dragon's Blood are obtained.

加工血竭　加入辅料（如达玛树脂等）加工而得的，称为加工血竭。

Processed Dragon's Blood　Processed by adding auxiliary materials (such as Dama resin, etc.).

【商品特征 / Commodity characteristics】

原装血竭　呈扁圆形、圆形或不规则块状。表面红褐色，有光泽，附有因摩擦而成的红粉。质硬而脆。断面有光泽，破碎面黑红色，研粉为血红色。无臭，味淡。不溶于水，在热水中软化。

Original Dragon's Blood　Oblate, rounded or irregular block, externally reddish-brown, lustrous, attached with friction-caused red powder. Texture hard and fragile, section glossy, broken section blackish-red, ground powder blood red. Odour, not smelly; taste, plain. Insoluble in water, softened in hot water.

加工血竭　呈扁圆四方形，底部平圆，顶部有包扎成型时所成的纵折纹。

Processed Dragon's Blood　Sub-rounded square, flat and round at the bottom; longitudinal folds at the top formed during the packaging.

【规格等级 / Specification and grade】

血竭有原装血竭、加工血竭，再分等级或统装。

Dragon's Blood includes original and processed Dragon's Blood, which can be divided into different grades or unified grade.

【化学成分 / Chemical constituent】

主含红色树脂类成分，如血竭素、血竭红素、去甲基血竭红素、去甲基血竭素、(2S)-5- 甲氧基 -6- 甲基 -7- 黄烷醇、(2S)-5- 甲氧基 -7- 黄烷醇等。

Dragon's Blood mainly contains red resins of dracorhodin, dracorubin, nordracorubin, nordracorhodin, (2S)5-methoxy-6-methylflavan-7-ol, (2S)-5-methoxyflavan-7-ol, etc.

【检查 / Examination】

总灰分不得过 6.0%。醇不溶物不得过 25.0%。

Total ash, not more than 6.0%. Ethanol-insoluble solids, not more than 25.0%.

【质量要求 / Quality requirement】

外观质量 以表面黑红色、研末鲜红色、火烧呛鼻者为佳。

Appearance quality Good quality for blackish-red surface, bright red ground powder, and irritating smell being burnt.

内在质量 含量测定：按高效液相色谱法测定，本品含血竭素不得少于 1.0%。

Intrinsic quality Assay: It contains not less than 1.0% of dracorhodin according to HPLC method.

【功能主治 / Function and indication】

平，甘、咸。活血定痛，化瘀止血，生肌敛疮。用于跌打损伤、心腹瘀痛、外伤出血、疮疡不敛。

Neutral, sweet and salty. To active blood, relieve pain, resolve stasis, stanch bleeding, promote tissue regeneration and wound healing. For the treatment of traumatic injuries, stasis and pain in the heart and abdomen, traumatic bleeding, unhealing sore and ulcer.

【贮藏养护 / Storage and maintenance】

木箱或纸箱装，置阴凉干燥处。

Usually packed in wooden cases or cartons. Preserved in a cool and dry place.

【用法用量 / Administration and dosage】

研末，1~2g，或入丸剂。外用研末撒或入膏药用。

Ground into powder, 1~2g, or used in pills. For topical application, ground into powder for spreading or used in paste.

沉香 (Chenxiang) | Aquilariae Lignum Resinatum (Chinese Eaglewood Wood)

【基原 / Origin】

为瑞香科植物沉香 *Aquilaria agallocha* Roxb. 含有树脂的心材。

Chinese Eaglewood Wood is the resin containing wood of *Aquilaria agallocha* Roxb. (Fam. Thymelaeaceae).

【产地 / Producing area】

主产于印度尼西亚、马来西亚、柬埔寨及越南等国。

Main producing areas are Indonesia, Malaysia, Cambodia, and Vietnam etc.

【采制 / Collection and preparation】

全年均可采收，割取含树脂的木材，除去不含树脂的部分，阴干。

The medicinal material is collected all the year round, removed from the part without resin, and dried in shade.

【商品特征 / Commodity characteristics】

呈不规则块状、片状；表面凹凸不平，有刀削痕，黄棕色或灰黑色，可见黑棕色树脂斑纹。质坚实而重，能沉水。香气浓烈，味苦。

In irregular lumps and flakes. Externally lumpy, yellowish-brown or greyish-black, with scars of knife cutting, and showing streaks formed by black-brown resin. Texture tight and heavy, sinking in water. Odour, intensely aromatic; taste, bitter.

【规格等级 / Specification and grade】

进口沉香一般分绿油伽南香、紫油伽南香、黑油伽南香、青丝伽南香等规格。其等级标准为：

Specification of imported Chinese Eaglewood Wood is divided into Lvyoujiananxiang, Ziyoujiananxiang, Heiyoujiananxiang and Qingsijiananxiang, whose grading criteria are as follows:

一等：醇溶性浸出物含量 25%~30%。

First grade: The content of ethanol-soluble extractives is between 25% and 30%.

二等：醇溶性浸出物含量 20%~25%。

Second grade: The content of ethanol-soluble extractives is between 20% and 25%.

三等：醇溶性浸出物含量 17%~20%。

Third grade: The content of ethanol-soluble extractives is between 17% and 20%.

四等：醇溶性浸出物含量 15%~17%。

Fourth grade: The content of ethanol-soluble extractives is between 15% and 17%.

【化学成分 / Chemical constituent】

主要含有沉香螺萜醇、沉香萜醇、α- 及 β- 沉香萜呋喃、去甲基沉香萜呋喃酮、4- 羟基二氢沉香萜呋喃及 3,4- 二羟基二氢沉香萜呋喃、芹子烷等成分。

Chinese Eaglewood Wood mainly contains agarospirol, agarol, alpha- and beta-agarofuran, nor-ketoagarofuran, 4-hydroxydihydroagarofuran, 3,4-dihydroxydihydroagarofuran, selinane and others components.

【质量要求 / Quality requirement】

外观质量 以色黑、质坚硬、油性足、香气浓而持久、能沉水者为佳。

Appearance quality Good quality for black colour, tight and heavy texture, rich oiliness, strong and persistent aroma, and sinking in water.

内在质量 浸出物含量：乙醇浸出物（热）不得少于 15.0%。

Intrinsic quality Extract content: Not less than 15.0% of ethanol-soluble extractives (hot).

【功能主治 / Function and indication】

微温，辛、苦。行气止痛，温中止呕，纳气平喘。用于胸腹胀闷疼痛、胃寒呕吐呃逆、肾虚气逆喘急。

Mild warm, pungent and bitter. To move qi, relieve pain, warm the middle energizer, stop vomiting, absorb qi and relieve wheezing. For the treatment of distention, oppression and pain in the chest and abdomen, vomiting and hiccup caused by stomach cold, wheezing caused by qi counterflow and kidney deficiency.

【贮藏养护 / Storage and maintenance】

密闭，置阴凉干燥处。

Sealed and stored in a cool and dry place.

【用法用量 / Administration and dosage】

1~5g，后下。

1~5g, added when the decoction is nearly done.

重点小结
Summary

药材	主产地	商品规格	等级标准
血竭	主产于印度尼西亚及马来西亚，土尔其、叙利亚、埃及、索马里和波斯湾附近各国	原装血竭、加工血竭	分等级或统装
沉香	主产于印度尼西亚、马来西亚、柬埔寨及越南等国	分绿油伽南香、紫油伽南香、黑油伽南香、青丝伽南香等规格	按醇溶性浸出物分1~4等

Medicinal material	Main producing area	Commodity specification	Grading criteria
Draxonis Sanguis	Main producing areas are Indonesia, Malaysia, Turkey, Syria, Egypt, Somalia and countries near the Persian Gulf	Includes original and processed Dragon's Blood	Be divided into different grades or unified grade
Aquilariae Lignum Resinatum	Main producing areas are Indonesia, Malaysia, Cambodia, Vietnam and other countries	Includes specifications of Lvyoujiananxiang, Ziyoujiananxiang, Heiyoujiananxiang and Qingsijiananxiang	Be divided into four grades according to the content of ethanol-soluble extractives

题库

目标检测
Object Detection

一、选择题（Choice question）

（一）单项选择题（One-choice question）

1. 以外色黑似铁，研粉红似血为主要鉴别特征的中药是（　　）

A. 阿魏　　B. 苏木　　C. 血竭

D. 鸡血藤　　E. 赭石

Which of the following is distinguished mainly by externally dark like iron and ground powder red like blood (　　)

A. Ferulae Resina　　B. Sappan Lignum　　C. Draxonis Sanguis

D. Spatholobi Caulis　　E. Haematitum

2. 下面中药不能用火试鉴别是（　　）

A. 海金沙　　B. 血竭　　C. 沉香

D. 槟榔　　E. 青黛

Which of the following is not distinguished by fire (　　)

A. Lygodii Spora　　B. Draxonis Sanguis

C. Aquilariae Lignum Resinatum D. Arecae Semen
E. Indigo Naturalis

3. 燃烧时有松香气的是（ ）
A. 雄黄 B. 琥珀 C. 沉香 D. 血竭 E. 降香
Which of the following owes rosin smell when burning ( )
A. Realgar B. Ambrum
C. Aquilariae Lignum Resinatum D. Draxonis Sanguis
E. Dalbergiae Odoriferae Lignum

4. 血竭内服时用量为（ ）
A. 3~10g B. 5~15g C. 0.5~1g
D. 1~2g E. 10~20g
The dosage of Draxonis Sanguis when taken orally is ( )
A. 3~10g B. 3~5g C. 1.5~3g
D. 1~2g E. 10~20g

5. 沉香醇溶性浸出物（热浸法）不得少于（ ）
A. 15.0% B. 16.0% C. 14.0%
D. 17.0% E. 20.0%
The content of ethanol-soluble extractives (the hot extraction method) of Aquilariae Lignum Resinatum is not less than ( )
A. 15.0% B. 16.0% C. 14.0%
D. 17.0% E. 20.0%

（二）多项选择题（Multiple choice question）

下列哪些是我国主要进口药材（ ）
A. 番泻叶 B. 胖大海 C. 肉豆蔻
D. 西洋参 E. 西红花
Which of the following are the main imported medicinal materials in China ( )
A. Sennae Folium B. Sterculiae Lychnophorae Semen
C. Myristicae Semen D. Panacis Quinquefolii Radix
E. Croci Stigma

二、解答题（Thinking question）

1. 比较国产沉香和进口沉香的主要鉴别特征。

To compare the main identification characteristics between the domestic and imported Aquilariae Lignum Resinatum.

2. 比较国产血竭和进口血竭的主要鉴别特征。

To compare the main identification characteristics between the domestic and imported Draxonis Sanguis.

药 名 索 引
index

一、药材中文名笔画索引
I. Chinese name stroke index of Medicinal Material

二、药材拉丁名索引
II. Latin name index of Medicinal Material

三、植物、动物拉丁学名索引
III. Latin name index of plant and animal

参 考 答 案
Reference Answer

总论 (Overview)

第一章（Chapter 1）

一、填空题（Fill in the blanks）

1. 中药商品质量；经营

quality; management

2. 经营管理；质量控制；购销；贮存；商品规格；经营管理规律

management; quality control experience; purchase and sale; storage; commodities specification; management rules

3. 中医药理论；临床经验；防治疾病和医疗保健

prevention, treatment of diseases and medical care; CMM theory; clinical experience

4. 仅经过产地简单加工

simply processed in the producing areas

5. 来源；购销；贮存；商品规格；商品质量

the place of origin; purchase and sale; storage; commodities specification; commodities quality

6.《本草经集注》

Variorum of the Classic of Materia Medica

二、选择题（Choice question）

1. ABCD　2. ABC　3. ACD　4. ABCDE

第二章（Chapter 2）

一、选择题 (Choice question)

（一）单项选择题 (One-choice question)

1. D　2. A　3. B　4. E　5. E

（二）多项选择题 (Multiple choice questions)

1. ABCD　2. ABE　3. ABCD　4. BDE　5. ACD

二、解答题 (Thinking question)

略 (Omission)

第三章（Chapter 3）

一、选择题（Choice question）

（一）单项选择题（One-choice question）

1. D　2. D　3. A　4. B　5. C

（二）多项选择题（Multiple choice question）

1. ABCDE　2. CD　3. CD　4. AB

二、解答题（Thinking question）

略

Omission

第四章（Chapter 4）

一、选择题（Choice question）

（一）单项选择题（One-choice question）

1. D　2. B　3. E

（二）多项选择题（Multiple choice question）

1. ABDE　2. ABCDE　3. ABCDE　4. ABCDE

二、解答题（Thinking question）

略。

Omission.

第五章（Chapter 5）

一、选择题（Choice question）

（一）单项选择题（One-choice question）

1. A　2. D　3. A

（二）多项选择题（Multiple choice question）

1. ABDE　2. ABCDE　3. ABD　4. ABCE

二、解答题（Thinking question）

略

Omission

第六章（Chapter 6）

一、选择题（Choice question）

（一）单项选择题（One-choice question）

1. E　2. B　3. A　4. C　5. E

（二）多项选择题（Multiple choice question）

1. ABCDE　2. BCD　3. ABCDE　4. ABCDE

二、解答题（Thinking question）

略

Omission

第七章（Chapter 7）

一、选择题（Choice question）

（一）单项选择题（One-choice question）

1. B　2.C

（二）多项选择题（Multiple choice question）

1. ABC　2. BD　3. ABDE　4. ABCD　5. ACD

二、判断题（Judgment question）

1. Ture
2. True
3. False

各论 (Monograph)

第八章（Chapter 8）

一、选择题（Choice question）

（一）单项选择题（One-choice question）

1. E　2. A　3. A　4. B　5. A　6. B　7. E

（二）多项选择题（Multiple choice question）

1. ABCDE　2. ABCDE　3. ABCD　4. ABC

二、思考题（Thinking question）

略

Omission

第九章（Chapter 9）

一、选择题（Choice question）

（一）单项选择题（One-choice question）

1. A　2. A　3. C　4. B　5. C　6. C　7. C　8. B　9. C　10. A　11. D

（二）多项选择题（Multiple choice question）

1. ABCDE　2. ABCD　3. ABCDE　4. ABCDE　5. ABCD　6. ABC　7. ABCDE

二、思考题（Thinking question）

略

Omission

第十章（Chapter 10）

一、选择题（Choice question）

（一）单项选择题（One-choice question）

1. B　2. B　3. A　4. C　5. B

（二）多项选择题（Multiple choice question）

1. ABCDE　2. ABCDE　3. ABCDE　4. BE

二、解答题（Thinking question）

略

Omission

第十一章（Chapter 11）

一、选择题（Choice question）

（一）单项选择题（One-choice question）

1. D　2. D　3. C　4. B　5. C

（二）多项选择题（Multiple choice question）

1. DE　2. ABCDE　3. AE　4. AD

二、思考题（Thinking question）

略

Omission

第十二章（Chapter 12）

一、选择题（Choice question）

（一）单项选择题（One-choice question）

1. A　2. E　3. B　4. B　5. A

（二）多项选择题（Multiple choice questions）

1. ABCD　2. BC　3. ABC　4. ABC　5. BD

二、思考题（Thinking questions）

略

Omission

第十三章（Chapter 13）

一、选择题（Choice question）

（一）单项选择题（One-choice question）

1. A　2. A　3. B　4. C　5. A

（二）多项选择题（Multiple choice question）

1. ABCD　2. ABCD　3. ABC　4. ABC　5. BC

二、思考题（Thinking questions）

略

Omission

第十四章（Chapter 14）

一、选择题（Choice question）

（一）单项选择题（One-choice question）

1. C　2. E　3. B　4. B　5. C

（二）多项选择题（Multiple choice question）

1. ABCDE　2. ABCDE　3. AB　4. ABC　5. BCD

二、解答题（Thinking question）

略

Omission

第十五章（Chapter 15）

一、选择题（Choice question）

（一）单项选择题（One-choice question）

1. C　2. B　3. A　4. D　5. C

（二）多项选择题（Multiple choice question）

1. ABCDE 2. BC 3. BE 4. ABC

二、解答题（Thinking question）

略

Omission

第十六章（Chapter 16）

一、选择题（Choice question）

（一）单项选择题（One-choice question）

1. B 2. D 3. A 4. A 5. C 6. E 7. B 8. B

（二）多项选择题（Multiple choice question）

1. ABCD 2. ABCD 3. ABCDE 4. ABCDE 5. AC 6. AB 7. ABCDE

二、思考题（Thinking question）

略

Omission

第十七章（Chapter 17）

一、选择题（Choice question）

（一）单项选择题（One-choice question）

1. A 2. C 3. C 4. B 5. A

（二）多项选择题（Multiple choice question）

1. ABC 2. ABCDE 3. ABC 4. ABCDE

二、解答题（Thinking question）

省略

Omission

第十八章（Chapter 18）

一、选择题（Choice question）

（一）单项选择题（One-choice question）

1. C 2. D 3. B 4. D 5. A

（二）多项选择题（Multiple choice question）

ABCDE

二、解答题（Thinking question）

略

Omission

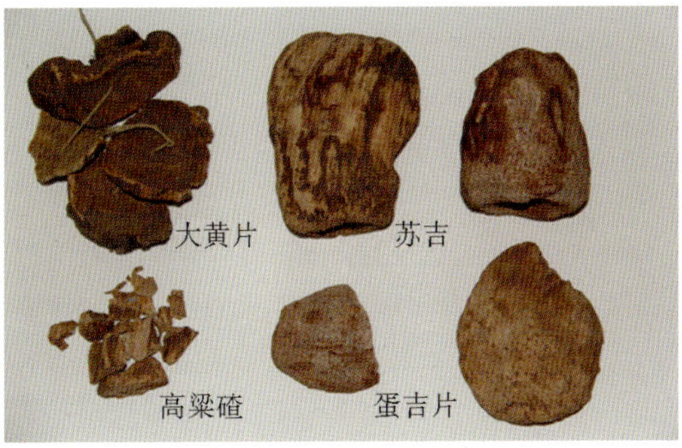

图 1　大黄药材商品规格

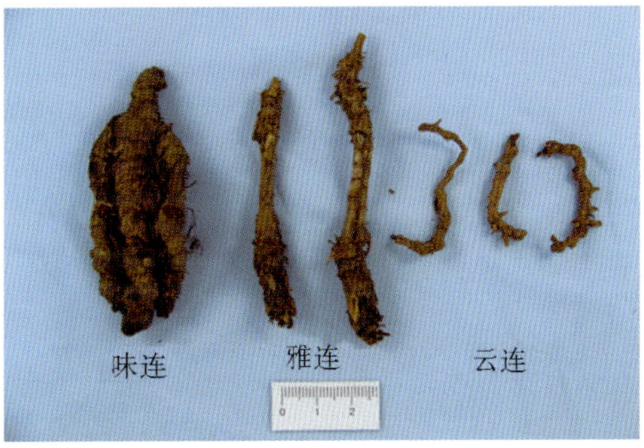

图 2　黄连药材商品规格

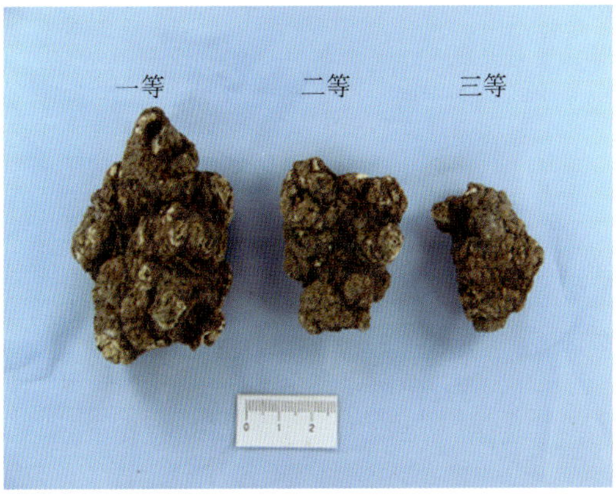

图 3　川芎药材商品规格

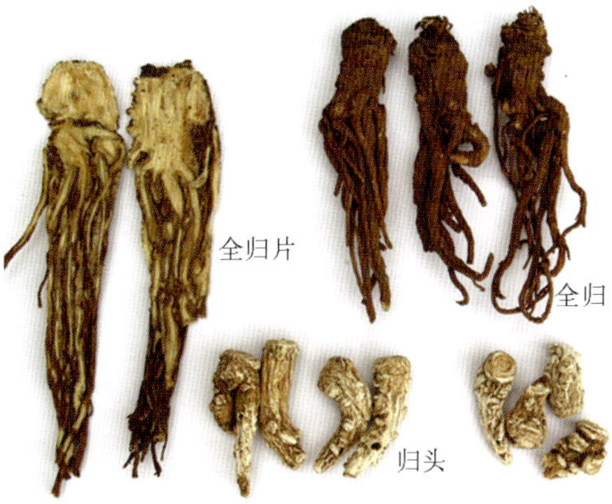

图 4　当归药材商品规格

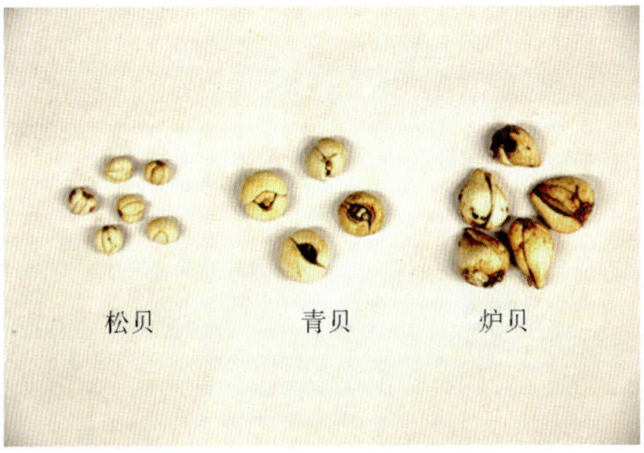

图 5　川贝药材商品规格

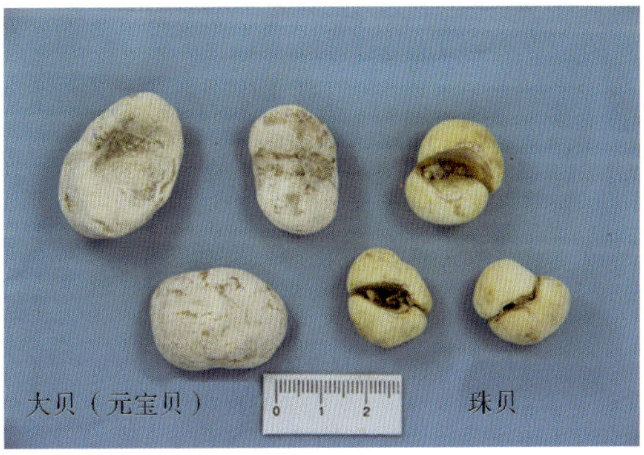

图 6　浙贝药材商品规格

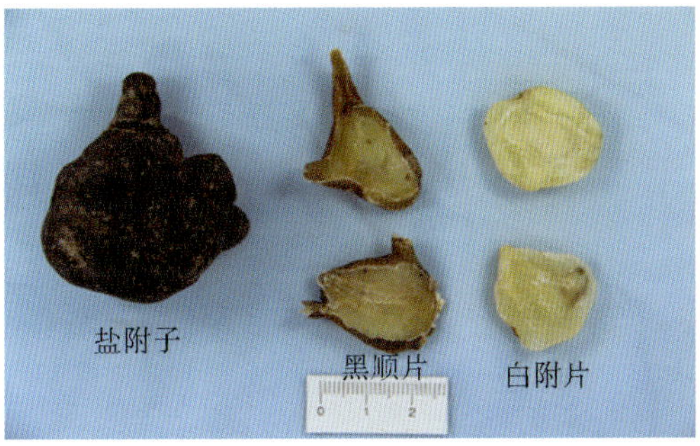

图 7　附子药材商品规格

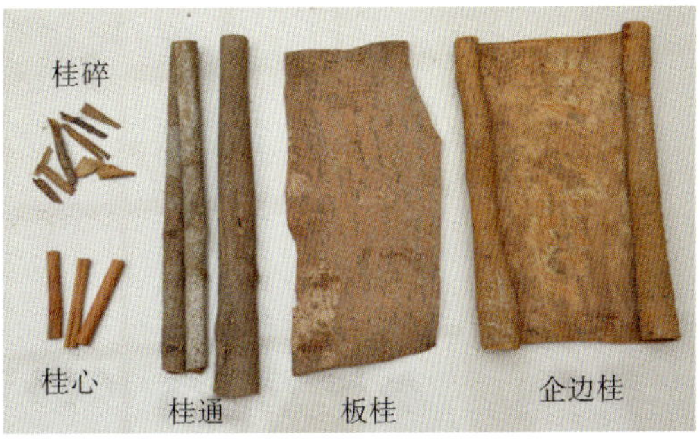

图 8　肉桂药材商品规格

图 9　安徽亳州中药材市场

图 10　河北安国中药材市场

图 11　四川成都荷花池中药材市场

图 12　江西樟树中药材市场

图 13　河南禹州中药材市场

图 14　山东鄄城舜王城中药材市场

图 15　广州清平中药材市场

图 16　广东普宁中药材市场